AF607971

CLANDESTINE PHILOSOPHY

New Studies on Subversive Manuscripts in Early Modern Europe, 1620–1823

THE UCLA CLARK MEMORIAL LIBRARY SERIES

CLANDESTINE PHILOSOPHY

NEW STUDIES ON SUBVERSIVE MANUSCRIPTS IN EARLY MODERN EUROPE, 1620–1823

Edited by Gianni Paganini, Margaret C. Jacob, and John Christian Laursen

Published by the University of Toronto Press in association with the UCLA Center for Seventeenth- and Eighteenth-Century Studies and the William Andrews Clark Memorial Library utorontopress.com

ISBN 978-1-4875-0461-8 (cloth)
ISBN 978-1-4875-3055-6 (EPUB)
ISBN 978-1-4875-3054-9 (PDF)

Library and Archives Canada Cataloguing in Publication

Title: Clandestine philosophy : new studies on subversive manuscripts in early modern Europe, 1620–1823 / edited by Gianni Paganini, Margaret C. Jacob, and John Christian Laursen.

Names: Paganini, Gianni, 1950– editor. | Jacob, Margaret C., 1943– editor. | Laursen, John Christian, editor. | University of California, Los Angeles. Center for 17th– & 18th-Century Studies, host institution, publisher.

Series: UCLA Clark Memorial Library series ; 27.

Description: Series statement: UCLA Clark Memorial Library series ; 27 | This volume is a result of a conference held on March 4–5, 2016 in Los Angeles at the UCLA Center for Seventeenth– and Eighteenth-Century Studies. | Includes bibliographical references and index.

Identifiers: Canadiana 20190099763 | ISBN 9781487504618 (hardcover)

Subjects: LCSH: Underground literature – Europe – History and criticism – Congresses. | LCSH: Underground literature – Europe – Manuscripts – Congresses. | LCSH: Philosophy, Modern – History – Congresses. | LCSH: Manuscripts, European – History – 17th century – Congresses. | LCSH: Manuscripts, European – History – 18th century – Congresses. | LCSH: Manuscripts, European – History – 19th century – Congresses.

Classification: LCC B801 C63 2020 | DDC 190.9/032 – dc23

This book has been published with the help of a grant from the UCLA Center for Seventeenth- and Eighteenth-Century Studies.

University of Toronto Press acknowledges the financial assistance to its publishing program of the Canada Council for the Arts and the Ontario Arts Council, an agency of the Government of Ontario.

Canada Council for the Arts   Conseil des Arts du Canada

Funded by the Government of Canada   Financé par le gouvernement du Canada

Contents

Part Five: Toleration, Criticism, and Innovation in Religion

Part Six: Spanish Developments

Preface

MARGARET C. JACOB

When it comes to the discovery of new clandestine texts, no end appears to be in sight. It is also the case that one person's heresy might need to be hidden, and another's deemed not particularly outrageous. To give but one example: the curious fate of an anonymous author who in the mid-eighteenth century attempted to articulate a self-controlled *via media* aimed at a happy life in society.[1] The actual author of *The Oeconomy of Human Life. Translated from an Indian Manuscript, written by an Ancient Bramin,* known in French as *Le Philosophe Indien,* is widely believed to be the British publisher and poet, Robert Dodsley. Safely ensconced in London, he claimed to have learned philosophy and religion from the ancient Brahmans and to have travelled to China and Tibet. Then the text moved to Catholic Europe.

While attributed to an English aristocrat, Lord Chesterfield, on the Continent the French version of *The Oeconomy* takes its place among a raft of clandestine texts, often materialist in inspiration and dating from the 1740s. It advocates an entirely natural religion, albeit a theistic one suitable for living a happy life in society. And it claimed to be composed by an ancient Brahman. Its heterodoxy and lack of identification with Christianity doomed it among the French censors.

True to the intellectual pedigree that belonged to the clandestine genre, there are Spinozist elements in the Indian philosopher's theism; he praises the wisdom of God by noting, "The marvels of his mechanism are the work of his hands. Listen to his voice …"[2] Thus anthropomorphized, "the Lord is just; he judges the world with equity and truth … The Great and the Small, the Wise and the Ignorant … are received equally in accordance with their merit."[3] This is not the God of the materialists, nor is he particularly identifiable with any of the three monotheistic religions. No text we can associate with the Enlightenment went through more editions and translations, printed and manuscript, with copies in German, Hungarian, Welsh, and so on. In the eighteenth century two hundred editions appeared and again half as many were produced after 1800.[4] We might describe the sentiments in *The Oeconomy of Human Life* as enlightened religiosity *light*, close to physico-theology but nowhere near as theistic. The creed being advocated by this anonymous author anchors itself in the secular, in worldly pursuits that discipline the individual. He or she has religion without the need for priests, churches, sermons, or the Testaments.

As various of the fine essays assembled here make clear, more texts are still being found by researchers working in a variety of national settings. Attempts are always being made to pigeonhole these texts as "radical" or "Spinozist" or the like, but as the case of the "Indian philosopher" makes clear, that is sometimes an exercise in futility. To be sure, the genre of "bad books," or what we have labelled "clandestine philosophical texts," was recognized by consumers as early as the 1770s in French, if not before.

We know about the genre because of the widow Stockdorf. In 1771 she made her way from her bookshop in Strasburg to Paris in search of bad books or manuscripts. For her trouble, she landed in the Bastille, where the police (kindly for us) left a copy of her shopping lists. She was on the trail after only heretical, irreligious, and scandalous books. Her book bag, as well as her shopping list, were confiscated by the authorities, and they offer a rare window into the universe of forbidden books and manuscripts.

The widowed bookseller knew what she was doing, and she assembled just about every forbidden book or manuscript known at the time. The genre of clandestine philosophical works must be broadly defined to include the rabidly anticlerical and anti-Catholic. Into that category fell works supposedly out of the English republican tradition – by the 1720s sometimes identified as the "country" opposition – found on the Continent and said to be written by the exiled Henry St John, 1st Viscount Bolingbroke. His British political life need not be recounted here, suffice it to say "complex" would be an understatement. What the widow and her buying public, who knew little about Bolingbroke's domestic politics, found in *L'examen important de Milord Bolingbroke* was an attack on religious fanaticism, priests, and Catholicism. Indeed, so central was religion that the discerning reader might have suspected the real author to have been none other than Bolingbroke's good friend, Voltaire. The book claimed to date from 1736 but in fact was published in 1771, the year the widow and her travelling companions, two abbés, started their Parisian buying spree. In the same year, the Roman Catholic Inquisition put *L'examen* on the Index of Forbidden Books, noting that "it judges, attacks, condemns and lacerates one after the other book in the Old and New Testament, the dogmas that are essential to the Christian faith, the doctrine of the Fathers of the Church."[5] We distort the meaning of the genre of the forbidden if we imagine that to qualify, the text must be materialist (although there were plenty in that category), or Spinozist, or deist, or pornographic, or simply anti-Christian.

It is doubtful that the widow knew about the condemnation of *L'examen*, but had she, the book would only have been more eagerly sought. The widow's list and inventory are among the best evidence we have that contemporaries recognized the *genre* of the forbidden and knew exactly what belonged in it. In short, historians have not invented the category; it was there at least by the 1770s and we suspect before.

To look at a few famous examples, we need only consult the lists of what Stockdorf owned and for what she was shopping. Of course, she wanted to buy the pornographic *Thérèse philosophe*, and under it she listed *La fille de joie*, the French title of Cleland's *Fanny Hill*. The only problem with that title is, as far as the French national library can ascertain, the first published edition of the French translation was in 1776. Either there is an earlier edition missed by bibliographers, or the widow had in mind a manuscript about which she had heard and that she knew she wanted to buy. Either way, her shopping list shows expertise and a keen eye for what would sell. And from the list it is not always clear if she was shopping for texts already in print or still hand-written. All were anonymous; all could offend political or religious authorities somewhere, and all, we may reasonably assume, could be sold at a profit.

The widow was not put off by the scandalous reputation of a text that discussed in detail the impostures committed by Jesus, Moses, and Mohammed, or described the heterosexual act so explicitly that it could have been a training manual. Stockdorf was also involved in international trafficking in the forbidden; she had business dealings with shops in Maastricht. Her two-year stint in prison probably cooled her ardour, but there were plenty of other *libraires* to take her place.

A long time ago Elizabeth Eisenstein reminded us that publishers were businessmen as well as "patrons of learning or sponsors of emigré intellectuals and protectors of heterodox refugees."[6] We have moved away from the simple-minded notion that being in the business of the forbidden meant that you were in it for the money. Contemporary scholarship gives much greater attention to publishing in general, and historians of the book have made a significant impact on the study of the clandestine genre. For sure there was money to be made, but there was also the possibility of imprisonment. Mixed motives abounded.

And religion cannot be ruled out entirely as one of those motives. Generally, "fringe" religions made their way to the clandestine circuit in Protestant countries, while prior to 1750 Jansenism and quietism were the most prolific offenders in Catholic lands. In either territory, the authorities took a dim view particularly when one or another sect was articulate in political matters. Indeed the French police when they went after "bad books" lumped works by Jansenists with materialist and pornographic texts, possibly being distributed by the same *libraire* and swept up in the same raid. As long as we keep our definitions fluid we stand a better chance of getting at the mindset both of the authorities and of the transgressive.

These essays attempt to give the reader a sense of the state of the field; it offers the most recent work, new discoveries, and rereadings of "classics" in the forbidden that can stand a second look. They give us access to what in early modern Europe could most offend or threaten. They could be written in Latin or the vernacular, and aimed at particular audiences. The consumer of Socinian works may be imagined as not the same person who read pornography. Or can we be sure? The multifaceted character of the genre suggests that when someone back then looked for the latter the former may have popped up from the same locked drawer. Censorship has a way of creating strange but interesting bedfellows.

NOTES

1 Bibliothèque d'Arsenal, Paris, MS 9528, with a preface dated 1749, Peking, and a dedication dated 1758. Facsimile edition available through Google Books and attributed, in the preface to the original manuscript and in the facsimile edition, to Robert Dodsley: https://play.google.com/books/reader?id=biBhAAAAcAAJ&printsec=frontcover&output=reader&hl=en&pg=GBS.PR23. There is a printed version of the text, [Anon], *Le Elixir de la morale indienne, ou Economie de la vie humaine* (Paris: chez Ganeau, 1760), authorized by a royal privilege. See also Harry M. Solomon, *The Rise of Robert Dodsley: Creating the New Age of Print* (Carbondale: Southern Illinois University Press, 1996).

2 MS 9528, f. 18.

3 Ibid. f. 110–13.

4 John Bray, "The Oeconomy of Human Life: An 'Ancient Bramin' in Eighteenth-Century Tibet," *Journal of the Royal Asiatic Society*, Third Series, 19, no. 4 (2009) 439–58; James E. Tierney, ed., *The Correspondence of Robert Dodsley 1733–1764* (Cambridge: Cambridge University Press, 1988), 10–11.

5 Laurence Macé-Del Vento, "'Lancer la foudre et retirer la main'. Les stratégies clandestines de Voltaire vues par la censure romaine," *La Lettre clandestine*, no. 16, 2008, 165–77, quoted on page 166, from Rome, ACDF, Index, Protocolli 1771–1773, dossier 17, f' 66r.

6 Elizabeth L. Eisenstein, *Print Culture and Enlightenment Thought: The Sixth Hanes Lecture* (Hanes Foundation, University of North Carolina at Chapel Hill, 1986), 1–2. And see also Eisenstein, "Print Culture and Enlightenment Thought," *Réseaux* 6, no. 31 (1988): 7–38.

Acknowledgments

The editors would like to thank the Director and Staff of the William Andrews Clark Memorial Library and the Center for Seventeenth- and Eighteenth-Century Studies at the University of California, Los Angeles, and the Centro Linceo Interdisciplinare "B. Segre" of the Accademia dei Lincei in Rome for their help and support, which made the original conference such a pleasure for everyone involved and made this volume possible. This book benefited also from a fellowship at the Paris Institute for Advanced Studies (France), with the financial support of the French State, program "Investissements d'avenir," managed by the Agence Nationale de la Recherche (ANR-11-LABX-0027-01 Labex RFIEA+).

CLANDESTINE PHILOSOPHY

New Studies on Subversive Manuscripts in Early Modern Europe, 1620–1823

Introduction: What Is a Clandestine Philosophical Manuscript?

GIANNI PAGANINI

Seventeenth- and eighteenth-century clandestine philosophical manuscripts became a field of study and historical research especially in the twentieth century.[1] These manuscripts form an appreciable *corpus*: more than 290 texts corresponding to some 2,000 manuscript copies owned by public and private European and North American libraries, most of them dating back to the seventeenth and eighteenth centuries, but some to the beginning of the nineteenth century.

To begin, it should be noted that the philosophical manuscript is an early modern literary genre *par excellence*: there is nothing like it either in the Middle Ages or in the Renaissance. It is only in the years straddling the sixteenth and seventeenth centuries that anonymous authors (e.g., the author of the *Quatrains du déiste*, around 1620, or of the *Theophrastus redivivus*, in 1659) or well-known ones like Jean Bodin (considered to be the author of the most famous deist work criticizing religion, the *Colloquium Heptaplomeres*) entrusted to this form of communication ideas and works that could never have been printed and published in their time.

Clearly, the existence of the "clandestine philosophical manuscript" itself is in part a consequence of and in part a reaction to historical circumstances that are typical of modernity: the invention and expansion of printing, against which the manuscript served as an alternative and surrogate channel for texts that were unquestionably impossible to print; the establishment of great institutional orthodoxies, both Protestant and Catholic, with their mechanisms of uniformity and control, from the Council of Trent to the synod of Dordt; the close alliance of throne and altar that significantly conditioned intellectual life, albeit in different ways depending on the state and the religion; the creation of increasingly efficient and restrictive forms of preventive censorship of books (think of the Inquisition and the *Index librorum prohibitorum* in a Catholic context, but also of the French *privilège du roi* and censorship system), which meant that new ways had to be found to circumvent the web of repression; the birth of forms of intellectual sociality that developed on the edges of the official circles of the churches and universities or juxtaposed with them; and, finally, the growing autonomy of minor or dominant "intellectuals," who were often forced to lead a double life or in any case to conceal their ideas, revealing them at the very most to a restricted and carefully selected group. All these factors led the heterodox authors to privilege manuscript expression and communication over the printed book.

Another "modern" characteristic of philosophical clandestinity was its transversality among the social classes of the *Ancien Régime.* The collectors and authors of philosophical manuscripts included princes (e.g., Prince Eugene of Savoy, general of the imperial Habsburg army and a prominent collector of forbidden works, both printed and in manuscript), nobles, soldiers, diplomats, magistrates fully integrated into the political structures (e.g., Jean Bodin, mentioned above), clergymen both Catholic (the parish priest Jean Meslier) and Calvinist (Yves de Vallone), abbés (Jean Terrasson), tutors and intellectuals (Dumarsais), and renowned academics (Fontenelle and Fréret).[2]

What, then, is a clandestine philosophical manuscript?[3] Naturally, different forms of clandestinity existed: there were erotic texts, political pamphlets, satires of court life and of the nobility, forbidden religious texts (from the Jansenist books to the Jewish or Protestant ones in Catholic countries, and vice versa), and books about alchemy and the occult.[4] These various types of clandestine works often relied on the manuscript form as a means of diffusion; this led to the clandestine printing, often in other countries, of books that were then circulated by the so-called *colporteurs* or sold surreptitiously. The studies of Robert Darnton shed light on the phenomenon of "forbidden books." Yet the status of "clandestine" is relative with regard to time, place, and situation and is therefore affected by events: what is clandestine in one era or in one country may not necessarily be clandestine in other eras and in other countries, under one regime or under another. In practice, the clandestine philosophical manuscripts are a specific species within a much wider genre, that of forbidden literature in general, whether printed or in manuscript. The boundaries therefore need to be drawn.[5]

Are there defining characteristics of the "clandestine philosophical manuscript"? We believe that the intersection of three terms – *clandestine* +

philosophical + manuscript – within the larger set of manuscripts and unpublished documents is sufficient to define the characteristics of this species within the "clandestine" genre.

Notwithstanding efforts to relativize the "ideological" meaning of the term "clandestine" – it is posited that recourse to the manuscript was the result of a series of circumstances linked to the sociology of *Ancien Régime* writing and reading – it remains true that a significant number of these texts absolutely could not be circulated openly, given the *Ancien Régime*'s censorship and repression of anti-religious and anti-metaphysical philosophical, moral, and political ideas. Thus Leibniz began his philological work with the intention of publishing the *Colloquium Heptaplomeres* but had to abandon that idea due to the clear impossibility of making public a work that contained fierce criticism of all the positive religions as well as an apology for natural religion and for religious tolerance.[6]

We can suggest a non-abstract but historically based definition of the "clandestine philosophical manuscript," distinguishing it from other forms of clandestinity (religious, political, erotic, satirical, purely literary, etc.) based on the intersection of three criteria: "clandestinity of expression," "clandestinity of ideas," and the "philosophical" nature of these ideas.

The first criterion is fairly clear. In the seventeenth and eighteenth centuries not all manuscripts were clandestine; there also existed manuscripts written for public circulation – first and foremost the epistolaries with semi-public characteristics, as well as certain collections of poems that circulated first in manuscript and then in printed form.[7] Yet it is undeniable that most of the resolutely "heterodox" authors found it useful to entrust their ideas to manuscripts both to protect themselves against the retaliation of the authorities and to circumvent the censorship to which printed books were subject. Hence the widespread use of anonymity, the recourse to pseudonyms and invented names (even in the case of the *Colloquium Heptaplomeres* none of the oldest copies bear the author's name), the frequent removal of the signature, and so on. In many cases this anonymity has never been broken, such as for the *Theophrastus redivivus*, the *Symbolum sapientiae*, *L'Art de ne rien croire*, the *Doutes des Pyrrhoniens*, and many other important works; in other cases the authorship was so well protected that even today there is debate over who the author or authors of *L'Esprit de Spinosa* or the *Traité des trois imposteurs* actually were.

One could object that a printed version of *Traité des trois imposteurs* was published in Holland in 1719. However, the entire run was immediately suppressed by the police, with the result that the work had to be circulated in manuscript, and today only four printed copies survive. Paradoxically, the exception proves the rule. A classic sentence with which one of these underground works begins (the *Symbolum sapientiae*) – a sentence that serves as exergue also to book I of David Hume's *Treatise of Human Nature* – clearly refers to the controls to which texts and ideas were subject: "Rare and happy are the times in which one is allowed to think whatever one wants and to say whatever one thinks" (Tacitus, *Historiae*, I, 1). Thus, also in the field of the "forbidden," the "clandestine" manuscript almost always preceded the "forbidden book." As the numerous cases of seizure by the police and of penalties confirm (think of Bonaventure de Fourcroy, whose text survives at the Bibliothèque de l'Arsenal only because it was confiscated by the police, or the misfortunes of the cleric Guillaume and of the more famous Diderot), it is not true that there was a certain tolerance of the clandestine manuscripts, that they were more "ignored than forbidden" by the authorities, and that their level of "toxicity" was inconsequential.[8] Even those scholars who minimize the importance of the manuscripts have to admit that the great *philosophes* not only drew inspiration from them but also undertook – above all in the second half of the eighteenth century – a large-scale campaign promoting the publication of these texts (naturally the printing of these texts was not authorized, so they were printed abroad and then circulated furtively).[9]

The second criterion is the "clandestinity of ideas": the clandestine philosophical manuscripts were messengers of a "full heterodoxy" that we could call "global," not "local." The exclusion did not regard one or another context but *all* (or almost all) of the contexts of the *Ancien Régime* – these manuscripts expressed a radical dissent that contrasted with *all* of modern Europe's orthodoxies. The *Colloquium*, like the *Theophrastus redivivus* and the *Mémoire* by Meslier, could not have been published in a Catholic country *or* a Protestant one, in an absolute monarchy *or* a republic. The clandestine authors were aware that it would be impossible to spread their ideas outside a circle protected by the manuscript form and often by anonymity. It could also be said that in certain situations the political pamphlets, the court satires, and the Jansenist texts were hunted down with even more determination, which placed the authors of these manuscripts in even greater danger. Yet texts of this type, albeit forbidden, did not advocate a total rejection of orthodoxy in all its aspects – philosophical, religious, moral, and political – as most of the "philosophical" manuscripts did.[10] Rightly, Martin Mulsow has coined the suggestive term "Moderne aus dem Untergrund" ("Enlightenment Underground")[11] to indicate forms of thought that were underground because they were peripheral to any "official" and "approved" culture, towards which they expressed a "radical" and "fundamental" dissent. In these cases clandestinity was not a contingent fact but a necessity intrinsic to the ideas they transmitted.

Finally, the last, but not least, criterion: these are clandestine *philosophical* manuscripts, even if the term "philosophy" is not meant here in the classical sense of the major systems of the seventeenth century. Rather, it is a philosophy opposed to most metaphysical systems because it reintroduces the "forgotten" currents of Classical-Renaissance naturalism and because in many aspects it anticipates the *philosophie* of the eighteenth century with its leaner, more polemical, almost warlike and propagandistic style. Moreover, while there was no lack of major systematic texts (such as, in different forms, the *Theophrastus redivivus* and Jean Meslier's *Mémoire*), their content was diametrically opposed to the "official" theologies and philosophies of the time. This does not mean that the clandestine authors were impervious to modern philosophical ideas. Indeed, while criticizing and contesting them, they also used, transformed, and adapted them for their own purposes, which were completely different from those of the original authors.

Certainly, the *corpus* of the philosophical manuscripts is varied and heterogeneous; it includes texts of just a few pages as well as much longer treatises (the thousand handwritten pages of *Theophrastus redivivus*!). Also, these manuscripts varied in terms of the quality of their philosophical arguments: in many cases those arguments are weak, almost propagandistic, but in other cases they deservedly accompany and at times boldly anticipate Enlightenment philosophical ideas. The case of atheism is exemplary:[12] the first treatise in the history of modern philosophy that openly, explicitly, and comprehensively supports the thesis of atheism is not a printed book but a clandestine manuscript, the *Theophrastus redivivus.* This manuscript dates back to 1659, more than a century before the era in which modern atheism, with D'Holbach, Diderot, and Naigeon, is often considered to have originated. The same thing could be said about "deism" or the idea of "natural religion," which appears first in the clandestine manuscripts (the *Colloquium*, the *Quatrains du déiste*, Challe's work) and not in the texts of Voltaire, Hume, and the early Diderot. Also, the program of a "natural history of religion," which traces the genealogy of religion in terms of completely natural and human factors, appeared and was developed brilliantly in the clandestine manuscripts well before the homonymous work by Hume published 1757.

These clandestine texts are "philosophical" in a broad sense; they discuss metaphysical, religious, and moral topics from a critical perspective and based fundamentally on what the authors consider to be the criterion of reason as opposed to authority, tradition, revelation. From the end of the Renaissance to the Libertine era and the birth of the Enlightenment, these manuscripts crossed eras of important cultural and philosophical transformations. We cannot speak of "clandestine philosophy" in the singular because the authors drew on different traditions and concepts: they referred to the scepticism of Montaigne and Bayle, to the rationalism of Descartes or Malebranche, to the metaphysics of Spinoza, or to the materialistic approach of Hobbes, or yet again to the empiricism of Locke. Likewise, there were different orientations: from scepticism to atheism, from deism to materialism, from Spinozism to pantheism. Had Leo Strauss ever taken into consideration the clandestine texts he would have realized that these "forbidden" manuscripts in modern times allowed freer, more direct, and more "radical" intellectual processing than the encrypted texts that had to be read "between the lines" and to which he devoted his study *Persecution and the Art of Writing* (1952).

The epoch in which the clandestine manuscripts were written and in which they flourished preceded what is viewed as the "official" start of the Enlightenment in the 1720s and 1730s, that is, the period between the publication of the *Lettres persanes* (1721) by Montesquieu and the *Lettres philosophiques* (1734) by Voltaire. Studying these clandestine texts allows us to work backwards to the sixteenth century (with the "deism" of the *Colloquium* by Bodin) and the early seventeenth century, with the rise of "libertine" philosophical dissidence, which would culminate in the "radical libertinism" of the *Theophrastus redivivus*. The clandestine communication of ideas certainly continued after the 1730s, but the impression is that it was more a quantitative expansion than a qualitative creation of original ideas. And after the 1750s, thanks also to the growing efficacy of the publishing industry abroad and to the spread of book trafficking, printed editions of the clandestine texts that had circulated as manuscripts (and continued to do so even after being printed) multiplied.[13]

One important lesson from a survey of the manuscripts is that there was no one single clandestine and heterodox philosophy being transmitted. From the ancients some of them drew on scepticism, some of them drew on cynicism, some of them drew on Epicureanism, and so on. Some of them drew on all of the above, oblivious to possible incompatibilities. From the medieval period and the Renaissance they harvested all sorts of heterodox ideas, stressing as a common denominator the fact that those ideas were in some way unwelcome to and subversive of prevailing and established theological, philosophical, and political dogmas.

In short, the answer to the question "What is a clandestine philosophical manuscript?" is neither solely empirical, referring back to the *corpus*, nor solely sociological or "ideological"; rather, it is historically founded, bearing in mind both the contents and the circumstances that prevented the publication of texts that were highly unorthodox and contrary to any orthodoxy. This clandestine and heterodox underground has been studied for more than one hundred years. To contextualize the significance of this new volume, it may be useful to define the various stages in the historical research on this topic.

(1) The first stage was pioneering, from the early discoveries of Gustave Lanson[14] in 1912 to Ira O. Wade's monograph in 1938.[15] The articles by Lanson, which retraced the university course he held in 1906–7, provided an ordered and systematic overview of the clandestine manuscripts for the first time, from Pierre Cuppé to Jean Meslier, from Boulainviller to Fréret and Dumarsais, even if he made numerous and at times glaring mistakes – for example, he attributed the *Promenade de Cléobule* to Boulainviller instead of Diderot; he claimed that the *Theophrastus redivivus* is "very similar and at times identical" to the *Traité des trois imposteurs*, which is patently incorrect; he considered Meslier a "Spinozist"; and so on. Above all, Lanson focused exclusively on France and the Enlightenment, since his aim was to study the formation of the "esprit philosophique." In his opinion there was no significant difference between Voltaire and Montesquieu on one hand and the much more radical authors of the clandestine manuscripts on the other. His articles also contain paradoxes: he includes a seventeenth-century text such as the *Theophrastus redivivus* in the context of the Enlightenment. This distortion in perspective, focused on eighteenth-century philosophy, would affect research for many years. Wade's book, which marked a real step forward, has a title that for the first time correctly defines the unity of its historiographical object – *The Clandestine Organization and Diffusion of Philosophical Ideas in France from 1700 to 1750* – even if it continues to include the *Theophrastus*, considering it to be the aggregation of other clandestine texts that are incorrectly presented as parts or translations of it. Regarding the repertory of the texts, Wade's step forward is significant: Lanson had found around thirty texts and a hundred or so copies; in 1938 Wade listed in his "Appendix" 102 titles and 392 copies, including, *inter alia*, manuscripts outside France and belonging to the British Library, the library of Leningrad, and Harvard University.

(2) The second stage can be seen as beginning with J.S. Spink's 1960 volume and as culminating with Margaret Jacob's, published in 1981.[17] The study of the clandestine works was now going beyond the link with the *Lumières*, and new historiographical categories were being born in which the clandestinity of ideas and documents played a primary role. Spink launched the "French free-thought" category, thus uniting the seventeenth and eighteenth centuries, and he had the fortunate intuition that it would be useful to work back to Gassendi and his legacy. Within this framework, the *Theophrastus redivivus* finally found its correct historical location. Jacob coined the new category "Radical Enlightenment," shifted attention to the Anglo-Dutch context, incorporated in the paradigm both the Newtonian scientific revolution and the English political revolution, and extended the study of the clandestine currents so that they formed a cosmopolitan arc that coincided not with the French *Lumières* but rather with the milieu between Holland and England, which in turn served as a bridge to Continental culture. In tandem with this new conceptualization contained in the notion of "Radical Enlightenment," the geography and chronology of early modern radicalism changed. The seventeenth-century milieu became even more important for understanding the birth of Enlightenment ideas. Two notable conferences relaunched research on clandestine texts: an Italian one held in Genoa, gathering Gregory, Canziani, Paganini, Ernst, and others and focusing on the seventeenth century and libertine culture; and a French one, assembled by Olivier Bloch (a key player in these studies), which concentrated on the eighteenth century.[18] It was during this period that the works of Meslier and Boulainviller[19] were published and that Miguel Benitez defended his pioneering thesis, which inaugurated a fuller and systematic cataloguing of the clandestine manuscripts.[20] In the 1980s Olivier Bloch began to develop an inventory of the clandestine manuscripts preserved in France, a task that today is being coordinated by Geneviève Artigas-Menant; the inventory (with material descriptions) of the numerous clandestine manuscripts kept at the Bibliothèque Mazarine (Paris) is now available online at http://www.bibliotheque-mazarine.fr/fr/impc.

(3) It could be said that the third stage, from the 1980s to the present, has been characterized by a veritable resurrection of the texts. Many have finally come back to light and have been printed. Fundamental texts that had never been published, such as the monumental *Theophrastus redivivus* (1659),[21] have now been edited, and new critical editions of what had been printed in the eighteenth century with significant modifications, such as *Militaire philosophe*,[22] have been issued. Other

major texts have finally been brought out in critical editions with notes and comments, first and foremost the *Traité des trois imposteurs ou L'Esprit de Spinosa.*[23] An important impetus has come from Richard H. Popkin, who has dealt above all with this last treatise but also with the circulation of Hebrew texts from a "philosophical" and "anti-Christian" point of view.[24] A great book series "Libre pensée et littérature clandestine," edited by Antony McKenna, has been assembled: this collection now has more than seventy titles (including studies and texts). Meanwhile, research is expanding into other areas; in Germany, for example, there are the book series edited by Winfried Schröder ("Philosophische Clandestina der deutschen Aufklärung" and "Freidenker der europäischen Aufklärung"). Two specialized journals are being published: *La Lettre Clandestine* (1992–) and *Libertinage et philosophie* (1996–), and the number of conferences and collections of studies is multiplying, especially in Europe. Miguel Benìtez has published the most complete repertory of the clandestine manuscripts,[25] along with some important collections of studies[26] and a weighty monograph on Meslier.[27] Winfried Schröder has refounded the history of modern atheism based on the clandestine texts.[28] Another key figure in this time of research and fresh editions is Gianluca Mori, whose critical edition of *L'Examen de la religion* by Du Marsais[29] and collection of texts edited with Alain Mothu, *Philosophes sans Dieu,*[30] deserve mention. Sergio Landucci has published a critical edition of *La Lettre de Thrasybule à Leucippe*, which he attributes to Fréret,[31] Antonella Del Prete has published the *Traité de l'infini créé* by Terrasson[32] and Bertram E. Schwarzbach the *Examens de la Bible* by Madame Du Châtelet.[33] These are just a few examples in a literature that is growing every year. These thirty-five years of catalogues, editions, and studies have greatly expanded and increased our knowledge of the clandestine world and have become the subject of specialized but at the same time interdisciplinary and pan-European studies. The geography of clandestinity now encompasses all of Europe, from Vienna to Helsinki and Saint Petersburg, from Parma to London, from Venice to Rouen, from Paris to Berlin, with areas of minimum intensity (Bavaria, most of Italy, and all of Spain are still dominated by inquisitorial control) and areas of maximum intensity, but all or almost all in contact with one another. Moreover, the seventeenth century has proved to be a very rich and important century for the production of clandestine texts; the principal progenitors of these *clandestina* certainly belong to this century. It cannot be claimed that the centre of gravity of the clandestine chronology has shifted completely, but the seventeenth century has certainly taken on an importance equal to if not greater than the eighteenth, including from the point of view of the originality of the contents. Recently, Jean-Pierre Cavaillé has published another important text of 1668: the *Apologie pour Machiavelle* by Louis Machon.[34]

(4) As a result of this quantitative and qualitative growth in studies and editions, current research has developed a wider and more mature vision of the clandestine phenomenon from the geographical, sociological, and chronological perspectives.[35] The fact that studies are now being conducted in previously unexplored or little-known areas such as Germany, the Netherlands, Denmark, and Spain is certainly a change. From a diachronic point of view, we can clearly see the continuity between the season of the "libertines" and that of the "clandestines," even before the advent of Spinoza. Moreover, we have become aware that Latin was an important language for clandestine communication for many years, even in the eighteenth century, as confirmed by the extraordinary good fortune of the *Colloquium Heptaplomeres*, one of the most widespread texts, of which almost a hundred copies survive. At the same time, the "philosophical" reputation of these manuscript texts, whose history is now included in what is still the most comprehensive and authoritative collective and general history of philosophy, the new *Ueberweg*, has been raised;[36] since then they have been included in their own right in the *Dictionnaire des philosophes français du XVIIe siècle*.[37] Moreover, starting with the Tenth International Congress on the Enlightenment (Dublin 1999),[38] every congress of the ISECS has included at least one session on the clandestine manuscripts.

This final stage has seen new historiographical categories flourish, partly due to the growth of the known clandestine corpus. The clandestines have found their place in the "radical enlightenment" of Jonathan Israel.[39] Studying mostly the German area, Martin Mulsow has established the category of the heterodox "underground," which includes not only the manuscript texts but also a vast amount of the anti-conformist and dissident university and academic production.[40] Gianni Paganini has proposed the category of "radical libertinism" to underscore the innovation and importance of seventeenth-century texts such as the *Theophrastus* and, more generally, to establish a link between libertinism and radical thought.[41] Work on published texts with subversive implications can now be situated in the larger context of the unpublished manuscripts.[42]

The research around the clandestine manuscripts has set out to fill libraries with new texts and new authors and to discover the "hidden" dimensions of other authors already known; but it has also done much more than that – it has forced us to rethink the big questions about the origins of the Enlightenment and its relationship with the previous era, and the multiplicity of trends and programs that crossed it. Likewise, the seventeenth century has turned out to be a crucial era for the innovation of philosophical ideas, besides the major systems. Crossing geographical, chronological, and ideological boundaries that once seemed deeply entrenched, the clandestine philosophical manuscripts have been one the great laboratories of our modernity. A powerful tool of research has recently become available: the digital platform "Philosophie cl@andestine."[43]

The time is now ripe to write a global history of European "clandestine" thought, as it is documented in the manuscripts, and the fundamental lines of that history are now beginning to be drawn. A synthesis has been provided by Gianni Paganini[44] that would have been impossible without the wide and cooperative research enterprise discussed above. This volume prepares the ground for further work.

This volume aims to contribute to a wider vision of the clandestine philosophical phenomenon. It is the result of a conference held on 4–5 March 2016 in Los Angeles, at the UCLA Center for Seventeenth- and Eighteenth-Century Studies, co-sponsored by the UCLA Department of History, the Dipartimento di Studi Umanistici (Università del Piemonte Orientale, Vercelli), and the Centro di Ricerca dell'Accademia dei Lincei, Rome. It was the first conference on the clandestine manuscripts held in English in the United States and, in general, outside Europe.

This volume's organization reflects the new trends that have been described in this introduction. Part One (Clandestinity, the Renaissance, and Early Modern Philosophy), with chapters by Winfried Schröder and Gianni Paganini, discusses the philosophical value of the clandestine texts, their sources in the sixteenth and seventeenth centuries, and the originality of their thought, above all as regarding a new way of expressing theories of philosophical atheism, which is quite different from the ways used at the end of the eighteenth century.

Part Two (Politics, Religion, and Clandestinity in Northern Europe), with chapters by Frederik Stjernfelt, Wiep van Bunge, and Rienk Vermij, explores the North European area (Denmark and the Netherlands), starting from a very early date, 1620, with special reference to radical clandestine reflection on religious and political themes.

Part Three (Gender, Sexuality, and New Morals), with chapters by Inger Leemans and Karen Hollewand, shows that the topics of sexual morality, gender, and relations between the sexes were the subject of special attention in clandestine circles, with results that had a significant impact on traditional concepts of the family and of individual and social ethics.

In Part Four (Clandestinity and the Enlightenment), with chapters by Whitney Mannies, Susana Seguin, Martin Mulsow, and Antony McKenna and Fabienne Vial-Bonacci, the volume enters the eighteenth century, from John Toland and Fontenelle to the Germany and Holland of Marc-Michel Rey, editor of numerous clandestine texts.

In Part Five (Toleration, Criticism, and Innovation in Religion), the chapters by John Marshall and Jeffrey D. Burson tackle general topics that held great significance for the Enlightenment: respectively, the concept of tolerance and early modern representations of Islam; and the pluralism of heterodoxies in the religious transformation of the eighteenth century. The clandestine manuscripts contributed greatly to both these topics.

Part Six (Spanish Developments), with chapters by Jonathan Israel and John Christian Laursen, extends the research to Spain and the early nineteenth century, when the circulation of clandestine philosophical literature contributed to the first liberal revolutions in a country that had long been on the margins of the "radical enlightenment."

NOTES

1 An important predecessor to the twentieth-century scholarly work was *Le Testament de Jean Meslier*, ed. Rudolf Charles (Amsterdam: A la Librairie Etrangère, 1864; repr. Hildesheim and New York: G. Olms, 1974).

2 On this question see the rich dossier in *La Lettre Clandestine*, vol. 12, 2003, 13–222, on *Lecteurs et collectionneurs de textes clandestins à l'âge classique.*

3 In general, on the status of manuscripts, see Roger Chartier, "Le manuscrit à l'âge de l'imprimé," *La Lettre Clandestine*, vol. 7, 1998, 175–93; for the English-language world, Harald Love, *Scribal Publication in Seventeenth Century England* (Oxford: Clarendon, 1993). On clandestinity, cf. Geneviève Artigas-Menant, *Du secret des clandestins à la propagande voltairienne* (Paris: Champion, 2001).

4 On this, see Alain Mothu, *La Pensée en cornue. Matérialisme, alchimie et savoirs secrets à l'âge classique* (Paris and Milan: S.E.H.A. – Archè, 2012).

5 The issue of the "limits" of the corpus was discussed at a round table that was published in *La Lettre Clandestine*, vol. 7, 1998, 343–98, on *Limites du corpus des manuscrits philosophiques clandestins.* It did not arrive at definitive conclusions. In the conclusion, Geneviève Artigas Menant recommended

the use of "empirical" criteria (398), while we are trying to arrive at better definitions and limits of the genre. On the relations between the unpublished and the clandestine, see the dossier in *Le clandestin et l'inédit à l'âge classique* in *La Lettre Clandestine,* vol. 11, 2002, 13–131.

6 Cf. Günther Gawlick and Friedrich Niewöhner, eds, *Jean Bodins Colloquium Heptaplomeres* (Wiesbaden: Harrasowitz, 1996); and Ralph Häfner, ed., *Bodinus Polymeres. Studien zu Jean Bodins Spätwerk* (Wiesbaden: Harrassowitz, 1999).

7 The case of Toland is interesting because this author played deliberately with the distinction between printed and circulated. Cf. Justin Champion, "Publiés mais non imprimés: John Toland et la circulation des manuscrits," *La Lettre Clandestine,* vol. 7, 1998, 301–42. On the techniques of writing in an age of censorship and persecution, see Jean-Pierre Cavaillé, *Dis/simulations. Jules-César Vanini, François La Mothe Le Vayer, Gabriel Naudé, Louis Machon et Torquato Accetto. Religion, morale et politique au XVII*[e] siècle (Paris: Champion, 2002).

8 We refer to the thesis of Alain Mothu in "Le manuscrit philosophique existe-t-il?," in Jean-Louis Lebrave and Almuth Grésillon, *Ecrire aux XVIIe et XVIIIe siècles* (Paris: Editions du CNRS, 2000), 59–74. The mentioned cases, among others, actually support the opposite thesis.

9 As examples we supply a selective and not exhaustive list of publications in the eighteenth century of manuscripts that had previously circulated only in manuscript: *Traité des trois imposteurs*: 1719, 1721, 1768, 1775, 1776, 1777, 1780, 1793; *Nouvelles liberté de penser*: 1743 ; *Examen de la religion*: 1745; *Extrait del Testament* di Meslier: 1762; *Evangile de la Raison*: 1764, 1765, 1768; *Lettre de Thrasybule à Leucippe*: 1765 (in *Œuvres* of Fréret: 1775, 1776, 1787–92; *Le Militaire philosophe*: 1768; *Examen critique des apologistes de la religion chrétienne*: 1766, 1767, 1768, 1775, 1777; *Le Ciel ouvert à tous les hommes*: 1768, 1783; *Traité de l'Infini créé*: 1769; *Israël vengé*: 1770; *Jordanus Brunus redivivus*: 1771; *Dialogues sur l'âme*: 1771; *La fausseté des miracles des deux Testaments*: 1775. A list of the clandestine works published by the famous editor Marc-Michel Rey may be found in the chapter in this volume by Antony McKenna.

10 On the nexus between clandestinity and repression of ideas, see the dossier *Le délit d'opinion à l'âge classique: du colporteur au philosophe,* in *La Lettre Clandestine,* vol. 17, 2009, 15–194. There are interesting remarks on the heterodoxy of the clandestine manuscripts in Olivier Bloch, "Matérialisme et clandestinité: tradition, écriture, lecture," in idem, *Matière à histoires* (Paris: Vrin, 1997), 273–86.

11 Martin Mulsow, *Moderne aus dem Untergrund. Radikale Frühaufklärung in Deutschland 1680–1720* (Hamburg: F. Meiner, 2002). English translation: *Enlightenment Underground: Radical Germany, 1680–1720* (Charlottesville:

University of Virginia Press, 2015). See also the reviews by Gianni Paganini: "Modernità dalla clandestinità, " *Giornale Critico della Filosofia Italiana*, vol. 84, 2005, 172–80; and John Christian Laursen, *Journal of the History of Philosophy* 41 (2003): 419–20. Martin Mulsow has now reissued a revised edition of that volume and added a second volume, under this general title: *Radikale Frühaufklärung in Deutschland 1680–1720*, vol. 1: *Moderne aus dem Untergrund*; vol. 2: *Clandestine Vernunft* (Göttingen: Wallstein, 2018).

12 As illustrated in the chapters by Paganini and Schröder in this volume.

13 Sometimes the printed version was a fundamental distortion of the original manuscript. This was the case with the deistic work of Robert Challe, *Difficultés sur la religion proposées au père Malebranche*, which was transformed into an atheistic text by Naigeon and published with the aggressive title *Militaire philosophe*. Voltaire did the opposite with the atheistic *Mémoire* of Meslier, published as a deistic *Extrait du Testament du curé Meslier* (1762).

14 Gustave Lanson, "Questions diverses sur l'histoire de l'esprit philosophique en France avant 1750," *Revue d'Histoire Littéraire de la France*, vol. 19 (1912), 1–29, 293–317.

15 Ira O. Wade, *The Clandestine Organization and Diffusion of Philosophic Ideas in France from 1700 to 1750* (Princeton: Princeton University Press, 1938). Cf. also Wade, *Voltaire and Madame du Châtelet* (Princeton: Princeton University Press, 1941); Norman Torrey, *Voltaire and the English Deists* (New Haven: Yale University Press, 1930; (new ed., 1967); Rudolf Brummer, *Studien zur französischen Aufklärungsliteratur im Anschluss an J.A. Naigeon* (Sprache und Kultur der germanischromanischen Völker, C. Romanistische Reihe, Bd XI, Breslau, 1932); and Paul Vernière, *Spinoza et la pensée française avant la Révolution* (Paris, PUF, 1954).

16 John S. Spink, *French Free-Thought from Gassendi to Voltaire* (London: Athlone Press, 1960).

17 Margaret C. Jacob, *The Radical Enlightenment: Pantheists, Freemasons, and Republicans* (London, Boston, and Sydney: 1981; second ed., The Temple Publishers, 2003). Cf. also Antoine Adam, *Le mouvement philosophique dans la première moitié du* XVIIIe *siècle* (Paris: Société d'édition d'enseignement supérieur, 1967).

18 Tullio Gregory, Gianni Paganini, Guido Canziani, et al., *Ricerche su letteratura libertina e letteratura clandestina nel Seicento* (Florence: La Nuova Italia, 1981); Olivier Bloch, ed., *Le matérialisme au XVIIIe siècle et la littérature clandestine* (Paris: Vrin, 1982).

19 Jean Meslier, *Œuvres complètes*, ed. Roland Desné, Jean Deprun, and Albert Soboul, 3 vols (Paris: Anthropos, 1970); Henry de Boulainviller, *Œuvres philosophiques*, ed. Renée Simon, 2 vols (The Hague: M. Nijhoff, 1973 and

1975). In 1970 Roland Mortier edited *Les difficultés sur la religion* (Bruxelles: Presses de l'Université de Bruxelles, 1970), and in 1969 Alain Niderst edited *L'Ame matérielle* (Paris: Nizet, 1969; new ed. Champion: Paris, 2003). In 1981 Paolo Cristofolini edited *Le Ciel ouvert à tous les homme* by Pierre Cuppé: *Il Cielo aperto di Pierre Cuppé,* con un'edizione critica del *Ciel ouvert à tous les hommes* (Florence: L.S. Olschki, 1981). On Boulainviller, see Stefano Brogi, *Il cerchio dell'universo. Libertinismo, spinozismo e filosofia della natura in Boulainvilliers* (Florence : Leo S. Olschki, 1993).

20 Miguel Benitez, *Contribution à l'étude de la littérature matérialiste clandestine en France au XVIIIe siècle* (thesis, Paris: Nanterre, 1978).

21 Guido Canziani and Gianni Paganini, eds, *Theophrastus redivivus,* first and critical edition with commentary, 2 vols (Florence: La Nuova Italia, 1981–2), now distributed by Franco Angeli Editore, Milan. See also the study by Tullio Gregory, *Theophrastus redivivus. Erudizione e ateismo nel Seicento* (Napoli: Morano, 1979).

22 Robert Challe, *Difficultés sur la religion proposte au Père Malebranche,* ed. F. Deloffre and F. Moureau (Genève: Droz, 2000).

23 Françoise Charles-Daubert, *Le "Traité des trois imposteurs" et "L'Esprit de Spinosa." Philosophie clandestine entre 1678 et 1768* (Oxford: Voltaire Foundation, 1999); cf. Silvia Berti (ed.), *Trattato dei tre impostori* (Turin: Einaudi, 1994).

24 Cf. esp. Silvia Berti, Françoise Charles-Daubert, and R.H. Popkin, eds, *Heterodoxy, Spinozism, and Free-Thought in Early Eighteenth-Century Europe: Studies on the "Traité des trois imposteurs"* (Dordrecht: M. Nihoff, 1996); R.H. Popkin and A. Vanderjagt, eds, *Scepticism and Irreligion in the Seventeenth and Eighteenth Centuries* (Leiden: Brill, 1993).

25 Miguel Benítez, *La Face cachée des Lumières. Recherches sur les manuscrits philosophiques clandestins de l'âge classique* (Paris and Oxford: Universitas and Voltaire Foundation, 1996), 20–61; the list of manuscripts is brought up to date in idem, *La cara oculta de las Luces. Investigaciones sobre los manuscritos filosóficos calndestinos de los siglos XVII y XVIII* (Valencia: 2003), 33–82.

26 Miguel Benitez, *La face cachée*; idem, *Le Foyer clandestin des Lumières: nouvelles recherches sur les manuscrits clandestins* (Paris: Champion, 2013), 2 vols. Benítez also published a modern edition of *Doutes sur la religion. L'œuvre libertine de Bonaventure de Fourcroy* (Paris: Champion, 2005).

27 M. Benitez, *Les yeux de la raison. Le matérialisme athée de Jean Meslier* (Paris: Champion, 2012).

28 A rich body of manuscripts was analysed in Winfried Schröder, *Ursprünge des Atheismus. Untersuchungen zur Metaphysik- und Religionskritik des 17. und 18. Jahrhunderts* (Stuttgart: Fromman-Holzboog, 1998), 395–526.

29 Cesar Chesneau Du Marsais, *L'Examen de la religion*, ed. Gianluca Mori (Oxford: Voltaire Foundation, 1998).

30 Alain Mothu and Gianluca Mori, eds, *Textes athées clandestins du XVIIIe siècle* (Paris: Champion, 2005).

31 Nicolas Fréret, *La Lettre de Thrasybule à Leucippe*, ed. Sergio Landucci (Florence: Olschki, 1986). The text was republished in *Philosophes sans Dieu*, 51–186.

32 Jean Terrasson, *Traité de l'infini créé*, ed. Antonella Del Prete (Paris: Champion, 2007).

33 Gabrielle-Émilie Le Tonnelier de Breteil, marquise Du Châtelet-Lomond, *Examens de la Bible*, édités et annotés par Bertam E. Schwarzbach (Paris: Honoré Champion, 2011).

34 Louis Machon, *Apologie pour Machiavelle*, ed. Jean-Pierre Cavaillé (Paris: Champion, 2016). An important conference directed attention to the Italian sources of much of heterodox thought: Jean-Pierre Cavaillé and Didier Foucault, eds, *Sources antiques de l'irréligion moderne: le relais italien* (Toulouse: Collection de l'ECRIT, 2001).

35 Important contributions to this phase can be found in Antony McKenna and Alain Mothu, eds, *La philosophie clandestine à l'âge classique* (Oxford and Paris: Voltaire Foundation–Universitas, 1997); and Alain Mothu and Antonella Del Prete, eds, *Révolution scientifique et libertinage* (Turnhout: Brepols, 2000). Cf. also Marie-Hélène Cotoni, *L'Exégèse du Nouveau Testament dans la philosophie française du* XVIIIe *siècle* (Oxford and Paris: Voltaire Foundation–Touzot, 1984); Antony McKenna, *De Pascal à Voltaire. Le rôle des* Pensées *de Pascal dans l'histoire des idées entre 1670 et 1734* (Oxford: Voltaire Foundation, 1990).

36 For the seventeenth century, see Gianni Paganini, "Haupttendenzen der clandestinen Philosophie," in *Ueberweg. Grundriss der Geschichte der Philosophie. Die Philosophie des 17. Jahrhunderts*, ed. Jean-Pierre Schobinger, vol. 1 (Basel: Schwabe, 1998), 120–95. For the eighteenth century, see Antony McKenna, "Die frühe Aufklärung, §4: Die philosophische Clandestina", in *Ueberweg, Grundriss der Geschichte der Philosophie, Die Philosophie des 18. Jahrhunderts*, 2/1: *Frankreich*, ed. J. Rohbeck und H. Holzhey (Basle: Schwabe, 2008), 47–83.

37 *Dictionnaire des philosophes français du XVII*[e] *siècle*, ed. Luc Foisneau (Paris: Classiques Garnier, 2015). See G. Paganini, "La Pensée clandestine," 59–63; G. Canziani, "Theophrastus redivivus," 1681a–5a; G. Paganini: "Anti-Bigot ou Le Faux Dévotieux," 141b–143b; "Art de ne rien croire," 169b–71b; "Doutes des Pyrrhoniens," 576b–80a; "Fourcroy, Bonaventure de," 740a–41b; "Vallone, Yves de," 1724a–7b.

38 Gianni Paganini, Miguel Benitez, and James Dybikowski, eds, *Scepticisme, clandestinité et libre pensée / Scepticism, Clandestinity, and Free-Thinking* (Paris: Champion, 2002).

39 Jonathan Israel, *Radical Enlightenment: Philosophy and the Making of Modernity, 1650–1750* (Oxford: Oxford University Press, 2001), 684–703.

40 See Martin Mulsow, *Moderne aus dem Untergrund. Radikale Frühaufklärung in Deutschland 1680–1720* (Hamburg: F. Meiner, 2002).

41 Gianni Paganini, "Wie aus Gesetzgebern Betrüger werden. Eine philosophische Archäologie des 'radikalen' Libertinismus," in Jonathan Israel and Martin Mulsow, eds, *Radikalaufklärung* (Berlin: Suhrkamp, 2014), 49–91; idem, "Qu'est-ce qu'un 'libertin radical'? Le *Theophrastus redivivus*," in *Libertin ! Usage d'une invective aux XVIe s XVIIe siècles*, ed. Thomas Berns, Anne Staquet, and Monique Weis, eds (Paris: Classiques Garnier, Paris 2013), 213–30. Recently the *Theophrastus redivivus* has been the subject of Nicole Gengoux, *Un Athéisme philosophique à l'âge classique: le Theophrastus redivivus* (Paris: Champion, 2014), 2 vols.

42 See, e.g., Lynn Hunt, Margaret Jacob, and Wijnand Mijnhardt, eds, *Bernard Picart and the First Global Vision of Religion* (Los Angeles: Getty Research Institute, 2010); Lynn Hunt, Margaret C. Jacob, and Wijnand Mijnhart, *The Book That Changed Europe: Picart and Bernard's* Religious Ceremonies of the World (Cambridge, MA: Belknap Press, 2010). The book by Maria Susana Seguin, *Science et religion dans la pensée française du XVIIIe siècle. Le mythe du Déluge universel* (Paris: H. Champion, 2001), is extensively based on clandestine authors and texts (Challe, Maillet, Fréret, Boulainvilliers, Boulanger, Dumarsais, many anonyms).

43 See ch. 8, Appendix by Susana Seguin.

44 Gianni Paganini, *Les philosophies clandestines à l'âge classique* (Paris: PUF, 2005); Italian expanded edition: *Introduzione alle filosofie clandestine* (Roma and Bari: Laterza, 2008).

PART ONE

CLANDESTINITY, THE RENAISSANCE, AND EARLY MODERN PHILOSOPHY

Chapter One

Why, and to What End, Should Historians of Philosophy Study Early Modern Clandestine Texts?

WINFRIED SCHRÖDER

Among historians of philosophy the clandestine philosophical texts of the seventeenth and eighteenth centuries do not enjoy the highest reputation. They are often deprecated as works of poor theoretical quality far below the level of serious philosophical works of that era such as, for instance, those of Leibniz, Bayle, or Locke. They may be appreciated as relevant sources by historians of mentality, social historians, and the like, but historians of *philosophy* do not view them as worthy of study. Of course, one could counter that there are at least *some* clandestine texts of good quality.[1] A number of those treatises, which are allowedly not equal in rank to those of the prominent philosophers just named, do meet the normal criteria of theoretical substance and argumentative elaboration. However, it should in fact be admitted that the greater part of the clandestine *corpus* exhibits considerable shortcomings in these respects. In particular, the (so to speak) technical, argumentative deficits are often palpable. For evidence, we only need take a cursory glance at the flagships of the "philosophical underground," the two treatises *Of the Three Impostors.* The author of one of them – the French *Traité des trois imposteurs* – reduces the elaborate ontology of Spinoza's *Ethics* to a popular atheistic metaphysics or rather *Weltanschauung.* The remark with which he introduces the sketch of his "clear and simple ideas" on metaphysics (*idées … claires* [*et*] *simples*)[2] is revealing: "there is no need for lofty speculations […]; it requires only a little common sense [*un peu de bon sens*] to perceive that" anthropomorphism is false, that there is no such God as the divine person found in the teachings of Christian philosophers and theologians. Without any serious philosophical justification, he dogmatically declares that there is no theistic God, but instead an immanent material cause of the universe.[3] Many other clandestine texts fare no better.

Matthias Knutzen, the first known atheist (at least in Europe) and thus a prominent figure of the philosophical underground, was aptly branded a "Hyde Park atheist" by Don Cameron Allen in his *Doubt's Boundless Sea.*[4] Allen's polemical label – "Hyde Park atheist"– fits perfectly with many other underground philosophers or *dilettanti* philosophers. Take for example the awkward composition of the clandestine "bible" of atheism, Jean Meslier's *Mémoire de pensées* or *Testament.*

Needless to say, most of the clandestine authors were no academic professionals. Some of them sharply repudiated the academic style of delivery and chose instead a popular, manifesto-like approach to articulating their philosophical messages. So these deficits in academic elaboration and articulation can easily be explained. Even so, they are there. Thus we have little choice but to explain how and to what extent the study of the clandestine philosophical literature may profit the historiography of philosophy and why it is worth studying even those texts of admittedly poor quality. This is what I am going to do in the first part of this chapter. In the second and final part I shall address some texts that illustrate that in some cases the "literary underground" provided the appropriate setting for developing well-thought-out theories and arguments – theories that in those days could not have been advanced anywhere else but in the *milieu clandestin.*

I

As historians of philosophy we might ask ourselves – and this is my first question – why we should not just ignore the *Traité des trois imposteurs*, Meslier's and Knutzen's pamphlets, and the like, and leave research on them to historians of mentality or social historians. Let me begin with what I have to admit is a somewhat trivial statement: the period to which the clandestine texts belong – the early modern era and the age of the Enlightenment – was a period of unprecedented dynamics, particularly in the fields of philosophy of religion and of metaphysics. What we encounter in the philosophical documents of these centuries is a more or less radical break with the previously uncontested philosophical and religious/theological tradition, ranging from a break with Christian dogmas, the rejection of divine revelation, and the denial of the immortality of the soul and of divine providence (with its political implications), to the repudiation of metaphysical theism.

Now, as historians of philosophy our task is not simply to study and reconstruct sophisticated high-level philosophical theories, but to try to understand the *process* of modernization just mentioned. When did this break with tradition commence? How far did its protagonists go? Did they go to the extremes? More concretely, did they entirely reject any form of theism and adopt atheism? And if so, when and why did they choose these options? Was this spectrum of alternatives to the tradition subject to change? Was it possible to be an atheist at any time between 1600 and 1800? In answering these questions, we may form an adequate picture of the spectrum of philosophical innovations in the early modern era and the dynamics within this spectrum. And having done so we will find ourselves in a position that enables us to rectify several current myths concerning the origins of modernity, of the Enlightenment, of secularism, et cetera. And needless to say, there are lots of myths, legends, and dubious "grand narratives" about the sources of modernity on offer in the academic market.

One of these literally "grand narratives" is set forth in Charles Taylor's impressive volume *A Secular Age.* As a matter of course the emergence of the most radical variety of secularism – atheism – is dealt with extensively in this book. In this respect Taylor draws on Michael Buckley's *At the Origins of Modern Atheism.* This book, published in 1987, is still held in high regard by anglophone scholars.[5] Now, what did Taylor learn from Buckley's – as he praises it – "penetrating book"[6]? Well, we are told that Diderot, d'Holbach, and the mid-eighteenth-century French materialists were "the first of the atheists, not simply in chronological reckoning."[7] Buckley's complete attention is focused on the later eighteenth-century French materialistic atheists (except Meslier; e.g., 269); he makes no mention whatsoever of texts prior to Diderot and d'Holbach, simply because he ignored the clandestine literature and apparently had not even read Ira O. Wade's classic monograph.

If we narrow our view to the *corpus* of printed publications and philosophical "classics," as did Buckley and his readers, our perception of the process whereby the traditional philosophical and religious world view was ultimately overcome is distorted. Yet for quite some time several clandestine sources of early atheism have been readily accessible. To start, we must mention the anonymous *Theophrastus redivivus,* a text composed a hundred years before Diderot and d'Holbach. It is thanks to Tullio Gregory, and to Guido Canziani and Gianni Paganini, who published the *Theophrastus*[8] several years before Buckley's book, that we have learned that atheism dates back to the middle of the seventeenth century, which means it emerged in an intellectual environment significantly different from that of eighteenth-century France.

Considering this historiographic and editorial work, it is all the more surprising that some of the old myths about the emergence of atheism persist. Barry Allen, who relies on Michael Buckley's book and hence is not familiar with pre-1750 sources, does not stand alone in affirming that "atheism was a politically driven attack upon ... Christian theology."[9] Of course, a fair number of atheists of the *Siècle des Lumières* were fervent anticlericals who opposed the *Ancien Régime* and who battled Catholicism as the ideology that stabilized it. These radicals in fact used the propagation of atheism as an instrument in their political campaign; most prominent among them was Jean Meslier, who in his *Testament* expressed his ardent desire "that all the mighty on earth and all noblemen would be hanged and strangulated with the intestines of priests."[10]

Likewise Matthias Knutzen, who was something of a late baroque anarchist, understood himself as a spearhead against both the celestial and the terrestrial authorities. However, examples like these are not representative of all the early atheists and therefore do not provide a serious basis for a genealogy of atheism altogether. But this is exactly what Barry Allen and the historians who share his view assume: according to them, atheism is rooted in political motivations and therefore lacks a rational, philosophical justification. Yet on the basis of a non-selective inspection of the pertinent sources, this general view cannot be maintained: beginning with the *Theophrastus redivivus* and later on the *Symbolum sapientiae* up to several eighteenth-century French treatises, there are numerous atheistic texts in which theism is rejected on epistemological, psychological, or metaphysical grounds and in which a political (let alone revolutionary) agenda is totally absent. The overall picture of early atheism is not as simple as the above-named historians assume. Atheism had many fathers. Anticlericalism combined with the struggle against the *Ancien Régime* was only one of them. If we look not only to the philosophers who were visible to the public and belonged to the widely accepted canon of philosophy, but also to authors of the clandestine *souterrain*, the aforementioned genealogy of atheism must at least be relativized, or even dismissed as conjecture plucked out of thin air.

It is not only the issue of the emergence of atheism that requires recourse to the *corpus* of clandestine philosophical texts. Take, for example, the dynamics in early modern and Enlightenment moral philosophy. What were the consequences of the anti-traditional movements in this field? Was moral *nihilism* the final result of the critique of morality, as atheism was in the realm of metaphysics? Or to put it rather bluntly: was the marquis de Sade the legitimate heir to the Enlightenment, as

Horkheimer and Adorno once maintained and many others echoed? Charles Taylor[11] comes to mind again, as does Lester G. Crocker, who summed up this view with the following pointed remark: "There is nothing in Sade's nihilism which, in essence or in embryo, is not also found" in "eighteenth-century philosophy."[12] I cannot go into this here in detail, but let me make a few very brief remarks.

Objections to morality were not infrequently raised in texts of the philosophical underground. Some of them went very far indeed: the *Theophrastus redivivus* launched extraordinarily bold attacks against sacrosanct norms and institutions.[13] For example, its author challenged the institution of monogamous marriage.[14] He did not recommend polygamy in its stead, and this – in 1659 – for a remarkable reason: "polygamy gives freedom only to men, and not to women, who according to nature must enjoy the same right to a free conduct."[15] It is no anachronism to say that the author of the *Theophrastus* propagated sexual liberation: "the greatest injustice is that which restricts natural freedom and suppresses bodily love by laws."[16] And he adds that we must not forget that women have "the same lust" as men. Therefore, he (or she? Who knows whether this anonymous text was not written by a woman?) concludes that "the unification of a man and a woman must be free and unconstrained, so that both may have intercourse which whoever they wish and as often as they want."[17]

Of course, these audacious reflections have little to do with philosophy in the strict sense. I have quoted them because they reveal strikingly that the author of *Theophrastus* obviously stopped at nothing and was ready to go all the way. Therefore one might wonder which views he and his like entertained in ethical *theory*. For the sake of brevity, I confine myself to a text that is, for the most part, in line with the *Theophrastus*, but whose author sets out his position in a more succinct way. That text is the anonymous late-seventeenth-century treatise *De origine boni et mali*, probably composed by the author of the atheistic *Symbolum sapientiae* and one of the most radical texts in this respect. First, his (so to speak) meta-ethical position is in fact radical: "good" and "evil," the principles of justice, and the *ius naturae* are "ex conventione"[18] – nothing but human inventions.[19] Second, in normative ethics, too, the author goes far beyond the moderate critique of morality we normally encounter in texts of that period that challenge Christian morality, its ascetism and demonization of pleasure, and so on. According to the author of *De origine*, moral norms need not be obeyed *in principle*. We need not and should not restrict our desires by moral imperatives and the so-called *ius naturae*.[20] The instincts ("instinctus naturales")[21] we share with animals suffice for us to live peacefully together. Humans do not rely on larger social associations like civil societies or states. Small groups ("minores societates"[22]) such as the Aristotelean *oikos* ("societas domestica")[23] are sufficient to guarantee survival; indeed, they are the only natural association, a fact he sees corroborated by accounts of the (as he believes) peaceful way of life of the "peoples we call savages [*gentes quas feras vocamus*]."[24] The anonymous author may be charged with naivety, but he is certainly no anti-moralist.

Again we benefit from a favourable hermeneutical position when we turn towards clandestine philosophers. Writing under the protection of anonymity, the author of *De origine*, like the other underground writers, had no reason to hide his real views. Now, as we have just seen, he did *not* go to the extreme in the realm of morality, although he was not prevented from doing so by the threat of sanctions. Therefore we may conclude that moral nihilism – unlike atheism – was no option, even for the most radical intellectuals of the underground.

II

In order to present a specimen of a well-thought-out theory developed in the philosophical underground, I refer to a peculiar variety of atheism. The relevant texts are the late-seventeenth-century *Symbolum sapientiae*[25] and three texts dating from the subsequent century: the *Lettre de Thrasybule à Leucippe*,[26] the *Lettres à Sophie*,[27] and the *Jordanus Brunus redivivus*.[28] The kind of atheism their authors advocate is not a politically motivated denial of the existence of God, as in the case of Meslier, nor does it have anything to do with the dubious naturalism of d'Holbach, who promised scientific explanations likely to make a divine creator superfluous but was in fact unable to deliver. I am referring to the question of the origin of life and the structures of the biosphere, a central topic in eighteenth-century debates. For this phenomenon d'Holbach – a century before Darwin – had no explanation, whereas theists – by inference to the best explanation – could appeal to God the creator. The wording "dubious naturalism" may seem somewhat polemical. But we have to keep in mind that even Richard Dawkins stressed that the enterprise of developing a naturalistic anti-theistic world view was a futile undertaking in the eighteenth, let alone the seventeenth century. "I could not imagine," so we read in his *The Blind Watchmaker*, "being an atheist at any time before 1859."

Unlike Meslier or d'Holbach, some clandestine philosophers rejected theism on the basis of methodological reflections. Instead of simply trumpeting forth or dogmatically asserting that God does not exist, they carefully considered the possibilty of proving the non-existence of a given entity. All of these authors begin by admitting that the non-existence of any entity can only be proved if contradictions within its concepts can be detected. "L'Athéisme ne se prouve pas mieux que le Théisme"[29] – "There is no definitive proof of either atheism or theism," as the *Jordanus Brunus redivivus* succinctly put it. Therefore, if the discussion is about "*a* God" (whatever his attributes may be), we cannot demonstrate that such a God does not exist. And hence we should – so it seems – suspend our judgment.[30] Since there is no way to prove either theism or atheism, the appropriate stance is something like what today we call agnosticism.

But according to these authors we must go a step further. For whenever two opposing claims are supported by equally strong or equally weak evidence, a procedural principle decides the issue, namely, *Affirmanti incumbit probatio*[31] – that is, the burden of proof lies upon the proponent of the strong claim, not upon the opponent. And this means that if there is no positive evidence in favour of the strong claim, it is always the weaker claim that has to be affirmed, whereas the stronger claim has to be rejected. This principle is structurally identical with the juridical presumption of innocence in court (one is considered innocent unless proven guilty). Applied to the dispute on the agenda (atheism versus theism), it yields the following consequences:

First: There is a probative asymmetry between the assertion and the denial of theism (and of any other thesis): "La non-existence d'une chose n'a pas besoin de preuves: c'est l'existence qui doit être démontrée."[32] So the atheist (who makes the weaker claim) is entitled to reject theism (unless sufficient evidence is produced in favour of theism).[33]

Second: The atheist need not prove the non-existence of God by producing counter-evidence. In other words, the claim that God does not exist is a *pre*sumption based on methododological considerations (*praesumtio*[34] / *presomtion*[35], as these authors explicitly express themselves). It is not an *as*sumption that has to be supported by evidence.[36]

Third: The position of the atheist is even much stronger, if the theistic God – a God with specific attributes – is in question. In that case the atheist can claim that he has proved the non-existence of God if he is able to detect contradictions in the concept of a perfectly good and omnipotent God.[37]

Fourth: The atheist is not required to offer a naturalistic metaphysics as an alternative to theism. He need not provide better answers to the great metaphysical questions. He may simply remain sceptical about them and leave them open. The authors I am referring to clearly speak out in favour of such a "metaphysical ascetism." Nicolas Fréret, who wrote the *Lettre de Thrasybule à Leucippe*, explicitly restricts his criticism to the "rejet"[38] of theism without any pretension to a philosophical explanation of the totality: "nous ne pouvons [pas] expliquer les causes de tous les effets."[39] An alternative materialistic metaphysics is neither possible nor required in order to defeat theism. If we can prove the arguments in favour of God's existence to be invalid, the presumption is valid that God does not exist, and hence we are entitled to "reject" (*rejetter*) theism.[40] But we should abstain from switching to an atheistic dogmatism: "If we have rejected the false ideas of theism, we should leave it at that. We should not bother with substituting another opinion in the place of the opinion we have relinquished" (contentons-nous de rejetter les chimères que l'on nous débite sur ce sujet et ne nous embarrassons point de mettre une autre opinion à la place de celle que nous quittons[41]). The supporters of this kind of atheism were immune to a most problematic temptation to which d'Holbach and his like succumbed, namely, to developing naturalistic theories that in fact they could not seriously offer in those days. Instead, the author of the *Symbolum* and kindred spirits chose an approach based on methodological considerations.

As I have said, this was not the way in which atheism was brought forth by prominent philosophers such as d'Holbach. It was actually about three hundred years later that it was advocated, in the 1970s, by Antony Flew in his famous article (and afterwards, book) *The Presumption of Atheism.*[42]

By contrast, the atheistic theories of Meslier or d'Holbach are not very attractive, either from a philosophical point of view or from a scientific one. Yet normally these naturalistic atheists are presented to us as *the* representative figures of early atheism. One may be left with the suspicion that for historians sympathizing with Christianity (like both Buckley and Taylor), d'Holbach must have been a preferred opponent. Certainly, the French baron was the most prominent and most successful propagandist of atheism in that period. But he is testimony to the – what they would have us believe is ubiquitous – theoretical weakness of early atheism. To rectify this view – and the other historiographic myths mentioned earlier – we in fact need to study the clandestine *corpus*. For the *littérature clandestine* comprises substantial and innovative theories that were not developed anywhere else during that period. It is to these texts that historians of philosophy should pay particular attention in order to achieve a more adequate understanding of the history of metaphysics[43] and philosophy of religion.

NOTES

1 Antony McKenna and Alain Mothu, eds, *La philosophie clandestine à l'âge classique* (Oxford: Voltaire Foundation, 1996); Olivier Bloch, ed., *Le matérialisme du XVIIIe siècle et la littérature clandestine* (Paris: Vrin, 1982); Miguel Benítez, *La face cachée des Lumières: recherches sur les manuscrits philosophiques clandestins de l'âge classique* (Paris: Universitas, 1996); Gianni Paganini, *Les philosophies clandestines à l'âge classique* (Paris: Presses Universitaires de France, 2005); idem, *Introduzione alle filosofie clandestine* (Rome: Laterza 2008).

2 Anon., *Traité des trois imposteurs. Traktat von den drei Betrügern*, ed. Winfried Schröder (Hamburg: Meiner, 2nd ed., 1994), ii.11, 36: "Ces idées sont claires, simples & les seules mêmes qu'un bon esprit puisse se former de Dieu."

3 Anon., *Traité des trois imposteurs*, i.4, 8: "Pour en venir à bout, il n'est besoin ni des hautes spéculations, ni de pénétrer fort avant dans les secrets de la nature. On n'a besoin que d'un peu de bon sens pour juger que Dieu n'est ni colère ni jaloux; que la justice & la miséricorde sont des faux titres qu'on lui attribue; & que ce que les Prophêtes & les Apôtres en ont dit ne nous apprend ni sa nature ni son essence."

4 Don C. Allen, *Doubt's Boundless Sea: Skepticism and Faith in the Renaissance* (Baltimore: Johns Hopkins University Press, 1964), 241. In fact, Knutzen profusely professed his atheistic views. In his three surviving treatises arguments are nearly altogether absent, replaced by an all the more radical rhetoric. See Matthias Knutzen, *Schriften und Materialien. Dokumente*, ed. Winfried Schröder (Stuttgart-Bad Cannstatt: Frommann-Holzboog, 2010) [Philosophische Clandestina der deutschen Aufklärung, ed. Winfried Schröder, I.5].

5 Michael Buckley, *At the Origins of Modern Atheism* (New Haven: Yale University Press, 1987; 2nd ed., ibid., 2010). The rather recent *Cambridge Companion to Atheism* includes Gavin Hyman's article on atheism in early modern and modern history, which is mainly framed by Buckley's basic historiographic assumptions: "Atheism in Modern History," in *The*

Cambridge Companion to Atheism, ed. Michael Martin (Cambridge: Cambridge University Press, 2007), 27–46. But see also James E. Force's critical remarks in his "The Origins of Modern Atheism," in *Journal of the History of Ideas* 50 (1989): 153–62.

6 Charles Taylor, *A Secular Age* (Cambridge, MA: Harvard University Press, 2007), 225.

7 Buckley, *At the Origins of Modern Atheism*, 249: "in many ways, Diderot is the first of the atheists, not simply in chronological reckoning, but as an initial and premier advocate and influence." Cf. Louis Dupré, "On the Intellectual Sources of Modern Atheism," in *International Journal for Philosophy of Religion* 45 (1999): 1–11.

8 Anon., *Theophrastus redivivus*, ed. Guido Canziani and Gianni Paganini (Florence: La nuova Italia), 1981. See also Tullio Gregory, *Theophrastus redivivus. Erudizione e ateismo nel seicento* (Naples: Morano editore), 1979; Marcelino Rodríguez Donís, "El ateísmo en el Theophrastus redivivus," *Themata* 21 (1999): 243–61; Olivier Bloch, "Theophrastus redivivus," in *Grundriss der Geschichte der Philosophie, Die Philosophie des 17. Jahrhunderts, Frankreich und Niederlande*, vol. 2, ed. Jean-Pierre Schobinger (Basel: Schwabe, 1993), 258–61; Nicole Gengoux, *Un athéisme philosophique à l'âge classique: le Theophrastus redivivus, 1659* (Paris: Champion, 2014); *Entre la Renaissance et l'Âge classique, le Theophrastus redivivus, 1659*, ed. Nicole Gengoux and Pierre-François Moreau (Paris: Champion, 2014); Gianni Paganini, "Le premier traité philosophique athée de l'âge moderne: le Theophrastus redivivus (1659)," in *Athéisme voilé/dévoilé aux temps modernes*, ed. Anne Staquet (Brussels: Acad. Royale de Belgique, Classe des Lettres et des Sciences Morales et Politiques, 2013), 199–214.

9 Barry Allen, "Atheism, Relativism, Enlightenment, and Truth," in *Studies in Religion / Sciences religieuses* 23 (1994): 167–77 (reprinted in *Walking the Tightrope of Faith*, ed. Hendrik Hart [Amsterdam, Rodopi, 1999], 70–81), 176: "atheism was a politically driven attack upon … Christian theology seen by its opponents as contrary to the tolerance and freer forms of political government they favored."

10 Jean Meslier, *Mémoire des pensées et sentiments*, in *Oeuvres complètes*, ed. Roland Desné, Jean Deprun, and Albert Soboul (Paris: Éditions Anthropos, 1970–72), vol. 1, 23: "[…] que tous les grands de la terre, et que tous les nobles fussent pendus, et étranglés avec des boiaux des prêtres."

11 According to Charles Taylor, de Sade's anti-moralism represents "the most consistent … liberation from the tradition": "What Sade's views bring out, as a foil, is the usually invisible background of Enlightenment humanism."

Taylor, *Sources of the Self: The Making of the Modern Identity* (Cambridge, MA: Harvard University Press, 1989), 335–6.

12 Lester G. Crocker, *Nature and Culture. Ethical Thought in the French Enlightenment* (Baltimore: Johns Hopkins University Press, 1963), 398: "Sadism is a dark pool formed by those streams of eighteenth-century philosophy which flow into it. There is nothing in Sade's nihilism which, in essence or in embryo, is not also found in the writings we have examined."

13 See Olivier Bloch, "La contestation libertine des normes et valeurs traditionnelles du Theophrastus redivivus au médecin Gaultier," in *Ordre et contestation au temps des Classiques*, ed. Roger Duchêne and Pierre Ronzeaud (Paris: Papers on French Seventeenth Century Literature, 1992), 307–20; Guido Canziani, "Morale, politica e religione in alcuni testi della letteratura filosofica clandestina," in *I filosofi e la società senza religione*, ed. M. Geuna and G. Gori (Bologna: Il Mulino, 2011), 301–22; Gianni Paganini, "Bonheur, passions et intérêts: l'héritage des libertins," in *L'état classique. Regards sur la pensée politique de la France dans le second XVIIe siècle*, ed. Henri Méchoulan and Joël Cornette (Paris: Vrin, 1996), 71–92; John Christian Laursen, "Cynicism in the Theophrastus redivivus," in *Entre la Renaissance et l'Âge classique, le Theophrastus redivivus, 1659*, ed. Nicole Gengoux and Pierre-François Moreau (Paris: Honoré Champion, 2014), 47–64.

14 Anon., *Theophrastus redivivus*, 895. Cf. the polemic against monogamy in a 1674 pamphlet by the atheist Matthias Knutzen: *Schriften*, 53.

15 Anon., *Theophrastus redivivus*, 893: "polygamia viris tantum indulget, non vero mulieribus, quae eodem libertatis iure secundum naturam frui debent, quo viri ipsi."

16 Anon., *Theophrastus redivivus*, 893: "omnium quidem iniuriarum saevissima ea est, quae eiusmodi libertati naturali illata est quaeque venerem legibus coercuit."

17 Anon., *Theophrastus redivivus*, 893: "Itaque libera et soluta esse debet viri mulierisque coniunctio, ut uterque, cui et quantum voluerit, misceri possit."

18 Anon., *De origine boni et mali*, in *Symbolum sapientiae*, ed. Guido Canziani, Winfried Schröder, and Francisco Socas (Milan: FrancoAngeli, 2000), §13, 275.

19 Anon., *De origine boni et mali*, 274: "Firmo igitur talo subsistit principium natura libertatem nostram agendi nulla lege a Deo restrictam apparere, proinde nullas actiones originarie malas esse, sed malum demum ex societatibus, indeque ex pacto oriri."

20 Anon., *De origine boni et mali*, §14, 275.

21 Anon., *De origine boni et mali*, §10, 274.

22 Anon., *De origine boni et mali*, §10, 272.

23 Anon., *De origine boni et mali*, §10, 272.

24 Anon., *De origine boni et mali*, §20, 277.

25 Anon., *Symbolum sapientiae*, ed. Guido Canziani, Winfried Schröder, and Francisco Socas (Milan: FrancoAngeli, 2000). A Spanish translation was published by Francisco Socas in 2015: Anon., *Symbolum sapientiae* (Wien: Österreichische Nationalbibliothek, cod. 11539). *La clave de la sabiduría (Un tratado clandestino del siglo XVII)*, edición bilingüe de Francisco Socas, in *Exemplaria classica*, vol. 6, 2015, 1–242. Cf. Guido Canziani, "Critica della religione e fonti moderne nel 'Cymbalum mundi' o 'Symbolum sapientiae,'" in idem, ed., *Filosofia e religione nella letteratura clandestina secoli XVII e XVIII* (Milan: FrancoAngeli, 1994), 35–81; Gianni Paganini, "Haupttendenzen der clandestinen Philosophie," in *Grundriss der Geschichte der Philosophie. Die Philosophie des 17. Jahrhunderts*, ed. Jean-Pierre Schobinger, vol. 1 (Basel: Schwabe, 1998), 120–95, esp. 168 ff. and 189; Winfried Schröder, "Das 'Symbolum Sapientiae' / 'Cymbalum Mundi' und der 'Tractatus theologico-politicus,'" in *Studia Spinozana* 7, 1991, 227–39; idem, *Ursprünge des Atheismus. Untersuchungen zur Metaphysik- und Religionskritik des 17. und 18. Jahrhunderts* [1998] (2nd ed., Stuttgart–Bad Cannstatt: Frommann-Holzboog, 2012), passim, esp. for the philological and historical aspects: 408–16; Jonathan Israel, *Radical Enlightenment: Philosophy and the Making of Modernity, 1650–1750* (Oxford: Oxford University Press, 2001), 470–71, 689–91, 702–3; Franco Giacone, "Une réception du ‚Cymbalum mundi' en Allemagne au XVIIe siècle," in idem, ed., *Le Cymbalum mundi* (Geneva: Droz, 2003), 103–13.

26 Nicolas Fréret, *Lettre de Thrasybule à Leucippe*, ed. Sergio Landucci (Florence: Olschki, 1986).

27 Anon., *Lettres à Sophie. Lettres sur la Religion, sur l' âme humaine et sur l'existence de Dieu*, ed. Olivier Bloch (Paris: Champion, 2004) [*Libre pensée et littérature clandestine*, ed. Antony McKenna, 17], 90; cf. Bloch, "Les 'Lettres à Sophie' ou 'Lettres sur la religion, sur l'âme humaine, et sur l'existence de Dieu': questions de source," in *La philosophie clandestine*, ed. McKenna and Mothu, 459–72.

28 Anon., *J. Brunus redivivus, ou traité des erreurs populaires, Ouvrage Critique, Historique & Philosophique, Imité de Pomponace*, n.p. 1771 [also in *Philosophes sans dieu. Textes athées clandestins du XVIIIe siècle*, ed. Gianluca Mori and Alain Mothu (Paris: Champion, 2005), 277–36].

29 Anon., *J. Brunus redivivus*, 96.

30 Cf. Anon., *Symbolum sapientiae*, 225: "nec Deum negare nec credere debemus, sed materiam hanc ad incognita referre praestat, de quibus nostrum judicium est suspendendum."

31 Anon., *Symbolum sapientiae*, 223. See my *Ursprünge des Atheismus*, 376ff.

32 Anon., *J. Brunus redivivus*, 96; Anon., *Symbolum sapientiae*, 223: "Omnis rei existentia probari debet, nec credere cogor, hoc vel illud existere, esse, reperiri, nisi probetur. Nos igitur Deum non esse demonstrare nullo jure sumus obligati, sed quia affirmanti incumbit probatio, demum, qui Deum esse contendunt, istud argumentis evincere constringuntur."

33 Anon., *Symbolum sapientiae*, 226–7: "In re maxime dubia et astrusa minor temeritas est, si ad negationem inclinemus, quam si affirmativa χέρσιν τε πόσιν τε defendatur."

34 Anon., *Symbolum sapientiae*, 223.

35 Anon., *Lettres sur la religion*, 90.

36 Anon., *Symbolum sapientiae*, 223: "tamdiu militat praesumtio, rem vel non existere vel istud a nobis ignorari, donec existentia illius probetur atque doceatur."

37 Anon., *Symbolum sapientiae*, 227: "[Deicolae] Deum talem effinxerunt, qui per rerum naturam Deus esse non potuit. Pertinent huc attributa Dei et quae de Deo et doctrinis suis revelatis praedicare solent Christiani, quae uti ut plurimum contradictionem involvunt, ita non possunt non atheum seducere, ut Deum esse omnino neget. Nam talis Deus, qualis a Christianis et ethnicis in scenam producitur, utique dari nequit in hoc universo." In spite of these uniquivocal statements, Gianluca Mori regards the author of the *Symbolum* not as an atheist, but as a sceptic; see his *L'ateismo dei moderni. Filosofia e negazione di Dio da Spinoza a d'Holbach* (Rome: Carocci editore, 2016), 200–1. Similarly, the anonymous *Lettres sur la religion, sur l'âme humaine et sur l'existence de Dieu* or *Lettres à Sophie*, 90, argue that although there is sufficient reason to deny the specific Christian (or the philosophers') God, we cannot conclude that there is no God at all. A theist could still insist that there may be a God not defined by specific attributes, a God according to the premises of negative theology, an "Etre indéfinissable." If the theist thus abandons the philosophical definition of God and retreats to a vague idea of a Supreme Being or to the doctrines of revelation, he faces the presumption-argument. So the author of the *Lettres* concludes that, if the existence of God is not supported by philosophical argument, but only by the testimony of the fraudulent so-called Holy Scriptures, there is a strong presumption that theism is false.

38 Fréret, *Lettre de Thrasybule à Leucippe*, 353, 405. See Winfried Schröder, "From Doubt to Rejection: The Impact of Ancient Pyrrhonism on the Emergence of Early Modern Atheism," in *Scepticisme, clandestinité et libre pensée. Scepticism, clandestinity and free-thinking*, ed. Gianni Paganini, Miguel Benítez and James Dybikowski (Paris: Champion, 2002), 67–77.

39 Fréret, *Lettre de Thrasybule à Leucippe*, 353.

40 Fréret, *Lettre de Thrasybule à Leucippe*, 353: "Les philosophes partisans du système religieux prétendent que, parce que nous ne pouvons expliquer les causes de tous les effets ni parcourir la suite infinie des causes, il faut que nous admettions leur opinion de l'existence d'une Cause universelle. Mais tant qu'ils ne pourront me la rendre probable, tant qu'elle impliquera contradiction dans mon esprit et n'y entrera qu'accompagnée du sentiment de la fausseté, je serai en droit de la rejetter, quoique je ne puisse rendre raison de tout et qu'il y ait bien des choses dans l'univers, au sujet desquelles je demeure dans l'ignorance."

41 Fréret, *Lettre de Thrasybule à Leucippe*, 405.

42 Antony Flew, "The Presumption of Atheism," in idem, *God, Freedom, and Immortality: A Critical Analysis* (Amherst: Prometheus Books, 1984), 13–30; also in *Philosophy of Religion: A Guide and Anthology*, ed. Brian Davies (Oxford: Oxford University Press), 2000, 36–41. See also Kai Nielsen, *Philosophy and Atheism: In Defence of Atheism* (Buffalo: Prometheus Books, 1985), ch. 7: "The Burden of Proof and the Presumption of Atheism," 129–44; Alvin Plantinga and Nicholas Wolterstorff, eds, *Faith and Rationality. Reason and Belief in God* (Notre Dame: University of Notre Dame Press, 1983), 25ff.

43 See Winfried Schröder, "Critique de la métaphysique et fabrication de la modernité," in *Qu'est-ce que les Lumières "radicales"? Libertinage, athéisme et spinozisme dans le tournant philosophique de l'"âge classique*, ed. Catherine Secretan, Tristan Dagron, and Laurent Bove (Paris: Éditions Amsterdam, 2007), 277–87.

Chapter Two

The First Philosophical Atheistic Treatise: *Theophrastus redivivus* (1659)

GIANNI PAGANINI

1. Introduction: Clandestinity and Radical Libertinism

Over the last fifty years, knowledge about the clandestine world of ideas has improved significantly and has brought about a real historiographical revolution, giving rise to new interpretive paradigms. To name just two, we owe to the works of Margaret Jacob[1] the term and the idea of "radical Enlightenment" based on the Anglo-Dutch context, while Martin Mulsow has coined the term "heterodox underground" as a melting pot of modernity in the "Frühaufklärung."[2] Another paradigm, born from this kind of research, is that of "radical libertinism," to which I will return at the end of this chapter. In practice, these new proposals have supplanted older categories such as "crisis of the European conscience," "pre-enlightenment," and "erudite libertinism." Jonathan Israel, in his turn, has taken up again the idea of "radical Enlightenment" and developed it into that of "democratic Enlightenment,"[3] stressing above all the universality and public use of reason – with all its consequences – that distinguishes "radicals" from "moderate" thinkers. Thus we have witnessed a propitious moment for studies during which the quantitative growth of knowledge (documented by two specific book series dedicated to the *clandestina* in France and in Germany, respectively led by Antony McKenna[4] and Winfried Schröder)[5] has resulted in a qualitative mutation of paradigms in the history of ideas.[6]

When we focus specifically on manuscripts (a special subset of the clandestine world, distinct from clandestine printed books), we come to see that an important change in scholarship has generated a different chronology of the phenomenon. The first discoverers of clandestine texts (Gustave Lanson and Ira O. Wade) looked mainly at the eighteenth century; much of the recent research has shifted attention to the seventeenth century, and in this connection, a close relationship to Renaissance philosophy has emerged. This implies also a kind of linguistic turn, from French (or German or English) to Latin: this was the language of the "clandestinity" at its very beginning, as in Bodin's *Colloquium*, Seidel's *Origo et fundamenta religionis christianae, Theophrastus redivivus,* and some other early texts.[7]

In terms of their approach to philosophical and religious issues, we can classify the manuscripts roughly into three large families: the deist tradition, the pantheist, and the atheist. The former is grounded in the *Colloquium Heptaplomeres,* attributed to Jean Bodin, and the *Origo et fundamenta religionis christianae* (both at the end of the sixteenth century), and a little afterwards (around 1620) in the so-called *Quatrains du déiste*: two Latin texts and a French one. The second tradition culminates in *L'Esprit de Spinosa,* which circulated in different versions under the title *Traité des trois imposteurs.* The third tradition has as its archetype *Theophrastus redivivus,* anonymous and dated to 1659, conserved in four different manuscripts, all in Latin, and not published until 1981–2.[8]

2. *Theophrastus redivivus*: Atheism as a Counter-History of Philosophy

This chapter will focus on *Theophrastus redivivus,* which is still little-known or, better, almost unknown in the anglophone world, even though, among the first scholars to deal with it, one was an American (Ira O. Wide)[9] and the other was English (John Stevenson Spink).[10] The first comprehensive studies, however, and the first and critical edition, have been made by three Italian scholars.[11] French scholars have been following in their footsteps.[12] It seems that Anglo-American scholars have not yet realized or have underestimated the importance of this text.

Let us start with some unquestionable facts: the anonymous *Theophrastus redivivus* is one of the longest, most ponderous, and most reasoned philosophical manuscripts (1,090 folios, nine hundred pages in the printed edition) in the entire history of philosophy,[13] both ancient and early modern. It is also the first systematic and explicit treatise on atheism, even though its author rarely uses the words "atheism" or "atheist."[14] So it is surprising that *Theophrastus redivivus* has not taken its rightful place in the history of philosophical atheism, except in the valuable work of Winfried Schröder.[15]

Theophrastus redivivus contests religion in general and especially the four main historical religions (paganism, Christianity, Judaism, Islam), with a comparative glance at Asian and American religions. The author aims

Hi omnes negaverunt Dominum, & dixerunt non est ipse. Ierem. 5°

Protagoras | Diagoras | Theophrastus Eresius | Theodorus Cyrenæus | Eumerus Tegæus | Plato | Aristoteles

THEOPHRASTUS REDIVIVUS SIVE *Historia de iis quæ dicuntur* De Diis, De Mundo, De Religione, de Anima, Inferis & Dæmonibus, De Contemnendâ Morte, De Vitâ secundum Naturam,

OPUS Ex Philosophorum opinionibus constructum, & doctissimis Theologis, ad diruendum propositum.

PARS PRIMA

Epicurus | Lucretius | M.T.Cicero | Annæus Seneca | Plinius Secundus | Lucianus | Galenus | Sextus Empiricus | Pomponatius | Cardanus | THEOPHRASTUS REDIVIVUS | Joannes Bodinus | Jul. Cæsar Vaninus

Figure 2.1 Title page of *Theophrastus redivivus* (1659): ms copy preserved in Wien, Oesterreichisce Nationalbibliothek cod. 10405.

to replace religion with a positive atheist philosophy articulated in terms of epistemology, psychology, cosmology, morals, and politics. We thus encounter three different aspects in the same work: the *destructive* aspect of radical criticism; the *constructive* aspect of a philosophical alternative, based on what the author calls "true and natural reason" (vera et naturalis ratio); and, finally, the *reconstructive* aspect, which sets out to elucidate the history of religions. Confronting the errors made by philosophy and religion, the author of *Theophrastus* tries to explain their origins and developments, turning to history, psychology, and politics. Taking a completely humanistic and fact-based approach, he presents the first "natural history of religion" (even though he does not use that expression) – this, long before Hume's work brought this kind of analysis into renown.

This "natural history" is above all a "history of opinions," although rites, behaviours, and ecclesiastical organization are not left out of its scope. A "history of what has been said about gods, the world, religion, the soul, the afterlife, demons, disregard of death, and life according to nature": thus reads the title page of the manuscripts. Ostensibly, this doxography is presented to the "most learned theologians" for them to rebut, as declared on the frontispiece. In truth, this invitation to debunk atheistic reasoning is entirely a façade, so tenuous that it reads like a parody of certain defensive techniques used during the Renaissance and Counter-Reformation to defend the author from the condemnations of Church and Inquisition. For example, Pomponazzi demonstrated the mortality of the soul from the philosophical standpoint throughout the text of his *De immortalitate*, but at the end he declared himself to be in matters of religion a faithful believer who submitted to Church authority. In the case of *Theophrastus*, between the very short preamble dedicated to the theologians and the final peroration aimed at "real men of wisdom, followers of the Christian religion" (TR 3–8, 930–1), in which the anonymous author professes to be a believer (six or seven pages in total), there is the whole body of nine hundred pages expounding anti-religious theories on all relevant topics (the existence of God, revelation, soul, morals, etc.), upheld with conviction and without the slightest hint of criticism addressed at the unorthodox theses.[16]

Following the order of the treatises into which the work is divided, we see an outline of the main theories backed by the anonymous author:

- Treatise I ("Qui est de diis"): not only is atheism possible, it is also the necessary conclusion of any sound reasoning. Religious beliefs arose from the observation of the constant and regular movement of the celestial bodies: these, not any sort of intelligences, were the

Figure 2.2 Title page of *Theophrastus redivivus*: ms copy preserved in Oesterreichische Nationalbibliothek, cod. 11451.

first divinities worshipped by men, who mistook astral bodies for gods (TR 27–174).

- Treatise II ("Qui est de mundo"): the world is eternal and not created; the chronicles of all the ancient populations (Chaldeans, Egyptians, Chinese, and Americans) are infinitely longer than the biblical chronology; the supposed beginnings of the world and of humanity are lost in the mists of time. Every account of the world's origin is a pretence invented by a people or a kingdom with the aim of boasting about being the first. (Vico would later write about the arrogance of nations – in a different vein, however, in that his theory was not intended to back atheistic theses about the eternity of the world, as does *Theophrastus redivivus.*) (TR 175–340).[17]
- Treatise III ("Qui est de religione"): an analysis first of religion in general, then of the four principal religions (paganism, Christianity, Judaism, Islam), with reflections on their "causes." Starting from primitive astral myths, the priesthood has transformed religious beliefs into a tool to control and dominate the people. Religion has thus become a "political art," "created by men and not delivered by god." Taking a comparative approach, one chapter deals with the supposed supernatural that can be found in all religions: oracles, miracles, prophecies, myths of every kind. All of these widespread phenomena can be traced back to natural causes (such as exhalations, for some oracles), to imagination, and especially to political and economic exploitation (TR 341–558).[18]
- Treatise IV ("Qui est de anima et de inferis"): being neither immortal nor spiritual, the soul coincides with the life of the body. Heaven and hell, angels and demons, are fantasies invented by theologians and used by priests, who lead the people, infusing in them fear of punishment and hope for rewards. Anthropocentrism is an illusion; the belief in immortality derives from a thoroughly human yet excessive passion: "the desire to never cease from existing" (*numquam desinendi libido*) (TR 559–716).
- Treatise V ("Qui est de contemnenda morte"): one must not fear death; rather, one must despise it. Life has to be assessed in itself and enjoyed for everything it can give, in spite of mortality. The wise man can commit suicide when it is necessary; but even in this extreme choice, "there is more good than evil" when too much pain is avoided (TR 717–82; for the praise of suicide, see 758–82).
- Treatise VI ("Qui est de vita secundum naturam"): a compendium of morals and politics "according to nature." The state of nature actually

existed; it is not a literary fantasy or myth. The "golden age" is not a metaphor, because there was a time long ago when men really did enjoy full freedom and equality, without any oppressive authority. Coarse and primitive, these men used only their "natural intellect," and they were not deceived by any imposture. The first law of nature is self-preservation, in a broader sense that includes not only pure life but also pleasure and well-being. In the state of nature there was neither property nor power; conflicts were inevitable but could be resolved following the simple rule of reciprocity (*alteri ne feceris quod tibi fieri non vis*). Discord and human stupidity by degrees established disparities, hierarchies, and permanent authorities, which in turn produced new and greater differences of rank and wealth, until societies turned into mere agglomerations of "convicts for life," though they are nowadays described as "civil." It was in the civil or political state, not in the state of nature, that "man became wolf to man," thus reversing the application of Hobbes's famous maxim. The anonymous author of *Theophrastus redivivus* applies the phrase (dating back to Plautus) not to the state of nature but to civil society. Religion came into this dark story of degeneration too, because – the author notes – "it is always easier to command by persuasion than by violence" (TR 783–926).

Few seventeenth-century authors and texts are mentioned in *Theophrastus redivivus*: Giulio Cesare Vanini (1585–1619), Thomas Brown (*Religio medici*, 1642), Guy Patin (1601–1672), Cyrano de Bergerac (*La mort d'Agrippine*, 1654), Tommaso Campanella (1568–1639), and above all this latter's Parisian editions of *Atheismus triumphatus, De gentilismo non retinendo* (1636), and *Metaphysica* (1638). Also Cardinal Richelieu (1585–1642) is mentioned. Much more impressive is the legion of ancient and Renaissance authors on which *Theophrastus redivivus* relies, including the clandestine manuscript of *Colloquium Heptaplomeres*, which is extensively cited and commented on. Many of the author's contemporaries are not even mentioned: Descartes, Galileo, Hobbes, Mersenne, Pascal, just to give some examples, are absent from the text. The author's scientific world view is outdated. He refers to Copernicus and his astronomical theory in sceptical tones, as Montaigne did earlier in his *Essais*. Both Montaigne and the anonymous author of *Theophrastus redivivus* mention Copernicanism and its classical forerunners to indicate that the coming and going of astronomical hypotheses over the centuries do not allow for definitive certainty in the sciences (TR 307, 322). The bibliography of the sources quoted and commented on by TR occupies thirty pages of the edition (TR 933–62).

The composition style recalls the mainstream of European humanism between the sixteenth and early seventeenth centuries: the author quotes lavishly from his cherished sources and joins them together in a sort of *tapisserie*, developing his own considerations out of the texts that are his starting point. A work that employs a similar technique of composition is the famous *Anatomy of Melancholy*, by Robert Burton (1577–1640), first published in 1621, three more times in the author's life, and then posthumously in 1651 by Henry Cripps.[19] Outwardly, Burton's book is a thick collection of *authoritates*, authoritative phrases and arguments taken from classical and Renaissance authors, behind which the real author, Burton himself, seems to hide. In reality, he never abandons the thread of his "anatomy," which is to provide the reader with a complete and almost encyclopedic analysis of his own crucial topic: the nature, causes, circumstances, ramifications, symptoms, and remedies of this particular passion. In a way, *Theophrastus* shows off an encyclopedic ambition; it strives to be an encyclopedia of atheism, yet its structure is much more systematic and philosophical, avoiding digressions (which are frequent in Burton) and aligning the whole mass of his erudition to a very clear aim: not to destroy atheistic opinions, as he pretends in the preamble, but to demonstrate their truth. This composition technique, of borrowing from other authors (ancient classics, Renaissance and libertine writers), was very common in the clandestine manuscripts, including the most celebrated, such as *L'Esprit de Spinosa*, *Traité des trois imposteurs*, and *L'Ame matérielle*. What distinguishes these later products from the early ones, such *Theophrastus*, is that modern authors (like Spinoza, Hobbes, Descartes, and the Cartesians) start to be used, albeit with aims that are very different from their original intent. Several of these clandestine treatises were printed in the eighteenth century, usually by clandestine publishers, and introduced under cover in France.[20]

3. "True and natural reason"

The use of this collage technique does not mean that *Theophrastus* has no clearly defined stance. The text is more than a rich sourcebook of atheist and irreligious arguments, as it might seem at first glance. The author's overriding concern is to judge various "opinions" by applying the "real and natural intellect," which in turn draws on the certain and constant data of general experience. These data unmask the uncertainty and fickleness of "opinions," as first revealed by their variety and inconstancy. Any rational generalization derives from empirical observation; on this point, the author of *Theophrastus* notices that Epicurean epistemology with its "anticipations" confirms Aristotle's empiricist method, which is based on the uniform and permanent experience of nature (TR 10–24). This is why it can happen that the same conclusion is reached even though different philosophical paths are followed. For instance, though proceeding from different assumptions, Epicureans and Aristotelians like Pomponazzi shared in the idea of mortality of the soul (TR 628–58). This convergence between such different philosophical schools is not due to pure eclecticism; on the contrary, it means that "natural reason" in the end necessarily prevails, for all the differences between systems. Therefore, the criterion of "natural reason" allows us to distinguish, in the vast panorama of philosophical opinions, between what is real and what is "fake" or invented.

Another important criterion *Theophrastus redivivus* pointed out may be considered "ideological," if it is permitted to use that anachronistic word. Of a doctrine, one should assess not only the philosophical content but also the practical aims and interests it supports, be they individual or collective. Thus a sharp distinction is drawn between what regards "truth" and what, instead, refers to "utility." A true philosopher should look only at truth (TR 133–5). By contrast, the prevalence of "utility" transforms an idea into an "ideology," because what is useful is accepted and propagated even if it is false (TR 349–63). For example, *utilitas* could be to the philosopher's personal advantage when he invents myths and fantasies to please the people, to enjoy the support of the powerful, or simply to defend himself against persecution by concealing his real convictions (TR 219–21, 228–9). Moreover, a doctrine in itself false can be useful if it serves to guarantee the social order, to keep the people in obedience, or more simply to defend the political power and the privileges of the ruling class. Thus the first duty of a true *sapiens* is to tell apart truth and utility, even though there were over time very few wise men (*sapientes*) who searched solely for the truth. Too many "philosophers" mixed instead the truth and the useful, supporting, basically for practical reasons, opinions that contradict the "natural intellect."

The anonymous author of *Theophrastus redivivus* is one of the first early modern philosophers to theorize and practise this approach to doctrines, investigating not only what they say but also what they can aim at in terms of utility. Pomponazzi had already distinguished between *veritas* and *utilitas,* especially referring to the myth of the immortality of the soul, which can be useful to control human passions and above all those of the people (TR 629–36, 709–13). His analysis, however, was mainly restricted to the "interests" of religion and did not take into account finer distinctions between the different social figures that nourish and exploit the myth: political authorities, priests, even philosophers – all the figures that *Theophrastus* attentively reviews.

Being fully aware of this "ideological" function of doctrines, the anonymous author is encouraged to read his sources "between the lines," detecting the true meaning, often irreligious, that lies behind the "orthodox" appearances of the philosophical discourses. Until Leo Strauss, he was one of the first – with different aims of course – to practise this reading "between the lines." He was anticipated only by some sceptical philosophers, like Montaigne, who often unmasked the dogmatic confidence of the ancient philosophers, e.g., Plato, Aristotle, Epicurus, and others, who concealed the intrinsic incertitude of their doctrines behind professions of strong dogmatism. Yet Montaigne's aims were merely sceptical, sometimes even fideistic, and not irreligious as in *Theophrastus.* In this way the anonymous author created a whole genealogy of atheism, explicit and implicit, the first and the most original of his time, as well as one of the most detailed and rich. When we compare it with another genealogy drawn twenty years later and represented on the title page of Cudworth's *True Intellectual System of the Universe,* we realize how rich and unusual *Theophrastus*'s is. Before being explained and commented on in the text, this genealogy is graphically represented on the manuscript title page (see fig. 2.1, p. 39 and fig. 2.2, p. 41).

4. The Genealogy of Atheism

At the top of the title page, a declaration of the prophet Jeremiah reads thus: "All these denied the Lord and said He doesn't exist." In other words, they were all atheists. Below, the ancient Theophrastus (Theophrastus of Eresus, author of a lost work, *On the Gods*) is surrounded by the four famous Greek philosophers considered to be atheists (Protagoras, Diagoras, Evemeus, Theodorus of Cyrenes) and linked to the modern *Theophrastus redivivus* by two chains of philosophers. In these chains, some names are predictable: Epicurus, Lucretius, and Lucian first and foremost. Others are easy to explain: Seneca and Pliny were much appreciated for their naturalism, pantheism, and worldly morality; Galen posited the existence of a close relationship between body and soul; Cicero, in *De natura deorum,* prepared the ground for discussing the problem of religion, setting forth sceptical and Epicurean arguments about gods; Sextus Empiricus raised doubts about the validity of theology. Other choices, though, are quite astonishing, such as the two names placed at the beginning of each chain: Plato and Aristotle.

This choice can be explained if one considers the two procedures evoked earlier in this chapter: reading texts "between the lines," and looking at "ideological" motives. Bearing in mind that philosophy often developed in a hostile climate, the author of *Theophrastus* supposes that thinkers desiring to avoid persecution or to enjoy the benefits of public approval had to adopt cover strategies, hiding the real meaning of their teachings behind outward professions of orthodoxy, for the intelligent reader to uncover. According to *Theophrastus*, Plato and Aristotle were two such thinkers.

Of course, Plato and Aristotle had both learned from Socrates's fate, seeing the danger philosophy runs when it challenges popular opinions and authorities. They both interiorized this lesson, reacting however in different ways to it. Plato's case is the most interesting, because his philosophy had by then been christianized and was considered a pillar of any sort of idealism and spiritualism. Nevertheless, he is viewed in *Theophrastus redivivus* as an "absolute atheist" (TR 29). This surprising label can be gleaned from many clues. First, Plato made use of myths that, being the opposite of sober and rational doctrine, should repel a great philosopher, whereas this technique of writing can be justified when one's aim is to guide "the men of the people," who are always fond of fables and consolatory explanations. In fact, according to TR's author, Plato took on a task that usually belongs to a politician rather than to a philosopher: in his case, *utilitas* prevailed over *veritas*, as is revealed when he recommends to legislators that they use "fables," rites, and religion to educate the people. Even the care with which, in *Laws*, he banned the atheist from the city is a revealing clue that Plato was personally well aware of the strength of this doctrine and, it follows, concerned about the danger it posed to the political order. The myth-maker and politician Plato, then, represents the opposite of what a true philosopher should do, which is, search solely for truth and explain it using only rational arguments. All of this means that Plato had a double doctrine, and also a double way of writing. Outwardly he professed a politically and religiously useful doctrine, one that supported the idea of a god demiurge, immortality of the soul, and punishments and rewards in the afterlife: for this kind of doctrine, mythical stories, metaphors, and literary inventions are the best way to speak to the people. Inwardly, he practised a covert atheism, allowing myths to take the place of philosophical reflection when he cared more about *utilitas* than *veritas* (TR 28–33).

Aristotle's case is a little different, and not only because he had long been suspected of heterodoxy for his doctrine of the eternity of the world and for his ambiguous stance on the active intellect and its relationship with the passive, individual, and therefore mortal intellect. Instead of resorting to myths and practising a philosophy that mixed rational arguments with storytelling, he systematically distinguished between two different audiences, which brought about a double philosophy (TR 34–9). Even the "popular" one has at least the appearance of being a philosophical discourse, yet it is contradicted by the "true" one, which is actually addressed to professional philosophers. Thus in *Metaphysics* he spoke of God merely to gratify popular religion, while in *Physics* and *De caelo* he exposed his real thought, claiming that the world is eternal. His intent, "between the lines," was to express the point that divinity is not necessary to the existence and order of the world; by consequence, he was saying that all of his theology was a cover-up (TR 336–7).[21] Regarding the theory of a separate and supposedly immortal intellect, the author of *Theophrastus* notes that this is highly controversial, even in Aristotle's doctrine; he thinks that the obscurity of the related passages in *De anima* is specifically intended to mask Aristotle's personal bent towards the idea of the mortality of the soul. Here, *Theophrastus* follows Pomponazzi's interpretation of Aristotelian psychology (TR 591–2, 629–35), echoing also a widespread *topos* of Renaissance criticism, which compared Aristotle to a squid protecting itself within a cloud of black ink. But unlike most Renaissance interpreters, he does not blame Aristotle for not having clearly asserted immortality; rather, he realizes that the Stagirite had to keep hidden his own mortality thesis, fearing the same kind of persecution that led Socrates to drink poison.

Symmetrically to the ancient Theophrastus, at the bottom of the title page the modern *Theophrastus redivivus* is surrounded by four Renaissance philosophers, whom the author apparently classifies as atheists: Bodin, Pomponazzi, Cardano, and Vanini. None of these men was really an "atheist,"[109] but each was suspect for religious reasons, and most of all, each contributed to the author's personal atheism. To start with Bodin: It is noteworthy that the author of *Theophrastus* deeply knew and repeatedly quoted *Colloquium Heptaplomeres*, which at the time was circulating in manuscript. His reading is, as usual, highly selective. Leaving aside Bodin's Neoplatonic and esoteric background as well as his idea of natural religion, the author of *Theophrastus* especially values two other aspects of Bodin's thought: his religious tolerance, and his anti-Christian criticisms as set forth by Toralba and the Hebrew character of the *Colloquium*, Salomon, even if TR's author does not consider Judaism superior to other religions. Cardano is another highly praised author in TR, especially as regards morals, the immanent concept of nature, and his criticism of the doctrine of immortality. From Pomponazzi are taken natural explanations for miracles, as well as the idea of the mortality of the soul and the cyclical conception of history as applied to religions. Regarding this last aspect, which is at the heart of the "natural history of religion" developed in *Theophrastus*, we can measure both its author's debts to and distance from Renaissance philosophy.

5. Secularizing Renaissance Philosophy: Pomponazzi and Cardano in *Theophrastus redivivus*

Borrowed from Arabic astrology, which had begun to write horoscopes not only of individuals but also of kingdoms and empires, the cyclical theory of history was imported to the West and daringly applied to religions during the late Renaissance. Referring to heavenly motion as the primary cause in the universe, philosophers like Pomponazzi and Cardano attempted to compare the cycles of Judaism, Christianity, and Islam. Aware of this theory's secularist potential, however, they admitted behind natural causes some divine and providential preordination, mediated by the action of celestial intelligences, especially in the case of Christianity. In the first half of the seventeenth century, these concepts must have been firmly rooted, given that Campanella claimed that the stars were not "causes" but only "signs" of events within the order of the cosmos. Again, Gassendi felt obliged to confront astrology as well as the doctrine of fate. The most detailed and audacious astrological explanation was certainly Cardano's. In his famous commentary on Claudius Ptolemy, he went so far as to write the "horoscope" of Christ himself ("Servatoris genesis") – a project so troubling that he had to rewrite the chapter several times for the various editions of this work, with the aim of softening its extreme heterodoxy (see fig. 2.3, p. 51).

Pomponazzi and Cardano are widely quoted and commented on in *Theophrastus*, whose author nevertheless submits their theories to a triple secularization. First and foremost, against both astrology and divine providence, *Theoprastus* claims the existence of a full and absolute free will in man. Any kind of determinism, be it astrological or theological, is rejected. The ancient sceptic Sextus Empiricus, the modern one Agrippa von Nettesheim, and the humanist Giovanni Pico della Mirandola are all summoned as patrons of the fierce polemic against astrology fully developed in Treatise II (TR 94–132).

Second, all the celestial intelligences, including the first (God), are removed from the heavens. *Theophrastus* reduces the causality of heavenly "motors" to pure physical action. In this connection its author draws heavily on Giulio Cesare Vanini, who had materialized and desacralized the celestial vault, eliminating the celestial intelligences. This decisive move filters the influence of Renaissance authors like Pomponazzi and Cardano. When quoting their passages, *Theophrastus* significantly omits all references not only to God and divine providence but also to celestial intelligences (TR 241–65). In the end, only two basic ideas survive its deflationary approach: first, the idea of "the order of the universe and the power of the celestial bodies" as a kind of physical superior cause; and second, the belief that their circular motions impact the equally circular trend of all terrestrial events, starting from the biological cycles of birth and death and eventually covering all of history and religion. All of these events, including religions, have a birth, rise, decline, and fall. As *Theophrastus*'s world is eternal, the cycles of history must recur periodically – "infinite times" (TR 409) – following always the same circular pattern.

Third, thanks to these astrological explanations, the secularization of religion is confirmed also *ex hypothesi.* Even if the arguments of astrology were true – which the author does not admit – it would follow that religion is a natural event, insofar as it is submitted to the physical causality of the heavens. Reading Cardano's horoscopes and especially "Servatoris genesis," the author of *Theophrastus* (TR 460–6) becomes more convinced of his main thesis: the humanity of the founders of religions and of Christ in particular, which in turn involves the full historicity of all religions, natural and psychological explanations for extraordinary phenomena such as miracles, oracles, and prophecies, the psychology of popular credulity, the political exploitation of this bent, and so on. All religious events must belong to the "order of nature" and thus do not depend on supernatural causes, even when they occur "over very long periods" (*in longissimis periodis*), just to foster "great" and "the greatest changes" in history, such as the coming or the falling of a religion. Being highly exceptional, however, especially religious events require the coincidence of rare and occult factors, which are no less natural than any other events. Also, the declining number of miracles over the history of Christianity can be explained in a natural way. As Pomponazzi said, when

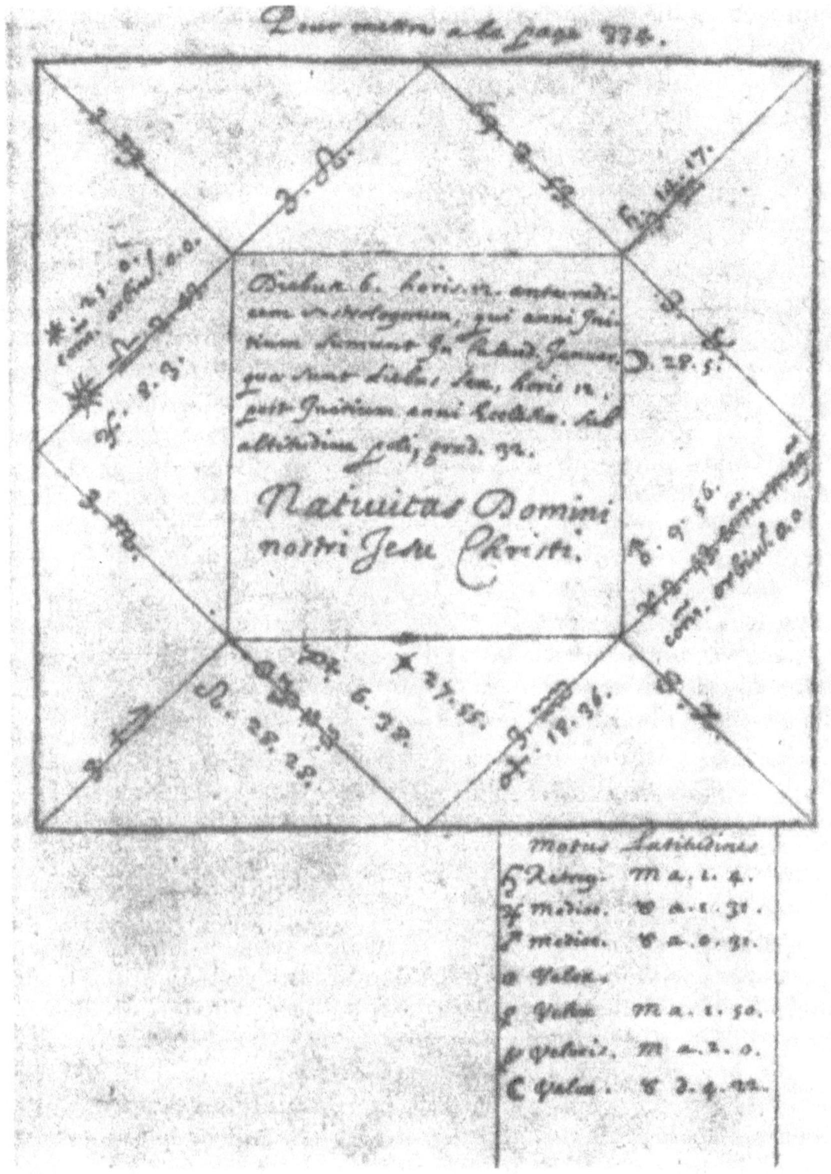

Figure 2.3 Oesterreichische Nationalbibliothek, cod. 11451, f. 334 ("Servatoris Genesis," from H. Cardanus, in *Cl. Ptolomaei Pelusiensis IIII de Astrorum Iudiciis … libros commentaria*, II, text. 54).

approaching the end, "everything dies down" ("omnia frigescunt"). All of these secularist explanations are strengthened by the theory of climates taken from Bodin's *Republic.* Bodin derived the various characteristics of peoples and religions from their geographic locations (see the long section "De religione christiana," TR 457–512).

6. *Theophrastus redivivus* and the History of Early Modern Atheism

Having examined the principal contents of *Theophrastus redivivus* and their connections with some Renaissance philosophies, we can conduct a wider historical evaluation of this text and its importance for the history not only of atheism but also of "radicalism." I shall focus now on the former issue and in the following section on the latter.

First, the mere existence of this text in the mid-seventeenth century should change our view of early modern atheism and lead us to reject two still widespread theories about it: the older one supported by Lucien Febvre,[22] and a more recent one maintained by Alan C. Kors. According to Febvre, real atheism would have been impossible before the coming of modern science and philosophy, especially if the author wrote in Latin! *Theoprastus redivivus* shows precisely the opposite: its author became an atheist without apparently having any knowledge either of Descartes or Hobbes or Spinoza, using basically classical and Renaissance "intellectual tools" (*outillage mental*), and what is worse for Febvre, he wrote one thousand pages in pure Latin! Kors's theory is more sophisticated. In his book *Atheism in France, 1650–1729,* published nine years after the edition of *Theophrastus redivivus,* he contended that seventeenth-century atheism was not a real philosophical position upheld by atheists in the flesh; rather, it was basically a polemical construction made by apologists and theologians in conflict with each other and therefore eager to reveal the possible atheist leanings of their adversaries. Thus, according to Kors, at least until the beginning of eighteenth century (with Jean Meslier), atheism would have been a mere ghost invented by theologians![23] This historical reconstruction of the "sources of disbelief" is highly questionable; we need merely summon the massive bulk of theoretical arguments in favour of atheism offered by *Theophrastus* just at the beginning of the period considered by Kors (1650–1720) in order to realize that the anonymous author was neither an atheist "by consequence," nor an invention of the apologists, nor a parasite of the theological debate, as Kors's history claims in general for early modern atheism. This is why, to maintain his theory, Kors needed to minimize the importance of this text and of the heterodox culture of which it is a clear and flamboyant symptom.

The issue is twofold: the first concerns the possible circulation and consequent influence of a work of which only four copies remain; the second straightforwardly concerns the contents, that is, whether they are modern or pre-modern, compilations or original. As to the issue of influence, it is true that the sheer length of the work (almost one thousand pages *in folio*) and thus the cost of manuscript copies seriously limited its circulation to the high nobility and their milieu (we know that one copy was owned by Prince Eugene of Savoy, another by his aide-de-camp, the baron von Hohendorf, and a third by Le Tellier, minister of Louis XIV; we have no clue as to the owner of the fourth).[24] In an intellectual world dominated by censorship and the persecution of ideas, this is exactly what happened to the most dangerous and inconvenient works that were circulating, and these inconveniences affected as well the culture surrounding manuscripts and printed books. To give a couple of examples: the first Italian and English editions of Giordano Bruno's work became extremely rare after their suppression by the Inquisition, and it often happened that even noble and upper-class amateurs, willing to pay any price for these books, had in the end to give up and turn to manuscript copies.[25] Later, in the eighteenth century, the circulation of another massive work, this one in French rather than Latin, the original text of *Mémoire* by Jean Meslier, underwent a similar process. We know that before dying, the priest Jean Meslier made three manuscript copies of his work, and that today only eleven copies are extant. The summary prepared by Voltaire had a happier fate, for it was printed in 1762 as an *extrait* of the original *Mémoire*. However, in addition to drastically cutting it, Voltaire disfigured it by turning it into a deist pamphlet that lacked any trace of atheism and political protest.

To return to *Theophrastus redivivus* as it features in Kors's *Atheism in France*: First of all, Kors minimizes the importance of its classical and Renaissance sources, viewing them as outdated and out of fashion: "they were authors who quickly seemed anachronistic in France, irrelevant to new dates," "not to be taken seriously as naturalists and materialists in terms relevant to the late seventeenth and eighteenth centuries." Yet substantial historical research has shown that (just to mention some relevant examples) Descartes and Mersenne were both interested in their contemporary Campanella; and that a work infused with Neoplatonism like Jean Bodin's *Colloquium Heptaplomeres* was one of the most cherished clandestine texts, a true bestseller, deep into the Enlightenment, with more than one hundred surviving copies. Furthermore, "radical" eighteenth-century philosophical historiography played a major role in the birth of the Enlightenment, as any visitor to an eighteenth-century library can guess and as Jonathan Israel, Martin Mulsow, and many other scholars have shown on a more scientific basis than pure historical insight. After all, Pierre Bayle, one of the most innovative and provocative authors of the late seventeenth century, loved by Enlightenment *philosophes*, was extremely interested in the same Renaissance figures that stand out as sources of *Theophrastus*: Pomponazzi, Cardano, and Bodin. They are all the subjects of relevant entries in the *Dictionnaire historique et critique* and are taken seriously by Bayle, who also dealt extensively with Vanini in his *Œeuvres diverses*.[26] Kors reproaches TR for this attention to those Renaissance authors, yet he praises Bayle for it; what is more, the attention of Bayle's reading was drawn to their heterodoxy, along similar lines as in *Theophrastus*, even though Bayle did not go so far as to reach explicit atheistic conclusions.

Regarding circulation or fame, one must take into account that the massive *Theophrastus redivivus* was mentioned – of course with scorn – in the apologetic treatise of Louis Ferrand, *De la connoissance de Dieu* (Paris, 1706).[27] It occupied a top rank on the shelves of Prince Eugene of Savoy in Vienna, at the Belvedere Palace,[28] and when he passed it to the Hofbibliothek it drew the attention of the imperial librarian, Nicolao Forlosia,[29] and through him, most probably, the attention of the Italian radical deist Pietro Giannone (1676–1748) at the time he was writing *Il Triregno*, one the most audacious and profound works of the Italian and European radical Enlightenment.[30] If all of this is not enough to reassess the place of *Theophrastus redivivus* in the history of the transmission of the clandestine texts,[31] we still have to consider that the work left behind some memory of its contents, given that its title appears in a constellation of other, later French clandestine manuscripts that claim to be partial translations of some of its chapters (see, for instance, fig. 2.4, p. 55).[32] It is not true that *Theophrastus redivivus* was "ignored almost totally" by the philosophical milieu[33]; the filiation we have illustrated, partly real and partly fictional, bears witness to the memory of *Theophrastus* as a highly subversive work all the way into the high Enlightenment.

Leaving aside quantitative considerations about the spread of this work (considerations that could also affect other provocative and innovative works that had very little and only narrow circulation at the time), let us come back to the contents as they are (negatively) assessed by Kors. First of all, Kors considers the work a mere compilation (speaking of

I

Theophrastus
Redivivus

Traduction des quatre pre=
=miers chap.^{es} du Theophrastus
redivivus.

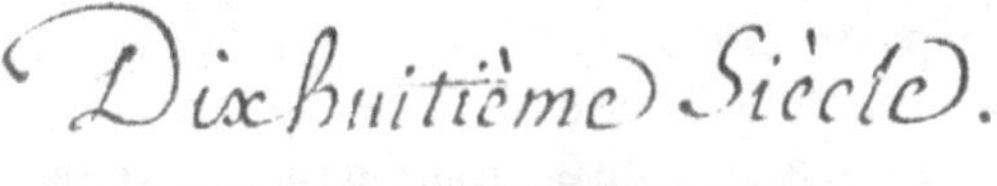
Dix huitième Siècle.

Figure 2.4 Paris, Bibliothèque Mazarine ms 1195.

its author as an "author/compiler"), denies its originality, reduces its sources to the classical inheritance, and presents the first treatise "as a mere catalogue of the names and assertions of the traditional atheists,"[34] which is absolutely untrue, considering the original developments and conclusions presented in *Theophrastus*, as we shall see below. Kors thinks that "if one had read Sextus Empiricus and Lucretius, one learned nothing new about such ancient attitudes."[35] One may not like the philosophical and literary genre practised by *Theophrastus*, even though it is a little paradoxical in a scholar like Kors, who devoted so many years and so many pages to the study of obscure ecclesiastical authors who also practised the compilation genre, with lengthy repetition of old and medieval arguments, albeit con and not pro atheism. One would expect a more balanced assessment and above all a historical approach truer to the real contents of the work and based on an attentive reading, whether he liked or not it.

To give just a few examples of serious misunderstanding that affects Kors's reading of *Theophrastus*: (a) It is not true that *Theophrastus* "was a work that did very little indeed with the formal issue of atheism,"[36] considering that 365 pages (the first and the third treatises) are entirely dedicated to demonstrating – with all sort of philosophical arguments – that "gods [including the monotheistic God] do not exist" and that religion has only human and natural origins. (b) It is not true that "there were no significant epistemological claims about belief or disbelief in God in the *Theophrastus redivivus*" and that, if there were any, they were reducible to "Epicurean and Aristotelian sensationalism."[37] Certainly, these latter play a major role in *Theophrastus*'s epistemology, but one should not forget that there are also more "formal" and sophisticated interrogations about the epistemological issue of theology, as it happens with sceptical arguments that exclude any possibility of reaching the knowledge of divinity, either by reason or by faith. This is one of the earliest and most radical uses of scepticism aimed not at a fideistic goal but at an atheistic one, as Richard H. Popkin, for all his bent towards a more religious interpretation of early modern scepticism, had the scholarly integrity to admit.[38]

To rebut Kors's thesis that in *Theophrastus* there are no "significant epistemological claims about belief or disbelief," we could provide the reader with plenty of passages where the formal issue of the "epistemological" status of faith is seriously addressed with many philosophical arguments and with the help of various sources. But that would take too much space, and it is enough here to refer to the studies mentioned above.[39] Nevertheless, at least one example is worth mentioning, one that also highlights the different and innovative approach of *Theophrastus redivivus* in comparison with its Renaissance sources.

In *Theophrastus* some elements are to be found that are completely missing in works like Pomponazzi's *De immortalitate*, for all his "radical" Aristotelianism, and that make the stance of the former much more clearly definable than that of the latter. First, the anonymous clandestine author develops an entire critique of *fides* and of revelation, on which doubt is never cast as such by Pomponazzi. In *Theophrastus*, *fides* can only hold among Christians, who are already convinced of their beliefs, whereas it has no effect on those who "have gone beyond those boundaries" and who only employ "natural reason" (TR 7).[40] This is why the anonymous author requires a discussion between "philosophers" and "Christian theologians" "on equal terms" ("paribus, ut dicitur, armis"), without invectives ("maledictis") and arguments already prejudiced in favour of faith ("rationibus tantum ab authoritate fidei petitis") (TR 7). It is hard to imagine an approach more distant from the fideistic one. Furthermore, as early as the first treatise, *Theophrastus redivivus* demolishes the probative value of revelation, using sceptical arguments. What is more significant, he reappraises the original epistemological structure of those arguments against the changes they underwent during the Reformation and Counter-Reformation, when they were often associated with positions of a fideistic type. In so doing, he applies to Christian theology and to the idea of revelation, which was absent in the pagan world, the critical arguments that Sextus Empiricus had conceived for the Epicurean and Stoic philosophies. Let us briefly summarize this crucial point of the "epistemological" attack of *Theophrastus redivivus* on faith.

After summarizing Sextus's reasoning concerning the arguments of proof (demonstration, hypothesis, conjecture), the clandestine author brings to light that "gods cannot be demonstrated in any way," neither "per evidens ac manifestum" nor "per incertum et non manifestum" (TR 142–6). One easily recognizes in this dichotomy the basic duality of the sceptical counter-epistemology. The author of *Theophrastus* then takes the floor himself and, significantly, drops the role of simple expositor to develop his own personal considerations, which strike at the remaining means of proof: faith. Still, he says, the possibility remains that God can be known by faith ("Superest ergo ut ex fide deus cognosci possit"). In this connection, he goes further than ancient scepticism and addresses a typical "modern" issue, that of revelation and the means to pinpoint the true one. First, he rejects the idea that revelation may come about by illumination or apparition: the former because it would have the paradoxical effect of making knowable what by definition is supposed to be incomprehensible; the latter because God cannot appear or manifest himself, not having a body. In that they stress these "logical" impossibilities, the arguments in *Theophrastus* recall some similar, albeit less audacious, observations of Hobbes in *Leviathan*, which pointed out that every supposed revelation, including the "true" one, is always mediated by "human" means (prophecies are basically dreams, texts still need interpretations because they are controversial, God does not speak himself but rather through legislators or prophets, so that "faith" is basically trust in those who speak in the name of God, etc.).[41] Much more blatantly than in *Leviathan*, it is the reasons for the doubtful credibility of matters of faith that dominate in *Theophrastus*, since every "revelation" takes the concrete form of "a thought in the mind conceived by the force of the imagination, and augmented and confirmed in the soul due to its very credulity, without any divine influx or contribution." The miracles that support the claim of revelation are only lies and frauds ("figmenta et mendacia fraudesque ad credulos decipiendos"). And since "fides ex auditu" (faith by hearing) in turn depends on the credibility of the primary revelation, it follows that the former's strength collapses together with the latter (TR 147–8). By the way, note that this position, which is taken in the first person (together with many others at decisive points of the work), belies the thesis that TR is entirely "compilative" in nature.

The conclusion drawn by the author of *Theophrastus* could hardly be more frank or more explicit: it throws into crisis the very idea of revelation and therefore also the idea that faith can be a way to revelation. "Those who proclaim to have had a revelation, pretend; those who preach a revelation taken from people who pretended, either believe or pretend to believe." Indeed, "revelation" was excogitated by legislators and princes, whose political interest was to instil religious doctrines in the people with the sole purpose of ensuring their obedience: "Therefore, no one with a sound mind could doubt that faith is only an invention of lawgivers and princes" (TR 148).[42]

7. The Disenchantment of the Supernatural: Vanini, Hobbes, and *Theophrastus redivivus*

The many chapters devoted by the author of TR to the "supernatural" (miracles, prophecies, apparitions, angels and demons, witchcraft, magic, etc.), which accompanies the world of the sacred as an inevitable corollary, show that, again more daringly than Hobbes[43] and almost twenty years before the provocative work by Balthasar Bekker, TR demolished the "enchanted world" and, what is more, drew on an important late Renaissance heterodox thinker: Giulio Cesare Vanini. This is yet another example of "modern" use by an author who is supposedly "premodern," according to too rigid and artificial categorizations.

Not by chance does *Theophrastus* dedicate a long and detailed chapter to "oracles, sybills, prophecies, and miracles" (TR 364–96) within the more extensive treatment "De religione." In this chapter the selective use of Vanini plays a major role, despite the oscillations affecting the whole frame of his approach. TR actually seems to hesitate between two lines of argument that are not coincident, although they converge on the same effect of demythologization. The marvel (be it miracle, oracle, or prophecy) may be traced back from supernatural event to natural effect in two different ways: either by making it a product of occult causes of nature (this was the main approach followed by Pomponazzi in *De incantationibus,* Cardano, and Bodin, this last having a stronger propensity for Neoplatonic demonology) or by taking it as mere deceitful mystification.

In this connection, it is interesting to compare the line of argument in this crucial chapter in *Theophrastus redivivus* with the parallel argument in Vanini's *De admirandis*[44]. The former's chief passages may be summed up as follows. A quotation from Herodotus against the impostures perpetrated in the sanctuaries of antiquity is followed immediately by a declaration of principle that reduces most such phenomena to "frauds" of which the "populace" easily falls victim; only the "philosophers" are able to unmask them, even though they cannot do so openly for fear of reprisals from above (political power) or from below (envy of the people)[45]. Throughout this chapter, TR gives considerable space to "naturalistic" explanations of miraculous phenomena developed by Renaissance authors, yet the author privileges the explanations oriented towards the thesis of imposture (political or ecclesiastical), conceding much less to the hypothesis of the occult powers of nature (magical, astrological, psychological). Thus, while mentioning Cardano's remarks concerning the "natural" causes of oracles (astral influx, particular exhalations of the locality), *Theophrastus* emphasizes that oracles ceased because the underlying fraud perpetrated by priests was unmasked; it was not a result of Christ's coming (TR 365).[46] Also in the case of miracles, Cardano's text provides a variety of explanations, all of which fall into the extended category of "naturalness." Having cleared the ground of phenomena that appear entirely "impossible," the Italian writer points out that most "miracles" are due either to unknown causes of nature or to disturbed senses, or to the force of the imagination; this, however, still leaves room for the "influence of stars" (TR 382–3). It is significant that in introducing this review of Cardano's opinions, the author of *Theophrastus* is quite deflationary, reducing all possible explanations to a clear-cut alternative: either natural causes, or fraud by the priesthood – adding, however, "but above all this latter" (TR 381–2).[47] Cardano himself, the manuscript continues, wrote that "miracles" in the main come about when religious *leges* are founded or at the time of the constitution of empires; therefore, "either they come about through causes unknown to us, but well known to nature, or else they are faked, to make men believe that they came by God's will" (TR 383).

A similar selective filter underlies the interpretation of the other great author interested in "enchantments" (*incantationes*): Pomponazzi. In this case, too, alongside the explanation "per occulta," *Theophrastus* turns to the simpler hypothesis that people's credulity is exploited to make them believe. Thus, a matter of fraud or deceit is stated with increasing force. The author concludes with Machiavelli that miracles ceased occurring when men became incredulous or diffident – as Campanella put it, "religion is the art of reigning and taking people in control and obedience." In this broader Renaissance context, Vanini's contribution is still important to *Theophrastus*, yet the latter stresses much more than his source the imposture thesis. We observe a simplification that is at the same time a demythologization.

Vanini's chapters "De oraculis" and "De Sybillis" indulge rather more in astrological explanations, evoking the power of celestial intelligences over the "imagination" of the prophets; he dwells at length on astral providence, although in the end the conclusions drawn by the character of Julius Caesar himself (Vanini's *De admirandis* takes the form of a dialogue) incline towards a brusque simplification of the issue, opting for the imposture thesis. In connection with oracles, the concluding exchange of the dialogue is explicit: "Alexander: What do you think about oracles? Julius Cesar: they were impostures made up by the priesthood. Alexander: How was it that the fraud was not uncovered? Julius Cesar: Because philosophers did not dare to speak because of fear of public power."[48]

Thus *Theophrastus*'s emphasis on a single aspect, the explanation of the "political" imposture contrived by the government and the priesthood, was already available in this late Renaissance source. Bringing about a more marked "purification" of all magical-occult aspects of the medieval and Renaissance world, the seventeenth-century clandestine author straightened out and strengthened a line of argument already carried out by Vanini.

After a wide review of all the arguments put forward by Pomponazzi, Cardano, and Vanini, *Theophrastus redivivus* draws a conclusion that apparently goes much further towards a complete demythologization of the supernatural sphere:

> Therefore, it is clear from the authoritative sources quoted above, that neither predictions and divinations made by soothsayers and foretellers, nor even oracles, sybills, and prophets are of any value, and that they contain nothing but much vanity, fraud, and superstition; only an ignorant populace could be made believe them by means of frauds, whereas the wise could not. These latter did not believe these things by any means, when they understood that all were priestly fables and deceptions, as Vanini says [*in dial. Cap. 55*], aimed at and for the sake of praise and gain, and inventions of princes helpful to bring the people into obedience, using the fear of the surpernatural god. (TR 379)[49]

Nocturnal apparitions likewise lend themselves to being explained as artificial excogitations, without turning to the deceptive idea of angelic messengers;[50] similarly, some cases of presumed resurrection are due rather to awakening from situations of apparent death, syncope, or sleeping sickness (TR 606–7).[51] The so-called demonomania may also be explained, echoing a fine passage from Vanini, as a sort of "disease" due not to the presence of the "daemon" but rather to an excess of melancholy humour. Nor does *Theophrastus* pass up a roguish hint at "cultural" factors, such as the abundance of cases of presumed possession by the devil in Spain and in Italy would show, in comparison to a very small number in France and almost none at all in Germany or Britain[52]: this, at least, is *Theophrastus*'s thesis (TR 687). Lastly, in a sort of demythologizing crescendo, magic and necromancy themselves are compared by the author to "sleight of hand," although Vanini's related passage still leaves room, somewhat ambiguously, for psychological phenomena such as "faith" and "force of imagination" (TR 695–6),[53] which certainly are not reducible to mere prestidigitation. Compared to the extreme demystification made by *Theophrastus*, Hobbes's reading of these burning questions (the reality of miracles, angels, and demons) seems to be more cautious: he does not deny the existence of angels, but only their incorporeity: they are "aerial bodies."[54] As to demons, he tends to think that demonic possession is about mental illness ("madmen"),[55] yet he has to cope with several passages of the Bible where Jesus addresses the evil spirits and frees men, and also pigs, of them. For all his critique of pagan and Catholic demonology, displayed especially in the fourth part of *Leviathan*, and for all his declared temptation to consider "improper" the language of the Gospels when Jesus commands the spirits to go out of a man, since they are mostly "a disease (as frenzy or lunacy),"[56] Hobbes concludes his long and somewhat tortuous argument against "demonology" with a statement that is at least partly orthodox. He admits the existence of angels and even demons, provided that they are not "incorporeal," and denies that there is such a phenomenon as possession.[57] On this, ch. V of Treatise III of TR is much bolder and clearer, without a compromise of any kind, since it starts from the title "In quo nullos esse daemones sive angelos ostenditur" (TR 676–716).

What emerges from the more straightforward strategy of *Theophrastus redivivus* is thus not only an "atheist" world view but also a disenchanted presentation of the whole biblical story. Being an enemy of every kind of the supernatural, inclined to medical, psychological, or "political" explanations of all these phenomena, the author of *Theophrastus* assigns an extensive value to conclusions that in the original authors (Pomponazzi, Cardano, and even Vanini) are more cautious and circumscribed, not explicitly and radically attacking the Christian supernatural (TR 388). Nearly the same comparison can be made with a "modern" author like Hobbes, who is much less explicit about the thesis of imposture (except for the fourth part of *Leviathan*, mainly dedicated to Catholicism). One cannot find either in Hobbes or in other seventeenth-century authors a statement so clear-cut and explicit as the one we read in *Theophrastus*: "If the same miracles that Pagans consider true are deemed false by Christians, why cannot we consider as fake also the miracles that Christians deem true? Necessarily, all these miracles must have the same origin and credibility, as they overcome the strengths of nature. Therefore, one must admit that all the miracles (if they are really happened) are either the work of nature or human deceitfulness" (TR 388).

8. The Modernity of *Theophrastus redivivus* and the Natural History of Religion

After just the few examples we have given about the use of sources made by the author of *Theophrastus*, we cannot but disagree with Kors when he presents the manuscript as just "a summary of a whole ancient tradition concerning the origin of ancient gods," claiming that it "seems far less an anticipation of the new than merely a repetition of the generalities of the Epicurean tradition." According to Kors, the "author/compiler" would be "quite singular in his almost exclusive reliance upon the ancients ... and in the seriousness with which he takes Cardan, Pomponazzi, and Vanini."[58] Leaving aside the many counter-examples of people (first of all, Pierre Bayle) who "took seriously" and debated at length the same Renaissance authors as *Theophrastus*, we shall focus now on some misunderstandings and overlooked matters that prevented Kors from correctly assessing the historical significance of a work like *Theophrastus redivivus*.

(a) Kors did not realize the cultural novelty of a text that, reading classical authors in tandem with Renaissance philosophers, managed to dissolve the synthesis of natural and supernatural, philosophical and theological, human and divine that almost a century of Christian humanism and concordism had brought about. This major intellectual change made it possible to write the eighteenth-century "critical history of philosophy," starting with Bayle's *Dictionnaire*. To Kors, this true intellectual revolution is reducible to the discovery of the fallacy of "universal consent."[59] That is too little, historically speaking. The new historiography was preceded by the radical criticism of clandestine authors such as *Theophrastus redivivus*.

(b) Kors did not realize that in so doing the anonymous author did not repeat Renaissance philosophers, but went much further. Before him, the tradition of atheism – basically the ancient one – was poor, scanty, and fragmentary, and even if none of his modern sources were "formally" atheistic (Vanini was at worst a pantheist, his *Deus vel Natura* reads like Spinoza's *Deus sive Natura*), the author of *Theophrastus* was able to infer "formal" atheistic conclusions, expanding, developing, and even combining their arguments. As we have already remarked, its writing technique was not unique – like many, TR used other authors as mouthpieces. Nevertheless, TR often speaks in the first person, especially in the work's most topical passages, when it is necessary to draw conclusions, as we saw above. In any case, even when speaking through a third person, it is clear where TR is going and the point the author is making. The author of *Theophrastus* is not a passive collector of "opinions," as TR ironically self-presents starting with the title page, even though – I reasonably suppose – the anonymous never thought that they would be believed.

(c) Kors focused almost exclusively on the issue of atheism and did not realize that *Theophrastus redivivus* enshrines much more than a denial of the existence of God or a demonstration of atheism. The clandestine author takes into account all the ramifications of the religious world view (cosmology, psychology, ethics and politics, history and phenomenology of various religions); and moreover, every topic is provided an alternative conception so that the reader is able to ponder the world, man, his destiny, his happiness, his fears, hopes, and other passions without any theological assumptions. TR was the first to do so with such breadth and radicalism, going literally to the roots of the world view it was intended to debunk. Furthermore, TR outlines a genealogy of society and a reconstruction of human history that erases any religious basis; in so doing the author offers a version of the natural law devoid of theological or metaphysical grounds. This is what we called the *reconstructive* aspect of *Theophrastus*, which cannot be overlooked if one is to understand the aims and the peculiarities of this work.

(d) Kors flattens *Theophrastus*'s discourse on the origins of religion to the level of ancient sources and thus does not realize how its approach is original when compared to them. One could easily object that the same remarks should be addressed to Hobbes, Spinoza, and Hume, who turned sharply to ancient and classical concepts (mostly Epicurean) of religion. In reality, eight years after *Leviathan* and eleven before *Tractatus theologico-politicus*, thanks to a wide variety of sources, the author of *Theophrastus redivivus* was the first and for a long time the only one to write an extensive genealogy of religion in general and of the main religions in particular from a purely human and natural point of view, and from a wider perspective than the other two authors just mentioned: we might say a global perspective, for TR includes in the genealogy not only the three monotheisms but also paganism, which it is considered to be the most ancient religion, and even American and Asian religions; whereas Hobbes and Spinoza focused exclusively on Jewish and Christian traditions. Like Hobbes and Spinoza, the author of *Theophrastus* casts doubt on the Mosaic authorship of the Pentateuch (TR 433, 446),[60] and – despite having no special expertise in biblical philology – deals with the Bible as a wholly human and historical document (see, for example, TR's commentary on the creation story at TR 218–22). The author's methodological principle is clearly stated. Theologians are accustomed to adopt a principle of adaptation to explain biblical expressions, but they do so in a contradictory way; they invoke this principle when Genesis tells the creation story in six days, but not for the idea that the world was created out of nothing. This is contradictory: "Moses either had to speak always according to the human discourse (*more humano*), or he had never" (TR 219). The author of *Theophrastus* adopts consistently an anthropological way of reading the Bible: "Let us keep speaking in a human way. We are men, Moses was a man; therefore, nothing else but the human way of speaking is appropriate both to us and him" (TR 219). Moses being a pure man, we should think that he told his story "in a human way" (*more humano*). In its attempt to explain the origins, development, decline, and fall of religions resorting only to human, psychological, political, and natural factors, *Theophrastus redivivus* is the only early modern text that can be closely compared to David Hume's *Natural History of Religion*; yet this comparison turns out favour of the former, notwithstanding the brilliancy and greater readability of the latter. One century earlier than Hume (*Natural History of Religion* was published in 1757), the author of *Theophrastus* is much bolder (he firmly declares the non-existence of God, whereas Hume often writes of a natural belief in "a supreme spirit," an "invisible and intelligent power" that ordained the whole construction of the nature), and is more global (Hume relies basically on classical sources) as well as more direct and explicit (Hume cautiously keeps away from the biblical religions, saving all his sharp criticisms for paganism and superstition). On one point, however, both the clandestine author and the famous Enlightenment philosopher agree: the most ancient religion (not really the first, according to *Theophrastus*, because the world is cyclically eternal) was polytheism and not monotheism; in this, TR goes against against the wider tendency to favour deism from the time of Bodin until that of Voltaire.

(e) Another remark deserves to be added, one that points to a strange paradox in Kors's book. Just one page after his harsh criticism of *Theophrastus*, Kors starts studying another topic that he apparently likes much more: "Far more important for the dynamic life of seventeenth-century French educated culture than this manuscript without progeny, however, was an emerging genre, the history of 'atheistic' philosophy."[61] He then examines some seventeenth- and eighteenth-century authors (Campanella, Valerianus Magnus, Spizelius, Reimmann, Cudworth, Buddeus, etc.) who wrote "histories of atheism," most of them apologetic of theism and aimed at refuting atheism (Bayle is a case apart). For all this examination, Kors does not realize that (1) the *very first early modern history of atheism*, which moreover was written *from an atheistic standpoint* and not from an apologetic one, was … *Theophrastus redivivus*, which he has just torn apart; (2) the range of *Theophrastus*'s knowledge about the history of atheism is far richer, broader, and more insightful than that of the authors most valued by Kors; and (3) the scope of the author of *Theophrastus*'s research in this field is much more challenging than that of the other apologetic histories, for TR places the development of religions against the background of the general history of humanity and its civilizations. Furthermore, this history is closely related by TR to a theory of physical catastrophes affecting various regions of the planet; in this the author anticipates the Enlightenment histories of the earth, based on geological sequences of catastrophic events.

More recently, Kors has published a two-volume work on atheism and unbelief in France over the same period (1650–1729).[62] Especially in one of them he comes back to the issue of the origins of early modern atheism,[63] with a brief mention of "the now celebrated *Theophrastus redivivus*."[64] It seems that compared to the previous book, Kors has profoundly changed his mind regarding the main thesis of his research: instead of viewing atheism mainly as a "ghost" projected by theologians and controversialists in order to attack their adversaries as willing or rather unwilling promoters of atheism with their wrong philosophies, he thinks now that there were real "lay" atheist thinkers – something he finds especially among the clandestine writers, and not only among theologians beset with a kind of paranoia. Kors describes these atheists in the flesh as people "who rejected all proofs of God and who explicitly proclaimed and embraced a belief that we inhabit an undesigned, unplanned universe, the product of unthinking matter and fortuitous accidents, not of a perfect being, intelligence, or intention. Those authors believed that we indeed found ourselves left to our own devices and expedients in a world that reflected no wisdom and no love of us."[65] Regarding this profound change, Kors declares his debt to the current and wide research on clandestine,[66] even if "the actually atheist texts were largely synthetic repetitions, reworkings, and rearrangements of themes and specific arguments already circulated in the culture."[67] One who has studied or simply had the patience to read the thousand pages of *Theoprastus redivivus* should be relieved: the summary definition of atheism quoted above perfectly fits this work; also, the reappraisal of the clandestine composition style should help the reader better understand its peculiarities. What is more, it appears now that, judging from the titles of the two-volume set, one dedicated to Epicureanism and the other to Naturalism, ancient traditions strongly contributed to the birth of the Enlightenment, and this is another vantage point for understanding a text like *Theophrastus*. By the way, this clandestine author was fond of Epicurus and Lucretius, yet not only of them, and besides being an atheist, TR could be also described as a naturalist, according to many of the various definitions of naturalism given in the seventeenth century and aptly commented on by Kors.[68] These changes of perspective actually would require more explanation than what is given in the new work, all the more so since in the introduction to *Epicureans and Atheists*, Kors mentions again from time to time his old thesis and stresses the continuity with the older volume.[69] The result is, to say the least, a bit confusing. For instance, in the volume in which he studies clandestine texts for more than fifty pages he still declares in the introduction that there is little new to find there, thus reaffirming his old conviction that atheism had theological roots, because "orthodoxy begat heterodoxy from its own substance." According to his introductory remarks: "Atheism was an eclectic synthesis, in positive form, of ideas ubiquitous in the theistically orthodox world."[70] Later, before examining "Historians' Atheists and Historical Atheism," however, he presents theism and materialistic atheism as "two mutually exclusive and fundamental choices," so that "almost all (if not all) fundamental philosophical and theological conclusions, ancient and modern, could be placed in one or those two alternatives."[71] The opposition thesis seems not to be consistent with the previous "ubiquity" thesis.

Despite all these changes, Kors does not seem to have changed his mind about *Theophrastus redivivus*. He still dismisses this work in a few lines as "essentially a compilation of the naturalistic views of ancient philosophers, at first, second, and third hand."[72] To avoid repeating what we have already said against this interpretation, we shall add only that having studied for years the text and its sources, we have found quotations at second hand to be, in fact, very few, because the clandestine author, being a true erudite and lover of his cherished philosophers, made it a point of honour to go straight to the sources; as is not the case with many other eighteenth-century manuscripts, we have not yet found a quotation at third hand. It is noteworthy, on the other hand, that in a footnote in his book, Kors mentions "three copies of the *Theophrastus redivivus* in all of Europe,"[73] when in fact there are four, as was clearly indicated in the first edition of the text, published more than thirty-five years ago.

9. The Author of *Theophrastus redivivus* as a "Radical Libertine"

Coming now to the other issue, that of radicalism, we can ask: Is the modern *Theophrastus* a "radical philosopher"? If so, in what sense? And if he is, how far does this radicalism go? Obviously the answer depends largely on the historical meaning we give to this word. One good historical definition has been provided by Jonathan Israel in his first book on the "radical Enlightenment." To quote him: "the Radical Enlightenment, whether on an atheistic or deistic basis, rejected all compromise with the past and sought to sweep away existing structures entirely, rejecting the Creation as traditionally understood in Judaeo-Christian civilization, and the intervention of a providential God in human affairs, denying the possibility of miracles and reward and punishment in the afterlife, scorning all forms of ecclesiastical authority, and refusing to accept that there is any God-ordained social hierarchy, concentration of privilege or land-ownership in noble hands, or religious sanction for monarchy."[74] I suppose that even the first statement ("to sweep away any structure") must be meant in an intellectual sense, at least for the period considered (1650–1750), because no one, before the French Revolution, thought to put into practice his own "radical" convictions. It is easy to see that all of these requirements are met, and strongly met, by *Theophrastus redivivus*.[75]

I suggest, however, that the author is better understood as a "radical libertine" and not as a "radical Enlightenment philosopher," not only for evident chronological reasons but also because the author of *Theophrastus* had mixed feelings about three basic premises that are usually tightly associated with "radicalism": I mean the egalitarian concept of reason, the ideal of universal emancipation, and therefore the preference for republican and democratic governments. Actually, *Theophrastus* neither totally rejects nor totally accepts these ideas, but often qualifies them.

Let us commence from the bottom: the author is not a republican, yet he tries to trace the origins of power and its legitimacy not from above, but from below, starting from the state of nature, where everyone is equal to everyone else (TR 841–8). Thus human equality is for him the starting point of human history. In this regard, *Theophrastus* strongly supports the equality of reason, given that every man is endowed with the same natural intellect and therefore can have easy access to the truth. Thus two of the three basic requirements are met, at least in principle: the clandestine author supports human equality and thinks the use of reason is open to all and moreover easy to practise. Being adulterated and the result of artificial techniques, the world of false *opiniones* is much more complicated, requires particular skill, and presupposes the division of society into hierarchical groups. By contrast, "true and natural reason" is an inborn faculty and does not depend on any particular training. Difficulties with its use arise solely from prejudices and opinions that have only the appearance of reason ("falsa et degeneris ratio"). If the metaphysical contexts of the two works were not so different, or rather opposite, one might compare the democratic praise of "vera et naruralis ratio" made by *Theophrastus* with Descartes's famous claim in *Discours de la méthode*: "le bon sens ou la raison est naturellement égale en tous les hommes." As in Descartes, there is the other side of the coin, and this is not only about epistemology, as in *Discours*, but involves the whole settlement of politics and society. For Descartes, the variety of opinions and the misuse of reason have their roots in not following the right intellectual conduct; for *Theophrastus*, the supremacy of "false reason" is connected to the fact that in the present situation the great majority of people are prevented by impostures and illusions from using right reason, and even more they are deeply hostile to the few philosophers who do make use of it. All of this has serious consequences for the possibility of spreading right ideas and the right use of natural reason. Despite the author's conviction that truth, in principle, is easily accessible and within reach of everyone, the *sapiens* (wise man) in practice will not popularize his ideas and will instead restrain their circulation to the closed milieu of those who in seventeenth-century France were called *esprits forts* or *libertins*. Nearly the same might be said about the idea of freedom: the author of *Theophrastus* claims "absolute freedom" for all (TR 901–2), but only in the state of nature and in the inner circle of the author's peers; in the civilized state, TR keeps this kind of liberty only for the wise and – for reasons of prudence and self-preservation – the author does not oppose the authorities.[76] We could consider TR a seventeenth-century libertarian who tried to experiment with natural reason, equality, and freedom in the closed world of the private sphere, practising for the rest of the world an original mix of intellectual radicalism and political realism: TR never gave up criticizing all the aspects of the *Ancient Régime* – intellectual, religious, social, political – yet the clandestine author never tried to put in practice this criticism in the open space of society.

10. Cosmological "Revolutions" and the "Demolition of the Laws"

It would be tempting to assimilate this stance to that of the so-called French *libertins érudits*. After all, their motto was "intus ut libet, foris ut licet," exactly the same the one adopted and recommended by the author of *Theophrastus* from the very first pages of the manuscript (TR 35). However, the author's mix of radicalism and realism is different from that of the other libertines. Three outstanding features distinguish TR from people like Naudé, Le Vayer, Patin, and Sorbière (there are many others, but I think the following are the more important).

The first distinguishing feature is *Theophrastus*'s stronger attachment to the idea of a state of nature, and therefore to the notion of natural liberty. Actually, a state of nature and natural liberty were neither myths, nor hypotheses, nor pure ideals; they were and still are historical realities (TR 841 ff.). There was natural liberty in the past, and there will be in the future, after the breakdown of false civilizations and a return to our primitive origins (TR 266–301). In the present situation, we are told in *Theophrastus,* it is impossible, even dangerous, to enlighten the people, because the introduction of property and the establishment of authorities have completely changed its nature. But this will not last forever, because, thanks to the catastrophes provoked by historical cycles, men are going to recover freedom and equality, and again begin to use sound intellect, once social hierarchies and adulterated opinions disappear. This kind of human rebirth will be due to "revolutions": not political revolutions, but "*revolutiones*" in the original Latin meaning – that is, in great cyclical and cosmological returns that are going to restart human history from the very beginning. Of course, this conviction, supported in great length and detail in *Theophrastus,* can be considered a form of primitivism, yet not that far from the theorists of the state of nature like Hobbes and Locke. This point of view allows the author to better contrast original equality and freedom with the perversions of the political state.

The second distinguishing feature is a consequence of the first and specifically regards the assessment of politics. A "radical" Renaissance Aristotelian like Pomponazzi[77] was already aware that "laws lie and pretend" and that all religions, considered as *leges* – that is, political and religious regulations at the same time – abound in impostures, starting with the myth of the immortality of the soul. For all his radicalism, however, he was still ready to "justify" politicians in the name of the "common good": the politician "should not be condemned" even when he lies, like the doctor who pretends to a good purpose, according to Plato's old metaphor. One century later, the French libertines were more disenchanted about the real origins and exercise of power and could no longer share in this Aristotelian ideology of the "common good." They still considered lies "useful" – not, however, for the public utility but rather for the power and dominance of a few people. At the same time, living in a time of social and political revolutions (the many *Frondes* and the English civil wars), they feared for peace and social order. Thus they still would have partly agreed with Pomponazzi, saying that the politician can be justified in the name, not of the common good, but of reason of state, in order to help avoid disorder and popular upheavals. Accordingly, most libertines acted as state officers: Naudé as Mazarin's secretary, La Mothe Le Vayer as a writer on commission for Richelieu and the Dauphin, Sorbière as an apologist of absolutism. Compared to them the author of *Theophrastus redivivus* is much more "radical": TR no longer "justifies" the politician, either for moral reasons, like Pomponazzi, or for political reasons, like Naudé and Le Vayer. TR fully practises the right to criticize and blame the authorities, recommending retreat from official responsibilities and the denial of any political solidarity (TR 888–90). TR advises no involvement in public life, no compromise between "truth" and "utility," no apology for power. The author retains the liberty to say that an opinion is "false," even if it turns out to be "useful" and unmasks the ideological status of many doctrines, revealing to whom and for what purpose they are useful. Even if the work remains clandestine and reserved, in this concern about total freedom of thinking, expression, and also behaviour, the author of *Theophrastus redivivus* follows in the footsteps of the ancient cynics (TR 898 ff.), as the final "icon sapientis" amply shows and as J.C. Laursen has aptly remarked.[78] *Theophrastus*'s ideal posture in the face of power is not that of the "counsellor of the prince," like Naudé and Le Vayer, but on the contrary that of Diogenes the Cynic before Alexander the Great, in the famous episode that is mentioned with praise in the manuscript (TR 903).[79]

The third distinguishing feature of the clandestine author regards the actual extent of their program. Among the libertines, the author of *Theophrastus redivivus* is the only one to suggest the "demolition of the laws" as a remedy to inequalities and injustice. Having described all the constraints on natural liberty and natural reason that have transformed civil association in a "prison for life" through the establishment of private property, social and political hierarchies, marriage, army and war, and so on (TR 854–60), the author suggests that regulation through the natural law, based on the Golden Rule, would be better and much fairer than the civil law even in its present state (TR 865 ff.). This is the most "radical" angle of *Theophrastus*, whereas its "libertine" angle consists in realism regarding the origins of power, realism the author shares with most of the other French *libertins érudits*. Like Naudé and Le Vayer, as earlier Montaigne and Charron, the author of *Theophrastus* cannot imagine a "rational" construction of power, for example through the political contract as it is suggested by Hobbes and later by Locke. To be more precise, TR is too disenchanted to accept that one could freely and rationally give up his natural rights, his natural freedom, unless he is forced to do so by tricks, impostures, and violence. Keeping eyes open on the real nature of power prevents TR from seeing another possible source of authority that could consist in a rational and mutual agreement aimed at obtaining the advantages of security and protection. If in abstract the exchange between obedience and protection might be profitable, the big problem is that for the clandestine author the protection of the state is much more an oppression than a benefit. That politics could be matter of voluntary subjection and scientific knowledge, as Hobbes would have it, is what a "radical libertine" like the author of *Theophrastus redivivus* would never have accepted.

Since TR does not even mention the doctrine of the political covenant, it is clear that the clandestine author rejects as unrealistic and impossible the idea of grounding politics on an original contract as a conscious and voluntary stipulation. Like the French sceptics and libertines, he subscribes to the very opposite formula of the "mysterious foundations"[80] of any political authority. Of course, that formula must be read ironically: "mysterious" does not hint at the "divine" origin of authority, it rather means that the original spring of political power must be kept hidden because it is always plunged into violence and cheating. After all, how can a reasoned consensus about authority be settled, if the society derived from it is much worse than the state where natural liberty prevails? J.C. Laursen has qualified the author of *Theophrastus redivivus* as a "proto-libertarian,"[81] and I think this definition, however anachronistic for that time, fits well enough the "radical libertine." In fact, the author of *Theophrastus* most emphasizes the evil provoked by losing natural liberty, in comparison with the political state described as a systematic power of oppression that denatures man with all his natural rights and skills. Accordingly, the analogy between *Theophrastus* and some trends of modern libertarianism can be developed further. Both are committed to the promotion of individual liberty, even if the clandestine author is necessarily more cautious in practice, due to the political situation of his time, and more inclined to absolutism than to liberalism; both rest on a theory of human rights according to which every individual has free disposal of himself and his resources; both consider that government is not a necessary evil, but a largely unnecessary evil (TR 854–8); both, being enemies of the "big state," would reduce government to a minimum, and in this, the author of *Theophrastus* is of much more consequence than some "modern" libertarians. The latter, like Nozick, not only support a theory of the right entitlement to legitimate private property but also accept at least a "minimal" state for protecting property rights. The early modern libertarian is even more radical: instead of a permanent government, TR accepts only provisional authorities for temporary purposes (as in times of war), sees human associations as spontaneous gatherings without any need for an institutional and lasting hierarchy, attacks marriage as a harsh submission to an unnatural law (891), and thinks that children and women should be held in common, as the Cynics did and as Plato and the Stoics claimed. Most of all, TR supports equality of rights, including sexual freedom, between men and women, and this is the reason the author considers polygamy an unfair arrangement when it is not accompanied by polyandry (TR 891, 893). The "radical libertine" was much more radical than a modern libertarian.

Appendix: A Comparison between a "Radical" Renaissance Philosopher and a "Radical Libertine"

Pomponazzi, *De immortalitate animae.* The politician as the doctor of the soul; religions were established aiming at the common good.	*Theophrastus redivivus* comments on this same passage and reaches a very different conclusion, speaking in the first person: the ruin of laws and religions.
The politician is like a doctor of the soul, his aim is to render the man more obedient than learned. To reach this end, one must proceed according to the differences between men, on the basis of their different tempers [...] Most of them, if they behave well, do it much more for fear of eternal punishment than for hope for eternal good, because we know more about evils than about eternal rewards. As this tendency can be helpful to all men, no matter what their nature, the legislator, seeing the general bent towards evil and aiming at the common good, established the immortality of soul. For this, he did not care about the truth, but only about morality, in order to lead men to virtue. Nor should one blame	It should therefore come as no surprise if the politician used similar arts, yet philosophers, looking not to public utility but only to the truth of the thing, scorn all this and using natural intellect demolish the inventions of all laws. They follow nature alone, which does not require such pretences to divert men from evil and push them towards good: indeed, according to nature, no one is bad, there is nothing that is not good, just, legitimate. [...] Things being so, legislators, stop with your pretences, "stop deceiving the ignorant people with vain enticements" (Ovid, Metamorphoses, V, 308–9). May the gods you so easily contrived step back, may the religion

the politician for that; just as the doctor pretends in order to heal the sick person, so the politician invents things to lead citizens along the righteous path.	with all this baleful mechanism with which you have adorned it go to ruin, laugh at the immortality of the soul as a delirium of an old woman, consider the demons and underworld as lies and once these monsters have been eliminated, let us look directly at natural joy (TR 712).

NOTES

1 See esp. Margaret Jacob, *The Radical Enlightenment: Pantheists, Freemasons, and Republicans* (London: Allen and Unwin, 1981).

2 For the German *Frühaufklärung*, see Martin Mulsow, *Moderne aus dem Untergrund. Radikale Frühaufklärung in Deutschland 1680–1720* (Hamburg: Meiner, 2002), now in English: *Enlightenment Underground: Radical Germany, 1680–1720* (Charlottesville: University of Virginia Press, 2015); and my review article: "Modernità dalla clandestinità, " *Giornale Critico della Filosofia Italiana* 84 (2005): 172–80.

3 Jonathan Israel, *Radical Enlightenment: Philosophy and the Making of Modernity, 1650–1750* (Oxford: Oxford University Press, 2001); idem, *Enlightenment Contested: Philosophy, Modernity, and the Emancipation of Man, 1670–1752* (Oxford: Oxford University Press, 2006). On the specific topic of clandestine literature, see the numerous articles by M. Benitez, collected in his volumes *La Face cachée des Lumières. Recherches sur les manuscrits philosophiques clandestins de l'âge classique* (Paris and Oxford: Universitas–Voltaire Foundation, 1996); and *Le Foyer clandestin des lumières* (Paris: H. Champion, 2013), 2 vols.

4 Series: "Libre pensée et Littérature clandestine" (Paris: H. Champion). McKenna edits with Pierre-François Moreau the specialized periodical *La Lettre Clandestine* (Paris: Presses de la Sorbonne) as well as "Libertinage et Philosophie au XVIIe siècle" (Presses de l'Université de Saint-Etienne; now Paris: Classiques Garnier).

5 Series: "Freidenker der deutschen Aufklärung" (Stuttgart: Frommann-Holzboog).

6 For an overview of research on this topic see these collections of articles: Catherine Secrétan, Tristan Dagron, and Laurent Bove, eds, *Qu'est-ce que*

les Lumières "radicales"? Libertinage, athéisme et spinozisme dans le tournant philosophique de l'âge classique (Paris: Editions Amsterdam, 2007); Jonathan Israel and Martin Mulsow, eds, *Radikalaufklärung* (Berlin: Suhrkamp, 2014); and Steffen Ducheyne, ed., *Reassessing the Radical Enlightenment* (London: Routledge, 2018).

7 For the history of clandestine philosophies in the seventeenth and eighteenth centuries, let me refer to my previous syntheses: Gianni Paganini, "Haupttendenzen der clandestinen Philosophie" in *Űberwegs Grundriss der Geschichte der Philosophie. Die Philosophie des 17. Jahrhunderts,* ed. Jean-Pierre Schobinger, Band 1/1. Hrsg. v. Teil 1 Allgemeine Themen (Basel: Schwabe, 1998), 121–95; *Les Philosophies clandestines à l'âge classique* (Paris: P.U.F., 2005); *Introduzione alle filosofie clandestine,* Italian expanded ed. (Roma: Laterza, 2008).

8 Guido Canziani and Gianni Paganini, eds, *Theophrastus redivivus,* first and critical edition with commentary, 2 vols (Florence: La Nuova Italia, 1981–2, CXXIV-998), now distributed by Franco Angeli Editore, Milan. The pagination is continuous between the two vols. Hereafter cited in the text with the initials "TR" and the page numbers. The edition is accompanied by a wide commentary concerning sources, comparison with other contemporary authors, historical and philosophical explanations, etc. In order not to overburden this chapter, I will only occasionally refer to this commentary, which in any case may be found in the edition at the corresponding pages of the text.

9 Ira O. Wade, *The Clandestine Organization and Diffusion of Philosophical Ideas in France from 1700 to 1750* (Princeton: Princeton University Press, 1938), ch. 7, "The Theophrastus redivivus," 222–8. This chapter, however, is seriously vitiated by the idea that TR was a mere collection of texts derived from other clandestine manuscripts, which is not true.

10 John Stevenson Spink, "La diffusion des idées materialists et antireligieuses au début du XVIIIe siècle: le *Theophrastus redivivus*", *Revue d'histoire littéraire de la France,* 49, 1937, 248–55; idem, *French Free-Thought from Gassendi to Voltaire* (London: Athlone Press, 1960), 66–71.

11 See Tullio Gregory, *Theophrastus redivivus. Erudizione e ateismo nel Seicento* (Napoli: Morano, 1979); Gianni Paganini, "La critica della civiltà nel *Theophrastus redivivus.* I. Natura e cultura," in T. Gregory, G. Paganini, G. Canziani, O. Pompeo, F.-D. Pastine et al., *Ricerche su letteratura libertina e letteratura clandestina nel Seicento* (Florence: La Nuova Italia, 1981), 49–82; Guido Canziani, II. "Ordine naturale e legalità civile," in ibid., 83–118; Gianni Paganini "L'anthropologie naturaliste d'un esprit fort. Thèmes et problèmes pomponaciens dans le *Theophrastus redivivus,*" *Dix-septième siècle,*

38, 1985, 349–78; Canziani, "Une encyclopédie naturaliste de la Renaissance devant la critique libertine du XVIIe siècle: le *Theophrastus redivivus* lecteur de Cardan," in ibid., 379–406. Recently, the ENS in Lyon organized a conference on TR: Nicole Gengoux, ed., *Entre la Renaissance et les Lumières, le* Theophrastus redivivus (Paris: Champion, 2014), with a complete critical bibliography.

12 TR has now entered "La Pléiade," with the French translation of Treatise VI, regarding "life according to nature," and therefore morals and politics: *Libertins du XVII*[e] siècle, vols I–II, ed. Jacques Prévot, Thierry Redouelle, and d'Étienne Wolff (vol. I), and Prévot, Laure Jestaz, and Hélène Ostrowiecki (vol. II) (Paris: Gallimard, 1998–2004). The most recent study on TR is that of Nicole Gengoux, *Un Athéisme philosophique à l'âge classique: le Theophrastus redivivus* (Paris, H. Champion, 2014), 2 vols. This study is extremely rich and also has the great merit of stressing the philosophical content of the work, putting it against the background of Renaissance naturalism and other seventeenth-century philosophies, especially those of Spinoza and Hobbes. Furthermore, the author places TR's political thought in the context of the general crisis of politics in France at that time (see esp. ch. 22, 665–704). On the interpretive theses expressed in this book, I have two major points of disagreement: (a) Gengoux minimizes the importance of the thesis on religion as imposture, which is one of the main strengths of TR; and (b) according to her, TR makes a sharp distinction between a "pure religion" and the others, whereas one of the boldest statements of TR is that "omnis religio esse bona osternditur" (TR 530 ff.) provided that it rightly performs its political function of control over the people. Even Gengoux must admit that this supposed "pure" religion comes down to the simple natural law and thus again to atheism. Among the many aspects that contradict the thesis of the "pure religion" is the circumstance that TR does not take up but rather completely neglects all the passages and arguments referring to "natural religion" in a source well-known to the author, the *Colloquium Heptaplomeres,* that could have played in favour of Gengoux's thesis. For a more developed examination of this work, see my review in *La Lettre Clandestine,* 23, 2015, 329–42.

13 Cf. Gianni Paganini, "Le premier traité philosophique de l'âge moderne: le *Theophrastus redivivus* (1659)," in *Athéisme devoilé aux temps modernes,* ed. Anne Staquet (Bruxelles: Académie Royale de Belgique, 2013), 199–214.

14 He borrows these words, at that time still often written in Greek, from *La République* of Jean Bodin.

15 Winfried Schröder, *Ursprünge des Atheismus. Untersuchungen zur Metaphysik- und Religionskritik des 17. und 18. Jahrhunderts* (Stuttgart:

Frommann-Holzboog, 1998), 404–8. For a debate on the historiography of atheism, see Gianni Paganini, "Un athéisme d'ancien régime? Pour une histoire de l'athéisme à part entière: l'héritage de la pensée de la Renaissance et l'incrédulité modern," in *La question de l'athéisme au dix-septième siècle,* ed. Pierre Lurbe and Sylvie Taussig (Turnhout: Brepols, 2004), 105–30. An important debate on modern atheism took place at the conference evoked above: Staquet, ed., *Athéisme devoilé aux temps modernes,* where the stance of TR is represented. In the book edited by Michael Hunter and David Wootton, *Atheism from the Reformation to the Enlightenment* (Oxford: Clarendon Press, 1992), TR is strangely absent. Michel Buckley, *At the Origins of Modern Atheism* (New Haven: Yale University Press, 1987), makes atheism start with Diderot and d'Holbach. When it is mentioned, TR is often misunderstood, as in Georges Minois, *Histoire de l'athéisme: Les incroyants dans le Monde Occidental des Origines à Nos Jours* (Paris: Fayard, 1988), where TR is considered "agnostic" on the existence of God. TR is missing in the other compilation by the same author: Minois, *Dictionnaire des athées, agnostiques, sceptiques et autres mécréants* (Paris: A. Michel, 2012). Even though TR is out of the chronological scope of Gianluca Mori, *L'ateismo dei moderni. Filosofia e negazione di Dio da Spinoza a d'Holbach* (Roma: Carocci, 2016), there are some scattered references to it.

16 An attentive analysis of these "paratexts" (preamble and "peroratio ad fideles") was made by Hélène Ostrowiecki in two essays: "Le paratexte du *Theophrastus redivivus,*" in *La philosophie clandestine à l'Age classique,* ed. Antony McKenna and Alain Mothu (Paris and Oxford: Universitas, 1997), 267–78; and "Le jeu de l'athéisme dans le *Theophrastus redivivus,*" *Revue philosophique de la France et de l'étranger,* 186, 1996, 265–77. After stressing the "dialogic" or "polyphonic" composition of the work, as it makes several authors speak in the text, Ostrowiecki reached a highly controversial conclusion, claiming that TR is not atheistic, but represents a sort of "third party" between atheism and belief. In reality, the "orthodox" professions of faith commented on by Ostrowiecki were usually shields used by heterodox authors to hide and protect themselves from persecution, even if the shield was ridiculously tenuous, as it was both in TR and Pomponazzi. For a comparative analysis, see Gianni Paganini, "Early Modern Atheism and Renaissance Philosophy: The Play of Paratexts in *Theophrastus redivivus* and Pomponazzi's *De immortalitate,*" *Intellectual History Review,* 26, no. 1 (2016): 25–31. Afterwards, Ostrowiecki changed her mind, acknowledging the overall atheistic nature of TR. See Hélène Bah-Ostrowiecki, *Le "Theophrastus redivivus": érudition et combat antireligieux au XVIIe siècle* (Paris: Champion, 2012). Mori, *L'ateismo dei moderni,* 14, seems to relaunch a distinction

between "atheus" and "sapiens" in TR; in reality, he rather stresses the fact that the appellation "atheist" was so uncommon and so hot at that time that even true atheists avoided it. Actually, the definition that Mori (14) gives of the author of TR ("a *sapiens* who lives 'according to nature,' denying the existence of any transcendent divinity") comes down to true and simple atheism.

17 For an analysis of TR's cosmology, see Gianni Paganini, "Voyage dans le Monde du *Theophrastus redivivus*," in *Entre la Renaissance et les Lumièrs…*, ed. N. Gengoux, 109–37.

18 On the role played by the thesis of the imposture of religions, see Gianni Paganini, "Quand, comment et pourquoi les législateurs sont-ils devenus des imposteurs? Averroïsme et libertinisme 'radical' dans le *Theophrastus redivivus (1659)*," *La Lettre Clandestine*, 24, 2016, 103–32; idem, "Pour une archéologie de l'imposture à l'époque moderne: L'imposture des 'leges' dans le *Theophrastus redivivus* et son inscription dans l'histoire de l'humanité," in *Figures de l'imposture. Entre philosophie, littérature et sciences*, ed. Jean-Charles Darmon (Paris: Editions Desjonquères, 2013), 29–53.

19 Robert Burton, *The Anatomy of Melancholy* (Oxford: Clarendon Press, 1994), 3 vols.

20 For a rough list of publications that contained manuscript texts, taken from my *Introduzione alle filosofie clandestine*, 152: *Traité des trois imposteurs*: 1719, 1721, 1768, 1775, 1776, 1777, 1780, 1793; *Nouvelles liberté de penser*: 1743; *Examen de la religion*: 1745; *Extrait* of Meslier's *Testament*: 1762; in *Evangile de la Raison*: 1764, 1765, 1768; *Lettre de Thrasybule à Leucippe*: 1765 (in Fréret, *Œuvres*: 1775, 1776, 1787–92); *Le Militaire philosophe*: 1768; *Examen critique des apologistes de la religion chrétienne*: 1766, 1767, 1768, 1775, 1777; *Le Ciel ouvert à tous les hommes*: 1768, 1783; *Traité de l'Infini créé*: 1769; *Israël vengé*: 1770; *Jordanus Brunus redivivus*: 1771; *Dialogues sur l'âme*: 1771; *La fausseté des miracles des deux Testaments*: 1775.

21 For the complex transformation of Aristotle's "first philosophy," which included also theology, into "naturalism without pantheism" by TR, see Paganini, "Voyage dans le monde du *Theophrastus*," esp. 129–37.

22 Lucien Febvre, *Le problème de l'incroyance au XVI*[e] *siècle. La religion de Rabelais* (Paris: A. Michel, 1942). See the new edition (Paris: A. Michel, 2003), 381, 498.

23 See Alan Charles Kors, *Atheism in France, 1650–1720*, vol. 1: *The Orthodox Sources of Disbelief* (Princeton: Princeton University Press, 1990), 222–5 on TR. This same idea about the genesis of early modern atheism can be found in Kors's entry "Atheism" in *Encyclopedia of the Enlightenment*, ed. Kors

(Oxford: Oxford University Press, 2003), vol. 1, 94–7. For a very different idea, see Gianluca Mori, "Ateismo e religione naturale," in *Illuminismo,* ed. Gianni Paganini and Edoardo Tortarolo (Torino: Boringhieri, 2008), 33–45.

24 See the description of manuscripts in the edition of TR: lxiii–lxviii.

25 For example, the aide-de-camp of Prince Eugene von Savoy, Baron von Hohendorf, succeeded only in getting a manuscript copy of Giordano Bruno, *Spaccio della bestia trionfante,* which he obtained from John Toland, who let his own printed copy be copied by an amanuensis (see TR lxxxi).

26 For an analysis of the important entries dedicated to Renaissance philosophers (Pomponazzi, Cremonini, Cesalpino, Taurellus, Zabarella, Valla, Lascaris, Barbarus, Fernel, Huarte, Sylvius, Patrizzi, Cardano, Giordano Bruno, Kepler, Bacon, Corbinelli, Puccius, Socinus, Agrippa H.C., Agricola, Berigardus, Charron, Erasmus, Guicciardini, Ochin, Mariana, Rorarius, Charron, etc.) in Bayle's *Dictionnaire,* see Gianni Paganini, *Analisi della fede e critica della ragione nella filosofia di Pierre Bayle* (Florence: La Nuova Italia), 331–47. Renaissance philosophy and culture was still alive, and often provocative, at the end of seventeenth century

27 See TR lxv.

28 See TR lxxviii–ci for the description of the extremely rich and heterodox libraries owned by Prince Eugene and his aide-de-camp Hohendorf.

29 In his "Recensio" of the manuscripts present in the Hofbibliothek in Vienna, Nicolao Forlosia gives a detailed account of the contents of TR. See TR ci–ciii.

30 On Giannone's connection with Forlosia, when he stayed in Vienna, with a detailed comparison between some sections of Giannone's *Triregno* and *Theophrastus,* see Gianni Paganini, "Pietro Giannone, Nicola Forlosia et le *Theophrastus redivivus* à Vienne," *Lias,* 12, 1985, 263–86.

31 On this aftermath of TR, Kors relies uniquely on Jeroom Vercruysse, "Le *Theophrastus redivivus* au 18e siècle: mythe et réalité," in Gregory et al., "Ricerche su letteratura libertina e letteratura clandestine," 297–304. Kors seems to ignore the more detailed information afforded by the introduction to TR, ciii–cxi.

32 There are many eighteenth-century French manuscripts that keep a trace of TR in their titles, even if they were not truly affiliated with the Latin work: *Des miracles. Traduction d'un chapitre du mscr. Intitulé Theophrastus redivivus*; *Theophrastus redivivus. Traduction des quatre premiers chapitres du Theophrastus redivivus*; *L'Ame mortelle ou réponse aux objections que font les partisans de son immortalité, ouvrage traduit du manuscrit qui a pour titre: Theophrastus redivivus.* There is also a printed book titled *La Fausseté des miracles des deux Testaments,*

Prouvée par le parallèle avec des prodiges opérés dans diverses sectes. Ouvrage traduit du manuscrit latin intitulé: Theophrastus redivivus 1775, published by M.M. Rey (Amsterdam). Another manuscript, published in 1771, *J. Brunus redivivus ou Traité des erreurs populaires. Ouvrage critique, historique et philosophique, imité de Pomponace,* attests to the interest in Renaissance philosophy, even at a later date, contrary to what Kors contends.

33 Kors, *Atheism,* 222. Vercruysse's conclusion is, however, a bit different from Kors's. See Vercruysse, "Le *Theophrastus redivivus* au 18e siècle," 303: "dans ce cas [TR] le mythe et la réalité se conjuguent en une seule et même dynamique." It is not only about myth, there is also some reality in this chain on witnesses.

34 Kors, *Atheism,* 223.

35 Kors, *Atheism,* 224.

36 Kors, *Atheism,* 224.

37 Kors, *Atheism,* 224.

38 See the reviews of the edition of TR made by Richard H. Popkin, *Renaissance Quarterly* 37 (1984): 630–4; and Charles B. Schmitt, *History of European Ideas* 6 (1985): 367–9.

39 Notes 11, 13, 15.

40 "sed infirma prorsus at debilior [fides] videtur adversus eos qui hos fines transiliunt, quique rationibus naturalibus ad pugnam nos lacessunt et provocant."

41 See Thomas Hobbes, *Leviathan,* 32, esp. 5 ("How God speaketh to man"), ed. Edwin Curley (Indianapolis: Hackett, 1994), 246–7. Unlike TR, however, Hobbes admits, at least in principle, that God can speak to man "immediately," as happened to Moses.

42 TR 148. For the use of sceptical arguments (taken from Sextus Empiricus) from an atheist perspective already in the seventeenth century (an approach later codified by Bayle), I refer the reader to my essay "Avant la *Promenade du sceptique*: Pyrrhonisme et clandestinité de Bayle à Diderot," in *Scepticisme, Clandestinité et Libre Pensée / Scepticism, Clandestinity and Free-Thinking,* ed. Gianni Paganini, Miguel Benitez, and J. Dybikowski (Champion: Paris, 2002), 17–46; see also Paganini, *Skepsis. Le Débat des modernes sur le scepticisme* (Paris: Vrin, 2008).

43 In principle, Hobbes does not deny that miracles as supernatural events could occur, even while remarking that they almost disappeared in post-biblical times (see *Leviathan,* 37, 292–300).

44 Giulio Cesare Vanini, *De Admirandis Naturae Reginae Deaeque Mortalium Arcanis. Libri quatuor* (Lutetiae: Apud Adrianum Perier, 1616; anastatic reprint, Galatina: Congedo, 1985), dial. LII "De oraculis," 379–92 and LIII "De Sybillis," 392–405.

45 "Itaque soli philosophi has fraudes detegere possunt, quas in vulgus edere non audent ob metum publicae potestatis quae semper patitur ut populus in religione decipiatur, quin etiam sedulo prospicit ut sic fiat."

46 For the passages from Cardano cf. TR 371–2, 379, and the related comments. On the relations between the libertines and Renaissance thought, see Lorenzo Bianchi, *Rinascimento e libertinismo. Studi su Gabriel Naudé* (Bibliopolis: Napoli, 1996). More in general, see Tullio Gregory, *Etica e religione nella critica libertina* (Guida: Napoli, 1986).

47 "De miraculis in religionibus tantopere celebratis par extitit ratio. Ea enim aut ad causas naturales referre necesse est, aut ad fraudes sacerdotumque deceptiones, sed praesertim ad has."

48 Vanini, *De admirandis,* 391.

49 Cf. Vanini, *De admirandis,* 412. TR 387 refers to the passage where Vanini explains as "political" fraud the so-called miracles of Vespasian, aimed – he writes – "ad fraudem et deceptionem" (Vanini, *De admirandis,* 441–2). TR goes further, wondering: "Quid vetat caetera miracula istis similia pari modo conficta fuisse existimare?" A heated excursus follows on the claimed resurrections of the dead, which likewise are compared to "praestigiationes et illusiones" (TR 387–390).

50 TR 603, who refers to Vanini, *De admirandis,* 368–9, with the exemplary story of the mystification put in place by Cenechus, King of the Scots.

51 Cf. Vanini, *De admirandis,* 456–7.

52 Cf. Vanini, *De admirandis,* 406–7.

53 Cf. Vanini, *De admirandis,* 478.

54 Hobbes, *Leviathan,* 34, 261–71.

55 Hobbes, *Leviathan,* 8, 26 (45–6); see also 45, 4 (437–8).

56 Hobbes, *Leviathan,* 45, 5 (438).

57 Hobbes, *Leviathan,* 45, 8 (440–1): "To conclude: I find in Scripture that there be angels and spirits, good and evil, but not that they are incorporeal [...] And I find that there are spirits corporeal (though subtle and invisible), but not that any man's body was possessed or inhabited by them."

58 Kors, *Atheism,* 223.

59 Kors, Atheism, 223.

60 Moses is considered a cunning and tyrannical political legislator (TR 433–47): "saevissimus tyrannus" (445), Egyptian magician (436); even the disappearance of his corpse after his death was organized as a trick (446). "Sic igitur vixit Moses, sic mortuus est, astutus in morte ut in vita" (447). For the "clandestine" pattern of secularization of Jewish history compared to Spinoza's view, see my article: "*Moïse clandestin, Moïse Spinoziste,* in "La Lettre Clandestine", n° 26 (2018), 21–32.

61 Kors, *Atheism,* 225.

62 Alan C. Kors, *Epicureans and Atheists in France, 1650–1729* (Cambridge: Cambridge University Press, 2016); idem, *Naturalism and Unbelief in France, 1650–1729* (Cambridge: Cambridge University Press, 2016).

63 Kors, *Epicureans*, ch. 4 ("Historian's Atheists and Historical Atheists"), 139–97, mostly dedicated to the philosophical clandestine literature.

64 Kors, *Epicureans*, 147.

65 Kors, *Epicureans*, 140.

66 Kors, *Epicureans*, 145–7.

67 Kors, *Epicureans*, 146.

68 Kors, *Naturalism*, 5 ff.

69 Kors, *Epicureans*, 1 ff.

70 Kors, *Epicureans*, 3.

71 Kors, *Epicureans*, 139.

72 Kors, *Epicureans*, 148.

73 Kors, *Epicureans*, 148n22.

74 Israel, *Radical Enlightenment*, 11. For the discussion of Israel's overall thesis, in connection with *clandestina*, cf. Paganini, *Introduzione alle filosofie clandestine*, 149–61.

75 According to his main thesis, which is focused on the Spinozistic origins of the radical Enlightenment, Israel tends to exclude from his genealogy of "radicalism" the contribution of libertinism (see Israel, *Radical Enlightenment*, 15); and in his ch. 36 ("The Clandestine Philosophical Manuscripts," 684–703) he does not grasp the role of forerunner played by TR. Afterwards, TR was readmitted to the "big picture" of the "radical Enlightenment" under the rubric of "Radical Renaissance": Israel, *Enlightenment Contested: Philosophy, Modernity, and the Emanicipation of Man, 1670–1752* (Oxford: Oxford University Press, 2006), 481. In the chapter "Radical Renaissance" (481–95), Israel remarks that eighteenth-century thinkers and historians of philosophy "lent a wholly new significance to late Renaissance philosophical naturalism which, though Aristotelian, looked also subversive and atheistic in orientation" (481). This assessment is rightly extended to TR. We would, however, add the warning that Aristotelianism, though relevant, is not the only inspiring philosophy in TR.

76 For a broad illustration of TR's "radicalism," cf. our recent articles: Gianni Paganini, "Qu'est-ce qu'un 'libertin radical'? Le *Theophrastus redivivus*," in *Libertin! Usage d'une invective aux XVIe s XVIIe siècles*, ed. Thomas Berns, Anne Staquet, and Monique Weis (Paris: Classiques Garnier, 2013), 213–30; idem, "Wie aus Gesetzgebern Betrüger werden. Eine philosophische Archäologie des 'radikalen' Libertinismus," in *Radikalaufklärung*, ed. Martin Mulsow (Berlin: Suhrkamp, 2014), 49–91.

77 For this label of "radical," extended to a Renaissance Aristotelian philosopher, see Martin Pine, *Pietro Pomponazzi: Radical Philosopher of the Renaissance* (Padova: Antenore, 1986).

78 For the "cynical" vein in TR, see J.C. Laursen, "Cynicism in the Theophrastus redivivus," in Gengoux, ed., *Entre la Renaissance et les Lumières*, 47–66.

79 For a comparison between a "radical" Renaissance philosopher (Pomponazzi) who "justifies" the laws and a "radical libertine" (*Theophrastus redivivus*) that argues for their abolition, see the appendix to this chapter.

80 Cf. Montaigne, *Essais*, III, xiii, 1072: "Or les loix se maintiennent en credit, non parce qu'elles sont justes, mais parce qu'elles sont loix. C'est le fondement mystique de leur authorité; elles n'en ont point d'autre, qui bien leur sert. Elles sont souvent faictes par des sots, plus souvent par des gens qui, en haine d'equalité, ont faute d'equité, mais toujours par des hommes, autheurs vains et irresolus." There are many other passages in the same vein. Cf. e.g., I, xliii, 270. For the relations between the French sceptics and Hobbes's political philosophy, see Gianni Paganini, "Hobbes and the French Skeptics," in *Skepticism and Political Thought in the Seventeenth and Eighteenth Centuries*, ed. John Christian Laursen and Gianni Paganini (Toronto: University of Toronto Press, 2015), 55–82.

81 Laursen, "Cynicism," 53.

PART TWO

POLITICS, RELIGION, AND CLANDESTINITY IN NORTHERN EUROPE

Chapter Three

Danish Clandestina from the Early Seventeenth Century? Two Secret Manuscripts and the Destiny of the Mathematician Christoffer Dybvad

FREDERIK STJERNFELT

In the year 1620, legal proceedings were undertaken in Copenhagen against the mathematician Christoffer Dybvad. The court was convened in the Academic Senate of the University (the "Konsistorium"), which since the 1536–7 Danish Reformation had been the organ responsible for state censorship as well as the proper court for an academic citizen like Dybvad. Among the evidence in the possession of the council were two handwritten papers seized during a raid on Dybvad's home. Both can be found at the State Archives in Copenhagen.[1] In the standard academic use of the term "clandestine writings," reference is most often made to early-Enlightenment tracts of the later seventeenth and eighteenth centuries. In this volume, Dybvad's two papers form an interesting borderline case. They are earlier than most papers in the standard lists of clandestine writings; moreover, they cannot be said to be Enlightenment papers in any standard use of the word. Still, they are strongly political in nature, attacking the mixed constitution of Denmark with its king and its State Council of noblemen ("Rigsraad") and advocating instead the introduction of absolutism. This was long before the eighteenth-century heyday of "enlightened absolutism," but still, it seems to be something in that direction that Dybvad had in mind, with his proposal that the State Council be extended to cover other estates than the nobility (so as to include also the peasants, the townsmen, and the learned estate), as well as with his emphasis on academic reform. Simultaneously, Dybvad strongly attacked the leading clergy as well as the Lutheran orthodoxy of his time and indulged in libertine fantasies. In that sense, Dybvad may still seem to count as a sort of forerunner of the early Enlightenment. Both manuscripts are informed by currents such as Jean Bodin's political philosophy and Justus Lipsius's neo-Stoicism and thus constitute radical, clandestine versions and developments of contemporaneous philosophies.

Christoffer Dybvad (ca 1578–1622; also Christopher Dibwad, Christophorus Diwadius, etc.) was a talented mathematician who had been further educated in medicine and theology during a seven-year journey (1599–1606) that had taken him to, among other places, Leiden and Paris.[2] In Caen, he took the doctoral degree in medicine, probably in 1602.[3] In Leiden, academic life was blooming since the foundation of the university in 1575; here, he became acquainted with Arminian circles on the non-predestination "left wing" of Calvinism, which fostered in him a more liberal theology than the Lutheran orthodoxy developing in Denmark – as well as a more liberal view as to the coexistence of theologies. Perhaps it was in Paris that he became acquainted with Jean Bodin's *Six livres de la république* (1576), which gave him the idea of absolutist rule, where one ruler took possession of all of the seven basic rights of majesty[4] – and of the prince as an objective and dispassionate political figure elevated above the tensions and strife between factions of society and able to contain potential struggles between them, thus guaranteeing the unity of the state. Dybvad published widely on mathematical matters and introduced decimal numbers to Denmark with his *Decarithmia* (1602), inspired by the Dutch mathematician Simon Stevin.

Dybvad's Father Jørgen Dybvad

A prerequisite to understanding Dybvad's clandestine writings is the destiny of his father, Jørgen Dybvad (?–1612), whose fate in several ways anticipated that of his son. Also a mathematician, Jørgen was a professor at the University of Copenhagen from 1578 and a theology professor from 1590; he also served as rector for the year 1596–7 and again 1605–6. Trained in Wittenberg and Leipzig and an admirer of Melanchthon, Jørgen viewed Calvin as well as Luther as modern church fathers. In 1605, Jørgen planned to publish a book titled *Theses de Juramento* on the taking of oaths, which also contained a criticism of a recent Danish reform of measurements, which he claimed was unjust against peasants. He did not secure permission to print and was forced to withdraw the book. In 1607 he published the uncensored *Theses de sanctificando Sabbatho,* which contained criticism of the nobility's tax-exempt status, of certain church rules, and of the Jesuits – simultaneously attacking the Spanish Crown. For this offence, in 1607 a case was opened against Jørgen at the

Konsistorium of the university. During the trial, he refused to withdraw his criticisms and even maintained he should be thanked for presenting them. Like his son, he seems to have conceived it as a duty for academics with their special knowledge to support, inform, and even correct political rulers. His attack on the Spanish Crown seems to have been decisive in the case, for he was seen as meddling in the king's foreign policy and disrespecting political authority in one and the same move. Despite his illustrious career, Jørgen was dismissed from his professorship. He never found another position, and died in poverty five years later in 1612. The 1607 court case followed immediately his son's return from abroad in 1606 and probably effectively blocked Christoffer's promising university career. Simultaneously, he inherited and even expanded on his father's viewpoints, regarding both criticism of the nobility's political role and a more liberal stance than the Lutheran orthodoxy, which was tightening its grip on Denmark during the same period. Jørgen's professor colleague, the theologian Hans Poulsen Resen (1561–1638), was at the time introducing many of the strict principles of the Lutheran "Formula of Concord" of 1577, which had originally been rejected by the Danish king Frederik II, but many of whose ideas Resen was now able to spread in the clergy and state apparatus after the young Christian IV ascended to the throne in 1588. Resen was particularly on guard against so-called crypto-Calvinists, and even Luther's old partner Melanchthon was increasingly branded a crypto-Calvinist. Thus, it now may have seemed that the Academic Senate could not risk hiring yet another of those crypto-Calvinist Dybvads.

Christoffer went abroad again to France in 1608–10. Back in Denmark, he tried to intervene in politics in 1614 with a manuscript intended for Christian IV titled *Observationes politicæ*,[5] written in a mix of Latin and Danish. It promoted an absolutism inspired by Bodin as well as by Louis XI's advisor Philippe de Commines, who related how his king had dismissed the French State Council of Nobles.[6] The text also sketched a conspiracy against the king, supposedly led by Professor Resen, who was now in the process of becoming a bishop. It saw the ongoing Danish series of court cases against crypto-Calvinist clergy as part of an undermining of the king's position, and it directly warned the king that Resen and the State Council might seek to end the king's life.[7] It is unknown whether the king ever read Dybvad's alarmist *Observationes*. In 1618, however, Christoffer was appointed royal mathematician at Christian's court, where his principal duty would be to compute horoscopes. What sealed his fate was an event during his visit, in 1619, to the large Norwegian provincial town of Bergen. There, Christoffer for some reason felt free to present his political views: absolutism should be introduced, and now that he himself had a position at court he was confident that the time was ripe. He added, perhaps jokingly, that the execution of no more than eight hundred noblemen would suffice for the purpose. He further

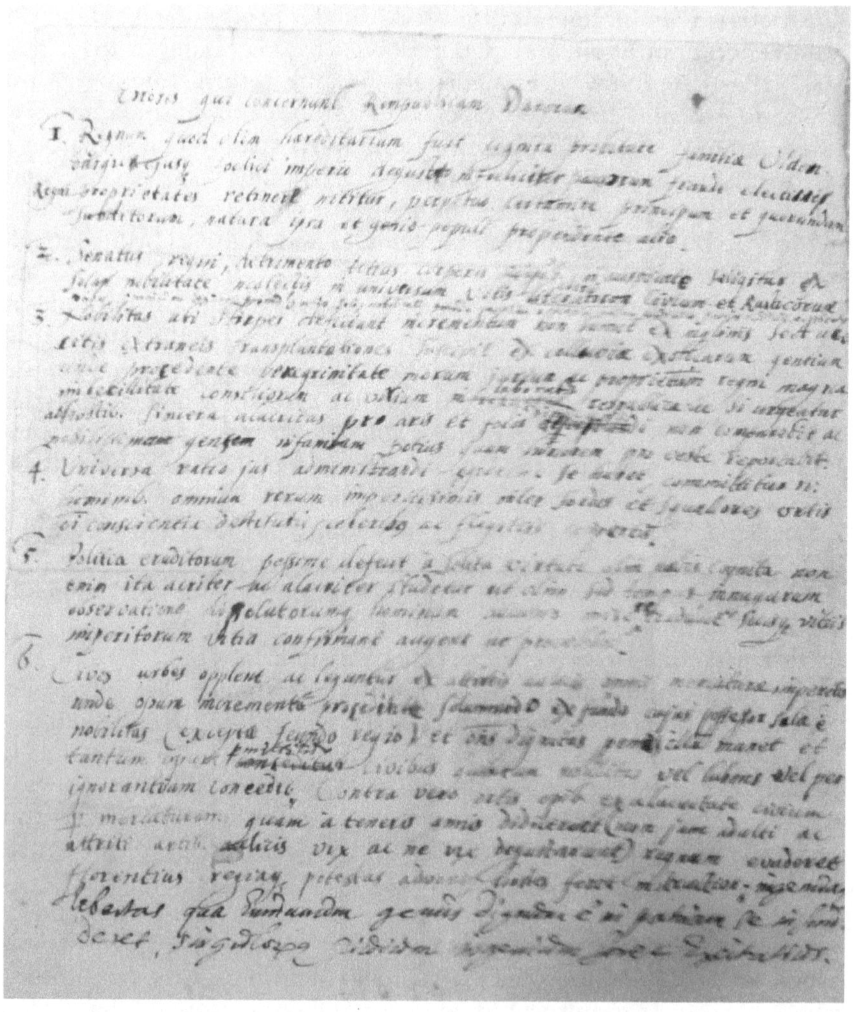

Figure 3.1 Dybvad's political one-pager *Errores qui concernunt Republicam Danorum.*

ridiculed Resen, who had in the meantime risen to Bishop of Zealand in 1615, the highest position in the Danish-Norwegian Church.

The host of the meeting was Christoffer's old fellow-student Niels Paaske, now bishop of Bergen. To the king, however, Paaske told the tale of what had happened in Bergen, and when Christoffer returned to Denmark, he was imprisoned in the Blue Tower of the Royal Castle in central Copenhagen and questioned by the leading noblemen of the State Council. Simultaneously, authorities ransacked Dybvad's home, where they found two clandestine manuscripts titled *Errores, qui concernunt rempublicam Danorum* and *JOCI AULICI,* respectively – both of them in his own meticulous handwriting. Along with detailed witness reports from Bergen, the two manuscripts became central pieces of evidence in the ensuing court case against Dybvad because of their radical character. The former is a political one-pager with six bullet points (handed down in at least three copies in the State Archives in Copenhagen); the second is a twenty-eight-page booklet with poems, notes, and jokes – particularly the latter proved fateful in court.

The *Errores*

The political one-pager is so concise that we can reproduce it here in its entirety.[8] A raw English translation goes as follows:[9]

> Errors concerning the state of the Danes
>
> 1. The kingdom was formerly hereditary, but even if it has learnt to know the righteousness of the Oldenburgian house and enjoyed the advantages of its fortunate government, it assumes more and more, to its ruin, the character of an elective state. This is due to the treacherous behaviour of a few men, but has been accompanied by an ongoing strife between the princes and certain subjects, and the very nature and tendency of the people points in another direction.
>
> 2. The council of state, unfortunately and to the harm of the whole of the state, is elected solely from the nobility, while no consideration is given to the wishes of the clergy, the commoners, and the peasants. For that reason, the whole legislation only aims toward the benefit of the nobility, and the roots of the trees of the fatherland are subdued by miserable servitude.
>
> 3. When lineages perish, the nobility does not seek replenishment from the natives, but takes in strangers and transfers groups of foreigners into the state. Therefore alien customs and laws increase, estates come into foreign possession, and the state will for that reason come to suffer from foolish decisions and lack of strength. When it is attacked by enemies, no real

zeal to fight for home and hearth will emerge, and the lot of the nobility will be shame rather than honour.

4. The administration of justice is generally bad, for it is entrusted to completely unexperienced persons, coming from raw and uneducated homes, who are unscrupulous and besmirched by crime and misdeeds.

5. The worst thing is that the learned class of society is deeply lacking in the traditional virtue we once knew, for they do not seek energetically and eagerly to do as before, but now they miserably teach the observation of bits and disconnected pieces to the quibbling of men, and from their ignorant fallacies they increase and spread error.

6. Citizens fill the cities and are taught by shameless courtiers about how to trade with the inexperienced, so wealth depends only on growth from the estates whose owners are exclusively the nobility (except for the king's estate) and is continually in the hands of the elite, and only so much wealth accrues to the citizens as the nobility yields, either voluntarily or by ignorance. On the other hand, it is by means of riches originating from the activity of the citizens through trade, which they learned from their earliest years (now adult and weary, they have barely tasted the courtly arts), that a kingdom escapes [war] if it blooms. The royal power would be better armed against the enemy, just like the noble freedom which dignifies the human race, if the fatherland is not defeated and the skills of the single citizens are stimulated.

The treatise condenses some of the points already addressed in the *Observationes*, in a more concise and systematic way. The six points may be summarized as follows:

(1) Against noble influence in government, and in favour of preservation of hereditary rule rather than elective kingdom.
(2) All estates should be represented in the State Council.
(3) The introduction of foreign noblemen into the state government should cease.
(4) The court system should be reformed and use educated and non-criminal personnel.
(5) Academia should go back to the old striving for the integration of knowledge.
(6) Trade and individual skills should be encouraged in order to make the state richer.

As to the first point, Dybvad argues with tradition and points to the deeds and virtues of the ruling Oldenburgian house on the Danish throne. It is clear, however, that his real argument is political rather than traditional: the present situation is one of detrimental strife between king and noblemen, which is what should be avoided. So speaking about the hereditary kingdom here is really an indirect way of expressing support for absolutism and the ensuing removal of the nobility from political power.

The second point displays a surprising proto-democratic idea, that of the representation of a plurality of estates. Dybvad adds three estates to his conception of a reformed State Council: the learned/the clergy, the commoners, and the peasants. It is remarkable that he first, as in the *Observationes*, chooses the more general notion of "the learned" ("litteratorum") before settling on "cleri, civium et rusticorum," thus narrowing his first supplementary estate to the clergy. Perhaps this was a tactical move to seek support among clergy and theologians, the leading professors at the university.

The third point introduces a standard complaint in the medium-sized state of Denmark, whach at the time was on the margins of European political developments: the introduction of foreign noblemen in state administration. This was a traditional item of grievance over the centuries for Danish noblemen, who saw what they perceived as their native rights to state office forfeited with the introduction of better trained foreigners, often Germans. In particular, it was claimed that foreign noblemen lacked the patriotism needed to defend the state in the event of war – an argument seemingly directed at the king as head of the army.

The fourth point makes a damning judgment of the state of the Danish courts of law: justices are deemed uneducated, not to mention unprincipled and downright criminal themselves. Dybvad would of course have had, as warning instances in the back of his mind, the conviction of his own father and the actual persecution of crypto-Calvinists in Denmark.

The fifth point criticizes the state of the learned society, that is, the learned estate as a whole, primarily the clergy, as well as its educational centre, the University of Copenhagen, Denmark's only academic institution at the time. Here as well, Dybvad would have had both his father's and his own example to substantiate his charge; however, his more detailed criticism is less than clear, even if Dybvad with his knowledge of the new university in Leiden was in a good position to judge the standard of academia in Denmark. Some unspecified earlier state of the learned estate is judged superior, compared to which the present state is one of decay: now the learned merely "teach the observation of bits and disconnected pieces to the quibbling of men, and from their ignorant fallacies they increase and spread error." This hairsplitting accusation is perhaps aimed indirectly at the already mentioned series of famous court cases against crypto-Calvinist theologians of the immediate Danish past – against Iver Stub (1609), Oluf Kock (1613), Niels Michelsen Aalborg (1614), and Hans Knudsen Vejle (1615), all of whom had been dismissed from their positions and some of whom had been driven from Denmark.[10] That being so, the "bits and pieces" giving rise to complaints could refer to the list of unalterable basic dogmas of the Lutheran orthodoxy, which were used as standards against which to measure other points of view. This leaves unsaid, however, what really characterized the "traditional virtue" that had gone before.

The sixth point represents a sort of early trade liberalism. Again, a central target is the nobility for their quasi-monopoly over commerce, and it is argued that the real source of wealth in a society is "the activity of citizens through trade." This proto-liberal idea is given a political frame when it is argued that such wealth is what really buttresses society against military defeat. Dybvad's emphasis on the skills of the citizens makes it clear, again, that he is basing, from below, his political doctrine on the townsmen and the learned (a classic social alliance for liberals), whereas from above, he is basing it on a king, strengthened by absolutism.

It is not known whether the one-pager of the *Errores* was intended for circulation; nor do we know whether it indeed did circulate, and if so, in what circles. The existence of three copies of the paper in the State Archives indicates that more may exist or once existed, but it is also important to realize that the three copies seem to stand in a clear relation of ascendancy. Of two virtually identical copies, one seems to have been selected for corrections, of which two in particular should be mentioned. One is the removal of the specific Danish references in the text – through the deletion of the words "Danorum" in the title and "Oldenburgica" in the first bullet point. This makes the paper no longer a specific complaint about something rotten in the state of Denmark, but rather a more general political program potentially applicable to other European states at the time. The other is the deletion of bullet point 5 about "academia," indicated by the crossing out of the text. A third copy of the *Errores* now displays the text afresh after the inclusion of these corrections – thus the three copies constitute one original, one proof sheet, and one corrected version.[11]

An interesting note commenting on the corrections appears on the flip side of the proof sheet version with deletions. Written in a quick hand, it is rather hard to read, and several words remain illegible, but it seems to express the idea that all souls are subjected to servitude imposed by their corporeal incarnation. For that reason, embodied souls must be kept in servitude by a ruler who conceives of his state as indivisible ("Indiuidua"). It follows that corrupt elements must be expelled from the state through the vigilance of princes. And the basic form of the state, indivisibility, must be proclaimed. The note thus does not refer to the particular character of the proof corrections of the text (its Danish character, the complaint about academia); rather, it adds a further Lutheran theological argument for absolutism, unity of the state, and even the persecution of those who deviate from these.[12] What is interesting, however, is that the note concludes with the following postscript or signature: "Corrigebantur R. Maiestati Anno 1619" – "This has been corrected for [or to] R. Majesty in the year 1619."

It is difficult to judge whether the much more hastily written note is by the same or another hand as the much more carefully written text of *Errores* and *JOCI*. In any case, the writer seems to be indicating that the corrections on the front side of the sheet have been made on behalf of, as proposed by, or as intended for the Royal Majesty, that is, Christian IV, at whose court Dybvad was now employed. Until further corroboration of this, it might, of course, be Dybvad's or the note writer's own supposition that he knew the king's mind – or, perhaps he introduced the text changes on the page himself after less binding or less explicit discussions with the king, who need not even have seen or known about the actual written document. Christian IV, it should be noted, was one of the strongest supporters of Lutheran orthodoxy on the list of Danish kings, so the Lutheran-sounding note might not be far from his views. In any case, if the king did know about or to some extent approve of Dybvad's political ideas, or even know the manuscript itself, this would explain why Dybvad was so confident that absolutism might be introduced in the near future.

Dybvad the younger did not commit the errors of his father: that of entrusting his thoughts to the printing press. Moreover, the very nature of those thoughts would have made it impossible for them to pass censorship. The court case against his father had probably cautioned Christoffer Dybvad to keep his thoughts in private, hidden, handwritten manuscripts. Even if *Errores* or some of its contents might have been known to the king, Dybvad must have realized the risks he would face from the nobility and the clergy if he expressed such ideas in a more public forum. We are not in a position to know whether a more restricted circulation, in certain circles, of the political program of *Errores* took place.

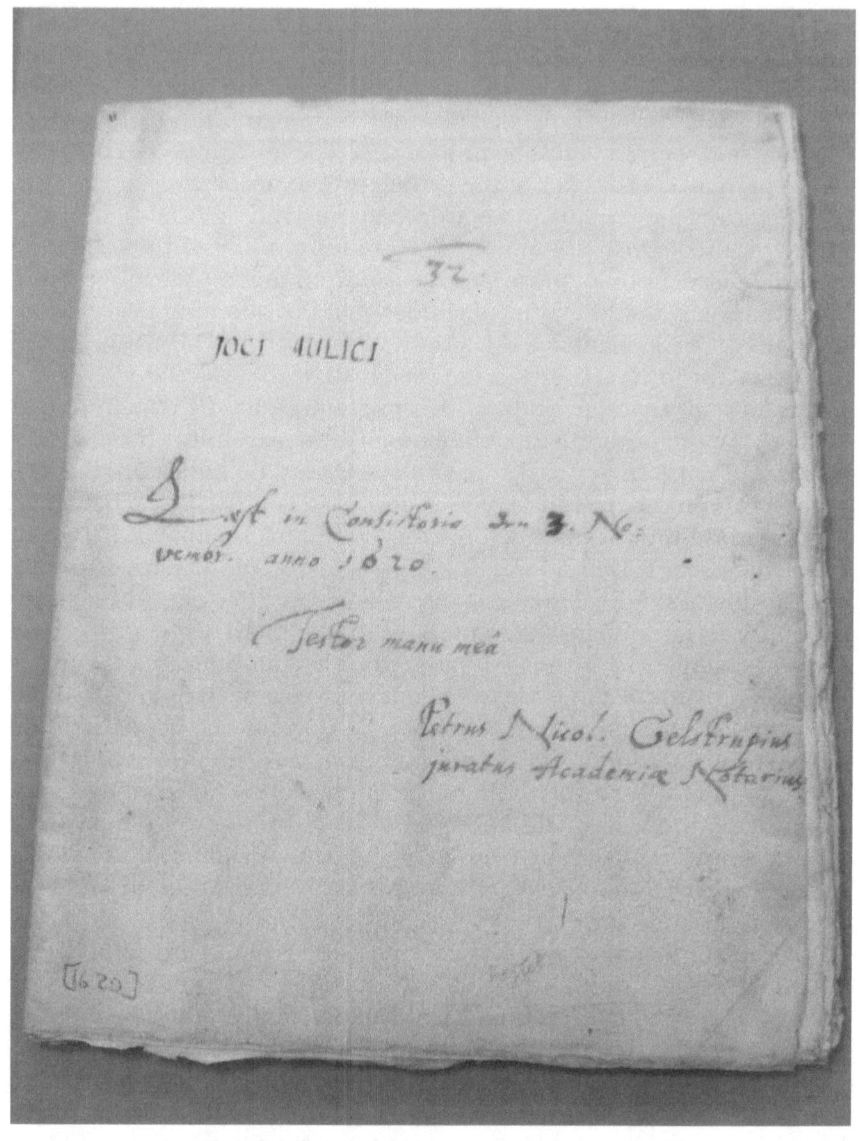

Figure 3.2 Dybvad's twenty-eight-page booklet *JOCI AULICI.*

The *JOCI AULICI* – First Half

As to the second of the clandestine manuscripts found at Dybvad's home, it can be said almost with certainty that circulation was not intended, nor did it occur. *JOCI* bears all the hallmarks of a private notebook, one with few of the argumentation strategies aimed at different recipient groups that are visible to us in *Errores.*

The booklet has seven folded sheets – twenty-eight pages, of which four serve as a cover, with only the title *JOCI AULICI* appearing in capital letters on the front page. The remaining unpaginated twenty-four pages fall in two halves, one largely a collection of quotes, the other containing the jokes mentioned in the title. The first twelve pages and some lines of the next consist of mixed brief texts, most of them quotes. Some of them address court life and thus support the booklet's title. They are introduced under a header that roughly states: "Amusements we propose together with really great geniuses, affecting some people in these sheets, as joking as they are serious, either to ridicule or to be considered literally."[13]

These brief texts include the following:

1. A Latin verse by the British poet Thomas Chaloner (page 3) with a brief introduction by Dybvad.
2. An anonymous Italian verse (by Giovanni Batista Guarini) (page 4).
3. A Latin verse by Justus Lipsius (page 4).
4. A Latin verse by Seneca.
5. Four brief pieces under the headers RECTE MONIT QUIDAM; ACTIUS SINCERUS. HOC DIXIT; SIMILIS HIC JACET: and "Hac respexit magnus ille Galliæ Cancellarius Hospitalius," respectively (pages 5–6).
6. An anonymous Latin verse (by Michel de l'Hospital) (page 6).
7. An anonymous Latin prose text (from the conclusion of Lucian's satire "Libellus de iis qui mercede conducti, in divitum familiis vivunt," in the translation of Erasmus of Rotterdam) (pages 6 and 7).[14]
8. An anonymous Latin prose text (from the German polyhistor Philippus Camerarius's *OPERAE HORARVM SVBCISIVARVM,*[15] (pages 7 and 8) – a book from which Dybvad apparently also took several of the other quotes in the first half of *JOCI,* cf. below).
9. An anonymous Latin prose text beginning with "Memini cum apud Anglos" – which cannot be identified as a quote, so most probably it

is Dybvad's own prose, again referring to Thomas Chaloner (pages 8 and 9).

10. An anonymous Latin prose text (from the 1591 Latin version of the *Six Livres* of Jean Bodin: *Andegavensis, de republica libri sex*) (pages 9 and 10).[16]
11. A series of brief epitaph quotes, with the headlines EPITAPHIUM GLAPHYRÆ; LUCRETIÆ EPITAPHIUM IN EPISCOPATI VITERBIENSI; and MONUMENTUM RAVINNÆ (page 11); INSCRIPTIO SARDANAPALI; IN ARAGONIA URBE; ROMÆ ALIUD; IBIDEM; PATAVII; and "Othocarus Rex Bohemia" (page 12); "Andronicus Imperator Constantinopolitanus";[17] SACRAMENTUM SENATORIUM ROMANI (this text seems to stem from Valerius Maximus's "Factorum et Dictorum"); and INSCRIPTIO ELEGANS ET PIA IN CURIA RATISBONENSI (pages 13 and 14, as the title indicates from a plate at the town hall of Regensburg).
12. A Latin prose text with the header "P. Camer. Cent. 3 cap. 6.," as indicated, again from Camerarius's *Operae* (page 14).
13. An anonymous Latin prose text beginning with "Cura vetusta eruditio in contemplum" (which cannot be identified as a quote, and seems to be Dybvad's own transition text from the first to the second half of the *JOCI*) (pages 14 and 15).[18]

Many of the quotes also appear in Camerarius's *Operae*, which Dybvad seems to have used as a principal source. Camerarius's book appeared in several versions beginning in 1591, and it became widely circulated as a sort of *vademecum* lexicon of knowledge pertaining to both human and natural history, with plenty of facts and quotes, expressed from his own perspective.[19] It enjoyed widespread use and was translated into French, German, Italian, and English. For most of his long life, Camerarius (1537–1624) was a high-ranking professor at the University of Altdorf near Nuremberg, but he had also lived in Leiden before Dybvad's arrival there. Given that so many of Dybvad's quotes can be found in the 1609 version of Camerarius's major work, often with the exact same demarcations, the conclusion is natural that Dybvad used a copy of that book for inspiration.

The first half of *JOCI* as a whole gives the idea of a sort of repository book with a collection of small texts and quotes that the owner treasured and wished to keep. This part of *JOCI* played no role in the court case, and existing treatments of Dybvad such as those by Pontoppidan[20] and Rørdam[21] all but ignore this part; an exception is Fink-Jensen, who cogently points out that in the short introduction to the pamphlet's first verse, the influential British courtier and chancellor of Prince Henry, Thomas Chaleron (1559–1615), is mentioned by Dybvad as his friend.

From the text "Memini cum" later in the pamphlet, Fink-Jensen concludes that Dybvad may even have visited Chaleron in Britain; and he suggests that the conspicuous absence from the court case of this connection – with its intimation of Dybvad's meddling in international politics – may have been ordered by the king.[22] There is some confusion here, however. The verse quoted is not by the Chaleron who was active at the British court during Dybvad's lifetime, but by his stepfather and namesake Thomas Chaleron, statesman and poet (1521–1565), and was published in his *De rep. Anglorum instauranda libri decem* (1579).[23] To make matters more complicated, this collection of poetry was published posthumously by his young stepson. So it seems that Dybvad may have confused the two namesakes and actually thought that the verse was written by his London contact.

In any event, Chaleron the elder's verse begins with a pastoral scene of calm, faith, and love amid woods and streams, presumably at court, then continues by stating that the halls of Penelope are ripe with suitors, that fraud and treason are everywhere, and for that reason, "Ergo nec aspectu tutum est divertere" (i.e., no aspect of the whole should be diverted away from the whole). In short, this is a plea for unity of state, for absolutism at court. *JOCI* thus begins by restating absolutism, this time in a lyrical-pastoral manner.

The next poem, by Giovanni Battista Guarini, continues the pastoral theme: happy is he who turns his back on city work to indulge in wandering studies and merry hunting in forests, like the ancients. Dybvad was fond of Stoicism, and the next two texts pertain to that – a verse by the leading Dutch neo-Stoicist, Justus Lipsius, followed by a stanza by Seneca himself. Lipsius's poem begins with the Stoic maxim that he is higher than gods and mortals who neither lightly chooses the uncertain day of destiny nor fears it. Security is a spring day, it falls and dies, the third verse teaches. The author, if asked, would prefer to spend his life not pursuing riches but instead safe in a remote rural place devoted to tranquility and poetry. Thus, Lipsius is being quoted for a pastoral idyll and not for his famous political support for a strong, absolutist state; yet it is far from unthinkable that such a state is resonating in the background as a sort of ultimate guarantee of the tranquil life. Also, the next quote – from Seneca's drama *Phaedra* – is about leaving the city behind and preferring the forests, now in the mouth of the character of young Hippolyte (implicitly, as he is not mentioned by Dybvad). Dybvad, like Camerarius, quotes the first thirteen lines of Hippolyte's monologue, leaving out, for example, his concluding attack on the female gender for being behind all sorts of trouble in society. An English translation of Dybvad's quote (which seems to be a common passage to cite, for we find other authors doing so as well): "No Life so happy, none from Ill so free, / So near the elder Times Integrity. / As that which, leaving Towns in Fields is led: / No avaricious Fury fills his Head, / Who lives the harmless Guest of Hills and Wood. / No Breath of People, faithless to the Good, / No rancorous Spleen, nor Favour's fickle Grace, / Affect his Soul. – / He's no Court Vassal: gapes not for a Crown, / Nor toils go compass it: fears no man's Frown, / Ne'er couzen'd is with flatt'ring Hopes; nor yet / By the base Tooth of black-mouth'd Envy bit. [/] Nor of those Ills which reign in Cities knows. [/] Nor conscious fears how the loud Rumor goes."[24] The line on kingdoms, "Non ille regno servit; aut regno invidet" (the last word softened by Dybvad from the original's "imminens," threatening) literally means: Nor is he a slave to kingdom, nor kingdom does he envy. The free person envisioned by Dybvad through Seneca's Hippolyte is devoid of ambitions to royal power and thus does not add to tensions within the state.

Dybvad's Stoic quotes celebrating the peaceful rustic life at a distance from the perpetual quarrels of city life thus seem to connect to the theme of absolutism insofar as the unity of the state appears to be the only possible security against never-ending wars between factions of society – and thus the guarantee of a carefree life. Ideal court life in pastoral peace is attainable only by avoiding the division and contestation of unified state power, which would immediately open the gates to strife, if not civil war.

Some of the following texts continue the pastoral theme. Thus Michel de l'Hospital's four-liner celebrates summer life during which the poet – while people go about their usual business – has seen the very days when the sun lived. The quote from Lucian provides an allegorical conclusion to his satirical picture of what it is like to live as a salaried philosopher in a wealthy house – exactly what Dybvad was doing himself after 1618. It is no pretty picture: a person in this state of dependence is lured by the golden gates at the top of a hill, where he is taken in by Hope, soon to give him over to Despair and Servitude, leading him to Toil. Finally, "Naked, potbellied, pale and old" he is kicked out through some obscure back door, having wasted his life, and is left to Regret. Conclusion by proverb: blame not the heavens, but your own choices.

Dybvad seems to reason that such a destiny depends also on the ruler of the house, for now a new theme is introduced – the issue of just kings versus tyrants – and even the theme of tyrannicide. Quoting Camerarius, Dybvad recounts Aelianus's tale of the tyrant Trizus, who ordered his subjects not to speak to one another. Then, when they began using gestures, he forbade sign language. When they assembled to weep together in the marketplace, the regent sent out his guard to stop even their tears. Finally, they wrested the weapons from the soldiers and killed Trizus. Given that Dybvad knew about the suppression of expression from the case against his father, this of course would have been a telling tale for him to recount. After this quote, Dybvad in his own words returns to Thomas Chaleron, whom he now recalls meeting for a discussion in England; this leads him to refer to Bodin's distinction between kings and tyrants. This in turn sets the scene for the long quote from Bodin himself, which begins as follows: "The most notable distinction between the king and the tyrant is that the king conforms to the laws of nature and the tyrant tramples them underfoot. The one is guided by piety, justice, and faith. The other denies his God, his faith, and the law." In passing, Bodin addresses how the just king allows for freedom of expression: "The one encourages free speech on the part of his subjects to the point of wise rebuke when he has failed in his duty. The other dislikes none so much as the serious, free-spirited, and virtuous citizen."[25] After this, some pages filled with Roman epitaphs to wise rulers follow; these lead up to the final, explicit quote from Camererius, who contends that the persecution of the early Christians was possible only because of infighting between their vain and ambitious bishops. The quote concludes with a reference to the complicated strife at the Byzantine court of the twelfth century, seemingly pointing to the fact that the patriarchate gave the emperors full powers to bind and loose, traditionally associated with the church – again sounding the theme of destructive warring factions as against the unity of a strong state. Dybvad's argument for absolutism rarely points to the interests of regents, but rather to the societal need for peace granted by the strength of the state.

Overall, the text selections in the first half of *JOCI* weave together a number of themes in political philosophy, which can be summarized as follows: in order to live a peaceful life, protected against civil wars and rebellions, there must be a strong state capable of suppressing such disorder. The ruler of that state, however, must be a just king who allows freedom of speech; if he is not just, his subjects may legitimately commit tyrannicide.

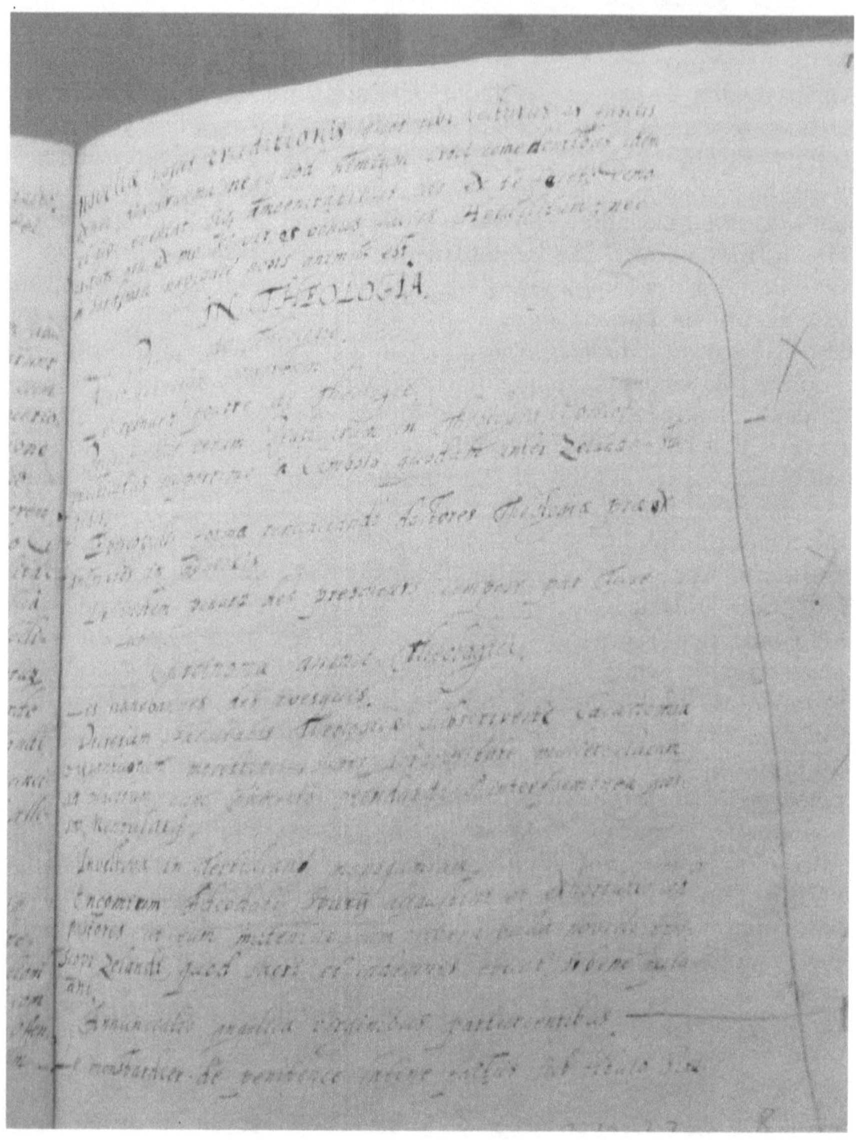
IN THEOLOGIA

Figure 3.3 The first page with jokes in *JOCI AULICI*, here "In Theologia."

A final remark, seemingly by Dybvad himself, celebrates the reborn pagan muses and – in the only place in *JOCI* that makes an appeal to a reader – advises the reader to close his ears if he wishes to avoid being offended. This trigger warning seems to serve as the introduction to the second half with its list of jokes: Dybvad tells the reader that if the amusements offered here will make of him a Democritus, he begs him, in turn, if he is a good man, not to make of Dybvad himself a Heraclitus. It is not our intention to sail to Sardinia, he concludes. This probably refers to Heraclitus praising Bias of Priene, who recommended to the Ionians, after their defeat of the Persians, that they collectively emigrate and found a new city in Sardinia. It is not completely clear whether this should be taken literally as saying that Dybvad would not want to emigrate – or, more generally, as an assurance that he intends nothing drastic with what now follows: the collection of jokes.

The *JOCI AULICI* – Second Half

Pastoral themes, court life, Stoicism, and a strong state, however, disappear all but completely in the last eleven pages of text. It is they that contain the "courtly jokes" of the booklet's title. The adjective does not refer to the content of the jokes: none of them deal with courtiers or their behaviours. Given Dybvad's recent position at court, the title might instead suggest the idea of jokes that had circulated in court circles; given their character, however, this also seems quite unlikely. The jokes comprise 124 brief units of text, separated by means of indentation, and many of them are one-liners. After them, the book closes with a long quote from Polybius. None of the joke texts are longer than twelve lines, and they are grouped under the headers IN THEOLOGY (jokes 1 to 37, pages 15 to 18; from joke 7, they are subheaded "Carcinomi animi Theologici," the cancers of the minds of theologians); IN LAW AND POLITICS (jokes 38 to 64, pages 18 to 20); IN MEDICINE AND PHILOSOPHY (jokes 65 to 116, pages 21 to 24); and IN MAGIC (jokes 117 to 124, page 24). The dominant issues, however, are theology and sex, and the themes reflect the headers only approximately.

The court proceedings in the case against Dybvad in 1620 refrained from quoting any of the jokes: "while the larger part is so unseemly, improper, and un-Christian etc. that courteous ears could by no means tolerate such, we have not inserted it here, but decided to keep it, testified by the hand of our notary, along with the sentence; yet, when the aforementioned unseemly points had been read aloud, Dr Christopher said that it was nothing but some *jocularia* and pastimes."[26] The court could not tolerate quoting such abominable expressions in its proceedings, which is probably why we now have *JOCI* handed down as a piece of legal evidence from the archived proceedings.

Despite their role in the court case against Dybvad, most of the jokes have remained unknown to the Danish public. Two eighteenth-century historians took an interest in the Dybvad case. The pietist theologian Erik Pontoppidan in *Annales Ecclesiæ Danicæ Diplomatici Oder nach Ordnung der Jahre abgefassete und in Urkunden belegte Kirchen Historie des Reichs Dännemarck* (1747) published the whole of *Errores*[27] but none of *JOCI*. His younger public opponent, the historian Jacob Langebek, in his handwritten source collection of Danish historical materials, "Excerpter" (probably from the 1760s and 1770s),[28] copied lengthy passages from *JOCI*. More recent papers quote several of the jokes – for example, Holger Fr. Rørdam (1873) provided a selection of the jokes in Latin.[29] But the most important recent piece of Dybvad scholarship, by Morten Fink-Jensen (2005), refrains from quoting them.[30]

There seem to be two reasons for not translating a representative selection of the jokes: (1) some are very crude and explicit, to say the least; and (2) many of them are notoriously difficult to understand. Written as they are in a Latin tossed with French and Italian words as well as neologisms, and with references to contemporary persons, teachings, and situations, it is often very difficult to assess what is really at stake in them. Also, though the jokes were carefully handwritten in printed style, almost calligraphy, the decomposition of the ink has added to the difficulties of interpretation.

The genre of the jokes has not really been elucidated before: all of them are fictitious book titles in the manner of Rabelais's famous grotesque novel *Gargantua et Pantagruel* (1530–40s), book II, ch. VII, which contains a list of 141 fictitious book titles of the Saint-Victor Library, expressed in a jumble of French and Latin. Most of Rabelais's titles are parodies of existing books, as shown in Lacroix and Brunet's book-length *Catalogue* (1862), an investigation of that Rabelais chapter.[31]

Some of Dybvad's joke titles, especially the first ones, are direct quotes from Rabelais's list; several are modelled on items on that list; but most of them are Dybvad's own concoctions, especially the ones that are a bit longer.

When Rabelais writes, for instance,[32]

(4) "Malogranatum vitiorum"
(8) "Les Hanebanes des evesques"
(26) "Les fanfares de Rome"
(10) "Decretum Universitatis Parisiensis super gorgiasitate muliercularum ad placitum,"

Dybvad elaborates these inspirations like this:

(2) "Malo granatum vitiorum"
(7) "Les hanebannes des evesques"
(18) "Les fanfares de Wittenberg"
(9) "Gargantuorum meretripoli super gorgiasitate muliercularum ad placitum, cum commento stendardi & interfoeminea glossa mentularij."

The first two examples are virtually identical; in the third example Dybvad substitutes Wittenberg for Rome, so as to target the Lutherans rather than the Catholics; the fourth one quotes a sequence from Rabelais but adds Dybvad's own, bawdier context. Rabelais writes about the coquetry of small prostitute girls; to this, Dybvad coarsely adds: with the learned explanation by the prick in the pelvic floor.[33]

Many of Dybvad's examples address theology:

(14) An argument regarding the removal of Rasenism from the church compared to that of Papism, and it is apologetically concluded that the former is necessary for the time being, encouraging pressingly that both are wished for.[34]

"Rasenism" is Dybvad's nickname for the orthodox Lutheranism of bishop Resen. Here he is probably also playing on the Danish verb *rase* (rage). So this book title is arguing that the expulsion of Resen's orthodoxy from the church is even more urgent than that of Catholicism.

A long and complicated joke with additional canned laughter strikes deep into what Dybvad obviously took to be a serious theological problem with Resen's position:

(17) Tartaretus on Hell in the middle of the Heavens (in this book appears a sophisticated argument of surprising subtlety in this way. For heaven is infallibly driven into hell by the Brentian decree: as God relates to heaven, so the Devil relates to hell: But God fills up all of Heaven: Ergo the Devil

also fills up hell. And because heaven is ubiquitous and thus also in hell, as was first said: Ergo God is necessarily in the Devil. But then, wonderfully, absurdity follows: how then can the Devil do evil? Dear friends, not all doubts can be solved in this life, and to the non-enlightened minds a mixed stew is miraculous: pray to God to be enlightened in the devil with the Rasenians) ha ha ha he.[35]

Let us try to disentangle the contents of this fictive title. The inspiration for the author seems to be one Pierre Tartaretus (d. 1522), a commentator on Aristotle, probably chosen merely because of his name's similarity to the Greek *tartaros* (hell). The theme of the book is how Hell is found in the Heavens. The explanation of this refers to the "Brentian decree," that is, to the doctrine of Johannes Brenz, one of the German Lutherans behind the Formula of Concord that attempted to unite the quarrelling German Lutherans in 1577–80. Brenz had specifically advocated the doctrine of Christ's omnipresence, so-called "ubiquitism." The argument is that if Christ is indeed present at all Eucharists, as claimed by the Lutherans, he must be ubiquitous, because there may be several Eucharists in different churches at the same time. This became part of the Formula of Concord, which had been refuted by the Danish king Frederik II at the time because the king did not want to disturb the peace that had by then been achieved in the Danish church. Resen, however, was known to subscribe to a strong and mystical variant of the omnipresence of Christ beyond time and space, and had even been forced by the council of Danish bishops, in 1614, to modify this idea before he could be promoted to Bishop of Zealand the following year. So this joke constitutes another, deeper attack on Resen and one of his well-known weaknesses. The basic argument is that as God takes up all of Heaven and the Devil all of Hell (and as Christ is part of the Trinitarian godly unity), Resen's ubiquitism entails that God is also in Hell, and thus even in the Devil himself. So, the conclusion: Resen's supporters, the Rasenians, pray to God to become enlightened in the Devil. This depiction of the head of the Danish–Norwegian church as a leader of devil-worshippers thus called down the conclusive laughter of the joke.

Ubiquitism is a central means by which Dybvad targets Resen:

(75) The holy Medicine book about the ingredients & composition of the wafers with the Papal lightning into them which gives quid pro quo, like dog-fat for geese; even if the mystery of ubiquitarianists rather makes a man fat, wherefore its symbolization is cannibalism. [36]

This invented treatise addresses the composition of the host, and the crypto-Calvinist Dybvad (Calvinists saw the Eucharist as a symbolic commemoration meal only, with no divine participation) makes no distinction between the Catholic doctrine of transubstantiation and the Lutheran one of "Real Presence" in the Eucharist: eating the body of Christ is a sort of cannibalism, and when the ubiquitists do so, it makes them fat – probably a satirical reference to the wealth of the clergy.

The following is the title of a fictive meeting announcement, targeting no less than two theologians in one strike:

> (122) The provincial meeting of all devils of the city Merchante-Golfo in the brain of Master Raisnard written by Master Brodman.[37]

The meeting summons all the devils of Copenhagen (meaning "Merchant's Harbour") in the mind of Resen: Dybvad often associates French "Raisnard" or "Renard" (fox) with Resen, while Master Brodman is probably Resen's theology professor colleague (later to become his successor as Bishop of Zealand), Jesper Brochmand.

One of Dybvad's strongest and most dangerous satirical ideas was probably to go directly after Luther himself, as in this joke:

> (36) Question whether Luther was always thinking; And the answer is no because he wrote invectively against the king of England and humiliatingly called the duke of Braunschweig "Wursthans" [Sausage-John] and called James the Apostle crazy, about Christians that they could not keep the decalogue better than the Thuringians keep the Swiss constitutions & wrote against the truth to painfully make a devil of Andreas Karlstadt, which is not a Christian and even less Theologian thing to do. With these manifest signs of madness it is marvellous that he became the Elias of the Germans and the God of the Northern Hemisphere.[38]

This book title considers whether Luther was sane at all – and it answers in the negative with reference to a series of proofs: he wrote evil things about the king of England, the duke of Braunschweig (thereby transgressing his own doctrine about the unconditional obedience of state authorities), and even James the Apostle, about the Christians as such, and about his own fellow reformer Andreas Karlstadt. The conclusion is nothing less than that Luther displayed "manifest signs of madness." This joke alone would probably have sufficed to have Dybvad convicted for calumny or even blasphemy, at a point when the extensive

Danish centenary celebrations of Luther and the Reformation in 1617 were fresh in memory, including Resen's glowing tribute piece, the *festschrift* "Lutherus Triumphans."

Theology as such is a target in several jokes:

(33) The eternal apostasy of theologians.[39]

(25) The vessel of the theological brain is filled with ire, hatred, envy, evil. Therefrom they fill more generously the chalice of the Lord than with the blood of Christ.[40]

Theologians as such are taken to tend towards apostasy and to spend their mental powers on strife, struggle, and evil rather than on the teachings of Christ. Dybvad even goes so far as a fictive book title toying with preferring the devil over god:

(38) A Political-Theological consideration whether it is preferable to be without God rather than without the Devil: and it concludes, from theological evil, affirmatively for the first alternative of the question [...][41]

A considerable number of the jokes head in another dangerous direction: seduction and sex. There are many short titles after the following manner:

(80) How to white-taw female breasts.

(95) The tambourine of buttocks.

(109) The way to sponge on ladies.

(110) How to lift the skirt.

(111) The counting of virgins and how to take their virginity after the manner of Photide in Apuleius.

(115) Questions about snail shells [female parts] discussed in the middle of the night with large earthquakes of beds. The cock presides, the cunt responding.[42]

Some fictive books address the particular issue of the size of sexual organs, how to measure them, and how to bring them into suitable relative proportions:

(85) The widening of cunts for those who can hardly with their cock marry virgins but only command widows.

(86) The narrowing of cunts for widows to be married, as ordinary members are delicate and refined.

(91) From the petitioning council of doctors to Kings of the earth, not to consummate any marriage before an experiment of the proportionality clubs-caves.

(101) The measuring of cunts, two vols.[43]

Here, Dybvad mockingly assumes the style of a medical doctor recommending anatomical and political action for sexual health purposes. The connections between sex and religion even take him in a quasi-serious direction of reviving certain Roman religious ceremonies, and mapping religious customs across Europe – a daring degree of religious liberalism for his time:

(87) The old Romans' celebration of cocks to be revoked, a most serious proposal.

(88) The new art called lectisternium gathered from the observations of all the nations of Europe, a work preserving these species to the divine nature, happily perfected, written to the Lord by Roquelaure, of the Basque country.

The "lectisternium" refers to a Roman custom: the public presentation of a meal to the bust of a god on a couch. The duke of Roquelaure participated as an official of King Henry in the Wars of Religion in France in the sixteenth century and is said to have been the one who persuaded Henry to convert to the Catholic faith with the aim of obtaining the French throne – so the joke may indirectly be comparing the Catholic Eucharist to the antique customs of the heathens, in a surprising piece of comparative religion.

A special preoccupation with excrement in Dybvad might be inherited from Luther, who was famous for his obsession with feces and scatological expressions in his pejorative portrayals of the Papacy. Dybvad, again, directs his satire against the Protestant clergy instead:

(8) The Cacademy subscribing to the decree of the Theological faculty.

(73) The universal Shithouse of Doctors.

(23) The priests dressed in woolen cloaks and their robes by the altar or in the Sacristy honorably, if at least the robes mentioned are not pissed or shit upon, requiring at least to be washed beforehand, with repeated blessed apology in bribes.[44]

The Academy becomes a Cacademy when subjecting itself to the dominance of theology, and the cleansing of priests of excrement seems possible only by means of corruption – harsh charges against the clergy.

Notwithstanding Dybvad's header MEDICINE AND PHILOSOPHY and his obvious love for the Stoics, there are only few jokes that delve explicitly into philosophy, such as these:

(79) Argument contra atheism Anno Humanae Salutis, sinfully stating the eternity of the world, in passing denying the penetration of dimensions introduced to defend the ubiquity of the spatially limited, monstrously thought out with new delirium for the admirers.

(94) The daubing of Thomas Aquinas with additional stains from Scotus, the most subtle Doctor, directed towards the Sorbonists of all difficulties with drinks.[45]

The first book title here presents an argument against atheism that commits the sin of claiming the world to be eternal (i.e., non-created). The argument being mocked seems to be a ubiquitarian one arguing against spatial dimensions by claiming the existence of something (Christ) that transcends the spatially limited world. Dybvad's position, by contrast, seems to be a sort of space-time realism, one claiming the infinity of the dimensions of space and time – and that reality pertains to non-ubiquitous beings within this continuum. Thus, Dybvad is arguing against an argument against atheism, thereby avoiding the explicit embrace of atheism. The "difficulty with drinks" at the Sorbonne is probably again a joking way of addressing discussions of the Eucharist, simultaneously associating the priesthood with alcoholism. Duns Scotus had indeed indicated problems in the doctrine of the Eucharist: if new flesh and blood of Christ may appear by means of transubstantiation after the pronouncement of the *verba testamenti*, how can these new holy matters simultaneously share any part in the sacrifice of Christ, which has already taken place, once and for all? Scotus believed himself to possess the solution in his complicated theory of the Eucharist, but that did not prevent Dybvad from playing him against the Paris theologians.

The most powerful effect Dybvad probably achieved was when mixing a cocktail of his two favourite subjects, theology and sex. The following book title strangely works its way from a scholarly dispute between medical doctors and law scholars to outright pornography:

(58) The action of medical doctors against lawyers to acquire the right to investigate the belly of those accused for corruption. It follows that the whole of the process is cast into doubt. E.g. the mother-mirror constructed by surgeons fits the investigation of the belly. So the doctor does not stick out

> his nose when the woman pees. C. of Spreading the Legs should truly be printed on walls, posts, doors, jars, stairs, chests, with the most elegant pictures when they lean backwards the most, such pictures are freely allowed by the new wives of bishops.[46]

The belly is investigated for corruption, and the surgeon's invention of a mirror instrument turns attention towards the female parts. This, in turn, is associated with representations of those parts. The abbreviation "C." could be "cerae," (wax) images, or "conflatiles," cast idols – in any case such images of spread female legs should be presented all over town, thereby depicting particularly bishops' wives in the most revealing, backwards-leaning positions. Again, Dybvad's arch-enemy, Bishop Resen, recently married, could not be blamed for feeling targeted by this singular fictitious piece of medical science. Resen, again, is explicitly associated with sex in the following:

> (11) Praise to Adeodato, the false Augustine, and encouragement to the priests to imitate him, by the free decree of the new bishop of Zealand, that they shall be holy and free of condemnation if they fuck well.[47]

Adeodatus was, according to legend, an early and illegitimate son of Saint Augustine, from before his Christian conversion – a child who turned out to be a prodigy but who died young. This product of illegitimate intercourse, this "child of sin," and his sinful father, are praised in this fictive treatise and elevated to figures of imitation. The "new bishop of Zealand" is again Resen, and he is intimated to have encouraged the priests of his diocese to engage in good sex in order to be saved, like his false predecessor. The implication seems to be that Augustine's sin did not prevent him from later rising to sainthood. It is not known if there was any actual pretext for fitting Resen into this picture, but it was evidently designed to question the self-righteous orthodoxy with which Resen pursued theological opponents in court.

After the 124 jokes, the end of the booklet follows with page 25, which can be read as a closing statement. That page's centred header roughly translates as "Printed in the city of the whole wide world, these pages are stated in the workshop of Furies, are sold under the sign of ignorance in the lazy roads" (if Erÿnnidis is taken to be an alternative spelling of Erinnydis, Furies), and thus forms a sort of mock title page. After that follows a quote from the Hellenistic Greek historian Polybius (his *Historiae,* vol. I, Dybvad's quote probably again taken from Camerarius

1609, 333, from which Dybvad leaves out the first couple of lines). The quote highlights the conclusion that human beings may suffer wounds not only in their bodies, but also in their souls, and if these latter are not cured, they may spread to infect the whole human being. That may make human beings worse than animals, and this condition has it roots in the early years of education.[48] This quite sober conclusion to a series of burlesque jokes may surprise; Dybvad's intention is probably to characterize those soul-sick persons who have been ridiculed in many of the jokes: the theologians.

These examples give us a picture of the overall character of *JOCI AULICI*. Its 124 fictive book titles cover, in a playful way, a vast ground of possible satire, but with a strong focus on sex and theology, ridiculing theologians, particularly the Lutheran orthodoxy and its Danish representative in the person of Bishop Resen. In that sense, *JOCI* bears comparison to the French libertine tradition of the seventeenth century, which also often turned to Rabelais for inspiration.[49] There is even a tendency to mock theology as such, as well as a whiff of atheism. Thus, several themes that would emerge in full bloom in later early-Enlightenment *clandestina* are already present here. It can be said with some certainty, however, that Dybvad's secret writings were without further influence in his own time. The *Errores* were not printed in Denmark until the 1740s, and then in the academic, non-subversive context of a church history, and the first known copying of (some of) *JOCI* had to wait until the 1770s, also in the historiographic context of source materials.

The Case against Dybvad

Regarding the case against Dybvad, the court of the Academic Council in Copenhagen was set for 3 November 1620, as we can see from the front cover of *JOCI*, where the notarius of the council has meticulously noted that it was "Read aloud in Consistorio" on that date. Here, Dybvad faced an impressive row of Copenhagen professors including the physician, collector, and natural historian Ole Worm, the anatomist and theologian Casper Bartholin, rector Cort Aslakssøn, astronomer and linguist, and not least the two leading theologians Hans Poulsen Resen and Jesper Brochmand, both of whom he had targeted. It must have been a strange scene, with the painstaking reading aloud of every single one of the 124 joke book titles to the grave attendance of this learned assembly. Resen, as representative of the theological profession, lead the accusation against a man who must now have appeared as a theological and political arch-enemy of his, and as the leading expert he determined that Dybvad had indeed transgressed the limits of academic theology.

As to *Errores*, Dybvad claimed in his defence that all of his political ideas were but quotations from Bodin, whose ideas were already known. Referring to praise he had offered Christian II during the dinner in Bergen (which does not appear in either of the two secret texts), he said he had only stated what was known to be true.[50] *JOCI*, he claimed, was but idle jocularities. He added that he had not at all intended to publish his writings; to this, the prosecutor Axel Arenfeld replied that he could prove from private correspondence of Dybvad's that he had, in fact, intended to show parts of them to the prince.[51] The proceedings tell us that Dr Christopher at that point fell silent – implying this was a tacit admission of guilt.

The court considered the following different excuses presented by Dybvad's defence, regarding various parts of his critical utterances:

They were quoted from another, well-known source
They were true
They were only jokes
They were never published

All of these arguments – which have since been repeated many times in court cases involving crimes related to freedom of the press, in Denmark as elsewhere – were rejected by the *Konsistorium.* Dybvad was found to have grossly committed an offence against no less than "God, against His Christian Religion and Church, Ceremonies, against the Royal Majesty Our most gracious Lord, against the State and State Council, even against the Dead [chancellor], against ordinary Nobility and the Estates of the State."[52] Christoffer Dybvad was expelled from academia on 22 December 1620; his further punishment was left to the king's mercy.

This followed in early 1621, when Christian IV sentenced his courtier to imprisonment for life. A month later, on 27 January 1621, Dybvad was sent to serve the sentence at the tower of "Folen" in Kalundborg Castle on the west coast of Zealand. Remains of the massive tower can still be seen in central Kalundborg. Fifteen months later, on 22 April 1622, Christoffer Dybvad died – perhaps from a carbon monoxide poisoning, due to a badly burning lamp – at the age of forty-four. The orthodox Lutheran confession state of Denmark had proved itself capable of applying harsh means to marginalize challenging utterances, even non-public utterances in the form of secret manuscripts on philosophy, theology, politics, and sex – and even concerning talented, educated, and high-ranking individuals such as Christoffer Dybvad.

Clandestine Manuscripts?

Do the two secret, handwritten manuscripts analysed here qualify as clandestine writings? They were certainly kept secret; they contained philosophical inspirations, politically rebellious ideas, and gross insults against the nobility, clergy, and established religion alike; and they were explicit about sexual matters to a degree rarely found in those days.

As to *Errores,* it went against the nobility and their current political privileges, as well as the current institutions of justice and academia, and it supported absolutism, estate representation, the development of trade, and the empowerment of townsmen. In that sense, it constituted an explosive political program. Whether the king was made aware of (some of) its contents is unclear, but in any case the current position of the nobility made it highly revolutionary, and absolutism would only be introduced in Denmark forty years later, in 1660, by the king's son Frederik III.

JOCI AULICI does not contain any explicit political program, and it completely lacks the quasi-public character of the approach to influential power factions of *Errores.* Its first half with its series of quotes presents an indirect argument that the ideal, in neo-Stoic philosophy, of pastoral life is best protected by an undivided state headed by a just king – as opposed to a tyrant, who merits tyrannicide. The second half, with its Rabelaisan book title jokes, intermixes, among other things:

(1) ridicule and attacks on theologians, particularly bishops Resen and Brochmand, as well as theological ubiquitism, even on Luther himself;
(2) scatological jokes;
(3) sexual jokes and quasi-serious sexological proposals; and
(4) some degree of religious pluralism, and a comparative accounts of religions.

Do these two documents qualify as clandestine writings? They surely were kept secret, and for very good reasons, but they did not circulate and were not copied – with the possible exception of *Errores.*

Today's discussions of clandestine manuscripts have flowed from from a research tradition first triggered by the existence of secret eighteenth-century French manuscripts, with Gustave Lanson in his papers around 1910; then with I.O. Wade's 1938 book *The Clandestine Organisation and Diffusion of Philosophical Ideas in France from 1700 to 1750*, including his famous inventory of 102 such papers;[53] and finally with the recent efforts of Miguel Benitez, who expanded Wade's list to 139 papers in 1988 and then, after intensive archival research, to no fewer than 269 papers by 1996. Those 269 papers were written in a multiplicity of languages, including English, German, Italian, Spanish, and Portuguese, besides French and Latin.[54] And that list now stretches well back into the mid-seventeenth century with important early *clandestina* like *Theophrastus redivivus* and *Ineptus religiosis*, both supposedly from the 1650s. Twentieth-century research into *clandestina* thus developed from a prototypical core involving French philosophical manuscripts of the eighteenth century to embrace a broader localization in time and space – further fuelled by Jonathan Israel's *Radical Enlightenment* (2001) with its focus on the mid-seventeenth-century early Enlightenment.[55] The Dybvad manuscripts would extend this time frame even earlier, to include early-seventeenth-century Danish examples.

Dybvad's manuscripts, however, are not philosophical in a narrow sense, and unlike many of the core French eighteenth-century examples, they hardly attack religion as such. They *are* based, however, on Dybvad's further development of philosophies such as those of Seneca, Bodin, Lipsius, and Camerarius, and they did set out to foment radical academic, political, and theological change, even with a certain representative and liberal tendency. But in no sense do they take full Radical Enlightenment positions such as philosophical monism, theological deism, atheism, or criticism of religion as such, nor do they support political republicanism or democracy, or related positions.

My tentative conclusion is that they should indeed be counted as *clandestina* and thus be candidates for the lists of such writings. It would seem too narrow a criterion to admit only writings explicitly connected to full-blown early Enlightenment currents or ideas. Christoffer Dybvad's two manuscripts are politically radical and philosophically informed; they target religious orthodoxy, and they embrace libertinism in addressing tabooed issues in the sexual realm. They were kept secret until their originator paid for his authorship with his liberty and, ultimately, his life.

Thanks to Bodil Due, Morten Fink-Jensen, and Jonathan Israel for comments on versions of the manuscript.

NOTES

1 The former is *Errores qui concernunt respublicam Danorum,* Danish State Archives (Rigsarkivet), Københavns Universitets Arkiv, 12.01.24, Sager henlagt efter 1633, læg 3–12–33. Another version with corrections is in the same file. A third version, complying with the corrections, is in file 3–12–31. The latter is *Joci Aulici,* Danish State Archives, Københavns Universitets Arkiv, Sager henlagt efter 1633, 12.01.24, læg 3–12–33.1.

2 The recent and most thorough account of Dybvad's life and destiny – along with those of his father, uncle, and brother – can be found in Morten Fink-Jensen: "De Lærde Dybvader: Bogtryk og Samfundskritik i det 16. og 17. Århundrede," in *Fund og Forskning,* vol. 44, 2005, 63–106. See also his "Enevældens ensomme fortrop. Christoffer Dybvads systemkritik under Christian 4," in *Oprørere: Skæbnefortællinger om danmarkshistoriens tolv største rebeller,* ed. Morten Petersen, Kbh. 2006: Aschehoug, 37–64. Important also is Rørdam, Holger Fr., 1873: "Efterretninger om Jørgen og Christoffer Dybvad," *Danske Magazin,* 4. rk., 2–3, 1873, 105–44 and 211–64. A shorter presentation of Dybvad in the context of the history of freedom of speech in Denmark can be found in Jacob Mchangama and Frederik Stjernfelt, *MEN – ytringsfrihedens historie i Danmark* ("BUT – the History of Free Speech in Denmark") (Copenhagen: Gyldendal, 2016), 44–55.

3 Cf. Fink-Jensen, "De Lærde Dybvader," 81.

4 The seven rights are to give laws, to wage war, to make peace, to appoint the highest state officials, to serve as superior appeal judge, to coin money, and to levy taxes.

5 The *Observationes* can be dated to either 1614 or 1615 and exists in copies only; it is transcribed in Rørdam 1873, 226. It did not appear in the court case against Dybvad and so does not seem to have been found during the raid on his home.

6 Cf. Fink-Jensen, "De Lærde Dybvader," 87.

7 Dybvad possessed a copy of Commines's *Les Memoires de Philippe de Commines sur les principaux faicts et gestes de Louis XI et Charles VIII* (Fink-Jensen, "De Lærde Dybvader," 87).

8 This and the following are my own photographs from the Danish State Archives (Rigsarkivet).

9 This and the following translations are my own, helped by Kristoffer Bahrenscheer and Bodil Due. I thank them for their assistance.

10 On the general persecution of crypto-Calvinists, see Mchangama and Stjernfelt, *MEN,* 51ff.

11 Here, I agree with Fink-Jensen's account of the relations between the three versions (Fink-Jensen "De Lærde Dybvader," 89n86).
12 To Luther, it was the bodily incarnation of souls that made (most of) them evil and entailed the politically necessary subjection of them to a strong public authority ("The Sword"), which should be unconditionally obeyed by all subjects.
13 "FESTIVITATES CUM IMPENSE PRÆCLARA INGENIA AFFICIANT NONNULLAS IN HAS CARTAS CONJECIMUS TAM JOCOSAS QUAM SERIAS, UT UTRINQUE RIDENDI ET CONSIDERANDI IN PROMPTU SIT MATERIA."
14 *Omnia opera Des. Erasmi Roterodami, quaecunque ipse autor pro suis ...* ex officina Frobeniana, 1540, vol. 1, 268 (https://books.google.es/books?id=RrA_AAAAcAAJ) – known in English versions under the title "On Salaried Posts in Great Houses" (http://www.sacred-texts.com/cla/luc/wl2/wl202.htm).
15 Philippus Camerarius, *OPERAE HORARVM SVBCISIVARVM. SIVE MEDITATIONVM HISTORICARVM*, 3 vols (Frankfurt: 1602, 1606, and 1609). The book exists in several different versions, 1591/1599/1602–9/1658, etc. The quote is from CAPVT XXV, *Exsuspicionibus plerunque Reges et principes, praesertim accedente senio, meticulosos et crudeles fieri*, images s125–6 of the 1609 Internet version. (http://www.uni-mannheim.de/mateo/camenahist/camer6/Camerarius_meditationes_3.html). 1591 version: http://reader.digitale-sammlungen.de/resolve/display/bsb10160131.html.
16 *Andegavensis, de republica libri sex*, apud Jacobus Dupuy, 1591 (first version 1586); http://www.e-rara.ch/gep_g/content/titleinfo/1752392 – the quote is from bk II, ch. IIII, 263.
17 Some of these brief texts are also excerpts from Camerarius, cf. below.
18 The whole of this text: "Cura vetusta eruditio in contemptum venit prisciq-ævi mores irrisui [samme som derisui] sunt, absq- minore labore et sumptu, renascentibus musis barbaris, novitate sua orbi admirationi forie sunt futuræ, tanquam hilaviores, et si dis placet comptiores, auribus ita hebetatis, quod nulla scabrositate offendantur: En itaque farraginem autenticorum scriptorum Novellæ hujus Eruditionis quos ubi lecturus es fasciis excipe diaphragma, ne quod nimium croci comedentibus idem et tibi eveniat, siq- amoenitatibus his ex te fecero Democritum non ex me si vir es bonus, facies Heraclitum; nec in Sardiniam navigare nobis animus est." A passage from this text is also quoted in the court proceedings, which thus also took it to form an introduction to the jokes immediately following it: "D anden D. Christophers scrifftlige concept findes iblant Jocos ipsius aulicos, in farragine authenticorum scriptorum novellæ erudtitionis." (The second

of Dr Christopher's writerly conceptions is found among the Very Courtly Jokes, in a mixture of authentic writings of the new learning.) Quoted from Langebek *Excerpter*, 218.

19 Thus, the Chaloner poem (341), the Lipsius poem (342), the Seneca quote (341), the Guarini poem (341), the l'Hospital poem (343), the EPITAPHIUM GLAPHYRÆ (295), the first half of the "Othocarus Rex" quote (296), and the "Andronicus Imperator" quote (224 f.) can be found in Camerarius's *Operae* (1609), vol. III.

Also, in Camerarius (1602), vol. I, can be found the Valerius quote of SACRAMENTUM SENATORUM (158), the "In Aragonia Urbe" (450), the INSCRIPTIO SARDANAPALI (Ibid.), ROMÆ ALIUD (451), the IBIDEM (Ibid.), the PATAVII (452). (All three vols, 1602–9: http://www.uni-mannheim.de/mateo/camenahist/camer4/te08.html.)

20 Erik Pontoppidan, *Annales Ecclesiæ Danicæ Diplomatici Oder nach Ordnung der Jahre abgefassete und in Urkunden belegte Kirchen Historie des Reichs Dännemarck*, vol. III (Copenhagen: J.P. Anchersen, 1747) (https://archive.org/details/annalesecclesia00pontgoog).

21 Rørdam, "Efterretninger om Jørgen."

22 Cf. Fink-Jensen "De Lærde Dybvader," 94.

23 Thomas Chalonerus, 1579, *De rep. Anglorum instauranda libri decem* (https://archive.org/stream/bub_gb_rqNcO2YmfrcC/bub_gb_rqNcO2YmfrcC_djvu.txt).

24 *The Tragedies of L. Annaeus Seneca the Philosopher* (London: S. Smith and B. Walford, 1702), 155–6.

25 Quoted from the English translation, http://www.yorku.ca/comninel/courses/3020pdf/six_books.pdf, 61–2, corresponding to 246–7 in Bodin's 1576 French original version: https://fr.wikisource.org/wiki/Livre:Bodin_-_Les_Six_Livres_de_la_République, 1576.djvu.

26 My translation from the original: "... hvor udaf effterdj dend største part er saa usømlig, utilbørlig og u-Christelig etc. at höfske Ören ingenlunde saadant taale kunde, have Vi icke dend hidinfört, men for got anseet, samme med Voris Notarii Haand paaskreven saa og hos Dommen at være gifven, dog at de forn.te usømlige Puncter waar oplæste, sagde Doct. Christopher, at det waar icke uden nogle jocularia og Tids-fordrifv" Quoted from the Process against Dybvad, GKS 1466 Kvart, Royal Library, Copenhagen.

27 Pontoppidan, *Annales Ecclesiæ Danicæ*, vol. III, 722.

28 Jacob Langebek, *Excerpter* 218 4°: "Collectanea," Royal Library, Copenhagen.

29 Holger F. Rørdam, "Efterretninger om Jørgen og Christoffer Dybvad," *Danske Magazin*, 4. rk., 2–3, 1873, 105–44 og 211–64 (Latin joke quotes on 254–6).

30 Fink-Jensen, "De Lærde Dybvader," "DE LÆRDE DYBVADER. BOGTRYK OG SAMFUNDSKRITIK I DET 16. OG 17. ÅRHUNDREDE," in *Fund og Forskning*, vol. 44, 63–106.

31 Paul Lacroix and Gustave Brunet, *Catalogue de la bibliothèque de l'abbaye de Saint-Victor au seizième siècle, rédigé par François Rabelais, commenté par le bibliophile Jacob et suivi d'un essay sur les bibliothèques imaginaires par Gustave Brunet* (Paris: J. Techener, 1862).

32 The consecutive numbering of the Dybvad jokes in brackets is mine.

33 I apologize for the expletives in the translations, but they are necessary to give an idea of Dybvad's Latin crudenesses.

34 (14) Disputatio de auferabilitate Rasenismi ab Ecclesia collata cum alia de Papismo, & Apologetice concluditur primam tempore hoc magis esse necessariam, ad urgendam instantius licet ambo optentur.

35 (17) Tartaretus de Inferno in medio Coelorum [in hoc libro extat stupendæ subtilitatis alembicati argumentatio in hunc modum. Quia detrusum est coelum in infernum infallibiliter ex decreto Brentiano: ut autem Deus se habet ad coelum, ita Diabolus ad infernum: Sed Deus replet totum Coelum: Ergo et Diabolus infernum. Atqui coelum ubique est et quidem in inferno ut initio dictum fuit: Ergo Deus necessario in Diabolo. Sed mirabilie sequitur absurdum: quomodo ergo Diabolus potest male facere? Rx amici non omnia dubia solvi possunt in hac vita: et est mirabilis Ollipodrido mentibus non illuminatis: orate Deum ut vos illuminet in diabolo cum Rasenianis] ha ha ha he.

36 (75) Sanctus codex Medicinalis de ingredientibus & compositione hostiarum cum fulmine Papali in eos qui ponunt quid pro quo, ut apidem canum pro anserum: quanquam ex mysteriis ubiquitariorum rectius poneretur hominum pingvedo, propter Symbolÿsationem anthropofagias.

37 (122) Chapitre provincial de tous les diables tenu a la ville de Merchante-golfo dans le cerueau du mestre raisnard escritte par mestre brodman.

38 (36) Quæstio an Lutherus omnibus horis fuerit sapiens; Et respondentur quod non quia scripsit invectinaliter in regem Angliæ et vursthansum ducem Brunsuicensem contumelialiter ac Jacobum Apostlum delirum vocat, de Christianos non magis teneri decalogo, quam turingos constitutionib. helveticis & contra ueritatem scripsit ut ægre faceret diabolo Carelostadio: quod non est Christianum multo minus Theologicum. Quæ cum manefesti delirij signa sint mirum qui sit Elias Germanorum ac Deus Septentrionaliam.

39 (33) Apostasia perpetua Theologorum.

40 (25) Dolium Cerebri theologici plenum ira, odio, invidia, malitia. Ex quo calicem dominicum replent libentius, quam Christi Sanguine.

41 (38) Consideratio Politico-Theologica, an præstabilias sit carere Deo quam Diabolo (at foretrække at være uden gud eller uden djævel): Et concluditur ex malitia theologica affirmativa pro prima parte quæstionis; (...)

42 (80) Modus blancandi Mammellas.

(95) Le tembourin des fesses.

(109) Le maniere de queufer les dames.

(110) Fason de leuer le chemise.

(111) Le depoullement de pucelles et le fason de le depuceller selon la maniere de Photide d'Apulee.

(115) Problemata Cochleatoria disputata media nocte ad magnas terræmotum lecTorum. Præside il Cazo respondende la potta.

43 (85) Cunnodilatatorium pro ijs qui parum valide mentulatè virgines ducere nolunt, sed solummodo viduas expetunt

(86) Cunnoarctatorium pro viduis maritandis ut mediocribus boardis gratiores et delicatiores sint.

(91) Ex consilio medicorum supplicatorium ad Reges terræ, ne ullæ perficiantur nuptiæ ante experimentationem proportionalitatis antro-palorum.

(101) Cunnometriæ libri duo.

44 (8) Decretum facultatis Theologicæ subscribente Cacadomia

(73) Universale Cacatorium Medicorum

(23) Ex cottis velutis doncellarum earumque chemisis Præstras habiliandi apud altare vel in Sacerstia modus honorificus, modo prædictæ chemisæ non sunt perpisatæ aut merdatæ requiritur ut ad minimum prælaventur cum Apologo benedictionis redundantis in largitrices.

45 (79) Disputatio contra Atheismum Ahs statuentis æternitatem mundi piaculariter, interim negantis penetrationem dimensionum introduita pro defendenda ubiquitate circumscriptiva monstrose excogitata cum delirio novo admirantium.

(94) Barbovillamenta Thomæ de Aquina cum Embrocatione Scoti subtillissimi Doctoris, adjectis Sorbonistariens difficultatum omnium absorptionibus.

46 (58) Actio Medicorum Contra Iureconsultos ut vindicent titulum ad eis de Inspiciendo ventre intendato Crimine peculatus. Incipit Ex hic verbis quæ totum litem contestantur: Ex. l. speculum matricis à Chirurgis Excogitatum aptum est inspectioni ventris. Si ne medicus nasam ponat cum foemina mingit. C. de Separandis Cruribus Imprimitur vero ad parietes Tapetia, Postas, Portas,dolia, scalas, cistas, chaminos elegantissimis tÿpis transcendentaliter resupinatissime cubatur quos tÿpos libenter admittunt les novelles euesquesses.

47 (11) Encomium Adeodati spurij augustini et exhortatio ad pastores ut eum imitentur, cum libera bulla novelli episcopi Zelandi, quod sacri et indemnes erant, si bene futuant.

48 An English translation of the Polybius quote: "No one looking at this would have any hesitation in saying that not only do men's bodies and certain of the ulcers and tumours afflicting them become so to speak savage and brutalized and quite incurable, but that this is true in a much higher degree of their souls. In the case of ulcers, if we treat them, they are sometimes inflamed by the treatment itself and spread more rapidly, while again if we neglect them they continue, in virtue of their own nature, to eat into the flesh and never rest until they have utterly destroyed the tissues beneath. 7 Similarly such malignant lividities and putrid ulcers often grow in the human soul, that no beast becomes at the end more wicked or cruel than man. In the case of men in such a state, if we treat the disease by pardon and kindness, they think we are scheming to betray them or deceive them, and become more mistrustful and hostile to their would-be benefactors, but if, on the contrary, we attempt to cure the evil by retaliation they work up their passions to outrival ours, until there is nothing so abominable or so atrocious that they will not consent to do it, imagining all the while that they are displaying a fine courage. Thus at the end they are utterly brutalized and no longer can be called human beings. Of such a condition the origin and most potent cause lies in bad manners and customs and wrong training from childhood, …" – from bk 1, ch. 81, 219–21, of the English translation, *The Histories of Polybius*, published in Vol. I of the Loeb Classical Library edition, 1922–7; http://penelope.uchicago.edu/Thayer/E/Roman/Texts/Polybius/home.html

49 An open issue for further research, of course, is which international influences and network connections Dybvad may have entered into on his many European travels, for example, in the relatively liberal Leiden of the early seventeenth century. In 1603–5, Dybvad published four comments upon Euclid with dedications to the Danish king and chancellor as well as to James 1 of England and Henry, Prince of Wales (Fink-Jensen "De Lærde Dybvader," 83), the intention probably being to collect support for a professorship in Copenhagen. To emphasize his abilities, Christoffer also had several Leiden professors compose celebratory poems for himself, underscoring his scientific qualifications – the philologist Janus Dousa, the mathematician Ludolph van Ceulen, and the historians Daniel Heinsius and Paulus Merula (Ibid.). Dousa was the first librarian of the Leiden University Library, one of the first Dutch historians, and conspired with

other noblemen against Spanish rule; van Ceulen famously prolonged al-Kashani's sixteen-digit calculation of the decimal expansion of Pi to thirty-five digits; Heinsius was a leading poet and poetic scholar as well as the world's first professor of political science; and Merula was Dousa's successor as librarian and a historian, philologist, and legal scholar. Dybvad was thus well-connected to a network of illustrious Leiden professors, and it is probable something similar holds for Paris, where he spent several periods.

50 Christian II was famous for the "blood-bath in Stockholm" during which he lured the Swedish high nobility to a meeting where he had them all executed – an event it is easy to see Dybvad sympathizing with.

51 Perhaps referring to the young crown prince Christian (1603–47).

52 "… Gud, imod Hans Christelige Religion og Kircke, Ceremonier, imod Kongl. May.t Vor allernaadigste Herre, imod Riget og Rigens Raad, endog imod dend Döde, imod meenige Adelskab og Rigens Stænder." – quoted from the verdict of Dybvad, GKS 1466 Kvart, The Royal Library, Copenhagen.

53 I.O. Wade, *The Clandestine Organisation and Diffusion of Philosophical Ideas in France from 1700 to 1750* (New York: Octagon Books, 1967; orig. Princeton: Princeton University Press, 1938).

54 Miguel Benitez, *La face cachée des Lumières: recherches sur les manuscrits philosophiques clandestins de l'âge classique* (Oxford: Voltaire Foundation, 1996).

55 Jonathan Israel, *Radical Enlightenment: Philosophy and the Making of Modernity 1650–1750* (Oxford: Oxford University Press, 2001).

Chapter Four

"Qui toujours servent d'instruction": Socinian Manuscripts in the Dutch Republic

WIEP VAN BUNGE

Introduction

There are at least two reasons not to be interested at all in the fate and possible significance of the transmission of Socinian manuscripts in the Dutch Republic. To begin with, many of the most important Socinian *books* were *published* in Amsterdam, including Christopher Sandius's (1644–1680) *Bibliotheca anti-Trinitariorum* (1684) and Stanislaus Lubienietzki's (1623–1675) *Theatrum Cometicum* (1666–8) and *Historia Reformationis Polonicae* (1685), as well as the famous, hefty *Bibliotheca Fratrum Polonorum*, issued in Amsterdam between 1665 and 1692, which contains the works of Johann Crell (1599–1630), Jonas Schlichting (1592–1661), Faustus Socinus (1539–1604), Johann Ludwig von Wolzogen (1599–1661), and Samuel Przypkowski (1592–1672).[1] In addition, as the *Bibliographia Socinana* compiled by Philip Knijff and Sibbe Jan Visser makes abundantly clear, pre-Socinian anti-Trinitarian treatises had been published on Dutch soil in abundance ever since the sixteenth century, when dozens of texts by, for instance, Castellio (1515–1563) were issued in Dutch and Latin in Utrecht, Rotterdam, Gouda, Haarlem, and Amsterdam.

What is more, between 1652 and 1684 the Rakow catechism of the *Ecclesia minor* was published in seven separate editions, in Dutch – by Jan Knol (?–1672) – English, and Latin, and several hundreds of texts by major Socinian authors and a host of minor ones were also printed in the Dutch Republic.[2] This no doubt served as a source of inspiration to many anti-Trinitarian indigenous authors such as Lancelot van Brederode (1583–1668), Daniel de Breen (1599–1665), and Adam Boreel (1603–1665). As will be only too familiar, by the middle of the seventeenth century this had provoked a massive Calvinist anti-Socinian polemic, which turned Socinianism into the most hotly disputed theological school of thought in the seventeenth-century Dutch Republic. It very much remains to be seen what role manuscripts can have played in a marketplace on which so much printed material appears to have been readily available.

Since 1653, Socinianism had been officially outlawed, after a fervent campaign led by Calvinist ministers across the country, which by the early 1650s was about to embark on its first *stadholderless* period – the age of "True Freedom." But even such an agile politician as Johan de Witt (1625–1672), pensionary of Holland until his gruesome death in 1672, was in no position to stem the tide: in 1653 the States of Holland and West Friesland banned Socinianism, and well into the eighteenth century, any Dutchman accused of sympathizing with the "Polish Brethren" had a serious legal problem. So the publication of, for instance, the *Bibliotheca Fratrum Polonorum* was a perfectly *clandestine* affair. It remains difficult to account for the fact that Frans Kuyper (1629–1691) and his Collegiant friends, who served as the principal editors of the *Bibliotheca*, actually managed to pull it off. Let's not forget that the bulk of the *Bibliotheca* was printed and first sold in 1668 in Amsterdam – the same year in which Adriaan Koerbagh (1633–1669) was arrested and put in jail in that same city for preparing the publication of *Een Ligt schynende in duystere plaatsen.*

It's especially tempting to make this connection, as Adriaan and his brother Johan (1634–1672) were widely known to share anti-Trinitarian feelings, and the library of the Koerbagh brothers was indeed packed with Socinian titles.[3] The successful production of the *Bibliotheca* is the more perplexing as it followed the arrest, in July 1668, of Adriaan Koerbagh: the appearance of the *Bibliotheca* in Amsterdam bookshops was only brought to the attention of the Reformed Church council in March 1669.[4] Indications are that the liberal Amsterdam alderman Hans Bontemantel (1613–1688), who in the end refused to intervene in the Koerbagh affair, actively sought to sabotage the Calvinist campaign against the Socinians. The *Bibliotheca* was only prohibited by the States of Holland in 1674.[5] It would seem, then, that although the Dutch Republic served as a crucial *bibliopolis* of Socinian books, this does not imply that the production and dissemination of these texts was without serious risks. Perhaps Socinian manuscripts continued to play an important part in the proliferation of anti-Trinitarianism. Françoise Weil's warning not to overestimate the difference during the early modern age between printed and handwritten clandestine philosophical texts could well hold also for theological manuscripts.[6]

There is a, however, a second reason why the presence and circulation of Socinian manuscripts in the Dutch Republic may seem an issue of only minor historical relevance, for Martin Mulsow has eloquently argued that "it makes little sense to conduct research on the Socinians from the point of view of national-state culture, or to restrict our views to 'Socinianism in England' (McLachlan) or 'Socinianism in the Netherlands' (Kühler, van Slee). The research must now take on the international character of its subject matter."[7] Mulsow reaches this conclusion after having brilliantly demonstrated the way in which during the second half of the seventeenth century "New Socinians" emerged as "transfer products" from the cultural "melting pot" of the Netherlands, where texts produced by Middle and Eastern European theologians such as Johann and Samuel Crell (1660–1747) as well as Christopher Sandius, Johann Völkel (1565–1616), and Andreas Wissowatius (1608–1678) were picked up by Samuel de Sorbière (1615–1670), Charles Le Cène (1647–1703), Noel Aubert de Versé (1642/5–1714), and Jean Le Clerc (1657–1736), and further exported to England, where for instance John Locke (1632–1704) made good use of them.[8] In a sense, by doing so, Mulsow reiterates and further elaborates the third chapter of his *Moderne aus dem Untergrund*, which deals with Samuel Crell's "European Network."[9]

What is more, Mulsow's insistence on the need to study "cultural exchange and transfer" rather than "influences" turns his work on Socinianism into an early and particularly eloquent example of the recent, massive turn among intellectual historians towards *the circulation of knowledge*.[10] In France, the CNRS currently runs the research theme "The Circulation of Knowledge in Humanist Europe";[11] in October 2016, Paris 3 hosted a conference on "Circulation of Knowledge and Copyright";[12] in the Netherlands, the Huygens Institute has launched its program "Circulation of Knowledge and Learned Practices in the 17th-Century Dutch Republic";[13] in Germany, the Wissenschaftskolleg zu Berlin hosts "Circulation of Knowledge" as a joint initiative of a wide variety of German and Austrian "Transregional Studies."[14] Not to be outdone, in Belgium, FWO, the Flemish Organisation for Scientific Research, has initiated its scientific network "Circulating Knowledge in Early Modern Science."[15] Much as I appreciate and admire Mulsow's work, the emphasis on the circulation of ideas, which to an entire generation of intellectual historians has become something of a mantra, cannot hide from view the fact that all movement presupposes space. More specifically, every single book and every single manuscript is produced and kept in a certain place, and if it moves, it moves from one place to another. Precisely because the Dutch

Republic served as such a crucial place in the publication of printed Sociniana, it also served as a hub for Socinian manuscripts, as they must have played a pivotal part in the production of so many Socinian books and pamphlets in the Dutch Republic.

Traces of Circulation: *Maxima Polonica*

Research into the impact the circulation of manuscripts may have had in the Dutch Republic is seriously hampered by the scarcity of materials available today: very few Socinian manuscripts have survived in the Netherlands. To my knowledge, no attempt has ever been made to locate the surviving manuscripts in any systematic manner, and it remains to be seen whether such an exercise is worth the effort. Having perused the main catalogues, I fear that today the main Dutch libraries have hardly any Socinian manuscripts on offer. Leiden owns a 1633 copy of Johan Crell's *De Spiritu Sancto Tractatus*, first published in 1650, and there is an anonymous Dutch translation of the very rare 1609 Socinian catechism published in Rakow, kept in the former provincial Library of Friesland.[16] But I couldn't trace a single relevant manuscript in the Royal Library at The Hague or in the university libraries of Utrecht, Nijmegen, and Groningen.[17] One would expect the library of the University of Amsterdam to be the exception as it keeps the manuscript collections of both the local Remonstrant and Mennonite communities. But the Mennonite collection does not list a single Socinian item, and the Remonstrant collection keeps only a small number of very minor Sociniana, including some personal papers, largely in Polish, of Stanislaus Lubienietzki and some notes on Daniel Zwicker's (1612–1678) *Irenicum Irenicorum.*[18] Unfortunately, the archives of the Amsterdam Collegiant orphanage "De Oranjeappel," preserved at the municipal archives of Amsterdam, do not contain any Sociniana either.[19] The same holds for the archives of the Mennonite community.[20]

The collection of manuscripts kept by the Remonstrant community of Rotterdam is slightly more interesting. It is presently located in the municipal library of Rotterdam, and besides a number of manuscripts of texts by Servet (1511–1553) and Castellio, its catalogue contains various manuscripts of works by Socinus and Schlichting as well as a massive, 1,154-page collection titled *Maxima Polonica*, carrying the signature, or so it would seem, of one Thomas Litaurovicz, 1657.[21] The date is spurious, however, as this collection contains a host of material dating from the 1660s. In fact, the youngest item I've been able to identify dates from

1670.[22] What is more, the name "Thomas Litaurovicz," or "Litorovicz," does not produce a single hit in Google, so as long as we're unable to identify this name, it does not carry much significance. In view of the many texts related in some way or another to Stanislaus Lubienitzki, it is tempting to assume that it must have originated among his closest friends and relatives.[23] The only printed material included in the *Maxima Polonica* is a copy of a short, anonymous, and now extremely rare pamphlet titled *Morientis Poloniae servandae ratio certissima,* which was composed by Lubienietzki and published in Gdansk in 1665 on Prince Jerzy Sebastian Lubomirski's (1661–7) rebellion against the Polish King John II Casimir (1609–1672).[24] It also includes Lubienietzki's *Vindicia pro Unitariorum in Poloniae Religionis Libertate,* which was only published in 1684 as an appendix to Sandius's *Bibliotheca Anti-Trinitariorum.*[25] Some of these materials are unique – for example, many letters by Lubienietzki, such as those to an unnamed French Catholic.[26] K.E. Jordt Jorgensen, who studied the *Maxima Polonica* during the 1960s, edited Lubienietzki's account contained in the manuscript of the debate on the Trinity he held in Copenhagen on 12 February 1661 with the Jesuit Hieronymus Müllmann (1606–1666) who, incidentally, was the son of a Lutheran professor of theology in Leipzig.[27] The frequent occurrence of Polish clearly suggests a Polish collector, and the uniformity of the handwriting appears to indicate a single hand.

Let us take a closer look at this unique document. It contains many dozens of separate items, mostly in Latin, but also in Polish. It starts with excerpts from Grotius's (1583–1645) *De veritate religionis Christianae,* but it also includes the text of a poem by Grotius, *De Susanna* (on the chaste Susanna in Daniel 13) as well as his letter, from 10 May 1631, to Johann Crell.[28] Other "Dutch" contributions include several collections of Erasmiana,[29] Thomas à Kempis's (1380–1471) *Alphabeticum spirituale,*[30] several excerpts from Justus Lipsius (1547–1606),[31] a section titled *Epistola aliquot D. Sam. Przypk. Ad Fratres Batavos,* dated 1665,[32]and a stirring Latin elegy composed by Nicolaas Heinsius (1620–1681) on the admiral Michiel de Ruyter (1607–1676), dated 12 June 1666, following the Four Day's Battle in the Second Anglo-Dutch War, and only published in the nineteenth century.[33] There are more texts by Przypkowski, such as his *Demonstratio quod neque pater domini nostri Jesu Christi per metaphoram filius dici queat aut debeat,* which would only be published in the 1692, tenth volume of the *Bibliotheca Fratrum Polonorum.*[34] Przypkowski's *De Christianorum Summo Bono Dissertatio,* a text of which I have been unable to locate any printed copy, is also included.[35] The collection ends with a Latin translation of Daniel de Breen's remarks on chapter 17 of Acts of the Apostles.[36]

On the whole, the *Maxima Polonica* looks very much like a Socinian *Vade mecum.* It contains for instance a brief essay on the Unitarian credentials of the early fathers of the Church: *Antiqui Patres Filium Dei Ipsum Summum Deum esse, non crediderunt,* which in Sandius is only listed as an anonymous manuscript.[37] One of the earliest documents is a letter, written in June 1571 by the Catholic Polish astronomer Andreas Dudith (1553–1589) to the historian Johannes Lasiciki (1534–1602): by the end of his life Dudith had started to display considerable sympathy for the Socinian cause.[38] Most of the Polish material is concerned with the political position of the *Ecclesia minor* in Poland. It also holds several collections of excerpts from Classical and Renaissance philosophers such as Agrippa,[39] Apuleius,[40] Virgil,[41] Livy,[42] and Pico della Mirandola (1563–1594).[43] In view of the importance of the Peripatetic tradition for Socinian theology, it's odd that the *Maxima Polonica* does not contain any excerpts of Aristotle.[44]

In all fairness, the *Maxima Polonica* is a sad document as it mainly bears testimony to the gradual destruction of Polish Socinianism. One of its most curious sections is a collection of epitaphs of famous crowned heads, including the Polish Princess Anne of Sweden (1568–1625), the half-Polish King Sigismund III of Sweden (1566–1632), and Prince Christoph Radziwill (1549–1616).[45] A special section is devoted to epitaphs of major scholars and theologians: Vives (1493–1540), Copernicus (1473–1543), Vesalius (1514–1564), Bucerus (1491–1551), Melanchton (1497–1560), Schwenckfeldt (1489/90–1560), Calvin (1509–1564), and many more.[46] In conjunction with the *Epitafium Libertatis Polonica*[47] – a text that is not even listed in Sandius's *Bibliotheca anti-Trinitariorum* – this Rotterdam manuscript bears all the hallmarks of being an epitaph on the *Ecclesia minor* itself. As a handbook it was probably designed mainly to serve its copyist, whoever he or she may have been. Frustratingly, nothing is known about the history of this manuscript – how it ended up in the collection of the Remonstrant community of Rotterdam remains a mystery.

Politica Ecclesiastica

Sometimes, however, the relevance of a Socinian manuscript can be gauged even long after its disappearance.[48] This appears to be the case with Jean-Frédéric Bernard's (1683–1744) chapter on Socinianism in the sixth volume (1736) of the *Cérémonies et coutumes religieuses de tous les peoples du monde*, at the end of his account of Protestantism. By this time Socinianism had definitely turned into an object of historical inquiry: Samuel Crell, often referred to as "the last Socinian," was in his late sixties, living in Amsterdam, and about to join the Remonstrants. I fully appreciate that bringing up Picart (1673–1733) and Bernard's *Cérémonies et coutumes religieuses* in Los Angeles of all places is like carrying coal to Newcastle, but at this occasion I can at least dispense with an elaborate introduction of this massive *Encyclopaedia of World Religions*, published in Amsterdam from 1723 to 1743.[49] Even though Bernard obviously depends on a wide variety of sources, his analysis of Socinianism reveals a remarkable coherence.[50]

First, Bernard claims not to be interested in Socinian theology since its denial of the divinity of Christ is simply "too odious" to be elaborated upon yet again.[51] Instead, he prefers to regard Socinianism as a historian.[52] Bernard presents himself as no more than a "compilateur fidelle," who does not have to worry about the numerous "errors" made by the Socinians, now that they have been exposed and refuted by such eminent theologians as the seventeenth-century Groningen professor of divinity Samuel Maresius (1599–1673). Samuel des Marets, who was French by birth and who had been educated in Saumur and Geneva, was indeed a theologian of international repute whose three-part *Hydra socinianismi expurgata* (1651–2) was widely held to be an authoritative piece of reformed orthodoxy.[53]

Having established his credentials, Bernard sets out to "roughly sketch" the "blasphemous" views of the Socinians on the divinity of Christ: apart from the fact that the Trinity destroys God's unity, it lacks any Scriptural basis: "Si, dissent-ils, le salut du genre humain eut dépendu de la nécessité de croire le mystère de l'Incarnation, elle seroit rapporté, aussi distinctement et aussi claire dans la Bible que les autres vérités nécessaires au salut."[54]

In addition, Bernard continues, Socinians reject the notion of primordial sin and uphold the freedom of the will. There is no divine predestination either, and the idea of Christ's satisfaction is simply unnecessary: if God had wanted to pardon mankind he could easily have done so at any given moment. We revere Christ only because God expects it of us, not because He is His "Son." Some Socinians even go so far as to deny God's creation *ex nihilo*.[55] The best way, Bernard muses, to silence these "prequ'Athées," would be to ignore them altogether, but apparently the author of the *Cérémonies et coutumes religieuses* is not done yet, for he happily continues his discussion of their "monstrous opinions" and highlights the internal "discipline" of what its adherents hold to be a "*culte raisonable.*"[56] Since they feel Christ should be deemed the sole "monarch" of the kingdom that is His Church, and Christ did not issue commands in the way Moses did regarding the manner in which His Church was to be organized, Socinians feel obliged to follow only the Gospel. They are guided by two principles: respect for the truth, and concern for the well-being of the Church.

In what follows, Bernard quotes abundantly from a manuscript compiled by a Unitarian, dating from 1642 or so he tells us, titled *Politica Ecclesiastica*.[57] Apparently, Bernard had acquired a copy of Petrus Morscovius's (or: Piotr Morzkowski/Moskowski) *Politica Ecclesiastica*, which was actually written in 1646 at the behest of the Synod of Dazhva in Volhynia, today's Western Ukraine. Morscovius (?–post 1646), a Polish nobleman, was a pupil of Johann Crell. Morscovius seems to have had little contact with Dutch theologians, although in 1633, in Krakow, he encountered the Remonstrant minister Johannes Naeranus (1608–1679).[58] The history of this manuscript is not uninteresting, for his grandson Samuel Crell, who lived in Amsterdam from 1727 to his death in 1747, handed it over to Johan Grashuis (1699–1772), a medical doctor from Groningen, trained in Leiden, who practised in Amsterdam during the 1730s and subsequently moved to Hoorn. Grashuis passed it on to one Christopher Brückmann from Nuremberg, who allowed the Lutheran minister Georg Ludwig Oeder (1694–1760) to finally publish it in 1745.[59] So here we have an example of a very well-travelled manuscript indeed, and as it turns out, its presence for a while in Amsterdam turned it into an *interesting* manuscript, allowing Bernard to add an insider's perspective to his essay on Socinianism. Incidentally, Bernard's acquaintance with Grashuis is hardly surprising, for the doctor was a prominent figure in Amsterdam: he had taken his doctorate in 1722 with Herman Boerhaave (1668–1738), and he was the author of a considerable number of medical treatises and a member of several learned societies, as well as a fervent Collegiant. His friends included the historian Jan Wagenaar (1709–1804) and the famous novelist Betje Wolff (1738–1804), with whom he exchanged letters, in one of which he praises her for her courage to defend a "pure" Christianity, "free of all human additions." In 1760, Betje Wolff, that is Elizabeth Wolff-Bekker, was one of the last Collegiants to be baptized at Rijnsburg.[60]

Correspondences

While very few Socinian manuscripts that once must have been brought to the Netherlands appear to have survived, a pretty substantial correspondence between Socinian authors and their Dutch friends can still be consulted in Dutch libraries. Recently, Sibbe Jan Visser has studied the correspondence of Samuel (1582–1641) and Johannes Naeranus – again: two Remonstrant theologians – with Socinians such as Martinus Ruarus (1588–1657), Schlichting, Joachim Pastorius (1611–1681), and Przypkowski – but these letters are mainly concerned with the issue whether the Socinians could be admitted to and adopted by the Remonstrant Fraternity now that their position in Eastern Europe was becoming increasingly precarious.[61] One of the Arminians or Remonstrants who at a very early stage were suspected and accused of harbouring Socinian sympathies was of course Grotius. Much has been written already about Grotius's alleged Socinianism.[62] As early as his *Ordinum pietas* of 1613 he actively intervened in the first stages of the Dutch debate concerning Socinianism by arguing that the States of Holland had been wrongfully accused of Socinianism following their decision to offer Conrad Vorstius (1569–1622) a Leiden chair.[63] Four years later Grotius felt compelled to publish his *Defensio fidei catholicae de satisfactione Christi adversus Faustum Socinum.*[64] Living in exile in Paris did not stop him from entering into epistolary relationships with Socinian leaders such as Johan Crell and Martin Ruarus during the early 1630s, and in particular Grotius's irenic engagement with the establishment of a broad Church based on a dogmatic minimum ensured his continuing association with the Socinian cause.[65] Until well into the eighteenth century, French scholars were referring to "ce prétendu commerce de lettres de Grotius avec les Freres Polonais."[66] In the early eighteenth century Richard Simon (1638–1712) recorded a rumour apparently circulating in Paris that a large correspondence between Grotius and several Socinians was being kept in the local Jesuit library. Simon, however, was sceptical: "Ces Jesuites n'en ont jamais fait parler."[67]

All this will be only too familiar. Much less well known, however, is the enduring relationship with Socinian theologians of the De Groot *family*, who operated very much in unison, like a scholarly clan of relatives.[68] Hugo's son Pieter (1615–1678), and his nephew Jacobus de Groot (1628–1694), son of Hugo's brother Willem (1597–1662), both corresponded with senior Polish Socinians such as Lubienietzki. During the late 1660s Pieter served at the Dutch embassy in Stockholm, mobilizing his Scandinavian contacts as much as he could in support of his friend.[69] It would seem much of the correspondence has been lost, as a letter kept in the Royal Library in The Hague strongly suggests an intimate relationship: De Groot assures Lubienietzki of his gratitude for his letters, "qui toujours servent d'instruction."[70]

Lubienietzki was very well connected indeed: preparing the publication of the *Theatrum cometicum*, he corresponded for instance with

Dutchmen such as Isaac Vossius (1618–1689), Nicolaas Heinsius, and Christiaan Huygens (1629–1695).[71] Once the *Theatrum cometicum* had been published, however, Lubienietzki got into a nasty quarrel with its publisher, Frans Kuyper, upon which Johannes Naeranus and his Mennonite friend the Rotterdam poet Joachim Oudaen (1628–1692) did what they could to help his Polish friend, who had probably indeed been cheated by Kuyper.[72] As time went by the Socinians grew more dependent on their Western European correspondents, and as a consequence they were no longer in a position to offer their friends instruction. Benedictus Wissowatius (1650–1704), Andreas's son, edited Sandius's *Bibliotheca* as well as Lubienietzki's *Historia.*[73] He was in touch with Van Limborch, exchanging letters from 1691 to 1704, but in this correspondence Van Limborch is very much the professor, and Wissowatius the student, as they discuss the technical details involved in the interpretation of 1 Tim 3:2, 1 Cor 5:9–11, and 2 Thess 3:6 and 14.[74] Van Limborch, however, occasionally took a more active interest, supervising for instance the posthumous publication in 1692 of Samuel Przypkowski's *Cogitationes Sacrae* as part IX of the *Bibliotheca Fratrum Polonorum.*[75]

Finally, as noted above, Samuel Crell lived in Amsterdam from 1727 until his death in 1747. He had already been on very friendly terms with Philippus van Limborch prior to his arrival in the Netherlands – he had studied at the Remonstrant seminary during the late 1670s – and the two would keep up a correspondence, parts of which have been preserved.[76] While Van Limborch's successor at the Remonstrant seminary, Adriaan van Cattenburgh (1664–1743), was anxious to keep his distance,[77] Crell's joining of the indigenous theological landscape turned him into the "last" Socinian: by the end of his life he had joined the Amsterdam Remonstrants, and he probably felt perfectly at home as well among the Amsterdam Collegiants. By the 1730s, however, the Collegiant movement itself was in decline, with many of its members being drawn towards Pietism.

Conclusion

Despite the seventeenth-century evaporation of Socinianism as a movement, guided and inspired by its "own" theologians, in the Dutch Republic accusations of Socinianism would continue to be hurled at, for instance, Johannes Stinstra (1708–1790), the Mennonite author of *De mutua Christianorum tolerantia* (1745). As late as 1742 he was suspended from his ministry for fifteen years.[78] Until the end of century, long after

Crell has passed away, and a reasonable, tolerant Christianity was becoming part and parcel of the cultural make-up of the enlightened Dutch "burger," orthodox Calvinists would continue to use the term to denote ungodliness in general. See, for instance, Betje Wolff's *De onveranderlijke Santhorstsche Geloofsbelijdenis* (1772), and her epistolary novel *Sara Burgerhart* (1782), as well as its sequel, *Brieven van Abraham Blankaart* (1787–9): again and again, Wolff complained, enlightened, pious Protestants were accused of being Socinians.[79] The huge success her work enjoyed appears to indicate, however, that in Dutch society the accusers were becoming a minority. It should be added that by the end of the century, orthodox Calvinists were facing much more dangerous opponents: as early as 1784 Joseph Priestley's (1733–1804) *History of the Corruptions of Christianity* (1782) was translated into Dutch, and in 1798 Thomas Paine's (1737–1809) *Age of Reason* (1794) appeared in a very popular Dutch translation as well.[80]

During the 1780s, some Orangist Calvinists such as Johannes Le Francq van Berkhey (1729–1812) had attempted to link the dreaded "Patriots" with the Socinian cause, but the label did not stick.[81] As late as 1793 the reverend Jan Scharp (1756–1828), fulminating against "the so-called Enlightenment," singled out "Socijn en Crellius" as having triumphed at last, but by this time Scharp, another ardent Orangist, could no longer claim to represent the Dutch Reformed Church in the way that for instance Maresius had been able to do in the middle of the seventeenth century.[82] Following the Batavian Revolution, in 1798 the *Staatsregeling* was issued, the first Dutch constitution ever, according to which – Article 19 – each and every citizen was free to serve God as he or she saw fit.[83] By the end of the eighteenth century, theology no longer served as the principal issue of debate in the Dutch Republic.[84] By this time, politics had taken centre stage and Socinianism had indeed become an object of historical research, just as Bernard had approached it already in the 1730s.

It seems doubtful that many manuscripts survived the Dutch Republic, although the sheer volume of Socinian books it had produced amply testifies to its importance for the proliferation of Socinianism once it had been outlawed in Eastern Europe. The manuscripts on the basis of which such monumental enterprises as the publication in Amsterdam of the *Bibliotheca Fratrum Polonorum* were carried out must have disappeared soon after Dutch printing presses had done their work. Occasional finds such as the Rotterdam *Maxima Polonica* and the way in which Bernard took advantage of Morscovius's *Politica Ecclesiastica* appear to suggest that Socinian manuscripts continued to play at least some part in the conservation and transmission of the views cultivated by the exiled members of the *Ecclesia minor*. But in view of the evidence available today it would seem the crucial manuscripts involved were the letters exchanged between Socinian theologians and their Dutch friends, quite a few of which have survived. From the mid-seventeenth century onwards, however, wherever they went as exiles, Socinians were at the mercy of others. Yet by the same token it could be argued that when the Dutch Republic was itself about to collapse and some Calvinist hardliners would continue to warn against what Maresius had dubbed the *Hydra Socinianismi*, "enlightened" Dutchmen were now at last ready to embrace the vision of a broad, tolerant Reformed Church that the Polish Brethren had been denied both in Eastern and Western Europe.[85]

NOTES

1 The volumes I and V–VII (1665, 1668) contain the works of Johann Crell; II (1665) those of Schlichting; II–IV (1668) those of Socinus; VIII–IX (1668) those of Wolzogen; X (1692) those of Przypkowski. The entire text is available at http://www.sbc.org.pl/dlibra/docmetadata?id=3075&from=publication&tab=3.

See Jerome Vercruysse, "Bibliotheca Fratrum Polonorum, tables et index," *Tijdschrift voor de studie van de Verlichting* 5 (1977): 379–403; and "'Bibliotheca Fratrum Polonorum.' Histoire et bibliographie," *Odrodzenie I Reformacja w Posce* 21 (1975): 197–212. Janusz Tazbir, "Die Sozinianer in der zweiten Hälfte des 17. Jahrhunderts," in *Reformation und Frühaufklärung in Polen. Studien über den Sozinianismus und seinen Einfluss auf das Westeuropäische Denken im 17. Jahrhundert*, ed. Paul Wrzecionko (Göttingen: Vandenhoeck & Ruprecht, 1977), 9–77, 63–4.

2 Aart de Groot, "Die erste niederländische Übersetzung des Rakower Katechismus (1659)," in *Socinianism and Its Role in the Culture of the XVIth to XVIIIth Centuries*, ed. Lech Szczuchi (Warsaw and Lodz: PWN, 1983), 129–37; Piet Visser, "Kritisch commentaar van een collegiantse kwelgeest. Twee manuscripten en een pamflet van Jan Knol uit de jaren 1655–1659 ingeleid en van aantekeningen voorzien," *Doopsgezinde Bijdragen* 38 (2012): 285–349.

3 Cis van Heertum, "Reading Johannes Koerbagh. The Auction Catalogue of His Library as a Reflection of His Life," *Lias* 38 (2011): 1–57.

4 Vercruysse, "'Bibliotheca Fratrum Polonorum,'" 200–2. See also my introduction to Adriaan Koerbagh, *A Light Shining in Dark Places*, ed. and trans. Michiel Wielema, intro. Wiep van Bunge (Leiden: Brill, 2011);

Bart Leeuwenburgh, *Het noodlot van een ketter. Adriaan Koerbagh 1633–1669* (Nijmegen: Vantilt, 2013), ch. 2.

5 See also Ingrid Weekhout, *Boekencensuur in de Noordelijke Nederlanden. De vrijheid van drukpers in de zeventiende eeuw* (Den Haag: SDU, 1997), 92–5.

6 Françoise Weil, "La fonction du manuscript par rapport à l'imprimé," in *De bonne main. La communication manuscrite au XVIIIe siècle*, ed. François Moureau (Paris: Universitas, 1993), 17–27.

7 Martin Mulsow, "The 'New Socinians': Intertextuality and Cultural Exhange in Late Socinianism," in *Socinianism and Arminianism: Antitrinitarians, Calvinists, and Cultural Exchange in Seventeenth-Century Europe*, ed. Martin Mulsow and Jan Rohls (Leiden: Brill, 2005), 49–78, 64. Crucial to Mulsow's analysis is Jeroom Vercruysse, "Crellius, Le Cène, Naigeon ou les chemins de la tolérance socinienne," *Tijdschrift voor de studie van de Verlichting* 3–4 (1973): 244–85.

8 The most recent analysis of Locke's engagement with Socinianism is to be found in Sascha Salatowsky, *Die Philosophie der Sozinianer. Transformationen zwischen Renaissance-Aristotelismus und Frühaufklärung* (Stuttgart-Bad Cannstatt: Frommann-Holzboog, 2015), esp. 43–53; 186–94; 327–39; 446–53.

9 Martin Mulsow, *Moderne aus dem Untergrund. Radikale Frühaufklärung in Deutschland, 1680–1720* (Hamburg: Felix Meiner, 2002).

10 Just a handful of recent examples: Sven Dupré and Christoph Lüthy, eds, *Silent Messengers: The Circulation of Material Objects of Knowledge in the Early Modern Low Countries* (Berlin: LIT, 2011); Bernard Lightman, Gordon McOuat, and Larry Stewart, eds, *The Circulation of Knowledge between Britain, India and China: The Early-Modern World to the Twentieth Century* (Leiden: Brill, 2013); Leandro Rodriguez Mendins, *The Circulation of European Knowledge: Niklas Luhmann in the Hispanic Americas* (London: Palgrave Macmillan, 2015).

11 http://www2.cnrs.fr/en/278.htm.

12 http://www.univ-paris3.fr/copyright-and-the-circulation-of-knowledge-358583.kjsp.

13 http://ckcc.huygens.knaw.nl.

14 http://www.wiko-berlin.de/en/institute/projects-cooperations/archive/circulation-of-knowledge-transregional-studies/.

15 http://www.circulatingknowledge.ugent.be/mission.

16 Jacob van Sluis, ed., *Inventaris van de handschriften van de voormalige Provinsjale Biblioteek fan Fryslan* (Leeuwarden: Tresoar, 2007), 108: Sign. 762 Hs. The collection is now in the possession of Tresoar, in Leeuwarden.

17 There is, however, in typescript, a pretty impressive inventory of printed Socinian texts available in Utrecht: E.G. Arnold, *Sociniana Ultraiectina*.

Inventaris van gedrukte werken van sociniaanse tint en toon in de collectie van de Universiteitsbibliotheek Utrecht en de collectie "Thomaasse"– daarin apart begrepen (S.l., 1978). For Groningen, see S. Krikke, *Bibliotheca Unitariana. Keuze van werken uit de collectie betreffende vrije religiositeit* (Groningen: Universiteitsbiblibliotheek, 1994).

18 The relevant texts were described in the *Catalogus der handschriften VII. De handschriften krachtens bruikleencontract in de universiteitsbibliotheek berustende.* Eerste gedeelte. De handschriften van de Remonstransche kerk beschreven door den conservator Dr M.B. Mendes da Costa. De handschriften van het Evangelisch-Luthersche seminarium en van de Vereenigde Doopsgezinde Gemeente, beschreven door den conservator Dr J. Berg (Amsterdam: Bibliotheek der Universiteit, 1923), I, #23; 244; 249–51; 629–30; 701–2.

19 https://stadsarchief.amsterdam.nl/archieven/archiefbank/inventaris/169.nl.html.

20 https://stadsarchief.amsterdam.nl/archieven/archiefbank/inventaris/1120.nl.html.

21 IJ. Rogge, *Catalogus der handschriften op de bibliotheek der remonstrantsch-gereformeerde gemeente te Rotterdam* (Amsterdam: IJ. Rogge, 1869), 46–50; 49, #527: "Maxima Polonica." I should add that I have not been able to locate this signature myself. Unfortunately, Rogge does not give a page number. The municipal archives of Rotterdam keep the archives of the Remonstrant community, which also contains a small collection of manuscripts: no Socinian texts, however. See: http://www.archieven.nl/nl/zoeken?mivast=0&mizig=210&miadt=184&miaet=1&micode=326&minr=988926&miview=inv2.

22 Rogge, *Catalogus*, #527, 581.

23 K.E. Jordt Jorgensen, *Stanislaus Lubienicki. Zum Weg des Unitarismus von Ost nach West im 17. Jahrhundert* (Göttingen: Vandenhoeck & Ruprecht, 1968). For Lubienietzki's correspondence in Rogge, *Catalogus*, #527, see 855ff and 868ff.

24 Worldcat holds only two copies: Jagiellonski University library in Krakow and the Provinzialbibliothek in Amberg, Germany. A Dutch translation appeared in Amsterdam in 1667: *Het stervende Polen.* (Knuttel 9446). See *Bibliographia Sociniana*, 83; Jorgensen, *Stanislaus Lubienicki*, 99–101.

25 Rogge, *Catalogus*, #527, 84–104.

26 Rogge, *Catalogus*, #527, 855–9 ; Jorgensen, *Stanislaus Lubienicki*, 30 and 91–2.

27 Rogge, *Catalogus*, #527, 819–40: *Brevis et fidelis relatio.* See K.E. Jordt Jorgensen, ed., "De antitrinitariske Kollokvier i Kobenhavn i februr 1661," *Kirkehistoriske samlinger* (1973): 46–86; and Jordt Jorgensen, *Stanislaus Lubienicki*, 62–70.

28 Rogge, *Catalogus*, #527, 125–7; 269–70. See Hugo Grotius, *Poemata*, ed. Guil. Grotius (Leiden: Brill, 1639), 190–2.
29 Rogge, *Catalogus*, #527, 118–21; 131–52; 612–30.
30 Rogge, *Catalogus*, #527, 545.
31 Rogge, *Catalogus*, #527, 490ff.
32 Rogge, *Catalogus*, #527, 886–90.
33 Rogge, Catalogus, # 527, 816–17. See G.D.J. Schotel, ed., *Theodori Ryckii, Joh. Georgii Graevii, Nicolai Heinsii, ad Adrianum Blyenburgum et Adriani Blyenburgi ad diversos Epistolae ineditae* (Den Haag: P.H. Noordendorp, 1853), 99–100.
34 Rogge, *Catalogus*, #527, 843–52.
35 Rogge, *Catalogus*, #527, 417–24. According to Christopher Sandius, *Bibliotheca anti-Trinitariorum* (Freistadt [Amsterdam]: Johannes Acontius, 1684), 123; there was once a 1636 edition. Not in WorldCat.
36 Rogge, *Catalogus*, #527, 1104ff, apparently based on Daniel de Breen, *Breves in Vetum et Novum Testamentum Annotationes* (Amsterdam: Hendricus Dendrinus, 1664), 105–27.
37 Rogge, *Catalogus*, #527, 185–6; Sandius, *Bibliotheca anti-Trinitariorum*, 179.
38 Rogge, Catalogus, #527, 43–57. See Gábor Almási, *The Uses of Humanism: Johannes Sambucus (1531–1584), Andreas Dudith (1533–1589), and the Republic of Letters in East Central Europe* (Leiden: Brill, 2009), 306.
39 Rogge, *Catalogus*, #527, 327–43.
40 Rogge, *Catalogus*, #527, 104–11.
41 Rogge, *Catalogus*, #527, 215.
42 Rogge, *Catalogus*, #527, 741–51.
43 Rogge, *Catalogus*, #527, 111–18.
44 See most recently Salatowsky, *Die Philosophie der Sozinianer*, esp. ch. 2.
45 Rogge, *Catalogus*, #527, 752ff.
46 Rogge, *Catalogus*, #527, 288ff.
47 Rogge, *Catalogus*, #527, 810–19.
48 This part is taken from my "Jean-Frédéric Bernard's Global Perspective on Socinianism and Deism" (forthcoming).
49 Jean-François Bernard and Bernard Picard, *Cérémonies et coutumes religieuses de tous les peoples du monde*, 8 vols (Amsterdam: J.-F. Bernard, 1723–43). See of course Lynn Hunt, Margaret C. Jacob, and Wijnand Mijnhardt, *The Book That Changed Europe. Picart and Bernard's* Religious Ceremonies of the World (Cambridge, MA: Harvard University Press, 2010); and Lynn Hunt, Margaret Jacob, and Wijnand Mijnhardt, eds, *Bernard Picart and the First Global Vision of Religion* (Los Angeles: Getty Publications, 2010).
50 It is titled *Dissertation Qui contient (a) la Discipline des Freres (b) Polonois (c) connus aussi sous les noms d'Unitaires, Antitrinitaires, (c) Sociniens, etc.*; VI, 287–328.

51 Bernard and Picard, *Cérémonies et coutumes,* VI, 287.

52 Bernard and Picard, *Cérémonies et coutumes,* VI, 288, note (a), in which Bernard briefly discusses the comparison between Socinianism and Islam made by Mathurin Veyssière de La Croze: "Réflexions historiques et critiques sur le mahométisme, et sur le socinianisme," in his *Dissertations historiques sur divers sujets* (Rotterdam: Reinier Leers, 1707). See Martin Mulsow, "Socinianism, Islam, and the Radical Uses of Arabic Scholarship," *Al-Qantara* 31 (2010): 549–86, esp. 563–5.

53 Samuel Maresius, *Hydra socinianismi expurgata,* 3 vols (Groningen: Joannes Nicolaus, 1651–62). See Doede Nauta, *Samuel Maresius* (Amsterdam: H.J. Paris, 1935), 349–53.

54 Bernard and Picard, *Cérémonies et coutumes,* VI, 289.

55 Bernard and Picard, *Cérémonies et coutumes,* VI, 290, referring to Johannes Volkelius, *De vera religione,* which was included in Maresius' *Hydra socinianismi expurgata.*

56 Bernard and Picard, *Cérémonies et coutumes,* VI, 291.

57 Bernard and Picard, *Cérémonies et coutumes,* VI, 287, note (a).

58 Piet Visser, *Samuel Naeranus (1582–1641) en Johannes Naeranus (1608–1679). Twee remonstrantse theologen op de bres voor de godsdienstige verdraagzaamheid* (Hilversum: Verloren, 2011), 158.

59 Petrus Morscovius, *Politica Ecclesiastica, quam vulgo Agendam vocant, sive Forma Regiminis Exterioris Ecclesiarum Christianarum in Polnia …, Tribus Libris* (Frankfurt and Leipzig, 1745). See G.H. Williams, ed. *The Polish Brethren: Documentation of the History and Thought of Unitarianism in the Polish–Lithuanian Commonwealth and in the Diaspora, 1601–1685,* 2 vols (Missoula: Scholars Press, 1980), vol. 1, 424. This appears to contradict Marian Skrzypek's suggestion that manuscript copies of Morscovius's work circulated in France: "Le libertinisme polonaise et la littérature clandestine," in *La Philosophie clandestine à l'Âge classique,* ed. Antony McKenna and Alain Mothu (Paris: Universitas, 1997), 509–20, esp. 515–16.

60 *De briefwisseling van Betje Wolff en Aagje Deken,* 2 vols, ed. P.J. Buijnsters (Utrecht: HES, 1987), 129: "het zuivere Christendom, buiten alle menschelyke byvoegzelen en bepaalingen." See also 823–4 and J. Hartog, "Uit de aantekeningen van Joännes Cuperus," *Doopsgezinde Bijdragen* N.S. 2 (1868), 85–111, esp. 93–4; J.C. van Slee, *De Rijnsburger collegianten* (Utrecht: HES, [1980]1895), *passim.* Grashuis was also involved in popularizing experimental philosophy: Huib J. Zuidervaart, "Science for the Public: The Translation of Popular Texts on Experimental Philosophy into the Dutch Language in Mid-Eighteenth Century," in *Cultural Transfer through Translation: The Circulation of Enlightened Thought in Europe by Means of Translation,* ed. Stefanie Stockhorst (Amsterdam: Rodopi, 2010), 231–62.

61 Visser, *Samuel Naeranus (1582–1641) en Johannes Naeranus (1608–1679)*, ch. 6. See also Sibbe Jan Visser, "Het heldere licht der waarheid. De briefwisseling tussen Samuel Naeranus en Martinus Ruarus," *Doopsgezinde Bijdragen* 30 (2004): 292–312.

62 See most recently Henk J.M. Nellen, "In Strict Confidence: Grotius' Correspondence with his Socinian Friends," in *Self-Presentation and Social Identification: The Rhetoric and Pragmatics of Early Modern Letter Writing* ed. Toon van Houdt, Jan Papy, Gilbert Tournoy, and Constant Mattheeussen (Leuven: Leuven University Press, 2002), 227–46; *Hugo de Groot. Een leven in strijd om de rede 1583–1645* (Amsterdam, 2007), 429–35; and "Minimal Religion, Deism, and Socinianism: On Grotius' Motives for Writing *De Veritate*," *Grotiana* 33 (2012): 25–57; Hans W. Blom, "Grotius and Socinianism," in *Socinianism and Arminianism*, ed. Martin Mulsow and Jan Rohls, 121–47; Florian Mühlegger, "De reactie van Hugo de Groot op het socinianisme," *Doopsgezinde Bijdragen* 30 (2004): 210–36.

63 Hugo Grotius, *Ordinum Hollandiae ac Westfrisia Pietas* (1613), critical ed. with English translation and commentary by Edwin Rabbie (Leiden: Brill, 1995).

64 Hugo Grotius, *Defensio fidei catholicae de satisafctione Christi adversus Faustum Socinum Senenesem*, ed. with intro. and notes by Edwin Rabbie, with English trans. by Hotze Mulder (Assen-Maastricht: Van Gorcum, 1990).

65 See most notably Grotius's *De veritate religionis Christianae* (1627), of which no modern edition is available. See J.P. Heering, *Hugo Grotius as Apologist for the Christian Religion* (Leiden: Brill, 2004).

66 [Louis-Anatase Guichard], *Histoire du Socinianisme* (Paris: François Barois, 1728), 538.

67 [Richard Simon], *Bibliothèque critique*, 4 vols (Paris and Amsterdam: Jean Louis de Lormes, 1708–10), III, 124. According to Simon, the Rouen bibliophile Louis-Émery Bigot (1626–1689), a dear friend of Nicolaas Heinsius, had been responsible for spreading this rumour.

68 Martine J. van Ittersum, "Knowledge Production in the Dutch Republic: The Household Academy of Hugo Grotius," *Journal of the History of Ideas* 72 (2011): 523–48.

69 Jorgensen, *Stanislaus Lubienicki*, 84. See UBL: HS PAP2, Lubienietzki to Pieter de Groot, April 1669.

70 KB: HS 72D20: Pieter de Groot to Lubienietzki, 17 April 1669.

71 Stanislaus Lubienietzki, *Theatrum cometicum*, 3 vols (Amsterdam: Franciscus Cuperus, 1666–8). On his exchange with Huygens, see Yoella Yoder, *Catalogue of the Manuscripts of Christiaan Huygens: Including a Concordance with His Oeuvres complètes* (Leiden: Brill, 2013), 183; Christiaan Huygens, *Oeuvres complètes*, 22 vols, eds, D. Bierens de Haan et al. (Den Haag: Martinus Nijhoff, 1888–1950), V, #1486, 1487, 1480, and VI, #1577.

72 UBA: HS N59: Lubienietzki to Naeranus, 27–10–1671 and UBA: HS 134 Dh: Lubienietzki to Oudaen, 5–12–1668. See Jorgensen, *Stanislaus Lubienicki*, 83–4; Visser, *Godtslasterlijck ende Pernicieus*, 18–20; Visser, *Samuel Naeranus (1582–1641) en Johannes Naeranus (1608–1679)*, 182–4. See also the three letters Lubienietzki wrote to Oudaen in 1668–9, kept at Leiden: UBL: HS BPL 246; BPL 2899; PAP 15. Curiously, J. Melles, *Joachim Oudaan. Heraut der verdraagzaamheid, 1628–1692* (Utrecht: Kemink & Zoon, 1958), remains silent on Oudaen's Socinian contacts. Individual Mennonites occasionally sympathized with Socinianism, but on the whole their congregations took a very defensive stance: S. Zijlstra, *Om de ware gemeente en de oude gronden. Geschiedenis van de dopersen in de Nederlanden, 1531–1675* (Hilversum: Verloren, 2000), 330–9.

73 Martin Schmeisser, ed., *Sozinianische Bekenntnisschriften. Der Rakower Katechismus des Valentins Schmalz (1608) und der sogenannte Soner Katechismus* (Berlin: Akademie Verlag, 2012), 52–3.

74 UBA: HSS III D17: 158, 159, 80, 162. See P.J. Barnouw, *Philippus van Limborch* (Den Haag: Mouton & Co., 1963), 52–3.

75 UBA: HSS K88 a-d. See Luisa Simonutti, "Resistance, Obedience and Toleration: Przypkowski and Limborch," in Mulsow and Rohls, eds, *Socinianism and Arminianism*, 187–206.

76 The letters stretch from 1666 to 1704: UBA HSS J21a-c and III D17. See also Eric H. Cossee, "Meer verschil dan overeenkomst; remonstrantisme en socinianisme vergeleken door Adriaan van Cattenburgh in zijn *Specimen controversiarum inter remonstrantes et Socinum* (1728)," *Doopsgezinde Bijdragen* 30 (2004): 141–52. On Crell's joining the Remonstrants: W.J. Kühler, *Het Socinianisme in Nederland* (Leeuwarden: De Tille, [1912]1980), 256–7.

77 Aart de Groot, "Het kusje. Samuel Crellius op de grens tussen socinianisme en piëtisme," in *Geschiedenis, godsdienst, letterkunde*, ed. E.K. Grootes and J. den Haan. Opstellen aangeboden aan dr. S.B.J. Zilverberg ter gelegenheid van zijn afscheid van de Universiteit van Amsterdam (Roden: Nehalennia, 1989), 186–95.

78 See on Stinstra: Joris van Eijnatten, *Mutua Christianorum Tolerantia: Irenicism and Toleration in the Netherlands: The Stinstra Affair 1740–1745* (Firenze: Olschki, 1998).

79 E. Bekker and A. Deken, *Historie van Mejuffrouw Sara Burgerhart*, ed. P.J. Buijnsters, 2 vols (Den Haag: Martinus Nijhoff, 1980), I, 188, 225, 305; *Brieven van Abraham Blankaart*, ed. E. Wolff and Agatha Deken, 3 vols (Den Haag: Isaac van Cleef, 1787–9) I, xlii–xlv. On Betje Wolff's religious attitudes, see P. van der Vliet, *Wolff en Deken's Brieven van*

Abraham Blankaart. Een bijdrage tot de kennis van de Reformatorische Verlichting (Utrecht: HES, 1982), esp. 245–6; Ernestine van der Wall, "Religious Pluralism, Toleration, and the Enlightenment: The Dutch Novelists Elisabeth Wolff-Bekker and Agatha Deken," in *La Formazione storica della alterità. Studi di storia della tolleranza nell'età moderna offerti a Antonio Rotondò*, ed. Henry Méchoulan, Richard H. Popkin, Giuseppe Ricuperati, and Luisa Simonutti (Firenze: Olschki, 2001), 1069–83; André Hanou, "Het meisje, God en vaderland. Een ideale religieuze opvoeding volgens Wolff en Deken," in *Een veelzijdige verstandhouding. Religie en Verlichting in Nederland, 1650–1850*, ed. Ernestine van der Wall and Leo Wessels (Nijmegen: Vantilt, 2007), 309–24.

80 Joseph Priestley, *Historie van den verbasteringen van het Christendom*, 2 vols (Dordrecht: Fr. Wanner, 1784); Thomas Paine, *De eeuw der rede, zynde eene nasporing van ware en fabelachtige Godgeleerdheid* (Den Haag: J.C. Leeuwestyn, 1798).

81 See, for instance, Johannes Le Francq van Berkhey's leaflet of 1785 titled *Order van Bataille. Of Staat der Sociniaansche, en Overheid-dwingende Legermagt der Onafhankelyke vry-corpsen* (Knuttel 21187) and the anonymous *Patriottisch alphabeth of A.B.C. boek voor de vry-corpsen*, 1.

82 J. Scharp, *Godgeleerd-historische verhandeling over de gevoelens, de gronden, het gewigtige voor de eeuwigheid en burgermaatschappijen, den voortgang, en den tegenstand der hedendaagsche zoogenaamde verlichting en godsdienst-bestrijding* (Rotterdam: Johannes Hofhout en zoon, 1793), 4, quoted by Joris van Eijnatten, "Orthodoxie, ketterij en consensus, 1670–1850. Drie historische vertogen over religie en Openbaring," *Bijdragen en mededelingen betreffende de geschiedenis der Nederlanden* 119 (2004): 468–90, esp. 478.

83 https://www.denederlandsegrondwet.nl/9353000/1/j9vvihlf299q0sr/vi48khzkt9ys. See L. de Gou, *De Staatsregeling van 1798. Bronnen voor de totstandkoming*, 2 vols (Den Haag: Instituut voor Nederlandse Geschiednis, 1988–90); M. van de Vrugt, "De Staatsregeling van 1798 en de kerkgenootschappen," in *De Staatsregeling voor het Bataafsche Volk van 1798*, ed. O. Moorman van Kappen and E.C. Koppens (Nijmegen: Gerard Noodt Instituut, 2001), 169–82.

84 Peter van Rooden, *Religieuze regimes. Over godsdienst en maatschappij in Nederland, 1570–1990* (Amsterdam: Bert Bakker, 1996), ch. 3; Edwina Hagen, "Een zaal van staatsmannen, niet van godgeleerden. Godsdienstige sentimenten in de Nationale Vergadering," in *Het Bataafse experiment. Politiek en cultuur rond 1800*, ed. Frans Grijzenhout, Niek van Sas and Wyger Velema (Nijmegen: Vantilt, 2013), 125–53.

85 The most detailed assessments of the way in which the Enlightenment affected the Dutch Reformed Church are still to be found in Jan Willem Buisman, *Tussen vroomheid en Verlichting. Een cultuurhistorisch en -sociologisch onderzoek naar enkele aspecten van de Verlichting in Nederland (1755–1810)*, 2 vols (Zwolle: Waanders, 1992); and Jelle Bosma, *Woorden van een gezond verstand. De invloed van de Verlichting op de in het Nederlands uitgegeven preken, 1750–1800* (Nieuwkoop: De Graaf, 1997).

Chapter Five

"The political theory of the libertines": Manuscripts and Heterodox Movements in the Early-Eighteenth-Century Dutch Republic

RIENK VERMIJ

The study of eighteenth-century clandestine manuscripts has focused in particular on manuscripts with a "philosophical" content, but these were not the only ones, or even the largest group among them. Radical philosophical thinkers were only a small minority in society. Most opposition to the orthodox establishment took a different form and was religiously rather than philosophically inspired. The French Jansenists are a case in point. They left behind several hundreds of thousands of manuscript pages, containing the transcripts of tens of thousands of ceremonies and discourses.[1]

Moreover, it would be a mistake to make a clear-cut distinction between religious and philosophical ideas. Obviously, there are many cases of a purely religious or philosophical discourse, but in other cases, the distinction is more blurred and the discourses overlap. A case in point is the "antinomianism" as it existed in the Dutch Republic in the first half of the eighteenth century. Antinomians had all the characteristics of a religious sect, or rather a group of sects, but the boundaries with radical strains of freethinking appear often blurred. Historians have noticed that in the revolutionary movements in the Dutch Republic in the first half of the eighteenth century, antinomians often played a leading part and formulated radical political ideas.[2] Most interestingly, their piety and religious orientation show a clear impact of Spinoza's philosophy.

Both in Church history and in the history of philosophy, this movement has largely been ignored, mainly, it would seem, because it was something of a blind alley. It was repudiated by the Church for its libertine and Spinozist tendencies and by later philosophical thinkers for being too religious. Moreover, there appears hardly any connection between

Dutch vernacular Spinozism on the one hand, and the libertinism that developed in the francophone "Republic of Letters" on the other.[3] So, in the course of the eighteenth century, antinomianism largely disappeared from the scene without leaving apparent heirs. Still, antinomianism represents an intriguing aspect of the impact of Spinoza's ideas on eighteenth-century thought that needs to be studied more seriously.

In the following, I will focus on one particular episode, the so-called Hattemist controversy in Middelburg in the early 1700s, and then on one particular manuscript, *De staatkunde der vrijgeesten* (The Political Theory of the Libertines). Although coming from a religious group rather than from what most people would regard as the "philosophical" movement, it presents a frontal attack on the power of the clergy, very much in the vein of the early Enlightenment. This text circulated in manuscript in the second decade of the eighteenth century. Its circulation appears to have been local, mainly restricted to the Dutch province of Zeeland. It did not make it into the canon of famous manuscripts of the Enlightenment period. However, this limited scope does not make it uninteresting. It should be deemed representative of a much larger army of similar manuscripts that may be considered more representative of manuscript culture than such famous texts as the *Traité des trois imposteurs* and the *Examen de la religion*. Below the well-known underworld of the famous clandestine texts, these little-known manuscripts constituted a still deeper underworld, a layer that remained mostly invisible. These lesser manuscripts informed the philosophical and religious debates of the period, perhaps even more so than their famous counterparts.

In the following, my main interest is not in the philosophical significance of the text itself, but rather in the way it functioned as a vehicle for ideas in its historical context. Before entering into a discussion of the contents, I will therefore first briefly discuss the context in which it was written, as well as provide a more general sketch regarding the use of various types of texts, manuscript or printed, in the political and religious debates in the Dutch Republic at the time.

Hattemism and Religious Controversy at Middelburg

In 1700, Willem Spandaw, a reformed minister in the province of Zeeland, published a book wherein he accused his ex-colleague Pontiaan van Hattem of covertly propagating the ideas of Spinoza. Van Hattem had been minister in Sint Philipsland, in the same province, until deposed for heterodoxy in 1683. After his removal, Van Hattem left the province, but he continued to teach his religious views in the nearby city of Bergen op Zoom. He gained a circle of followers who came to be known as "Hattemists."

Although Van Hattem's ideas certainly were regarded as unorthodox, the dispute so far had been purely theological, mostly concerning Van Hattem's interpretation of Christ's atonement as freeing us from sin and from subjugation to the law of God. Nobody so far had openly accused him of Spinozism. Spandaw's work thus launched a new round in the religious polemics in the Dutch Republic. Earlier, the Reformed Church had regarded Spinozism mainly as an external threat, an enemy at the gates against which the ministers manned the walls. It was not viewed as something that had been bred and nurtured in their very midst. It appears, however, that around 1700, Church leaders became aware of Spinozist propaganda cloaked, as they saw it, in the guise of Reformed orthodoxy. Accusations of Spinozism came to be made almost routinely against many groups and persons who, like the Hattemists, had their roots in the Reformed Church. Other examples are the Zwolle minister Fredcrik van Leenhof and the lay preacher Jacob Brill. Van Leenhof indeed had been the focus of controversy before, but Brill had died as a respected member of the Church.

People like Van Hattem considered themselves perfectly orthodox. They called the Bible the foundation of their faith and subscribed to all the articles of the Reformed creed. Moreover, they would clearly and plainly reject Spinoza's tenets. Still, Spandaw was not spinning tales out of the blue, for Spinozist elements were clearly there. The Hattemists and similar movements had appropriated Spinoza's thought to a high degree. Though strictly speaking not adhering to Spinoza's tenets, they used his concepts and principles to reformulate or reinterpret traditional church doctrine. This probably was much more threatening to orthodoxy than the formulation of a clearly opposed view, and it partly accounted for the fierce hostility they encountered throughout the eighteenth century. In the eyes of the defenders of orthodoxy, the Hattemists' professions of faith did not exculpate them, but rather showed their perfidity.[4]

Middelburg, Zeeland's capital city, became a major focus of the controversy. Van Hattem's main local champion was a shoemaker, Marinus Booms. In the 1690s, Booms came into conflict with the local church authorities. In 1712 and 1713, anonymous writings almost certainly written by Booms were distributed in Middelburg attacking the Church Council. In 1714, Booms was thereupon banished from the city. However, from his various places of exile, he (or his friends) continued to harrass the Church of Middelburg with his writings, which included both letters and printed pamphlets. These writings were answered by Carolus Tuinman, a local minister who took it upon himself to expose the Hattemist heresies. With the support of the Church Council, between 1712 and 1719 he published six books against the Hattemists, generally in reply to the successive works by Booms and his supporters. In these books, Tuinman followed Spandaw's lead, denouncing Hattemists as Spinozist wolves in Reformed sheep's clothing. His work apparently appealed greatly to his colleagues in the Church.[5]

Tuinman was a fiery polemicist. His writings, though not particularly subtle or modest, show zeal and emotion and are generally well written. (Besides being a minister, Tuinman was a skilled amateur of the Dutch language and a rather prolific poet.)[6] We discuss his work here at some length not for its own sake, but because it offers us a portal into the Hattemist literary underground. Tuinman discussed several Hattemist writings, and the better to refute them, he went so far as to include in his work complete treatises by his opponents. On one of these occasions, Tuinman explained: "I have included [the text] in full to prevent the accusation or the suspicion that I changed the sense or twisted the context."[7] On another occasion, he admitted that it was "with a great repulsion of the heart, and reluctantly, that we discover such horror-doctrines and blasphemies to the world. We would like that nobody was in need of reading it, and we will urge nobody to do so who does not meet such seducers, or their writings."[8]

Printing dangerous ideas seems a somewhat dubious method of combating them, but it was actually not an uncommon practice among theologians. Jacob du Bois, a Reformed minister in De Rijp in northern Holland who engaged in a polemic against the locally dominant Mennonites, included in his work the full text of one of their writings (with a paragraph-by-paragraph rebuttal), which until then had been available in manuscript only. He had this text by his opponent printed on learning that it had been "copied by several, was regarded highly and divulged widely."[9] Perhaps this same reason held in the case of the Hattemist texts as well. If Tuinman was not afraid to print them, that was apparently because he could be pretty sure that they were already well known among his intended audience.

It is from his writings that the text of "The Politics of the Libertines" can be recovered. But Tuinman's importance for our understanding of the Hattemist movement extends beyond the fact that he faithfully reproduced their writings and commented on their ideas. He also went into some detail about his dealings with the libertines (as he labelled them: "vrygeesten") themselves. We thereby get some idea of the situation in which these works were written and of the means by which they were circulated. This throws some light on the general role of manuscripts, especially such lesser-known manuscripts, in the intellectual debates of the period.

Spreading Heterodoxy

As far as we can tell, heterodox ideas spread mainly within conventicles, small circles of like-minded people, who often convened around some charismatic preacher. Typically, such conventicles had an edifying purpose, focusing on piety and the reading of the Bible, but as they convened without formal church oversight, they could easily enter philosophical or heterodox territory. Church authorities tended to regard them warily, and tried to impose rules and subject them to supervision or, if conventicles proved unwilling, to get them disbanded.[10] Of course, there were various ways to circumvent such restrictions. Van Hattem himself was accused at the South Holland synod of 1694 of spreading his ideas under the pretext of "drinking coffee with the friends."[11]

Within these groups, books and other writings circulated and were discussed. Apart from the Bible, the works of Van Hattem and other spiritual leaders held a prominent place. To show his thorough documentation, in 1715 Tuinman published the list of works, both in print and in manuscript, that he had consulted for his review of Hattemist opinions.[12] The number of manuscripts is actually rather small. He mentions two manuscript texts by Van Hattem, titled "Verbeterde lessen" (Improved Lessons) and "Eenige stellingen" (Some Theses), as well as an anonymous treatise on the relationship between man and God. Tuinman also mentions manuscript "Letters to P. Vervest" by Booms, but this appears to have been a private correspondence. Tuinman got these letters directly from Vervest, so it is doubtful whether they circulated more widely. The same is true for some manuscripts Tuinman retrieved from the church archives concerning Van Hattem's earlier conflict with the Church.

The list of *printed* works is longer. Besides works by Spinoza and Bredenburg, Tuinman lists two works by Booms, four treatises by Van Hattem, and the collected works of Jacob Brill. There are also seven anonymous works, as far as can be assessed from their titles, which are all of a religious nature. Three of these titles can also be found on a list of seven Hattemist books prohibited and publicly burned by the city of Middelburg in March 1714. Two other works appear to be hinted at at the end of this list; probably the authorities were aware of them but did not have actual copies.[13] These books may well have had a rather ephemeral character, as they cannot be found in modern catalogues. It looks pretty much like a reading list for the religious meetings at Middelburg.

It is of course not unlikely that Tuinman overlooked certain texts, especially ones that had not been printed. For a theologian, it would have been simpler and more obvious to refer to printed books than to lay his hands on clandestine manuscripts. Even so, it is evident that Hattemist ideas not only circulated in manuscript but were available in printed form as well. Van Hattem's collected works were posthumeously printed in four volumes between 1718 and 1727 by his follower Jacob Roggeveen, a respected citizen of Middelburg, despite severe opposition by the Church Council.[14]

The fact that some of the texts remained in manuscript apparently was *not* because they could not be printed in principle. It probably just meant that nobody with the necessary means and connections had found it worthwhile to undertake the effort. It is probable that many treatises first circulated in manuscript (Spinoza's writings are a case in point); later, once they were deemed useful enough, it would not have been too hard to have them printed. Printing presses were everywhere in the Dutch Republic, and communications were excellent. The boundary between print and manuscript literature appears to have been somewhat blurred.

An interesting case of "hybrid distribution" – that is, both printed and in manuscript – relates to the lectures on Job by Willem Deurhoff, another sectarian leader. It seems that the text first circulated in manuscript form only, but in 1741, twenty-four years after Deurhoff's death, his followers undertook to publish the work. In this case, the authorities intervened and interrupted the printing process, so the book remained unfinished. The editors then took to the manuscript form again and distributed the book with the missing parts completed in manuscript.[15]

Intermezzo: Print and Manuscript in the Dutch Republic

It is of course well known that even highly controversial texts might be printed in the Dutch Republic. This was due not to the inherent liberalism of the Dutch, but in the first place to the country's large number of print shops, and in the second place to very lax oversight.[16] Authorities might sometimes crack down on a specific work, but there was no real attempt to track down and destroy all copies of a forbidden book. Forbidden books (or even manuscripts) frequently turn up in printed auction catalogues, albeit sometimes under a special rubric.[17] Spinoza's works, though forbidden, remained available, even in Dutch translation, and not just in major cities. For instance, we find them in 1746 in the probate inventory of Jan Geresteyn, a surgeon in the village of Ouderkerk aan de IJssel in the Krimpenerwaard.[18] Since so many texts were readily available in print, there was less need to resort to manuscripts.

Even defamatory libels were printed, as many examples attest. A well-documented example is offered by the widespread disturbances in Rotterdam in 1690, the so-called "Costermanoproer." That event saw the production of many *paskwillen* or lampoons, most of them attacking the local bailiff, Jacob van Zuylen van Nievelt. Many of these lampoons appear to have been distributed in manuscript. The house of a certain Pieter de Mey was transformed into a virtual lampoon mill, with numbers of people in long sessions writing and copying pasquinades. Such texts were then posted in public view or in other ways distributed or "strewed."[19] However, some of them were printed as well, probably after a certain demand had been created. Among the printed copies preserved is one by the young Bernard Mandeville, addressing the bailiff as "[h]ypocrite atheist, love-making whore's skin, tyrant greedy for money, product of hell ..." and ending: "O city fathers, bring down this rascal, before one of your children will do so himself."[20] It goes without saying that such defamation was much more offensive than any form of philosophical speculation could have been. It certainly would have brought Mandeville to the gallows, had he not in time fled to England.

The term "strewed" (*uitgestrooid*), which was used to describe the distribution of these pasquinades, probably should sometimes be taken literally, for such lampoons could turn up at unexpected places. On 3 March 1746, Paulus Hageman, a wine merchant and deacon of the Dutch Reformed Church in The Hague, testified before the Council of Holland that when on Sunday morning (27 February) after church service (in the Kloosterkerk), he and two fellow deacons went to count the money in the collection pouch, they had found a *paskwil*. The nature of this piece is not specified. Obviously, given that it had been smuggled into a collection pouch, it cannot have been very big. Given the date and place, it most likely referred to the war with France and the position of the Prince of Orange. Interesting is what followed. There were three deacons, one of whom immediately made two copies. Two of the deacons took one new copy each, and Hageman kept the original. He took it home, keeping it in his study. Apparently, someone tipped off the authorities, for on Wednesday evening, Hageman was summoned before the bailiff of Wassenaar, who reproached him and to whom he turned over the piece. In his testimony before the Council of Holland, he emphasized "that he had not kept a copy for himself, and read it only two times, and was of the intention to burn it."[21]

In these cases too, whether a text was printed or (preferably) distributed in manuscript was determined not by the content of the text itself, but in the first place by circumstances. For private use, and for fast and easy production, manuscripts were the obvious choice. When demand proved strong enough, printing became an option. In some cases people might want to see a work printed so as to convey status and respectability. Concerning the circulation of heterodox ideas, it was rather a matter of convenience and time whether a text was printed immediately, printed later, or not printed at all. However, this was largely due to the country's special circumstances and need not have been true elsewhere.

Distributing Hattemist Polemics

Tuinman accused the Hattemists of "strewing" their works among the public: "The libertines are used to strew their trash among the people anonymously, or under pseudonym, and watch as if from a hiding place how the world takes them. If it serves their cause, they deny knowledge of the booklets' origin, and pretend that it does not concern them."[22] Of course, this did not hold for all texts or all circumstances. On another occasion, in April 1714, Tuinman wrote against a (probably printed) work by Booms that was "secretly put into the hands of confidents."[23] But some works indeed were deliberately brought to the attention of people outside their own circle. This is especially true of the writings by which they hoped to justify themselves before the authorities.

Tuinman explains in detail (he even mentions the postage) how on 29 August 1714 an unknown man delivered to his house a parcel that (as this man claimed) came from Nijmegen. It contained a booklet and five leaves of anonymous writing, clearly of Hattemist origin.[24] Tuinman wrote a reply, and after he finished it (it is dated 1 March 1715), another "rather big letter" was delivered by the mailman from Goes (on the nearby island of Zuid-Beveland). His colleague Breukeland received one as well. This letter contained two booklets, which included the text of the earlier letter, now in printed form. Tuinman commented: "My guess was not bad that that letter would have been distributed among your gang and beyond. You saved me the trouble of having it printed, because remaining in uncertainty whether I would do so took you too long."[25]

The mailman explained that the letters had been put under his door at night by an unknown person. "From the bargeman who had ferried him over, he had heard that he too had on board such booklets in letters to deliver at Middelburg. Others too, even persons in the city government, have received these. Later, a parcel of these has been recuperated at the post office [*postcomptoir*]. This the city fathers in the townhall have thrown into the fire. The man to whom they had been sent was impudent enough to reclaim them from the magistrate."[26]

After the publication of his book *De liegende en bedriegende vrygeest* (The Lying and Deceiving Libertine), Tuinman got a letter from Booms wherein the latter denied that he was the author of some of the earlier treatises. The content of the letter, according to Tuinman, "is known among his sympathisers, who maybe knew of it earlier than I did."[27] Tuinman is less explicit about a text that was written against this book, but evidently, this was also sent to him as a letter, as he talks about the signets and the handwriting on the envelope, comparing it to the earlier ones.[28] In the case of these writings too, it clearly was mainly due to circumstances whether they were printed in the end or remained in manuscript.

Several of the anonymous and pseudonymous pamphlets and letters that defended Booms's case were printed with the false imprint "Altena," or gave Altena as their place of writing. This was generally understood as referring to Altona near Hamburg, a notorious hotbed of sectarianism. People in Middelburg would probably be familiar with the name, as the sectarian leader Jean de Labadie, who had earlier been a Protestant minister at Middelburg, had died there. Tuinman was not fooled and felt certain that this Altena was close to Middelburg: "Let each beware that he does not get too close to the mill of Altena."[29] In order to understand this allusion, one should know that supposedly Booms got his introduction to Spinoza's and Van Hattem's ideas from a certain doctor Bliek, a physician who lived in a mill near Middelburg. Tuinman claimed that Booms spent long days with that man at the mill.[30] Probably, this Bliek was well-versed in the philosophy of Spinoza. He also seems to have performed alchemical experiments. Among Tuinman's poetry there are some verses on the death of an anonymous person, apparently Bliek, who "had long given [his] Altena as a breeding-place for the rabble of atheists" and who died as a result of the explosion of a distillation vessel full of nitric acid.[31]

Tuinman intuited that this "Altena" was the place of origin of many of the anonymous and pseudonymous works that emerged during these years. Indeed, it is not improbable that Bliek was at the centre of a circle of like-minded thinkers. However, little is known about Bliek or the group that convened at his place. It appears that he was not a member of the Reformed Church, so he was not bothered by church censorship and hardly turns up in the records.[32]

"The Political Theory of the Libertines"

Turning now to our main text, "The Political Theory of the Libertines" is not its original title. It is the title that Tuinman gave it when he included it in his book *Het helsche gruwelgeheim der heillooze vrygeesten* (The Infernal Atrocious Secret of the Godless Libertines).[33] Having exposed the libertines' ideas regarding theology, Tuinman now felt urged, "because of the similarity of the material" (267), to include something on their political ideas, especially with regard to church politics. The *Staatkunde* is a polemical text attacking the Reformed clergy, not an edifying text to be studied in conventicles. The text is anonymous, and even Tuinman appears to have had no real clue as to its authorship, except that it must have originated in the same breeding place as earlier works.

It is dated 22 January 1714. There is no reason to doubt this date, given that the text presents itself as a reaction to a then recent affair, a petition of the *classes* (regional church assemblies) of Zeeland to the States.[34] However, Tuinman does not mention the text in the abovementioned list of Hattemist writings in *Sibboleth*, published in 1715. Most likely, he had only laid hands on it shortly before he printed it in 1717. Tuinman writes: "This is certain, that this piece of writing has secretly been distributed under great and small. Before we knew that it was in the world, some of us, so now and then, have heard the matter of it objected from the one or the other, also from people for whom this was not appropriate" (267).

Apparently the text was not written to justify the Hattemist cause before the ministers of the Reformed Church; rather, it was a text that circulated among the libertines themselves. They themselves never printed it. Most sectarians probably were less interested in political than in religious texts. Also, the fact that it discussed a recent event may have made it obsolete rather quickly, although the text definitely raised some more general points as well. All original copies appear to have been lost. The only version extant is the one in Tuinman's book, with his "short comments" (which are not short at all) after every section. In the following, I ignore Tuinman's comments and discuss only the text itself. Since

Tuinman could assume that his readers would be familiar with the text, there is no reason to doubt that he printed it, as he said, "zo als wy dat magtig geworden zijn" (as it came into our hands) (268).

The text has the form of a letter. The author refers to an earlier conversation and now sends his considerations on the question "What harm can the political order [*de Politie*] suffer by allowing the Churchmen [*de kerkelyke*] their six articles?" The reference is to a petition by the three *classes* of the Reformed Church in Zeeland to the States, wherein they formulated six requests to curb the growth of libertine thought. Such petitions by churches to the government were actually fairly standard in the seventeenth and eighteenth centuries. Several of the demands we find repeated throughout the years over and over again. The *classes* of Zeeland were at this time particularly insistent, however. In 1713–14, they submitted no fewer than five petitions against the libertines. This led to an anti-Hattemist decree by the Middelburg magistrate in March 1714 and the banning of Booms from the city. In January 1714, therefore, the dissidents had some reason to worry.

The six articles in the petition of the churches can be summarized as follows: (1) Only persons who have been confirmed in the Reformed Church and who are still accepted as members should be eligible for, or accepted in, public office. (2) All schoolteachers, principals, and so on should be required to subscribe to the articles of faith as formulated by the National Synod. (3) All conventicles and all theological books that have not been approved should be prohibited. (4) All practising doctors of medicine should subscribe to the Reformed faith. (5) The practice of Roman Catholicism should be suppressed. (6) The churches should be given permission to have a general meeting to decide upon measures to obtain these pious goals.

Our text discusses, and refutes, these six points in succession. The general tenor is that with these points the churches, or rather the ministers, are trying to extend their power over politics and public life. So for instance, if persons who do not profess the Reformed religion are denied public office, the ministers will be able to kick anybody out of government who is not to their liking. To accomplish that, they only would have to declare that this person's ideas are not sufficiently orthodox.

The sixth point, of keeping a general assembly, is less common. Our author states: "Allow them this, with the five preceding points, and I assure you that within a short time their sovereignty will be no less than that of Rome. Your tribunals will be no less stained and denuded of their justice, as the governance will be brought into a continuous confusion" (300).

Instead of going over the refutations of the various points one by one, it seems more convenient to discuss the letter's introduction, where the author states his principles in a somewhat more general way. He starts off with a strong anti-ecclesiastical tone: "Mylord, you know, and all old clever politiques know, that the intent of the Churchmen has always been to obtain as much power as ever possible" (269). It is thanks to the actions of some past regents that their power has been curbed, otherwise we would have to fear the churches more than a harsh government. The author states that a citizen who lives according to the laws of his country has nothing to fear from its government, even if its regents were tyrants, for they know that their continuation in office depends on the citizens. However, a citizen who obeys the laws and tries to teach his neighbours what brings peace and happiness to his soul offends against the goal of the churchmen, for they recognize that this would undermine their reputation in the state.

The author then discusses the common objection that a civil society (*Borgerstaat*) cannot exist without an established religion and an ordained priesthood. He does not want to dispute this point. "To the contrary, I maintain the necessity not of one, but of many religions. The regents should be part of only one of these, and be required to maintain it. [However, they should do so] not by suppressing other people's religions, but by favouring the citizens who profess [that religion], are born in it and therefore adhere to it, giving offices and positions, especially political ones, exclusively to them, as long as there are enough qualified persons among them" (271–2). The author feels that a plurality of religions will stabilize the government and make the state prosper, as is the case in Amsterdam. If there were only Reformed people in Middelburg, and of the kind that believe everything the ministers say, the ministers would be masters not only of the citizenry but also of governance (*Politie*) (274). The regents would not be able to execute a resolution disliked by the Church, "for the Churchmen bring the regents into disrepute with the common people, they even spit into their faces, and thereby even are praised by the riffraff" (274). Any resolution that would tax the people would have to be coordinated with the churchmen, so that they can soothe the feelings of the common people. By contrast, in the case that the population of Middelburg was only one-third Reformed, with the other two-thirds adhering to the Lutheran, Mennonite, Remonstrant, Catholic creeds and so on, the regents would have nothing to fear, "for the tolerated sectarians depend for their protection on the government, and are in continuous fear of the Reformed clergy. Therefore, they will always be ready to obey. And by them, as well as by those among the Reformed who are honest and prudent subjects, the government will always be able to have its resolutions executed" (277).

At this point, before entering the discussion of the six articles, the author summarizes his statements. For one, he emphasizes that the Churchmen are trying to make themselves masters of governance. This point serves as the basis for his following refutation of the six articles. His second point is that, for the sake of government stability and the general welfare, it is useful and necessary to have many religions in the state (280). This point does not appear to be important for his refutation of the six articles; apparently he includes it because he feels it is important more generally.

At the end of the letter, the author asks why in the Reformed Church some of the city fathers are made elders or presbyters. He explains that in church affairs, the ministers have precedence over such regents. "They show off with a regent at their left hand, demonstrating to the common people that they stand higher than the regents, and therefore deserve the highest respect" (302). Moreover, they normally select those regents who are least competent and most willing to do the ministers' wishes. It is to these regents, then, that the affairs of the Church are often relegated. "These are all cancers for good governance, and breaches in the solidity of the government" (303). In a general conclusion, the author states: "I do not believe that any harm has ever befallen to a monarchy or a republic, which it could not be demonstrated that the clergy have been the direct or indirect causes" (304).

There is in this text much that sounds familiar from mainstream Enlightenment thought, in particular the accusation that clerics lust for power, and the support of a strong state against clerical interference. However, this anticlericalism is not so much philosophically inspired; rather, it has its roots in the traditional wariness of the Dutch ruling elites concerning ecclesiastical pretentions.[35] This anticlericalism does not translate into a general dismissal of the supernatural as such. When the author claims that citizens should not be disturbed by the established clergy in teaching to others what has given them inner peace and happiness, he is arguing for a private, non-institutional form of religion. Actually, this is well in line with tendencies of the period. However one values it from a philosophical point of view, the "privatization" of religion and its separation from politics can be regarded as more constitutive of eighteenth-century Enlightenment culture than philosophical radicalism.[36] The author's solution of allowing as many religions in the state as possible is unusual, but it would not have seemed so very utopian in the Dutch Republic.

Overall, his views, though outrageous to the orthodox, seem intended not so much to shock or provoke as to contribute in a serious way to the political debates of the time.

Conclusion

There are two general points to be made. First, the Hattemist controversy should make us wary about drawing too sharp a distinction between a strictly secular Enlightenment on the one hand and the sectarian religious movements on the other. There is no doubt that the motivation of the Hattemists and other antinomians was primarily religious. It is also clear that these people particularly welcomed Spinozist ideas and, as shown above, defended radical ideas in their time with regard to curbing the power of the clergy and the place of the Church in society.

The second point has to do with the function of manuscripts in the intellectual debates of the period. I wrote above that there appeared to be little overlap between the clandestine manuscripts of the high Enlightenment and the heterodox Dutch texts in the vernacular. After the above discussion, that should probably not surprise us. The two types of texts were quite distinct, not just in their content, their readership, and their language, but also in their functions. A relatively large number of French manuscripts have been preserved in part because they were collector's items. They sold for relatively high prices, and people kept them in their libraries. In a sense, they were curiosities rather than contributions to current political or philosophical debates. People relished them because of their provocative character, but they provoked in the private sphere only. As the Dutch knew, if you really wanted to provoke, you should go public – in print, or by "strewing" lampoons.

The *Staatkunde der vrijgeesten*, by contrast, was a contribution to an ongoing debate among a group of libertines reflecting on an actual situation. It was a weapon in the battle for hearts and minds. The manuscript form was more or less accidental. It was a natural form for communicating one's thoughts within a specific group, but if people were sufficiently interested, such works might end up being printed as well. On the other hand, once the main conflict was over, or once it was superseded by other work, few people would have bothered to keep the manuscript. It is impossible to say how many of these manuscripts circulated, but most of them probably were disposed of after some years. Manuscripts like these were of little monetary or sentimental value. But they certainly attest that manuscript culture was still vibrant in daily life.

NOTES

1 C.-L. Maire, ed., *Les convulsionnaires de Saint-Médard. Miracles, convulsions et prophéties à Paris au XVIIIe siècle* (Paris: Gallimard-Julliard, 1985), 25 (with footnote at 255–6), 183.

2 Murk van der Bijl, *Idee en interest. Voorgeschiedenis, verloop en achtergronden van de politieke twisten in Zeeland en vooral in Middelburg tussen 1702 en 1715* (Groningen: Wolters-Noordhoff, 1981), 166. See also Roelof van Gelder, *Naar het aards paradijs. Het rusteloze leven van Jacob Roggeveen, ontdekker van Paaseiland (1659–1729)* (Amsterdam: Balans, 2012), 97–100.

3 One Dutch text, by Dirk Santvoort, indeed made it into a clandestine French manuscript, the "Recherches curieux de philosophie," but it did so only by a long and tortuous road.

4 Michiel Wielema, *The March of the Libertines: Spinozists and the Dutch Reformed Church 1660–1750* (Hilversum: Verloren, 2004), 163–204; Jonathan Israel, *Radical Enlightenment: Philosophy and the Making of Modernity 1650–1750* (Oxford: Oxford University Press, 2001), 406–35; Rienk Vermij, "De boeventaal der vrijgeesten. Carolus Tuinman (1659–1728) en het hattemisme," in *Verlichting in Nederland 1650–1850. Vrede tussen rede en religie?*, ed. Jan Wim Buisman (Nijmegen: Van Tilt, 2013), 31–49; Roelof van Gelder, *Naar het aards paradijs*, 85–96.

5 On these controversies, see Van Gelder, *Naar het aards paradijs*, 137–46.

6 On Tuinman, see Gerrie Wisse, "Aan de vruchten kent men de boom; Carolus Tuinman (1659–1728)," in *Archief. Mededelingen van het Koninklijk Zeeuwsch Genootschap der Wetenschappen*, 2008, 121–70.

7 Carolus Tuinman, *Het helsche gruwelgeheim der heillooze vrygeesten, open gelegt door den vermomden Pius Fidelis, met het opschuimen van zijn eigen schande, in de missive aan den heer I.M.H.V.H … Mitsgaders de staatkunde der vrygeesten, omtrent de religie en kerkelijken, met korte aantekeningen …* (Middelburg: W. Eling, 1717), preface to the reader.

8 Carolus Tuinman, *De liegende en bedriegende vrygeest, ontmaskert in een andwoord aan den vermomden Constantius Prudens* (Middelburg: J. Boter, S. Clement and W. Eling, 1715), preface.

9 Jacob du Bois, *Kinder-doop bewezen en verdedigt vyt des apostels woorden …* (Amsterdam: M.J. Brandt, 1642), dedication.

10 Several examples in Jori Zijlmans, *Vriendenkringen in de zeventiende eeuw. Verenigingsvormen van het informele culturele leven te Rotterdam* (The Hague: Sdu, 1999) 68–9, 72–80, 95, 101–3.

11 Ingrid Weekhout, *Boekencensuur in de noordelijke Nederlanden. De vrijheid van drukpers in de zeventiende eeuw* (The Hague: Sdu, 1998), 149.

12 Carolus Tuinman, *Sibboleth, of leugen en bedrog, van den vermomden vrygeest Marinus Booms* (Middelburg: J. op Somer, 1715), 542–3: "Schriften der Ongodisten en Vrijgeesten, welker uittrekzels hier voor by-gebragt zijn."

13 This list is printed in Carolus Tuinman, *De heilloze gruwelleere der vrygeesten … ontmaskert, en wederlegt,* (Middelburg: J. op Somer, 1714), 237–8.

14 Van Gelder, *Naar het aards paradijs,* 147–58, 286.

15 The Dutch Royal Library has a description on its website with a reproduction of where the book is continued in manuscript: https://www.kb.nl/themas/gedrukte-boeken-tot-1800/willem-deurhoff-het-voorbeeld-van-verdraagzaamheid-onder-de-goddelyke-bezoekingen-vertoond-in-de. The copy at Utrecht University Library also is continued in manuscript. See record in STCN: http://picarta.nl/xslt/DB=3.11/SET=1/TTL=21/SHW?FRST=25.

16 Weekhout, *Boekencensuur in de noordelijke Nederlanden.* See also the contribution by Inger Leemans in this volume.

17 A catalogue of books to be auctioned at Luchtman's in Leiden in 1689 has a rubric of "Libri prohibiti, qui privatim in fine Auctionis venales exhibuntur."

18 Johan A. Kamermans, *Materiële cultuur in de Krimpenerwaard in de zeventiende en achttiende eeuw. Ontwikkeling en diversiteit* (PhD diss., Wageningen, 1999), 126.

19 Weekhout, *Boekencensuur in de noordelijke Nederlanden,* 217–18.

20 "Schijnheylig Atheist, liefhebbent hoere vel, / Geltsuchtigh dwingeland, uytbroedsel van de Hel… O Borger Vaderen ligt dees Schelm de voet, / Eer dat het iemand van u kinderen self doet." A reproduction of the printed version of this lampoon, as preserved in Rotterdam City Archives, can be found in Rudolf Dekker, "Schijnheilig atheïst. Bernard Mandeville als pamflettist tijdens het Costermanoproer in Rotterdam in 1690," *Holland: regionaal-historisch tijdschrift,* 26, 1994, 9. Reproductions of other lampoons, ibid., 12.

21 The Hague, Nationaal Archief, Hof van Holland, criminele papieren, 5453:9.

22 Tuinman, *Liegende en bedriegende vrygeest,* preface.

23 Tuinman, *Heilloze gruwelleere,* dedication.

24 Tuinman, *Liegende en bedriegende vrygeest,* 1.

25 Tuinman, *Liegende en bedriegende vrygeest,* 182.

26 Tuinman, *Liegende en bedriegende vrygeest,* 181. Cf. Wisse, "Aan de vruchten," 139.

27 Tuinman, *Sibboleth,* 530.

28 Tuinman, *Helsche gruwelgeheim* (1717), 3.

29 Tuinman, *Liegende en bedriegende vrygeest*, 2. The pun "al te na" (too close) gets lost in translation.

30 Tuinman, *Sibboleth*, 205.

31 Carolus Tuinman, *Rijmlust: behelzende [...] Noch een byvoegsel van gedichten* (Middelburg: M. Schryver, 1729), Bijvoegzel van eenige gedichten, 13, no. 20 (NN, Doodelyk gebrand door 't springen van een distileerglas met sterk water): "Gy had, ô NN, tot een broednest van 't gespuis / der ongodisten, lang uw Altena gegeven. / De vlam, door 't bersten van een glas, benam u 't leven. / Gy quaamt den Duivel dus wel gaar gebraaden t'huis." This kind of accident was not uncommon in alchemical practice; see Lawrence M. Principe, *The Secrets of Alchemy* (Chicago: University of Chicago Press, 2013), 123.

32 For the little information available on Bliek, see Wielema, *March of the Libertines*, 175, 179.

33 Tuinman, *Het helsche gruwelgeheim ... Mitsgaders de staatkunde der vrygeesten, omtrent de religie en kerkelijken, met korte aantekeningen*, 265–314.

34 On this affair, see Tuinman, *Sibboleth*, 164–6. The petition was submitted in 1713. In the same year, Marinus Booms published a reply.

35 Cf. Heinz Schilling, "'Afkeer van domineesheerschappij': ein neuzcitlicher Typus des Antiklerikalismus," in *Anticlericalism in Late Medieval and Early Modern Europe*, ed. P.A. Dykema and H.A. Oberman (Leiden: Brill, 1993), 655–68.

36 Leszek Kolakowski, *Chétiens sans église. La conscience religieuse et le lien confessionel au XVIIe siècle* (Paris: Gallimard, 1969), remains a classical study. For a more general argument, see Rienk Vermij, *De geest uit de fles. De verlichting en het verval van de confessionele samenleving* (Amsterdam: Nieuwezijds, 2014).

PART THREE

GENDER, SEXUALITY, AND NEW MORALS

Chapter Six

The Science of Sex: Passions and Desires in Dutch Clandestine Circles, 1670–1720

INGER LEEMANS

> "Grotius explains all those indecent passages in the Bible. Joseph revealed the crime of his brothers; that was to say that they buggered one another or gave each other a hand job."

In the years 1678 and 1679 a young Dutch libertine sat down to make notes of interesting and outrageous things he had read and heard. His notebook developed into a fascinating collection of heterodox philosophical insights, libertine ideas, impudent readings of the Bible, humorous anecdotes, political opinions – mainly anti-Orangist sentiments – and plain gossip. The notebook ended up in the library of Utrecht University, where it was recently discovered. It has since received its first public notoriety through an edition of the original Latin text with an English translation, supplied with an extensive introduction.[1]

Although the editors have not been able to establish the notebook's authorship, its author evidently was a man of letters – the notes are written mostly in Latin – and of standing. He presumably played an active role in Utrecht politics, where he sided with the republican party. Possibly he had some connection to the circles around Spinoza, for he provides some intimate details of Spinoza's deathbed, and he may have been acquainted with Lambert van Velthuysen (1621/2–1685), one of Spinoza's main correspondents.[2]

Judging from the somewhat rough and often uncorrected Latin, the author did not intend his compilation for publication. The small size of the notebook suggests that he carried it in his pocket in order to make on-the-spot notes of interesting events and quotes. But he could also consult it in order to locate the underpinnings of a spirited argument.

Figure 6.1 Merry company, probably in a brothel (1699). Print by Jan van Somer (after Johann Liss & Jeremias Falck). Rijksmuseum Amsterdam RP-P-1895-A-18667.

Other famous notebooks from the same period served this function – for example, those of the radical pamphleteer Ericus Walten (1662–1697) and the jester Aernout van Overbeke (1632–1674).[3]

The Dutch Republic as the Sex Shop of Europe

This tiny notebook opens up a world of underground manuscript practices in the Dutch Republic at the end of the seventeenth century. Initially it may seem surprising that the early modern Dutch Republic, with its relatively open and highly developed international book market, still relied on clandestine manuscript production and circulation.[4] Many famous clandestine manuscripts originated from within the Republic – Spinoza's *Ethics* (published 1677), the anonymous *Traité des trois imposteurs* (published 1712/1719), Adriaan Koerbagh's *Een Ligt schijnende in duystere Plaatsen, om te verligten de voornaamste saaken der Gods geleertheyd en Gods dienst* (almost published in 1688, but censored before it was printed and distributed).[5] These examples highlight that many clandestine manuscripts eventually were also published clandestinely. In the highly competitive Dutch book market, in which publishers and printers were fighting for their livelihood, one could always find a daredevil who would accept a challenging manuscript and turn it into a publication, hoping to smuggle it onto the international book market.[6] Publishers could always employ the fictitious imprint of Pierre Marteau of Cologne to hide their trails.[7]

Even in the libertine underground of pornography the printed form seems to have been dominant. In the second half of the seventeenth century, Italian, Latin, and French pornographic texts – for example, Pietro Aretino's *Ragionamenti* (1534), *L'École des filles ou la philosophie des dames* (1655), and *L'Academie des dames* (first Latin edition *Aloisiae Sigaeae, Toletanae, Satyra sotadica de arcanis Amoris et Veneris,* 1660) – were printed or reprinted in the Dutch Republic and from there distributed all over Europe.[8] The Netherlands had become "the sex shop of Europe."[9] *Liefhebbers* (curious "lovers" of erotica, or lovers of loving) shared and exchanged the volumes of erotic novels among one another. Sometimes "liefhebbers" even happened upon complete pornographic illustrated volumes in the bushes.[10] The less fortunate could buy printed volumes of pornographic novels and copies of erotic engravings from street peddlers, who roamed the Dutch cities and countryside selling to young customers.[11] While Dutch Reformed ministers and churches tried to ban these blasphemous texts, and even personally visited publishers they suspected of being the brains behind these obscenities, booksellers kept on advertising new *snakerijen* (smut, rogueries) and hanging title pages with suggestive engravings in their shop windows to attract buyers.

The basic form for "livres philosophiques" seems to have been print. As printed texts were censored (which happened regularly in many of the Dutch provinces), confiscated, and even burned, new editions were printed in other cities or provinces so that copies remained in circulation. In this vibrant print climate there seemed to be less need for the manuscript form than in, say, France, Italy, or Spain, where book markets and distribution channels were less developed or more heavily regulated.

Manuscript Culture in the Dutch Republic

Still, manuscripts seem to have played an instrumental role in the development of radical enlightened thought in the Netherlands. The Dutch cities offered every philosophical text imaginable in print, and Amsterdam publishers like the Huguenot Pierre Mortier kept catalogues of manuscripts on offer.[12] Not all manuscripts made it into print, however, and some had to wait to be printed. Before being published, texts could be circulated among groups of friends and colleagues, to test their quality and potential for scandal. In the world of letters, this was standard practice: authors were obliged to help one another in striving for the best. This became even more important in the classicist poetical practice that was introduced in the 1670s. Sociability, shared effort, and criticism became cornerstones of the ideal of good authorship.[13] Manuscript production and circulation in this way became entrenched in social and literary practices.

In this essay I will explore the dynamics of Dutch clandestine manuscript practices between 1670 and 1720 by zooming in on two specific manuscript forms: notebooks (or books of compilations) and letters. I will analyse how these textual forms helped formulate new and radical ideas about sex and the passions. Up until now the history of philosophy has often only indirectly touched on the history of sexuality. Eroticism and attitudes towards sex have long been researched largely within studies on libertinism. Foucault's *History of Sexuality* tied sexuality research more closely to the history of philosophy as he described how sex developed from a primarily moral category into a category of knowledge, which eventually led to a vision of man as a complex psychological system driven by sexual impulses. The "scientia sexualis" that began to develop in the eighteenth century is distinguished by Foucault from the "ars erotica." The history of philosophy has recently set to out narrow the gap between discourses on sex intended for sexual arousal and those intended for theorizing sexual behaviour.[14] This chapter follows that line of research. I will argue that in the context of the new urban sociability, letters and notebooks helped piece together an initial coherent body of sexual knowledge, one that can be labelled "scientia sexualis" which combined eroticism with truth finding and thereby helped conceptualize sex as a distinct category of practice. Through its description of the development of a science of sex in the context of the Dutch

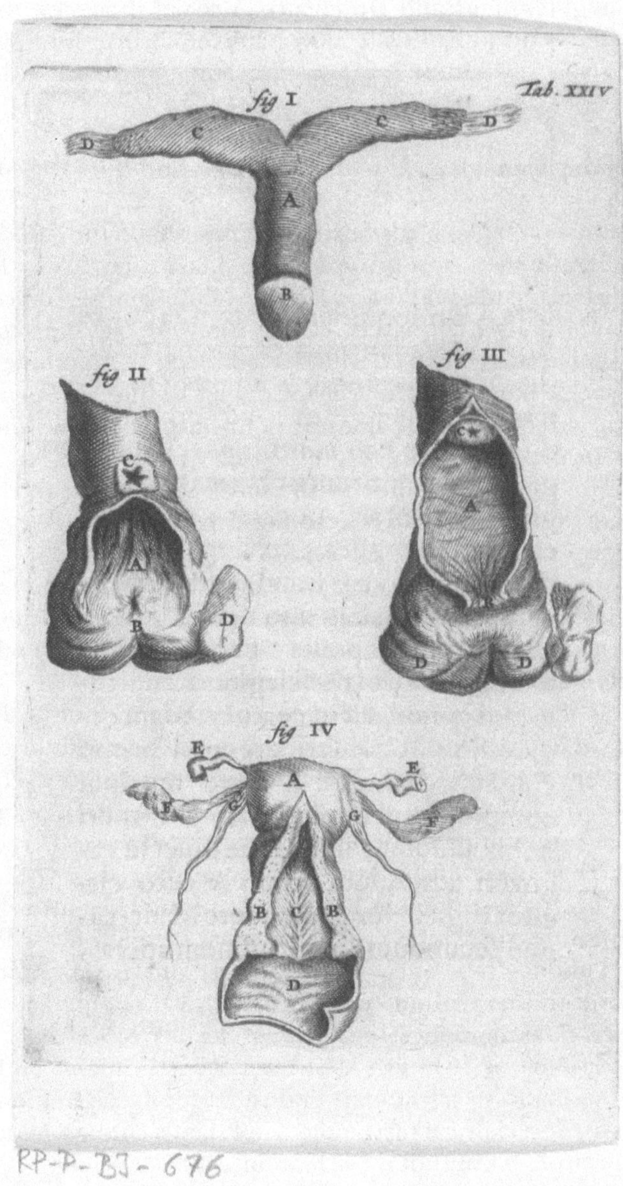

Figure 6.2 Anatomical analysis of the clitoris, vagina, and uterus. Book illustration for Reinier de Graaf, *De mulierum organis generationi inservientibus tractatus novus* (1672). Rijksmuseum: RP-P-BI-676.

radical Enlightenment and Dutch urban social practices, the chapter will also take issue with the all too exclusively British interpretation of "the first sexual revolution," as it was proclaimed by Dabhoiwhala in *The Origins of Sex.*[15]

Scheming Orangists, Unruly Clitorises, and the Original Sin

The Utrecht notebook places us in the middle of the fast-developing radical Enlightenment in the Dutch Republic of the 1670s. The beginning of the decade was marked by a radical shift from republican politics to more authoritative, monarchical rule, after the elevation to power of William III of Orange in 1672, which heightened the prominence of the more orthodox branch of the Calvinist church. Intellectual differences swiftly radicalized along the lines of political parties, and the number of clashes in the public sphere grew quickly as a result. As censorship became more strict, opposition to the suffocating power of church and government grew, and on both sides the debate intensified and became more aggressive.

The Utrecht notebook seems to reflect this cultural climate. The author is keen to collect any kind of smut he can find on the House of Orange, who are all tyrants in his eyes: "When William II of Orange died, the Italians believed that he had been poisoned, and they said: '*The Dutch are coming to their senses.*' On the death of a tyrant, Pluto's *The Prince's descent into hell,* in order to break the god of the Styx with love. Boozing is rampant among the wicked" (66). He has also found the secret meaning of the word Orange in this anagram: go Nero! (167). Many persons cited by the author are men of higher ranking, of former Utrecht regent circles, who had been ousted from office after the rise of William III.

Overall, however, the tone is light, exploratory. The author seems fascinated by all the secrets he is able to unveil through his social circles. Apart from politics, he seems to have a special interest in Spinozist Bible criticism and in many other bodies of radical thought. The notebook also displays a fascination with all things sexual. More than one third of his entries (60 of 167) are about sex, sexual organs, and the centrality of the libido in all human endeavours. His fascination with sex focuses in part on classical mythology: on Priapus cults and Bacchanalia. Another part of the author's fascination with sex seems to be rooted in his open attitude towards new scientific approaches, for example, anatomical research. He is curious about natural phenomena, such as the clitoris. The organ had just been "discovered" in medical research.[16]

The very first occurrence of the word in the Dutch language is from 1650, in a book by the famous medical doctor and anatomist Nicolaes Tulp: "hoewel dese Clitoris niet altijdt uythingh, soo quamse somwijlen voor den dagh" (although the clitoris was not always externally visible, it sometimes appeared").[17]

Some twenty-five years later, the author of the Utrecht notebook is fascinated by this female organ and especially by the size it may acquire, providing a woman with the opportunity to assume the male role in sex and become a tribade (lesbian). The notebook author gossips: "The wife of Jan Lammersen, the envoy of this magistrate, is a lesbian, and if the French had not protected her, she would have been expelled from the city by the magistrate. She has an enormous clitoris" (115). Entry 17 narrates: "From Van Someren: There was some lesbian here, who had such a protruding clitoris, that she had fucked many decent married women. For fear of being discovered, she ran away." Entry 120 educates: "Gerard Blasius in his notes: Often the clitoris sticks out like the male penis, particularly among those who either as ignorant girls or as very lascivious adults touch and rub it frequently. Sometimes it grows to a very big size; there is example in Platter and Tulp. Mr Panqrall saw it extended and stretched out to such a size in a prostitute that it would equal the dick of a boy of twelve years old."

The author thus shows a great deal of interest in various aspects of the female sexual organ: its normal and aberrant proportions, its relation to sexual behaviour.

This sexual curiosity becomes truly radical when the author takes a materialist turn and declares that the libido is the driving force behind all human endeavours: "The poet Abba, treating of the cunt and coitus, said: 'If this mill would come to a halt, the world would soon perish'" (106). Since Adam and Eve and the original sin, he posits, sexual desire has propelled us forward. The author probably derived these ideas from the writings of the Dutch libertine Adrian Beverland (1650–1716), a student at Leiden, whose learned but highly scandalous work was censored and led to its author's imprisonment and banishment. Around 20 of the 167 entries in the Utrecht compilation manuscript can be traced back to Beverland's unpublished master's thesis titled *De prostibulis veterum*, a radical compilation of humanist knowledge, specifically about sexuality. Beverland's main thesis in this erotological compilation is that the libido is the driving force in human behaviour. Karen Hollewand's chapter in this volume provides an in-depth analysis of Beverland, his work, and the censorship of his manuscript and printed texts.[18]

The author of the Utrecht notebook almost certainly had a direct connection to Beverland or one of his friends, since he seems to have had access to the manuscript of *De prostibulis veterum*, not just to the printed text, which was published in a small number of copies in the autumn of 1678.[19] The manuscript had been circulating during the first months of 1678 among a select circle of Beverland's friends. It was not until October 1679, after Beverland published a second version of the text as *De peccato originali*, that he was arrested, censured, and banned from the university and the provinces of Holland. By then, his ideas had spread through printed text, manuscript versions, notebooks, and conversations.

Figure 6.3 Merry Company. Jan van Somer (after Johann Liss, after Jeremias Falck), 1699–1700. Rijksmuseum Amsterdam RP-P-1937-1720.

The First Sexual Revolution: Manuscripts and "Merry Companies"

The Utrecht Notebook opens up questions about the development of *scientia sexualis* in the seventeenth century and the role that manuscripts played in this process. In his recent study *The Origins of Sex*, Dabhoiwala states that around 1700 a first sexual revolution took place, a groundbreaking change both in the way people thought about sex and in the ways they behaved sexually. Although Dabhoiwala presents this as a shift in Western European civilization in general, nearly all of his research materials and arguments relate to England.[20] It is in England that he traces a radical shift in the discourses on sexuality and in the disciplining of sexual behaviour. Urbanization and the Reformation, as well as Enlightenment philosophies regarding the autonomy of men and reason, had all paved the way for more sexual freedom. As church and government control slackened, people began to act and talk more freely, celebrating and researching sexual passion in images and texts as well as through their actions. No longer was lust regarded as a sin; now it was a useful impulse for human actions, and one to be celebrated.

Dahoiwala's book presents a convincing account of the fundamental shift in attitudes towards sex and the accompanying development of the science of sex. But it is far from clear that this development should be restricted to England, whose neighbour across the North Sea was another highly urbanized commercial society where the Reformation and the early Enlightenment paved the way for new attitudes towards sexuality. As related above, in the second half of the seventeenth century the Dutch Republic developed into the sex shop of Europe, with its own home brand of erotic literature and visual depictions.[21] This fast-expanding body of texts encompassed pleas for openness about sex, for open and tolerant laws on prostitution, and for treating men and women as equals, since they had basically the same body/mind structure and the same libido.[22]

What role did manuscripts play in this process? As the Utrecht notebook indicates, manuscripts were a means to collect information. Since no coherent body of thought was available in textual form, those interested in *scientia sexualis* had to collect bits and pieces of information from various sources. The Utrecht author used both published texts and manuscripts, not only Beverland's but also those of other scholars. For example, in entry 7 the author indicates that he gleaned information from a manuscript by "Liefting" (perhaps this points to Jacob Lieftinck, a Utrecht city councillor and a critic of the Orangist faction). Most of his information, though, seems to have been derived directly from people.

Although some of the proverbs, epigrams, and jokes in the notebook can be traced back to (classical) texts, the author nearly always stipulates a different source: one of his friends or colleagues, who presumably told him this anecdote. Entries usually start with indications – for example, "from Beverland," "from Van Someren," "from De Witt."

The author uses strategies from the commonplace book tradition.[23] In this respect his notebook closely resembles the one kept by Aernout van Overbeke. A lawyer in The Hague, and later an admiral with the VOC (the Dutch East India Company) and a literary author, van Overbeke collected jokes, anecdotes, and noteworthy quotes and wrote them down in a notebook.[24] His collection of nearly 2,500 entries is strongly biased towards all things sexual and scatological. As van Overbeke seems to have intended to ultimately publish his work, he was cautious in naming people and sometimes even censored his own work. The notebook was never published, but its contents were almost certainly distributed among his friends and colleagues, as he used the notes for lively conversation in the merry companies he attended. Wherever he went, van Overbeke was sure to be able to entertain the company.

As these notebooks indicate, merry companies were an important social context for the development and distribution of libertine thought. In the seventeenth century, the "merry company" also fascinated painters and authors. In the Dutch Republic, it even evolved into a specific genre. It seems that in the collective imagination, the merry company and the brothel scene provided social contexts for erotic explorations, both in action and in words, as is clear from the many depictions of songs and poems being sung and read by young people during their merry gatherings.[25]

The merry company, with its sparkling conversation, provided a popular format for erotic prose. One of the most radical examples of this is the pornographic novel *De doorluchtige daden van Jan Stront, opgedragen aan het kakhuys* (Mighty deeds of John Shit, Dedicated to the Shithouse, 1680; Part II, 1696).[26] In both volumes of this novel, merry companies serve as vehicles for pornographic explorations. In the first volume the protagonist Jan Stront joins a group of friends at an inn to eat, drink, and discuss "everything that comes to our mouths." To hide their real names, the friends constantly borrow different ones from both famous and less familiar people: classical authors, *philosophes*, lawyers, kings, famous ladies. Thus a "dialogue of the dead" unspools between such different persons as Aristotle, Spinoza, Erasmus, Cardinal Cusa, Gravelle, Anna Viterbitensis, Galenus, Pliny, Ronsard, Magdalena, Rabbanus Maurus, Sophanisba, Caesar, Herodotus, and so on. This short list reveals

Figure 6.4 Jan van Somer, a jester embraced by a lady (around 1690). Rijksmuseum RP-P-1890-A-15454.

that women were already playing an important role in merry knowledge production.

Most of the knowledge discussed by Jan Stront and his friends in the first volume is taken from the baroque satire *Le Moyen de parvenir* by Béroalde de Verville.[27] This famous knowledge compilation and joke book was reprinted in the Netherlands in 1675. The author of *Jan Stront* may have owned a copy, but another option is that bits and pieces of the book were handed down to him in manuscript form. In *Jan Stront* little is left of the original structure of the *Le Moyen de parvenir*. Structured dialogues are taken apart, scrambled, sampled, and pieced together again, sometimes so as to form a completely different line of thought. The original text seems to have been intended as a satire on humanist learning, constantly defying logic and structure; the author of *Jan Stront* seems to have taken the next step by again mixing together all the pieces of the "encyclopedia" and reassembling them in his own knowledge collage.

Scientia Sexualis: *Jan Stront* and the Utrecht Notebook

The second volume of *Jan Stront* is a completely original piece of work that focuses more exclusively on sex. In this volume the protagonist Jan Stront sits with some of his colleagues (lawyers like himself) and female friends (some of whom are schooled prostitutes) to discuss things sexual. During these conversations a highly overt form of sexual materialism is formulated. The author declares over and over that sex is the most important driver of human conduct. He attempts to paint a new universe composed of animated bodies in motion, mechanisms driven by the laws of pleasure.[28] The genitals are described as separate entities, acting autonomously. Jan Stront thinks marriage is an insult to the genitals, which have professed such tender love to one another that they would be saddened to know they were mistrusted. In the end, the genitals do indeed take over. The conversation concludes with a merry group sex scene.

Jan Stront seems to be rooted in the same social and intellectual realm as the circles of Aernout van Overbeke and the Utrecht notebook author. We encounter the same kind of light-hearted sexuality, with the same kind of curiosity about all things sexual, and with sex employed as a form of criticism of traditional authorities and axioms. *Jan Stront* also tell jokes about van Overbeke, and some of the related anecdotes and puns are quite similar.

I think there is a distinct possibility that the author of *Jan Stront* was also the author of the Utrecht notebook. There are many similarities between the texts and between their social contexts. As I have argued before, the author of *Jan Stront* may have been Pieter Elzevier, one of the very last – and not so successful – descendants of the once mighty Elzevier publishing family.[29] Pieter was raised in the world of books and even practised publishing for a while in Utrecht. Between 1668 and 1675 he published several books in Latin and French. Pierre Bayle criticized Elzevier for publishing a Priolo's *Ab excessu Ludovici XIII. de rebus Gallicis, historiarum* in Latin; according to Bayle, a French-language version would have given the book notoriety. During his short span as a publisher, Pieter Elzevier obviously favoured the scandalous side of the book market: he published *Journal du journal, ou censure de la censure* (1670) and the *Traitté de la politique de France* by Paul Hay Marquis de Chatelet, under the fictitious imprint of Pierre Marteau.[30] After his brief time as a publisher, Pieter Elzevier embarked on a career at the bar, swiftly making his way into politics as a city councilor. In 1684, conflicts with William III caused his downfall as a regent, after which his public life seems to have ended.

These episodes place Pieter Elzevier in the same circles as the notebook author, with his overt dislike of Orangist politics and his bookish interest in clandestine literature. Both authors share a fascination with sex and aim to gather as much information as possible to piece together a *scientia sexualis.* Both have a special interest in the language of sex, duly listing current terms, synonyms, and playful ways to describe the male and female genitals and the act of sex. See for example entry 151, which deals with the linguistic aspects of Dutch names such as *Trullaert* (Dickens), *Clootwyck* (Ballwick), and *Miss Contstorf* (Arseton). While entry 151 explains that *futuere* (to fuck), originally meant "to plant, to sow," this is further explained in *Jan Stront* through an anecdote of someone who first shits in a woman's lap (fertilization), after which he can plant and harvest. Some of the named persons also overlap – for example, "Wesel." The second volume of Pieter Elzevier's book of bawdy songs and poems, *Den lacchenden Apoll* (first volume, 1667; second, 1669), was edited by Dominicus van Wesel. In the Utrecht notebook two entries (46 and 123) indicate a certain "Wesel" (not identified) as the source of information.

But even if the texts were not written by the same person, it is interesting how the same fascination with all things sexual found its way in these different textual forms, and how the two different texts overlap in their radical obscenity, formulated in the context of a new form of sociability. As Joan DeJean has recently argued, during the seventeenth century a new form of obscenity was developed, a radical epistemological form of the obscene that was perceived as a serious threat to traditional authorities.[31] The threat posed by this body of thought lay not just its blasphemous

Figure 6.5 Arnold Houbraken, Engraving of Orginal Sin, in *Verzameling van uitgeleezene keurstoffen* (1713). Amsterdam, Rijksmuseum Research Library: 318 F 23:1.

nature and its possible consequences for moral ideals, for the sanctity of marriage and other cornerstones of religious life; it also raised the danger that this kind of overt sexuality would now spread across all social groups. Eroticism and materialist philosophy had long been the province of noblemen and restricted groups of scholars; with the development of print culture and new forms of sociability, a new form of obscenity now threatened to spread across the urban community, and not only among men.

Similar observations are made by Jonathan Israel and Margaret Jacob in their studies of the radical Enlightenment: libido is a possible instrument of radical equality, for the male and female libidos basically function in the same way.[32] In terms of sex, everyone can be an expert, a lowly prostitute even more so than a noble or wise man. These claims, which are put forward in obscene publications and manuscripts, formulate an egalitarian vision of mankind.[33] The Dutch Republic played an important role in the development of this new attitude towards sex.

Scientia Sexualis in Letters and Correspondences

Sexuality, original sin, hermaphrodites, and clitorises were also topics in another manuscript form: letters. In early modern correspondences, numerous letters can be found that are concerned with the science of sex. Medical doctors and researchers in anatomy corresponded on all aspects of the human and animal body and their sexual organs.[34] Beverland is discussed – for example, by Constantijn Huygens, who visited the man in England in 1692: "J'ay esté l'autre jour chez ce Beverland, qui a demeuré quelque temps avec Vossius, et a escrit le livre que vous scaurez de Peccato Originali, pour lequel il fust banny de l'Hollande. A l'intercession de Monsieur Halewijn et autres il aura sa grace du Roy. Il me fist voir sa Bibliotheque qui est de livres choisis, et un grand nombre de tailles douces parmy les quelles il y en a de belles. de desseins il n'en a point."[35]

Many of these letters remained unpublished, but some of them were collected and printed in order to expand their audience. This was the case with a correspondence I would like to discuss as a case study. The letters were written by the Dutch painter Arnold Houbraken and sent to several of his male and female friends and pupils. Houbraken published a collection of these letters anonymously in 1712 under the title *Philaléthes' Letters*. The same year, he published a follow-up: a tractate on religion and the passions, this time in the form of a dialogue he conducted with his pupil "Eusebius." Together, these were published under a new title in 1713.[36]

As Jonathan Israel has written, *Philaléthes' Letters* can be seen as "especially symptomatic of the underground Radical Enlightenment of the early eighteenth century." In his very first letter, to a certain "G.L," Houbraken references Beverland's work with a rereading of the role of the snake in the seduction of Eve to original sin. Houbraken was a painter and a theorist of art, yet here he departs from his interest in visual depictions of biblical scenes. He scorns painters like Rembrandt and De Lairesse for painting biblical fantasy stories. Embracing accommodation theory, he declares that the Bible should not be taken literally when dealing with original sin. The snake is just a figure that has been woven into the historical tapestry, according to Houbraken. The essence of the episode lies in Eve's act, which was induced by desire. He states that desire is a necessary element of human life and credits a certain J. Pel with this opinion.[37]

Houbraken praises the famous Dutch playwright Joost van den Vondel, who apparently did understand the essence of Eve's act and who highlights her physical attractiveness in his play *Lucifer* (1654). This intriguing reading of Vondel's work (he is not often seen as a radical thinker)[38] can also be found in the Utrecht notebook, where the author praises Vondel for his radical insights: "*The fall of the angels* was written very elegantly by Vondel, and about the tree of life in paradise it also hints tacitly that it was not a tree but a penis" (134). And Vondel was not the only poet who was inspired by the radical potential of the first act of physical love between Adam and Eve. One of Beverland's friends wrote a pornographic poem about the first sexual act:

But actually; his Wife, egged on by t' Devil's talk
Is eager now to know the powers of that tree
She comes with hollow hand, and at her Husband's Stalk
Most eagerly she grasps, she tempts him thus to feast,
To sample of the fruit hidden between her thighs.
Good Adam stands perplexed, but to her winks and nods
He finally gives in; He sees the red so shy,
He sees her luscious flesh, perfected by the gods
He sees her tender face, and hears her sweet voice laugh.
His chastity is raped. And underneath it all,
His hellish firebrand rears, his miracle-working staff.
Go to and fight, the long eternity is thine,
Engendered in your seed; you'll be God's equal,
O, Adam had been caught; Before him, Eve, supine,
Gives herself up to him; he finds he is unable
To resist, receives her, and she him; And at the height
Of ecstasy body joined soul, separate no more,
Together ate the fruit, the sweet but banned delight,
One body God created, where two had been before.[39]

Figure 6.6 Arnold Houbraken, erotic engraving of satyrs spying and preying on nymphs (ca 1700). Rijksmuseum: RP-P-1885-A-8991.

Figure 6.7 Arnold Houbraken, erotic engraving of satyrs spying and preying on nymphs (ca 1700). Rijksmuseum: RP-P-OB-48.944.

Figure 6.8 Arnold Houbraken, erotic engraving of satyrs spying and preying on nymphs (ca 1700). Rijksmuseum: RP-P-OB-48.946.

Figure 6.9 Arnold Houbraken, erotic engraving of satyrs spying and preying on nymphs (ca 1700). Rijksmuseum: RP-P-1885-A-8995.

Houbraken's Radical Eroticism

Houbraken's interest in the workings of sexual desire is evident in his other work. He designed engravings for love poems and kissing songs by his colleague Jan van Hoogstraten (1710),[40] and he composed several explicitly erotic engravings. Voyeurism especially fascinated him. Many of his engravings depict peeping satyrs, cats and dogs, and artists with eyes full of lust. His interest in voyeurism seems to have stemmed from its being inherent in artistic practice. The artist's observing gaze is turned sexual by the mimicking behaviour of the peeping cats and dogs.

Houbraken's interest in things sexual was linked to his general interest in the passions and sensations. The second part of *Philaléthes' Letters* is a long treatise on the centrality of the passions. Taking a Cartesian turn, he begins by breaking down all known truths. Unlike Descartes, however, he rebuilds a system of information not from reason but from the passions: *I feel, therefore I am.* To acquire knowledge about man, nature, and God, we need a sensitive body, one that brings us information through seeing, feeling, sensing, smelling, and tasting.[41] As a true classicist artist, Houbraken thus weaves the passions and sensations into a fabric for truth finding. He derives some of his ideas from the writings of the Académie Royale on the passions but combines them with completely different types of texts, such as the Spinozist logic of Petrus van Balen and the Cartesian medical theory of Dutch physician Cornelis Bontekoe.

Houbraken seems to be well read in radical Enlightenment philosophy – in Spinoza, Bayle, Deurhoff, and Balthasar Bekker. He agrees with Bekker that biblical references to miracles and other supernatural phenomena should not be taken literally. Together with the radical Reformed minister Frederik van Leenhof, he argues that heaven is not a place but a state of mind, a state of happiness. Yet Houbraken is also clearly a deist, declaring that God is a watchmaker, the "designer of the world." To one "Miss N.N." he writes that it is impossible to prove that one religion is truer than another, since they all make mistakes. Houbraken concludes that he must start all anew, for "we all have learned to echo the articles of faith like parrots, and therefore have no real knowledge of God or religion." He compares religion to a marketplace: as proper merchants, ministers sell their services to the public. From their pulpits they all shout: this is the path, walk it!

Small wonder that the Dutch Church Council immediately tried to censor *Philaletes' Letters.* The Holland synod drew up a list of all the "afschouwelijcke gevoelens [horrible sentiments] van Philaletes." When the Dutch government could not be convinced that the book should be banned, the Church Council decided to drop the case, since it had heard that the publisher was having a hard time selling copies of the letters. It did, however, pay a visit to the author to set him straight. Houbraken apparently confessed his "groot leedwesen" (deepest regret) and said he was prepared to offer satisfaction. He never did, because shortly after the churchmen's visit, he left the country, for England.

Figure 6.10 "The Artist and His Model." Print designed by Arnold Houbraken and engraved by Nikolaas Verkolje (c. 1690). Rijksmuseum RP-P-OB-17.59.

Figure 6.11 "The Artist and His Model." Anonymous copy after the print by Arnold Houbraken. Rijksmuseum SK-C-15.

Letters, Manuscripts, and Radical Sociability

Houbraken's case can tell us more about the role of manuscripts in radical Enlightenment culture in the Netherlands around 1700. Apparently, most of his ideas originated in discussions with pupils, colleagues, and other interested men and women. Sending one another letters was one way for them to exchange ideas. Houbraken also talks about manuscripts that were sent to him. And from a letter to an anonymous lady, we learn that he had sent her the manuscript of *De gemeene leiding tot de godsdienst afgebroken* (1713). She sent it back to him, and through further letters they engaged in discussion on the topics of his tractate.

As the case of the notebooks revealed, manuscripts functioned within various urban, sometimes underground forms of sociability. In his youth, Houbraken had belonged to Prodesse et Delectare, one of the many artistic societies founded in that period. After moving to Amsterdam, he began to participate in more underground kinds of gatherings, where theology and philosophy were discussed. He attended Collegiant gatherings in Amsterdam and Rotterdam, where he witnessed "word battles." He was delighted when his friends won and the "enemy" was forced to sound the retreat, utterly defeated.

The military imagery is striking and intentional. Houbraken brings up this story of the Collegiant meetings in the middle of a paragraph on natural law, contract theory, and the development of governance. He describes how after an initial peaceful state, mankind started to quarrel and seek the rule of law. However, governance turned into tyranny, with church and monarchy supporting each other. This church/government arrangement, according to Houbraken, is the reason why people are raised in only religion only and enjoy no opportunity to seek what is the best religion for themselves. To free the people from the monopolization of knowledge, a real fight is necessary. Thus, Houbraken learned to "arm" himself with logic, to flank his enemies' ambushes, to attack their fortifications.

Houbraken paints a lively picture of the underground debates in Amsterdam. One night a certain Jan Prik debated with Lemmerman, who held meetings behind the Rozengracht. Prik was a disciple of the famous Socinian author Daniel Zwikker ("a man of notorious scholarship, forced to practice in secret in Amsterdam because of his strange opinions"). Lemmerman apparently was quite famous by then as one of the sharpest debaters of Amsterdam. Prik felt compelled to attend

Lemmerman's meetings to test him out. Prik won the debate, which was on "whether God will punish men for sexual immorality."

Houbraken talks about a public debate on whether the devil did physically appear before Christ, or whether he was just a mental image. The debate was held between a friend of the Houbraken circle and a certain Mr Van Kuik, over two days, 13 and 27 January 1693. Van Kuik lost the argument to reason, for "reason does not need scripture, but the Bible certainly needs reason."[42]

By his own account, the no-holds-barred debates started to bore Houbraken. He understood that they were more a matter of *overdwarsen* (one-upmanship), fuelled by vanity and the wish to become famous among one's peers in the underground. So he opted for another form of sociability more in line with the ideal of "brotherly love" and the desire to gain insight into complex matters. That is how he ended up writing letters, circulating manuscripts, and engaging in more private small-group discussions. Eventually he tried to expand his public by looking for a printer to publish his manuscripts.

This last step was not taken lightly. When Houbraken finally decided to publish his letters and manuscripts, he did so cautiously and reluctantly. In a letter to one D.v.S., he wrote:

> You seem to think that I should (as my good friends have long been pressing me to) make some of my writings available to the public in print; but is it not enough that you (in your role as friend) have access to them? What would I expect from such a move, in a world of diverse passions? Do you wish me to give anger the opportunity to soil my writings with its poisonous bile?[43]

But in the end, Houbraken felt it his duty to inform the public of how they were being kept ignorant by church and state. People, he believed, should start to school themselves. So this manuscript ended up in print, and on the doorstep of the censoring bodies of the Dutch Republic.

Conclusion

The Dutch Republic as "Magazine de l'Univers" hosted a highly developed market for printed works, yet manuscripts still played an interesting role in the development and distribution of radical thought. Notebooks

Figure 6.12 Arnold Houbraken (design) and Nikolaas Verkolje (print), "Two different versions of a man who tries to seduce a woman with an erotic drawing" (ca 1700). Rijksmuseum RP-P-1911-196 and RP-P-1911-195.

and letters were important elements in the knowledge dynamics of new and partly underground kinds of sociability. Private notebooks served as compilations of different bodies of knowledge, passed on in manuscript form, in printed publications, or orally, through personal contact or social gatherings.

Figure 6.12 Continued

Manuscripts functioned in various social contexts. They were used in merry companies, where libertine conversations could be held. Here, notebook jokes could be tested and the new knowledge could be gathered. In this context, the science of sex was explored, sometimes in combination with the *ars erotica* of seduction. As well, scholars and interested *liefhebbers* helped build up the *scientia sexualis* through letters, schooling one another on everything that concerned sex and the passions. Another kind of sociability in which manuscripts functioned was that of artistic societies. In art societies, sociability and a critical attitude were seen as central to the ideal of good authorship. Manuscripts were used to register the findings of the companies and the progress made, and were passed on to the next generation as a means for instruction in the arts and the passions. Manuscript circulation was thus also entrenched in the social practices of the art world. But the development of radical thought seems to have been strongest in the social world of the heterodox underground, of religious and philosophical groups convening for debates in the urban environments of the Dutch Republic. Here too, manuscripts fuelled the discussion.

All of this strongly suggests that manuscripts were not primarily private documents. In the Dutch Republic, they functioned within various forms of sociability, distributing knowledge that often could not enter the printed public sphere. In line with existing radical ideals regarding open debate and the need to educate the public, Dutch scholars and *liefhebbers* experimented with different forms of knowledge exchange. The new *scientia sexualis* that was compiled by means of these different knowledge routes, as well as in the collective imagination, was a product of egalitarian knowledge exchange. The example of *Jan Stront* exemplifies this statement, in that it imagines various groups of men and women from different social backgrounds exchanging knowledge about sex, from classical and modern sources, from personal experience to hearsay. These novels and notebooks can be read as indications of a sexual revolution that developed in relation to the radical Enlightenment in the Dutch Republic.

NOTES

1 P.M.L. Steenbakkers, J.J. Touber, and J.M.M. van de Ven, "A Clandestine Notebook (1678–1679) on Spinoza, Beverland, Politics, the Bible and Sex: Utrecht, UL, ms. 1284," *Lias* 38, no. 2 (2011): 255–65. The quote about Grotius is from entry 28. For a scan of the MSS, visit http://bc.library.uu.nl/nl/seks-politiek-en-godsdienst-zeventiende-eeuws-utrecht.html.

2 About Velthuysen, see his entry in Wiep van Bunge et al., eds, *The Dictionary of Seventeenth- and Eighteenth-Century Dutch Philosophers* (Bristol: Thoemmes Press, 2003). See also Henri Krop, "Spinoza en het calvinistisch

cartesianisme van Lambertus Van Velthuysen (1622-1685)," in *Spinoza en het Nederlands cartesianisme*, ed. Gunther Coppens (Leuven: Acco, 2004), 61–78.

3 Rindert Jagersma (University of Utrecht) is preparing an edition of the *Memoriael* by Ericus Walten in the context of his PhD project on this radical pamphleteer.

4 On censorship in the Netherlands, see I. Weekhout, *Boekencensuur in de Noordelijke Nederlanden: de vrijheid van drukpers in de zeventiende eeuw* (Den Haag: SDU, 1998); M. Matthijssen, ed., *Boeken onder druk. Censuur en persónvrijheid in Nederland sinds de boekdrukkunst* (Amsterdam: AUP, 2011).

5 On the Dutch radical Enlightenment, Spinozism, and clandestine culture, see M.C. Jacob, *The Radical Enlightenment: Pantheists, Freemasons, and Republicans* (2nd rev. ed., Lafayette and Los Angeles: Cornerstone, 2006); Jonathan Israel, *Radical Enlightenment: Philosophy and the Making of Modernity 1650–1750* (Oxford: Oxford University Press, 2001); Wiep van Bunge, *From Stevin to Spinoza: An Essay on Philosophy in the Seventeenth-Century Dutch Republic* (Boston and Leiden: Brill, 2001); Michiel Wielema, *The March of the Libertines: Spinozists and the Dutch Reformed Church 1660–1750* (Hilversum: Verloren, 2004); W. van Bunge, *Spinoza Past and Present: Essays on Spinoza, Spinozism, and Spinoza Scholarship* (Boston and Leiden: Brill, 2012). Koerbagh's work has recently been translated: *Adriaan Koerbagh: A Light Shining in Dark Places, to Illuminate the Main Questions of Theology and Religion*, trans. M. Wielema (Boston and Leiden: Brill, 2011).

6 C. Rasterhoff, *The Fabric of Creativity in the Dutch Republic: Painting and Publishing as Cultural Industries, 1580–1800* (Amsterdam: Amsterdam University Press, 2013).

7 *Pierre Marteau's Publishing House, Cologne Virtual Publisher for over 340 Years* (http://www.pierre-marteau.com); Olaf Simons, *Marteaus Europa oder Der Roman, bevor er Literatur wurde: Eine Untersuchung des deutschen und englischen Buchangebots der Jahre 1710 bis 1720* (Amsterdam: Rodopi, 2001). A short introduction to Pierre Marteau can be found in M.C. Jacob, *The Enlightenment: A Brief History with Documents* (Boston: Bedford/St Martin's Press, 2001).

8 Lynn Hunt, ed., *The Invention of Pornography: Obscenity and the Origins of Modernity, 1500–1800* (New York: Zone Books, 1993); Inger Leemans, *Het woord is aan de onderkant. Radicale ideeën in Nederlandse pornografische romans 1670–1700* (Nijmegen: Vantilt, 2002).

9 Inger Leemans, "De Sexshop van Europa. Nederlandse productie en verspreiding van pornografische romans in de zeventiende eeuw," *Jaarboek voor Nederlandse boekgeschiedenis*, 7, 2000, 81–96.

10 The example of the "found" pornographic texts is an anecdote from the manuscript diary of Constantijn Huygens Jr. Huygens notes that Adriaan

van Borssele showed him a pornographic work with engravings by Romeyn de Hooghe "in the manner of *L'École de la Filles.*" By his own accord, Van Borssele had found this curious book (probably a copy of the Dutch translation of *La Puttana Errante*) in the gardens of the Royal Palace in Dieren. Leemans, *Het woord is aan de onderkant*, 108, 164. For Huygens's diary see Rudolf Dekker, *Family, Culture, and Society in the Diary of Constantijn Huygens Jr, Secretary to Stadholder-King William of Orange*, Egodocuments and History Series vol. V (Leiden: Brill, 2013).

11 Leemans, *Het woord is aan de onderkant.*

12 Israel, *Radical Enlightenment*, ch. "The Clandestine Philosophical Manuscripts."

13 I. Leemans and G-J. Johannes, *Worm en donder. Geschiedenis van de Nederlandse literatuur 1700–1800. De Republiek.* Geschiedenis van de Nederlandse literatuur, vol. 4 (Amsterdam: Bert Bakker/Prometheus, 2013).

14 M.C. Jacob, "The Materialist World of Pornography," in Hunt, ed., *The Invention of Pornography*, 157–202. Jonathan Israel devotes a chapter to the philosophy of libido and sexual equality, also taking pornographic texts into account. Israel, *Radical Enlightenment*, ch. 4: "Women, Philosophy, and Sexuality."

15 F. Dabhoiwala, *The Origins of Sex: A History of the First Sexual Revolution* (London: Allen Lane, 2012).

16 K. Park, "The Rediscovery of the Clitoris: French Medicine and the Tribade, 1570–1620," in *The Body in Parts: Fantasies of Corporeality in Early Modern Europe*, ed. D. Hillman and C. Mazzio (New York and London: Routledge, 1997), 171–93.

17 N. Tulp, *De drie boecken der medicijnsche aenmerkingen*, translated from the Latin (Amsterdam: J.J. Bouman, 1650); E. Sanders, "Clitóris en vagína," *NRC* 1–2-2014. Many thanks to Ewoud Sanders, who sent me his column on the earliest occurrences of the term clitoris in the Dutch language.

18 See Karen Hollewand's chapter in this volume "Expert of the Obscene." See also K. Hollewand, "Between Books and Brothels: The Sexual Scholarship of Hadriaan Beverland (1650–1716)," in *Framing Premodern Desires: Between Sexuality, Sin, and Crime*, ed. M. Heinonen, T. Linkinen, S. Lidman, and M. Kaartinen (Amsterdam: Amsterdam University Press, 2017); R. de Smet, *Hadrianus Beverlandus (1650–1716): non unus e multis peccator: studie over het leven en werk van Hadriaan Beverland* (Brussel: Paleis der Academien, 1988).

19 Steenbakkers et al., "A Clandestine Notebook," 18–19.

20 Dabhoiwala, *The Origins of Sex.*

21 Leemans, *Het woord is aan de onderkant*; I. Leemans, "Arousing Discontent: Dutch Pornographic Plays, 1670–1800," *Journal for Early Modern Cultural Studies* 12 (2012): 117–32.

22 S. Stuurman, *François Poullain de la Barre and the Invention of Modern Equality* (Cambridge, MA: Harvard University Press, 2004). Israel, *Radical Enlightenment.*

23 A. Moss, *Printed Commonplace-Books and the Structuring of Renaissance Thought* (Oxford: Clarendon Press, 1996); F. Büttner, M. Friedrich, and H. Zedelmaier, eds, *Sammeln, Ordnen, Veranschaulichen: Zur Wissenskompilatorik in der Frühen Neuzeit* (Münster: LIT Verlag, 2003).

24 Aernout van Overbeke, *Anecdota sive historiae jocosae. Een zeventiende-eeuwse verzameling moppen en anekdotes,* ed. R. Dekker, H. Roodenburg, and H.J. Van Rees (Amsterdam: P.J. Meertens-Instituut, 1991).

25 Elmer Kolfin traces different "modes" or traditions in the depiction of merry companies: idealistic, moralistic, and satirical. Sometimes the company is idealized, in many instances it is ridiculed, sometimes the intent is to warn the audience of sinful behavior. Elmer Kolfin, *The Young Gentry at Play: Northern Netherlandish Scenes of Merry Companies 1610–1645* (Leiden: Brill, 2005). See also Lotte C. van den Pol, "The Whore, the Bawd, and the Artist: The Reality and Imagery of Seventeenth-Century Dutch Prostitution," *JHNA* 2, 2010. DOI: 10.5092/jhna.2010.2.1.3. See also J.H. Böse, *"Had de mensch met èèn vrouw niet konnen leven": Prostitutie en overspel in de literatuur van de zeventiende eeuw* (Zutphen: Walburg Pers, 1985).

26 [Anon.], *De doorluchtige Daden van Jan Stront, Opgedragen aan het Kakhuis Bestaande In een uitgelezen Gezelschap, zo[wel] van Heren als Juffers. Tweede Deel. Gedrukt voor de Liefhebbers,* ed. Inger Leemans (Utrecht: IJzer, 2000).

27 Béroalde de Verville, *Le Moyen de parvenir,* ed. Michel Renaud (Paris: Gallimard, 2006). About De Verville: Emily Butterworth, *Poisoned Words: Slander and Satire in Early Modern France* (Oxford: Legenda, 2006); Neil Kenny, *The Palace of Secrets: Béroalde de Verville and Renaissance Conceptions of Knowledge* (New York and Oxford, Clarendon Press, 1991)

28 Cf. Jacob, "The Materialist World of Pornography."

29 I. Leemans, "Een verloren zoon. Uitgever, drollige poëet en pornograaf Pieter Elzevier," *De boekenwereld,* 18, 2001–2, 70–82.

30 G.A. Evers, "Pieter Elsevier te Utrecht," *Het Boek* 5, 1916, 337–43; A. Willems, *Les Elzevier: Histoire et annales typographiques* (Nieuwkoop: B. de Graaf, 1974; reprint of Brussels: G.A. van Trigt, 1880), ccliii–ccix, 412–14.

31 Joan DeJean, *The Reinvention of Obscenity: Sex, Lies, and Tabloids in Early Modern France* (Chicago: University of Chicago Press, 2002).

32 Israel, *Radical Enlightenment;* Jacob, *The Radical Enlightenment.*

33 I. Leemans, "'This Fleshlike Isle': The Voluptuous Body of the People in Dutch Pamphlets, Novels and Plays 1660–1730," in *In Praise of Ordinary People: Early Modern Britain and the Dutch Republic,* ed. M.C. Jacob and C. Secretan (New York: Palgrave Macmillan, 2013), 181–202.

34 E.g., letter by Jan Bruynestein (1642–1686) to C. Huygens in 1668 about hermaphrodites and extended clitorises; or Henry Oldenburg (1619–1677) in 1672 from London to Jan Swammerdam on the same topic.

35 Constantijn Huygens (from Whitehall, 30 December 1692) to Christiaan Huygens. This letter can be found in the excellent collection of Dutch digitized learned letters at Huygens ING: Epistolarium (http://ckcc.huygens.knaw.nl/epistolarium/).

36 Anon. [Arnold Houbraken], *Philalétes Brieven [...]* (Amsterdam: P. Boeteman, 1712); Anon. [Arnold Houbraken], *De gemeene leidingen tot den Godsdienst afgebroken en weder opgebouwt op vasten grond door een Redenvoeringe over de Hertstogten* [...] *Dienende tot vervolg van Philaléthes Brieven* (Printed for the Author; Amsterdam: G. onder den Linden, 1712); Anon. [Arnold Houbraken], *Verzameling van uitgeleezene keurstoffen, handelende over den Godsdienst, Natuur- Schilder- Teken- Oudheid- Redeneer- en Dichtkunde* (Amsterdam: J. Oosterwijk & H. van de Gaete, 1713). I. Leemans, "'Zie ons vry voor uwe wetsteen aan'. Frans-classicisme en de Radicale Verlichting," in *Een groot verleden voor de boeg. Opstellen voor Joost Kloek*, ed. J. de Kruif, G.-J. Johannes, and J. Salman (Leiden: Primavera Pers, 2004), 213–36. For an extensive treatment of Houbraken, his work, his theories, and the censorship of his works, see H.J. Horn, *The Golden Age Revisited. Arnold Houbraken's Great Theatre of Netherlandish Painters and Paintresses* (Doornspijk: Abebooks, 2000).

37 The mysterious autodidact Pel merits more research. One study that certainly inspired Houbraken was J. Pel, *De wonderdaden des Alderhoogsten (Wonders of the Supreme Being, in which it is proved that it is far more likely that the temptation of men came from himself, and not by some fallen spirit)* (Amsterdam: W. de Coup, 1693).

38 The exception in this regard is F.W. Korsten, *Vondel belicht: voorstellingen van soevereiniteit* (Hilversum: Verloren, 2006).

39 J.v.B, *Lof-digt ter eeren van Mr. Adriaan Beverlant* (S.l: s.n., s.a.).

40 J. Van Hoogstraten, *Minnezangen kusjes drinkliederen,* 3rd enl. ed. (Gouda: L. Kloppenburg, 1708).

41 [Houbraken], "Redenvoering over de hartstochten," in *De gemeene leidingen,* 1–15.

42 Similar debate clubs also appear in the Dutch spinozist novel *Het leven van Philopater & Vervolg van 't leven van Philopater.* Ed. en inl. G. Maréchal (Amsterdam: Rodopi, 1991).

43 [Houbraken], *Verzameling,* 178.

Chapter Seven

Expert of the Obscene: The Sexual Manuscripts of Dutch Scholar Hadriaan Beverland (1650–1716)

KAREN HOLLEWAND

> In fact, I have decided to deliver the three books of De Prostibulis Veterum soon ... I would not commit this difficult work to print, if your courtesy and inborn kindness would not promise your favour to my temerity... Because only you, Ilias of the learned, can assist me with my endeavours, [thus] I beg that you may not refuse to help me with them.[1]

In the late 1670s, scholar Hadriaan Beverland sent his latest study to scholarly friends, asking them to read it carefully and respond with their criticism. He was planning to publish his work on original sin in the foreseeable future and was looking for advice, not just concerning the style of his writing but also regarding the content of his study on sex and sin. At the same time, Beverland allowed his closest friends to have a look at a much larger work he was completing. Segments of his "De Prostibulis Veterum," a manuscript too large to be sent round in full, circulated among Dutch scholars. He requested humanists like Nicolaas Heinsius and Jacobus Gronovius to comment on the text and asked, in addition, if they could send him material from their private libraries to complement his grand thesis.[2]

This chapter introduces Hadriaan Beverland, one of the lesser-known yet most rebellious members of the Dutch intellectual elite in the last decades of the seventeenth century, and discusses two of his manuscripts, which circulated among humanist scholars in the late 1670s.[3] In the context of this collection of articles on clandestine manuscripts, I will focus in particular on the circulation of Beverland's studies in relation to the dissemination of his ideas and the development of his works and scholarship. Although he circulated his manuscripts with the best intentions, sharing his studies did more than provide Beverland with honest critiques from his friends. It also got him into a lot of trouble.

Beverland and His Studies

In December 1679, Hadriaan Beverland (1650–1716), a talented classical student, was banished from the province of Holland by the academic court of the University of Leiden. Beverland's scholarly career had commenced in 1669, when he started studying at the University of Franeker. In the decade that followed, he was also enrolled at the universities of Leiden and Utrecht and spent a year in Oxford, where he dedicated his time to reading books and manuscripts in the Bodleian Library. Although he became a Doctor of Law at the University of Utrecht in 1677, Beverland did not pay much attention to legal matters. During his student years, he became fascinated by the subject of sex. He read and collected all he could find on the topic, visiting university libraries, browsing the collections of his friends, and purchasing many works and manuscripts himself. His studies of the sexual slowly developed from youthful play into a more serious endeavour and by the late 1670s he was ready to publish.[4]

In 1678 and 1679 Beverland published *De Peccato Originale* and *De Stolatae Virginitate Iure*, two previews of the master's thesis, titled "De Prostibulis Veterum," he was completing at the same time.[5] After a decade of studying all he could find on the subject, concentrating in particular on the obscenities he had encountered in ancient sources and classical literature, the young scholar revealed his grand theory. He argued that sexual lust was the original sin: Adam and Eve had engaged in sexual relations in the Garden of Eden against God's will and were consequently banished from Paradise. After the Fall of Man all descendants of the first humans, Beverland argued, were dominated by sexual desire. Based on his own philological studies of ancient texts and the biblical criticism of other scholars, he underscored the validity of his argument on sexual lust by exploring ancient and (early) Christian history.[6] In his first study, *De Peccato Originali* (hereafter the DPO), Beverland focused on the relation between the original sin and sexual lust, and in his work on women he depicted the overbearing influence of sexual desire on the female nature. The three-volume "De Prostibulis Veterum" (hereafter the DPV) was to be his master's thesis, in which he described the importance of sex in universal human nature by concentrating on an array of different subjects – discussing for example the sexual misbehaviour of the clergy of the early Church, sexual euphemisms in classical literature, and obscene subjects in ancient art. Beverland's works were denounced by both friends and foes, by his own scholarly community as well as religious and secular authorities in the Dutch Republic.[7] He was tried before the academic court of the University of Leiden and in December 1679 was convicted of publishing blasphemous, heterodox, and perverse works and banished from the provinces of Holland and Zeeland.[8]

After his banishment, Beverland moved across the Channel. He would spend the rest of his life in exile in England. He kept working on his DPV for a few more years but in the end gave up on his sexual subject. He continued to study his beloved classics, however, and also worked as a sort of secretary, librarian, and broker in the service of Dutch friends, such as Isaac Vossius, and new English contacts, such as the physician and collector Hans Sloane.[9] In the course of the 1680s, Beverland planned to return to the Dutch Republic. He received a pardon for his crimes, signed by King William III, in 1693, after he had assisted in the sale of the library of Isaac Vossius to the University of Leiden. Yet Beverland never returned to his fatherland, since he felt that the atmosphere in the Dutch Republic had remained greatly hostile towards him.[10] Even a long apologetic work, *De Fornicatione Cavenda Admonitio*,[11] published in London in 1697 and 1698, had not changed his reputation, he concluded. After the early 1690s, his financial situation deteriorated, as did his mental health. In 1714, Beverland's DPO was adapted in French, the first of many popular adaptations of his infamous work that were published in France and Germany in the eighteenth century.[12] Beverland would never know. He died in London, lonely and destitute, in 1716.[13]

Since the early eighteenth century, Beverland's story has been recounted many times. Different scholars have commented on the fate of the talented libertine, who was exiled due to the obscene nature of his intellectual interests. Although these studies often allude to his DPV, little attention has been paid to the circulation of this manuscript; moreover, the manuscriptal history of Beverland's most notorious work, the DPO, is usually overlooked.[14]

Two Sexual Manuscripts

In 1678 Beverland was ready to publish his first work and reveal his argument on sexual desire. He dedicated the first chapters of his study on sex and sin to the story of Adam and Eve as depicted in Genesis 1–3, explaining that careful philological study had revealed the true, sexual meaning of this biblical text. There had been no trees, there had been no apple: Adam and Eve had given in to the sexual lust that God had told them to

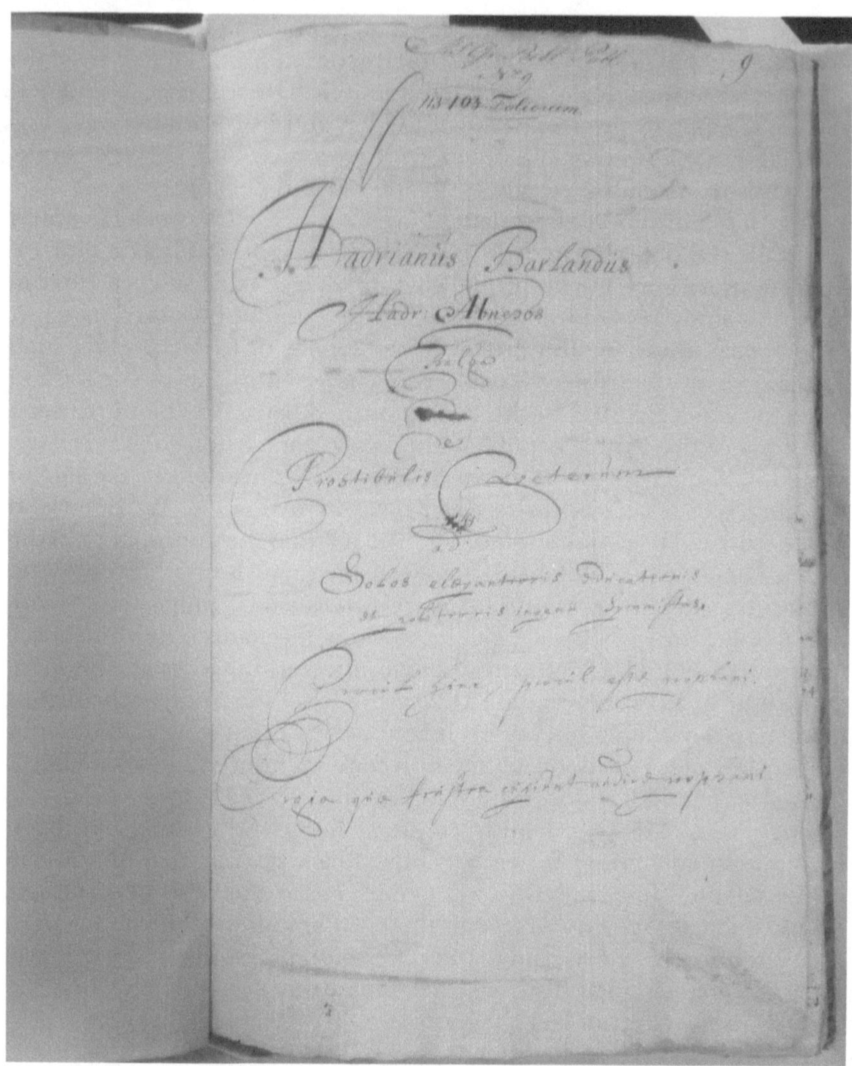

Figure 7.1 Title page and folio 87r of the first book of Beverland's DPV, preserved in the Library of the University of Leiden (BPL 1994).

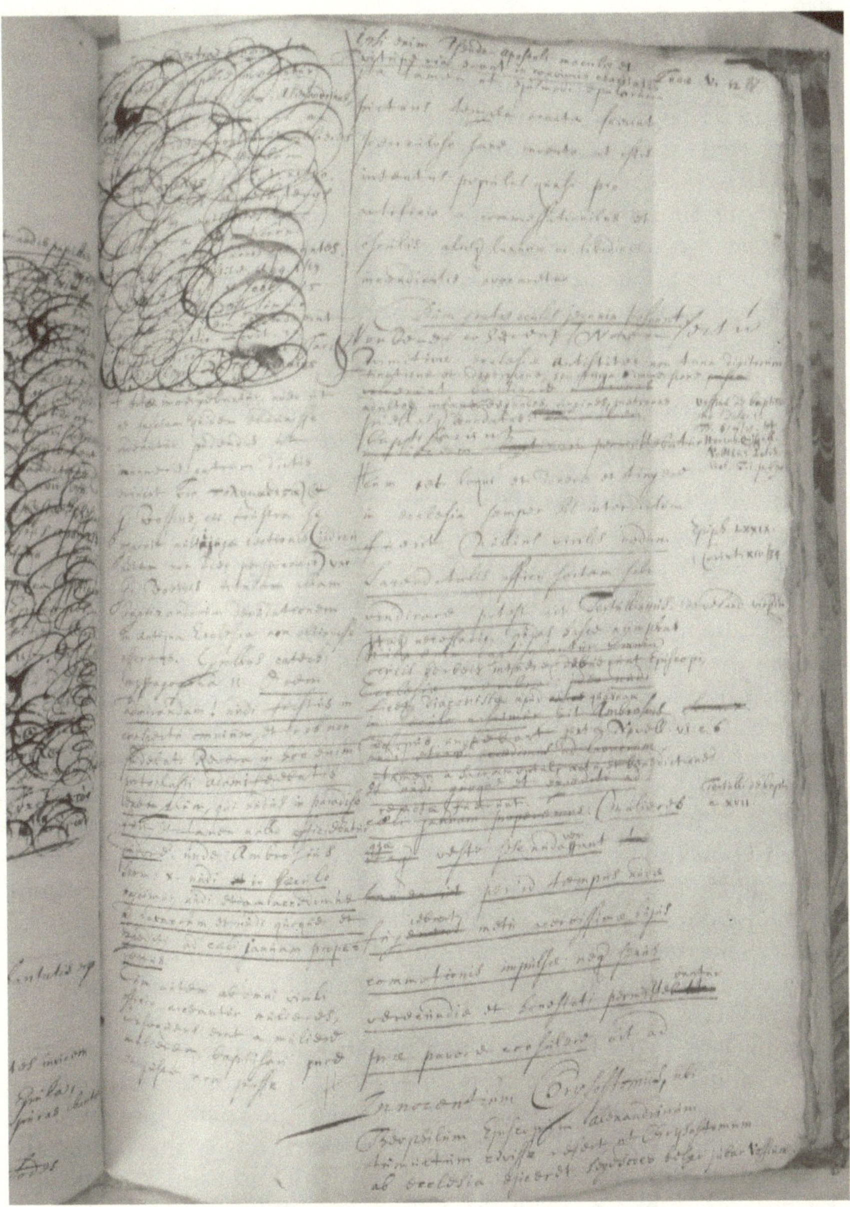

Figure 7.1 Continued

ignore. In his DPO, which was published in three different editions in 1678 and 1679,[15] Beverland approached his sexual subject without holding back, recapturing the story of the first humans in obscene detail. He vividly described, for example, what happened when Eve, after her lust was aroused by the snake, noticed Adam:

> the young girl with devouring eyes, to whose side the lethal weapon clung, fixed her eyes on the stiff, exceedingly desirable wood, suitable to and desired by her private parts, and while she approached her husband with a mischievous face and invaded her husband's neck with an embrace, overloading him with kisses, which he did not resist, with her piercing bite tormenting now his legs now his arms, with sinful hand and soothing words, which possessed fingers, she solicited his most innocent part, She laughed and by pulling with sinful hand his manly parts, the stolen love gave them pleasure, *"husband," she said, "use the gift that nature has given: I am not so strict to condemn the fire that I feel."*[16]

As a result of the Fall of Adam and Eve, Beverland argued, sexual desire became a universal and dominant characteristic of human nature. In his work, he used excerpts from the Bible, classical literature, and other well-known pagan and authoritative Christian texts to establish this theory. He underlined his argument on sex and sin by focusing on cultural artefacts, which exhibited the human obsession with lust; by recounting historical events, which revealed how often (the longing to have) sexual relations had shaped human history; and by reinterpreting the meaning of certain words, which unfailingly betrayed hidden sexual connotations. In the end, he also urged his readers to examine themselves, since no human being could deny that sexual lust ruled their body and soul. "My conscience and the light of my heart taught me that our opinion is more consistent with the words of God. And indeed, nobody fails to experience and discover such a vehement and frequent sin in their own instrument."[17]

In the late 1670s Beverland was not just contemplating the publication of his DPO; he was also completing a much longer work. In his DPV[18] he presented his sexual argument in its full glory, exploring the subject of sex as discussed in a wide variety of texts, from the books of the Bible and the works of Saint Paul and Saint Augustine to the obscene publications of the Italian writer Pietro Aretino and the verses of the Dutch poet Aernout van Overbeke. His main focus was

Table 7.1 Subjects discussed in the second book of Beverland's "De Prostibulis Veterum"*

Chapter	Subject
1	Unnatural sex (introduction of the work)
2	Masturbation by men
3	Ejaculation of semen at night
4	Masturbation by women
5	On women having sex with castrated men and young men
6	Abortion (references, methods, and consideration as murder)
7	Obscene worship (secret sects that concentrate on certain sexual sins)
8	Homosexuality (pederasty and sodomy)
9	Lesbianism (tribadism)
10	Oral sex (given by women to men)
11	Bestiality (sex with devil-like creatures and the personification of people in animals)

* The content of these chapters was summarized in the "Goyeri Paralipomena" (see notes 41 and 42).

the classics, however – in particular, the history of the Roman Republic and Empire (roughly 200 BCE to 200 CE). He paid special attention to explicit words, lewd phrases, and sexual passages in classical literature, with as his favourites the works of Ovid, Juvenal, Martial, Lucretius, and Horace.

In the DPV Beverland described in great detail how the dominant presence of sex exhibited itself in everything: from religion and politics to art and literature. Using his years of studies, he explored his subject by describing obscene plays, sculptures, and coins, referring to religious sects with specific ideas on sexual morality, and noting particular sexual preferences. In the second book of the DPV he compiled various unnatural sexual acts, discussing not only oral sex, homosexuality, and lesbianism but also ejaculation by night, bestiality, and masturbation (see Table 7.1).[19]

Besides the text, Beverland's grand thesis would also contain images. Unfortunately, the prints he commissioned have not been preserved: financial difficulties compelled him to sell many prints in his collection in the 1690s. In two collections of his personal notes, however, we do find images he collected at this time, which give us some indication of what the pictures for the DPV might have looked like.[20] Representative is Figure 7.2.

Figure 7.2 Collected pictures in connection to Baalpeor (DPV, book I, chapter IV), as collected by Beverland in a document of personal notes ("Crepundia Lugdunensia," © British Library Board, Add MS 30384, 68r).

We see a heap of flesh, a mound of naked men, women, and animals in all kinds of positions. Next to the Priapus-like statue at the top, of a man with an erect penis, Beverland has written "Baalpeor" – the name of the Lord of Mount Peor: a God referred to in the Torah and New Testament who was associated with an obscene cult. This assembly of pictures is just one example of Beverland's creative combining of images he cut from published works. In his notebooks we find collages like this one, but also individual images, which Beverland might have preserved in his personal collection in order to one day feature them in a published DPV.[21]

Before printing any of his sexual studies, Beverland sent his manuscripts to trusted friends. His social network was profoundly humanist in character: he corresponded regularly with other scholars, above all with Dutch classicists affiliated with the University of Leiden.[22] He could count men like Nicolaas Heinsius, a renowned classical scholar,[23] Jacobus Gronovius, a professor in law, Latin, and Greek,[24] and Johann Georg Graevius, a professor of history and eloquence,[25] among his close acquaintances. His friendships with these fellow humanists were based on a shared fascination with classical scholarship, and when he contemplated publishing the DPO and DPV, he appealed to his friends for advice, criticism, and support.[26]

He started sharing early versions of (parts of) the DPV years before he was ready to publish the work. To Gronovius he wrote in 1676: "I do not doubt that you also often repeat in your mind the conversations we had in The Hague, where in our spare time you kindly promised to supply me with concealed and secret [literature], when I had submitted the undigested digressions of my nature … De Prostibulis Veterum to your critical opinion, so that you could indicate faults in these books with asterisks and, if I had wandered or omitted something, you could note down suggestions of new teachings."[27] Although his own studies must have supplied him with more than enough obscenities, Beverland asked his friends for additional material. Heinsius's learned library could greatly improve the DPV, Beverland wrote to his patron in 1678. He asked his friend for "a list of men and women who masturbate, perform oral sex, of the active and the passive men who have sexual intercourse, the bold sodomites, and similarly cursed species."[28] He also appealed to Gronovius: "If you have anything in your notes concerning wanton lesbians who masturbate, relying on you I ask that you may send it to me."[29]

While it is safe to assume that before its first printing in 1678 Beverland sent the DPO to some of his closest friends, who allegedly pressured him to publish it,[30] his correspondence reveals that the work circulated most frequently between its first publication sometime in 1678 and its second in early 1679.[31] When discussing the manuscript with Graevius, for example, Beverland focused mainly on issues of style. Because his friend did not approve of the style of the first edition of the DPO,[32] Beverland worked hard to improve his writing. "I am entirely immersed in polishing the unfinished product of my feeble intellect mind and in softening the expressions which had become worse on account of haste ... This [first] edition reeks most foully of a goat, but the second [edition] will breathe a more elegant style."[33] While he previously modelled his text after the baroque and pompous style of humanist scholar J.F. Gronovius, the father of his friend Jacobus, Beverland aimed to style the second edition in a clearer and more fluent manner.[34] "It is typical of young people to have a flowery style, to use lascivious language, and therefore to exaggerate," he wrote to Graevius, yet "the more I adapt my writing to the language of ancient authors, the more I strengthen my mind."[35] Beverland greatly appreciated the help of his friend in editing the text for its second edition: "Your advice has been very helpful to me and it will be even more so if you continue to offer it."[36]

The archives reveal to us that the manner in which Beverland shared his works with friends and acquaintances varied. To some of his friends, he sent complete manuscripts.[37] Hadriaan Molenaer, for example, received the first edition in print in April 1679. "Although I am almost completely overwhelmed by endless cares and work, which are the reason why I could not consult you regarding the publication of this writing," Beverland stated in the accompanying letter, "nonetheless I did not want to keep you deprived of my already printed and published text."[38] Graevius received a revised manuscript of the DPO around the same time, to read and criticize before Beverland printed the second edition.[39] Figure 7.3 shows how in this bound text, written by Beverland himself, he carefully presented his plan for the amended edition to his friends, including page numbers and notes in the margins.

With other friends Beverland shared particular parts of his works, asking them to comment on specific sections or sending them summaries of certain chapters. At the University of Leiden a manuscript titled "Goyeri Paralipomena ad libros de Prostibulis Veterum" has been preserved (see Figure 7.4).[40] The text not only provides a summary of the three books of the DPV but also contains comments on the work, most likely written by Jacob de Goyer, a lawyer in Utrecht and friend of Beverland, together with French scholar Paul Colomesius.[41] Because the manuscript is constructed in Beverland's own handwriting, it seems that Beverland copied his friends' summary and comments from a different document, to use himself and/or to share with others. The manuscript exemplifies the different ways in which the DPV was commented upon, copied, and summarized, as a whole and in parts, by its author and by its readers.

From Exchange to Exile

The circulation of Beverland's manuscripts in the Dutch Republic in the second half of the 1670s had important consequences for the development of his ideas and the future of his scholarship. In 1678 and 1679, Beverland's DPO became widely known in the Dutch Republic.[42] The work's argument was even summarized in a Dutch publication. In a *Poem of Praise in honour of Mr. Adriaan Beverlant* an anonymous author presented an overview of Beverland's views and defended him against his critics.[43] Not just the DPO was debated, however: Beverland's master's thesis was discussed by people who did not directly belong to his inner circle, which suggests that this unprinted manuscript circulated widely.[44] We for instance find Beverland in an anonymous notebook preserved in Utrecht. The author of this brief collection of notes was a student at the University of Utrecht, who stated for instance that Beverland discussed how venereal disease featured in the Bible and who repeated arguments from the DPO: "From Beverland: The tree in paradise was Adam's dick, a phallus extending from his groin, for God did not want human beings to propagate through carnal copulation – since he knew very well that all evils come from sexual intercourse."[45] The notebook reveals that the Utrecht student not only read Beverland's published works but also had access to the DPV; for example, he referred to Beverland's argument on the obscene cult of Baalpeor – a subject not discussed in the DPO but only in chapter 4 of the first volume of the DPV.

Beverland himself referred to the notoriety of his unpublished master's thesis during this period. In the dedication to the second edition of his DPO, he recounted his surprise on discovering that people were talking about his DPV. After he had decided to publish it and was discussing the content of the work with friends, he discovered that lies were being spread about his argument.[46] It seems that his manuscripts changed hands often, yet Beverland did attempt to control the circulation of his texts and was unhappy when they travelled too far out of his reach. When he heard that Graevius had forwarded a manuscript of the DPO without permission, he expressed his dismay: "You did not have any regard for my honour, my Graevius, because allegedly you have sent my Milesian stories to Magliabechi while they were still hot off the press. The rumour that my writings had even arrived in the hands of the pope himself horrified me. How much I wish that you had restrained yourself until the second edition saw the light of day."[47] Disappointed that certain friends could not be trusted, he insisted that Heinsius, to whom Beverland sent a

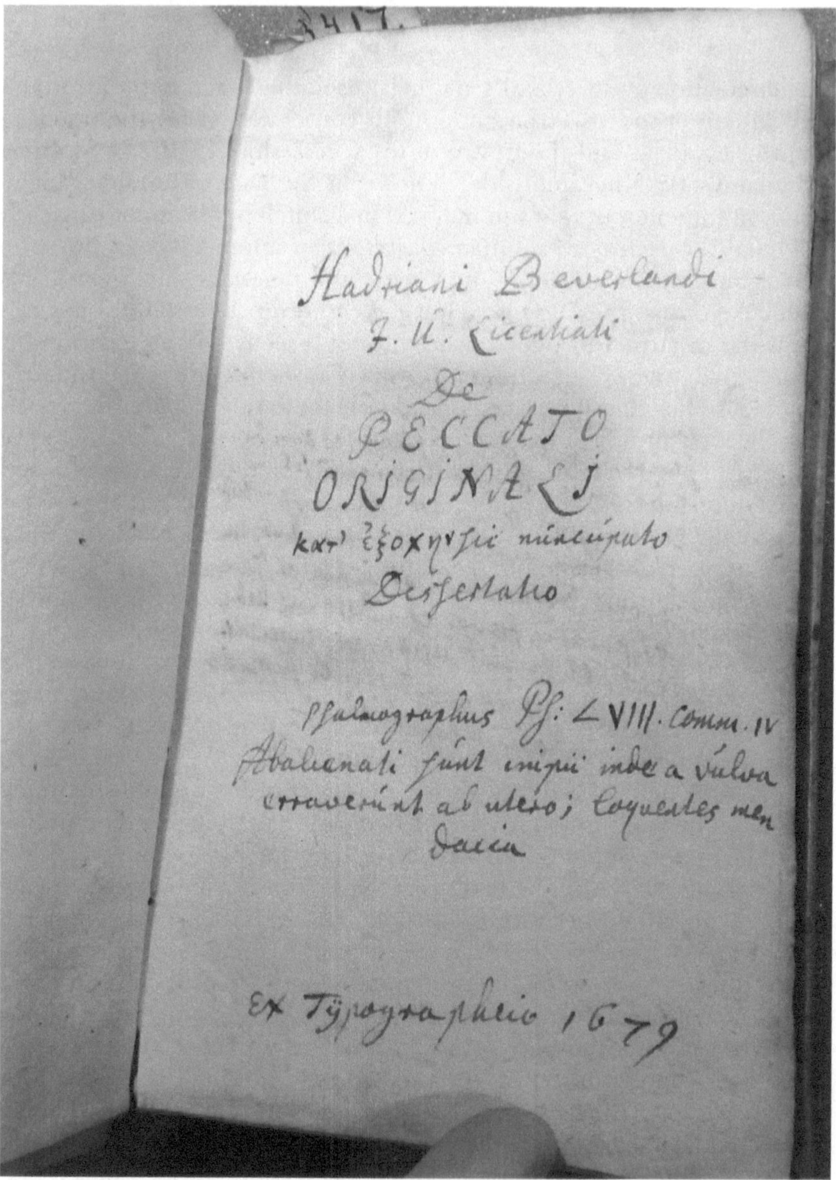

Hadriani Beverlandi
J. U. Licentiati
De
PECCATO
ORIGINALI
κατ' ἐξοχὴν sic nuncupato
Dissertatio

Psalmographus Ps: LVIII. Comm. IV
Abalienati sunt impii inde a vulva
erraverunt ab utero; loquentes men
dacia

Ex Typographeio 1679

Figure 7.3 Title page and page 51 of a manuscript version of the DPO, written by Beverland. It is preserved in the Royal Library of Copenhagen (GKS 3417 8 oktav).

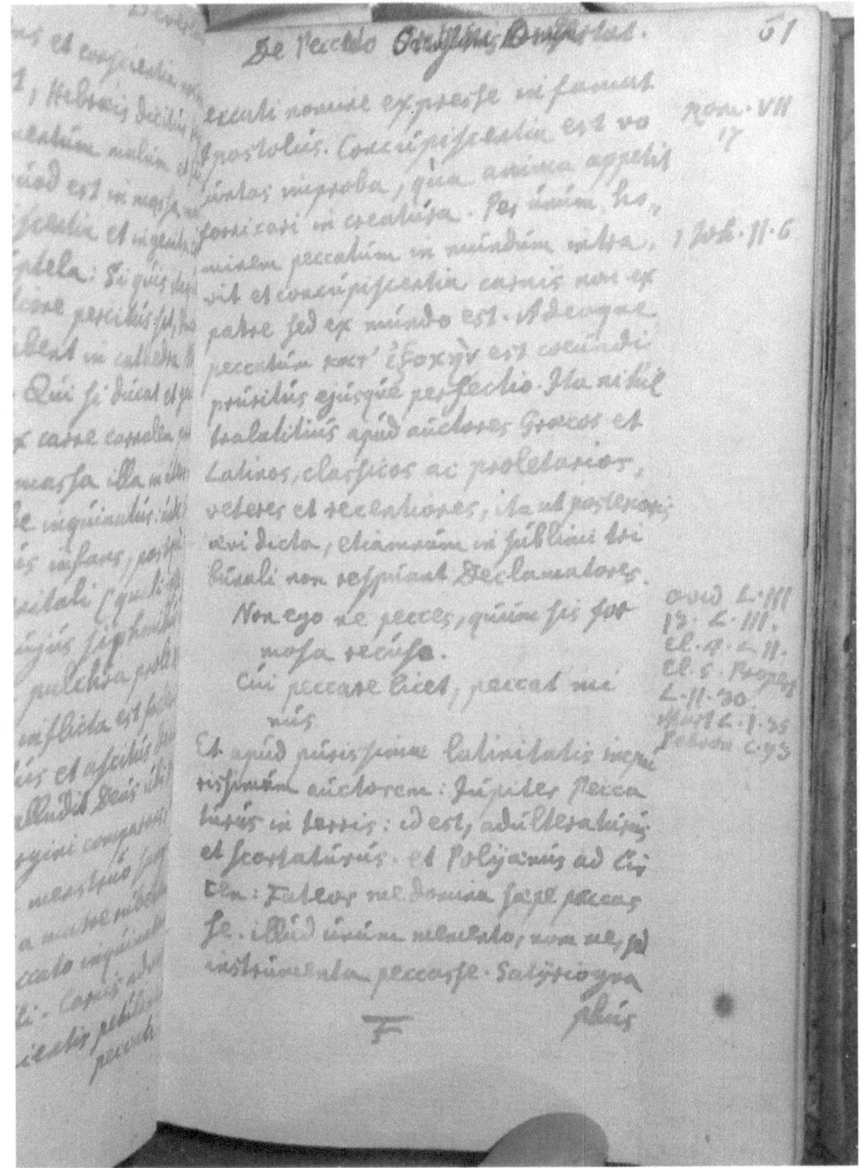

De Peccato [illegible]

[illegible] nomine expresse infamat
Apostolus. Concupiscentia est vo
luntas improba, qua anima appetit
fornicari in creatura. Per unum ho
minem peccatum in mundum intra
vit et concupiscentia carnis non ex
patre sed ex mundo est. Adeoque
peccatum κατ' ἐξοχὴν est coeundi
pruritus ejusque perfectio. Ita nihil
[illegible] apud auctores Graecos et
Latinos, classicos ac proletarios,
veteres et recentiores, [illegible]
[illegible]
[illegible] Declamatores.

Non ego ne pecces, quum sis for
mosa recuso.
Cui peccare licet, peccat mi
nus

Et apud purissimae latinitatis [illegible]
auctorem: Jupiter pecca
turus in terris: id est, adulteraturus
et scortaturus. Et Polyaenus ad Cir
cen: Fateor me, Domina, saepe peccas
se. Illud enim [illegible], non me, sed
instrumenta peccasse. Satyricon

Figure 7.3 Continued

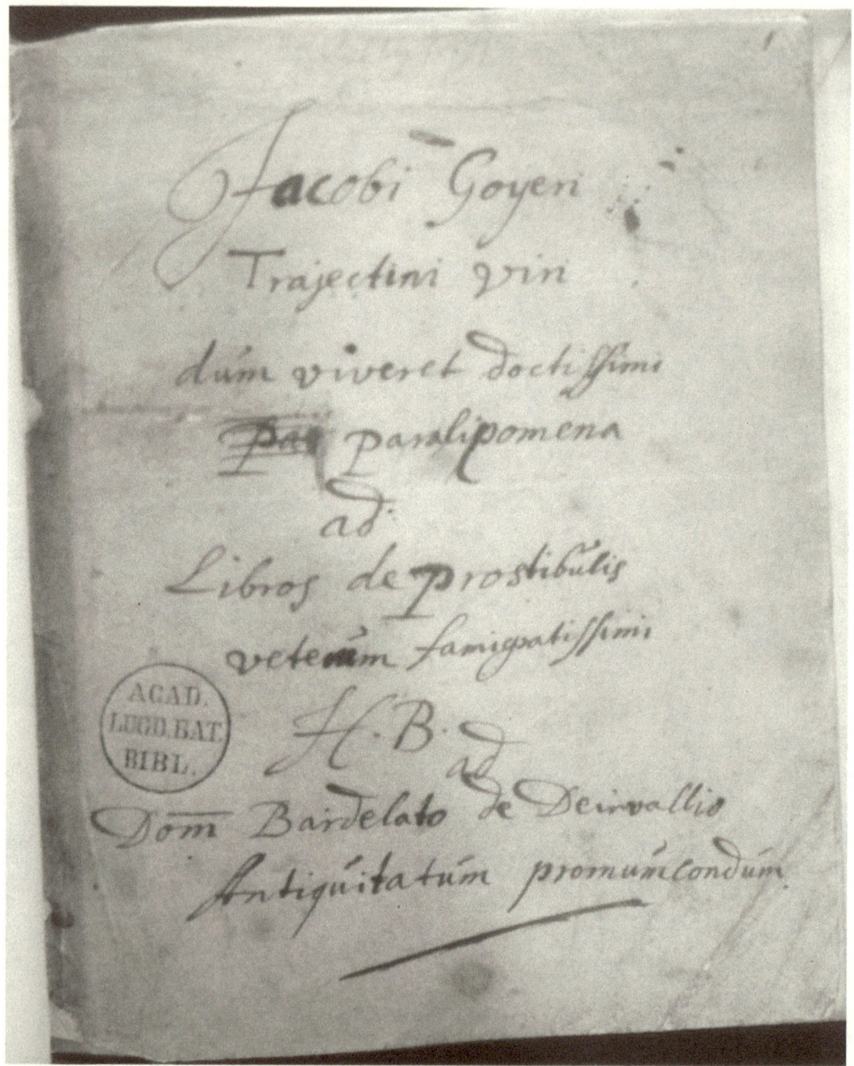

Jacobi Goyeri
Trajectini viri
dum viveret doctissimi
~~Par~~ paralipomena
ad
Libros de prostibulis
veterum famigeratissimi
H. B.
ad
Dom Bardelato de Deirvallio
Antiquitatum promumcondum

Figure 7.4 Title page and page 40 of the "Goyeri Paralipomena," which consists of summaries of and comments on chapters of the DPV. The text is preserved in the Library of the University of Leiden (BPL 1716).

Caput 10.

Fellatrices ad oris stuprum parata

Caput 11.

Quadrupes cum bestiis.

Dicit fabulas e quod dicantur coisse cum
avibus et capreis. illa esse intelligenda de
pene humano, qui vocatur coturnix hirundo
et Luscinia. ut passer lesbiae et [illegible]
columba [illegible] aves apponitur
mentula Mart. VII/13 Lux mea non capitur
nigris nec amoribus illis

Nec dominae pectus talia damna movent.
Scaliger interpretatur si mihi dederis basia
Catulliana dabo tibi elegans carmen non
minus argutum do quod de lesbiae passere
scripsit. passer deliciae carrionem hi sentiente
Pollionem et plagiarum vocat Scaliger cum
tamen et idem ante Scaligerum observarunt
partenius passeribus lusitasse puellas constat
ex Hiob. XL/24 Manibus totumque per orbem
Qui gestant caveat volucres ad jussa paratos,

Figure 7.4 Continued

manuscript of his DPO in September 1679, keep it to himself: "I demand urgently that not any mortal see this edition ... [especially] not Lord Graevius, because he will notify Gronovius, whom I trust less than the maid who cleans the toilet."[48]

But it is clear that however much he complained about the wide dispersal of his texts and the rumours surrounding his person and ideas, part of the blame falls on Beverland himself. The wide reception of his work on sex and sin and the extensive dispersal of his writings in European archives today belie his assurances to friends and foes that he intended his sexual studies to be read only by close colleagues.[49] His actions spoke louder than his words. François Halma (1653–1722), bookseller and printer in Utrecht, noted that when Beverland stayed in the city in the first months of 1680, "with his acquired skill in debauchery, in the company of unruly youth and in taverns, he threw his weight around in a peculiar way, boasting about his burned manuscript, as the most principal of his works, and revealing several parts of it, with great flamboyance and a smooth tongue."[50] Halma also recounted that Beverland showed off the title page of his DPV, which consisted of "a temple of Venus, or the inside of a Brothel, full of obscene behaviour, with [Beverland] himself sitting in the foreground with a whore on his lap. [Beverland] showed this image regularly to his intimates, with titillating delight."[51]

The wide dispersal of Beverland's manuscripts in the late 1670s, besides adding to his fame, drew strong criticism to the young scholar. This was precisely why he had circulated (parts of) his studies among members of his scholarly network: he counted on their guidance and commentary to improve his texts. But although he welcomed their critiques, it is doubtful that he anticipated their negative responses.[52] Exemplary is the reaction of Heinsius, one of his most important patrons. Heinsius had not liked the first edition of the DPO, and Beverland tried to address his patron's disapproval. "Because you urged me, from the kindness and affection of our heart towards an inexperienced and truly reckless protégé, to change my opinion, [while] they [urged me to do so] because of the ambition and arrogance of their obligation. I will make sure that in the second edition all that causes offence is expunged, so that a castrate comes forth to please the decrepit sons of the Stoics."[53] He hoped Heinsius would endorse his DPV,[54] but as it turned out, he failed to gain his patron's approval for the work: "From the bottom of my heart, it would please me to present [my three books of the DPV] to you, the solace and sole sanctuary of those who devote themselves to studies, if I did not already know that you would not like them."[55] And despite

Beverland's efforts to improve the text of the DPO, in the end Graevius too condemned his studies. In a letter to Heinsius, Graevius stated that he considered the DPO a most disgusting work: "And truly it must be deplored that such filthy and impious books are published and tolerated in these lands."[56]

The wide dispersal of his manuscripts meant that Beverland did not just receive harsh criticism from his inner circle. Members of the Dutch Reformed Church in particular denounced the DPO for its obscene and profane contents. Theologian and preacher David Knibbe (1639–1701) wrote to Beverland in the spring of 1679[57] that "[a]ll preachers and [even] those who have but a very small bit of piety in their heart must condemn your treatise as deeply harmful and scandalous."[58] Knibbe warned Beverland that a number of theologians were planning to take action against him and advised him to direct his talents towards more pious themes.[59] In letters to friends Beverland often discussed the harsh critiques launched at him by Dutch theologians.[60] For instance, he wrote to Heinsius in September 1679 that orthodox theologian Johannes Vollenhove (1631–1708) had told secular authorities "that I am irreligious and an atheist, and he has even demanded that the first edition [of the DPO] should be burned."[61]

Taken aback by the comments he was receiving from friends and foes, Beverland decided against publishing the DPV for the time being.[62] He was determined, however, to refute the lies going around about his studies and therefore edited the text of the DPO. "Even I know myself what should be done to the book," he explained to Heinsius. "I am not so drunk on hellebore nor so irreconcilable due to prejudices that I would object to being taught by others who know better."[63] Early in 1679 he published the work anew: "Everything that seemed too harsh and rustic in the first publication I have erased and reworked, even to the extent that I have written new material."[64] While the second edition of the DPO differed from the first, with Beverland paying some attention to the critiques of his friends, his main argument on sex and sin remained the same. He refused to appease the majority of his critics, specifically those who did not belong to his group of close friends. Many of these "censors" were ignorant men, he argued, who disapproved of his studies based on hearsay; and regarding those who had actually read the work, their reproach showed that they had not understood his argument at all. With his second edition Beverland intended to convince all of the validity of his theory of sexual desire.[65] Despite his alterations – for example, he deleted some obscene quotations and provocative passages – the second DPO might be considered even more rebellious than the first. For instance, he added a *Pia Meditatio* in which he asked God to free him from the priestly hate of Dutch theologians and stated that he hoped the eloquence and honesty of his work would expose their hypocrisy.[66]

"I was afraid that a second edition of your treatise might incite fresh commotion at the wrong moment and that it, to some extent, could open wounds, which were already closed. But the die is cast."[67] Heinsius wrote thus to Beverland in September 1679. Beverland had changed the text of his DPO but had failed to convince his audience. The publication of the second edition had serious and immediate consequences: concluding that Beverland's "filthy" study would cause more trouble, deputies of the Dutch Reformed Church informed the States of Holland about his "horrible and offensive" book. After discussing Beverland's works, the States of Holland decided that the University of Leiden should take action. Beverland was arrested in October, tried in November, and banished in December 1679 by the academic court in Leiden. His DPO was banned, he had to hand over the DPV manuscript, and he was exiled from the provinces of Holland and Zeeland.[68]

Conclusion

Much more can be said about Beverland and his clandestine manuscripts, in relation to his own scholarship and in the intellectual context of the Dutch Republic and England in the last decades of the seventeenth century. The story of Beverland's two texts demonstrates the importance of the circulation of manuscripts for the dissemination of early Enlightenment ideas; it also highlights the precarious balance between toleration and censorship in the Republic of Letters. Beverland's contention that sexual lust was the original sin bothered Dutch theologians, but it was his broader philosophy on sexual liberty that got him into serious trouble. By highlighting the importance of sex in history, focusing on biblical passages but mainly on ancient literature, he aimed to address the problem of lust in contemporary society. He proposed a radical solution to the gap between the exalted doctrine of the Calvinist Dutch Reformed Church, which restricted all sexual activity to matrimony, and the depraved morality of seventeenth-century Dutch society, in which premarital sex was broadly tolerated, prostitution was on the steady increase in cities, and the market for pornography was flourishing. Beverland's solution – greater sexual liberty for the male elite – was accompanied by calls for practical adjustments to Dutch policies: he for instance commented on the benefits of legalizing prostitution, which would provide an outlet for lustful men while keeping honourable women safe. This liberal philosophy regarding sex, which could not be tolerated in the Republic of Letters in the late seventeenth century, would become the central argument of the eighteenth-century adaptations of Beverland's works, which enjoyed great popularity in France and Germany.

Looking at the circulation of Beverland's manuscripts in the late 1670s, we can first conclude that in the period leading up to his banishment, the DPO and DPV were eagerly read by and exchanged among scholars in the Dutch Republic in different forms. Beverland shared his manuscripts with members of his inner circle, on whom he counted for feedback on his work, and he altered his texts and his strategies for publication in response to the reception of his studies. It is clear that the circulation of manuscripts was of vital importance for the dissemination of heterodox ideas in the underground circles of the early Enlightenment of the late seventeenth century; that said, the relationship between circulation and the development of these ideas must not be underestimated. The two editions of the DPO published in 1678 and 1679 were directly influenced by the feedback Beverland received from his inner circle and the wider public. Friends and colleagues read the manuscript and sent it back with comments, and their criticisms impacted the content and composition of the DPO. Due to the negative response to his DPV in its unprinted form, Beverland decided against publishing the work. In the end, his master's thesis was never printed. As part of his sentence, he handed in an unfinished copy of the first book to the University of Leiden in 1680.[69] He did send copies of all three volumes to England, yet he abandoned the project in the course of the 1680s.[70] During his exile in England, Beverland played an important role in the circulation of texts. His correspondence indicates he was a central figure in the exchange of manuscripts between English, Dutch, and French scholars. Being in close contact with many of the major players in the field, he functioned as an intermediary, who received and dispatched, copied and summarized, bought and sold manuscripts, prints, and books for his friends and colleagues.[71]

Beverland's banishment highlights the crucial distinction between public and private, between the underground circulation of manuscripts and the public dissemination of texts, in the eyes of early modern scholars. The same scholars who considered Beverland to be a talented, erudite, promising scholar on the basis of his sexual manuscripts denounced his scholarship and rejected his works after he published them. Over the course of the 1670s, Beverland sent around his erotic encyclopaedia without getting into trouble. His inner circle actually seemed to enjoy reading his works, sent him additional materials, and commented freely on his style and content. Yet as soon as Beverland mentioned publishing his studies, things changed: his colleagues strongly discouraged him from publishing on the topic of sex, arguing that printing his ideas would only bring him trouble. After the publication of his works, during his trial and exile, most of Beverland's humanist friends abandoned him. Heinsius had supported his young patron with advice for years, yet he disapproved of the publication of the DPV. In the private collection of classical scholar Graevius a handwritten version of the DPO can be found today, yet in 1679 Graevius told everyone who wanted to hear it that he despised Beverland's work on sex and sin. And the first book of the DPV, which Beverland publicly surrendered to the rector of the University of Leiden, Friedrich Spanheim, was not burned, as the prosecutor of the student court had pleaded during the trial; instead, Spanheim preserved the copy in his private collection.[72]

Beverland himself was well aware of this paradox between private encouragement and public denunciation, and he observed it with great frustration. He criticized his scholarly friends and humanist colleagues for their hypocrisy and insincerity. In a letter sent from jail in 1679, he wrote to his friend De Goyer: "the stupid herd believes in investing their strength not in their erudition but in their wealth ... I do not doubt that if all honourable men became acquainted with supporting themselves with bread and polenta instead of the insult of wealth (like Dodwell in England), adorned with the scanty persistence of frugality, they would actually be able to debate with the gods themselves."[73]

NOTES

1 "Constitui enim brevi typis mandare libros tres De Prostibulis Veterum... arduum hoc negotium stylo haud committerem, nisi temeritati meae veniam promitteret tua humanitas ac innata comitas ... Tu autem, eruditorum Ilias, cum solus conatibus nostris opitulari posses, precor ut eorum adiutor esse haud dedigneris," in Beverland to Nicolaas Heinsius, 15/10/1678, from Beverland's Correspondence with Nicolaas Heinsius, Library of the University of Leiden, Burm. F 6a, letter no. 2. This collection of letters is hereafter referred to as EH.

2 He asked friends for their criticism on the content and style of his manuscripts and inquired after additional material. Many epistles in the "Epistolae Tullianae" collection (letters from Beverland to different friends, sent between 1679 and 1685, preserved in the Library of the University of Leiden, BPL 204, hereafter ET) attest to this, as do EH 1, 11/02/1678; EH 2, 15/10/1678. For more on the ET collection, see R. de Smet, "Epistolae Tullianae. Brieven van Hadriaan Beverland," *De Gulden Passer*, 64, 65, 68 (1986, 1987, 1990): 83–124, 70–101, 139–67.

3 Beverland, his works, and his banishment are discussed in great detail in my PhD thesis: K.E. Hollewand, "The Banishment of Beverland: Sex, Scripture, and Scholarship in the Seventeenth-Century Dutch Republic" (PhD diss., Oxford University, 2016), which was published by Brill as *The Banishment of Beverland: Sex, Sin, and Scholarship in the Seventeenth-Century Dutch Republic* (Leiden: Brill, 2019). This thesis will hereafter be referred to as Hollewand, 2016.

4 For more on Beverland's life, see Hollewand, 2016, 40–60, 283–97; K.E. Hollewand, "Hadriaan Beverland (1650–1716)," *Oxford Dictionary of National Biography* (Oxford: Oxford University Press, 2017).

5 Beverland's *De Peccato Originali* (DPO) was published in Leiden in three different editions in 1678 and 1679 (see n15). His work on women, *De Stolatae Virginitatis iure Lucubratio Academica*, was published in Leiden in 1679. Beverland's "De Prostibulis Veterum" (DPV) originally consisted of three books (see n18).

6 For more on Beverland's argument and studies, see Hollewand, 2016.

7 For the discussions of Beverland's studies by the Dutch Reformed Church and the States of Holland, see Hollewand, 2016, 49–51; W.P.C. Knuttel, ed., *Acta der particuliere synoden van Zuid-Holland 1621–1700* (The Hague: Instituut voor Nederlandse Geschiedenis, 1908–16), vol. 5, 283, 321–2, 495; "Resoluties van de Staten van Holland en West-Friesland," National Archive of the Netherlands, 1679–1727, 851.

8 For more on his trial, see Hollewand, 2016, 50–60, 317; National Archive of the Netherlands, Vierschaar der Universiteit te Leiden, Crimineele klachtboeken, 1631–1810, pt 13, Litt. E, 1647–95, 115r–116d.

9 For more on his services for Vossius and Sloane, see Beverland's correspondence with both as preserved in the British Library (Sloane MSS 1985, 3963, 3395, 4042) and in the Library of the University of Amsterdam (MS OTM: hs. E 10: a-u; E127).

10 See Hollewand, 2016, 285–8.

11 H. Beverland, *De Fornicatione Cavenda Admonitio Sive adhortatio ad Pudicitiam at Castitatem* (London: Christopher Bateman, 1697, 1698). See R. de

Smet, "Hadrian Beverland's De Fornicatione Cavenda: an adhortatio ad pudicitiam or an ad impudicitiam?," *Éros et Priapus: érotisme et obscénité dans la littérature néo-latine,* ed. I. de Smet and P. Ford, Cahiers d'Humanisme et Renaissance, 51 (Geneva: Droz, 1997), 113–39.

12 J.F. Bernard published the first of these: *Histoire de l'état de l'homme dans le péché originel* (Paris: n.p. 1714). This edition was followed by French and German alterations. See Hollewand, 2016, 304–6, 324.

13 For more on Beverland's exile and the last years of his life, see Hollewand, 2016, 283–97.

14 Biographies of Beverland have been printed in the Netherlands, Germany, France, and England since the early eighteenth century. For an overview of these, see R. de Smet, *Hadrianus Beverlandus (1650–1716): non unus e multis peccator: studie over het leven en werk van Hadriaan Beverland, Verhandelingen van de Koninklijke Academie voor Wetenschappen, Letteren en Schone Kunsten van Belgie. Klasse der Letteren,* 50, no. 126 (Brussels: Paleis der Academien, 1988), 9–14; E.J. Dingwall, *Very Peculiar People: Portrait Studies in the Queer, the Abnormal, and the Uncanny* (London: Rider, 1962), 169–72. In the twentieth century, Beverland's works have been studied by a handful of scholars, yet the circulation of his manuscripts has been a relatively unexplored subject.

15 The first edition, *Peccatum Originale,* was printed in 1678, the second edition, *De Peccato Originali,* followed in the late summer of 1679, and *Poma Amoris,* the third edition, was published during Beverland's trial in October or November 1679. Unfortunately, no copies of the third edition have been preserved. See: Hollewand, 2016, 47–53, 324–6.

16 "devorantibus oculis virguncula, cujus lateri haerebat lethalis arundo, arborem tentam, summopere desiderabilem, sexui suo aptam gratamque contemplata, protervaque fronte maritum petens, ejusque cervicem amplexu invadens, & non repugnanti oscula fingens, ferratoque morsu nunc crus nunc lacertos vexans, manuque improba & blandis, digitos habentibus, dictis innocentissimam sollicitans partem, Risit & immunda tractando virilia palma, His quoque furta placent, *conjux ait, utere donis, Quae natura dedit: nec sum tam tetrica, quales Sensi ignes, damnem.*" In DPO 1679, ch. VI, 29–30. Quotation from J. Barclay, *Euphormionis [Lusinini] Satyricon* (Amsterdam: Schmidlinus, 1629), vol. 5, 442.

17 "Nostram sententiam Dei eloquiis magis congruam conscientia & lux cordis docuit. & in proprio vase quisque nullum adeo vehemens & frequens ubicunque sentiet reperietque, vitium." In DPO 1679, ch. XI, 58.

18 Beverland composed the three books of his "De Prostibulis Veterum" in the 1670s. Today only an unfinished copy of the first book, which he handed over to the University of Leiden as part of his sentence, has been preserved

(see n70 and n71). The contents of all books were described at the time, however, in a manuscript titled "Goyeri Paralipomena" (see n40 and n41). For more on the DPV manuscript, see R. de Smet, *Hadriani Barlandi (Hadriaan Beverland) "De prostibulis veterum": een kritische uitgave met inleiding en commentaar van het handschrift BPL 1994* (PhD diss., Vrije Universiteit Brussel, 3 vols, Brussels: Peeters, 1984); R. de Smet, "The Realm of Venus"; "Hadriani Barlandi" [H. Beverland], "De Prostibulis Veterum," MS Leiden BPL 1994, *Quaerendo* 17, no. 1 (1987): 45–58.

19 The second book of the DPV was not preserved, but its contents were summarized in "Goyeri Paralipomena" (see n40 and n41).

20 These collections of Beverland's notes are preserved in the British Library, London ("Crepundia Lugdunensia," Add MS 30384), and the Bodleian Library, Oxford ("Inscriptiones singulares hactenus ineditae," MS D'Orville 540).

21 For more on the images Beverland collected, see the manuscripts cited in n20 and Hollewand, 2016, 243–57; J. Zelen, "Blinded by Curiosity: Hadriaan Beverland (1650–1716) and His Radical Use of the Printed Image," (PhD diss., Radboud University, Nijmegen, forthcoming 2019).

22 For more on Beverland's social network, see Hollewand, 2016, 40–60, 141–8, 200–10, 283–97.

23 For more on Nicolaas Heinsius (1620–1681), see F.F. Blok, *Nicolaas Heinsius in dienst van Christina van Zweden* (PhD diss., University of Leiden, Delft: Ursulapers, 1949); J. Papy, "Heinsius, Nicolaus," in *Brill's New Pauly: Encyclopaedia of the Ancient World*, ed. H. Cancik, H. Schneider, and M. Landfester, trans. C.F. Salazar and F.G. Gentry (Leiden: Brill, 2002), Supplements I, vol. 6.

24 For more on Gronovius (1645–1716), see B.J. Blok and P.C. Molhuysen, eds, *Nieuw Nederlandsch biografisch woordenboek* (10 vols, Leiden: Israel, 1911–37), vol. 1, 986–7; W.J.J.C. Bijleveld, "Het geslacht Gronovius," *De Nederlandsche Leeuw*, 60, 1942, 95–109; Papy, "Gronovius, Johannes Fredericus," *Brill's New Pauly*, Supplements I, vol. 6.

25 For more on Graevius (1632–1703), see Blok and Molhuysen, *Nieuw Nederlandsch biografisch woordenboek*, vol. 2, 669–70; J. Leonhardt, "Graevius, Johann Georg," *Brill's New Pauly*, Supplements I, vol. 6.

26 See the references in n2.

27 "Etiamque tuae inhaerere menti sermones nostros Hagae reciprocatos nullus dubito, ubi inter otia benignitas tua recondita arcanaque mihi suppedi[ta]turam spoponderat, cum crudas ingenii… digressiones De Prostibulis Veterum tuo iudicio κριτικωτάτῳ submisissem, ut in iis [s] phalmata asterisci nota indicares et, si quid errassem aut omisissem, signa

novis poneres praeceptis." In Beverland to Jacobus Gronovius, 12/12/1676, from Beverland's Correspondence with Jacobus Gronovius, University Library of Munich, 2e Cod. Misc. 627, letter no. 1. This collection of letters is hereafter referred to as EG.

28 "Denique mastrupatorum, frictricum, fellatorum ac labdarum, cunnilinguorum, cinaedorum pariter ac pathicorum similiumque execrandarum divisionum brutorumque sodomitorum catalogum mihi exhibere facile poteris." In EH 1, 11/2/1678. See also EH 2, 15/10/1678; EH 13, 29/6/1681.

29 "De frictricibus lesbiatoribus Cynaedis si quaedam in adversariis habeas, eadem opera transmittas subnixe peto." In EG 1, 12/12/1676.

30 As Beverland claimed in ET 2, 28/04/1679, to Molenaer; ET 10, 1679, to Heinsius.

31 See the references in n2 and sources cited in the notes below.

32 See ET 3, 1679, to Gronovius; ET 4, 1679, to Graevius.

33 "Iam totus sum in ingenioli abortum lambendo, horridioremque quam ex celeritate contraxerat, emolliendo locutionem ... Redolet haec editio hircum: secunda Veneres spirabit elegantiores." In ET 5, 1679, to Graevius. See also his other letters in the "Epistolae Tullianae" collection (see n2).

34 See his discussions in, for example, ET 3, Gronovius, 1/6/1679; ET 7, Heinsius, 1679; EH 13, 29/06/1681.

35 "Flosculis nitere, sententiolis lascivire, subindeque turgescere adolescentum, est. Magis expeditam animi mei vim exsequor, quoties veteris scriptoris sententiam in suffragium adopto." In ET 5, 1679, to Graevius.

36 "Gratissima mihi fuit tua instructio eritque eo gratior quo crebrior ..." In ET 4, 1679, to Graevius.

37 His correspondence reveals that he sent editions of his DPO to, among others, Nicolaas Heinsius (see EH 4, 9/1679; EH 8, 8/10/1679, and ET 10, 1679, to Heinsius); Isaac Vossius (see ET 8, 1679, to Vossius); and Nicolaas Blanckaert, professor in history at the University of Franeker and a friend of Beverland (see ET 11, 7/7/1679, to Blanckaert).

38 "Quamquam infinitis propemodum obruar vuris negotiisque quae in causa sunt quominus te de scripto hoc publicando potuerim consulere, nolui tamen te iam impressi ac vulgari schedii exsortem permanere." In ET 2, 28/4/1679, to Molenaer.

39 The text is preserved in the Royal Library Copenhagen (GKS 3417 8 oktav).

40 The manuscript is preserved in the Special Collections of the University of Leiden, BPL 1716.

41 For more on this manuscript, see De Smet, "The Realm of Venus," 50–1; De Smet, *Hadrianus Beverlandus,* 98–104.

42 The work was for instance discussed by the Dutch Reformed Church, the States of Holland, in a student's notebook, and in a Dutch pamphlet (see nn7, 43, 45). Beverland himself discussed the commotion around his work in, for instance, EH 13, 1681; EG 8, 12/11/1685; DPO 1679, letter to De Goyer, A7r, B2r.

43 *Lof-Digt ter eeren van Mr. Adriaan Beverlant* (1679). De Smet has argued that the poem was probably written by Johan van Baelen, or Jan van Balen, a lawyer in The Hague who assisted Beverland during his trial. See De Smet, *Hadrianus Beverlandus,* 42–3.

44 The DPV and DPO were usually mentioned together, in, for instance, the documents discussed in nn7, 43, 45, 58.

45 "ex beverland, arbor in paradiso erat mentula Adami porrectus ab inguine palus, nam Deus nolebat homines propagare per copulam carnalem, bene gnarus ex coitu omnia mala provenire ...," in Utrecht University Library, ms 1284. See P. Steenbakkers, J. Touber, and J.M.M. van de Ven, "A Clandestine Notebook (1678–79) on Spinoza, Beverland, Politics, the Bible and Sex: Utrecht UL, ms. 1284," *Lias* 39 (2011): 225–365.

46 See DPO 1679, letter to De Goyer, A7r.

47 "Non bene consuluisti honori meo, mi Graevi, quod fabellas nostras Milesias ad Magliabequium miseris adhuc calentes. Perculit aures nostras rumor eas in ipsius Pontificis Max[imi] pervenisse manus. Quam vellem te inhibuisse hoc tuum propositum usque dum editio secunda...," in ET 5, 1679, to Graevius.

48 "Hanc editionem flagito ne quisquam mortalium videat ... Nec Dom[inus] Graevius, quia notificaret Gronovio, cui non magis fido quam ancilla, quae latrinam lavat," in EH 4, 09/1679.

49 See, for his excuses, ET 2, 28/04/1679, to Molenaer; ET 3, 01/06/1679, to Gronovius; ET 4, 1679, Graevius; ET 8, 1679, to Vossius; ET 14, 15/10/1679, to Heinsius; ET 21, 11/1679, to De Goyer.

50 "met zijne ingezoge kundigheit van ontucht, in gezelschappen van onbandige jongelingen, en herbergen, wonderlijk den baas speelde, breedt opgaf van zijn verbrandt handschrift, als het hoofdtstuk zyner werken, en daar uit verscheide stukken, met veel zwiers, en eene gladde tonge, opsneedt," in F. Halma, *Tooneel der Vereenighde Nederlanden en onderhoorige landschappen* (Leeuwarden: Hendrik Halma, 1725), 135.

51 "De Tyteltekening hadde hy ook van dit werk bewaart, zynde een Venustempel, of Bordeel van binnen, vol ontuchtig gebaar, waar in hy zelf op den voorgrondt zat met eene hoer op zyn schoot: welke tekening hy dan

menigmaal, met een kittelend genoegen, aan zyne vertrouwelingen onder doogen bragt," in Halma, *Tooneel*, 135.

52 Beverland comments on and responds to these negative reactions from friends and family in letters of his ET collection (see n2).

53 "Tu enim ex animi candore et amore erga inexpertum adeoque et temerarium clientem, illi ex muneris ambitione et arrogantia me compulere ut sententiam mutaverim. Curabo in editione secunda, ut offendicula expungantur utque castratus in exoletorum Stoicidarum gratiam prodeat," in EH 3a, 08/07/1679. With the "exoletorum Stoicidarum" Beverland referred to the Dutch theologians, who had most harshly criticized his works.

54 See EH 2, 15/10/1678 (this line is quoted in n1).

55 "Hos ex animi candore tibi, studiis dicatorum solamen ac asylum unicum, offerrem lubens, si non ingratos fore praescirem," in EH 2, 15/10/1678.

56 "Et sane dolendum est tam foedos ac prophanos libros in his terris publicari ac tolerari ...," in Letter Graevius to Heinsius, n.d., in P. Burman, *Sylloges Epistolarum*, Part IV (Leiden: Samuel Luchtman, 1727), 598.

57 David Knibbe (1639–1701), who studied at the same Latin School as Beverland and his brother in Middelburg, was probably an old acquaintance of Beverland. For more on Knibbe, see J. van Eijnatten and F. van Lieburg, *Nederlandse Religiegeschiedenis* (Hilversum: Verloren, 2005, 2006), 218; J.P. Bie and J. Loosjes, eds, *Biographisch woordenboek van protestantsche godgeleerden in Nederland* (6 vols, The Hague: M. Nijhoff, 1919–49) vol. 5, 55–8.

58 "Alle de predicanten en die maer een graentje godsalicheyt in't hert overhebben moeten u tractaet seer schadelyck en schandelyk keuren," in Knibbe to Beverland, 07/1679, EH 3b.

59 See Knibbe to Beverland, 07/1679, EH 3b. See also EH 3a, 08/07/1679.

60 See ET 4, 1679, to Graevius, and other letters in the ET collection (see n2).

61 "Dom[inus] Vollenhoven patriae proceribus retulit me impium et atheum adeoque petiit ut scriptum istud primum Vulcano mancipetur, sed facili negotio illud omen a me avertam," in EH 7, 15/9/1679.

62 He discussed this with his friends in, for instance, ET 37, 03–1680, to Gelder; ET 38, 03/1680, to Godin; EH 10, 11/02/1680.

63 "Quid fieri libro debeat, ipse moneo. Non adeo sum veratro ebrius nec praeiudiciis irreconciliabilis, ut meliora ab aliis doceri recusarem," in EH 3a, 08/07/1679.

64 "Quaecunque in prima nimis acre et rustice videbantur typis mandata, ea litura expunxi, ita tamen ut nova debuerim perarare, si iustus saltem libellus manibus teri posset," in EH 5, 18/07/1679.

65 He explained this in DPO, Letter De Goyer; EH 7, 07/10/1679; and in other letters written in 1679 (see the ET and EH correspondences, referred to in nn 1, 2).

66 See DPO 1679, Pia Meditatio, N6r.

67 "Altera scripti tui editio ne novos excitaret fluctus et vulnus iam quoddammodo obductum rescinderet parum tempestive metuebam. Sed iam iacta est alea," in Heinsius to Beverland, 12/09/1679, EH 6b.

68 See nn 7, 8.

69 This the only part of the DPV that has been preserved and can today be found in the Library of the University of Leiden (BPL 1994). See nn 18, 71.

70 What happened to his own copies of the work is unknown: Beverland states in different letters that he sent it back to the Dutch Republic, that he gave parts of the work to friends, but also that he threw it in the fire. See: Hollewand, 2016, 284, 316; De Smet, *Hadrianus Beverlandus*, 104–7.

71 See the references in nn 9, 10, 13.

72 For more on the changed attitudes of Beverland's friends and the role their abandonment played in his banishment, see Hollewand, 2016, esp. 200–11.

73 "Quae assentatio effecit ut bruta illa Armenta putaverint virtutem non in eruditione sed in divitiis consistere ... Certe si didicissent viri boni pane et polenta contra fortunae insultus se tueri (ut in Anglia Dodwellus) iam patientia parcae frugalitatis ornati, ipsis etiam diis controversiam facere potuissent," in ET 21, 11/1679, to De Goyer. For more on Beverland's frustration regarding the hypocrisy and dishonesty of his contemporaries, see Hollewand, 2016, 257–82.

PART FOUR

CLANDESTINITY AND THE ENLIGHTENMENT

Chapter Eight

The Style and Form of Heterodoxy: John Toland's *Nazarenus* and *Pantheisticon*

WHITNEY MANNIES

In 1711, Joseph Addison narrated a short episode about John Toland (1670–1722) in *The Spectator*. Laying on his deathbed, Toland uncharacteristically requests a curate to hear his confession.[1] Toland is penitent: his works subverted religion and belief in God, he admits, and, sadly, they will continue to do so long after his death. The curate, however, reassures him: your cause is so weak, your books are so poorly argued, and what is more, only your friends and acquaintances read them anyway, so there is no real danger of doing any mischief. Toland, whom Addison reports "had still so much the frailty of an author in him," is galled back to health, sends away the curate, and indignantly asks his friends "where they had picked up such a blockhead."

Addison's story is obviously apocryphal, but Toland, a top-notch manufacturer of apocrypha in his own right, probably had it coming. In any case, Addison's pithy Whiggish sarcasm succeeds in getting to the heart of the matter: How influential was Toland? Did anyone actually take his books seriously? Did his influence travel via a radical, clandestine network of friends, or was he also, as Justin Champion argues, "mainstream"?[2]

I consider the perspective, elaborated by Champion, that Toland's influence on mainstream culture lay in his ability to appropriate the style and form of religious knowledge, with the consequence that he was also able to appropriate the authority of religion for his own, heterodox works. This perspective on language and power echoes Pierre Bourdieu, who argues that linguistic practices reflect and reproduce social power.[3] Successful institutions, he argues, establish and maintain linguistic practices that symbolically reproduce power. Replicating the linguistic practices of dominant institutions (such as the Church or the State) allows a speaker or author to arrogate to herself the legitimacy and authority of those institutions. For example, when scholars speak and write with footnoted historical objectivity, they communicate more than just content – they convey the authority of the university, and thus their own status as an authoritative knowledge-creator.

This Bourdieuan perspective on language and social power is reflected in other scholarship on the clandestine literature as well. Jean-Pierre Cavaillé, for example, has argued that libertinism emerged in the sixteenth and seventeenth centuries as a *culture philosophique* that managed to overcome Christianity, not merely by providing alternative beliefs, but also by providing alternative practices and forms of knowledge.[4] If libertine philosophy succeeded, it was because it created an alternative culture – a social basis that could operate as a "mode de vie et mode de connaissance affranchis de la sujétion aux religions institueés."[5] The practices and forms of knowledge – the *mode de connaissance* – are conveyed, in part, through style and form. Because style and form can be deployed for subversive ends, it is arguably a more salient topic with regard to the clandestine *corpus* than with mainstream texts.

I consider Champion's perspective – that Toland was adept at appropriating the style and form of religious knowledge and was therefore able to appropriate the authority of religion for his own works – with respect to two of Toland's texts that pursued heterodox ends through conservative means. *Nazarenus* (1718)[6] and *Pantheisticon: or, the Form of Celebrating the Socratic-Society* (1720)[7] assumed the form of biblical criticism and liturgy, respectively. Was Toland successful in attaching his own texts to the legitimating discourses of his day, as Champion argues? Do these texts demonstrate that dominant discursive forms – and the authority they confer – are vulnerable to appropriation, even by the most heterodox of content?

Based on the content of these texts and the responses they received, I suggest that taking on the style and form of orthodoxy can only take an author so far. The responses to *Nazarenus* were uniformly negative; apparently, employing the form of (or masquerading as?) biblical criticism was insufficient as a tactic to appear as a credible voice in the dominant, Christian discourse. *Nazarenus,* I argue, did not *appropriate* so much as it *exposed* the facile nature of biblical criticism and ecclesiastical authority while promoting individual reason as an alternative authority. Likewise, *Pantheisticon* did not successfully appropriate the divine authority of a dominant discourse by employing a liturgical style. Instead, I argue that *Pantheisticon* was a genuine attempt to get back to the foundational and benevolent purpose of liturgy: the notion that society is an indispensable element of reason. If these texts succeeded, it was not, as Champion would argue, because they were able to navigate and appropriate the linguistic tactics of the dominant discourses of Church and State. Rather, if these texts were successful at all, it was because they were able to latch on to or even construct an alternative basis for authoritative knowledge.

When grafted onto heterodox content, styles and forms that normally act as a symbolic indicator of the legitimacy and authority of a text might import that legitimacy and authority as well; if readers treat the text as legitimate and authoritative, or at least seriously grapple with the text's claims, we might reasonably infer that the orthodox style and form successfully fulfilled their symbolic function. If, on the other hand, a heterodox text fails to convince or elicit serious response despite its orthodox style and form, we might reasonably find that there is a limit to the ability of style and form to perform this symbolic function.

Background

John Toland was born in Ireland in 1670 in humble circumstances. He died in England in 1722 in still humbler ones. In between, he was educated in Glasgow and Oxford before moving to the Netherlands and falling in with a radical set that revolved around Benjamin Furly's well-stocked library. Returning to England, Toland embarked on a career as a radical and prolific contrarian after his first major work, *Christianity Not Mysterious* (1696), provoked scandalized responses. Throughout his life, Toland corresponded with royalty, the Whig elite,[8] and influential thinkers of his generation; he was a polarizing figure among his contemporaries, who described him as a libertine, atheist, freethinker, pantheist, and Spinozist. Voltaire would later describe Toland as a principled radical: if only he'd been more moderate, the impoverished Toland could have made a fortune, but instead he chose to vociferously oppose Christianity's hate and vengeance.[9] Whatever one thought of his ideas, Toland's poverty at least testified to his sincerity.

His success was not primarily due to the originality of his thought.[10] Incredibly well read, Toland excelled at packaging elite scholarship in ways that reflected the concerns and literary style of the public sphere, and it was primarily by repopularizing and adapting the ideas of earlier, mid-seventeenth-century republican authors such as James Harrington, Algernon Sidney, and John Milton that Toland had political impact.[11] Toland was influential in part because he was able to employ different literary styles and forms, tailoring his rhetoric to suit different social milieux.[12] Rhetorical style and form was, for Toland, a means to negotiate the social milieux in which he sought influence.

The legitimating discourses of Toland's own day were those of orthodox Protestantism and the State, and the fact that the State's relationship to religious authority was being vigorously contested at this time only presented Toland with a greater opportunity to appropriate and challenge the dominant legitimating discourses with his own heterodox interventions.[13] Christianity was the hegemonic authority to which knowledge had to conform if it were to be legitimate and authoritative, and the styles and forms of one's discourse signalled conformity to the rituals and processes of the production of orthodox discourse and knowledge. Writes Champion, "the hegemonic authority of Christian culture meant that there was a defined structure for the production of orthodox discourse and knowledge. Conformity to that set of speech-codes was the process whereby legitimate (and therefore potentially successful) discourses became authorized … Transgressive projects were then both conceived and articulated within the idiom of orthodoxy."[14]

In this context, conformity to Scripture was the criterion of truth and authority – but what exactly conformed to Scripture was not clear. For Protestants, history presented an especially daunting hermeneutic challenge, as generations of ritualistic, heretical accretions had to be carefully scraped away to reveal a purer, more original religion.[15] The Church's authority rested on its perceived proximity to the true beliefs of the early Church, so it was paramount to purge the false doctrines appended by a superstitious line of papists.[16] However, establishing exactly what this primitive church looked like was a tricky historical task. Philology, linguistics, and history became the cornerstones of legitimate scriptural interpretation; if biblical criticism could wield these hermeneutical tools effectively, it could effectively guard against the willy-nilly interpretations of enthusiasts.[17] Toland employed the hermeneutical methods, but crucially, he did not do so for the (legitimate, Christian) purpose of *understanding* heresy, but rather for the purpose of *advancing* heresy.[18] Toland's manipulation of discursive techniques was an ironic demonstration of the artificiality and superficiality of these biblical hermeneutics. In this way, Toland's writings were proposing something far more radical than heterodox doctrines; they were a much more fundamental attack on the rituals and methods by which religious power presented itself as legitimate and authoritative.

Toland's *Nazarenus*

Toland was in Amsterdam in 1709 when a diplomat showed him an odd document, in Latin with Arabic interpolations. This "discovery," Toland claimed, was a newly recovered Mahometan gospel – the lost Gospel of Barnabas. Christians ought to accept this new gospel as divine, Toland argued, since they had long acknowledged that Barnabas wrote a lost gospel, and anyway, Mahometans acknowledge the same god as Christians. Toland proceeded to circulate this manuscript among his fellow freethinkers, eliciting their feedback and revising his own comments accordingly so as to produce a text that would be broadly appealing. This text would eventually become *Nazarenus* (1718).

Nazarenus presents the Gospel of Barnabas along with Toland's own commentary. In it, Toland articulates a familiar complaint about manipulative clergy: they themselves are to blame for the existence of atheists, not sober philosophers. Toland celebrates true humanity and argues for the proximity, socially, philosophically, and religiously, of Christians and Muslims. Toland's stated purpose is to reveal true Christianity, rescuing it from its endless divisions, and proposing in its stead a civic, pluralistic religion.[19] Finally, he elaborates on the historical and textual processes necessary to discern true, uncorrupted religion, drawing on Spinoza, Hobbes, and Simon.

Nazarenus is at once biblical criticism and a critique of biblical criticism. In the First Letter of *Nazarenus*, Toland, playing the sincere theologian, makes the altered, profane nature of Scripture obvious while claiming to defend Scripture vis-à-vis Islam:

> The minute the learned may alter, add, or substitute, what to them shall seem most becoming the divine spirit, there's an end at once of *Inspiration*, (according to these gentlemen) and the book becomes thenceforth their own: meaning that it is then the production of different times and diverse authors till nothing of the original be left, tho the book continues as bulky as ever. But it must be carefully observed, that the Mahometan *system of inspiration*, and that of the Christians, are most widely different: since we do not so much stand upon words, phrases, method, pointing, or such other niceties; as upon the matter it self, and the design of the whole, tho circumstances shou'd not be always so exact. Tis here we cast our sheet-anchor, and tis here we are confirm'd by matter of fact: notwithstanding the 30000 variations, which some of our Divines have discover'd in a few copies

> of the New Testament: nor have the copies of the Alcoran escap'd such variations (which is impossible in nature for any book to do) whatever the Mahometans pretend to the contrary, and even some of themselves have produc'd such different readings.[20]

Here Toland turns the style and form of biblical criticism against itself. By highlighting textual inaccuracy and cultural variation, he casts doubt on Scripture and, by extension, the Church's legitimacy and authority.

In addition to this dismantling, however, Toland has a positive project. He posits another, alternative source of credibility: reason, uncramped by partiality, will allow "men of candor [to] accurately judge of the things themselves, without regarding whether he be a Clergyman or a Layman that delivers them."[21] Toland's own legitimacy as a biblical scholar ought to rest on impartial reason alone, indifferent to his institutional status.

Another way Toland replaces religious authority with the authority of individual reason is by emphasizing clarity of style in writing. Rhetorical flourishes obfuscate and manipulate; clear language facilitates clear reasoning for every individual. Toland writes,

> But my text is plain and perspicuous enough, even to the meanest capacity … every man who clearly conceives any subject, may as clearly express it. Witty conceits and harmonious florishes [*sic*] are for another-guess sort of writing: but obscurity is to be avoided in all sorts, and nothing to be affected but not to be misunderstood; if too great a care of being intelligible, can be reckon'd affectation.[22]

Criticizing the clergy, he argues:

> If the Stile of the man they love not, be chaste and unaffected, stript of the enthusiastic cant of the Fathers, the barbarous jargon of the Schools, and the motly dialect of later Systems, then his Principles are vehemently suspected; and by how much more they are intelligible, judg'd to be by so much the more dangerous.[23]

Indeed, throughout *Nazarenus*, Toland repeats the theme that the Church is unnecessary for establishing truth. Individual reason is sufficient:

> Nothing in the Scriptures was plain and incontestable but a few moral precepts, which are more amply perspicuously, and methodically delivered in other books as they are very easy and intelligible without books at all.[24]

Privileging the role of individual reason, Toland inverted the source of authority in biblical criticism: the authority of a text depended more on the individuals *spoken to* rather than the person speaking.[25] Thus by appropriating the mode of biblical criticism, Toland challenged the very institution that made biblical criticism a credible mode of knowledge production.

Toland spilled plenty of ink in *Nazarenus* communicating his pious inquisitiveness and sincere desire to learn. But no one believed that Toland was pious or sincere; indeed, no one believed that Toland *could believe that they would believe it.* For at least a decade after its publication, the most positive public reference to *Nazarenus* was arguably Desmaizeaux's factual report that Toland wrote it.

But if success cannot be gauged by positive responses, it can perhaps be gauged by the volume of negative ones. The year *Nazarenus* appeared, it elicited several comprehensive rebuttals. Thomas Brett rejected Toland's argument against the genuineness of the New Testament canon; after all, how could the early Church, so close to the apostles, have gotten it wrong?[26] In a lengthy rebuttal, James Paterson criticized Toland for trying to reconcile Christianity and Islam.[27] The most comprehensive negative response came from Thomas Mangey, who was aghast that Toland could be so stupid as to think the Gospel of Barnabas was real.[28] Not only did Mangey argue that the text was intolerable, but he also dismissed *Nazarenus* as pedestrian (probably the worst critique, from Toland's point of view). *Nazarenus* and Mangey's rebuttal were summarized for francophone audiences in the *Bibliothèque Angloise* that same year.[29]

Other responses in the first year discussed *Nazarenus* with reference to a hubbub caused by the unacceptably latitudinarian disposition of the Bishop of Bangor, whom Toland had defended. Thomas Dawson took Toland's praise of the bishop as the basis for attacking the latter's impiety,[30] as did one Mathias Earberry.[31] Gilbert Dalrymple intervened to rescue the bishop from the unjust association, attacking Toland in the process.[32] Five years later the *Bibliothèque Germanique* would lament that the bishop had ever been tangled up in Toland's nonsense.[33]

These responses demonstrate that in the year of its publication, *Nazarenus* elicited only negative responses, although some of them were very substantive. After 1718, however, the attacks seem to descend to the *ad hominem,* save for two: In 1726, Jeremiah Jones defended the canonicity of the New Testament against *Nazarenus* – specifically, he objected to Toland's argument that a Turk could be a genuine Christian.[34] And in 1737, Carl Gottlob Hofmann also defended the authenticity of the New Testament against Toland.[35] *Nazarenus* was disliked by all who bothered to respond publicly to it, and those responses were quick to appear, numerous, and often substantive. Indeed, nineteen years after its publication, the arguments in *Nazarenus* were still eliciting lengthy, if critical, engagement. By contrast, *Pantheisticon* (as we shall see) did not provoke a comprehensive rebuttal until twenty years after its (deliberately discreet) publication.[36]

What might we conclude from the example of *Nazarenus* with respect to the close connection between social authority and ideas? *Nazarenus*, though it was an erudite work of biblical criticism, was nevertheless excluded from the social authority to which biblical criticism normally referred. Though Toland appropriated the style of biblical criticism, the responses to *Nazarenus* indicate that he was not able to appropriate the authority of biblical criticism. He was successful, however, in using biblical criticism to ironically demonstrate the fallibility of biblical hermeneutics, promoting individual reason in its stead.

Toland's *Pantheisticon*

Pantheisticon was conceived at least as early as 1711, when Toland indicated in his correspondence to Baron Hohendorf his intention to complete a liturgy.[37] It has been argued that it was inspired by Giordano Bruno, though one commentator has cited the Presocratic Anaxagoras as the central inspiration.[38] When Toland published it nine years later, in 1720, it was at his own expense, and very few copies were printed. *Pantheisticon* is straightforward about its intended audience: it was written for the use of members of a clandestine organization – the "Socratic-Society" mentioned in the subtitle.[39] He controlled the distribution personally.[40] Even as a published text, *Pantheisticon* was intended to be kept under wraps.

There is some debate over the intended audience of *Pantheisticon*. Margaret Jacob argues that it was a liturgy written for a Masonic lodge, and she links Toland to Freemasonry by way of a document in Toland's possession but written by Prosper Marchand circa 1710, in which he records the drunken shenanigans of a secret society of philosophically inclined men.[41] Philip McGuinness has discovered that two prominent Belfast citizens (as well as a Presbyterian church) owned *Pantheisticon*, a fact that is compatible with Jacob's hypothesis that *Pantheisticon* was a serious liturgy for a Masonic lodge, since it would not be surprising to find it in the possession of that city's leading citizens.[42] While there is no evidence that Toland was a Freemason, there is some that he associated with many known Freemasons, and even if he was not part of the organization himself, Freemasons helped circulate his ideas.[43]

It would be prudent, however, to differentiate between Toland's "Socratic-Society" and Masonic lodges. As Stephen Daniel points out, pantheist associations and other philosophical societies were widespread, and Toland certainly participated in small philosophical groups; these groups, though, were not necessarily Masonic in nature.[44] Toland describes his "Socratic-Society" as being in number "about the number of the muses," while Masonic lodges could have many more; and there is no suggestion of levels of membership – a characteristic of Freemasonry.[45]

More to the heart of the matter, there were philosophical differences between this pantheist Socratic-Society and Freemasonry. Toland was resolutely anti-Newtonian; in *Pantheisticon,* nature itself is worthy of praise and does not require a god or prime mover to set it in motion or give it order. By contrast, Freemasonry was officially Newtonian and was mostly populated with Newtonians. God, not nature, was central to the Masonic universe, and indeed, Jacob speculates that this was a reason why *Pantheisticon* was never officially adopted by Freemasons.[46] Finally, at least two accounts distinguish between Freemasons and *Pantheisticon*'s intended audience. Desmaizeaux, Toland's close friend and posthumous biographer, reports that Toland crafted *Pantheisticon* for the use of the members of a philosophical society where the worshippers were, as the title implies, *pantheists,* whom Desmaizeaux defines as people who "acknowledge no other God than the Universe."[47] Finally, in his *Dieu et les hommes,* Voltaire clearly distinguishes between Freemasons and a sect called Freethinkers (*les Francs-pensants*) who are "beaucoup plus étenduë que celle des Francs-maçons." Among the Freethinkers, Voltaire lists "pour les principaux chefs de cette secte, milord Herbert, les chevaliers Raleig[h] and Sidney, mylord Shaftsburi, *le sage Loke* moderé jusqu'à la timidité, le grand Neutown, qui nia si hardiment la Divinité de Jésu-Christ, les Colins les Toland, les Tindal, les Trenchard, les Gordon, les Wolston, les Wolaston, et surtout le célèbre mylord Bolingbroke."[48] In Voltaire's view, then, Freethinkers were more numerous than Freemasons, and since he included Newtonians and anti-Newtonians in their number, we can infer that it was a broader, more inclusive category.[49] Ultimately however, whether or not people were Freemasons seems less important than whether or not they were able to circulate texts, and it is obvious enough from the historical record that Freemasons like Jean Rousset de Missy and Prosper Marchand did help to popularize Toland's ideas.[50] Ultimately, whether or not the intended audience of *Pantheisticon* was

Freemasons or some other clandestine philosophical society, its purpose was to encourage social and philosophical camaraderie via eating, drinking, and formal ritual.

By and large, Toland succeeded in keeping *Pantheisticon* under wraps: compared to *Nazarenus, Pantheisticon* garnered little attention – it did not even elicit much invective from the religious establishment. In the years following its publication it was never advertised in newspapers, though booksellers continued to consistently advertise Toland's *Amyntor* (1699), *Nazarenus* (1718), and *Tetradymus* (1720). This was intentional: published for personal distribution, it was simply not for sale. Since Toland's other, less radical texts had routinely elicited many reviews in addition to vehement and widespread negative reaction, it is reasonable to infer that the lack of response was a result not of the public's failure to object to the radical nature of *Pantheisticon*, but rather of Toland's strategically restricted publication and circulation. Voltaire would later wonder how a text as radical as *Pantheisticon* could create so little hubbub. In his *Lettres à Son Altesse Monseigneur le prince de* ***, he notes that in Ireland, Toland was oppressed for his more cautious work (*Christianity not Mysterious*), but in England he was never troubled even by his boldest books – *Nazarenus* and the *Pantheisticon*.[51] It was not the case that Toland "ne fut jamais troublé" as a result of *Nazarenus*, but Voltaire was likely less interested in factual niceties than he was in strategically praising English freedom so as to implicitly criticize the illiberality of the *ancien régime*. If Toland was not troubled on account of *Pantheisticon*, it was because few people outside of his circle were reading it, not because English institutions were so enviably liberal. Indeed, this is how Desmaizeaux describes it: Toland was simply being cautious, given the radical and anti-Christian character of the text. Toland "seems to have been sensible," he writes, "that he had too much indulg'd his loose imagination; for he got it printed secretly, at his own charge, and but a few copies, which he distributed with a view of receiving some presents for them."[52]

Notwithstanding this limited publication and distribution, parts of *Pantheisticon* were translated into French and disseminated in both published and manuscript form.[53] Segments also reached the francophone public via book reviews.[54] In its French translation, *Pantheisticon* was tailored slightly to appeal to an aristocratic audience uncomfortable with the term "republican," and its natural philosophy was corrupted, probably as a result of the French translators' lack of scientific knowledge.[55]

Toland's choice to package his ideas in the liturgical form could seem surprising for two reasons. First, he is opposed to systematization. In *Letters to Serena*, Toland criticizes Spinoza for, among other things, being "too in love with his world." Moreover, because systems require all the parts to work in concert, they come apart when even the least fault is demonstrated.[56] Second, one of Toland's most important intellectual influences, John Milton, was vehemently opposed to liturgy in all its forms.[57] Milton had denounced the liturgy as evil in 1641.[58] An entire chapter of his *Eikonoklastes* (1649) is dedicated to attacking the Prayer Book and its royalist supporters; in that chapter he calls the Prayer Book "superstitious, offensive, and indeed, though English, yet still the Mass-Book." Even a reformed liturgy smacked of popery; true Christians ought not admit of a Prayer Book at all. Milton argues in *De Doctrina Christiana* (1660) that the liturgy is actively anti-religious: "Also opposed to true religion is hypocritical worship, where the external forms are duly observed, but without any internal or spiritual involvement. This is extremely offensive to God."[59] A liturgy was by definition a public and therefore sociopolitical expression of faith, so it implied a potential conflict between private and public belief. In contrast to Hobbes, for whom private belief existed separately – and safely – away from the civic realm, Milton viewed this bifurcation as an insincere, even schizophrenic, element. Certainly, a liturgy might seem a strange choice for a man like Toland, who, like Milton, decried Anglicanism's "residual popery."[60] Wasn't a pantheist liturgy inserting popery where there was none to begin with?

Indeed, Toland echoes the Miltonian suspicion of a public belief:

> Inasmuch as ... Philosophy is divided by the *Pantheists*, as well as other antient Sages, into *External*, or popular and depraved; and *Internal*, or pure and genuine; no Discord arises among them ... [S]hould the Religion derived from one's Father, or enforced by the Laws, be wholly, or in some respects, wicked, villainous, obscene, tyrannical, or depriving Men of their Liberty, in such Case the Brethren may, with all the Legality in the World, betake themselves immediately to one more mild, more pure, and more free.[61]

The philosophy of *Pantheisticon* itself seems to mitigate against a liturgical form. Toland writes in the beginning:

> To use our utmost Efforts, that Cattle-like, we might not follow the Herd of those that go before; going not where we should go, but where they go ... Since every Man chuses rather to believe than judge, Life then is never brought to a Scrutiny, Credulity has always the Ascendant, Error handed down from Father to Son, embarrasses our Thoughts in its Mazes, we give headlong into it: In a word, it is the dull Infatuation of being led by the Examples of others, that exposes us to Ruin.[62]

How could a liturgy – uniform, communal, ritualistic – be an appropriate form for a philosophy that extols individual reason and eschews tradition? Perhaps Toland employed the liturgical form as a means to import the symbolic authority of the Church for his heterodox pantheist philosophy. But the evidence cannot sustain such a proposition: there is none that *Pantheisticon*'s liturgical form lent it even a patina of authority. Given the blatantly un-Christian content of *Pantheisticon*, the idea that Toland employed liturgy as a strategy for appropriating religious authority is untenable. Legitimate reform of the liturgy was left to the moderate, Newtonian faithful like Samuel Clarke and William Whiston, whose Newtonian and Lockean liturgical reforms fell within the scope of reasonable dissent.[63] *Pantheisticon* is not masquerading as Christian doctrine; it is unabashedly pantheist and is directed towards the already converted, so to speak. The second liturgy begins:

PRESIDENT: Keep off the prophane People.
RESPONDENTS: The Coast is clear, the Doors are shut, all's safe.
PRESIDENT: All Things in the World are one, And one is All in all Things.
RESPONDENTS: What's All in all Things is GOD, Eternal and Immense, Neither begotten, nor ever to perish.
PRESIDENT: In him we live, we move, and exist.
RESPONDENTS: Every Thing is sprung from him, And shall be reunited to him, He himself being the Beginning, and End of all Things.[64]

In this excerpt, Toland is alluding to the New Testament teaching that "In Him we live and move and have our being" as well as to the Judeo-Christian notion that God is "the Alpha and Omega." Even so, it is hard to imagine a reader mistaking this for a Christian text – and indeed, no reader did.

Instead, *Pantheisticon*, I argue, was attempting something Milton had written off: a recovery of true, uncorrupted liturgy. Readers are informed on the first page that "Man, as a sociable Animal, can not live well, nor happy, nor at any rate, without the Help and Concurrence of Others," and that this was the original impetus for sorting ourselves into families, cities, and voluntary associations, such as those ancient Greek and Roman voluntary associations called "*Brotherhoods, Friendships, Societies,*" which were established "either for the Pleasure or Instruction of the Mind."[65] What made liturgy a promising style and form was its sociable expression of reason – the quintessentially Tolandian notion that philosophy's natural habitat is in society.

By and large, these lofty, sociable ambitions were lost on the reading public. It is not entirely clear how *Pantheisticon* was received among its intended, clandestine audience – the "Socratic-Society" mentioned in the subtitle, and possibly the secret society in The Hague that Jacob describes. However, the public's response to *Pantheisticon* fell into two categories: negative, and none at all. Edmund Curll – Toland's first (and sympathetic) biographer – falls into the latter category. He declines to comment on Toland's *Nazarenus, Tetradymus,* and *Pantheisticon,* "lest I should be stigmatized with the opprobious Name of a *Free-Thinker,*" he explains.[66]

Predictably, most reviews were negative for religious reasons. In the *Bibliothèque Germanique*'s review of *Histoire de la Vie et des Ecrits de M. Toland* by Mosheim, the scandalized reviewer notes, "It is audacious that such a profane book saw the light of day, that it was titled PANTHEISTICON, and that it ridicules the Divine service."[67] This scandalized reviewer sees *Pantheisticon* only as a derisive satire of religion. Moreover, the reviewer refers to an appalling prayer to Bacchus infamously interpolated into Toland's text.[68] Though this interpolation is not attributed to Toland himself – it was probably added by someone sympathetic to his ideas – the reviewer reasons that Toland is guilty by association. Finally, that there were very few copies attests not to Toland's caution, but to a less noble intention "d'en tenir le prix fort haut."[69]

Francis Hare's 1721 defence of orthodox Anglicanism rejects Locke's too-liberal religious tolerance, remarking with horror that under the Lockean scheme, just about anyone could set up a church: "none are excluded from this privilege but downright *Atheists,* such as the impious Author of the *Pantheisticon**, and a few such *Infidels,* who are either too stupid to understand an Argument, or too thoughtless to attend to one, or too vicious to give a practical assent."[70] Taking his complaint further in a footnote, Hare perpetuates the rumour about Toland being the author of a scribbled prayer to Bacchus interpolated in the published text. The heretical prayer is reprinted – with a slight omission (lest the reader's soul be inadvertantly imperiled by a fuller account?). "Thus prays this *Pantheist,*" accuses Hare, "whose impudent Blasphemies loudly call for the Animadversions of the Civil Power."[71] Despite its liturgical form, *Pantheisticon* clearly failed to amuse in the slightest the royalist, High Anglican Hare. Jakob Brucker's *Historiae critica philosophae* (1734) labels *Pantheisticon* "profane" and "full of impudence." It sows the seeds of a wicked Spinozism and satirizes in the vein of Bruno's *Expulsion of the Triumphant Beast.*[72]

The review of *Pantheisticon* in the *Bibliothèque Angloise* in 1720 is negative but for a different reason. Instead of taking it to be a derisive parody, the reviewer conceives Toland's motivation as a sincere attempt to put forth a clear version of his pantheist religion, pointing out that Toland had earlier promised to do so.[73] Unfortunately, he complains, Toland's universal religion is too hastily sketched; pantheist philosophy is given in "gros Caracteres."[74] If, as *Pantheisticon* claims, pantheistic societies are already such an expansive sect, existing in great numbers in London, Paris, Venice, Holland, and Rome, then this book is not really anything original; if, on the other hand, it is a *secret* society, then why is Toland publishing it? [75] Toland is unoriginal at best, disingenuous at worst.

William Warburton, who is generally negative towards Toland in *The Divine Legation of Moses Demonstrated* (1738), echoes the *Bibliothèque Angloise*'s disappointment. Noting that Toland's purpose in life was "to shed his venom on every thing that was great and respectable,"[76] Warburton nevertheless concedes that he approached *Pantheisticon* optimistically, hoping to uncover a brand of religion uncorrupted by idolatry. "But I had the mortification to find nothing there but an indigested heap of common-place quotations from the *ancients*," writes the disillusioned Warburton, "and an unmeaning collection of common-place reflections from *modern* infidels, without the least seasoning of logic or criticism, to justify the waste of time to the reader, or to make the labour supportable to one's self. And the authority of the man, which is nothing, could not engage me to any farther notice of his book."[77]

Apparently, by the time *Pantheisticon* was translated into English thirty-one years after its original publication, the anti-Toland climate had tempered. Warburton's attitude is arguably positive in his commentary on the works of Alexander Pope (who, incidentally, occasionally wrote favourably of Toland). With respect to Pope's line, "That NATURE our Society adores, / Where Tindal dictates, And Silenus snores," Warburton comments, "See the *Pantheisticon,* with its liturgy and rubrics, composed by Toland."[78] Milquetoast, to be sure – but an improvement over "indigested heap." Warburton then equates Toland's pantheist philosophy to Saint Paul's refrain, "In Him we live and move and have our being."[79] While he assumes *Pantheisticon* to be atheistic, he nevertheless seems to consider its pantheistic philosophy an expression of a reasonable belief system.

Judging from readers' responses and the content of the text itself, it is evident that *Pantheisticon* did not succeed in arrogating to itself the authority of religious discourses, despite its liturgical form. Still, *Pantheisticon* pursued and constructed another form of authority, rooted in individual reason and sociability. *Pantheisticon* aimed to provide the ritual glue for the construction of an alternative form of sociability – a recovery of true liturgy as an expression of the idea that reason is inseparable from social association. The best setting for philosophy is in a simple environment, in the company of friends, over a good meal.

Conclusion

Appropriating the style and form of power does not always bring it about. *Nazarenus* employed biblical criticism to promote individual reason; *Pantheisticon* employed liturgy to animate an alternative form of sociability. Too radical to be perceived as a sincere if reform-minded Christian, Toland forfeited the opportunity to benefit from the legitimacy and authority of hegemonic discourses, but he gained an opportunity to posit alternative sources of authority.

NOTES

1 Joseph Addison, *The Spectator* (London: Thomas Bosworth, 1854 [10 September 1711]), no. 166, vol. 2, 45–6. Perhaps this story prompted a letter that was printed in *The Spectator* two months later: A contributor complains of a "freethinking" figure (Toland) who recently arrived in Devonshire: he lacks common sense, he is an "infidel thinker" and pretends to the vague and conceited title of "freethinker" just because he is an atheist. *The Spectator,* no. 234, vol. 2, 253.

2 Justin Champion, *Republican Learning: John Toland and the Crisis of Christian Culture: 1969–1722* (Manchester: Manchester University Press, 2003), 11.

3 Pierre Bourdieu, *Language and Symbolic Power* (Cambridge, MA: Harvard University Press, 2003), 5.

4 Jean-Pierre Cavaillé, "Libertinage et dissimulation: Quelques éléments de réflexion," in *Sources antiques de l'irreligion moderne: le relais italien,* ed. Didier Foucault (Toulouse: Université Toulouse-Le Mirail, 2001).

5 Cavaillé, "Libertinage et dissimulation," 59.

6 John Toland, *Nazarenus,* ed. Justin Champion (Oxford: Voltaire Foundation, [1718]1999). Two editions appeared in the first year of publication; there was another run in 1732. A summary of both *Nazarenus* and its most vocal

critique appeared in French in 1718 in the *Bibliothèque Angloise,* and a complete French translation, perhaps by d'Holbach, appeared in 1777.

7 The original 1720 edition of *Pantheisticon* was in Latin and circulated clandestinely. In his *Tolandiana,* Carabelli identifies three Latin editions appearing in 1720. Giancarlo Carabelli, *Tolandiana: materiali bibliografici per lo studio dell'opera e della fortuna di John Toland (1670–1722),* 2 vols (Florence: La nuova Italia, 1975–8); John Toland, *Pantheisticon: Sive Formula Celebrandae Sodalitatis Socraticae* (Cosmopoli, 1720). Part of *Pantheisticon* was translated into English in 1740 by Arthur Ashley Sykes, whose extended refutation of *Pantheisticon* (unintentionally?) provided a detailed summary of its arguments and reprinted long, newly translated segments of the text itself. Arthur Ashley Sykes, *The Principles and Connexion of Natural and Revealed Religion Distinctly Considered* (London: J. and P. Knapton, 1740), 64–84. *Pantheisticon* was translated into English in its entirety in 1751. John Toland, *Pantheisticon: or, the Form of Celebrating the Socratic-Society* (London: Sam. Paterson, 1751) (hereafter cited as *Pantheisticon*). It was translated into German in 1856 (in part) and in 1897 (in full). John Toland, *Das Pantheistikon des John Toland* (Leipzig: J.G. Findel, 1897). In the years following its initial publication, sections were translated into French and circulated in both published and manuscript form. It was not published in French in its entirety until 1927. See the translation included in Albert Lantoine, *John Toland (1680–1722)* (Paris: E. Nourry, 1927). Interestingly, a newly reported manuscript of a French translation of Toland's *Pantheisticon* has been dated to sometime between 1757 and 1791, though the manuscript itself bears the false date of 1720. "Bulletin Bibliographique," *La Lettre clandestine* 25 (2017): 378–80. For more on *Pantheisticon*'s francophone fate, see Pierre Lurbe, "Traduire, trahir, se trahir: le cas du *Pantheisticon* de John Toland," in *Cultural Transfers: France and Britain in the Long Eighteenth Century,* ed. Ann Thomson (Oxford: SVEC, 2010), 233–42.

8 Champion's analysis of a "lent list" among Toland's manuscripts reveals him to be actively circulating ideas among a heterosocial, British Whig elite. Justin Champion, "'Manuscripts of Mine Abroad': John Toland and the Circulation of Ideas, c. 1700–1722," *Eighteenth-Century Ireland* 14 (1999): 9–36 at 27.

9 Voltaire, *Lettres à Son Altesse Monseigneur le prince de*** sur Rabelais et sur d'autres auteurs accusés d'avoir mal parlé de la religion chrétienne* (Amsterdam: Marc Michel Rey, 1767), 408.

10 For a contrary perspective, see Manlio Iofrida, *La filosofia di John Toland: spinozismo, scienza et religione nella cultura europea fra 600 e 700* (Milan: F. Angeli, 1983).

11 Justin Champion, "Introduction," in John Toland, *Nazarenus* (Oxford: Voltaire Foundation, 1999), 2.

12 Justin Champion, *Republican Learning: John Toland and the Crisis of Christian Culture: 1669–1722* (Manchester: Manchester University Press, 2003).

13 For an overview of the religious and political debates surrounding this period, see Margaret Jacob, "John Toland and the Newtonian Ideology," *Journal of the Warburg and Courtland Institutes* 32 (1969): 307–31.

14 Champion, "'Manuscripts of Mine Abroad," 12.

15 The hermeneutical problems confronting religious discourse were discussed widely within the clandestine corpus. Notably, Boulanger, Dumarsais, Challe, and Spinoza considered topics such as the conventional and arbitrary nature of language; the ostensibly natural or divine origin of language and its subsequent devolution; and the inadequacy of our own historical and linguistic knowledge to uncover the uncorrupted divine or natural message. See Claudia Stancati, "Éléments d'une 'linguistique clandestine,'" *La Lettre Clandestine* 14 (2005–6): 105–25.

16 Champion, "'Manuscripts of Mine Abroad,'" 39.

17 Champion, "'Manuscripts of Mine Abroad,'" 46.

18 Champion, "'Manuscripts of Mine Abroad,'" 47.

19 Champion, "'Manuscripts of Mine Abroad,'" 97.

20 *Nazarenus*, 140.

21 *Nazarenus*, 117.

22 *Nazarenus*, 122.

23 *Nazarenus*, 127.

24 *Nazarenus*, 289–90.

25 Steven Daniel, *John Toland: His Methods, Manners, and Mind* (Montreal and Kingston: McGill-Queen's University Press, 1984), 54.

26 Thomas Brett, *Tradition Necessary to explain and interpret the Holy Scriptures… Containing some remarks on Mr. Toland's* Nazarenus (London: James Bettenham, 1718), i–xxiii.

27 James Paterson, *Anti-nazarenus By way of Answer to Mr Toland; Or, A Treatise proving the Divine Original and Authority of the Holy Scriptures against Atheists* (London: S. Butler, 1718).

28 Thomas Mangey, *Remarks upon* Nazarenus. *Wherein the Falsity of Mr. Toland's Mahometan Gospel; And his Misrepresentation of Mahometan Sentiments, in respect of Christianity, Are set forth …* (London: William and John Innys, 1718).

29 *Bibliothèque Angloise* (Amsterdam, 1718), 301–26, 327–35.

30 Thomas Dawson, *An Introduction to the Bishop of Bangor's Intended Collection of Authorities …* (London: Jonah Bowyer, 1718), xliii.

31 Matthias Earberry, *The Old English Constitution Vindicated* … (London: J. Roberts, 1718), xxiv.

32 Gilbert Dalrymple, *A Letter from Edinburgh to Dr. Sherlock … With a Word or Two relating to Mr. Toland* (London: J. Roberts, 1718).

33 "Les éloges que M. Toland donna à l'Evêque de Bangor, fournierent à des gens soupçonneux un prétexte d'accuser ce Prélat de quelque conformité de sentimens avec lui. Rien n'étoit plus faux." *Bibliothèque Germanique* (1723): 54–5 at 54.

34 Jeremiah Jones, *A New and Full Method of Settling the Canonical Authority of the New Testament* … (London: J. Clark and R. Hett, 1726).

35 Carl Gottlob Hofmann, *Introductio In Lectionem Novi Testamenti* (Leipzig: Gleditsch, 1737), 23–6.

36 Arthur Ashley Sykes, *The Principles and Connexion of Natural and Revealed Religion Distinctly Considered* (London: J. and P. Knapton, 1740).

37 Toland to Hohendorf, 7 March 1712, BM Add. MS 4295.

38 Philip McGuinness, "'Perpetual Flux': Newton, Toland, Science, and the Status Quo," in *John Toland's Christianity Not Mysterious: Text, Associated Works, and Critical Essays*, ed. Philip McGuinness et al. (Dublin: Lilliput Press, 1997), 316; Jeffrey R. Wigelsworth, "A Pre-Socratic Source for John Toland's *Pantheisticon*," *History of European Ideas* 31 (2008): 61–5.

39 Margaret Jacob discovered among Toland's papers a record of a meeting authored by Huguenot bookseller Prosper Marchand that testifies to a meeting that refers to a Grand Master, brothers, and a constitution. It is reasonable to infer that Toland was inspired to write *Pantheisticon* for this or a similar group, especially since that was the impression of Desmaizeaux and *Pantheisticon*'s reviewers. See Margaret Jacob, *The Radical Enlightenment: Pantheists, Freemasons, and Republicans* (London: George Allen and Unwin, 1981).

40 Desmaizeaux attests to the limited distribution of *Pantheisticon*. John Toland, *A Collection of Several Pieces of Mr. John Toland*, ed. Pierre Desmaizeaux, 2 vols (London: Printed for J. Peele, 1726), lxxviii.

41 Jacob, *The Radical Enlightenment*, 267–9.

42 Philip McGuinness, "John Toland and Eighteenth-Century Irish Republicanism," *Irish Studies Review* 19 (1997): 15–21.

43 Jacob reports that Prosper Marchand and Jean Rousset de Missy were both Freemasons and associates of Toland's (Rousset having likely met Toland in the Netherlands in 1704), and they helped publish and circulate Toland's texts. Jacob, *The Radical Enlightenment*, 197–8. Note, however, that Rousset was integral in circulating Toland's *A Letter from an Arabian Physician*, a text that Daniel denies is authentically Toland's. Stephen Daniel, *John Toland:*

His Methods, Manners, and Mind (Montreal and Kingston: McGill–Queen's University Press, 1984), 213–14, 15.

44 Daniel, *John Toland*, 213–14.

45 Daniel, *John Toland*, 213; *Pantheisticon*, 12.

46 Jacob, *The Radical Enlightenment*, 24.

47 Desmaizeaux, "The Life of Mr. Toland," lxxviii.

48 Incidentally, Voltaire mentions Toland twenty-nine times in his works (by this author's count), and he always mentions him favourably. Usually, Voltaire lists Toland as part of a group of Freethinkers and notes that, for all their radical notions, they are far more preferable than theologians, who are actually to blame for social discord. Dr Obern, *Dieu et les hommes, œuvre theologique; mais raissonable*, trans. Jacques Aimon [Voltaire] (Berlin: Christian de Vos, 1769), 113.

49 Voltaire's inclusion of Newtonians – indeed, Newton himself – among the Freethinkers does not square with Jacob's description of Freethinkers as a resolutely anti-Newtonian group. Margaret Jacob, "John Toland and the Newtonian Ideology," *Journal of the Warburg and Courtland Institutes* 32 (1969): 307–31.

50 See above, n30. It is also interesting to note that Desmaizeaux, a close friend of Toland and an indefatigable popularizer of his works, also played a central role in popularizing the works of the members of the heavily Newtonian Royal Society in France and on the Continent. Moreover, Desmaizeaux's *Recueils de diverses pièces* was an important text for disseminating Newtonian notions abroad. Toland's radical influence was thus not necessarily dependent on an ideologically close-knit group of atheists or secret pantheist brethren, competing with Newtonian ideas. Rather, intellectual and social influence travelled through heterogenous networks. Elizabeth Grist, "Pierre Des Maizeaux and the Royal Society," in *Cultural Transfers: France and Britain in the Long Eighteenth Century*, ed. Ann Thomson (Oxford: SVEC, 2010).

51 "Dans son premier livre intitulé, *la Religion chrétienne sans mystères*, il avait écrit lui-même un peu mystérieusement, et sa hardiesse était couverte d'un voile. On le condamna, on le poursuivit en Irlande: le voile fut bientôt déchiré. Ses Origines judaïques, son Nazaréen, son Pantheisticon, furent autant de combats qu'il livra ouvertement au christianisme. Ce qui est étrange, c'est qu'ayant été opprimé en Irlande pour le plus circonspect de ses ouvrages, il ne fut jamais troublé en Angleterre pour les livres les plus audacieux." Voltaire, *Lettres à Son Altesse Monseigneur le prince de ****, 38.

52 Desmaizeaux, "The Life of Mr. Toland," lxxviii.

53 Lurbe, "Traduire, trahir, se trahir," 233–42. In *La Face cachée des Lumières,* Miguel Benítez lists nine extant French manuscripts. Miguel Benítez, *La Face cachée des Lumières: Recherches sur les manuscrits philosophiques clandestins de l'âge classique* (Oxford: Voltaire Foundation, 1996).

54 See Armand La Chappelle, *Bibliothèque Angloise, ou Histoire littéraire de La Grande Bretagne,* vol. 8 (Amsterdam: David Paul Marret, 1720), 285–322. See also *Bibliothèque Germanique ou Histoire littéraire de l'Allemagne, de la Suisse et des pays du Nord,* ed. Samuel Formey (Amsterdam: Pierre Humbert, 1723), vol. 6, 24–61. For more on the importance of book reviews to the circulation of British ideas to francophone audiences, see Rachel Hammersley, "The 'Real Whig' – Huguenot Network and the English Republican Tradition," in Thomson, ed., *Cultural Transfers,* 19–32. Armand de La Chapelle more than once publicized radical literature by way of denunciation: his hostility towards Huguenot pastor Jacques Saurin's claims for God's "beneficial lies" resulted in a vigorous and drawn-out debate with Saurin and Beaumarchais over Saurin's heterodox claims. See John Christian Laursen, "Impostors and Liars: Clandestine Manuscripts and the Limits of Freedom of the Press in the Huguenot Netherlands," in *New Essays on the Political Thought of the Huguenot Refuge* (New York: E.J. Brill, 1995).

55 Lurbe, "Traduire, trahir, se trahir," 233–42.

56 "But when a Man builds a whole System of Philosophy either without any first Principles, or on a precarious Foundation: and afterwards when he's told of the Fault, and put in mind of the Difficultys that attend it, yet neither supplies that Defect, nor accounts for those Difficultys by any thing he has already establish'd, nor yet acknoweldges his Mistake; we may reasonably suspect that he's too much in love with his new World (for such is a System of Philosophy) ever to admit of a better Creator: whereas a Person that proposes no other view but the manifesting and propagating of Truth, and that cannot rest satisfy'd with Fancys or Conjectures, wou'd in such Circumstances be nothing asham'd to confess and amend his Error." John Toland, *Letters to Serena* (London: Bernard Lintot, 1704), 137–8.

57 Timothy Rosendale, "Milton, Hobbes, and the Liturgical Subject," *Studies in English Literature* 44, no. 1 (2004): 149–72.

58 John Milton, "Animadversions," in *The Complete Prose Works of John Milton,* ed. Don M. Wolfe et al., 8 vols (New Haven: Yale University Press, 1953–82), 1: 661–735 at 691; Milton, "Of Reformation," in *CPW,* 1: 517–617 at 532.

59 Milton, *De Doctrina Christiana, CPW,* 6: 667.

60 Champion, "'Manuscripts of Mine Abroad,'" 4.

61 *Pantheisticon,* 56–7.

62 *Pantheisticon*, "To the Learned and Ingenious Reader." (There are no page numbers in this beginning section.)

63 Liturgical reform revolved around the necessity to defend the legitimacy of true Anglican ceremony from innovation. Whiston's and Clarke's proposed liturgical revisions questioned the doctrine of the Trinity. See Bryan D. Spinks, *Liturgy in the Age of Reason: Worship and Sacraments in England and Scotland, 1662–c. 1800* (Burlington: Ashgate, 2008).

64 *Pantheisticon*, 70–1.

65 *Pantheisticon*, 10–11.

66 Edmund Curll, *An historical account of the life and writings of the late eminently famous Mr. John Toland* (London: J. Roberts, 1722), 89.

67 "Il eut l'audace de mettre au jour son Livre Profane, qu'il a nommé PANTHEISTICON, et d'y tourner en ridicule le service Divin," *Bibliothèque Germanique*, 55.

68 "Omnipotens & sempiterne Bacche, qui hominum corda donis tuis recreas, concede propitius ut qui hesternis poculis egroti facti sunt, hodiernis curentur, per pocula poculorum, Amen!" Quoted in, among other places, Voltaire in his *Lettre à S.A. Monseigneur*, 38.

69 *Bibliothèque Germanique*, 55.

70 Francis Hare, *Scripture Vindicated from the Misinterpretations of the Lord Bishop of Bangor: In his Answer to the Dean of Worcester's Visitation Sermon Concerning Church-Authority* (London: Jonah Bowyer, 1721), xxi.

71 Hare, note on xxi.

72 Jakob Brucker, *Historia Critica Philosophiae*, vol. 4 (Bern[?]: Christoph Breitkopf, 1734), 702.

73 The reviewer quotes Toland's promise given in *Nazarenus:* He begins his article with a quote from *Nazarenus* (Preface, xiv), where Toland says "je donnerai, Dieu aidant, un compte de ma Religion, qui sera clair, dépouillé de toute Litterature & couché en Maximes simplement exprimées, sans Commentaire qui les obscuroisse. Je vous promets d'avance que ce ne sera pas une Religion de pure Machine, ou de grossier Artisan, consistant plus dans un respect stupide pour des Formulaires reçus & dans un Cercle languissant de Rites que l'on fait par routine, que dans un Service raisonnable & une Pieté sans affectation" *Bibliothèque Germanique*, 287–8. On Toland's ability to spread rumours in order to cultivate public anticipation for his publications, see Champion, "'Manuscripts of Mine Abroad,'" 18.

74 *Bibliothèque Germanique*, 288.

75 *Bibliothèque Germanique*, 291.

76 William Warburton, *The Divine Legation of Moses Demonstrated, On the Principles of a Religious Deist, From the Omission of the Doctrine of a Future State*

of Reward and Punishment in the Jewish Dispensation (London: Fletcher Gyles, 1738), 447.

77 Warburton, *The Divine Legation*, 565.

78 Alexander Pope, *The Works of Alexander Pope, Esq. Volume V, Containing* The Dunciad *in Four Books*, ed. William Warburton (London: J. and P. Knapton, 1751), 212.

79 William Warburton, the editor of Alexander Pope's collected works, makes an interesting comparison between the "Atheist's Liturgy" written by the "infamous Toland" and St Paul: the latter's "*In him we live and move and have our being*" smacks, he says, of Toland's (and Spinoza's) pantheism. Alexander Pope, *The works of Alexander Pope Esq., In nine volumes, complete. With his last corrections, additions, and improvements; … Together with the commentary and notes of Mr. Warburton* (London: A. Millar, 1760), vol. 3, 365–6.

Chapter Nine

Philosophical Clandestine Literature and Academic Circles in France

SUSANA SEGUIN

This chapter is dedicated to the paradoxical and complex relationship that philosophical clandestine literature had with the academic milieu in Paris, in particular with one of the royal institutions that contributed most efficiently to its organization, the Académie Royale des sciences. On first sight, the interrelation between the most "radical" ideas of "underground" thought (I will come back to these terms later) and the most official of the institutes that operated as political propaganda machines for the French monarchy could certainly come as a surprise. The polemic ideas of the eighteenth century have a heterogeneity and subtleness that seem paradigmatic to me. These terms, through which we attempt to structure and categorize intellectual production, should be applied with caution, for when these clandestine texts are removed from the context of their elaboration and their circulation, they don't always seem to fit the conceptual or historiographical categories we have since developed. I will thus permit myself a brief terminological and historical clarification, before offering you a series of observations, the object of which is less to apply a theoretical frame for interpreting past works and more to determine how clandestine thought penetrated the most official publications of eighteenth-century French and European intellectual life with regard to both the practices of the day and the texts themselves.

Thus, our first question is: What do we mean by philosophical clandestine literature? From a research point of view, the *corpus* of the philosophical clandestine literature is comprised of manuscripts that, since first being identified by Gustave Lanson (1912) and Ira O. Wade (1938), have continued to grow in number, to arrive at some 250 titles in 2,000 copies (according to the detailed study by Miguel Benitez[1]) preserved in European (predominantly French) libraries, and of which the covert circulation has been well documented. The consistency of this *corpus* is not based on any observable material criteria, such as that of being circulated clandestinely; otherwise we would need to include in this volume a large number of texts (from purely pornographic works to *poésies fugitives*, and also Jansenist writings) that share these same methods of diffusion and reception with our *corpus*.

Most but not all of these writings are handwritten. Some but not all were eventually printed. The intellectual and material history of the book and of reading shows us that the different forms that clandestine philosophy took (manuscripts, editions outside of France, clandestine editions within France, etc.) constituted a configuration unique to intellectual life of the eighteenth century in that these practices were exploited by works that, for various reasons, evaded the strict demands of the book market and the practice of royal and religious censorship to which the large majority of publications were submitted.[2] In fact, clandestine literature, and even more the choice of a handwritten format, not only was a response to the need for protection that authors and readers felt, thus creating a mode of dissemination unique to certain insider circles, but also constituted an economical and intellectual choice.[3] The handwritten format, which predominated in the *corpus* of clandestine philosophy, seems to have reflected a unique trait of this literature; besides being a favoured means of disseminating innately polemical thought, handwritten materials were malleable – they were reusable by other readers, who subsequently became authors and copiers. All of this was associated with the elaboration and diffusion of a way of thinking that was as much individual as it was collective, the simultaneous expression of leading figures and of a social phenomenon, the translation of a "crise des consciences" to borrow the title of Paul Hazard's book, where the names of the individuals concerned counted less than the network of meanings that structured the texts, and where the beauty of their form often mattered much less than the strength of their arguments.

What characterizes these texts, besides their covert diffusion and manuscript format, is the fact that they are "philosophical" in the broad sense that the Enlightenment bestowed upon this word: they treat topics that are essentially metaphysical or religious in a critical, subversive, or impious spirit, and they battle prejudice from a premise grounded in reason (philosophical, historical, scientific reason). For the most part this makes them heterodox or nonconformist writings in that the ideas they denounce are most often the truths of faith: God himself (his existence, his essence, and his relation to the world); the human soul (its spirituality, its immortality); Revelation (the authenticity and consistency of biblical Scripture, the validity of prophets and miracles, the power of biblical exegesis and criticism); historical religions in general (their origins, relation to the political world, crimes committed in their name over the course of history), and Christianity in particular, especially Catholicism, through its history, dogmas, mysteries, and morals. However, this constant in the overall theme of the critical approach can also be based on incredibly varied philosophical orientations, from naturalism to materialism, from atheism to pantheism or deism, and show the influence of Descartes, Bayle, Hobbes, or Spinoza, not to mention the erudite *libertins* of the seventeenth century.

It is because of its association with this unorthodox content, as well as its format, which was compatible with dynamic thought, in perpetual re-elaboration and easily adaptable to the conditions of clandestine circulation, that this *corpus* constituted a particularly strong weapon in "underground" philosophizing at the end of the seventeenth century and for at least the first half of the eighteenth. According to these features, Gustave Lanson was able to compile the first list of clandestine philosophical manuscripts: he recognized them, and rightly so, as a major source of the most polemical ideas of Enlightenment authors.

From this perspective, it seems difficult to extract from this collection a group of titles that are more "radical" than the others, precisely because the reach of these texts cannot be reduced to the nature of the topics that unite them, but must necessarily be associated with their circulation and their reception, which could result in equally "radical" transformations of the ideas expressed by their authors. It is precisely this that happened in the exemplary case of *Doutes sur la religion adressées au père Malebranche* by Robert Challe (who became a materialist and atheist pamphleteer) after Naigeon remodelled the text and Holbach made out of it a whole new work, *Le Militaire philosophique*, and in the case of *Mémoire des pensées et des sentiments* of the curé Jean Meslier, whom Voltaire made an apologist for pure deism.

Evidently, we cannot deny the importance that certain texts have had in and of themselves, such as the *Theophrastus redivivus* and the *Traité des trois imposteurs*; nor can we minimize the philosophical rigour with which some of these authors not only attacked the foundations of Christian theology but also provided entire philosophical systems that are coherent in themselves; in this respect, Dumarsais, Robert Challe, and the author of *Theophrastus redivivus* all offer very good examples. My intention is more to insist that the subversive efficacy of these texts is found not only in the virulence of the arguments they present but also in their capacity to make critical arguments heard among a public that at the outset was not inclined towards the most virulent philosophical thought. From this perspective, the radicalism of the texts must not be reduced to their static content but must be integrated into a dynamic reading that takes into account the multiple aspects of intellectual life of the time.

In this sense, the penetration of philosophical clandestine literature into academic circles was important not only because of the nature of the arguments that were diffused, but also because they prepared the public square for the most virulent ideas. This phenomenon is reinforced by the fact that numerous actors within the clandestine milieu mixed in academic circles, even occupying prestigious positions, which may seem especially paradoxical since these institutions were founded on a dual aim that specifically threatened clandestine thought. As we are well aware, the founding of the French Royal Academies constituted a strong political gesture that reinforced monarchial absolutism: they controlled intellectual production through the economic and social dependence of the *académie* members; at the same time, they placed these authors and scholars in the service of the French king, indeed, a *Catholic* king, to whose glory they were expected to contribute through their works. The various ministers of France under Louis XIV, beginning with Colbert, reinforced this policy, even while the elaboration and circulation of philosophical clandestine literature was intensifying.

Yet we are equally aware that if belonging to these institutions entailed political ties to the French monarchy, this was *not* a guarantee of religious orthodoxy (Voltaire was elected to the Académie française in 1746), even if the royal *compagnies* scrupulously respected that orthodoxy and counted among their members renowned churchmen (Bossuet was himself a member of the Académie française). Also, academicians acted just as much as censors within the system by supervising editorial activities, through which the French king intended to impose his prerogatives in precedence to the Roman Catholic Church, whose actions were thus limited to *a posteriori* censorship.[4] The secular French academicians scrupulously saw to it that no work contrary to the teachings of religion was published, at least without royal permission; even so, the system allowed a certain flexibility that the protagonists of philosophical clandestinity were able to exploit.[5]

While it is true that most academicians were not involved in the philosophical "underground," numerous authors of clandestine texts were regularly attending members or part of the *académies*. Fréret, for example, to whom is attributed the *Lettre de Thrasybule à Leucippe*,[6] and who was the name of choice during the campaign to systematically publish clandestine literature (it was under his name that Holbach published l'*Examen critique des apologistes de la religion chrétienne* in 1766), was above all else a prominent Orientalist, a member of the l'Académie des Inscriptions et Belles-Lettres since 1716, even becoming perpetual secretary in 1742. Fréret frequented the circles of the duke of Noailles and Count Boulainvilliers, much like Jean-Baptiste de Mirabaud, the probable author of *Opinions des anciens sur l'origine du monde*,[7] whose translation of *Jérusalem délivrée* by Tasso won him a seat at the Académie française. Mirabaud was received on 28 September 1726 by his *confrère* Fontenelle and was named perpetual secretary in 1742 (the same year as Fréret) of the prestigious institution, where he replaced the abbé d'Houteville. Jean Terrasson, who had links to clandestine circles, entered the Académie des sciences in 1707, then the Académie française in 1723. Nicolas Boindin, a master of discretion but one who, we are told, revealed traces of atheism at the Café Procope, joined the Académie Royale des Inscriptions et Médailles in 1706 (the future Académie des Inscriptions et Belles-Lettres). He was in line to be appointed royal censor by Pontchartrain – every indication says he had that position in his sights – but came up against the veto of Cardinal Fleury for election to the Académie française.[8] Levêque de Burigny only became *pensionnaire* of the Académie des Inscriptions et Belles-Lettres late in the game, in 1756. Despite Dumarsais's talents as a grammarian, he found no academic position.

Therefore, it is clear that the presence of some of the participants in philosophical clandestinity within the royal institutions is considerable enough to arouse curiosity and justify research into academic circles – into both the members of these institutions and the political leaders under whose authority the academicians were welcomed. For example, the attitude of the abbé Bignon, a nephew of Pontchartrain, reformer of the Académies des Sciences et des Inscriptions, member of the three Académies Royales, and protector of authors whose role in philosophical clandestinity is well known – such as Fontenelle and Fréret – certainly warrants further research.

Membership in the *académies* can be explained by the economic support and social recognition the institutions could offer to authors who otherwise would not have been able to earn a living from writing. Also, membership was often accompanied by the protection of a minister or a network of authority, or of someone close to the royal family; this could provide additional support in the event of ideological or religious clashes. It also often meant mingling in the scholarly circles in which numerous clandestine writings were composed and diffused. At the very least it offered a privileged position, and in certain cases it provided a fortuitous platform for ideas that otherwise would have been condemned to circuitous distribution.

The most significant example of this relates to one of the most discreet, but also most efficient, actors in the clandestine universe, whose name has already come up several times as if he were a common reference among authors of philosophical clandestinity: Fontenelle. Royal censor for a number of years, member of the Académie française since 1691, and elected to the Académie des Inscriptions et Belles-Lettres in 1701 (which, however, he left before the reform of 1717), Fontenelle was most notably a member of the Académie des sciences, which he joined in 1697. In 1699, after its reform, he became its first perpetual secretary, a role he continued until 1740, when Dortous de Mairan took his place.

For a long time, discussions of Fontenelle have reduced his academic work to a function of circumstance, a sort of official mask behind which the author hid to help him forget the *libertés* of his youth, and one that would enable him to lead a double intellectual life as a member of the "parti des discrets." And it is true that after Fontenelle joined the Académie des sciences he published many fewer works under his name and little of the importance of the *Histoire des Oracles* or *Nouveaux dialogues des morts.*[9] Most of his time there was spent preparing the annual volume of the *Histoire de l'Académie des Sciences*, the drafting of which became his responsibility after the Royal Statutes of 1699, and which he would oversee regularly between 1699 and 1740: forty-one volumes in total, corresponding to many thousands of pages that warrant close examination when it comes to an author of Fontenelle's standing.

I shall now formally present these volumes. Preceding the principal "mémoires" of the academicians for any given year, the secretary provided an "histoire" of the institution: a detailed presentation, with commentary and discussion, of scholarly works, in which Fontenelle assembled not only an account of the objective progress of knowledge, the life of academicians, and the collective construction of the institution, but also offered epistemological reflections in accordance with his conception of the history of the human mind. This transformed this element of the official publication of the Académie Royale des sciences into a space for personal expression, and indeed quite a free one, all the more so since the royal status bestowed on these writings added an additional privilege: they were published completely outside the orbit of royal censorship. And it is in this context that the word of the Académie des sciences, in its most official publications, offered some of the most polemic ideas of clandestine thought.

Writing the history of the Académie Royale des sciences gave Fontenelle the opportunity to test some of the principles supporting his most polemical writings, especially his conception of the natural mechanisms of the human mind, and introduced these ideas to a public space that was inaccessible to philosophical clandestine writings, publishing a book such as his *Histoire des Oracles.* This text reflects a double legacy of scepticism: that of Bayle, who, after Montaigne and La Mothe Le Vayer, sees in the past a tool for relativizing the present; and that of the freethinkers, who, since Gabriel Naudé but particularly since Spinoza, prioritized to varying degrees the idea that all forms of superstition from the fables of antiquity to the alleged Christian revelation amounted to stratagems used by the ruling classes and their religious supporters to impose and regulate the political order. Fables in all forms, including stories of the wonders and miracles in sacred history, were viewed as deceptions that a purely historical approach would allow us to expose.

In his *Histoire des Oracles,* which he presents as a translation of the work of Anton Van Dale, Fontenelle uses these two critical trends to distil new ideas, in the first place reversing the order of Van Dale's arguments. This enables him to inscribe his own theory on what he calls an "histoire de l'esprit humain."[10] The adjustments Fontenelle makes to the order of Van Dale's arguments profoundly change their logic but do not weaken it. The Dutch scholar showed first that oracles continued to provide predictions after the coming of Christ, and followed this by showing that we need to consider them simply as human *speech.* Fontenelle, by contrast, shows first that the oracles are merely human productions that we no longer consult once historical circumstance proves them to be of no utility. He thus contends that the conditions for exercising reason determine the beliefs of each society at a particular point in its history, which is to say that the oracles belong to a specific age in the development of the human mind, which "imposters" exploited to consolidate their political authority. He never mentions the Christian religion; in his overall logic he simply generalizes the argument that any religion is susceptible to this sort of development and that the defenders of the orthodoxy of the time understand this. I will not dwell on these aspects, instead referring readers to the work of Jonathan Israel.[11]

What is interesting here is that Fontenelle overturns the arguments that attribute a political origin to fables, and affirms, to the contrary, that they are the natural result of a mechanism of the mind. This idea appears even more clearly in another of his writings, most likely composed near the end of the seventeenth century – *De l'Origine des fables*, published in 1714, which was distributed clandestinely in the early years of the eighteenth century (the manuscript *Des Miracles* features whole paragraphs from it) – as well as in another, unfinished text, *Sur l'histoire*.[12] In these two works Fontenelle explains how, at certain moments in history, the human mind is forced to *imagine*, even *invent*, explanations of phenomena that are cannot be accounted for rationally. This is the first attempt at explaining the phenomena that give rise to fables, which he thus conceives as the first productions of the human mind. Politicization, and therefore fraud, subsequently follow; once the fables have been developed, malicious individuals find ways to use them for their own benefit. From Fontenelle's point of view, the origin of religions is not political in this sense, as Spinoza suggests, but gnosiological, since they result from misinterpretations frozen in time and transmitted from generation to generation, by virtue of the authority of tradition.

Thus two aspects of the human mind are *imagination*, as the first effort of interpretation, and *submission* to tradition, which allows the rising strength of fables over time, that is, their imposition as a fundamental frame for the history and beliefs of a people. Hence the need for the modern philosopher, Fontenelle says, to undertake the mission of an "histoire de l'histoire," which is less interested in the facts themselves than in the thought processes implemented to preserve the memory and the progress of these same mechanisms through time. History thus becomes a privileged terrain onto which the mind can be brought so that it can observe its own modes of action and analyse its own trajectory, as well as the risks it may encounter and that it must avoid. Such a conception of history, based on an analysis of its own modes of operation, necessarily leads to the creation of a space in which the mind attains full control of itself, of its productions, and therefore of its future, consequently released from any apocalyptic threat.[13]

Writing the *Histoire de l'Académie des sciences* allowed Fontenelle to study the mechanisms of the human mind in its endless search for truth, in constant tension with error, superstition, and scientific knowledge, and how freedom from any metaphysical influence is necessary for any real discourse on reason. It enabled him to complete the methodological transformation he had begun in the *Histoire des Oracles* by modifying his discursive strategy. For if it is solely the clandestine networks that allow the open presentation of ideas that only certain initiated minds are ready to hear, as he affirms in the *Traitee de l'âme,*[14] then it is necessary, in this public space created by the publications of the *académies*, to renounce the practice of learning that the erudite freethinkers, *libertins*, and authors of clandestine manuscripts draw from, and that he himself takes part in, in order to address another audience.[15] The secretary of the Académie des sciences thus tries to discuss issues traditionally reserved for scholars in a language that is accessible to the social classes that still need to be converted to the "parti de la philosophie" – such as the Marquise in *Entretiens sur la pluralité des mondes.*[16]

The influence of clandestine thinking in Fontenelle's academic writings is therefore very important. It initially led to the adoption of a method of writing history that sought not only to account for the objective results of science but even more to reveal the mechanisms whereby the mind manages to liberate itself from error. In other words, Fontenelle put into practice, in a domain removed from religious considerations, including pagan fables and oracles, the same method and the same principles on which he had formulated his demonstration in the *Histoire des Oracles* and whose consequences, when broadened as such, are the same. And this is but one example among many.

In 1723, Fontenelle comments on two *mémoires* by the naturalist Antoine de Jussieu about the nature and origin of "pierres figurées," that is, stones with visible imprints of things existing in nature (leaves, flowers, small creatures), or deriving from remains existing in the natural world (bones, teeth, or even small objects or tools that may have been made by humans). Long considered simply "jeux de la nature," the *pierres figurées* had attracted the attention of naturalists since the second half of the seventeenth century. Some of their number had, very early on, affirmed the organic nature of *pierres figurées,*[17] paving the way for the study of fossils as evidence of the natural upheavals the planet had faced throughout its history. The Académie des sciences adopted this position from the beginning, even if all of the scholars who participated in these debates did not agree on the nature of these "upheavals" of which said petrification was the result. If for some this was irrefutable evidence of the universal flood described in Genesis,[18] for a good number of scholars such as Jussieu and Réaumur it was more a question of partial transformations, spread out over an entirely different time frame than that of Biblical chronology.

Like Jussieu, Fontenelle did not believe that *pierres figurées* were the result of a plastic force of nature, let alone a singular, sudden disaster sent by God to punish a guilty mankind. Rather, they were traces of natural species that had once existed and were evidence of the many upheavals or "revolutions" that had marked the earth's history over the centuries.[19] This is the meaning behind the second *mémoire* by Jussieu that Fontenelle summarizes at the beginning of this account: he demonstrated that the *yeux-de-serpent*[20] (snake eyes) and the *crapaudines* (small semi-precious stones) [21] were in fact the remains of two distinct kinds of teeth from a fish native to the seas of Brazil and that their presence in a number of French quarries confirmed there had been changes in land and sea in the distant past. The naturalist also shows in his *mémoire* on *pierres de foudre* (lightning stones) that those he had seen – long believed to have fallen from the sky on stormy days and to which were attributed supernatural powers – were really only polished stones previously used as tools for hunting or defence by primitive populations (arrowheads, axes, sharp stones, etc.). Jussieu justifies his explanation using the example of the American Indians, who used polished stones in the same way as a substitute for iron, to which they had no access.

Fontenelle takes advantage of these two *mémoires* to establish a comparison, absent in Jussieu's works, between the "revolutions" of nature and the different stages in the history of human societies, which he calls "révolutions morales." In doing so, he presents principles that can also be found in *De l'origine des fables*, published clandestinely in 1714:[22] legends are based on a misunderstanding of natural phenomena and evaporate once reason is able to to explain them. We thus understand why the secretary of the *académie* chose to summarize the two *mémoires* in a single article – what applies to the natural sciences also applies to the human sciences. *Crapaudines* and *pierres de foudre* are not the same (organic or inorganic fossils, geological or archaeological), but their epistemological status is still quite similar when it comes to making that status the object of a rational discourse. The comparison between common European beliefs and American customs presents him with the opportunity to affirm the psychological and moral uniformity of human nature when faced with unexplained phenomena, the principle on which he was already constructing his explanation of fables and superstitions. His account of Jussieu's *mémoires* thus comes to support the *fontenellienne* conception of the origin of beliefs, and a privileged conception at that, for it awards scientific and institutional approval to a controversial hypothesis that has multiple consequences. Remember here that Fontenelle, from the supposed neutrality of his position, offered this principle teaching in his well-known history of the "dent d'or" (golden tooth): "Il est bon de s'assurer exactement des faits et de ne pas chercher la raison de ce qui n'est point."[23]

The practice of formulating a history of knowledge-in-development as part of the Académie des sciences also allowed Fontenelle to provide a scientific basis for some of the more complex debates in clandestine thought. I have shown elsewhere the importance that Fontenelle assigns to all debates concerning the human brain that reinforce the materialistic physiology that was developed in his *Traité de la liberté de l'âme,*[24] a clandestine text that began circulating in the early eighteenth century and that appeared in the *Nouvelles libertés de penser* in 1743. Editing the work of anatomists and correspondents of the *académie* for a good twenty years enabled Fontenelle to establish a direct relationship between matter and spirit (*sans cerveau pas d'idée*) and to affirm a sort of continuity between humans and animals, the difference between the two being found in the *quantity* of matter, and not the quality, let alone the existence of a spiritual soul.[25] We are therefore not surprised to note that, as Motoïchi Terada has shown, the article "âme" in the *Encyclopédie* is composed of many passages borrowed directly from Fontenelle's writings for the Académie Royale des sciences.[26]

In fact, if we follow the explanations given by the secretary of the Académie des sciences over the years, there is nothing in nature that cannot be explained by the action of matter. So he declares in an account of the reproduction of plants, in which he reverses the logic permitted under the scholastic argument that overlaps body and mind and thus makes from the soul a purely material principle:

> Ce bizarre principe de la philosophie scolastique sur la manière dont l'âme est dans le corps, que le tout est dans le Tout, et le tout dans chaque partie, est donc exactement vrai à l'égard des plantes, et il est assez remarquable qu'on trouve réellement dans la matière ce qui avait été imaginé comme une propriété particulière et incompréhensible de l'esprit.[27]

Fontenelle thus transforms academic writings into a privileged platform for his own ideas, but also for ideas that polemic thought can reappropriate, and to which the scientific dimension of the medium, and the apparently neutral role of Fontenelle's position, bring a guarantee. This strategy did not pass unnoticed among his watchful contemporaries, who made very good use of it in the polemic literature of the time. One example of its use is already well known to specialists, and we mention it here onl for its representative character.[28] Fontenelle reported that in the town of Chartres a young deaf-mute from birth, having "miraculously" recovered his hearing, began speaking at the age of twenty-four. He was questioned by "skillful theologians" on his ideas, in his former state, about God, the soul, and so on. Fontenelle noted, with a pleasant *litote*, or understatement, that the young man "ne parut pas avoir poussé ses pensées jusque là."[29] In Pierre Bayle we hear echoes of this anecdote in his *Réponse aux Questions d'un Provincial* of 1706, where he develops the implications of the *fontenellien* text: he attacks the innate idea of God by relating what he calls "un nouveau phénomène par lequel on peut comprendre qu'il n'est pas aussi facile que plusieurs l'assurent de parvenir à la connaissance de Dieu sans le secours de l'instruction." Bayle wryly points out that "[j]'ignore si tout le monde saura gré à Mr de Fontenelle d'avoir inséré ce fait-là dans l'Histoire de l'Academie royale des sciences. Mais quoi qu'il en soit, voilà un nouveau phénomène sur lequel Mr Bernard pourra s'exercer s'il le juge digne de son attention." This anecdote was subsequently used by several authors, notably in clandestine texts, to undermine the metaphysical foundations of Christianity (it is most notably found in the manuscript *l'Ame matérielle*, attributed to Du Marsais) and was the object of materialist interpretations by La Mettrie and Hevétius, to name but two. The anecdote even seems to have presaged some points made in Diderot's *Lettre sur les aveugles*.

Thus the case Fontenelle brought timely to light in 1703 demonstrates one of his favourite strategies: to disappear behind a supposed neutrality, that of the secretary of the Académie Royale des sciences, and to leave it to others – the closest or most astute readers – to find more controversial implications based on what he has been able to bring to light. The neutrality in religious matters claimed by the Académie Royale des sciences, the method of writing history adopted by Fontenelle, the choice of subjects discussed, and his unique philosophical style, ended up expressing in academic publications the image of Nature as constantly active – which replaced the idea of God, whose existence is never denied but whose effects are never called upon either.[30] Under the pen of Fontenelle, nature acts solely through unwavering principles (laws) whose infinite combinatorial processes produce an infinite number of possible structures.[31] In this creative dynamic, even random chance becomes a possible factor in the diversification of forms. It is moreover chance, the blind cause *par excellence*, that appears ultimately responsible for the existence of certain structures, including monsters – a recurrent theme in the *Histoire de l'académie des sciences*.[32]

To conclude. I emphasize three points:

1. It is clear that academic circles offered, for various reasons, a privileged terrain for the production and dissemination of clandestine

literature. This warrants a more systematic examination. But we can also state that Fontenelle's case is rather exceptional in this regard, not only because of the longevity of his academic involvement but also because of his efficiency as secretary of the institution: no other French academy can claim, like the Académie Royale des Sciences, the publication of an annual volume of its "histoire," let alone an account that stands as one of the first examples of what we would today call historical epistemology. The influence of Fontenelle in the first half of the eighteenth century must thus be measured by the quality of his ideas and his writings, but also by the power bestowed upon him in his position at the heart of one of the most prestigious institutions of the French monarchy, through which he erected a strategic platform for the development and circulation of new ideas. And let's not forget, moreover, that it was as secretary of the *académie* that Fontenelle advised Benoît de Maillet to explore the ideas on the origin of marine life he would later present in the *Telliamed.*

2. Certainly, the perpetual secretary of the *académie*, was, in his official function, the Historiographer Royal of the scientific achievements of the kingdom, and as such, he knew how to make pleasant reading of the driest research, make the experiments of chemists and the observations of astronomers accessible, all while providing the upper classes with the hero figure of modern times, the scholar, or *savant* (which is the role of the academic *Eloges*). But Fontenelle was also a free spirit, writing for a public that was not necessarily initiated into the new scientific knowledge of the times or the epistemological principles underlying them. Discreetly, he made of the *Histoire de l'Académie royale des sciences* an effective tool for converting his readers to the "parti de la philosophie." And for want of being able to openly present the philosophical foundations of new discoveries, at the very least he introduced new modalities of thought and new issues that would encourage the audience to be more open to certain presuppositions and consequences.
3. From the *Histoire des Oracles* to his academic writings, Fontenelle's historical method and his transformation of the discursive register revealed the consistency and efficacy of his publications. The lack of explicit moral considerations in the texts of the Académie Royale des sciences reflects a *fontenellienne* conception of the deterministic theory that the author exhibited in his clandestine writings: such a system cannot be disclosed to the public at large, and most people are not yet ready to receive and adopt such morals, which amount to a purely philosophical theory of happiness (which refers us back to

> the title of another well-known extract of his). The texts of the *académie*, addressed to a wide public in Europe, accustomed the reader, by the grace of pleasant language, to the foundations of a philosophical system; the clandestine treatises, written for the initiated, such as the *Traité de la liberté de l'âme* and the *Réflexions sur l'argument de M. Pascal et de M. Locke concernant la possibilité d'une autre vie à venir*, were published together in *Nouvelles libertés de penser* in 1743, explicitly to bring out the consequences of the author's radical thought.

The *Trésor de la Langue française* tells us that what is "radical" is that "qui concerne le principe premier, fondamental, qui est à l'origine d'une chose, d'un phénomène"; "qui va jusqu'au bout de chacune des conséquences impliquées par le choix initial." The question here is, which of the two methods – that of the explicit but clandestine manuscripts that only reached the already converted, or the writings disseminated by academicians and open to the public space – was more "radical" in the introduction of new ideas? I have made a case for the latter.

Appendix: "Philosophie cl@ndestine" – A Digital Platform at the Service of Research

The progress made in researching clandestine philosophical literature in just over a hundred years is without any doubt exemplary. After the *corpus* was identified Gustave Lanson in 1912 and the first systematic research was conducted by Ira O. Wade, the time of syntheses, of theses,[33] of first identifications, of important editions of text has come. The importance of underground literature for understanding the intellectual history of the seventeenth century and the Enlightenment has been confirmed. Special mention must be made, in this too brief history of research on clandestine philosophical manuscripts, of the systematic census of manuscripts by Miguel Benítez, which has become an essential tool for researchers around the world.[34] Since then, *La Lettre Clandestine*, a world-leading journal on the issue, has regularly reported the discovery of new copies of texts already identified or the existence of new titles likely to be integrated into the clandestine *corpus*.

The twenty-first century marks a turning point in research for all the human sciences, thanks to the development of digital tools, to which we cannot remain indifferent. Proof of this is the launching of the online digital platform "Cl@ndestine Philosophy" (philosophie-cladestine.

huma-num.fr), realized thanks to the support of ENS Lyon, LaBex COMOD, and the Institut Universitaire de France, under the responsibility of Antony McKenna and Maria Susana Seguin, within the framework of activities of IHRIM (UMR 5317 CNRS-ENS Lyon). This database, entirely publicly funded and hosted free of charge in a large research infrastructure,[35] is fully open and freely available as an open source. It has an endpoint for SPARQL queries.

Designed as a true digital research tool exploiting the latest features of the semantic Web, the "Clandestine Philosophy" database now provides access to the complete and regularly updated list of clandestine philosophical manuscripts,[36] and adds a series of features to make it easier to do dynamic data exploitation. In addition to a critical bibliography, the platform gives access to old and modern editions, and to biographical information on identified or supposed authors (through authoritative files common to French and European libraries),[37] and it will soon point to the editions already available online in the main digital libraries. The geolocation function makes it possible to visualize the places of conservation of manuscripts and to access information useful for their consultation; it also offers researchers a quick overview of the places where texts were circulated and received, which later research can confirm or correct. When transcriptions are available, they are accessible for reading and downloading: systematic transcription work, as part of an educational project for masters students, will very soon enrich the background of unpublished texts.[38] Finally, it is possible to do simple searches or access pre-established lists and obtain PDF extractions of all of this information.

We are now working on future developments of this research tool: the policy of digitization of heritage funds undertaken in most libraries makes it possible to work now towards the simultaneous display of images of manuscripts and transcripts using IIIF tools, which can be a means to facilitate the study of the variants of the texts, the families of the manuscripts, and can contribute to the identification of the authors and the editions of these unpublished texts, whether in a traditional version or in an edition TEI, which also remains to be developed. We will then be able to consider the textometric exploitation of the *corpus* and, finally, begin advanced research on the underground philosophical literature in the era of digital humanities.

For more information or to collaborate on the development of this platform, you can contact us through the platform or write to susana.seguin@ens-lyon.fr

NOTES

1 Mention must be made of the precise study by Miguel Benítez in *La Face cachée des Lumières* (Paris and Oxford: Universitas and the Voltaire Foundation, 1996), which is even more enriched in the Spanish version, *La Cara oculta de la Luces* (Valencia: Biblioteca Valenciana, Colección Ideas, 2003). The journal *La Lettre clandestine* regularly highlights the discovery of new copies of texts already identified or the existence of new titles eligible to be included in the clandestine corpus.

2 On this point, see H.-J. Martin et R. Chartier, eds, *Histoire de l'édition française*, tome II (Paris: Promodis, 1984).

3 François Moureau, "La plume et le plomb" et "Clandestinité et ventes publiques," in *De bonne main. La communication manuscrite au* XVIIIe *siècle*, ed. F. Moureau (Paris and Oxford: Universitas and the Voltaire Foundation, 1993), 5–16 and 143–75; and *La Plume et le plomb* (Paris: PUPS, 2006), preface by Robert Darnton. See also Alain Mothu, "Le manuscrit philosophique clandestin existe-t-il?," in *Écrire aux* XVIIe *et* XVIIIe *siècles. Genèse de textes littéraires et philosophiques*, ed. Jean-Louis Lebrave et Almuth Gresillon (Paris: CNRS Éditions, 2000), 59–74; *La L. C.* no. 7, 1998, *L'Identification du texte clandestin aux XVIIe et XVIIIe siècles*; G. Artigas-Menant, *Du secret des clandestins à la propagande voltairienne* (Paris: Champion, 2001).

4 According to Raymond Birn, in the eighteenth century, 40 per cent of censors belonged to a provincial or Parisian *académie*. See Birn, *La Censure royale dans la France des Lumières* (Paris: Odile Jacob, 2007), 105.

5 See Fabrice Charton, "Fontenelle, secrétaire perpétuel de l'Académie royale des Sciences," *Revue Fontenelle*, nos. 6–7, Publications des universités de Rouen et du Havre, 2010, 295–310.

6 N. Fréret, *Lettre de Thrasybule à Leucippe*, critical ed. by Sergio Landucci (Firenze: Olschki, 1986).

7 Manuscript edited by l'Abbé Le Mascrier under the title *Le Monde, son origine, son antiquité. De l'âme et de son immortalité*, [Paris] 1751.

8 Maurice Barthélemy, *Documents historiques. La Libre-Pensée et ses martyrs, petit dictionnaire de l'intolérance cléricale* (Paris: Librairie de propagande socialiste et anticléricale, 1904), 63.

9 Other than the works coming from his membership to the Académie des sciences such as *Éléments de la Géométrie de l'infini* (1727) and the *Éloges des académiciens*, of which there are numerous editions throughout the eighteenth century, we can single out *L'Histoire du Théâtre français* along with its *Réflexions sur la poétique* (1742) and the *Traité des Tourbillons* (appearing in 1752).

10 Jean Dagen, *L'histoire de l'esprit humain dans la pensée française de Fontenelle à Condorcet* (Paris: Klincksieck, 1977).
11 Jonathan I. Israel, *Les Lumières radicales. La philosophie de Spinoza et la naissance de la modernité (1650–1750)* (Paris: Editions Amsterdam, [2001]2005), 407–23.
12 *Suite des oeuvres diverses de Mr de F*** contenant les trois traités suivants De l'existence de Dieu, De l'origine des fables et Du bonheur*, Rouen, 1714. See also S. Akagi, "*Suite des OEuvres diverses de Mr de F**** de 1714: The First Edition of *L'Origine des fables* and Two Others of Fontenelle's *discours*," *Études de Langue et de Littérature françaises* 50, Tokyo, 1987.
13 See Mitia Rioux-Beaulne, introduction to "De l'origine des fables," in *Digressions sur les Anciens et les Modernes et autres textes philosophiques*, ed. S. Audidière (Paris: Garnier, forthcoming).
14 We refer here to the edition of *Traité* in the *Nouvelles libertés de penser*, Amsterdam [Paris], 1743, 150.
15 Scholarship as a philosophical weapon can also explain the presence of clandestine authors in academic circles.
16 Fontenelle, *Entretiens sur la pluralité des mondes* [1686], ed. Christophe Martin (Paris: Flammarion, 1998), xxx.
17 Nicolas Sténon (1638–1686): Swedish anatomist and naturalist, author of significant dissertations on the nature of fossils, *De solido intra solidum naturaliter contento dissertationis prodromus* (1669).
18 Johann Jakob Scheuchzer (1672–1733) and Johann Scheuchzer (1684–1738). Swiss naturalists, corresponding members of the Académie des sciences, authors of numerous dissertations dedicated to the nature of fossils and to the role of the biblical flood in the formation of ground relief, among which we can single out *Herbarium diluvianum*, (Zurich, Imp. D. Gesner, 1709, 44pp in folio) that Fontenelle discusses not without irony in *HARS*, 1710, 21–3.
19 This doctrine, known by the name of "actualism," and of which Jussieu and Réamur were the most significant proponents, characterized French geological thought for the first half of the eighteenth century and countered the catastrophist vision of natural history that made the universal flood the key moment in the geologic formation of the globe. On this topic, see: M.S. Seguin, *Science et religion au XVIIIe siècle. Le mythe du déluge universel* (Paris: H. Champion, 2001).
20 Œil-de-serpent: gemstone or precious stone formed from fossilized teeth.
21 Precious stone, so named because it was believed to come from the head of a toad.
22 *Des miracles.*

23 "Sur les singularités de l'Histoire Naturelle de la France," *HARS*, 1699, 23. It is with these words that the *Histoire des Oracles* (1686), opens, the story of the famous "dent d'or": "Assurons-nous bien du fait, avant que de nous inquiéter de la cause. Il est vrai que cette méthode est lente pour la plupart des gens qui courent naturellement à la cause, et passent par-dessus la vérité du fait; mais enfin nous éviterons le ridicule d'avoir trouvé la cause de ce qui n'est point." *OC*, t. II, 161.

24 Maria Susana Seguin, "Fontenelle, l'Académie des Sciences et le siège de l'âme," *La Lettre clandestine* 18, 2010, 162–79.

25 This principle also emphasizes the idea expressed at the beginning of the *Digression sur les Anciens et les Modernes* through which the philosopher affirmed the universality of human nature, since nature produces men, animals, and plants from the "même pâte": "La Nature a entre les mains une certaine pâte qui est toujours la même, qu'elle tourne et retourne sans cesse en mille façons, et dont elle forme les hommes, les animaux, les plantes ; et certainement elle n'a point formé Platon, Démosthène ni Homère d'une argile plus fine ni mieux préparée que nos Philosophes, nos Orateurs et nos Poëtes d'aujourd'hui." *Digressions sur les Anciens et les Modernes, œuvres complètes*, ed. Alain Niderst (Paris: Fayard, 1990–6), t. II, 413.

26 Motoichi Terada, "Une 'façon' copiée-collée de l'Encyclopédie?: avatars de textes de l'*HMARS* à l'*Encyclopédie* par l'intermédiaire de Chambers," *Recueil d'études sur l'Encyclopédie et les Lumières* (Tokyo), no. 1, 2012, 1–40.

27 "Sur une végétation singulière," *HARS*, 1712, 43.

28 See Jørn Schøsler, "'Le sourd et muet de Chartres.' Un épisode sensualiste oublié de la lutte philosophique au XVIIIe siècle," *Actes du XIIIe Congrès des romanistes scandinaves, Jyväskylä, 12–15 août 1996*, ed. O. Merisalo et T. Natri (Jyväskylä: Publications de l'Institut des Langues romanes et classiques,1998), t. 2, 621–34.

29 *HARS*, 1703, 18.

30 Maria Susana Seguin, "La Nature dans les écrits de Fontenelle pour l'Académie des sciences," *Dix-huitième siècle* 45, 2013, 97–113.

31 "Nous pouvons [...] avancer [...] qu'on ne saurait guère attribuer à la Nature trop d'uniformité dans les règles générales, et trop de diversité dans les applications particulières. Plus on étend son plan en y faisant entrer différentes combinaisons des mêmes principes, plus on est en droit de se croire dans la route de la vérité": "Observations botaniques," *HARS*, 1702, 52.

32 "Ce n'est que le hasard de la rencontre des fœtus [...] qui les détermine à quitter certains chemins et à en suivre toujours d'autres. Et comme ce

hasard est susceptible d'une infinité de combinaisons différentes, c'est une chose infinie que les monstres qui le sont par quelques parties doubles": "Observations d'anatomie," *HARS*, 1702, 28. "Ne reconnaît-on pas là [à l'origine des êtres exceptionnels que sont les monstres] les effets de causes accidentelles, irrégulières, aveugles, qui n'agissent pas de concert avec les lois générales et ne reviennent point deux fois à une même combinaison": "Sur les Monstres," *HARS*, 1740, 49.

33 Marie-Hélène Cotoni, *L'Exégèse du Nouveau Testament dans la philosophie française du* XVIIIe *siècle* (Oxford: Voltaire Foundation, 1984); Antony McKenna, *De Pascal à Voltaire. Le rôle des* Pensées *de Pascal dans l'histoire des idées entre 1670 et 1734* (Oxford: Voltaire Foundation, 1990).

34 Miguel Benítez, *La Face cachée des Lumières* (Paris and Oxford: Universitas and the Voltaire Foundation, 1996). The list of the philosophical clandestine manuscripts is enriched in the Spanish version: *La Cara oculta de la Luces* (Valencia: Biblioteca valenciana, 2003).

35 https://www.huma-num.fr, research infrastructure included in the European consortium dariah.eu.

36 This database gives access to the very rich list by M. Benítez, supplemented with all the manuscripts listed in *La Lettre clandestine* since 2003 (date of the publication of *La Cara oculta de las Luces*).

37 Through the projects data.bnf.fr and viaf.org.

38 Educational project conducted in the framework of the Masters seminar led by Maria Susana Seguin, Université Paul-Valéry Montpellier III. The results of this collective work will be published in the research archive https://philoclandes.hypotheses.org.

Chapter Ten

Joseph as the Natural Father of Christ: An Unknown, Clandestine Manuscript of the Early Eighteenth Century

MARTIN MULSOW

I

A treatise claiming that Jesus was merely Joseph's natural son, and not of divine origin at all, was in circulation as a clandestine manuscript in the early eighteenth century in Germany.[1] This manuscript and its copies have so far completely escaped the attention of research. They do not appear in Miguel Benítez's otherwise very complete catalogue of underground writings.[2] Yet as we will see, this text did have a small, though limited, circulation.

"The devil wrote this down on 13 March 1743." This sentence is found at the end of a manuscript written in a beautiful, decorative hand and held by the Herzog August Library in Wolfenbüttel.[3] It is titled *De Josepho Christi Parente Naturali Meditatio,* that is, "A Reflection on Joseph as the Natural Father of Christ." It is clear that we are dealing with a clandestine work, a text that circulated underground, because the library in Wolfenbüttel holds a second copy of the manuscript, which is bound with the *Meditationes de Deo, Mundo, Homine* by the Freethinker Theodor Ludwig Lau.[4] Lau was a philosopher and lawyer who had caused a furore in 1717 and 1719 with writings that were critical of religion.[5] Writings like these were collected, copied, and bound with other radical works. The resulting collections were then given titles such as "Scripta antichristiana," "Scripta atheistica," or similar.[6] The state and university library in Dresden, as we shall see, also holds a version of this manuscript.

The heterodox nature of the thesis expressed in the manuscript's title is evident: it asserts that Joseph is Christ's natural father, so the idea of a virgin birth is to be rejected. The contents of this manuscript can be recapitulated quickly. The story of Christ's begetting is reconstructed from *Matthew* and *Luke.* Joseph, who is betrothed to Mary, initially thinks that she has been unfaithful to him or is fantasizing when she tells him of the angel's Annunciation. Joseph, for his part, dreams that the angel exhorts him to sleep with Mary so that the spirit can purify the seed that is to redeem mankind. Joseph does this not out of desire, but "ex praecepto coelestis nuncio," on the instructions of the heavenly messenger.[7] Thereafter he ceremonially takes Mary home as his wife (*suam uxorem*) in the manner of the Jews, but does not sleep with her again in order not to defile the womb sanctified by the Holy Spirit with his merely human seed.

After the author rebuts a number of objections by reference to parallel passages and philological arguments, he comes to the main reason for his reconstruction: "If Joseph is not Christ's natural father, it follows that Christ is not the true Messiah."[8] But this is not the conclusion that he wishes to draw. "If Joseph is not Christ's natural father, I ask why Christ's genealogy is derived from that of Joseph. Why do Matthew and Luke list Joseph's ancestors so carefully?"[9] It is true that these two evangelists provide detailed family trees for Jesus, leading via Joseph back to Abraham and even Adam.[10] The author of the manuscript continues: "If he [Joseph] were not, in fact, the father of Christ, they should have provided Mary's genealogy. For who would seriously try to prove that I am a member of the Brunswick ducal family if the Duke of Brunswick is my stepfather? Especially if my mother had never even slept with the man? Enough of these jokes!"[11]

The fact that the author draws on the duke of Brunswick as an example is a clear indication that the text originated in the territory of Brunswick-Wolfenbüttel. The tone is relaxed and provocative, similar to what we find in the Latin treatise *De tribus impostoribus* by Johann Joachim Müller. At the same time it is rather scholastic in the way it is structured by objections and responses, as in the appended concluding part of *De tribus impostoribus.*[12] But it should be noted that the text is quite clearly not written with any anti-Christian intentions. Its aim is to demonstrate that the royal genealogy attributed to Joseph and the figure of Jesus as the Messiah are connected, so that Christ's claim is justified. At least as a legal title, as Fausto Sozzini and his followers believed, Christ's position as the Messiah would in this case be secure.[13]

The text also gives a Christological justification for regarding Christ as naturally begotten, presenting it as implied by the doctrine of the hypostatic union (two natures of Jesus): "If he was truly a man, he must have been conceived naturally."[14] It also uses the argument of the minimization of miracles:

> God tends not to work miracles where he can act by natural causes. But tell me why such a great miracle should have been necessary here, where a truly natural man, one who is not imagined and who can eat and drink, is to be formed? Could not Joseph have brought forth such a man? I think I know what is making you anxious and depressed: you are imagining that a Christ produced in this way would not have been immune to original sin. But your fear is vain and foolish because there is no such thing as original sin. And if there were, could not the Holy Spirit have sanctified Joseph's seed and made it pure?[15]

Here it becomes clear that, even going beyond his Christian foundations, the author is a radical. He does not believe in the doctrine of original sin.[16] From this it follows for him that Jesus does not have to be a "pure" being produced by a virgin birth who, by virtue of this quality, can save humanity from its sins. The doctrine of original sin had been rejected by the Socinians in particular because it did not agree with the premises of human freedom and rationality. And it was unnecessary if the dogma of satisfaction, of justification and salvation through Christ's sacrifice on the Cross was rejected, as the Socinians did.[17] The author of *De Josepho* seems to share this view. As we will see, not all the copyists who approvingly distributed this text went so far – they simply omitted this sentence. The author, however, leaves both possibilities open: the genuinely radical option that denies the existence of original sin ("there is no such thing as original sin"), and the weaker version ("And if there were") in which there *is* original sin, but no virgin birth because the construction of the "purificatio" of the seed makes it superfluous.

The treatise has now almost adopted the tone of a pamphlet. The assumption that the Messiah has no father, the author continues, is found nowhere among the prophets and is "insipida," foolish. The Church Fathers had devised this, he claimed, along with dozens of other jokes ("cum sexcentis aliis naeniis effinxerunt"), and imposed it on the credulous people as an article of faith ("obstruserunt").[18] This author no longer has any faith in Christianity. He considers the dogmas corrupt and a priestly fraud. This tone, too, is reminiscent of the Latin treatise *De tribus impostoribus*, whose author believes that the founders of religion are fraudsters and who uses his detailed knowledge of Jewish traditions to express his contempt for Christianity. The very first sentence of *De Josepho*, "Fabulas multas de Christo Messia nostro circumferri, non solum credo; sed ex plurimis rerum documentis compertum habeo," seems to be constructed along the lines of the first sentence of *De tribus impostoribus*. Similarly starting with an Accusativus cum Infinitivo, it begins: "Deum esse, eumque colendum esse, multi disputant [...]"[19] We are talking here about a criticism of mythical views, about Enlightenment.

II

The title page gives the author as "H. v. d. H." This abbreviation is easy to decipher as "Hermann von der Hardt" and is confirmed by the Dresden manuscript, which states explicitly: "Dni. Herm. van der Hardt." Whether "the devil" who wrote the manuscript is thus to be seen as von der Hardt himself, or whether "Diabolus descripsit" should be translated more precisely as "the devil copied it," remains to be seen. Hermann von der Hardt was a quarrelsome, disagreeable professor of Oriental languages at the University of Helmstedt.[20] In his time, he was famous, the luminary of his university and a long-standing vice-chancellor, but today he is forgotten. This is largely because later generations of theologians found von der Hardt's theories and his behaviour embarrassing. Coming from a Pietist milieu, von der Hardt became a rationalist interpreter of the Bible and speculated wildly about the origins of the books of the Bible, their authors, and when they were written. In his view, many ancient texts, and the biblical writings in particular, were written in an enigmatic style. They were encoded, he suggested, because their stories and myths contained, in reality, political and historical descriptions of wars, alliances between states, the founding of cities, and invasions, that is, arcane knowledge that could not readily be communicated. Even at that time, according to von der Hardt, instruction had been a "political" art, that is, commentators had formulated their works "pro indulgentia erga traditiones vulgi" out of consideration for popular traditions, so that ordinary people would *not* understand their meaning and become anxious.[21] "Thus this long, symbolic address, which contains a threefold riddle," von der Hardt explained, "provides the model for the enigmatic style in which the ancients had portrayed the destinies of the great kings. They did this in such a way that the story of an individual great hero paints a picture of another, equally famous deed by a different king. Thus a threefold image is created with the same symbolic words in a triple riddle."[22]

This was a complicated hermeneutics of decipherment that amounted to reducing the Bible to a secular, political text. For this reason, von der Hardt was reprimanded by the court in Wolfenbüttel on a number of occasions, especially after 1704, when the death of Duke Rudolf August meant that he lost the close protection of his ruler. After 1713 he was subjected to censorship, his most important books were confiscated, he was forbidden to interpret the Bible, and, in 1727, he was removed from his professorship.[23] This did not stop the old man from publishing his attempts at decoding under various pretexts and in small print runs until his death in 1746. These were daring and, by present-day standards, often wrong (although they sometimes hit the mark).

Was von der Hardt capable of writing a text such as *De Josepho*? In order to come closer to an answer, we will have to differentiate. Von der Hardt dealt almost exclusively with the Old Testament; he kept his distance from New Testament themes. Nor can we simply assert that he was a man of the Enlightenment, or even a deist; his exegesis and enthusiasm for the biblical tradition seem to have been much too dominant. The professor appears to have retained a belief in God's providence at least. He did, however, display a number of similarities with the author of *De Josepho*. As a student of Edras Edzardi, von der Hardt was very knowledgeable about rabbinical literature, and he drew much inspiration from it for his euhemeristic exegesis. It is easy to believe that like many Lutheran and Calvinist writers,[24] he was critical of the Church Fathers and their "credulity." It is even possible that he did not really believe in the doctrine of original sin; after all, he viewed the story of Adam and Eve in paradise merely as an urban myth from Miletus. On matters of dogma, however, all his life von der Hardt was not a man to give much away.

Yet it is difficult to believe that this professor, who punctiliously observed academic rules and maintained high standards, would write a treatise that mounted a frontal attack on a central dogma and permitted itself repeated polemical sorties. How can we reconcile these doubts with the clear attribution of this text to Hermann von der Hardt as the author? Perhaps by investigating whether the text was merely indirectly created or inspired by von der Hardt. From the tone of the work, we might conclude that we should look at the circle around von der Hardt. Perhaps we need to view the treatise as based on extreme versions of his spoken, throwaway comments, which were then used by students and listeners.

In order to substantiate this, we can look back at incidents in which something similar happened. As early as 1706, in the case of the *Histoire de Bileam*, a book had been put together from von der Hardt's oral statements.[25] The ghostwriter at the time was a prominent man, namely Gottfried Wilhelm Leibniz. Von der Hardt had been discussing with Leibniz and Queen Sophie Charlotte the passage from Numbers 22:28 where Balaam's donkey starts to speak.[26] Von der Hardt had suggested that this episode could be explained as a dream. They considered together whether Balaam had been a dreamer, who might have had visions of this sort on the journey. It was Leibniz who had written this explanation down on the spot, in French, so that the Electress could read it too. Von der Hardt published the text a short time later, Leibniz corrected it for a later edition,[27] and they continued to correspond about the subject. As far as von der Hardt was concerned, this text formed part of a small series of biblical interpretations, all written in French (out of consideration for the Electress) and all published anonymously, which offered rationalist or euhemeristic explanations of biblical passages.[28]

When the Jesuit *Journal de Trévoux*, responding to a petition from Trier, issued a warning about von der Hardt in June 1710, it pointed to these writings: "L'Allemagne n'a pas eté inaccessible a une certaine Critique audacieuse toujours prête a favoriser l'incredulité, malgre l'heureux penchant pour la Religion, qu'un esprit naturellement solide donne à ses peuples. Trois ou quatre Ecrivains impies la scandalizent depuis quelque tems par les conjectures, qu'ils oserit debiter. Ces sont Messieurs Thomasius, Gundlingius, van der Hard, &c."[29] The dangers of rationalist biblical exegesis had been noticed. In Helmstedt, too, rumours began to circulate. As early as 1703 a traveller, Gottlieb Stolle, reported what he had heard about von der Hardt: "Perhaps he has more courage to express his opinions than Abbot Schmidt, but as a smart man, he is careful, taking note of who is around and of the circumstances, and when he has said something paradoxical, asks his listeners to keep it to themselves, so that he is not condemned from the pulpit as a heretic. He is generally held to be a Socinian, and it is said that he became one in Holland, because he spent so much time with the Unitarians."[30]

A good deal in the way of "paradoxes" can thus be attributed to von der Hardt. But what seems important is that at this time it was often other people who turned the interpretations hesitantly articulated by von der Hardt into texts. This was also the case with another short work, the *Renards de Samson*, published in von der Hardt's small series. This speculates that the three hundred "foxes" hunted by Samson in Judges 15:4 were merely haystacks. This argument, put forward with the intention of ridding the Bible of its miraculous aspects, had been announced in Halle's *Observationes selectae* as *Metamorphosis vulpecularum Samsonis in stramivis manipulos* in 1704, shortly before it was printed in von der Hardt's series. This time it was possibly the young and ambitious Jakob Friedrich Reimmann from Halberstadt who had heard von der Hardt speaking and turned his thoughts into a text.[31] Reimmann remained an enthusiastic collector of von der Hardt's writings.[32]

Let us look at Reimmann more closely. Was he aware of the heterodox manuscript *De Josepho Christi Parente Naturali*? Yes, he knew this text and provides important information about its origins. Reimmann's *Catalogus Bibliothecae Theologicae Systematico-Criticus*, a comprehensive catalogue of theological works based on his own reading, contains a section on *De Josepho*,[33] right after his listing of the *Esprit de Spinosa* and the *Cymbalum Mundi/Symbolum Sapientiae*, two of the most important and infamous atheistic texts of the radical early Enlightenment.[34] In the section on *De Josepho* Reimmann describes the text and attributes it to Hermann von der Hardt: "I received it from a certain friend. He added that it had been secretly misappropriated from this scholar and that this is how it reached other people against its owner's will, and eventually also … the library of the famous prince."[35] Who might have been the friend who gave the treatise to Reimmann? It is not out of the question that this friend was Leibniz, as Reimmann kept up a lively exchange with him. Leibniz sometimes even visited Reimmann, a headmaster in Halberstadt, at home.[36] Leibniz also had a good relationship with Hermann von der Hardt, so that he could have heard of internal matters, such as a theft, from von der Hardt himself. But other intermediaries, right in Helmstedt, were also conceivable, such as Johann Andreas Schmidt or Johann Fabricius.[37] The "library of the famous prince," in any case, is almost certainly the Wolfenbüttel library, which was under Leibniz's supervision and where, as we have seen, the text ended up.

Yet even the information provided by the friend seems a little uncertain: "I cannot say with certainty whether all this is so," Reimmann admits. But he is by no means indifferent to the text, adding: "Here is my opinion: this *Meditatio* is repulsive, abhorrent and scandalous."[38]

III

The text must, indeed, have been abhorrent to an orthodox theologian, at least to an aging Reimmann. Sixty-three years old in 1731 when he published his *Catalogus*, he was perhaps no longer as intellectually curious as he had been in his mid-thirties, when he might himself have adopted ideas from von der Hardt. But once again: can we really impute the writing of a text as radical as *De Josepho* to von der Hardt? Although he was rumoured to lean towards Socinianism, it is known how careful this professor was as soon as anything became public. I have already suggested that somebody else might have written down von der Hardt's spoken statements and turned them into a text, as we have seen in the cases of *Histoire de Bileam* and the *Metamorphosis vulpecularum Samsonis.* Was somebody taking notes during a conversation von der Hardt had with a small group of people? Is the text the record of a private disputation exercise with an extremely provocative thesis? It did occasionally happen that radical positions were played out internally and that something of the radicalism then stayed with some of the participants in the exercise.[39] In this context, the rumour of a secret theft (*clanculum surreptam*) that Reimmann spread would make more sense. In this case von der Hardt would still be the originator of the ideas, but his arguments would have been stolen from him, so to speak, and misused to produce a text with a radical tendency and a provocative tone.

If von der Hardt was not the direct author of the text, who could have "stolen" his ideas in this case, written them down, and perhaps radicalized them? In this context, let us return to the "devil" who, according to the manuscript held in Wolfenbüttel, had written or copied the work. What if the word "Diabolus" is to be taken literally and does not simply mean the Prince of Darkness, to whom it naturally alludes? What if it is a name? Someone with the name of "Teufel"? Someone from von der Hardt's circle, who could transform his ideas into pamphlets? Von der Hardt did in fact have a student called Teufel. He was not just a normal, well-behaved student, but someone who shared von der Hardt's more radical thinking and pushed it forward. In 1706 this Christian Teufel published an extremely daring work, *Delicatissimum Salomoneum Epithalamium*, under the pseudonym of "Christianus Theophilus."[40] A poem written for the wedding of the Prussian crown prince, this work argued that Psalm 45 was not a theological text, but itself simply a wedding poem from ancient Israel, historically marking the marriage of King Solomon to the daughter of the King of Tyre.

The reaction of orthodoxy was anything but friendly. In Löscher's *Unschuldige Nachrichten* we read: "May God be merciful and tread Satan beneath our feet! May the hapless author and those who have brought him to this [he probably means von der Hardt and his friend Johann Fabricius] recognize this contritely before the millstone is hung around their necks, or even more severe judgements are passed on such offences."[41] This was an open threat, as the worst criminals were punished by being drowned with a millstone around their necks.

Biographical information about Christian Teufel is difficult to find. Elsewhere it is rumoured that von der Hardt had already protected Teufel "on the occasion of another heresy about Adam's naming of the animals."[42] This was probably in 1705, when the small epistolary treatise *Ad Paulum Martinum Noltenium [...] de vocatis ab Adamo animalibus epistola* was published.[43] In it von der Hardt claims, in dispute with Samuel Bochart, that the scene in Genesis 2: 18–20 does not describe the naming of the animals, from which who knows what metaphysical arguments about Adamic wisdom and language could be derived. Rather, he argues, it is an evocation, a summoning up in order to encourage the Israelites not to seek to associate with the spirits of the dead, but to make do with animals. Men of the Enlightenment such as Gundling quickly and easily adopted this interpretation into their rejection of theological/metaphysical constructions.[44]

As the epistolary treatise was published under von der Hardt's name, not Teufel's, there might have been some previous history here too, such as an oral disputation by Teufel, who perhaps put von der Hardt's theses forward in a more provocative form and was then attacked by Helmstedt orthodoxy, whereupon his teacher protected him. There was another rumour about Teufel, which Johann Bernhard Hassel, senior court chaplain in Wolfenbüttel, reported to Johann Vogt, namely, that he was said "to have become a Jew … in the end."[45] This casts an interesting if highly uncertain light on Teufel, especially with regard to *De Josepho Christi Parente Naturali Meditatio.* If this treatise had anything to do with Teufel, could its contents have suggested to the author that he should convert to Judaism? This is not completely out of the question. Like von der Hardt himself, the author is very familiar with Jewish customs, and he uses them as a yardstick for his interpretation. "You do not know the customs of the Jews, my friend", he says condescendingly in the manuscript. "There was almost no difference between betrothal and wedding, except for the solemn act of bringing the bride home. It was not a crime for a man to have slept with his betrothed."[46] He refers to the scholarly literature – Buxtorf, Selden, Lightfoot, and "old manuscripts," which could have indicated Jewish, that is, Rabbinic manuscripts.[47] It was not unknown for such knowledge of Rabbinica and Judaica occasionally to lead to a Judaising of Christians, or even a conversion. Von der Hardt himself reported about theologians who had converted to Judaism.[48] This report refers to three members of the Reformed church, thus not to his student.

IV

Before we speculate any further about a possible author, we must date the manuscript. One difficulty is the date on the copy on which we have based our examination: 1743. If the text was not written until that year, there would be a large time gap between Teufel's documented activities around 1706 and the date 1743. Teufel would have been almost forty years older; aged around sixty rather than around twenty. This is highly unlikely. If the text was written by Teufel, it is much older than the date 1743 would suggest.

And this can in fact be shown. The manuscript is referred to as early as 1725, in the first volume of Johann Christoph Wolf's comprehensive *Curae philologicae et criticae*, in which he presents the research literature on the books of the New Testament.[49] There was, he reported, "an attempt, as unfortunate as it was senseless," to prove that Joseph was Christ's natural father. Wolf had not seen the text in person, but he referred to a review in the *Unschuldigen Nachrichten von alten und neuen theologischen Sachen* of 1711. This journal, edited by Valentin Ernst Löscher, had been published since 1701, and was Lutheran orthodoxy's main publishing organ.[50] We have thus arrived at a time long before 1743, in the period when Teufel was active. Apparently Löscher, or a member of his staff, had received a copy of *De Josepho*, and he responded to it in an article in his journal. "One of us," we read, "has received a handwritten – and therefore untidy – essay, about Joseph as Christ's natural father. It is written in a dangerous style, with evil, biting remarks which destroy the goodwill that suggests it deserves to be mentioned here. We call on the author, whoever he may be, to repent so that, freed from his highly dangerous lack of spirit, he learns to think in the light of grace and to distance himself from his fantastical (to say nothing worse) and offensive stories."[51] This was the official and concerned tone of the church establishment.

The Saxon State Library in Dresden holds a copy of *De Josepho* that can be linked with the review in the *Unschuldige Nachrichten*.[52] This text differs from the 1743 copy that we have been looking at so far in many details, but not in its overall thrust. The Dresden copy seems like a revision that makes the text more flowing and readable.[53] It omits a number of sentences (the final section of the text, a final "objection," is also missing), but also adds some. It could be the work of the author himself, or of an editor who has taken liberties and perhaps shies away from the explicit denial of original sin, for this sentence is left out. That the *Unschuldige Nachrichten* was using this version of the text is suggested by the reference on page 626 to "Prolepsis, vel Hysterosis." In the Wolfenbüttel variant, this passage had been expressed as "ὕστερα ϖρωτερα"; but the Dresden manuscript used these terms. It is highly likely that the Dresden manuscript is the copy on which the reviewer – perhaps Löscher himself, who had lived in Dresden since 1709 as a pastor in the Kreuzkirche and was a senior judge in the consistorial court (*Oberkonsistorialassessor*) – based the review in the *Unschuldige Nachrichten.*

V

We can therefore assume that the text was created in 1711 or earlier. It had quite clearly originated in the territory of Brunswick-Wolfenbüttel, probably in the circle around Hermann von der Hardt, possibly, we suspect, written by one of the professor's students, who had put the professor's ideas together in a text that was then circulated to a limited group. It reached the library in Wolfenbüttel, and from there – or by other paths – a concerned contemporary conveyed it to the supervisory body of Lutheran orthodoxy in Dresden. There soon seem to have been at least two variants of the text in existence, one of which was probably a revision of the other.

At first, the text seems to have had a limited circulation. A copy went to Jakob Friedrich Reimmann, probably via mutual friends of von der Hardt and Reimmann. A number of other scholars in Helmstedt most likely also had a copy. Yet it proved possible to prevent a widespread distribution, such as had been achieved by *De tribus impostoribus* (a more attractive and radical work). For quite a while, all was quiet around the manuscript. Perhaps it was the publication of Reimmann's *Catalogus Bibliothecae Theologicae Systematico-Criticus* in 1731 that reawakened interest in it again. Collectors and admirers of forbidden and heterodox writings used catalogues of clandestine works like this one when they wanted to find their way on the black market.[54] But it was especially in the years around 1743, the date of the Wolfenbüttel manuscript, that *De Josepho* became visible again. Johann Christian Edelmann, a Freethinker who was well known throughout the Holy Roman Empire and knowledgeable about the German clandestine scene,[55] wrote in his *Glaubensbekenntnis* of 1746:

> Those who know which famous man the good Herr Reimmann, in his Catalogo Syst. Crit. Tom. I. p. 1030, means by the initial letters H.v.d. ..., and have seen and read his learned treatise on this matter (which still circulates as a secret manuscript among scholars) with their own eyes / they will be the last in many places to subscribe to Herr Reimmann's view / that these

> modest thoughts constitute a shameful, cursed, and offensive work which deserves to be forgotten for ever / especially when they take into account / that outside our fatherland, namely, in England / the same material, namely, arguing that Joseph was the natural father of our Lord Jesus / at present is on public sale / in London / bearing the name not only of the author (who is said to be dead), but also of the bookseller [...][56]

Edelmann here describes *De Josepho* as a clandestine work "that still circulates as a secret manuscript among scholars." Had he read the 1743 Wolfenbüttel copy when he wrote the *Glaubensbekenntnis*? Or a similar copy? If it was the Wolfenbüttel copy, could he do anything with the "Diabolus descripsit"? And a further question: if the copyist really wanted to point to Christian Teufel as the "Diabolus," why is the text at the same time attributed to "H. v. d. H."? And after so many years had passed since the text was written, how did he know about Teufel's role? We can see that much is still unclear here, and, in particular, that our hypothesis that Teufel had "stolen" the text, or written it down, must remain mere speculation as long as no more striking evidence emerges.

Translated from the German by Angela Davies

NOTES

1 A more extended German version of this essay is in *Aufklärung* 25, 2013, 73–112 ("Joseph als natürlicher Vater Christi"), with a critical edition of the text "De Josepho Christi Parente Naturali" at 101–10 and an edition of the refutation in the "Unschuldige Nachrichten" of 1711. On the phenomenon of clandestine literature see Gianni Paganini, *Introduzione alle filosofie clandestine* (Bari: Laterza, 2008); Ira A. Wade, *The Clandestine Organization and Diffusion of Philosophic Ideas in France from 1700 to 1750* (Princeton: Princeton University Press, 1938); Antony McKenna and Alain Mothu, eds, *La Philosophie clandestine à l'Age classique* (Paris: Voltaire Foundation, 1997). A survey of the most important texts can be found in Winfried Schröder, *Ursprünge des Atheismus. Untersuchungen zur Metaphysik- und Religionskritik im 17. und 18. Jahrhundert* (Stuttgart: Frommann-Holzboog, 1998). On the situation in Germany see Martin Mulsow, *Enlightenment Underground: Radical Germany 1680–1720* (Charlottesville: University of Virginia Press, 2015).

2 Miguel Benítez, *La face cachée des lumières. Recherches sur les manuscrits philosophiques clandestins de l'âge classique* (Paris: Universitas, 1996); latest

expanded version in Benítez, *La cara oculta de las luces* (Valencia: Generalitat Valenciana 2003).

3 Herzog August Library Wolfenbüttel (hereafter HAB), Cod. Extrav. 265.14. "Diabolus descr[ipsit] d. XIII. Martii 1743."

4 HAB, Cod. Extrav. 157.11.

5 On him see Martin Mulsow, *Prekäres Wissen. Eine andere Ideengeschichte der Frühen Neuzeit* (Berlin: Suhrkamp, 2012).

6 See Martin Mulsow, "Die Transmission verbotenen Wissens," in *Kulturen des Wissens im 18. Jahrhundert*, ed. Ulrich Johannes Schneider (Berlin: De Gruyter, 2008), 61–80.

7 HAB, Cod. Extrav. 265.14, 6.

8 HAB, Cod. Extrav. 265.14, 27: "Si Joseph non est Christi naturalis pater, sequitur, quod non sit verus Messias."

9 HAB, Cod. Extrav. 265.14, 32: "Si Jospeh non est pater Christi naturalis, quaeso cur Genealogia Christi ex Genealogia Josephi deducitur? Cur tam anxiè Matthaeus atque Lucas Josephi parentes recensent?"

10 Matthew 1:1–17; Luke 3:23–38.

11 HAB, Cod. Extrav. 265.14, 32ff: "Si enim Christi pater non fuisset, Mariae texere Genealogiam debuissent. Numquis sanus demonstrat, me esse ex familia Ducum Brunsvicensium si vitricus meus dux fuit Brunsvicensis? Inprimis cum mater mea nunquam cum viro cohabitavit? Absint nugae!"

12 Anonymous [Johann Joachim Müller], *De imposturis religionum (De tribus impostoribus); Von den Betrügereyen der Religionen; Dokumente*, ed. Winfried Schröder (Stuttgart: Frommann-Holzboog, 1999).

13 See Otto Fock, *Der Socinianismus* (Kiel: Schröder, 1847). On Socinian precursors of the treatise see Mulsow, "Joseph als natürlicher Vater Christi," 75–7.

14 HAB, Cod. Extrav. 265.14, 36: "Quia Christus quoad humanam naturam fuit verus et naturalis homo. Si fuit verus homo, naturali etiam modo debuit concipi."

15 Ibd. 38ff.: "Quia Deus non solet miracula edere ubi per naturales causas agere potest. Sed dic, cur tantum miraculum hic fuerit necessarium, cum homo verus naturalis non phantasticus, qui edere et bibere poterat, esset formandus? An Joseph talem hominem procreare forte non potuit? Sentio quid te angat prematque. Opinaris Christum hoc pacto non mansisse immunem â Peccato Originis. Sed vanus et stolidus est timor, quia plane non datur Peccatum Originis. Et si esset, num Spiritus semen Josephi sanctificare et purum reddere nequibat?"

16 On the criticism of the doctrine of original sin see Anselm Schubert, *Das Ende der Sünde. Anthropologie und Erbsünde zwischen Reformation und Aufklärung* (Göttingen: Vandenhoek, 2002).

17 See Fausto Sozzini, "De statu primi hominis ante lapsum disputatio," in *Bibliotheca fratrum Polonorum*, vol. 2 (Amsterdam: Pieter van der Meersche, 1668). See also Fock, *Der Socinianismus*, 655ff.; Kestutis Daugirdas, *Die Anfänge des Sozinianismus. Genese und Eindringen des historisch-ethischen Religionsmodells in den universitären Diskurs der Evangelischen in Europa* (Göttingen: Vandenhoek, 2016).

18 HAB, Cod. Extrav. 265.14, 43ff: "In historia Christi rursus nullum apparet vestigium de hac opinione insipida. Nunquam vel Pharisaei vel Sadducaei adversus illam disputarunt et locuti sunt, ne quidem in ore vulgi talem sermonem fuisse deprehendimus. Christus ipse nullibi de hac re quicquam commemoravit; Apostoli tacent de miraculoso hoc nativitatis genere. Donec post aliquod tempus ex falso et superstitioso interpretandi modo patres Ecclesiae communem de origine Christi sententiam cum sexcentis aliis naeniis effinxerunt, populoque incauto ceu Sanctum fidei Articulum obstruserunt."

19 *De imposturis religionum* (n12), 99n12.

20 On Hermann von der Hardt (1660–1746) see Hans Möller, "Hermann von der Hardt als Alttestamentler" (typescript Leipzig, 1962). See also A.G. Hoffmann, "'Hardt,'" in *Allgemeine Encyclopädie der Wissenschaften und Künste*, Zweite Section, H-N, Zweiter Theil (Leipzig: Gleditsch, 1828), col. 388–95; Ferdinand Lamey, *Hermann von der Hardt in seinen Briefen und seinen Beziehungen zum Braunschweiger Hofe, zu Spener, Franke und dem Pietismus.* Beilage I zu den Hss. der Großherzoglichen Badischen Hof- und Landesbibliothek Karlsruhe (Wiesbaden: Harassowitz, 1891); Dieter Merzbacher, "Die 'Herwiederbringung der herrlichen Schriften, so fast verloren gewesen.' Das 'concilium Constantiense,' ein Editionsprojekt Hermann von der Hardts und des Herzogs Rudolf August von Braunschweig-Lüneburg," in *Vom Mittelalter zur Neuzeit. Festschrift für Horst Brunner*, ed. Dorothea Klein et al. (Wiesbaden: Reichert, 2000), 569–92; Ralph Häfner, "Tempelritus und Textkommentar. Hermann von der Hardts 'Morgenröte über der Stad Chebron'. Zur Eigenart des literaturkritischen Kommentars im frühen 18. Jahrhundert," *Scientia Poetica* 3 (1999): 47–71; Häfner, "'Denn wie das buch ist, muß der leser seyn' – Allegorese und Mythopoesis in den 'Hohen und hellen Sinnbildern Jonae' des Helmstedter Gelehrten Hermann von der Hardt," in *Die europäische Gelehrtenrepublik im Zeitalter des Konfessionalismus*, ed. Herbert Jaumann (Wiesbaden: Harassowitz, 2001), 183–202; Martin Mulsow, "Sintflut und Gedächtnis. Hermann von der Hardt und Nicolas-Antoine Boulanger," in *Sintflut und Gedächtnis. Erinnern und Vergessen des Ursprungs*, ed. Martin Mulsow and Jan Assmann (München: Fink, 2006), 131–61; Mulsow, "Religionsgeschichte in Helmstedt," in *Das Athen der Welfen. Die Reformuniversität Helmstedt*

1576–1810, ed. Jens Bruning and Ulrike Gleixner (Wolfenbüttel: Harassowitz, 2010), 182–9; "Asaph Ben-Tov, Helmstedter Hebraisten," in *Das Athen der Welfen. Die Reformuniversität Helmstedt 1576–1810*, ed. Jens Bruning and Ulrike Gleixner (Wolfenbüttel: Harassowitz, 2010), 224–31; Martin Mulsow, "Harpocratism: Gestures of Retreat in early Modern Germany," *Common Knowledge* 16 (2010): 110–27; Mulsow, "Der Silen von Helmstedt" in *Die Sachen der Aufklärung*, ed. Franke Berndt and Daniel Fulda (Hamburg: Meiner, 2012), 300–13; Mulsow, "Politische Bukolik. Hermann von der Hardts Geheimbotschaften," *Zeitschrift für Ideengeschichte* 2013–14, 103–16; Mulsow, "The Bible as Secular Story: The Northern War and King Josias in the Interpretation of Hermann von der Hardt (1660–1746)," in *Scriptural Authority and Biblical Criticism in the Dutch Golden Age: God's Word Questioned*, ed. Dirk van Miert, Henk Nellen, Piet Steenbakkers, and Jesze Touber (Oxford: Oxford University Press, 2017), 351–73.

21 On the distinction of an elite from the simple folk see Gianni Paganini, "Wie aus Gesetzgebern Betrüger werden. Eine philosophische Archäologie des 'radikalen' Libertinismus," in *Radikalaufklärung*, ed. Jonahan I. Israel and Martin Mulsow (Berlin: Suhrkamp, 2014), 49–91. On early modern "political" thinking in general see Gotthard Frühsorge, *Der politische Körper. Zum Begriff des Politischen im 17. Jahrhundert und in den Romanen Christian Weises* (Stuttgart: Metzler, 1974).

22 Hardt, *Aenigmata prisci orbis. Jonas in Luce in Historia Manassis et Josiae, ex Eleganti Veterum Hebraeorum Stilo Solutum Aenigma* (Helmstedt: Schnorrius, 1723), 32.

23 See Möller, "Hermann von der Hardt als Alttestamentler," 87ff.

24 See Wilhelm Schmidt-Biggemann, "Die Entstehung der unitarischen Exegese und die philologische Destruktion des Trinitätsdogmas," in *Apokalypse und Philologie. Wissensgeschichten und Weltentwürfe der Frühen Neuzeit* (Göttingen: Vandenhoek, 2007), 79–122.

25 See Wilhelm Brambach, *Gottfied Wilhelm Leibniz: Verfasser der* Histoire de Bileam*: mit Vollständigem Abdruck der* Histoire de Bileam *in der von Leibniz gebilligten Form* (Leipzig: Barth, 1887).

26 On the exegetical problem of this passus and its history of interpretation see Bernd Roling, *Physica sacra. Wunder, Naturwissenschaft und historischer Schriftsinn zwischen Mittelalter und Früher Neuzeit* (Leiden: Brill, 2013), 9–64.

27 Badische Landesbibliothek Karlsruhe, Ms 320, 4.

28 *Histoire de Bileam; Renards de Samon; Machoire d'Ane; Corbeus d'Elie; L'antichrist*, [Helmstedt] 1707.

29 *Journal de Trévoux*, Juin 1710.

30 Gottlieb Stolle, Travel Journal (authored partly together with Hallmann), Biblioteka Uniwersytecka, Wroclaw R 766, 4f. On this journal see Martin

Mulsow, "Eine Reise durch die Gelehrtenrepublik. Soziales Wissen, Wahrnehmungen und Wertungen in Gottlieb Stolles Reisejournal von 1703/4," in *Kultur der Kommunikation. Die europäische Gelehrtenrepublik im Zeitalter von Leibniz und Lessing*, ed. Ulrich J. Schneider (Wiesbaden: Harassowitz, 2005), 185–202.

31 Observationes selectae ad rem litterariam spectantes vol. VIII, 14 (Halle: Renger, 1704). On the Observationes and Reimmann's contributions to it see Martin Mulsow, "Ein kontroverses Journal der Frühaufklärung: Die Observationes selectae, Halle 1700–1705," *Aufklärung* 17 (2005): 79–99. On Reimmann see Martin Mulsow and Helmut Zedelmaier, eds, *Skepsis, Providenz, Polyhistorie. Jakob Friedrich Reimmann 1668–1743* (Tübingen: Niemeyer, 1998).

32 See the numerous copies of Hardt's writings in the Staats- und Universitätsbibliothek Göttingen.

33 Jakob Friedrich Reimmann, *Catalogus Bibliothecae Theologicae Systematico-Criticus* (Hildesheim: Schröder, 1731), 1030f.

34 *Esprit de Spinosa*, 1719, in *Traktat über die drei Betrüger*, ed. Winfried Schröder (Hamburg: Meiner, 1992); Guido Canziani, Winfried Schröder, and Francesco Socas, eds, *Cymbalum Mundi sive Symbolum Sapientiae* (Milano: Angeli, 2000).

35 Reimmann, *Catalogus Bibliothecae*, 1030f.: "Quam esse Domini H v.d … ab Amico quondam accepimus. Qui et hoc addebat, eam a quodam discipulo huic Doctori clanculum surreptam, &, hac ratione invito Domino ad alios delatam, in illustrissimi quoque Principis … Bibliothecam transiisse."

36 On Leibniz's visits see Kurt Müller, *Leben und Werk von G. W. Leibniz – Eine Chronik* (Frankfurt: Klostermann, 1984). A first search in the Leibniz-Reimmann correspondence of the years before 1711 (which is mainly unedited so far) that Nora Gädeke was so kind as to do for me achieved no positive result.

37 On them see, for example, Horst-Rüdiger Jarck, Dieter Lent, et al., eds, *Braunschweigisches Biographisches Lexikon: 8. bis 18. Jahrhundert* (Braunschweig, Appelhans 2006).

38 Reimmann, *Catalogus Bibliothecae Theologicae*, 1030f.: "Quae Omnia an ita sint, nostrorum non est definire. Hoc nostrum; Meditationem hanc infandam esse, & diram, & scandalosam." And, he continues, the writing should please remain unedited: "*Ανέκδοτον* adhuc, & dignam, quae tenebris sempeternis prematur, ne occasionem habent όι ἔξω, religionem nostram exagitandi, & nova maledicta in eam conferendi."

39 See Martin Mulsow, "Der ausgescherte Opponent. Akademische Unfälle und Radikalisierung," in Mulsow, *Die unanständige Gelehrtenrepublik. Wissen, Libertinage und Kommunikation in der Frühen Neuzeit* (Stuttgart: Metzler, 2007), 191–216.

40 Delicatissimum Salomoneum Epithalamium in gratiam tanti Israelitar. regis ante tot secula cantatum, nunc in gratiam gloriamque serenissimi principis ac domini D. Frederici Wilhelmi et Don. Sophiae Dorotheae [...] cum auspiciatissimum inirent matrimonium, s.l. 1706. See fol. A4r sq.: "Hoc itaque elegantissimum hymenaeum, a quoqunque tandem profectum, carmen, ante quam ordiretur, quisquis illud descripserit, in ipso primum titulo modum indicat, ac circumstantias, quibus illud, purgatissimis, delicatissimisque, nec nisi suasissima aventibus, judicioque acerrimis, alacribusque curiosissimi Regis aestimandum auribus oblatum sit. Non solam cantoris vocem, humanique gutturis artem modulationemve, ac mirificam oris coarctationem et divaricationem, tonosque emissos vivos, suffecisse, sed musici insuper hexacordi cujusdam instrumenti strepitum suavissimum, auribus gratissimum, concentumque dulcissimum, ac tremulas, nunc submissas nunc accutas, nunc mediocres planasque sonorum variations, ac naturae convenientissimos nunc tenerissimos, nunc languidos lentosque, ac placidos, atque ad sedandos spiritus aptos, nunc citissimos ac vivaces, et ad gaudium proclives, nunc celerrimos interque se certantes, fugitivos et praeruptos harmonicos lusus, artificiosissima quadam alternatione, dimensisque interruptionum spatiis, gratiam cantatis ori, venustatemque affudisse."

41 *Unschuldige Nachrichten von alten und neuen theologischen Sachen auf das Jahr 1707* (Leipzig: Großens Erben & Braun, 1707), 265, 270. Johann Fabricius was seen as far too liberal and conciliatory towards the Catholics. On the polemics against him by the Lutheran orthodoxy – especially Sebastian Edzardi – see Ulrich Groetsch, "Sesatian Edzard's Epic Battle for Souls," in *Das Akademische Gymnasium zu Hamburg (gegr. 1613) im Kontext frühneuzeitlicher Wissenschafts- und Bildungsgeschichte,* ed. Johann Anselm Steiger (Berlin: De Gruyter, 2017), 137–62.

42 Groetsch, "Sesatian Edzard's Epic Battle for Souls."

43 Hermann von der Hardt, *Ad Paulum Martinum Noltenium* [...] de *vocatis ab Adamo animalibus epistola* (Helmstedt: Hammius, 1705).

44 Mulsow, *Enlightenment Underground,* 215ff.

45 Adam Rudolph Solger, *Bibliotheca sive supellex librorum impressorum in omni genere scientiarum maximam partem rarissimorum,* vol. 3 (Nürnberg: Endter, 1763), 310, no. 2035, under the rubric "Libri paradoxi et suspecti."

46 HAB Cod. Extrav. 265.14, 48f.: "Ignoras mores Judaeorum, amice: Inter sponsalia et nuptias nulla ferè intercedebat differentia, praeter solennitatem unicam deductionem in domum. Nec crimen erat sponsam cognovisse. Hinc sponsae alienae compressio jam adulterium vocabatur."

47 Ibid. 48: "Vid. Buxtorf. Seldenus Ligtfoot et MS. Antiquit. tit. sponsa."

48 Gottlieb Stolle (n30), 10f., reports: "Weil er [Johann Peter Speeth] nun unter diesen und andern, so er gesprochen, keine Einigkeit der Meinungen angetroffen, sondern ein jeder immer etwas gehabt, das des andern Meinung contrair gewest, habe er endlich geschlossen: omnia esse incerta, nisi hoc: unum scilicet esse Deum, und sey zu Befriedigung seines Gewissens zu den Juden übergegangen, als welche diese Warheit von anfange gehabt, und bißher erhalten. Der Abfall vom Christen- zum Juden-thum sey so gar seltsam nicht, denn er wisse selbst, daß vor wenig Jahren au[ch] 3 Theologi reformati sich beschneiden lassen, davon aber der eine, weil er den Schmertz der Beschneidung nicht verwinden können, bald gestorben." On the conversions see Martin Mulsow and Richard H. Popkin, eds, *Secret Conversions to Judaism in Early Modern Europe* (Leiden: Brill, 2004).

49 Johann Christoph Wolf, *Curae philologicae et criticae*, vol. 1 (Hamburg: Herold, 1725), 15: "Quamvis S. Matthaeus & ceteri Evangelistae satis professi sunt, quo sensu Josephus Mariae uxoris maritus, atque adeo Christi pater vocetur, fuit tamen, qui infelici non minus, quam vano, conatu, Josephum Parentem Christi naturalem fuisse, contenderet. Vide somnia ejus explosa in Relationibus Theolog. Innoxiis (Unschuldige Nachrichten) an. 1711. 622sqq."

50 See Martin Greschat, *Zwischen Tradition und neuem Anfang. Valentin Ernst Löscher und der Ausgang der lutherischen Orthodoxie* (Witten: Luther, 1971); Klaus Petzoldt, *Der unterlegene Sieger: Valentin Ernst Löscher im absolutistischen Sachsen* (Leipzig: Evangelische Verlagsanstalt, 2001).

51 *Unschuldige Nachrichten von alten und neuen theologischen Sachen auf das Jahr 1711* (Leipzig: Großens Erben & Braun, 1711), 622: "Pervenit ad aliquem nostrum scheda manu exarata, atque hince inde sparsa, de Josepho parente Christi naturali, pernicioso sane stylo scripta, pravisque dicteriis, quae bonos mores corrumpunt, merito accensenda. Auctori, quisquis est, seriam apprecamur μετνάνοιαν, utque, αταξία mentis periculosissima liberatus, sapere discat in luce gratiae, & a *teratologíais* scandalo plenissimis, nequid gravius dicamus, abstineat."

52 Mscr.Dresd.A.189.c.

53 It is difficult to say which text came first. Although the Wolfenbüttel manuscript (Ms. 265/14 extrav.) dates from 1743 and is thus highly likely to be later than the Dresden manuscript, I assume that it was copied from the original, which was probably created in Wolfenbüttel or Helmstedt and thus possibly represents an earlier stage of the text than the Dresden manuscript. On the other hand, it is not impossible that the Dresden version is the primary text. At one point there is a small change in the text: "It is unworthy to say that Christ was born of an illegitimate marriage: you call Christ

a bastard. What is there to say that Joseph, if it was him, did not have intercourse on the day of the wedding?" (46 in Wolfenbüttel text). Here the scribe puts a comment in the margin that comes later in the Wolfenbüttel text: "Maria that dahero keine Kirchen-Buße, ob sie gleich zu früh in die Wochen kam" (Maria did not do penance in the church, although she was confined too early). The other Wolfenbüttel manuscript (Cod. Extr. 157.11), on the other hand, is quite close to that of 1743, as there are only a few insignificant changes.

54 Mulsow, "Die Transmission."

55 See Johann Christian Edelmann, *Sechs Briefe an Georg Christoph Kreyssig*, ed. Philipp Strauch (Halle: Niemeyer, 1918); on Edelmann in general see Annegret Schaper, *Ein langer Abschied vom Christentum. Johann Christian Edelmann (1698–1767) und die deutsche Frühaufklärung* (Marburg: Tectum, 1995).

56 Johann Christian Edelmann, *Abgenötigtes, jedoch andern nicht wiederaufgenötigtes Glaubens-Bekenntnis*, s.l. 1746 (reprint Stuttgart: Frommann-Holzboog, 1969), 96f. The text in English was Edward Elwall, *The supernatural incarnation of Jesus Christ proved to be false: having no foundation in the prophets, nor in all the Old Testament; and utterly inconsistent with his being the Son of David. But the main Prop and Support of all the absurd Doctrines, both of Papists and Protestants; to the great Scandal and Reproach of the true Christian Religion. And that our Lord Jesus Christ, was the real son of Joseph and Mary* (London: author, 1742).

Chapter Eleven

Clandestine Philosophical Manuscripts in the Catalogue of Marc-Michel Rey

ANTONY McKENNA AND FABIENNE VIAL-BONACCI

In this chapter we would like to draw attention to an ongoing online publishing project concerning all the papers and correspondence of Marc-Michel Rey (1720–1780), the famous Amsterdam printer of the French *philosophes* who also distributed to select customers a whole catalogue of clandestine philosophical manuscripts: http://rey.huma-num.fr.[1] We must first pay homage to the extraordinary wealth of documents collected by Jeroom Vercruysse, Emeritus Professor at the Free University of Brussels, who entrusted them to the Saint-Etienne research team IHRIM (CNRS UMR 5317: http://ihrim.ens-lyon.fr). Fabienne Vial-Bonacci has recently discovered two new sets of important documents: the exchanges between Rey and the chevalier d'Eon and the archives of the Weissenbruch family (Rey's son-in-law). She has already established the critical inventory of the papers, which provides three distinct entries: active and passive correspondence between 1744 and 1780, the archives of the book trade, and family archives. The inventory covers all the available documents, including lost letters. It is presented in chronological order by default but can be organized according to any one of the headings. By means of the research motor, many simple or combined searches are possible: filters by date (a given year or over a given period), by recipient or by sender, by place, and so on, and it is possible to combine these filters. From the elements of the inventory, hyperlinks lead the user to a precise description of each document. Progressively, a critical edition of these documents will be made available online (free access) with a critical annotation identifying people, manuscripts, and books mentioned. The entire publication will make the public more familiar with the activities of an eighteenth century bookseller and with his vital role in the spread of Enlightenment ideas throughout Europe.

The documents give us a good idea of his workshop in Amsterdam, of the role played by the abbé Du Laurens[2] as reader and corrector of works printed, and of Rey's collaboration with Jacques-André Naigeon, the friend of Diderot and d'Holbach and prolific intellectual editor of the philosophical articles in Panckoucke's *Encyclopédie méthodique*.[3] We can read Rey's correspondence with his customers great and small: Rousseau, Voltaire, Diderot, Jacobi, Allamand, Du Peyrou, Court de Gébelin, Panckoucke, Malesherbes, and many others. We discover the list of works sent from Paris to Amsterdam by the printer Duchesne's widow and of those sent to her by Rey according to the orders received. We overhear the negotiations of Rey's agent Leclerc with Antoine de Sartine, lieutenant general of the Parisian police, regarding the publication of forbidden books,[4] and we even have the list of customers to whom Leclerc sold copies of *L'Antiquité dévoilée* by Boullanger.[5] We have the declarations of ship captains setting sail for Rouen and learn the names of the intermediaries and the details of books sent – "under the wing of the director general of postal services or another administrator" or "by the stagecoach or with the help of individual travellers" – by Naigeon to his younger brother, controller of victuals in Sedan, who sends them on to a certain Mme Loncin in Liège, who in turn packs them off to Amsterdam. We can thus construct the spiderweb of the international network of Rey's book trade, which leads from Amsterdam everywhere in the United Provinces, to London, Düsseldorf, and Münster, and to Hambourg, Darmstadt, and Saint Petersburg. It is an exceptionally rich collection of papers, comparable to the archives of the Société typographique de Neuchâtel, and several letters bear witness to exchanges between Rey and that Société.[6]

We enter into the world of printers, booksellers, and peddlers, of their intermediaries and clients. We are thus essentially concerned with the means of communication and diffusion constituted by manuscripts, printed books, periodicals, translations, correspondences, and networks and circles of sociability such as *salons* and clubs[7] or Freemasonry lodges.[8] We can have recourse to the catalogues of private libraries[9] to check certain declarations.

Marc-Michel Rey (1720–1780) was a printer and bookseller who played a decisive role in the diffusion of Enlightenment ideas.[10] He was born in Geneva of parents who came from Treschenu in the region of Die (now in the Drôme). He was an apprentice printer in Geneva, probably from 1737, working under the orders of Jean Balthazar Huttenrauch, director of the printing house belonging to Marc-Michel Bousquet, Rey's godfather. Rey became a citizen of the town of Amsterdam on 14 January

1746 and was admitted into the corporation of booksellers a fortnight later, on 31 January. In Bruiksloot (Amsterdam) on 24 April 1747, he married Elisabeth (1723–1778), daughter of the renowned bookseller Jean-Frédéric Bernard (1684–1746), whose stock he took over at his death. Among his children, we will mention Marguerite Jeanne, born on 10 June 1749, who was to marry Charles de Weissenbruch, the brother-in-law of Pierre Rousseau, director and chief editor of the *Journal encyclopédique* and a pillar of the Société typographique de Bouillon, and her sister Suzanne, born on 3 May 1762, goddaughter of Jean-Jacques Rousseau. Rey's first publications under his own name appeared in 1746, but he was above all a bookseller, and he earned his fortune through the sale of the books he had printed or that were distributed by his bookshop until his death in 1780. His correspondence, notes, and accounts with the booksellers of the period, Duchesne, Dessaint et Saillant, Neaulme, Luzac, bear witness to the importance of his commercial network.

Rey was a *protégé* of Prosper Marchand, who often mentions him in his correspondence with Rousset de Missy. His characteristic beehive imprint ("marque aux abeilles") was engraved by Jacob van der Schley (1715–1779), one of the best pupils of Bernard Picart, who had gone into exile with Marchand at The Hague. One might thus say that Rey was the "product" of a network: Marchand, Rousset de Missy, Douxfils, Fritsch and Böhm, the heirs of Marchand, and Jean-Frédéric Bernard, his father-in-law.[11] Rey made a name for himself through his edition of the *Journal des savants*, which he transformed with additions drawn from the *Mémoires de Trévoux* and subsequently from other periodicals. In 1754 he undertook an important trip: on 10 July, he arrived in Lausanne, where he met Polier de Bottens three days later; on 18 July, he left for Geneva, where he met Jean-Jacques Rousseau. From there, he intended to go to Lyon, to Marseille, to Bordeaux, and then to Paris before returning to Amsterdam at the end of September (letter from Polier de Bottens to Mme Rey, 7 August 1754), but in October of that same year he visited Malesherbes in Paris and had in hand Rousseau's *Discours sur l'inégalité.* Rey is known above all for his printing of works by Enlightenment philosophers: he ran into trouble after printing Voltaire's *Dictionnaire philosophique, Evangile de la raison,* and *Sermon des cinquante.* He became Rousseau's printer and friend, but finally cut short their relations in 1774. His exchanges with Voltaire are no doubt marked by complicity, as we shall see, if one reads between the lines Voltaire's letters in 1764 and 1769. Rey also printed a number of texts by Diderot and works sent by the baron d'Holbach – his own works and his translations.

To get an idea of Rey's publications in the field of clandestine manuscripts, one has only to skim through d'Holbach's bibliography[12]: no less than fifty publications of this kind were printed by Rey, who also subsequently issued numerous editions of these same works (see the appendix to this chapter).

Clandestine philosophical manuscripts were not, of course, his only publications: the list is long, and we will mention here only some of the names in his impressive catalogue: Polier de Bottens, Challe, Mandeville, Chauffepié, Claude Yvon, Lévesque de Burigny, Jean-Jacques Rousseau, d'Alembert, Voltaire, Diderot, Mme d'Aulnoy, Pecquet, Trublet, Saurin, d'Argenson, Charles Bonnet, Samuel Crellius, Toussaint, Robinet, and Marmontel, as well as the *Critique* and *Défense de l'Esprit des lois* and even the *Psalms of David* (1754, 1759, 1768, 1770).

Through the *General account of books sent to M. Rey in Amsterdam by the widow Duchesne*, which contains also "on the other side" the books sent by Rey to Paris, we learn that Rey sent twelve copies of the *Dissertations mêlées* and two copies of Boullanger's *Dissertation sur Elie et Enoch*; a list dated 15 November 1757 includes twelve copies of Locke's works and thirty of Rousseau's *Discourses* as well as twenty of his *Portefeuille* and fifty of Bossuet's l'*Histoire universelle.* In all, some £15,000 worth of books were exchanged in this way.

If we consult the inventory established after Rey's death in 1780, we find French and English copies of the monumental work published by his father-in-law Jean-Frédéric Bernard in collaboration with a friend of Prosper Marchand, Bernard Picart, one of the best engravers of his generation, and Bruzen de La Martinière, the nephew of Richard Simon: *Cérémonies et coutumes religieuses de tous les peuples du monde* (Amsterdam, 1723–43, 11 vols in-folio).[13] There figure also, besides various editions of Pierre Bayle's correspondence, a copy of La Mettrie's *Histoire naturelle de l'âme* (Oxford, 1747, 8°), the *Apologia pro Jul. Cæsare Vanino Neopolitano* (s.l. 1712, 8°), and two copies of the *Porte-feuille d'un philosophe, ou Mélange de pièces philosophiques, politiques, critiques, satyriques et galantes* (Cologne, 1770, 8°, 3 vol.) by the abbé Du Laurens. At first sight, given that we are dealing with a bookseller who distributed around fifty of the most aggressive clandestine philosophical manuscripts, this list is disappointing. Certainly, his stock cannot be reduced to such works, and we find literature of all sorts: Fréron's *Année littéraire*, Polignac's *Anti-Lucrèce*, Frédéric II's *Antimachiavel*, Fénelon's *Télémaque*, Bossuet's *Histoire des* variations, Ostervald's *Arguments de la Bible*, his Bible, that of Charles Le Cène, and that of Mme Guyon, Calmet's *Dictionnaire de la Bible*, Jean

Le Clerc's periodicals, the whole collection *ad usum Delphini* directed by the Dacier, the *Bibliothèque bleue*, Papillon's *Bibliothèque des auteurs de Bourgogne*, the works of Charles Bonnet, Montesquieu's *Considérations* and his *Lettres persanes*, d'Alembert's essay on the *Destruction des jésuites en France*, Pufendorf, Formey, Haller, Crousaz, Wolff, Le Sage, Mandeville, Beausobre, d'Argens's *Lettres cabalistiques*, the marquis de Lassay's *Recueil de différentes choses*, and a thousand other works; the *Satyre Ménippée*, the *Sorberiana*, not Bayle's *Dictionnaire*, but several copies of the *Encyclopédie*, the *Apologie de l'abbé de Prades* by Diderot, Helvetius's poem *Le Bonheur* ... Everything that an *honnête homme* might be looking for in Amsterdam in the 1770s ... except clandestine philosophical manuscripts.

However, several allusions in the correspondence suggest that Rey had a separate catalogue for forbidden philosophical works – works that Jacobi called his "impieties" (*impiétés*) – which he sent to customers who asked for it explicitly and in whom he had complete confidence. The inventory is therefore not a faithful reflection of the evolution of his printing and bookselling trade and certainly not of his trade in forbidden philosophical works. Despite his prudence, Rey is recorded by the police as early as 1752 as "an extremely suspect bookseller" ("un libraire des plus suspects": Paris BN, ms. fr.22507, f.209). We must therefore take a closer look at his correspondence to find traces of his trade in forbidden books.

Only two letters of his correspondence with Voltaire have survived. They have been read as evidence of Voltaire's "difficult" relations with Rey, but to my mind, this interpretation is based on a misunderstanding. Their relation must have been characterized by complicity, at least if one reads "between the lines" the irony and humour of the following letter, which Rey fully grasped – albeit after some hesitation:

au château de Ferney en Bourgogne par Geneve 24 nov[embre] 1764

Je viens d'apprendre par la chambre sindicale de Paris qu'on s'est servi du *nom de Marc Michel Rei libraire d'Amsterdam* pour envoier un volume in octavo intitulé *Collection complette* etc. *ouvrages philosophiques de m*[r] *de Voltaire.* On y trouve

- le *Testament de Jean Mélier*
- le *Sermon des cinquante*
- le *Catéchisme de l'honnête homme*
- l'*Examen de la relligion*

etc.

La plus part de ces pièces connues depuis plus de vingt années sont un tissu des plus horribles blasphèmes qu'on ait jamais vomis contre la relligion chrétienne. Il n'y a point d'homme de lettres à Paris qui ne connaisse le *Testament* de Jean Mélier, curé d'Etrépigni près de Rocroy en Champagne. Il mourut je crois en 1733 et il laissa trois exemplaires manuscrits de ce malheureux testament par le quel il désavouait la relligion dont il avait été le ministre.

Le *Sermon des cinquante* est un libelle non moins exécrable qui a toujours passé pour être de La Métrie et qui même a été deux fois imprimé sous son nom.

L'*Examen de la relligion* attribué mal à propos à St Evremont ne peut pas être plus de luy que de moy. C'est un mauvais ouvrage mal écrit, qui a été d'abord imprimé à Hambourg. Je ne connais point le *Catéchisme* mais je sçais que les auteurs et les imprimeurs de tous ces ouvrages affreux seraient condamnez au dernier supplice dans tous les tribunaux de l'Europe.

Mr Marc Michel Rey est intéressé plus que personne à faire cesser l'abus criminel qu'on fait de son nom et du mien, et à emploier l'autorité des magistrats qui doivent réprimer une licence si infâme. Je le prie instamment de se joindre à moy pour effacer jusqu'aux dernières traces de cette indigne calomnie qui nous outrage tout deux également.

Voltaire
gentilhome ord[inaire] de la chambre du Roy

A few years later, in February 1769, Voltaire addresses Rey once more and again in a tone of emphatic exasperation: he begins by warning him of typographical errors in the Genevan edition of his *Siècle de Louis XIV*, "which is now enjoying some success in Paris." In case Rey intends to publish a pirated edition of that work, Voltaire provides him with a list of errata and suggests that he pass it on to a colleague if he does not do the job himself ... And he adds: "I passionately hope that it is you who will do the *Siècle de Louïs 14* the honour of a publication." He then turns to more serious matters:

J'ai une prière plus sérieuse et plus importante à vous faire, c'est de vouloir bien empècher qu'on déshonore mon nom en le mettant dans la longue liste des ouvrages suspects qu'on débite en Hollande. Mon nom ne rendra pas ces ouvrages meilleurs et n'en facilitera pas la vente. J'aurais trop de reproches à me faire si je m'étais amusé à composer un seul de ces ouvrages pernicieux. Non seulement je n'en ai fait aucun, mais je les réprouve tous, et je regarde comme une injure cruelle l'artifice des auteurs qui mettent sous mon nom ces scandaleux écrits. Ce que je dois à ma religion, à ma patrie, à l'Académie française, à l'honneur que j'ai d'être un ancien officier de la maison du Roi, et surtout à la vérité, me force de vous écrire ainsi, et de vous prier très instamment de ne pas souffrir qu'on abuse de mon nom d'une manière si odieuse. Vous êtes trop honnête homme pour me refuser cette justice.

It seems obvious that Voltaire wrote these two letters to Rey knowing full well that they would be read by the police. Better still, we find in Prosper Marchand's correspondence with Rousset de Missy the following unexpected information:

L'affaire de Rey est sérieuse, il a affaire à deux coquins, mais il a une protection qui ne lui fait pas honneur. [...] Les deux coquins sont les abbés *Noncourt* Lorrain [Mathis, pseud. Denoncourt] et *Yvon* Pradiste [Claude Yvon], Rey a prêté un *Zeonikizul* [sur les amours de Louis XV] au premier, qui apparemment en a voulu faire sa cour à quelque[s] courtisans de Versailles; Rey, qui en a été averti par S[aint-] Sauveur (*son protecteur consul de France, dont Rey passe pour l'espion*) a redemandé son exempl[aire] à Noncourt, celui-ci l'a refusé, disant qu'il le lui avoit donné, Rey l'a fait redemander par un notaire, et le coquinisme a inspiré à Noncourt pour ruiner Rey, de mettre l'avertisse[ment] dans la gazette de Tronchin, Rey y a répondu par un avertisse[ment] contraire, Noncourt a voulu riposter, la Tronchin [imprimeur] n'a pas voulu continuer; sur cela Noncourt et Yvon s'adressent à mon fat [Isaac] Buyn et le persuadent soit par raisons [...] soit par argent, qu'il aime beaucoup, de mettre dans [le périodique] l'*Epilogueur* n° XVII après «on met volontiers etc. [un nouveau démenti].[14]

The affair of the publication of *Les Amours de Zeonzinikul*, a satirical work on the amorous exploits of Louis XV, was not really embarrassing for Rey; he needed only to save face. But it is interesting to us as evidence that Rey was notoriously in close contact with agents of the French court. Voltaire knew the man he was dealing with and knew his letters would be relayed to the court of Louis XV.

As so often in Voltaire's correspondence, we are faced with indignant denials that are all the more emphatic since Voltaire knows that his correspondent knows that he, Voltaire, is really the author of the works in question or that he has played a vital role in their publication.[15] Indeed, we need not insist on his role in the publication of the *Doutes sur la religion ou Examen de la religion dont on cherche l'éclaircissement de bonne foi*

(1745)[16] and of the *Testament* of the curé Jean Meslier (1762),[17] nor on the fact that he was himself the author of the *Sermon des cinquante* and of the *Catéchisme de l'honnête homme* ... Thus Rey, who printed these works, learned nothing from Voltaire's letters but must have grasped their function immediately and passed them on to the appropriate authorities – which is why the two letters have survived. And we should not take too seriously Rousset de Missy's term "spy," since Rey was constantly dealing with French agents and officials when negotiating authorization to distribute his publications in France with "tacit permission." There was nothing secret about his contacts with Saint-Sauveur: the term "spy" is due simply to Rousset de Missy's desire to malign him.

Voltaire often adopts the same emphatic tone:

> Savez-vous que Marc Michel Rey, imprimeur de Jean-Jacques, a eu l'abominable impudence de mettre sous mon nom le Jean Mêlier, ouvrage connu de tout Paris pour être de ce pauvre prêtre, le *Sermon des cinquante*, de Lamêtrie, l'*Examen de la religion* attribué à S[ain]t-Evremond ? Tout a été incendié à La Haye avec le *[Dictionnaire] portatif.* Voilà une bombe à laquelle on ne s'attendait point... (à Damilaville, 17 December 1764: éd. Best. D12.266; éd. Leigh, n° 3783)[18]
>
> On dit que c'est Marc Michel Rey, éditeur de Jean Jaques, qui a imprimé le *Recueil nécessaire.* Cela est très vraisemblable, puisqu'on y trouve une partie du *Vicaire Savoyard.* Je n'ai pas vérifié si la traduction de milord Bolingbrocke est fidéle. Les vrais philosophes, mon cher ami, ne font point de pareils ouvrages, ils respectent la religion autant qu'ils chérissent le roi. (à Damilaville, 17 November 1766: éd. Best. D13.675)

His humour and irony are blatant, but a few letters express his real attitude towards Rey. To the prince de Ligne, he suggests:

> Vous êtes d'ailleurs plus à portée que nous d'avoir tous les livres que l'on imprime en Hollande, on dit qu'il y a de fort mauvais, mais qu'on en trouve aussi d'excellent[s].Vous pour[r]iez faire donner vos ordres à quelque commissaire de ce païs là pour faire venir le livre intitulé *Recueil nécessaire,* dans lequel on trouve l'*Examen important de feu mylord Bolingbroke,* et plusieurs autres pièces très curieuses. Il y a aussi le *Testament de Jean Mêlier,* la comédie de *Saül et de David* traduite de l'anglais, un abrégé de l'histoire ecclésiastique sous le nom de l'abbé de Fleuri avec une préface du roi de Prusse, un *Avis au public* sur les Calas et les Sirven, un *Examen des apologistes de la religion chrétienne* par Fréret, un autre *Examen* par Boulanger. Le libraire

Marc Michel Rey d'Amsterdam pour[r]ait vous faire tenir tous ces livres qui doivent entrer dans une bibliothèque choisie telle que la vôtre, et qui ne sont pas faits pour le commun des hommes.

J'ap[p]rends qu'il y a aussi une sixième édition d'un livre intitulé *Diction[n] aire philosophique.* Ce livre est composé par une société de gens de lettres dans laquelle il y a quelques théologiens. Ce livre est imprimé par Marc Michel Rey. Cette nouvelle édition commence je crois par l'article «Abbé», et finit par celui de «Trans[s]ubstantiation». Je ne connais guères que les tîtres des livres. Mon métier de banquier me laisse à peine le temps de lire. C'est à un prince de vôtre génie à juger du fond des choses et du stile. (17 July 1767: D14.285)

In the same vein, he orders books from Henri Rieu:

Je vous suis bien oblige de toutes vos bontés; on aura bien de la peine à empêcher Marc Michel Rey d'être un fripon et un insolent. Pourriez-vous cependant me faire avoir les *Doutes sur la religion* suivi de l'*Analyse de Spinoza* par Boulainvilliers; *L'Esprit du clergé ou le christianisme primitif vengé*, traduit de l'anglais; la *Théologie portative* de l'abbé Bernier; le *Recueil de Passeran* [Radicati]. Vous pourriez aisément me faire avoir ces livres par votre ami Mr Cramer. (31 October 1767: D14.512)

And he follows closely Rey's productions:

Parmi une grande quantité de livres nouveaux qui paraissent sur cette matière il y en a un surtout dont on fait un grand cas. Il est intitulé *Le Militaire philosophe*, et imprimé en effét chez Marc Michel Rey; ce sont les lettres écrites au Père Mallebranche, qui aurait été fort embar[r]assé d'y répondre. (à Marin, 27 November 1767: D14.554; voir aussi son commentaire du 2 January 1768 au marquis d'Argence: D14.639)

To Damilaville, he sings the same song:

Il y a un autre excès bien funeste, c'est celui de l'acharnement à m'imputer tout ce que ce coquin de Marc Michel Rey imprime depuis dix ans. (21 March 1768: D.14.861)[19]

– while simultaneously contributing to the development of the clandestine book-trade:

Si votre aimable prince [de Hesse-Cassel] veut se faire une petite bibliot[h]èque de tous les rogatons nouveaux sur ces matières, il faut qu'il fasse donner ordre à Marc Michel Rey libraire à Amsterdam, de faire tenir à Cassel à un homme de confiance, tout ce qui a été imprimé depuis un an ou dix huit mois.

On m'a dit qu'il y a dans Genève un nommé Grasset, rue Verdaine, dont il faut taire le nom, qui vend en secret quelques unes de ces brochures aux honnêtes gens par lesquels il est sûr de n'être pas compromis. Voicy un petit billet qui servira de passeport à celui qui voudra acheter. (to Mme Louise Suzanne Gallatin, 23 March 1768: D14.877)[20]

– as also in a letter to d'Alembert:

Vous me demandez de ces rogatons imprimés à Amsterdam chez Marc Michel Rey, et débités à Genève chez Chirol; mais comment, s'il vous plaît, voulez-vous que je les envoie, par quelle adresse sûre, sous quelle enveloppe privilégiée ? Qui veut la fin donne les moyens, et vous n'avez aucun moyen. Je me servais quelquefois de M. Damilaville, et encore fallait-il bien des détours; mais il n'a plus son bureau; le commerce philosophique est interrompu. Si vous voulez être servi, dites-moi comment il faut que je vous serve. (2 September 1768: D15.199)

Once Voltaire has found a provocative formula, he tries it on all his correspondents, especially if it involves disclaiming one of his own works:

La Hollande est infectée depuis quelques années, de plusieurs moins défroqués, capucins, cordeliers, maturins, que Marc Michel Rey fait travailler à tant la feuille et qui écrivent tant qu'ils peuvent contre la religion romaine pour avoir du pain. Il y a surtout un nommé Maubert[21] qui a inondé l'Europe de brochures dans ce goût. C'est lui qui a fait le petit livre des *Trois imposteurs,* ouvrage assez insipide que Marc Michel Rey donne impudemment pour une traduction du prétendu livre de l'empereur Frédéric second.

Il y a un théatin qui a conservé son nom de Laurent [Du Laurens] qui est assez facétieux, et qui d'ailleurs est instruit; il est auteur du *Compère Mathieu,* ouvrage dans le goût de Rabelais, dont le commencement est assez plaisant, et la fin détestable.

Les libraires qui débitent tous ces livres, me font l'honneur de me les attribuer pour les mieux vendre. Je paie bien cher les intérêts de ma petite réputation. [...] Ce brigandage est intolérable, et peut avoir des suites funestes. [...] Je compte assez sur l'amitié dont vous m'honorez pour être sûr que vous détruirez autant qu'il est en vous ces bruits odieux. (to Chardon, 11 April 1768: Best. D14.938; see also D14.955 to Chabanon; D15.093 to the duc de La Vrillière)

But this is only the mask of the *philosophe* of Ferney: deep down, he was delighted at Rey's success in the trade of forbodden books:

Ce n'est que sur les lettres réitérées de Toulouse que j'y envoie les Sirven; ce n'est que parce qu'on me mande qu'une grande partie du parlement qui n'était qu'un séminaire de pédants ignorants est devenue une académie de philosophes. Il faut partout laisser pourrir la grand'chambre, mais partout les enquêtes se forment. Marc Michel Rey n'a pas nui à ce prodigieux changement. Il ne s'agissait pas de faire une révolution dans les Etats comme du temps de Luther et de Calvin, mais d'en faire une dans l'esprit de ceux qui sont faits pour gouverner. Cet ouvrage est bien avancé d'un bout de l'Europe à l'autre [...] (à d'Argental, 27 February 1769: D15.490)

– and he passed a very flattering judgment on the quality of his own publications:

L'Imposture sacerdotale est un recueil de quelques pensées anglaises et un tableau de quelques abominations des papes. Michel Rey a imprimé à Amsterdam trente volumes plus philosophiques. L'*Examen de milord Bolingbroke* [de Voltaire] est beaucoup plus profond, plus méthodique et plus fort. C'est l'histoire suivie et démontrée de dix-sept cents ans d'impostures. *Le Militaire philosophe*, adressé au père Malebranche, est plus abstrait; mais c'est une logique à laquelle il n'y a rien à répliquer. Les livres philosophiques sont actuellement sans nombre; tout cela fait du bien sans doute; mais un cordelier véhément qui prêche, qui confesse, et qui fait des enfants à ses dévotes, a plus de crédit sur le peuple que cent mille volumes bien écrits n'en ont sur les sots qui osent croire n'être pas peuple. (à d'Argental, 20 April 1769: D15.600)

Voltaire rejoiced at Rey's success and worked in confidence with him to the end, as is shown by letters written towards the end of his life, in which he asks Rey to forward his own letters (D18.080) and to lend money to his friends (D18.760, D18.842). The indignant posture was simply a disguise intended for the authorities and that might amuse his own friends.

If only similar exchanges had survived between Rey and d'Holbach! But so far our searches in that direction have not borne fruit. However, there is a substantial correspondence between Rey and Rousseau, whose works he published. No mention there of clandestine manuscripts, of course, since Rousseau was engaged in sharp negotiations concerning the publication of his own works and certainly did not want it to be known that he might be interested in publications of that kind.

La Beaumelle, about to launch his periodical *La Spectatrice danoise,* is much more relaxed on that score and sends long lists of books he requires from Rey, as well as from Laurent Durand, bookseller on the rue Saint-Jacques in Paris. Fontenelle, Toussaint, Montesquieu, Pluche, Lévesque de Pouilly, Burlamachi, Ramsay, l'abbé de Saint-Pierre, Polignac, Mme de Graffigny, Crébillon fils, Rémond de Saint-Mard; something of everything: the *Institutions physiques* by Mme Du Châtelet, Nollet, Privat de Molières, Reyneau's mathematics, besides Bouhours and *Le Portier des Chartreux* ...[22] Rey provides what Durand doesn't have in stock: Wolff, Crousaz, Beausobre, Challe, Prévost, Houtteville, but also two volumes of the *Dissertations mêlées*; Boureau-Deslandes's *Histoire de la philosophie* "can no longer be found."[23] Rey sends La Beaumelle the list of his publications available in 1750, and similar exchanges accompany their collaboration in the launching of the *Nouvelles littéraires* (LB725; voir aussi LBD 47). Rey et La Beaumelle were looking for correspondents for this periodical and made contact with Mathieu Maty; books were sent through Rouen (LBD 58).

Rey also asked Malesherbes for at least tacit permission to sell the *Défense de l'Esprit des loix* in Paris, but the director of publishing declared that it was a work in which "the author of the *Esprit des lois* is defended only with protestant maxims": "I am surprised that it didn't occur to you that such a book could not possibly be allowed to enter France." He did agree, however, not to seize the copies sent and to return them to the printer (LB748, 23 January 1751).

La Beaumelle was not the only Protestant seeking to work with Rey: on 26 September 1766, Antoine Court contacted Rey in order to launch a periodical entitled *L'Observateur protestant* (the project was finally abandoned); beginning on 12 November 1772, his son Antoine Court de Gébelin engaged in intense negotiations with Rey regarding the publication of his monumental work *Le Monde primitif analysé et comparé avec le monde moderne considéré dans son génie allégorique et dans les allégories auxquelles conduisit ce génie* (1773–82, 9 vols).[24]

We thus discover a host of contacts and book orders, but nothing really dangerous – so far. During this period, Rey is not active in the field of clandestine philosophical manuscripts, and the correspondence between Rey and La Beaumelle runs dry in the period when Rey's activity in this new field explodes.

Friedrich Heinrich Jacobi, who was born in Düsseldorf on 25 January 1743 and died in Munich on 10 March 1819, entered into a correspondence with Rey that struck a completely different tone, since he had a great appetite for "impieties."[25] From 1769 on, he enjoyed excellent relations with the Amsterdam printer: "I am yours heart and soul," "I trust that I have no need to tell you that during your stay here you will lodge in my house" (February 1769); Jacobi even sent Rey some (dead) boar and promised him recipes for preserving and preparing the meat. Jacobi himself dealt in books, at first in collaboration with his brother, then (after 1 March 1768) alone. His first order arrived in Amsterdam in December 1764:

> 1 Recueil des oraisons funèbres de Fléchier, Mascaron et Bossuet.
>
> 2 exemplaires des dernières horreurs du radoteur des Délices, s'entend de son *Diction[n]aire philosophique* et de ses *Œuvres philosophique[s]*[26], vous sçaurez pourtant que le bruit s'étant répandu à Genève que l'imprimeur de son *Dictionnaire* avoit été conduit de Lyon à Paris pied et poing lié, Mr de Voltaire a craint une pareille aventure, et s'est retiré promptement de Ferney aux Délices.

He orders the *Pensées philosophiques* by Diderot and then a second copy, having lost the first (16 December 1766), as well as the great work by Jean-Frédéric Bernard and Bernard Picart, *Cérémonies et coutumes religieuses de tous les peuples du monde* (Amsterdam, 1723–43, folio, 11 vols). He receives but sends back a copy of *Les Trois imposteurs* (Amsterdam, Rey, 1768) (28 June 1768): it's not that he is shocked by what he reads, as the editors of his correspondence suggest, but simply that he already has a copy (23 March 1768). He also orders *Les Prêtres démasqués ou des Iniquités du clergé chrétien. Ouvrage traduit de l'anglois* (Londres [Amsterdam, Rey], 1763, in-8°) by d'Holbach (28 June 1768) and requests: "Please send me a new catalogue of *impiétés*; I have given away the one you sent" (7 October 1768). He searches for the works of Toland and Shaftesbury (16 December 1766),[27] praises Moses Mendelssohn and his work on the immortality of the soul,[28] and examines other books that deal with this question – the treatises of Bonnet, Edward Young, *Night Thoughts*, the *Bigarrurues philosophiques* by Tiphaigne de La Roche – but:

> Pour moi il n'y a aucune vérité au monde dont je sois mieux persuadé que de l'immatérialité de l'âme, elle me paroit démontrée ; son immortalité ne l'est pas, mais elle est aussi certaine à mes yeux que l'existence d'un Dieu souverainement parfait. (25 November 1768)

On 24 January 1769, he orders:

Traité des imposteurs.
Christianisme dévoilé.
Examen critique des apologistes de la religion chrétienne.
De l'imposture sacerdotale.
Doutes sur la religion.
Le Catéchumène (de Charles Borde).
Théologie portative.
La Princesse malabare.
Alcibiade.

And he adds: "Please enclose two copies of your catalogue of *impiétés*" (24 January 1769).

The following month (about 14 February, ed. cit., letter LI), a new order:

Lettres à Eugénie.
Examen de la religion.
Prêtres démasqués.
Dictionnaire philosophique.
Sermons de Tillotson.

On 18 March 1769, he asks for twenty-three other "impiétés" on behalf of Marschal, official counsellor of the elector of Trèves, resident in Koblenz:

Lettres philosophiques sur l'origine des préjugés du dogme de l'immortalité de l'ame
Lettres à Eugénie
La Contagion sacrée etc.
Traité des trois imposteurs

Collection des lettres sur les miracles
Dictionnaire philosophique, nouvelle edition en 2 volumes
Fragment des instructions pour le prince royal du divorce etc.
La Pucelle
Christianisme dévoilé
Lettre de Thrasibule à Leucippe joint *La Moïsade etc.*
L'Imposture sacerdotale
[Charles Borde] *Catechumène*
Diner du comte de Boulainvilliers
Esprit du clergé ou le christianisme primitif
Théologie portative ou Dictionnaire abregé de la religion chretienne par Bernier
Defense du paganisme par l'empereur Julien etc.
Les Prêtres démasqués
Etat de l'Eglise et de la puissance legitime du pontife romain etc.
Sermons de Tillotson 8 volumes
Lettres turques
Therese philosophe
Imirse ou fille de la nature
Philosophie de la Bible.

Rey registers the prices of the books and adds volumes 1, 2, and 3 of the *Evangile [de la raison].*

In general, Jacobi settles his accounts without hesitation, but on at least one occasion, he is surprised:

> Dans votre catalogue de livres nouveaux je trouve *Les Prêtres démasqués* à £1,10. Vous m'avez fait payer le meme livre £2,10. Pourquoi cela? (28 June 1768; ed. cit., letter 95)

Interrogated by the police on 3 February 1767, Pierre Guy, an associate of the widow Duchesne, gives the names of his foreign correspondents:

> Paul Vaillant (Londres); Raye [*sic*], Arkstée, Changuion (Amsterdam); Wallner (Vienne), Reysseau, Guibert et Argens (Turin); Grasset (Lausanne); Bardin et Cramer (Genève); Pitra (Parme): Boubers (Liège); (Bouchery (Bruxelles).[29]

– and many other letters bear witness to Rey's contacts with booksellers in France, in Switzerland, and in Germany with a view to spreading the circulation of his books. We thus enter the heart of the European book trade. This suggests that more information on the trade in clandestine philosophical manuscripts might be found in the places of residence of Rey's correspondents.

Diderot first contacted Rey through the physicist Allamand and the journalist Leuchsenring; he then offered to publish the collection of his works and a "Library of the Undaunted" (*Bibliothèque des inconvaincus*), projects that were not realized. Rey published the *Lettre sur les aveugles* and the *Lettre sur les sourds et muets* (LB795); he also harvested twenty subscriptions to the *Encyclopédie.*[30]

Traces of other manuscripts are to be found in Rey's correspondence, as indicated by J. Vercruysse[31]: his fellow-printer Lochner offered him a manuscript copy of *Le Ciel ouvert à tous les hommes* by Pierre Cuppé; on 21 April 1771, an employee of the post office, Courtin, offered him a manuscript, which was returned to him on 2 May on the pretext that it was anonymous; on 11 January 1773, his son-in-law Weissenbruch, director of the Société typographique de Bouillon, told him of the existence of a manuscript by Voltaire and the marquise Du Châtelet on the Bible.[32]

Pierre Alexandre Du Peyrou, in Neuchâtel, a friend of Rousseau and Voltaire, was familiar with clandestine publications and took great interest in them. On 18 October 1766, he sent to Rey

1. *Examen critique des apologistes de la religion chrétienne*;
2. *Recueil nécessaire*;
3. Collection des lettres sur les miracles;
4. Commentaire sur le *Traité des délits et des peines.*

J'ai supposé que ces deux derniers morceaux de Voltaire vous feroient plaisir si vous ne les connoissiés pas.

In December 1766, he writes:

Mille graces de l'offre de quelques exemplaires du *Christianisme dévoilé.* Nous l'avons ici. Voila Monsieur *une bonne trouvaille pour la collection projetée,* si elle vous convient.

We thus learn that the idea of a specific collection of clandestine works was in the air at the time. However, Du Peyrou warns Rey to be careful:

Vous faites bien Monsieur, de prendre plus de tem[p]s, et d'aller avec securité. Il faut se soumettre aux foiblesses qui régissent le monde entier, et faire comme les medecins, avoir des egards à la foiblesse et au temperament de ses malades. (5 January 1767)

Du Peyrou himself plays an important role in the diffusion of philosophical works. On 20 February 1768, he orders "50 *Philosophes militaires* [*sic*], 50 *Prêtres démasqués*, 50 *Relations de la mort du chevalier de La Barre*," and a second letter of the same date adds to this order that of "50 copies of the *Théologie portative*." The following year, he orders the *Essai sur les préjugés*, *L'Esprit du judaïsme*, *L'Infini créé*, and *Système de la nature* (8 July 1769). He was on such good terms with the printer that Rey visited him and stayed in his house in Neuchâtel in 1771.

Among Rey's other customers, the prince Galitsin, Russian ambassador in The Hague, should be mentioned. He ordered the *Receuil nécessaire* and the *Evangile de la raison* (28 February and 3 October 1776); he maintained a considerable correspondence with Rey and often made orders for books of all kinds. The Benedictine monk Dom Henryon (or Henrion) in Metz also revealed himself to be a lucid and enlightened reader:

J'ai parlé de vos bons ouvrages à nos libraires mais ce sont des poltrons qui se bornent à vendre des livres de prières. Vous ne ferez jamais rien avec eux. (25 April 1778)

The abbé Coger,[33] professor of eloquence at the Collège des Quatre Nations, made an important order on 28 March 1770:

L'Esprit du judaïsme
Anthony Collins, *Essai sur la nature et la destination de l'âme*

Tableau philosophique
Diderot, *Pensées philosophiques*
Théologie portative
Les Prêtres démasqués
Le *Recueil nécessaire* avec *l'Evangile de la raison*
Traité des trois imposteurs
Crellius, *La Liberté de conscience*
Le Philosophe militaire, et *Le Philosophe ignorant*
Projet de réforme pour l'Italie
Toussaint, Les Mœurs "avec le second volume"

Vous enverrez le ballot à l'adresse de M. de Sartine, lieutenant de police lequel est prévenu. Vous écrirez en même temps audit M. Riballier le tem[p]s auquel lesdits livres pourront arriver à Paris et vous tirerez sur lui une lettre de change, valeur de l'envoy que vous lui aurez fait. (26 January 1771)

He was obviously in the habit of dealing with forbidden books – no doubt for purposes of censorship. The abbé Duprat, in The Hague, aspired to follow his example for other reasons:

> Je vous prie de me recommander particulièrement à votre comptoir, afin que si, avant de quitter la Hollande et dans votre absence, j'avois besoin que quelques livres réservés pour vos amis, on ne me les refuse pas chez vous. (28 March 1771)

Customers seeking forbidden fruit had to prove they were trustworthy: those interested in *impiétés* made up a specific circle of friends in whom Rey could have complete confidence.

This remark suggests a first conclusion regarding this remarkable *corpus*, which has in store many surprises for the historians of ideas, of books, and of censorship: Rey is careful. He separates the two aspects of his book trade: on the one side, official catalogues of all sorts of works, from *Les Mœurs* by Toussaint to the Psalms of David; on the other, the catalogue of his clandestine *impiétés*. The papers that have survived give us many clues as to the extent of his clandestine trade, but we notice that the letters that have survived are those of Jacobi in Düsseldorf and of Du Peyrou in Neuchâtel: two correspondents who reside abroad and thus run no risk of arrest. Voltaire, as we have seen, is a case apart. If we look for customers in France, we find only the abbé Coger and the abbé Duprat, of whom one was directly linked to the *lieutenant de police*. That's very few. No letters from d'Holbach, in particular, whereas he is in constant contact with Rey to ensure the publication of his own works from 1766 onwards. That seems to indicate that many letters have been destroyed and that Rey took care to throw a cloak over his clandestine trade.

That trade began in 1766: a commercial option, probably, as well as a philosophical choice. Clues to his clandestine trade date mainly from the period 1766–71, while his correspondence in the 1770s concerns the sale of "ordinary" works, the development of Pierre Rousseau's periodical, the *Journal encyclopédique*, and the great affair that marked the end of Rey's career: the rivalry between Panckoucke's *Encyclopédie méthodique* and the *Encyclopédie d'Yverdon* directed by de Felice.[34] This silence – whereas we know that his clandestine trade continued until 1778 – suggests that

Rey carefully sorted his papers, leaving few traces of the printing and sale of clandestine works.

The letters that have survived – and his very discretion – suggest also that Rey was perfectly aware of the "intellectual revolution" that was taking place and in which he was playing an important role. Voltaire underlines Rey's key position, which was to publish philosophical works not only for privileged aristocrats and for marginal intellectuals but also for those who were to direct and determine public opinion. This brief exploration of his clandestine publications suggests a complementary examination of the evolution of political thought over those same years, in order to grasp the state of mind of Rey's readers on the eve of the Revolution.

NOTES

1 The project is conducted by Christelle Bahier-Porte, Fabienne Vial-Bonacci, and Antony McKenna, with the collaboration of Wiep van Bunge (Rotterdam), Jens Häseler (Potsdam), Christine Jackson-Holzberg (Munich) and Gianluca Mori (Florence). The infrastructure of the database was set up and is maintained by Maud Ingarao, Valérie Beaugiraud, and Nathalie Arlin (IHRIM, ENS, Lyon).

2 See Voltaire to Damilaville, 3 March 1768: D14.803.

3 See Cl. Blanckaert and M. Porret, with collab. F. Brandli, *L'Encyclopédie méthodique (1782–1832): Des Lumières au positivisme* (Genève: Droz, 2006).

4 Letter from Leclerc to Rey, 24 January 1766, on the sale of *L'Antiquité dévoilée* by Boullanger and a second letter of the same date concerning his negotiations with Sartine.

5 Letters from Leclerc to Rey, 23 February, 20 March, 20 April, 17 May, 25 September, 23 November, 22 December 1766 and 2 July 1767. "J'ai vendu les 200 *Antiquités* que j'avais, mais je n'en ai pas d'autres[;] lorsque j'en ai demandé [l'autorisation d'en diffuser] d'autres à M. de Sartine, il m'a dit que j'en avais eu plus qu'il n'avait compté m'en donner et que je vous renvoyasse le reste; je lui dis que ce livre ne faisait pas de bruit, il me dit que si et qu'il lui en était revenu quelque chose, je lui dis qu'il allait en paraitre une refutation qui pourrait servir de contrepoison, et qu'ainsi ce livre n'aurait pas de danger[;] il consentit à suspendre le renvoi jusqu'à ce qu'il ait vu cette refutation et son effet[;] ainsi voilà encore un peu de repit, je crois en effet que cette refutation en conseille la lecture, le livre renfermant en lui-même sa refutation" (23 November 1766). "Je vous passe en avoir les

200 *Antiquités* que j'ai vendues moins cinq que j'ai donné[es] à M. Marin, Mercier, de Mande, d'Hemery, de Mairobert. Vous en connaissez trois, les autres en ont été censeurs" (22 December 1766).

6 See the public *Lettre* dated 1 August 1769; see also letters dated 14 December 1781 and 29 January 1782, sent after Rey's death.

7 For instance, the "chevaliers de la Jubilation" around Prosper Marchand, the Club de la Lanterne around Benjamin Furly, the salons of Mme Du Deffand and Julie de Lespinasse, the circle of the baron d'Holbach.

8 See P.-Y. Beaurepaire, *L'Autre et le Frère. L'Étranger et la Franc-maçonnerie en France au XVIII*[e] *siècle* (Paris: Honoré Champion, 1998), and other works by the same author: *L'Espace des francs-maçons. Une sociabilité européenne au XVIII*[e] *siècle* (Rennes: Presses universitaires de Rennes, 2003); *La Plume et le Compas au siècle de l'Encyclopédie. Franc-maçonnerie et culture de la France des Lumières à la France des notables* (Paris: Edimaf, 2000); *Franc-maçonnerie et sociabilité au siècle des Lumières* (Paris: Edimaf, 2013). See also C. Revauger and C. Porset, eds, *Le Monde maçonnique des Lumières (Europe-Amériques) Dictionnaire prosopographique* (Paris: Honoré Champion, 2003).

9 See J.A.I. Champion, "'The Fodder of Our Understanding': Benjamin Furly's Library and Intellectual Conversation c. 1680–c. 1725," in *Benjamin Furly 1636–1714: A Quaker Merchant and His Milieu*, ed. S. Hutton (Florence: Leo S. Olschki, 2007). See also the catalogue of Shaftesbury's library, established by Paul Crell: manuscript made available to us by Christine Jackson-Holzberg, editor of Shaftesbury's correspondence; H.H.M. van Lieshout, *The Making of Pierre Bayle's "Diction[n]aire historique et critique"* (Amsterdam: APA-Holland University Press, 2001), with a CD-ROM recording the "library of Bayle's *Dictionary*"; *La Bibliothèque de Voltaire: catalogue des livres* (Moscow and Leningrad: Academie des sciences de l'URSS, 1961).

10 See also J. Vercruysse, "Marc-Michel Rey, imprimeur philosophe ou philosophique?" *Documentatieblad werkgroep Achttiende eeuw*, 1977, 93–118.

11 See C. Berkvens-Stevelinck, H. Bots, P.G. Hoftijzer, and O.S. Lankhorst, eds, *Le Magasin de l'univers: The Dutch Republic as the Centre of the European Book-Trade* (Leiden: Brill, 1992); C. Berkvens-Stevelinck and J. Vercruysse, *Le Métier de journaliste au dix-huitième siècle. Correspondance entre Prosper Marchand, Jean Rousset de Missy et Lambert Ignace Douxfils* (Oxford: Voltaire Foundation, 1993).

12 J. Vercruysse, *Bibliographie descriptive des écrits du baron d'Holbach* (Paris: Minard, 1971); 2nd ed. (Paris: Garnier, 2017).

13 On this work, see Sylvia Murr, *L'Inde philosophique entre Bossuet et Voltaire*, 2 vols (Paris: École Française d'Extrême Orient, 1987); L. Hunt, M. Jacob,

and W. Mijnhardt, *The Book That Changed Europe: Picart and Bernard's* Religious Ceremonies of the World (Cambridge, MA: Harvard University Press, 2010); L. Hunt, M. Jacob, and W. Mijnhardt, *Bernard Picart and the First Global Vision of Religion* (Los Angeles: Getty Research Institute, 2010).

14 Rousset de Missy to Prosper Marchand, in *Le Métier de journaliste*, ed. J. Vercruysse and C. Berkvens-Stevelinck, letter 91, 176–7. It is true that Rousset de Missy had a grudge against Rey: a few months later, he qualifies him as a "j[ean] f[outre]," worthy to bear the initials of his father-in-law, Jean-Frédéric Bernard: letter 120, 222.

15 In the same period, Voltaire addresses a similar letter to the Genevan Council dated 12 January 1765: "Je suis obligé d'avertir le Magnifique Conseil de Genêve que parmi les libelles pernicieux dont cette viille est inondée depuis quelque temps, tous imprimés à Amsterdam chez Marc-Michel Rey, il arrive lundi prochain chez le nommé Chirol, libraire de Genêve, un ballot contenant des *Diction[n]aires philosophiques*, des *Evangiles de la raison* et autres sottises, qu'on a l'insolence de m'imputer, et que je méprise presque autant que les *Lettres de la montagne* [de Rousseau]. Je crois satisfaire mon devoir en donna t cet avis; et je m'en remets entièrement à la sagesse du Conseil, qui saura bien réprimer toutes les infractions à la paix publique et au bon ordre" (ed. Besterman, D12313).

16 See César-Chesneau Du Marsais, *Examen de la religion, ou doutes sur la religion dont on cherche l'éclaircissement de bonne foi*, ed. Gianluca Mori (Oxford: Voltaire Foundation, 1999), Postface.

17 Jean Meslier, *Œuvres*, ed. Jean Deprun, Roland Desné, Albert Soboul (Paris: Editions Anthropos, 1974).

18 See also D12.276, éd. Leigh, no. 3821; D13.599 and D13.600.

19 See also the letter to Choiseul, 1 April 1768: "je ne me suis pas encor[e] fait chartreux attendu que je suis trop bavard, mais je fais régulièrement mes pâques, et je mets au pied du crucifix toutes les calomnies fréroniques et pompignanes qui m'imputent toutes les gentillesses anti-dévotes que Marc Michel Rey imprime depuis trois ou quatre ans à Amsterdam contre les plus pures lumières de la théologie" (D14.906). And to Charles Bordes, 4 April 1768: "Je ne connais ni Laurent [Du Laurens], ni aucun de ses associez que Marc Michel Rey fait travailler à tant la feuille. Ils ont l'impudence de faire passer leurs scandaleuses brochures sous mon nom" (D14.915). "Je suis à peu près comme M. de Pourceaugnac à qui on veut faire ac[c]roire qu'il a épousé trois ou quatre femmes. On met plus d'ouvrages sur mon compte qu'on ne mit de femmes sur le compte de Pourceaugnac" (to Mme Denis, 3 July 1769: D15.727).

20 Same indications addressed to the marquise Du Deffand, 6 January 1769 (D15.416).

21 Jean Henri Maubert de Gouvest (1721–1767), editor of Durey de Morsan: see J. Vercruysse, "Joseph Marie Durey de Morsan chroniquer de Ferney (1769–1772)," *SVEC*, 230, 1985, 323–91; M. Benitez, "Philosophes et libertins: le cas Durey de Morsan," in *La Face cachée des Lumières. Recherches sur les manuscrits philosophiques clandestins de l'âge classique* (Paris: Universitas and Oxford: The Voltaire Foundation, 1996), 175–90.

22 Laurent Angliviel de La Beaumelle, *Correspondance générale*, ed. H. Bost et C. Lauriol (Oxford: Voltaire Foundation, 2005–14), 10 vols, LB486, 24 January 1749.

23 La Beaumelle, *Correspondance générale*, LB524, May 1749.

24 See also A.-M. Mercier-Faivre, *Un supplément à "L'Encyclopédie": le "Monde primitive" d'Antoine Court de Gébelin; suivi d'une édition du "Génie allégorique et symbolique de l'Antiquité" extrait du "Monde primitive," 1773* (Paris: Honoré Champion, 1999).

25 *Les Années de formation de F.H. Jacobi d'après ses lettres inédites à M.-M. Rey (1763–1771) [...]*, ed. J.T. de Booy and R. Mortier (Genève: Institut et Musée Voltaire, 1966).

26 *Ouvrages philosophiques pour servir de preuves à la religion de l'auteur*, recueil qui est le même que *L'Evangile de la raison, ouvrage posthume de M. D. M... y* (s.l.n.d., in-8° de 43.207 p.), printed by Rey towards the end of 1764. Cf. Barbier et Bengesco, II.386–389 (no. 1897).

27 M.-G. Dehrmann, *Das "Orakel der Deisten": Shaftesbury und die deutsche Aufklärung* (Göttingen: Wallstein, 2008), 78n270: Jacobi's copy is the pirate edition of 1733, printed by Thomas Johnson in The Hague, with a false place name: "London." This edition was "particulièrement appréciée sur le continent," according to Dehrmann. Jacobi's copy is now to be found at the Universitätsbibliothek in Halle, shelf-mark FA 3111. Thanks to Christine Jackson-Holzberg, who provided this reference.

28 *Phädon, oder über die Unsterblichkeit der Seele*, printed in 1764.

29 Paris, Arsenal, Ms.12282, fol.231–8r.

30 See letters dated 17 June and 2 August 1773, 24 August and September 1775, and 14 April 1777.

31 J. Vercruysse, "Marc-Michel Rey et le livre philosophique," in *Literaturgeschichte als geschichtlicher Auftrag: in memoriam Werner Krauss* (Berlin: Akademie-Verlag, 1978), 149–56.

32 See Gabrielle-Emilie Du Châtelet, *Examens de la Bible*, ed. B.E. Schwarzbach (Paris: Honoré Champion, 2011).

33 See J.Th. Booy, "L'abbé Coger, dit *Coge Pecus*, lecteur de Voltaire et d'Holbach," *SVEC*, 18, 1961, 183–96.

34 See documents dated 18 February 1769, 3 May 1769, and 20 May 1769.

PART FIVE

TOLERATION, CRITICISM, AND INNOVATION IN RELIGION

Chapter Twelve

The *Treatise of the Three Impostors*, Islam, the Enlightenment, and Toleration[1]

JOHN MARSHALL

The most famous of all clandestine manuscripts and then obscurely printed texts of the Enlightenment was the *Treatise of the Three Impostors.* It is a work that, as Mosheim put it in his *Ecclesiastical History,* "surpasses infinitely in atheistical profanity even those works of Spinoza which are regarded as the most pernicious." It was recently called by Georges Minois *The Atheist's Bible.* It is, of course, a clandestine work that has been illuminated brilliantly as a text and in wonderfully thick descriptions of its various editions and contexts by a host of scholars, including Richard Popkin, Peg Jacob, Chris Laursen, Abraham Anderson, Justin Champion, Sylvia Berti, Jonathan Israel, Miguel Benitez, George Minois, and Françoise Charles-Daubert. The *Treatise of the Three Impostors* famously identified Moses, Jesus, and Muhammad as three "impostors" whose claims to religious authority were false and superstitious; simultaneously, it undermined the grounds for belief in the most significant other elements of religion of the three Abrahamic religions – including the afterlife, the soul, heaven and hell, and the devil. And the *Treatise of the Three Impostors* challenged organized religion as "superstition" based in the "ignorance" and "credulity" of the masses; condemned self-interested manipulation of the population's ignorance and credulity by political rulers and priests; and provided an euhemerist account of the base of religion in hope and especially in fear and the irrational and vain hope to propitiate. It is, in the 1768 edition associated with the atheist materialist d'Holbach, a compound of scepticism and derision directed not only against all three Abrahamic religions but also against the human folly, credulity, ignorance, and fearfulness that made humans religious. As such, it is associated in the eighteenth century with atheistically inclined esoteric discussion of circulated manuscripts, and more or less scandalized discussion of print versions, by cognoscenti in the Republic of Letters, rather than with the liberation of the credulous masses themselves – rather as so much of the eighteenth century Enlightenment was predicated on disdain for and often active hostility towards the intellectual capacities and commitments of the majority of the population, a point to which I will return at the end of this chapter.[2]

I want here to focus on one element of the *Treatise* that has received somewhat less analysis by scholars than its Spinozist and Hobbesian structure and carapace, or than its depiction of Moses and Jesus: its depictions of Muhammad and Islam, centred on its figuring of Islam as a religion of imposture, superstition, fanaticism, and use of force. It is unquestionably the case that if one reads the *Treatise* consecutively and entire in its 1768 so-called definitive edition, then the *Treatise* discussed each of Moses, Jesus, and Muhammad after already having declared sweepingly that the Bible was a "tissue of fragments stitched together at different times, collected by different persons" and published on the authority of rabbis' "fancy," with such being men's "malice" and "stupidity" that they "pass their lives in quibbling and persist in respecting a book in which there is no more order than in the Alcoran of Mahomet; a book, I say, which no one understands, it is so obscure and ill conceived; a book which serves only to foment divisions." This is an undermining of the Judeo-Christian Bible that worked by declaring it as disordered and obscure as the Koran was then often being declared to be. In the 1768 version, multiply thereafter reprinted, Muhammad was described even before one reached the chapters dedicated to him as one of three legislators who gave laws, cults, and ceremonies "proper to nourish the fanaticism which they wanted to establish," and as having taken from the two preceding Abrahamic religions "the wherewithal to compose his own, and thereafter declared himself the enemy of both" – an inflection that posed Islam as the enemy, rather than as either the at least partially admiring successor to Christianity or the centuries-old protector to Judaism and Christianity, that it could just as easily have been described as being on the evidence of Islamic societies' toleration and Islam's own often positive attitudes towards Jesus and Christianity.[3]

The immediately prefatory declaration to the accounts given of the lives of Moses, Jesus, and Muhammad was that the judgment of their character was needed in order to see whose views were better founded: those who "revere them as divine men, or those who call them tricksters and impostors." And after the accounts of Moses, Jesus, and Muhammad it was declared that the "apparitions and the conferences [with God] of

Moses and Mahomet," like the allegedly "divine origin" of Jesus, were "the greatest impostures which anyone has been able to hatch." Their writings were not where "one must search for a true idea of the Divinity." They should instead be fled, the *Treatise* intoned, "if you love the truth." Moreover, the *Treatise's* discussion of Muhammad followed immediately after those of Moses and Jesus. Moses was first indicted as using "pretended Magic," "pretended prodigies," and "trickery" in claiming powers to do miracles, as having boasted of his "frequent conversations" with Divinity in order to gain power over the Hebrews, and as having ruled by force as an "absolute Despot" and Tyrant who executed his opponents, while the ancient Hebrews were described as an "imbecile Populace," with "never a people more ignorant" and "more credulous." The combination of Moses's imposture and use of force here was important, and the *Treatise* declared that "Trickery without arms rarely succeeds." Christ was then held to have "got himself followed by some imbeciles" accustomed to believe in "dreams and fancies" who were therefore willing even to believe the Virgin birth; "As the number of fools is infinite, Jesus Christ found Subjects everywhere." But Jesus, it was said, had lacked money and forces sufficient to found an empire; and if he had had "these two instruments" then "he would have succeeded no less than Moses or Mahomet."[4]

It was only after these sections on Moses and Jesus that readers of the *Treatise* encountered Muhammad and Islam in detail. The *Treatise* described the foundation of Islam as occurring when men had followed a new legislator "who raised himself up by the same ways as Moses, he took like him the title of Prophet and Envoy of God; like him he made miracles, and knew how to profit from the passions of the people." Followed by "an ignorant populace" he then explicated to them the "new Oracles of Heaven." These "wretches seduced by his promises and the fables of this new Impostor, spread his renown and exalted him to the point of eclipsing that of his predecessors." In some versions of the *Treatise*, including that of 1768, it was further declared that Muhammad seemed not "fit to found an empire," not knowing how to read or write or excelling neither in politics nor in philosophy, and that Muhammad was followed by "an imbecile crowd which believed him a divine man." And it was suggested in these versions that Muhammad had tricked a companion to declare, as though with the voice of God, to his "infatuated multitude" of followers that he was the divine prophet from whom they could receive the true law that Jews and Christians had adulterated, and that Muhammad had then had those people use stones to kill that concealed individual, using as legitimation for this act the memory of the stone that Jacob had raised up to mark the place where God had appeared to him (Genesis 3). This was thus simultaneously a false and deceiving declaration that Muhammad was the authentic voice of God, based simultaneously on Muhammad having tricked a companion to declare this and thereby tricking the audience that heard it, compounded with a wresting of a textual example from the Old Testament, and an act of foundational religious violence, of the supposedly religiously required use of stones to kill someone. The *Treatise* then declared that this was precisely the "pile of stones" on which the "last of the most famous impostors established his law." Depicting Muhammad as happier than Jesus or Moses in seeing his "law" established – a politic emphasis – the *Treatise* declared "Thus" was Mahomet "raised" up, and – perhaps obliquely referencing the many Enlightenment and preceding Christian attacks on Muhammad's lustful pursuit of sensual sexual pleasures – that he had "died with all his wishes gratified." He had died, moreover, "with some certainty his Doctrine would subsist" because it was "accommodated to the genius of his sectaries, born and raised in ignorance."[5]

In some other early versions of the *Treatise*, including *Le Fameux Livre des Trois Impostuers,* emphasis was placed instead on the use of the sword, with stress that Muhammad had originally tried to persuade people by his false claims of revelations and visions appealing to the credulity of the populace – what might be called the argument from superstition and trickery – but that when he had been forced to flee from Mecca to Medina, "Then he ceased to support his authority by argument, and persuaded his disciples to plant the Mussulman faith at the point of the sword." Muhammad was then described as having placed armies in the field "who subjugated" the populace, and thus by his "hypocrisy and imposture" was "elevated to the dignity of sovereign." Here, then, were two somewhat divergent but overlapping depictions of Muhammad. In one the emphasis was on superstition and trickery to gain support for his religion, completed with an image of the use of force combined with deceit that involved killing someone as an alleged foundational act of faith in Muhammad's status as a divine prophet, but without a more explicitly generalized declaration that Islam was propagated primarily by the point of the sword; in the other, there was an explicit declaration that from his exile from Mecca onwards Muhammad became not only an impostor but also a Legislator using armed force to spread his religion by the point of a sword.[6]

In both of these versions, for all their parallel assaults on the credulity of populations believing in false prophets, the contrast is in part to Jesus, who is said not to have used force in spreading his religion, and in part to Moses, who was said to have used force and to have founded a tyranny but not to have founded a long-lasting empire. Even as the overarching scheme of the *Treatise* was thus to associate Moses, Jesus, and Muhammad as impostors, there was in this set of arguments the potential to see Muhammad as the worst of the three impostors and Islam as the worst of the three religions, as the one that had most effectively, lastingly, and committedly wedded and glued the use of force to coerce belief to imposture, superstition, credulous multitudes, and fanatic followers willing to use violence to kill people or take up arms to impose their religion on others. Attack on all three Abrahamic religions simultaneously was surely the primary intent of those circulating the *Treatise*, and they were circulating the *Treatise* in largely Christian and Judeo-Christian Western Europe and were as such intended practically to undermine much more immediately the power of Christian priests than that of Islam. But one response called for by these passages was subscription to the long prevailing image of Muhammad as leader of a violent religion, and of Islam as quintessentially a violent, fanatical, and aggressively imperial religion, in contrast to Jesus and Christianity. It was possible to attack Islam and Muhammad as a way to criticize indirectly Christians who were said to have imitated Islam, but in such a way that Islam and Muhammad would be condemned even more fiercely than Christianity, and, even if the text itself canvassed no intent to reform Christianity, Christianity could be read as capable of reform into a gentle mildness while Islam was left irredeemably a religion of violence and imperial ambitions. It is important to note both potentials in the *Treatise* itself – the strongly asserted equivalence of Muhammad to Jesus and Moses as an impostor deceiving people, or that Muhammad was effectively rendered significantly worse than Jesus and Moses. In this important way, The *Treatise* could be said to have been conceptually and rhetorically Janus-faced, indicating equivalence of imposture and difference among the religions simultaneously.[7]

In 1768–9 Voltaire composed a verse epistle reacting directly to the newly printed edition of the *Treatise*. For Voltaire, who described the *Treatise* as a "very dangerous work, full of coarse atheism, without wit and devoid of philosophy," the *Treatise* had confused "Mohammed and the Creator / And the deeds of man with God, his author." When it should have criticized the servant who had served his master poorly, the *Treatise* had instead criticized the master. Voltaire thus declared that he approved of attack on the "hypocritical insolence" of "proud charlatans promoted to high honors" such as Muhammad, and he declared that he had "unmasked" religious violence with his own pen "for the past fifty years," as he was himself the "enemy of … fanaticism," but he declared that in contrast to the *Treatise* he had always "distinguished between religion and the misery bred of superstition." Celebrating both the advance of "happy toleration" as the "catechism of all well-made souls" and the coming time when "philosophy, enlightening humanity," would make "frightful fanaticism" tremble, Voltaire described a future in which "the children of Sarah, whom we treat like dogs / Will eat ham that has been cured by Christians" and when "the Turk, without asking whether the imam will pardon him / Will go drink with the abbé Tamponet at the Sorbonne." Here, then, was a response to the *Treatise of the Three Impostors* – an attack on all revealed religions equally in the name of a kind of theism or deism, intended to render Muslims capable of being tolerable but involving them in violating what many held to be an obligation of Islam and thereby also ignoring the commands of their imams in drinking alcohol. It imagined a future of toleration in which deism had not so much accommodated as triumphed over revealed religion.[8]

In places, including his *Treatise on Tolerance*, Voltaire called explicitly for tolerance for Muslims as for Christians and Jews as all were "brothers" united by a common "humanity." And in many places he pointed to Islamic practices of toleration for Christians and Muslims, including in the Ottoman Empire, and he suggested that "the Turk" should in this be imitated by all Europeans. But in many other places Voltaire adopted an especially strident attack on Muhammad and on Islam, and he explicitly supported conquering rather than imitating the Ottomans. In various works Voltaire suggested that Islam had been extended by preaching as well as by force of arms, but he nonetheless declared that the first Muslims had been "animated by Mahomet with the rage of enthusiasm" and that "[n]othing is more terrible than a people who, having nothing to lose, fight in the united spirit of rapine and of religion." Voltaire called Muhammed a "charlatan" and a "brazen impostor who deceived imbeciles," and he described the Koran as "a rhapsody, without connection, without order, and without art," as the period of the High Enlightenment frequently joined explicit mockery of the Koran as an unreasonable and superstitious text with attack on Muslim uses of force. It was this combination that Voltaire had expressed in his early play, *Fanaticism, or Mohammed the Impostor*. The scornful tone is captured in the preface: "for a camel driver to stir up sedition … to [claim] that he had spoken with the angel Gabriel" and to have received this "unintelligible book whose every page sets common sense ashudder; to bring fire and sword to his country so that the book would be respected, and murder fathers, and ravish their daughters, and give the vanquished the choice of his religion or death; surely, there is nobody who could excuse this, except a Turk [for whom] superstition [had extinquished] the light of nature." In the play Voltaire fictionalized many things in Muhammad's life, identifying him as a lasciviously motivated adulterer hypocritically fostering assassination by his followers with false claims that this was required by their religion, and identified Muhammad as an "impostor" tricking the "vulgar" by false claims to divine inspiration. He characterized Islam as essentially a religion of force and imposture, a credulous faith followed by "the vilest of people." Voltaire was unquestionably here in part criticizing Islam and Muhammad in terms that he intended to be applied collaterally to the Catholic church and priesthood, and the play was banned in eighteenth-century France for its implied criticism of Catholicism in the guise of criticizing Islam. Voltaire's *Mahomet* was simultaneously a smash hit in London, where it was performed in every remaining decade of the eighteenth century, and where translators' prefaces explicitly criticized the intellectual slavery of Catholicism and Islam simultaneously, and did so during decades when Catholics and Muslims were both being denied full religious toleration in England as alleged apostles of religious violence who could not be good subjects. Even if targeting Christianity indirectly through targeting Islam, Voltaire himself also clearly was targeting Islam itself.[9]

In the eighteenth-century "High Enlightenment" many entries in the *Encyclopedia* composed by Diderot and others (including Voltaire) similarly combined denunciation of Muhammad as a "false prophet" of a religion of enthusiasm, superstition, and fanaticism with denunciation of Islam as primarily or exclusively established by force; and many of these entries contrasted Christianity as peaceful in its principles with Islam as committed to force in its principles. The entry "Tolerance" thus contrasted Jesus, "your model, [who] employed only gentleness and persuasion," with "Muhammad," who "seduced some and forced others to be silent." It declared that Jesus "called people to take up his work, Muhammad to take up the sword. Jesus said see and believe, Muhammad commanded die or believe." The entry "Mussulman" described the name of Muslims as meaning saved or escaped from danger and thus as derived from their "having established their religion by weapons and fire, massacring all those who did not want to embrace it and granting their lives to all those who did embrace it." The entry "Mohammedanism," which closely echoed Voltaire's analysis in the *Essay on Manners* and elsewhere, declared that Muhammad had known the "character of his fellow citizens, their ignorance, credulity, and their disposition to enthusiasm," and had "feigned some revelations," and described the Koran as full of "contradictions, absurdities, and anachronisms." It declared that "through word and through arms" Muhammad had conquered Arabia and then extended his conquests, giving "a choice to those he wanted to subjugate, of embracing his sect or paying a tribute." It declared that of "all the legislators who have founded religions," he was "the only one who has extended his by conquests." It contrasted Muslims, who "thought themselves made to dominate," with Jews as fearful of being enslaved. The entry "Koran" declared it the book of the "false prophet Mohammed," and continued that one of its two fundamental points sufficed to demonstrate its falsity – its commitment "that the Mohammedan Religion should be established ... without dispute, without contradiction, such that all those who repugn it should be put to death; and that the Muslims who kill these unbelievers merit Paradise: and History makes us believe that it is always less established by seduction than by violence and the force of arms."[10]

Voltaire's play *Fanaticism, or Mahomet the prophet*, and many other of his works thus depicted Muhammad as committed to the use of force to spread his religion, and many entries in the *Encyclopedia* reinforced that interpretation strongly. Both repeatedly attacked Islam as violent and fanatical as well as enthusiastic, superstitious, and unreasonable, and often contrasted this to the alleged tolerance and gentleness of Christianity. Enlightenment texts often further associated Islam with "Oriental Despotism," depicting the enslavement of Muslim subject populations to their rulers as due in significant part to their religion in a period when criticism of the absolute monarchy of France was often voiced indirectly through commentary on the Ottomans or Persians. For Montesquieu, the most important and influential of the writers repeatedly associating Islam with Oriental Despotism, "[i]t is a misfortune for human nature when religion is given by a conqueror. The Mohammedan religion, which speaks only with a sword, continues to act on men with the destructive spirit that founded it." And Montesquieu declared similarly sweepingly – in a chapter title itself – "That moderate government is better suited to the Christian religion, and despotic government to Mohammedanism," as Christianity taught "gentleness," and one should "without further examination, embrace the one and reject the other" for it was much more evident that a religion "should soften the mores of men than it is that a religion is true." According to Montesquieu, despotic government, ruling "timid, ignorant, beaten-down people," had been reinforced by Islam, with "fear added to fear." Montesquieu made the case for religious toleration in part by attacking Christian Inquisitors by arguing that they should stop using force to establish Christianity, as thereby "[y]ou deprive yourselves of the advantage over the Mohammedans given you by the manner in which their religion was established. When they flaunt the number of their faithful, you say to them that only force has acquired that number for them and that they have extended their religion by iron; therefore, why establish yours by fire?"[11]

As Michael Curtis, Denise Spellberg, and others have shown recently, similar views were very prominently stated in many Enlightenment works, including Trenchard and Gordon's *Cato's Letters*, which depicted the religion of the Ottoman Empire as "founded on imposture, blended with outrageous and avowed violence," and its subjects as "abject slaves." For Trenchard and Gordon, the "[s]ervitude of the body" was "secured by the servitude of the mind," with "oppression fortified by delusion. This is the height of human slavery. By this the Turk and the Pope reign. They hold their horrid and sanguinary authority by false reverence, as much as the sword." Elements of this compound association of Islam with enthusiasm, superstition, unreasonableness, and obedience to despotism, were recorded in brief by Hume, who attacked the "wild and absurd performance of the Koran" and condemned the "pretended prophet" Muhammad for praising "instances of treachery, inhumanity, cruelty, revenge, bigotry as are utterly incompatible with civilized society." And Kant agreed, declaring in *Religion within the bounds of mere reason* that "Mohammedanism" was "distinguished by its pride, because it finds confirmation of its faith in victories and in the subjugation of many peoples."[12]

Even though some Enlightenment writers were themselves inclined to anti-Trinitarianism, deism, or atheism, and found some significant positive things to say for Islam as a religion closer to natural religion and more tolerant than Christianity for most of its history, this was usually embedded in still severe criticism of Islam as intolerant and irrational. Condorcet, who assaulted Judaism, Christianity, and Islam as three forms of imposture, described Muhammad in his *Outline of a historical view of the progress of the human mind* as a "man of ardent enthusiasm and most profound policy, born with the talents of a poet, as well as those of a warrior," and imposing himself by "erecting upon the ruins of the ancient worship a religion more refined" by promulgating "a mass of fables, which he pretended to have received from heaven," *and* by use of force in "battles." For Condorcet, Islam had involved initially "the fever of fanaticism," "zeal for the propagation of religion," "ardor for conquests," and the "unmitigated despotism of religion," and while there had been some developments of sciences and arts in later centuries of Islam, nonetheless, "[b]orn ... in the midst of despotism, and, as it were, in the cradle of a fanatical religion," the religion of Muhammad had "condemned to an eternal slavery, to an incurable stupidity, all that vast portion of the earth in which it has extended its empire." It was only in combination with such declamations that Condorcet noted that Islam was itself of all religions "the most simple in its dogmas, the least absurd in its practices, above all others tolerant in its principles."[13]

In his *Decline and Fall of the Roman Empire* Gibbon described the Koran as a "glorious testimony to the unity of God," and defended Islam from allegations that it appealed to the sensual, stressed its care for the "indigent and unfortunate," held that Muhammad's own precepts inculcated a "simple and rational piety," and suggested that "[a] philosophic theist might subscribe the popular creed of the Mahometans, a creed too sublime perhaps for our present faculties." But Gibbon still described Muhammad conquering "with the sword in one hand and the Koran in the other," appealing to the "fanaticism of the first Moslems," and having "consulted the spirit of fraud or enthusiasm." Gibbon declared that the "fragments of the Koran were produced" with "each revelation ... suited to the emergencies of his policy or passion" and that the claim that "God alone could dictate this incomparable performance" was "most powerfully addressed to a devout Arabian, whose mind is attuned to faith and rapture ... and whose ignorance is incapable of comparing the productions of human genius." It was "an incoherent rhapsody of fable, and precept, and declamation, which seldom excites a sentiment or idea."[14]

In the *Decline and Fall* Gibbon did recognize that to Christian subjects Muhammad himself had "readily granted the security of their persons, the freedom of their trade, the property of their goods, and the toleration of their worship." He recognized that Muhammad "[s]eems to have allowed some of the conquered to choose to pay tribute and be indulged in worship." He further declared at one point that "[t]he passages of the Koran in behalf of toleration, are strong and numerous." But Gibbon then explained away Muhammad's own tolerance as having been only temporary and circumstantial, as when "[c]onscious of his reason and of his weakness, he asserted the liberty of conscience, and disclaimed the use of religious violence," or as it had been "the interest of a conqueror to propose a fair capitulation to the most powerful religion of the earth," and asserted that Muhammad had assumed "in his new revelations, a fiercer and more sanguinary tone, which proves that his former moderation was the effect of weakness." Gibbon treated Muhammad as having ended his life commanding Muslims to "propagate his religion by the sword," and commanding them "to pursue the unbelieving nations of the earth," with "bloody precepts, so repeatedly inculcated in the Koran." For Gibbon, Muhammad – for whom he could not "decide whether the title of enthusiast or impostor" more "properly belongs" – had ended his life "stained" by his use of the methods of "fraud and perfidy, of cruelty and injustice," and by having approved the "assassination of the Jews and idolaters"; had fired his followers with "enthusiasm"; and had described the "Sword" as the "key of heaven and of hell," such that "a drop of blood shed in the cause of God" was "of more avail than two months of fasting or prayer; whosoever falls in battle, his sins are forgiven."[15]

Very often, High Enlightenment texts treated Islamic tolerance as Gibbon had thus treated it, as temporary, *politique*, and as having been rescinded by Muhammad himself in his move from Mecca to Medina. And by the time that Gibbon was composing the *Decline and Fall*, a century and more of similar treatments of Muhammad's tolerance as temporary, *politique*, and rescinded had been circulated in texts often described as those of the radical Enlightenment or early Enlightenment, which formed part of the background to the *Treatise of the Three Impostors* itself. These themes were all registered within very strong emphasis on "Mahomet" as a "false prophet" and "impostor" in the course of Pierre Bayle's extensive entry on Muhammad in the 1696 *Historical and Critical Dictionary*. While Bayle stressed there that many Christian allegations of Muslim immorality were false, that many Muslims practised charity and the golden rule, and that there was no reason to prefer Christians over Muslims on the basis of their morality, in the course of this twenty-three-page entry on Muhammad Bayle declared him "much tainted with fanaticism" and an "impostor," and repeated and handed on to the "High Enlightenment," often thereafter repeated, a long-standing form of hostile ridicule of the Revelation to Muhammad which declared him an epileptic who had concealed his disease by turning it into a claim of inspiration. Bayle further indicted Muhammad as the propagator of laws very harmful to women who was personally lewd and who beat his wives.[16]

It was within a series of such fierce criticisms of Muhammad that Bayle declared in the *Dictionary* that "[w]ithout doubt, the principal Cause of the great Progress he made, was the Way he us'd, to Force those, by

Arms, to submit to his Religion, who would not willingly embrace it." In a work in which the footnotes performed the crucial work, Bayle expanded in a footnote that this use of force was "the sole and entire Cause" of the spread of Islam. Bayle further declared that it was clear from history that "the Mahometan Religion was establish'd by way of Conquest," and he mocked the initial actions of "Mahomet's" forces as those of "bandits" who had robbed a caravan but were proclaimed "martyrs." Bayle's targets here were at least as much his fellow Christians as they were Muslims, as Bayle attacked many Christian justifiers of the use of force and condemned Louis XIV and the Catholic Church for using "Mahometan ways." Indeed, his discussion in his footnotes did not quote Islamic arguments, but instead extensively quoted the arguments of the Catholics Bellarmine and Bossuet, and of his fellow Protestant refugee but apologist for intolerance Jurieu, in order to argue that if their arguments were accepted, Christians then could not "reproach Mahomet for having propagated his Religion by Force." Bayle further punctured Christians' arguments for their use of force by allegation that the support of God for Christianity was shown by military victory by suggesting that Islam's "Victories, its Conquests, its Triumphs, are incomparably more illustrious than any thing the Christians can boast of in this kind of Prosperity. The Exploits of the Mahometans are without doubt the most glorious things that History can afford."[17]

While in this lengthy entry on Muhammad in the *Dictionary* Bayle recognized briefly in a note that "[t]here is a Passage in the Alcoran which promises Infidels Liberty of Conscience" and that he "at the beginning offered Peace to the Christians," Bayle did not then emphasize this passage of the Koran and the Meccan period of Islam. Instead he stressed strongly both the Medinan period of Islam and the incongruity of principle and practice, as he declared in the continuation of this extensive note that

> [t]he Mahometans according to the Principles of their Faith, are oblig'd to employ Violence to destroy other Religions, and yet they tolerate them now, and have done so for many ages. The Christians have no Order, but to Preach and Instruct, and yet, time out of mind, they destroy, with Fire and Sword, those who are not of their Religion. "When you meet with Infidels," says Mahomet, "kill them, cut off their Heads, or make them Prisoners, and put them in Chains until they have paid their Ransom, or you find it convenient to set them at Liberty. Be not afraid to Persecute them, till they have laid down their Arms, and submitted to you."

Nevertheless, "tis true, that the Saracens did quickly leave off the Ways of Violence, and that the Greek Churches, as well the Orthodox as the Schismatical, have been preserv'd to this day under the Yoke of Mahomet." For Bayle, the "Conclusion which I would draw from all this, is, That Men are little govern'd by their Principles. The Turks, we see, Tolerate all sorts of Religions, though the Alcoran enjoins them to Persecute the Infidels."[18]

Bayle here cited and drew heavily from a work by a late-seventeenth-century English ambassador to the Ottoman Empire, Paul Rycaut's *Present State of the Ottoman Empire*, a work that was also to be a central source for later Enlightenment thinkers such as Montesquieu in the *Spirit of the Laws* and Trenchard and Gordon in *Cato's Letters*. Rycaut's work included a chapter titled "The Toleration that Mahometanism in its Infancy promised to other Religions, and in what manner that Agreement was afterwards observed." Rycaut therein declared that "[w]hen Mahematanism was first weak, and therefore put on a modest Countenance and plausible Aspect to deceive mankind, it found a great part of the World illuminated with Christianity" and "guarded ... with the Fortifications, Arms and Protection of Emperors and Kings," and so had judged it "best policy to make proffers of truce and peace between the Christian and its own profession: and therefore in all places where its arms were prevalent and prosperous, proclaimed a free toleration to all Religions, but especially in outward appearance, courted and favoured the Christian ... and Mahomet says in his Alchoran thus: 'O infidels, I do not adore what you adore, and you do not adore what I worship; observe you your law, and I will observe mine.'"[19]

Rycaut, however, had then continued:

> But mark how well Mahomed in the sequel observed this Law: As soon as his Government increased, and that by Arms and bad Arts he had secured his Kingdom, he writes his Chapter of the Sword ... and another chapter ... called the Chapter of Battle ... and therein his modest words (if you adore not what I adore, let your Religion be to you, and mine to me) and other promises of toleration and indulgence to the Christian Religion, were changed to a harsher note; and his Edicts were then for bloud and ruine, and enslavement of Christians: "When you meet with Infidels, saith he, cut off their heads, kill them, take them prisoners, bind them, until either you think fit to give them liberty, or pay their ransom; and forbear not to persecute them, until they have laid down their Arms and submitted."

Holding, moreover, that Muslims offered only the "specious out-side" of "toleration," Rycaut declared that "the Turks ... know that they cannot force men's Wills, nor captivate their Consciences, as well as their bodies," and that such toleration as they did provide in the Ottoman Empire used "what means may be used to render them contemptible, to make them poor, their lives uncomfortable, and the interest of their Religion weak and despicable." And Rycaut declared that "[t]he propagation of the Mahometan faith having been promoted wholy by the Sword; that perswasion and principle in their Catechism, that the souls of those who die in the Wars against the Christians, without the help of previous acts of performance of their Law, or other works, are immediately transported to Paradise, must needs whet the Swords and raise the spirits of the Souldiers."[20]

Occasionally, rather less negative notes about Islamic and Ottoman toleration were struck in the period of the Enlightenment. Bernard and Picart's extremely influential *Religious Ceremonies and Customs of the World* derived parts of its arguments – as Hunt, Jacob, and Mijnhardt have shown in discussing it in *The Book Which Changed Europe* – from Adriaan Reland's early-eighteenth-century *The Muslim Religion* and its translation into English by the Huguenot refugee David Durand. Therein it was declared concerning the various religions of the world that there was a need for "full liberty for each to follow his own lights and to believe true that which appears to him to be such" and that "it is a shame for Christians to refuse to other Christians, as they do, the usage of this precious liberty and thus to oblige them by their bad ways to take refuge in the empire of the Turks, where they find more repose and charity than with their brothers." For Reland, it was more broadly necessary to examine the actual commitments of religions from their own texts, and not to accept the attacks of their religious enemies upon them. Reland repudiated many attacks on Islam and showed that very much that had been alleged of Islam was false, including such allegations as that Muhammad was an epileptic concealing his disease by claiming revelation, recirculated by Bayle, or the notion that in Islam women would not enter paradise. And Reland declared importantly that among the many principles *falsely* attributed to Islam was the allegation that Islam declared that those who kill enemies would gain paradise, whereas Muhammad had only promised that who who fell in battle specifically in resisting idolaters who had attacked them at Mecca would thus gain paradise. Reland declared that many were thus deceived in holding that when Muhammad had said, only of the attacking idolaters, "[k]ill them wheresoever you shall find them," that this had been extended to all, "as if it were lawful for the Turks at this day to kill Christians and other Enemys, secretly or openly."

Reland was clear: this was not, even though it was often alleged, a principle of Islam. It was, he declared, not "more lawful for a Mahometan than for a Christian to kill his Enemy."[21]

In a small number of works the broader Islamic traditions of tolerance of Christians and Jews and the tolerant principles of Muhammad himself were stressed by discussion of some of Muhammad's actual, or alleged, covenants supporting toleration. In the 1740s the Anglican clergyman Richard Pococke printed a text in the first volume of his *Description of the East* that he called "The Patent of Mahomet, which he granted to the Monks of Mount Sinai; and to Christians in general." This text asserted that by grant Muhammed had himself given "a secure and positive promise to be accomplish'd to the Christian nation" – and not just to the monks at Mount Sinai – that he would protect and preserve them, exempting monks from poll taxes and tributes, allowing poll taxes from ordinary Christians but nothing more, with a call to Muslims to "give of your good things to them, and converse with them, and hinder everyone from molesting them." There was provision for intermarriage between Muslim men and Christian women, who were to be allowed subsequently to maintain their religion. And there was declaration that no Muslim should "bear arms against" Christians and that "on the contrary, the Mussulman shall wage war for them." Anyone who opposed this was called "an apostate to God, and to his divine Apostle" who had granted them "this protection" by "this promise."[22]

This "patent" or covenant (the *Achtiname*) has recently been republished by John Andrew Morrow as one among a series of six such covenants of Muhammad in *The Covenants of the Prophet Muhammad with the Christians of the World*, and both Morrow and other contemporary Islamic scholars have pointed towards it as one of many statements and practices of Islamic tolerance that occur also within the hadith and in the Koran itself, both of which support religious tolerance and oppose intolerance. Whether the covenant to the monks of Mount Sinai is genuine or not – and its authenticity is questioned by some today – extensive toleration and protection was actually provided to the monks of Sinai and to many other Christians over many centuries under Islamic rulers on its basis, as it was declared genuine by Fatimids, Ayyubids, Mamluks, and Ottomans, *inter alia*, over the course of many centuries. And this history of toleration and protection is itself one part of an extraordinarily important tradition within Islamic societies, which have very often indeed and very extensively indeed provided toleration to Christians and Jews throughout many centuries in many locations. Very often indeed in the pre-modern world Islamic societies provided a much more extensive religious toleration than was being provided by contemporary Christian societies.[23]

Such support for both principles and practices of religious toleration has further and very considerable textual basis in many passages in the Koran, especially, but not only, from Muhammad's Meccan period. In the single most important passage for centuries of Islamic defences of toleration it is held that "there is no coercion in religion" (2:256). This passage is, moreover, dated from the Medinan period, and not the Meccan period of Muhammad's life. The Koran further declares "unto you your religion, unto me, mine" (109:6). The Koran declares that "truth is from your Lord, so let whomever wills, believe, and let whomever wills, disbelieve" (18.29). According to the Koran, "Had God willed He would have made you into one community; but [it was His will] to test you in what he gave you. So compete with each other in doing good works. To God you are all returning, and He will inform you about how you differed" (5:48). And the Koran states: "And if thy Lord had willed, whoever is in the earth would have believed, all of them, all together. Wouldst thou then constrain the people, until they are believers? It is not for any soul to believe save by the leave of God; and He lays abomination upon those who have no understanding" (10.99–100). As many Islamic scholars have stressed, many passages of the Koran supported defensive but not aggressive war, perhaps most notably: "Fight those who fight you, but aggress not, verily God loves not the aggressors" (2.190–3). Even many passages that recognize enmity stress the duty to seek peace whenever not under attack: "If your enemy inclines towards peace, then you too should seek peace" (8.61). "Had Allah wished," the Koran declares, "[h]e would have made them dominate you, and so if they leave you alone and do not fight you and offer you peace, then Allah allows you no way against them" (4.90). The Koran further stresses persuasion in religion in discussion with Jews and Christians, declaring, *inter alia,* "So argue not with the people of the book except in the best way … and say: we believe in that which was revealed to us as well as that which was revealed to you. Our God and your God is one and the same. We all submit to him" (29:46). The Koran indicates that "[t]hose who have believed – and the Jews, the Christians, the Sabeans, those who believe in God, the Last Day, and do good works – stand to be rewarded by God. No fear or grief shall befall them" (2.62). The Koran specifies that "[o]f the People of the Book there is an upright Party who recite God's messages in the night-time and they adore Him. They believe in God and the Last Day, and they enjoin good and forbid evil and vie with one another in good deeds. Those are among the righteous; whatever good they do, they will not be denied it. And God knows those who keep their duty" (3:112–16).[24]

There are a small number of verses in the Koran, some of which we have already seen emphasized by European Enlightenment writers discussed in this piece, that call for various forms of intolerance, and a number of passages of the Koran emphasize the importance of *jihad* (struggle) as warfare against others. In some periods of Islamic history, these texts were interpreted by many Islamic religious authorities as abrogating the preceding passages of the Koran calling for toleration and as justifying war to extend the territory of the faith. The single most influential, the so-called "verse of the sword" (9:5), was at points held to have abrogated no fewer than 114 Koranic verses in 53 suras. Conquests were legitimated in part in the name of religion, including many conquests involved in the expansion of the extraordinarily powerful Ottoman Empire in late medieval and early modern Europe. This history of emphasis on abrogation of the commandment to toleration by the "sword verse" and by other verses thus occurred before Islam was being discussed in the European Enlightenment texts quoted in this article. In the "verse of the sword" it is declared: "When the sacred months have passed, slay the idolaters wherever you find them, and take them, and confine them, and lay in wait for them at every place of ambush" (9:5). Further passages declare: "[K]ill them wherever you find them and turn them out from where they have turned you out, for sedition is worse than killing"; "Fight them, till there is no persecution and the religion is God's"; and "Fight them, till there is no persecution and the religion is God's entirely" (2:191; 2:193; 8:39). As the leading Islamic scholar John Esposito has put it in his *The Future of Islam*, passages such as the "verse of the sword" recently "have also been selectively used (or abused) by Muslim extremists to develop a 'theology of hate' and intolerance and to legitimate unconditional warfare against unbelievers." Atrocities have been committed recently by such extremist Muslims. And there have been other acts of religious intolerance towards those judged blasphemers or idolaters in various Muslim-majority countries, and also against Muslims of alternative commitments, over recent years. Such acts have, however, been the acts of a tiny minority of the world's Muslims, the vast majority of whom have been and remain tolerant and peaceful, and understand their faith to command toleration and to condemn aggression. Many Muslim faith leaders have condemned the actions of the tiny minority of Muslims and the atrocities they have committed, and these Muslim faith leaders have drawn extensively on the sources and resources supporting toleration in the Koran and hadith.[25]

Such Muslim leaders and the vast majority of peaceful and tolerant Muslims have, however, faced a chorus of attacks on Islam that are in part the heritage of the image of Islam developed in many Enlightenment texts discussed in this article. Both as scholars, and as engaged citizens of our world now, we should not, then, neglect Islamic toleration and tolerance in the way that the *Treatise on the Three Impostors* neglected the extensive history of principled and practical support for toleration in Islam by its emphasis on Muhammad the violent "impostor" followed by fanatics using force. Approached from this direction, there are very significant problems with the lack of appreciation for religious commitments of others in the pages of the *Treatise of the Three Impostors* and in many other works of the clandestine early and High Enlightenment. Attacking the founders of the three major Abrahamic religions as "impostors," the *Treatise* disrespected and disdained the founders of each of those religions as well as their followers. It treated ordinary Jews, Christians, and Muslims as at best fearful, superstitious, and credulous followers of impostors and at worst as ignorant imbeciles undeserving of respect. In treating Muhammad and Islam as in some ways the worst of the three Abrahamic religions, as allegedly the most essentially violent and imperial contrasted to the alleged gentleness of Christianity, the *Treatise of the Three Impostors* ignored the many tolerant and pacific elements and traditions of Islam. The *Treatise* therefore contributed, as one among many clandestinely and openly printed Enlightenment works, to fostering an image of Islam prevalent in Enlightenment and post-Enlightenment European culture that could stand as a foundation for intolerance towards Muslims then, and that still stands as a foundation for intolerance to Muslims now.[26]

NOTES

1 This chapter is dedicated to the memory of my mother, Eileen Marshall, who passed away suddenly in England on the day that I gave this as a conference paper in Los Angeles.

2 G. Minois, *The Atheist's Bible* (Chicago: University of Chicago Press, 2012); S. Berti, F. Charles-Daubert, and Richard Popkin, eds, *Heterodoxy, Spinozism, and Free Thought in Early Eighteenth Century Europe: Studies on the Traité des trois Imposteurs* (Dordrecht: Kluwer, 1996), *passim*; R. Popkin, "Spinoza and the Three Impostors," in *Spinoza: Issues and Directions*, ed. E. Curley and P.

Moreau (Leiden: Brill, 1990); M. Benitez, "La diffusion du Traité des trois imposteurs au XVIIIe siècle," *Revue d'histoire modern et contemporaine,* 40–1, 1993, 137–51; M. Jacob, *The Radical Enlightenment* (London: Geore Allen and Unwin, 1981); S. Berti, "La Vie et l'esprit de Spinosa," *Rivista Storica Italiana,* 98 (January 1986): 5–46; I. Wade, *Clandestine Organization and Diffusion of Philosophic Ideas in France from 1700 to 1750* (Princeton: Princeton University Press, 1938); J. Champion, "Toland and the Traité des trois imposteurs," *International Archives of the History of Ideas* 148 (1990): 333–56. For the text itself as well as context, see A. Anderson, *The Treatise of the Three Impostors and the Problem of Enlightenment* (Lanham: Rowman and Littlefield, 1997), 1–42; F. Charles-Daubert, ed., *Le "Traité des trois imposteurs" et "L'Esprit de Spinosa"* (Oxford: Voltaire Foundation, 1999); cf. *De Tribus Impostoribus AD 1230 / The Three Impostors,* trans. A. Nasier (Cleveland: 1904).

3 Anderson, *Treatise,* 12–13, 17–18; Charles-Daubert, ed., *Traité,* 724–5, 728–9.

4 *Treatise,* 18–33; *Traité,* 729–43.

5 *Treatise,* 31–3; *Traité,* 741–2. Cf. Bayle, *Historical and Critical Dictionary,* "Mahomet," note U, for a preceding account of the burying in a well "under a shower of stones" of a follower of Muhammad whom he had persuaded to announce him to the multitude as a prophet, and then the building of a mosque at the site.

6 *Le Fameux livre,* in Charles-Daubert, ed., *Traité,* 605; *De Tribus impostoribus,* ch. XI (now also available via the web at https://infidels.org/library/historical/unknown/three_impostors.html).

7 For an interpretation suggesting the possibility of "less aversion" to Muhammad than to Moses or Jesus, see A. Gunny, *Images of Islam in Eighteenth Century Writing* (London: Grey Seal, 1996), ch. 4.

8 Voltaire, *Oeuvres complètes de Voltaire,* ed. L. Moland (Paris: Garnier frères, 1877–95), vol. 10, 402–5, with English translation by J. Iverson at www.whitman.edu/VSA/trois.imposteurs.html; R. Pearson, *Voltaire Almighty* (New York: Bloomsbury, 2005), 337–8; A. Aldridge, *Voltaire and the Century of Light* (Princeton: Princeton University Press, 1975), 124–8. On this and the next paragraph see my "Voltaire, Priestcraft, and Imposture: Christianity, Judaism, and Islam," *Intellectual History Review* 28 (2018), 167–84.

9 Voltaire, *Treatise on Tolerance and Other Writings,* ed. S. Harvey and B. Masters (Cambridge: Cambridge University Press, 2000), 21; G. Noyer, ed., *Voltaire's Revolution* (Amherst, New York: Prometheus, 2015), 137; Voltaire, *Ouevres,* vol. 11, 203–22; Voltaire, *The Complete Works of Voltaire,* ed. T. Besterman (Oxford: Oxford University Press, 1968–), vol. 73, 389–411; Voltaire, *The Complete Works,* vol. 20b, 154 and *passim* (translation largely as in Voltaire, *Fanaticism,* trans. H. Burton (Sacramento, California: Litwin Books, 2013), 19–20, *passim*; Voltaire, *The Complete Works,* vol. 38, 339; M.

Dimmock, *Mythologies of the Prophet Muhammad in Early Modern English Culture* (Cambridge: Cambridge University Press, 2013), 200–6.

10 *The Encyclopedia of Diderot and d'Alembert Collaborative Translation Project*, Ann Arbor: Michigan Publishing, University of Michigan Library, 2010, Web; articles "Tolerance" by J. E. Rommily, trans. L. Tuttle; "Muslim" by E-F. Mallet, trans. S. Emanuel; "Mohammedanism" by E-F. Mallet, trans. S. Emanuel; "Qur'an," trans. S. Emanuel.

11 Montesquieu, *The Spirit of the Laws* (Cambridge: Cambridge University Press 1989), ed. A. Cohler, B. Miller, and H. Stone, 59–61, 461–4, 490; M. Curtis, *Orientalism and Islam* (Cambridge: Cambridge University Press, 2009), chapter 4; T. Kaiser, "The Evil Empire? The Debate on Turkish Despotism in Eighteenth Century French Political Culture," *Journal of Modern History*, 72 (2000): 6–34; J-P. Rubiés, "Oriental Despotism and European Orientalism: Botero to Montesquieu," *Journal of Early Modern History*, 9 (2005): 109–80.

12 Curtis, *Orientalism*, 57–102; D. Spellberg, *Thomas Jefferson's Qur'an* (New York: Knopf, 2013), 23–5; J. Trenchard and T. Gordon, *Cato's Letters* (Indianapolis: Liberty Fund 1995), ed. R. Hamowy, vol. 1, 469, and vol. 2, 907; Hume, "Of the Standard of Taste," in Hume, *Selected Essays*, ed. S. Copley and A. Edgar (Oxford: Oxford University Press, 1993), 135–6; Kant, *Religion within the Boundaries of Mere Reason*, ed. A. Wood and G. di Giovanni (Cambridge: Cambridge University Press, 1998), 177n.

13 Condorcet, *Outline of an historical view of the progress of the human mind* (Dublin, 1796), 124–8.

14 E. Gibbon, *The History of the Decline and Fall of the Roman Empire* (London, 1790), vol. 3, 260–2, 267–9, 273, 275–7, 279, 321.

15 Gibbon, *The Decline and Fall* (1790), vol. 3, 285–6, 294–5, 297, 316, 320, 322.

16 P. Bayle, *Historical and Critical Dictionary* (London, 1734), "Mahomet."

17 Bayle, *Dictionary*, "Mahomet," esp. nnN–P.

18 Bayle, *Dictionary*, "Mahomet," esp. nAA.

19 P. Rycaut, *The Present State of the Ottoman Empire* (London, 1668), 98–9.

20 Rycaut, *The Present State*, 102–5.

21 A. Reland, *Of the Mahometan Religion* (London, 1712), *passim*, esp. 5, 11, 77–8, 87–100; L. Hunt, M. Jacob, and W. Mijnhardt, *The Book That Changed Europe*, Cambridge, Massachusetts: Harvard University Press, 2010), 247–69 at 262–3.

22 R. Pococke, *A Description of the East* (London, 1743), vol. 1, 268–70; J. Hobbs, *Mount Sinai* (Austin: University of Texas Press, 1995), 158–61; J.A. Morrow, *The Covenants of the Prophet Muhammad with the Christians of the World* (Angelico Press / Sophia Perennis, 2013).

23 Morrow, *Covenants*, 65–98; M. Khan, "Muhammad's Promise to Christians," http://www.faithstreet.com/onfaith/2009/12/30/

prophet-muhammads-promise-to-christians/125. The history of practices of Islamic toleration and intolerance is extremely extensive and intricately complicated, and I examine it elsewhere in forthcoming work.

24 On Islam's support for toleration in the Koran and hadith and its interpretation through the centuries there is now an extremely extensive scholarly literature, but see as a beginning: Y. Friedmann, *Tolerance and Coercion in Islam* (Cambridge: Cambridge University Press, 2003); K.A. El Fadl, *The Place of Tolerance in Islam* (Boston: Beacon Press, 2002); A. Tyler, *Islam, the West, and Tolerance* (New York: Plagrave Macmillan 2008); A. Black, *The History of Islamic Political Thought* (Edinburgh: Edinburgh University Press, 2001); I. Goldziher, *Introduction to Islamic Theology and Law* (Princeton: Princeton University Press, 1981), 32–6; D. Forte, 'Religious Toleration in Classical Islam," in *International Perspectives on Church and State*, ed. M. Mor (Omaha: Fordham University Press, 1993); A.M. Khouj, *Religious Tolerance in Islam* (Washington, DC: The Islamic Center of Washington DC, 1992); R. Mottadeh, "Toward an Islamic Theology of Toleration," in *Islamic Law Reform and Human Rights*, ed. T. Lindholm and K. Vogt (Cophenhagen: Nordic Human Rights Publications, 1993); A. Sachedina, "Freedom of Conscience and Religion in the Qur'an," in *Human Rights and the Conflict of Cultures*, ed. D. Little et al. (Columbia: University of South Carolina Press, 1988); S. Hashmi, "The Qur'an and Tolerance," *Journal of Human Rights* 2 (2003): 81–103 ; F. Bowering, ed., *Islamic Political Thought* (Princeton: Princeton University Press, 2015); F.A. Rauf, *What's Right with Islam* (New York: Harper Collins, 2004), 14, 33–40; A. Hussain, "Muslims, Pluralism and Interfaith Dialogue" in *Progressive Muslims*, ed. O. Safi (London: Oneworld, 2003), 251–69; J. Brown, *Misquoting Muhammad* (London: Oneworld, 2015), 100–3; A. El-Fadl, *The Great Theft* (New York: Harper Collins, 2005); A. Meddeb, *The Malady of Islam* (New York: Basic Books, 2003), 191–4; M. Akyol, *Islam without Extremes* (New York: W.W. Norton, 2011); M.A. Haleem, *Understanding the Qur'an* (London: Tauris, 2011). For just a very few important works on intolerance towards Islam in the present, see in addition to many of the above W. Brown, *Regulating Aversion* (Princeton: Princeton University Press, 2006); M. Nussbaum, *The New Religious Intolerance* (Cambridge, MA: Harvard University Press, 2012); A. Iftikhar, *Scapegoats* (New York: Skyhorse, 2016).

25 J. Esposito, *The Future of Islam* (Oxford: Oxford University Press, 2010), 29–33, 48–50, *passim*; R. Bonney, *Jihad from Qur'an to bin Laden* (New York: Palgrave Macmillan, 2004), "Foreword" and *passim*.

26 See my "Voltaire, Priestcraft, and Imposture."

Chapter Thirteen

The Polyvalence of Heterodox Sources and Eighteenth-Century Religious Change

JEFFREY D. BURSON

As evinced by the many superb contributions to this volume, a quiet historiographical revolution of great significance is already well under way with respect to the clandestine and heterodox underground of the early modern European republic of letters, but much work remains to be done.[1] *Inter alia*, the history of clandestine texts affords a glimpse into the laboratory of what Vincenzo Ferrone has called the "cultural revolution" of the eighteenth century in which European elites erected "a universal morality founded on recognizing the common identity of all human beings, on equal rights, on the diffusion of a spirit of tolerance, on a non-arrogant use of reason as an instrument to ensure peaceful relationships among human beings," and on the "sacralization of the principle of sociability and human rights."[2] Clandestine texts not only reveal the eclectic origins and complex development of Enlightenment radicalization, they in fact allow us to consider the entanglement of both radical and more religious and apologetic works, as eighteenth-century writers worked out the sociocultural, historical, and political implications of what were, in many cases, originally theological and metaphysical debates.[3] As both Ann Thomson and Roland Mortier have noted, many if not most of the works comprising the clandestine *corpus* concerned or emerged from metaphysical or religious questions. These issues intersected with developments in political thought and medical science.[4]

In addition to my own research, this chapter is indebted to the work of many specialists whose original and painstaking textual research on the circulation of clandestine writings and the Radical Enlightenment is indispensable. This chapter should therefore be understood as at least in part a synthetic historical essay that underscores the entanglement of newly transformed secular and religious sensibilities we see emerging from clandestine texts themselves during the long *siècle des lumières.* From the reading, circulation, and recombination of clandestine texts one is often confronted, not just with a univocal Radical Enlightenment that neatly emerges from similarly radical and heterodox origins, but with an often polyvalent and eclectic origins story. At times clandestine texts are even found woven into the fabric of later eighteenth-century apologetical texts, just as the textual transmission of the heterodox underground often arose from religiously charged debates.

This chapter examines two case studies in which clandestine texts play a significant role. Each of these seemingly disparate but often loosely interconnected examples illustrates the entanglement of various styles of "Religious Enlightenment" and "Radical Enlightenment" throughout the long century of lights.[5] The first illustration focuses on the surprising use to which Giordano Bruno's argument that there might be other worlds beyond Earth was put. The second and lengthier illustration considers the evolution of debates surrounding the mind-body relationship and the nature of the human soul. Such discourses, combined and recombined by the authors of clandestine texts, effectively shaped discussions of atheism, materialism, and moral determinism, eliciting changes both to the writings of radical *philosophes* and to their critics. Taken together, these illustrations shed light on the complicated and evolving history of manuscript copying and circulation vis-à-vis the history of the book, showing the ease with which the context of one debate might be reinscribed into a completely different discursive field. As such, the history of the clandestine and heterodox underground is one of readers, copyists, authors, and publishers; much of the relationship between seventeenth- and eighteenth-century thought cannot be satisfactorily understood in isolation from these modes of transition. The writing, reading, and copying of manuscript texts, in ways that preceded, succeeded, or disseminated the printed word, constitutes a kind of laboratory for the cultural and intellectual revolution of the long eighteenth century – one that reaches back to radical strains of Renaissance Humanism, as Gianni Paganini's chapter shows us, and forward into the revolutions of the early nineteenth century, as the contributions of Jonathan Israel and Jonathan Christian Laursen argue. The complicated history of manuscript copying and circulation that evolved in parallel to, and perhaps as an integral part of, the history of the book shows the ease with which the context of one debate might be reinscribed into a completely different discursive field.

Polyvalence and the Plurality of Worlds

The fate of the originally clandestine text *Jordanus Brunus redivivus* exemplifies the quality of clandestine circulation as the polyvalent inspiration to both radical philosophy and *antiphilosophie*. *Jordanus Brunus redivivus*, later compiled and published in its final form by baron d'Holbach, revisits and defends Giordano Bruno's controversial opinion that the earth was not the only planet in the cosmos.[6] The notion of the plurality of worlds had been censured by the Inquisition, but its dissemination through clandestine manuscripts of *Jordanus Brunus redivivus* nevertheless found its way into other clandestine and radical texts, including another well-known heterodox manuscript published in 1735 and again in 1748. This text, the *Telliamed*, authored by Bernard Maîllet, moved beyond *Jordanus Brunus redivivus* to suggest that earlier beings may well have populated Earth before humanity and that the climate and geology of the earth are self-evolving.[7] The manuscript's heterodoxy notwithstanding, some scholars contend that portions of *Jordanus Brunus redivivus* are derived from one Thomas Brown, who seems to have emerged from an ongoing theological tussle over Bruno's position, and that those portions represented an attempt to demonstrate the compatibility of Christianity with any system of philosophy. The distance of these other worlds from the earth, Brown argued, made whatever might have happened in them completely irrelevant to God's plan of redemption for humanity. This hypothesis, argued Brown, explained the absence in the Bible of any reference to these other worlds.[8] The hypothesis of multiple worlds that is central to *Jordanus Brunus redivivus* was not without precedent in the references of the Latin Fathers. Maîllet in his *Telliamed* quotes no less an authority than Athanasius of Alexandria to the effect that just because the creator is one does not exclude the possibility that God created more than one world.[9]

The plurality-of-worlds hypothesis popularized throughout the republic of letters by *Jordanus Brunus redivivus* and *Telliamed* also informs the moral philosophy of the sometimes *philosophe*, sometimes *antiphilosophe* apologist, the abbé Claude Yvon. In Yvon's article "Manichéisme," a seemingly straightforward entry on the originally Persian religion of late antiquity evolved into a long and intricate defence of divine providence in the face of the problem of evil. Yvon's analysis of different species of evil, and his argument that the very existence of evil does not in itself contradict the supreme goodness, justice, or power of God, are together primarily a creative gloss on passages from Leibniz's *Theodicy*.[10] But in addressing moral evil, Yvon asks the readers of the *Encyclopédie* to hypothetically posit that the ills caused by human vice actually outweigh all virtue. Even if such a statement were true, Yvon contends, "the universe is not synonymous with planet Earth." As he explains:

> When even revelation has already taught me that there are created intelligences as different from one another by nature as they are from me, does not my own reason conduct me to believe that the realm of thinking substances might perhaps be as varied in its species as matter is in its parts? ... I might wish to believe that all of these minds are subordinate in the same sphere of perfection. Now since I can and I must suppose the existence of minds of different order from my own, I should immediately be led to new consequences, and thus be forced to recognize that there could be at least as much, if not very much more, goodness in the universe than moral evil.[11]

Yvon thus buttressed Leibnizian metaphysical optimism by venturing far beyond him in suggesting that other minds might well exist beyond this world. Yvon invoked the logical possibility of other worlds – a notion popularized by the printing of previously clandestine texts – in order to suggest that this world could still be the best one that a perfect God would elect to create. Nevertheless, in vindicating the omniscience and supreme goodness of God, Yvon's superficially orthodox remark introduced a principle of moral relativity into the cosmos – in effect, that what one perceives and defines as evil depends entirely on the vantage point of the observer.

Returning to the author of *Jordanus Brunus redivivus*, Thomas Brown is also thought by some to be the author of two other far more radical texts: *Dissertation sur la resurrection de la chair* (1743) and *Dissertation sur la formation du monde* (1738).[12] Paradoxically, the *Dissertation sur la formation du monde* built on many of Brown's earlier notions rooted in the apologetic enterprise of harmonizing Bruno with Christian doctrines. But the implications of Brown's "trilogy" of clandestine works moved readers towards a conception of matter as dynamic, as capable of self-movement and evolution. The inspiration for the *Dissertation sur la formation du monde*, or so claims Claudia Stancati, was largely anchored in theological debates, and it reached its conclusions primarily with reference to Cartesian physics rather than anything specifically Newtonian or Spinozan. Arguably theological in its origins, Brown's work nevertheless problematized the philosophical need for divine intervention by rendering potentially unnecessary the mediation of a substantially and metaphysically distinct soul governing the interactions of mind and body.[13]

What the entangled histories these manuscripts reveal is the still more surprising characteristic of the intellectual history of Europe between 1650 and the Revolutionary Era – that radical philosophical critiques of early modern confessional churches could and often did emerge from theological debates circumscribed within and among confessional milieux. Similarly, and at times with no less revolutionary implications, radical texts could also directly inspire later defensive arguments against Enlightenment radicalization.

The Soul, the Body, and the Fate of Theism and Moral Agency

The circulation of clandestine manuscripts served as a kind of crucible within which religious debates were abstracted, refuted, and transmuted into new theological interpretations, or alternatively, into new and more secular ways of viewing the transformative potential of humanity. Another dimension of this process concerns the singular importance of clandestine texts in generating new conceptions of the human mind. As this second case study elucidates, the generation and dissemination of clandestine texts can be construed as the "laboratory" for early Enlightenment concepts of materialism, atheism, and ethics. But these concepts were transformative in a way that transcended the radicalization of the Enlightenment itself.[14]

In the last decades of the seventeenth century, British Socinians (including, at least tacitly and privately, Newton and Locke[15]) took the Protestant notion of *sola scriptura* to its logical conclusion. In so doing, many of them began to question whether Scripture necessarily implied that immateriality was an absolute precondition for immortality. After all, the teachings of the ancients and even many within the early church itself suggested that the immortality of the soul and the bodily resurrection of the dead need not necessarily entail the immateriality of the human soul. Ironically, the response to the British Socinians offered by what Ann Thomson has called the "Christian Mortalists" – a group of writers including William Coward and Henry Dodwell – actually embraced their argument for the soul's likely materiality and the body's resurrection at the last judgment precisely *because* materiality comported well with early Christian teaching, even as much as it did so with new developments in medical science concerning neurophysiology and the natural vitality of organic matter. Despite its apologetic intent, the House of Commons condemned William Coward's work in 1704. However, some of his views on the soul were favourably adopted by John Toland in his pantheistic work *Letters to Serena* (1704); and Coward's fellow mortalist, Henry Dodwell, found his work defended by no less than Anthony Collins.[16]

As the magisterial works of Ann Thomson demonstrate, William Coward was far from unique, even if at first glance his biography seems paradoxical. A member of the Anglican clergy and indeed the author of an apology for the Christian doctrine of the resurrection of the body, Coward's argument was a blatant assertion that the soul could be a kind of material substance.[17] Britannic debates over the work of the Christian Mortalists made their way to France through the works of Jean Bouhier and Caspar Cuenz as well as exile Huguenot journals.[18] The common perception in both Britain and France that English Deists had been inspired by Christian Mortalists appears paradoxically to have strengthened the appeal of Cartesian arguments in favour of a sharpened substantial distinction between an immaterial and immortal soul, and a material body that worked, like the rest of the universe, by mechanical principles.[19]

Yet French Cartesianism was itself – almost from its inception – capable of implying both dualism and the vitality of matter. Descartes's *Discours de la méthode* (1637) and *Méditations* (1641&ff) affected a posture of Pyrrhonian doubt in order to deduce a new set of first principles in philosophy: that one cannot doubt but that the rational soul is an entity that thinks, that it is an essentially immaterial substance; whereas the body is by nature extension in space – a quality implying its own substantial materiality.[20] But the nature of that union of body and soul always eluded Descartes. Unable to account for seemingly rational behaviour in animals that were not, so he thought, possessed of an immaterial and rational soul with free will, Descartes instead posited in *Passions de l'âme* that most of the vital functions of the now redundant Aristotelian concept of the vegetative soul could be accomplished even by "animal spirits" that infused vitality and sensibility into the bodies of all sentient beings. In the case of humans, the immaterial and rational soul miraculously incited and regulated so-called animal spirits at the occasion of divine will.[21] Some Cartesians, however, latched on to Descartes's argument in *Passions de l'âme* that the soul was a vital principle or force that observably coincided with, and was perhaps directly emergent from, the organizational complexity of the *cerveau.*[22]

But there was still another species of materialism not at first beholden to the Cartesian inheritance: a Gassendo-Epircurean one.[23] Pierre Gassendi had offered one of the most influential rebuttals to Descartes's positions on the animal spirits, concluding – in this sense much as Spinoza did – that if soul and body were substantially distinct, there could be no reciprocal causality between the two, nor could one beget the other.[24] Gassendi thus surmised that soul must be a very fine species of matter capable of infusing thought, sensation, and movement directly into an organism, be it human or animal.[25] The Gassendo-Epicurean and Cartesian positions were to a large extent incompatible *in situ*; however, through the mediation of clandestine texts, especially *L'Ame matérielle, Sentiments des philosophes sur la nature de l'âme*, and Mirabaud's *De l'âme et de son immortalité*, aspects of these positions came to be casually synthesized. The composite materialism that resulted often merged Epicurean, Cartesian, and even Spinozan positions.[26] In *L'Ame matérielle* especially, idea formation, judgment, and memory effectively materialized the manifold states of the soul, leaving to readers the final judgment as to whether states of the soul were the fruits of materialist and physiological processes.[27]

Alongside the clandestine laboratories of innovation discussed above, and often directly influenced thereby, was the marriage of Cartesian, Spinozan, and Gassendo-Epicurean positions similarly evident in the work of divers physicians including David Hartley, Herman Boerhaave, Albrecht von Haller, and many within the medical faculty at the University of Montpellier.[28] As the research of a host of intellectual historians has variously affirmed, the eighteenth-century medical community was not uniformly the vanguard of Enlightenment radicalization. Nevertheless, many eighteenth-century medical writers adopted and disseminated the hybrid materialism of clandestine texts in order to "physiologize" mental states.[29] Medical writers increasingly spoke of the mind as though it functionally depended on the physiology of the nervous system – that is, on the properties of the material body itself.[30] As Boerhaave asserted, "[T]here is such a reciprocal connection and consent between the particular thought and affections of the mind and body, that a change in one also produces a change in the other, and the reverse."[31] Although Boerhaave maintained (as would his student, von Haller) that the exact means by which the body and mind reciprocally acted on each other was metaphysically beyond the purview of empirical reason, there could be no denying the evident correlation between the body's physical changes and the appearance of changes in mental states. This correlation suggested that the body possessed as much vitality as the mind.[32]

By the middle third of the eighteenth century, then, many practitioners and theorists of the revolution in medical knowledge, many theologians, and many philosophers were groping collectively towards a surprising consensus that today is often obscured beneath the din of eighteenth-century polemics: it seemed to many that at least animate matter (and very possibly *all* matter) possessed unique properties of sensibility and self-impulsion. This "vitalistic materialism" found itself affirmed rather than undermined by clandestine texts, which had become important spaces of synthesis for new ideas from a variety of sources.[33] The dialogue between Socinians and Christian Mortalists, and the selective use of both by English Deists, thus strengthened the appeal of Cartesian dualism in France. Yet from the beginning, Cartesianism too yielded polyvalent ramifications in that Descartes had been forced to delve into the latent potential of his own conclusion that the body might be as decisive an influence on the mind, as the mind on the body. Through the mediation of clandestine texts, then, empiricist implications of Cartesianism became increasingly wedded to Gassendi's largely Epicurean materialism, thereby creating hybrid discourses from which the vitalistic materialism of early medical theorists emerged.

A final and fascinating twist to our story is that the English Mortalists were not the only ones to forge theological discourses that shaped or otherwise paralleled the vitalistic materialism of medical writers in France. Nor were Cartesian, Spinozan, Gassendo-Epicurean, and the new physiology the only sources for the tendency to reduce the mind to physiological processes. Even prominent members of the Jesuit intellectual elite among the *scriptors* of the Collège Louis-le-Grand in Paris were not immune to the vitalistic materialism that during the earliest years of the eighteenth century was emerging in both medical and philosophical circles. The Jesuit editor of *Mémoires de Trévoux*, René-Joseph Tournemine, was already quite unsatisfied with the virtual union of soul and body that he thought characterized both Malebranche's occasional causes and Leibniz's pre-established harmony. In rebuttal to both, Tournemine's conjectures about the nature of the mind–body union, which widely circulated in the *Mémoires de Trévoux*, in effect de-emphasized the notion of soul as immaterial substance in favour of one that defined it as the motive force or vital principle of the human being. Tournemine in fact viewed the soul as simply the "motive force" that unites any individual human soul with its particular body such that "souls designed for different bodies are different."[34]

In the continuation of his serialized conjectures published in the June 1703 issue of *Mémoires de Trévoux*, Tournemine asserted that "experience teaches that the soul acts on the body just as it teaches that one thinks and wills."[35] But he further argued that the soul's ability to act on the body is reciprocal. When the designs and actions of the soul cannot be impeded by the body, the soul experiences pleasure; when the body resists the will of the soul, one experiences pain.[36] Tournemine's critics were quick to call out what seemed to them a dangerous, albeit implied, concession to materialism. As the abbé Languet de Montigny phrased it: "After having recognized the impossibility that the body should act on the soul, you nevertheless could not develop your conjectures without leaving to the body the capacity for some species of action on it."[37] Any activity on the part of the body, even the simple capacity to resist the state of the soul, must necessarily imply that corporeal matter is vital. So Tournemine appeared to be suggesting. [38]

The venerable old Jesuit never did manage a satisfactory way out of his accidental endorsement of vitalistic materialism, and it remains hard to determine whether Tournemine's insight was in any way informed by clandestine manuscripts or their published versions, although it is likely. The Jesuits, like many Catholic clergy of the day, had access to clandestine texts, most certainly read them, and often heard them discussed.[39] Tournemine's colleague, Buffier, frequented the salon of Mme de Lambert along with Fontenelle and the abbé Alary, the close confidant of Cardinal Fleury and a founding patron of Club d'Entresol. Alary was also very close to Boulainvilliers, whose manuscripts circulated at d'Entresol.[40] The *Memoires de Trévoux*, over which Buffier and Tournemine both presided, had reviewed the 1706 published version of *La Vie de Spinosa*. Tournemine was in fact editor when this happened. Clandestine manuscripts, in addition, have been found in Jesuit archives.[41] In point of fact, Paris police records indicate that copies of La Mettrie's *Histoire naturelle de l'âme* – a work heavily imbued with the conclusions of many clandestine sources – were quietly sold, however *sub rosa*, even at the University of Paris Faculty of Theology.[42]

The possibility that the soul might be so intimately and recursively correlated with matter as to be merely its *élan vital* or motive force paralleled and reinforced the striking proliferation of newly globalized comparative histories of philosophy as well as what Guy Stroumsa now recognizes as the eighteenth-century origins of a more modern comparative concept of human religious experience.[43] The rise of this more globalized sense of history, built in part on the missionary texts of the Jesuits throughout the world, often implied that the primitive, original, natural theology of humanity was rooted in the universal human recognition of matter's vitality. Thus, if one were to equate materialism with atheism – as was so often the consensus of Catholic apologists – then the conclusion could be perilously provocative. Theism could thereby be said to be nothing more than the decadent affectation of societies imprisoned by illegitimate religious corruption, while materialism, therefore, would constitute the basis for natural religion and natural law. This implication emerged from many sources, which clandestine texts slowly sculpted into a more coherent whole. The Jesuit Longobardi, for example, was among the first to discover that, contrary to the theism assumed by Ricci to have been characteristic of ancient Confucianism, the most ancient of the Chinese classics actually lacked any idea of a personal and immaterial deity; as Israel and others have argued, Longobardi's position was not far from the one espoused by writers like the young marquis d'Argens, who believed that primitive Confucianism possessed affinities with Spinoza and other materialists.[44] Even Jesuit classicism, as Alan C. Kors noted, contributed ironically to the ongoing debate over whether or not the most ancient philosophical systems were imbued with materialism.[45] The Jesuit d'Olivet's critical edition of Cicero's *De natura deorum* publicized exactly this point in spite of itself, and it is telling that both *De natura deorum* and Jesuit missionary texts inform, respectively, *Telliamed* and Bernard Picart's largely deistic *Cérémonies et coutumes religieuses des tous les peuples du monde*, the subject of path-breaking research by Margaret Jacob and Wijnand Mijnhardt.[46]

The Jesuits, however, were not immune from creative solutions to the impasse. If the most ancient forms of philosophy were materialistic, was it necessarily the case that the soul was mortal? The Christian Mortalists certainly did not think so. Thus, perhaps materialism did not necessarily imply atheism. At least some Jesuits were willing to entertain this question. Among them was, unsurprisingly, Tournemine, who thought that "there are no true atheists," not even among all materialists. He insisted that whether one conceived of the divine as spiritual or as material, if a philosopher or a cultural group continued to ascribe intelligence and free agency to supernatural beings, then they could not be called atheists. Tournemine reserved the label "atheist" only for those who wilfully ascribed to notions of a blindly deterministic cosmos in which the possibility of divine (and by implication, he thought, human) free will was excluded.[47]

Tournemine was somewhat atypical in his ability to decouple atheism from materialism, and his argument belies one of the most common anxieties of those who would argue against the diverse forms of materialism characteristic of the radicalizing Enlightenment.[48] The way in which the attributes of the metaphysical soul were brought down to earth and reframed as physiological properties of organic matter posed problems for the question of moral determinism versus free will – a question that sparked innovations in both the Radical Enlightenment and the Religious Enlightenment so called. David Hartley had insisted that vibrations within the central nervous system at the occasion of matter in motion cause human acts, and thus, thought and the passions that occasion moral judgment are reducible to material causes. Notwithstanding the very obvious vitalistic materialism that underwrote Hartley's *Observations on Man*, he remained convinced that free agency was possible.[49] But Joseph Priestly's *Disquisitions relating to Matter and Spirit*, and his *Discussion of the Doctrines of Materialism and Philosophical Necessity*, further problematized free moral agency by emphasizing the will's dependence on the mind, which was in turn dependent on the body. However much Priestly may have distanced himself from the irreligious implications of his own arguments, his *Disquisitions* made use of La Mettrie's *Histoire naturelle de l'âme* (1745) as one of its key sources.[50] And of course, La Mettrie was a voracious reader and popularizer of many clandestine texts. In *Histoire naturelle de l'âme*, La Mettrie's argument, in eliding the functions of animal and human souls together as mere manifestations determined by the properties of organized matter, betrays its debt to two clandestine works: *L'Ame matérielle* and the chapter on the soul contained in *L'Esprit de Spinosa.*[51]

As clandestine texts were composed, copied, recombined, and discussed, they became, in a sense, the laboratories in which originally unrelated and often transnational discussions (theological, philosophical, and ethical) forged new parameters of debate characteristic of the late eighteenth century. La Mettrie's avid use of clandestine texts, as well as his hybrid materialism, derived as much from Gassendo-Epicureanism as from medical vitalism and Spinoza, directly inspired him to dispense entirely with any notion of an immaterial soul.[52] Confronted with both the emergence of vitalistic materialism within medical discourse and the discourse of universal history, then, apologetically inclined writers attempted to reframe what was meant by natural religion and atheism. In short, the clandestine texts functioned again as a vital incubator in which many seemingly disparate religious, medical, and philosophical notions fused, thus giving rise to radicalized Enlightenment ideologies.

Conclusion: The Eclectic Origins of Radical Enlightenment and the Transformation of Religious Experience

From the reading, circulation, and recombination of clandestine texts one is confronted, not with a univocal Radical Enlightenment emergent from similarly radical origins, but with a polyvalent and eclectic origins story where different uses of clandestine texts are found interwoven into the fabric of texts written both for and against the new philosophy of the Enlightenment. As Vincenzo Ferrone has aptly summarized, "the language of the Enlightenment was adopted by both its friends and its enemies." If the Enlightenment was the "laboratory of modernity," then surely clandestine textual circulation constituted a kind of laboratory for the Enlightenment, in all its diverse modalities.[53]

Two phenomena associated with the clandestine texts and the heterodox underground are particularly worth emphasizing by way of conclusion. First, clandestine texts and their circulation reflected the emergence of the Radical Enlightenment, but in ways that illustrated the tremendous diversity of texts and debates at the origins of Enlightenment radicalization. The popularization of Spinoza is certainly an important part of this story, but the vitalistic materialism of medical theorists, empirical Cartesians, Gassendo-Epicureans, Christian Mortalists, English deists, and some Jesuits – and no doubt others not covered in this chapter – are all encountered at the origins of Enlightenment radicalization as well. The language of these disparate conversations evolved and fused throughout the process of clandestine circulation.[54] If anything, the history of the clandestine and heterodox underground reveals that it was often in the reading and reappropriation of seemingly prosaic religious or philosophical texts that the seeds of Radical Enlightenment were planted. As Ann Thomson's recent book stresses – and I think fruitfully so – the polyvalence of meaning that can emerge from the reading of these texts remains a vital and insufficiently studied part of the story.[55]

Second, the role of clandestine texts after 1650 and their polyvalent use by radical and religious authors alike lends insight into a long eighteenth century during which secularization emerged from part of a broader transformation in religious sensibilities.[56] Jonathan Sheehan's *The Enlightenment Bible* speaks in most respects of the same history that Guy Stroumsa has traced in his more recent work, *The New Science*: it is a story of secularization to be sure, but a secularization characterized less by "the disappearance of religion" than by "its transformation and reconstruction."[57] The Bible came to be viewed by many of the Protestant critics Sheehan studies (as well as Catholic and Radical Enlightenment writers) as capable of being approached as cultural artefact rather than as a record of sacred revelation or (for more radical writers) as a sham contrived by priests. Stroumsa writes that this awareness flowed from a complex process to which travellers, Catholic missionaries, radical philologists, and Protestant scholars contributed as they reflected on practices and beliefs from around the globe. This process made it possible to speak of a "comparative history of religions."[58] As I have argued in this chapter, the culture of the eighteenth century, including its various modes of Enlightenment, afforded new institutions, practices, and techniques for the critical study of ancient religious experience, and the fruits of such study injected new ideological connotations into transformations wrought by experimental science. Thus, human dignity and sociability became paramount values common both to the Radical Enlightenment and to those who would persist in faith down into the Post-Revolutionary Age. Apologetic and theological works throughout the later eighteenth century rhetorically valorized ancient revealed religions by affirming their necessity for the promotion of human dignity, social utility, and individual happiness, evinced through supposedly empirical and historical evidence.[59] In short, it was common even among the apologists to treat faith as legitimate only insofar as it might be affirmed by empirical facts and utility. At least at the level of rhetorical construction, such a position was not far from that of many of the most determined of anticlerical writers and publicists, who for their part sacralized the secular by inventing new social rites and investing newly confident faith in forms of egalitarian sociability, toleration, and benevolence precisely because they seemed to have been affirmed by the empirical evidence of history and social utility.[60] Such was the "faith" of Spinozan pantheists, Epicurean materialists, and the institutions of the earliest Masonic Lodges in Britain and the Low Countries.[61]

I am not intending to misread the evidence by too casually eliding distinctions between the most radical partisans of the Enlightenment and their detractors. But insofar as a the secular Enlightenment attempting to crush the infamy of an often equally militant, religiously-directed Counter-Enlightenment only gradually and contingently emerged from the cultural history of the long eighteenth century, I am proposing that one might just as fruitfully consider the emergence of this duality of Radical versus Religious Enlightenment (or, as Israel controversially maintains, the tussle of Radical, Moderate, and Counter-Enlightenments) as having resulted from the growth of entirely new and widely diverse religious sensibilities in the eighteenth century.[62] In essence, transformations in ritual, new forms of human spirituality, and new modes of affirming truth-claims ultimately brought about changes in European confessional religions, even as they allowed for the possibility of greater faith in the potency of human dignity and of nature itself. Isolated case studies are necessarily limited, but they do serve to illustrate just how significant was the clandestine and heterodox world of textual circulation to the secularization of the sacred and the sacralization of the secular so quintessential to eighteenth-century culture.

NOTES

1 The literature on the Radical Enlightenment, clandestine texts, and the heterodox underground is increasingly vast. The most significant past and present foundational works include the following: Margaret C. Jacob, *The Radical Enlightenment: Pantheists, Freemasons, and Republicans* (London: George Allen and Unwin, 1981); Jonathan I. Israel, *Radical Enlightenment: Philosophy and the Making of Modernity, 1650–1750* (Oxford and New York: Oxford University Press, 2001), esp. 684–704; Martin Mulsow, *Enlightenment Underground: Radical Germany, 1680–1720*, trans. H.C. Erik Midelfort (Charlottesville: University of Virginia Press, 2015); Miguel Benítez, *La Face cache des Lumières: recherces sur les manuscrits philosophiques clandestins de l'âge classique* (Paris and Oxford: Voltaire Foundation, 1996); and Miguel Benitez, *Le Foyer clandestine des lumières: nouvelles recherches sur les manuscrits clandestins*, 2 vols (Paris: Honoré Champion, 2013). See also the recent essays in the special issue on "The Radical Enlightenment" in *Diametros* 40 (June 2014): 1–200; Steffen Ducheyne, ed., *Reassessing the Radical Enlightenment* (London: Routledge, 2017); esp. Margaret C. Jacob, "The Radical Enlightenment: A Heavenly City with Many Mansions," in *Reassessing the Radical Enlightenment*, 48–60. See also Sylvianne Albertan-Coppola, "La littérature philosophique clandestine aux dix-huitième siècle: orientations de la recherché," *Revue d'histoire des religions* 126, 1999, 355–66.

2 Vincenzo Ferrone, *The Enlightenment: History of an Idea*, trans. Elisabetta Tarantino (Princeton: Princeton University Press, 2015), xiii, xiv; on the Enlightenment construction of human rights, see Lynn Hunt, *Inventing Human Rights* (New York: W.W. Norton, 2008).

3 The relationship between clandestine manuscripts and the history of printed texts continues to be complex. Ira Wade completed the first, most

complete list of around one hundred manuscripts located throughout French and other European repositories. This list, which has informed foundational work by Miguel Benitez, Margaret Jacob, and Jonathan Israel, continues to expand and presently includes more than two thousand manuscripts. Scholars continue to locate new manuscripts while also mapping their circulation, emendation, and relationship to print editions. Ira O. Wade, *The Clandestine Organization and Diffusion of Philosophic Ideas in France from 1700 to 1750* (New York: Octagon Books, 1967), 11–21; for list of repositories and an early approximation of when each manuscript was likely composed, see 263–75; for additional texts, see Benitez, "Liste et localization des traités clandestins," in *Le Matérialisme du XVIIIe siècle et la littérature clandestine: actes de la table ronde des 6 et 7 juin 1980 organisée à la Sorbonne à Paris avec le concours du C.N.R.S. par le Groupe de recherché sur l'Histoire du Matérialisme,* ed. Olivier Bloch (Paris: Libraire Philosophique J. Vrin, 1982), 17–25.

4 Ann Thomson, "Qu'est-ce qu'un manuscrit clandestine?" in Bloch, ed., *Le Matérialisme du XVIIIe siècle,* 15; Roland Mortier, "Conclusions," in *Le Matérialisme du XVIIIe siècle,* 275–7 at 275; Margaret C. Jacob, "The Enlightenment Critique of Christianity," in *The Cambridge History of Christianity,* vol. 8: *Enlightenment, Reawakening, and Revolution 1660–1815,* ed. Stewart J. Brown and Timothy Tackett (Cambridge: Cambridge University Press, 2006), 265–82.

5 On Religious Enlightenment, see David Sorkin, *The Religious Enlightenment: Protestants, Jews, and Catholics from London to Vienna* (Princeton: Princeton University Press, 2008); Helena Rosenblatt, "The Christian Enlightenment," *The Cambridge History of Christianity,* vol. 8, 283–301; for further details on the social spaces in which the genesis and circulation of clandestine texts occurred within France, see Françoise Weil, "La Diffusion en France avant 1750 d'éditions de textes dits clandestins," in Bloch, ed., *Le Matérialisme du XVIIIe siècle,* 207–11.

6 [Paul Henri Thierry, Baron d'Holbach], *J. Brunus Redivivus, ou Traité des erreurs populaires: ouvrage critique, historique, et philosophique, imité de Pomponace* (N.p.: n.l., 1771), 17–39.

7 [Gernard de Maillet], *Telliamed,* 2 vols (Amsterdam: L'Honoré, 1748), 1: x, xxxvii, lxvii–lxviv; for more on Maîllet and the *Telliamed,* see Benitez, *La Face cache des Lumières,* 213–304; and Mary Efrosini Gregory, *Evolutionism in Eighteenth-Century French Thought* (New York: Peter Lang, 2008), 1–17, 19–31; on *Telliamed* and the notion of the plurality of worlds, see Benitez, *La Face cachée des lumières,* 390–9; on Maillet's materialism, see Benitez, *Le Foyer clandestins des lumières,* 1: 241–75.

8 See discussion in Miguel Benitez, "La Tentation du gouffre: la pluralité des mondes dans la littérature clandestine," in Bloch, ed., *Le Matérialisme du XVIIIe siècle*, 115–23 at 122; on attribution of *Jordanus Brunus redivivus* to Thomas Brown, see Claudia Stancati, "La *Dissertation sur la formation du monde* et les origins du matérialisme: matière et movement," in *Le Matérialisme du XVIIIe siècle*, 109–13 at 109; on the apologetical face of *Jordanus Brunus Redivivus*, see Antonella del Prete, "Anges, bêtes, hommes: les inquiétants débats sur les extraterrestres à l'Age classique," *Libertinage et philosophie au XVIIe siècle* 9, 2005, 47.

9 "Nec enim quia unus est creator, id circô unus est mundus; poterat enim Deus & alios mundos facere." St Athanasius, *Contra Gentes*; qtd in [Maillet], *Telliamed*, 1: ixiv.

10 For more on Claude Yvon, see Jeffrey D. Burson, *The Culture of Enlightening: Abbé Claude Yvon and the Entangled Emergence of the Enlightenment* (Notre Dame: University of Notre Dame Press, 2019). Two of Yvon's principal sources for Leibnizian optimism were the "Preliminary Dissertation on the Conformity of Faith and Reason" and Part II of his *Theodocy*: see Leibniz, "Preliminary Dissertation on the Conformity of Faith and Reason," in *Theodicy: Essays on the Goodness of God and the Freedom of Man and the Origin of Evil*, ed. Austin Farrer, trans. E.M. Huggard (London: Routledge and Kegan Paul, 1951), 73–122, at sect. 34–5, 93–4; sect. 43–6, 99–9; *Theodicy*, 123–389 at pt II, sect. 130.xv, 201–2; pt II, sect. 134.xix, 205–7; pt III, sect. 158–60, 222–3.

11 "Quand même la révélation ne m'apprendroit pas déjà qu'il y a des intelligences créés, aussi différentes entre elles, par leur nature, qu'elles le sont de moi, ma raison ne me donduiroit-elle pas à croire que la region des substances pensantes est, peut-être aussi variée dans ses espèces, que la matière l'est dans ses parties? … Je voudrois croire que tous ces sprits sont enchaînés dans la même sphere de perfection. Or, n dès que je puis et que je dois supposer des esprits d'un autre ordre que n'est le mien, me voilà conduit à des nouvelles conséquences, me voilà forcé de reconnoître qu'il peut y avoir, qu'il y a même beaucoup plus de bien moral que de mal moral dans l'univers." [Claude Yvon], "Manichéisme," in *Encyclopédie, ou Dictionnaire raisonné des sciences, des arts et des métiers, etc.*, ed. Denis Diderot and Jean le Rond d'Alembert (University of Chicago, ARTFL Encyclopédie Project, ed. Robert Morrissey, Spring 2013 ed.), 10:22, http://encyclopedie.uchicago.edu, accessed 31 May 2012. On known attribution of "Manichéisme" to Yvon, see John Lough, *The Contributors to the* Encyclopédie (London: Grant and Cutler, 1973), 2–3.

12 *Dissertation sur la formation du monde; Dissertation sur la resurrection de la chair*, édition critique des manuscrits du recueil 1168 de la Bibliothèque Mazarine de Paris (Paris: Honoré Champion, 2001).

13 Stancati, "La *Dissertation sur la formation du monde* et les origins du matérialisme: matière et movement," 109–13.

14 The scholarship on the concept of the human soul, the origins of materialism, and the religious, ethical, political, and scientific ramifications of this transformation is vast. Indispensable and diverse interpretations of this issue are afforded by Margaret C. Jacob, *The Radical Enlightenment: Pantheists, Freemasons, and Republicans,* 2nd rev. ed. (New York: Cornerstone, 2006; 1981); Ann Thomson, *Bodies of Thought: Science, Religion, and the Soul in the Early Enlightenment* (2008; repr., Oxford: Oxford University Press, 2010), esp. 1–27, 135–248; Thomson, *L'âme des Lumières. Le débat sur l'être humain entre religion et science Angleterre-France, 1690–1760* (Paris: Champ Vallon, 2013); Thomson, "'Mechanistic Materialism' vs. 'Vitalistic Materialism'?," in *La Lettre de la Maison française d'Oxford* 14 (2001): 22–36. See also John Wright, "Materialismo e anima vitale alle meta' del XVIII secolo. Il pensiero medico," in *L'eta' dei Lumi. Saggi sulla cultura settecentesca,* ed. Antonio Santucci (Bologna: Mulino, 1998), 143–57; Thomson, "Déterminisme et passions," in *Matérialisme et passions,* ed. Pierre-François Moreau and Ann Thomson (Lyons: Ens Editions, 2004), 79–95; Jonathan I. Israel, *Enlightenment Contested: Philosophy, Modernity, and the Emancipation of Man, 1670–1752* (Oxford: Oxford University Press, 2006), esp. 3–60; Israel, *A Revolution of the Mind: Radical Enlightenment and the Intellectual Origins of Modern Democracy* (Princeton: Princeton University Press, 2010); Israel, *Democratic Enlightenment: Philosophy, Revolution, and Human Rights 1750–1790* (Oxford: Oxford University Press, 2011), esp. 1–35; Israel, *Revolutionary Ideas: An Intellectual History of the French Revolution from* The Rights of Man *to Robespierre* (Princeton: Princeton University Press, 2014).

15 John Marshall, *John Locke: Resistance, Religion, and Responsibility* (Cambridge: Cambridge University Press, 1994); Marshall, "Locke, Socinianism, "Socinianism," and Unitarianism," in *English Philosophy in the Age of Locke,* ed. M.A. Stewart (Oxford: Oxford University Press, 2001), 111–82; Stephen David Snobelen, "Isacc Newton, Socinianism and 'the One Supreme God,'" in *Socinianism and Arminianism: Antitrinitarianism, Calvinists, and Cultural Exchange in Seventeenth-Century Europe* (Boston and Leiden: Brill, 2005), 244–98; Maria-Cristina Pitassi, "Avant-propos"; "Le Christ Lockien à l"épreuve des textes: De la *Reasonableness* aux *Paraphrase and Notes*"; Jean-François Baillon, "La Reformation permanente: les Newtoniens et le dogme trinitaire," in *Le Christ entre orthodoxie et lumières: actes du colloque tenu à Genève en août 1993,* ed. Maria-Cristina Pitassi (Genève: Droz, 1994), 7–9; 101–22; 123–37.

16 Ann Thomson, "Toland, Dodwell, Swift, and the Circulation of Irreligious Ideas in France: What Does the Study of International Networks Tell Us about the 'Radical Enlightenment'?," in *Intellectual Journeys: The Translation of Ideas in England, France and Ireland*, ed. Lise Andries and Frederic Ogee (Oxford: Voltaire Foundation, 2013), 159–75 at 162–4; Thomson, *Bodies of Thought*, 29–65.

17 Thomson, *Bodies of Thought*, 29–65; for similar treatment of William Coward and his place in the history of French vitalism, see Fernando Vidal, *The Sciences of the Soul: The Early Modern Origins of Psychology*, trans. Saskia Brown (Chicago: University of Chicago Press, 2011), 83–4; J.S. Spink, "'Pyrrhonien' et "sceptique" sunonymes de "matérialiste" dans la littérature clandestine," in Bloch, ed., *Le Matérialisme du XVIIIe siècle*, 143–8 at 145.

18 Thomson, *Bodies of Thought*, 97–174; Thomson, "Toland, Dodwell, Swift," 159–75; Ann Thomson, *L'âme des lumières: Le débat sur l'être humain entre religion et science Angleterre-France, 1690–1760* (Paris: Champ Vallon, 2013), 161–238.

19 Thomson, "Toland, Dodwell, Swift," 162; Thomson, *Bodies of Thought*, 44–54; Paul Hazard, *La Crise de la conscience européene, 1680–1715* (Paris: Librairie Arthème Fayard, 1961), 165–99.

20 René Descartes, *Discours de la méthode pour bien conduire sa raison et chercher la vérité dans les* sciences, IV.32–6, in *Oeuvres philosophiques de Descartes*, ed. Ferdinand Alquié (Paris: Editions classiques Garnier, 1988), 1:603; Henry Phillips, *Church and Culture in Seventeenth-Century France* (Cambridge: Cambridge University Press, 1997), 137–9.

21 Dennis Des Chene *Life's Form: Late Aristotelian Conceptions of the Soul* (Ithaca: Cornell University Press, 2000), 168–9, 199–202; Descartes, *Passions de l'âme*, Art. IV in Alquié, ed., *Oeuvres philosophiques de Descartes*, 3: 959, 965, 973.

22 Aram Vartanian, "Quelques réflexions sur le concept d'âme dans la littérature clandestine," in *Le Matérialisme du XVIIIe siècle et la littérature clandestine*, 148–65 at 148.

23 Earlier work by Vartanian had insisted on the Cartesian origins of materialism by way of Spinoza: see Aram Vartanian, *Diderot and Descartes: A Study of Scientific Naturalism in the Enlightenment* (Princeton: Princeton University Press, 1953), 291–321.

24 [Baruch] Spinoza, *Tractatus theologo-politicus* (1679), vol. 3, *Opera quae suersunt Omnia, ex editionibus principus*, ed. Charles Hermann Bruder ([Leipzig]: Bernh. Trauchnitz jun., 1843–6), IV–VI, 62–103; on the Spinozan contribution to the genesis of the Radical Enlightenment throughout the eighteenth century, see Israel, *Enlightenment Contested*, 1–60; for a vital reassessment of the role of Epicureanism during the eighteenth

century, see Alan C. Kors, *Epicureans and Atheists in France, 1650–1729* (Cambridge: Cambridge University Press, 2015); see also Alan C. Kors, *Naturalism and Unbelief in France, 1650–1729* (Cambridge: Cambridge University Press, 2015).

25 Pierre Gassendi, *Metaphysical Colloquy, or Doubts and Rebuttals Concerning the Metaphysics of René Descartes with His Replies*, IV.2, in *The Selected Works of Pierre Gassendi*, ed. and trans. Craig B. Brush (New York: Johnson Reprint, 1972), 275–8.

26 [Mirabaud], *De l'âme et de son immortalité* (London: n.p., 1751), I, 6–8: "Most ancient of philosophers associated spirit with the breath of life animating nature. The soul or spirit (*âme*) was the animate principal, and was often thought of a subtle and delicate matter"; Vartanian, "Quelques réflexions," 162.

27 Anonymous, *L'Ame matérielle*, ed. Alain Niderst (Paris: Presses Universitaires de Rouen et du Havre, 1969), 50, 52, 118, 222–34; Vartanian, "Quelques réflexions," 151–4.

28 John P. Wright, "Substance versus Function Dualism in Eighteenth-Century Medicine," in *Psyche and Soma: Physicians and Metaphysicians on the Mind-Body Problem from Antiquity to the Enlightenment*, ed. John P. Wright and Paul Potter (Oxford: Clarendon Press, 2000), 237–54; for a related interpretation, see Charles T. Wolfe, *Vitalism without Metaphysics?: Medical Vitalism in the Enlightenment* (Cambridge: Cambridge University Press, 2008); on Hartley's impact, see Ann Thomson, "Déterminisme et passions," in *Matérialisme et passions*, ed. Pierre-François Moreau and Ann Thomson (Lyons: Ens Editions, 2004), 79–95 at 83–9; for additional interpretations of the role of animal and human physiology in redefining the human soul during the seventeenth and eighteenth centuries, see Ann Thomson, *Materialism and Society in the Mid-Eighteenth Century: La Mettrie's "Discours Préliminaire"* (Geneva: Droz, 1981); Jessica Riskin, *Science in the Age of Sensibility: The Sentimental Empiricists of the French Enlightenment* (Chicago: University of Chicago Press, 2002); Stephen Gaukroger, *The Collapse of Mechanism and the Rise of Sensibility: Science and the Shaping of Modernity* (Oxford: Oxford University Press, 2010); Jonathan I. Israel, "Enlightenment, Radical Enlightenment and the 'Medical Revolution' of the Late Seventeenth and Eighteenth Centuries," in *Medicine and Religion in Enlightenment Europe*, ed. Ole Peter Grell and Andrew Cunningham (Aldershot: Ashgate, 2007), 5–26.

29 Thomson, *Bodies of Thought*, 22–174; Roselyne Rey, *Naissance et développement du vitalisme en France de la deuxième moitié du siècle à la fin du Premier Empire* (Oxford: Voltaire Foundation, 2000), 1–18, 53–61; Vidal, *The Sciences of*

the Soul, 74–84, 94–127; Elizabeth A. Williams, *The Physical and the Moral: Anthropology, Physiology, and Philosophical Medicine in France, 1750–1850* (Cambridge: Cambridge University Press, 1994), 37–8; Elizabeth A. Williams, *A Cultural History of Medical Vitalism in Enlightenment Montpellier* (Aldershot and Burlington: Ashgate, 2003); Peter Hanns Reill, *Vitalizing Nature in the Enlightenment* (Berkeley: University of California Press, 2005), 1–16, 33–70, 119–42, 198.

30 Wright, "Substance versus Function Dualism," 237–8.

31 Herman Boerhaave, *First Lines of Physiology*, Proposition 27, 27.7–8, ed. William Cullen (Edinburgh, 1786); as quoted in Wright, "Substance versus Function Dualism," 242 and 242n10.

32 Wright, "Substance versus Function Dualism," 237–8.

33 On vitalistic materialism, see Thomson, "'Mechanistic Materialism' vs. 'Vitalistic Materialism'?," 22–36; Wright, "Materialismo e anima vitale," 143–59.

34 "Je suppose que l'âme humaine est crée de Dieu avec une force naturelle de contenir les parties du corps auquel elle est destinée, dans cette situation convénable aux fonctions humaines: cette force dans chaque âme est relative au corps qu'elle doit animer: que cette force étant identifée, c'est-à-dire étant une même chose avec la nature de l'âme; & qu'ainsi les âmes destinées à différents corps sont différentes autant que les corps auxquelles elles sont destinées sont différentes." [Tournemine], "Conjectures sur l'union de l'âme et de corps," *Mémoires de Trévoux*, mai 1703, 872–3.

35 "L'expérience vous apprend que l'âme agit sur le corps, comme elle vous apprend que vous pensez, que vous voulez." "Suite des Conjectures sur l'union de l'âme & du corps par Père Tournemine, jésuite," *Mémoires de Trévoux*, juin 1703, 1063–85 at 1063.

36 "Suite des Conjectures," 1066–7.

37 "Après avoir reconnu qu'il est impossible que le corps agisse sur l'âme, vous ne pouvez cependant developer vos conjectures sans laisser au corps quelque espèce d'action sur elle." "Lettre de Mr. L'abbé Languet de Montigny, Aumonier de Madame la Duchesse de Bourgogne au P. Tournemine, jésuite," *Mémoires de Trévoux* (octobre 1703): 1840–57 at 1842.

38 "Et par consequent le corps peut produire des impréssions dans la substance de l'âme." "Lettre de Mr. L'abbé Languet de Montigny," 1842.

39 Jeffrey D. Burson, "Between Power and Enlightenment: The Cultural and Intellectual Context for the Jesuit Suppression in France," in *The Jesuit Suppression in Global Context: Causes, Events, Consequences*, ed. Jeffrey D. Burson and Jonathan Wright (Cambridge: Cambridge University Press, 2015), 40–64.

40 Nick Childs, *A Political Academy in Paris, 1724–1731: The Entresol and Its Members* (Oxford: Voltaire Foundation, 2000), 3–16; on Buffier and Mme de Lambert, see Katharine J. Hammerton, "A Feminist Voice in the Enlightenment Salon: Madame de Lambert on Taste, Sensibility, and the Feminine Mind," *Modern Intellectual History* 7, no. 2 (2010): 216–20; see Jeffrey D. Burson, "Claude G. Buffier and the Maturation of the Jesuit Synthesis in the Age of Enlightenment," *Intellectual History Review* 21, no. 4 (December 2011): 449–72; Katharine J. Hammerton, "Malebranche, Taste, and Sensibility: The Origins of Sensitive Taste and a Reconsideration of Cartesianism's Feminist Potential," *Journal of the History of Ideas* 69, no. 4 (October 2008): 533–58; Kathleen Wilkins, *A Study of the Works of Claude Buffier* (Geneva: Institut et Musée de Voltaire, Les Délices, 1969), 101.

41 [Jean] Colerus, "La Vie de B. Spinosa, tire des écrits de ce fameux Philosophe, & du témoignage de plusieurs personnes dignes de foy qui l'ont connu particulièrement," *Mémoires de Trévoux* (juin 1707): 95–110; Ann Thomson and Françoise Weil, "Manuscrits et éditions de *l'Examen de la Religion*," in *Le matérialisme du XVIIIe siècle et la littérature clandestine*, 177–86, at 178.

42 Françoise Weil, "La Diffusion en France avant 1750," 209.

43 David Allen Harvey, *The French Enlightenment and Its Others: The Mandarin, the Savage, and the Invention of the Human Sciences* (New York: Palgrave Macmillan, 2012); Guy Stroumsa, *A New Science: The Discovery of Religion in the Age of Reason* (Cambridge, MA: Harvard University Press, 2010), 1–13, 145–57; see also Israel, *Enlightenment Contested*, 409–513, 615–99.

44 Jean Baptiste Boyer, le marquis d'Argens, *Lettres chinoises ou correspondence philosophique, historique et critique entre un chinois voyageur & ses correspondans à la Chine, en Muscovie & au Japon*, 6 vols, nouvelle édition augmentée de nouvelles lettres & de quantité de remarques (Lay Haye: Pierre Paupie, 1769), 1: 138–9; Israel, *Enlightenment Contested*, 640–62; see also Israel, "Admiration of China and Classical Chinese Thought in the Radical Enlightenment (1685–1740)," *Journal of East Asian Studies* 4.1.7 (June 2007), 1–25; see also Burson, "Between Power and Enlightenment," in *The Jesuit Suppression in Global Context*, 45–51.

45 Alan C. Kors, *Atheism in France, 1650–1729*, vol. 1: *The Orthodox Sources of Disbelief* (Princeton: Princeton University Press, 1990), 210–17, 296; Israel, *Enlightenment Contested*, 409–71.

46 [Gernard de Maillet], *Telliamed*, 2 vols (Amsterdam: L'Honoré, 1748), 1: iv–v, xvii–xxi, xxv–xxxiv; see also Lynn Hunt and Margaret Jacob, "Introduction"; Wijnand Mijnardt, "Jean Frédéric Bernard as Author and Publisher," in *The Book That Changed Europe: Picart and Bernard's* Religious

Ceremonies of the World, ed. Lynn Hunt, Margaret C. Jacob, and Wijnand Mijnardt (Cambridge, MA: Belknap, 20101–13), 117–34; Lynn Hunt, Margaret Jacob, and Wijnand Mijnardt, *Decoding the Divine: The Religious Ceremonies and Customs of All the Peoples of the World* (Cambridge, MA: Harvard University Press, 2010).

47 "Réflexions du Père Tournemine, Jésuite, sur l'Athéisme, sur la demonstration de Monseigneur de Cambray, & sur le Systême de Spinosa qui ont servi de Préface aux deux Editions precedents de la Démonstration," in François de Salignac de la Motte Fenelon, *Oeuvres philosophiques*, nouvelle édition augmentée des Réflexions du Pere Tournemine (Paris and Avignon: Pierre Delaire, 1776), 377–412 at 380–2 and 393–4.

48 Thomson, "Déterminisme et passions," 79–95 at 79–80.

49 David Hartley, *Observations on Man, His Frame, His Duty, and His Expectations in Two Parts* (London, 1749; London: J. Johnson, St Paul's Church-yard, 1791), 12, 33–4, 111; John W. Yolton, *Thinking Matter: Materialism in Eighteenth-Century Britain* (Minneapolis: University of Minnesota Press, 1983), 195–6.

50 Joseph Priestly, *Disquisitions Relating to Matter and Spirit*, xxvii, 7, 21; Priestly, *A Free Discussion of the Doctrines of Materialism and Philosophical Necessity, in a Correspondence between Dr. Price and Dr. Priestly* (London, 1778; rpt. Thoemmes, 1994), 146–7; cited in Thomson, "Déterminisme et passions," 88–9.

51 [Julian d'Offray de La Mettrie], *Histoire naturelle de l'âme, traduit de l'Anglois de M. Charp, par feu M. H.*** de l'Académie des Sciences, &c.* (Oxford, n.p., 1747), ch. I, 1–4; ch. II, 5–7; ch. V, 16, 20; ch. VI, 24–30; ch. X, 50–113; ch. XI, 114–16; ch. XII, 133–247 at 244–7; ch. XIV, 272–96; 335–43. See also Gianni Paganini, "Politique et religion dans *L'Esprit de Spinoza*," *Littérature classique: libertinage et politique au temps de la monarchie absolue* 55 no. 3 (2004): 105–17.

52 La Mettrie certainly refers his opinions to Spinoza with some frequency, but the vast bulk of his citations and arguments derive at least as much, if not more so, from Gassendo-Epicurean arguments drawn from medical vitalists that fused with other currents thanks to the mediation of clandestine texts. Thomson, "La Mettrie et la littérature clandestine," 241; Pierre Vernière, *Spinoza et la pensée française avant la Révolution* 2 vols (Paris: Presses Universitaires de France, 1954), 2: 361–564; Charles T. Wolfe, "A Happiness Fit for Organic Bodies: La Mettrie's Medical Epicureanism," in *Epicurus in the Enlightenment*, ed. Neven Leddy and Avi S. Lifschitz (Oxford: Voltaire Foundation, 2009), 69–85. For a very compelling summary argument

concerning the "Variety of Materialisms" see Thomson, *Bodies of Thought*, 219–23.

53 Ferrone, *The Enlightenment*, x–xi.

54 Jeffrey D. Burson, "Unlikely Tales of Fo and Ignatius: Rethinking the Radical Enlightenment through French Appropriation of Chinese Buddhism," *French Historical Studies* 33 (2015): 391–420.

55 Thomson, *Bodies of Thought*, 217–47.

56 Jeffrey D. Burson, "The Catholic Enlightenment in France from *fin de siècle* Crisis of Consciousness to the Revolution, ca. 1650–1789," in *A Companion to the Catholic Enlightenment in Europe*, ed. Ulrich L. Lehner and Michael Printy (Leiden: Brill, 2010): 63–125 at 114–15; see also Hisayasu Nakagawa, "J.-J. Rousseau et J.-G. Pompignan: La 'Profession de foi du vicaire Savoyard,' et 'De la religion civile' critiques par l'*Instruction pastorale*," *Dix-huitième siècle* 34 (2002): 67–76 at 72; the observation concerning the renewed religious sensibility of the Enlightenment is echoed in Margaret C. Jacob, "Epilogue: Dichotomies Defined and the Revolutionary Implications of Religion Implied," *Historical Reflections / Réflexions historiques* 40 (2014): 108–16; it is similarly implied in John Christian Laursen, "Hacia una visión equilibrada del cristianismo en los estudios sobre ilustración y republicanismo," *Ariadna histórica: lenguajes, conceptos, metáforas* 2 (2013): 15–32; the centrality of religious debates to the origins of the Enlightenment is also covered in Anton M. Matytsin, *The Specter of Skepticism in the Age of Enlightenment* (Baltimore: Johns Hopkins University Press, 2016); William J. Bulman, "Introduction: Enlightenment for the Culture Wars," in *God in the Enlightenment*, ed. William J. Bulman and Robert G. Ingram (Oxford: Oxford University Press, 2016), 1–41; Charly Coleman, *The Virtues of Abandon: An Anti-Individualist History of the French Enlightenment* (Stanford: Stanford University Press, 2014), 12.

57 Jonathan Sheehan, *The Enlightenment Bible: Translation, Scholarship, Culture* (Princeton: Princeton University Press, 2005), xi.

58 Stroumsa, *A New Science*, 5.

59 For a fascinating recent perspective on how philosophical "conversions" were often transformative in spiritual conversions, see Daniel Watkins, "The Two Conversions of François de la Pillonière: A Case Study of Rationalism and Religion in the Early Enlightenment," *Eighteenth-Century Thought* 6 (2016): 33–59.

60 Ferrone, *The Enlightenment*, xiii.

61 Margaret C. Jacob, *Living the Enlightenment: Freemasonry and Politics in Eighteenth-Century Europe* (Oxford: Oxford University Press, 1991), 174; see also Pierre-Yves Beaurepaire, *L'Europe des francs-maçons (XVIIIe-XXIe siècles)*

(Paris: Belin, 2002); Beaurepaire, *La République Universelle des francs-maçons: de Newton à Metternich* (Rennes: Ouest-France, de mémoire d'home – l'histoire, 1999); most recently, Beaurepaire, *Franc-maçonnerie et sociabilité au siècle des Lumières* (Paris: Edimaf, 2013); see also Charles Porset Cécile Révauger, ed., *Franc-Maçonnerie et religions dans l'Europe des Lumières* (Paris: Champion, 1998).

62 Jacob, "Epilogue," *Historical Reflections* 40, no. 2 (2014): 110.

PART SIX

SPANISH DEVELOPMENTS

Chapter Fourteen

The Spanish Revolution of 1820–1823 and the Clandestine Philosophical Literature

JONATHAN ISRAEL

I. "Radical" and "Moderate" Enlightenment in Post-1808 Spain

The thesis that the Western Enlightenment in general needs to be divided into two main categories with fundamentally different traits, moderate and radical, was first conceptualized in detail by Leo Strauss (1899–1973) around 1928.[1] The concept was later further developed by Strauss himself, Günter Mühlpfordt,[2] Henry May, Giuseppe Ricuperati, Margaret Jacob (who, however, largely rejects the interpretation presented here), Silvia Berti, and Wim Klever. As conceived by Strauss, "Radical Enlightenment" preceded the "Moderate Enlightenment" chronologically and outlived it. From the late seventeenth century onwards, "moderate Enlightenment" remained the mainstream as far as governments, churches, and educators were concerned, but beneath the surface, contended Strauss, the radical impulse proved the more robust, philosophically and culturally. It constituted the "real" or main Enlightenment especially with respect to shaping the Enlightenment's troubled legacy – the intellectual paradoxes and dilemmas of post-1800 modernity. Strauss accordingly classified *Radikale Aufklärung* as the "veritable" Enlightenment, casting Locke, Voltaire, Montesquieu, Moses Mendelssohn, and other "moderates" as cautious compromisers whose unworkable deistic and "Socinian" philosophical "fixes" unwittingly weakened rather than strengthened their ultimately untenable theses reconciling reason with religion.

Since *Radikale Aufklärung* for Leo Strauss meant essentially philosophical "atheism," he chiefly distinguished what by 1928 he already termed "moderate Enlightenment" by the latter's theistic premises and willingness to compromise with ecclesiastical authority.[3] By contrast, Henry

May, the first to introduce the "Radical Enlightenment" construct in English,[4] highlighted the American Enlightenment's abiding split between radicals and moderates principally in terms of support for or against the democratizing tendency in the American Revolution without linking this especially closely to critique of religion. My own approach to the Radical Enlightenment phenomenon combines the Straussian and May lines of analysis, placing the main stress precisely on the philosophical, ideological, and eventually political linkage of these two elements – eliminating religious authority tied to democratizing republicanism. In my *Revolutionary Ideas*, I argue that while from the standpoint of popular culture and society "at the beginning of the French Revolution, no apparent contradiction between the Revolution and religion" existed, from the perspective of that revolution's left republican leadership – a large slice of the revolutionary vanguard and pro-revolutionary newspaper editors, if not the populace – it was manifest from the outset that the revolution, given its radical intellectual background and priorities, would comprehensively assail the Church as an authority, autonomous institution, value system, and set of doctrines.[5]

Portraying the Radical Enlightenment as an ideological set of sails well-placed as it turned out to catch at least a modest proportion of the everywhere powerful but usually inchoate winds of social discontent, anger, and frustration, I identified 1789–93 as the juncture within the French Revolution when Radical Enlightenment as a set of slogans and values based on universal and equal human rights gave birth, for the first time, to an ugly and seemingly inevitable concomitant, a vigorous mass political anticlericalism expressly directed against the Christian religion characterized by persecution, widespread vandalism, and self-defeating results. The point at which modern Spanish militant mass political anticlericalism comparably – if at this point so far much more weakly – emerged as a tentative mass movement was with the Spanish Revolution of 1820–3.

The years 1814–20 in Spain were rife with conspiracy and a seething revolutionary underground.[6] Following six years of intensely reactionary royalist repression, the Cádiz Constitution of 1812 was powerfully revived by the insurrection of early 1820, commencing with the mutiny of 14,000 troops King Fernando VII (reigned: 1808–33) had gathered at Cádiz for his projected attempt to reconquer Buenos Aires and the Río de la Plata. At first, the peasantry and urban masses, especially in Andalusia where the insurgency began, evinced only indifference; but as the weeks passed, sufficient mass support materialized particularly in

Galicia and elsewhere in the north to enable the rebels to encircle the capital and finally the royal palace. The sporadic urban rioting extended to attacks on the recently reinstated Jesuits in Madrid and on the Inquisition's tribunals, prisons, and archives in Madrid, Santiago de Compostela, Zaragoza, Valencia, Barcelona, and elsewhere.[7] In the 1820s and 1830s the great majority of the Spanish people remained deeply loyal to traditional Catholic piety; however, some scholars have discerned the first seeds of later Spanish political mass anticlericalism. It is important, therefore, to examine the role of Radical Enlightenment in this much-neglected revolution and, in particular, to investigate the wave of vehemently anti-religious and anticlerical books that poured out in Spain during the three years 1820–3. Books and texts that had been vigorously banned and repressed earlier by the crown and bishops as well as by the Inquisition – albeit with a major interruption in 1808–14 – for the first time in Spanish history gained a firm grip during this revolutionary upsurge of 1820–3, usually known in Spanish as "the Trienio." This formidable wave of clandestine philosophical literature in Spanish was simultaneously generated by presses within Spain – and not only in Madrid, as we shall see – and abroad, especially London, Bordeaux, and Paris but also Lisbon, Philadelphia, and Geneva.

Trapped in his palace, Spain's fuming monarch hurriedly proclaimed the Constitution's reinstatement by decree of 10 March 1820, expressing his royal "satisfaction" with a show of hypocrisy that duped no one. For the remainder of the revolution, the king remained under virtual house arrest. The Holy Alliance and all of Restoration Europe were profoundly shocked by this fresh assault on monarchy so soon after the inception of the Restoration in Europe and not least by the open display of revolutionary exhilaration in Madrid and other parts of Spain; they were especially angered by the enthusiasm for this new Spanish revolution displayed by the country's intelligentsia and their eager ideological allies abroad. There was no "liberal ilustrado" (enlightened liberal) in Europe, declared one of the revolution's leading ideologues, the writer, educator, and political activist José Joaquín de Mora (1783–1864), in 1820, in a leaflet introducing the ideas of Jeremy Bentham in Spanish, "who did not look on this event as the 'predecessor y anuncio' of the regeneration of the civilized nations."[8]

By indiscriminately expelling both radicals and constitutional moderates, both *josefinos* and liberal loyalists, in 1814–15, and on a scale unmatched by any other monarch of the Restoration era,[9] Fernando had massively expanded the burgeoning pan-European exodus of revolutionary *émigrés*, thus creating an exceptionally large Spanish liberation movement in exile. Droves of defeated radicals, "moderates," and Napoleonists, driven from their homes, posts, and pensions in Italy, Germany, Austria, Poland, Britain, and Ireland and well as France and Spain, had migrated abroad.[10] But the total ejected from Spain, in 1814, estimated at around 12,000 families, was undoubtedly the largest contingent expelled from any European country.[11] Thousands of Spanish political fugitives and refugees had congregated in semi-permanent exile, often remaining committed political activists in France, England, Belgium, Switzerland, and other places of refuge. Among them were a number of leading Spanish American revolutionaries menaced with arrest in Spain, such as Ecuador's foremost enlightener Vicente Rocafuerte (1783–1847), who had spent many years studying in Spain and France, had first-hand experience of the French Revolution, and had been a *diputado* for Guayaquil at the Cádiz Cortes before being forced to flee.

In 1820, reversing direction, radicals, moderates, and *josefinos* banished from Spain in 1814 streamed back from exile while those silenced internally resumed their former writing and gatherings.[12] Mexican and some other Spanish American deputies present at Cádiz in 1810–13 also now returned to Spain, hoping to participate once again in the empire's much heralded revival on the basis of the 1820 constitution. For a time there were extravagant hopes that the Spanish American rebellions could now at last be quieted and resolved by equitable and peaceful compromise. A six-month ceasefire between the Spanish crown and the Spanish American revolutionaries was proclaimed, and new constitutional arrangements were proposed for the whole empire based on the principles of "Cádiz" and "1812."[13] Excited optimism at first prevailed. But much time was lost owing to the deep split between moderates and radicals, which led to stalled or ineffective debates in the legislature so that only excruciatingly slow progress was registered in nearly all legislative areas. Between 1820 and 1823 the Dirección General de Estudios, headed by Quintana, set up to revolutionize Spain's education system, likewise proved largely ineffective in secularizing education, owing the depth of the intellectual rift between the two enlightenments, just as had occurred in 1808–14, though in April 1822 it did finally produce a measure for dissolving monasteries and converting them into schools, which scored a few successes.[14]

The revolution was eventually crushed, in March 1823, with the aid of a French army sent by Louis XVIII acting on behalf of the conservative powers of the Holy Alliance. Those elements in Spain eager to suppress religious toleration and restore the Inquisition at that point seized with alacrity the opportunity for thoroughgoing repression of Enlightenment values, in some cases invoking Rousseau's *Contrat social* to prove that even the most read political philosopher of the age contended, like them, that the upkeep of viable civil religion requires organized, institutionalized intolerance and the expulsion of those who dissent.[15]

II. The Influx of Previously Suppressed European Political Thought

Like all the European revolutions of the early nineteenth century, the Spanish Revolution of 1820–3 was carried out in the name of the people but was only to a limited extent a revolution *of* the people. Mainly, it needs stressing, it was a revolution of intellectuals consciously striving to establish a *público ilustrado* (enlightened public) in conscious opposition to the traditionally minded *vulgo irracional*. The principal architects of the revolution of 1808–12, the revolutionary vanguard, had been intellectuals, artists, professors, and journalists, and after March 1820 these groups were again the main actors, the backbone of the Trienio. Immediately after the king and his reactionary ministers and policies were defeated, key political prisoners, including leading figures from the earlier revolution such as Agustín Argüelles (1776–1844), a former bishop's secretary estranged from the Church who had composed the preface to the 1812 Cádiz Constitution, and Manuel José Quintana (1772–1857), a successful poet, playwright, and enlightened essayist, were released – Argüelles on Majorca, Quintana at Pamplona – and free to rejoin the revolution. Spanish political exiles expelled in 1814 or who had fled abroad returned *en masse*, often in a state of great excitement.

Such men were simultaneously the symbols of "revolution" and "Enlightenment" in Spain. Argüelles had been one of the main promotors of Beccaria's egalitarian legal theories in the Spanish-speaking world and a key inspiration behind moves to abolish judicial torture, which had finally succeeded with a decree of the Cortes of 22 April 1811. Argüelles was also a leading opponent of the slave trade.[16] Likewise released in March 1820 were all the South American revolutionaries held in Spanish jails, such as the veteran enlightener Antonio Nariño (1764–1824) of New Granada (Colombia), an aristocratic admirer of Franklin and eager zealot for the American and French revolutions who as early as 1794 had disseminated in his own Spanish translation the 1789 French "Declaration of the Rights of Man and the Citizen" in Peru as well as New Granada.[17]

An uneasy alliance of moderate and radical Enlightenment ideologues, the revolution's vanguard was highly precarious politically, intellectually, and religiously. The Spanish Revolution of 1820–3 faced a massive external obstacle to its success – the Holy Alliance, backed by a deeply reactionary British government – as well as two major internal obstacles, one of which was the continuing and formidable resistance in many parts of Spain of the reactionary right, including the nobility, a large part of the ecclesiastical establishment and the Inquisition, and much of the populace. The other obstacle within Spain was the more recent split, evident since the years 1810–14, between pro-revolution "moderates," including the liberal wing of the Catholic Church in Spain, and Spain's openly anticlerical radicals. The moderates had the great advantage of enjoying the firm and consistent support of the primate of the Spanish Church since 1799, the Cardinal-Archbishop of Toledo, Don Luis de Borbón (1777–1823), the "cardinal of the liberals." On all three levels, among radicals, reactionaries, and moderates alike, the essential battle – and this requires special emphasis – was envisaged as a clash of fundamental principles, as a struggle between Enlightenment "philosophy" and religion – or, in the moderates' case, as a struggle over how to reconcile them.

A particular problem, in the view of the revolutionary vanguard, was the country's lack of exposure hitherto to such political writers as Rousseau, Paine, Price, Priestley, Helvétius, d'Holbach, Filangieri, Condorcet, Constant, and Bentham, a result of their being banned by the Inquisition owing to the conspicuously irreligious and anti-ecclesiastical elements present in much of their writing. Very few texts propagating the new political consciousness of the late Enlightenment enjoyed much circulation in Spanish prior to 1820.[18] Among its first actions, the reinstated Cortes ordered courses in political science introduced in the Spanish universities. A leading *josefino* resident in France since 1814, and supporter of revolutionary change in Spain, Juan Antonio Llorente (1756–1823) – former secretary of the Inquisition in the years 1789–91 and recent author of the first full-scale critical history of (and modern assault on) the Inquisition, the *Histoire critique de l'Inquisition espagnole* (Paris, 1817) – commented on this Spanish advent of political science in Marc-Antoine Jullien's *Revue Encyclopédique* (Paris).[19] The Spanish Revolution directed the universities to use Benjamin Constant's *Cours de Politique constitutionelle* (1818–20), recently published at Paris, to modernize and enlighten Spain's political consciousness. Translated by Marcial Antonio López, Constant's course appeared in three volumes, at Madrid in 1820, under the title *Curso de política constitucional*, and again, in the same translation, but in two volumes, at Bordeaux in 1823.[20] Less radical than in the 1790s, and now no revolutionary, the Constant of 1820 still energetically promoted reform, constitutionalism, freedom of the press, and the abolition of slavery.

The second Spanish Revolution began auspiciously, but before long the old rift between moderates and radicals reopened, with the former seeking to conciliate and palliate the Church and modify the unicameral Cádiz constitution by introducing a second, upper chamber and by safeguarding royalty and the royal veto as well as urging a continued political role for the Church and nobility.[21] Joseph Blanco White (born José María Blanco Crespo) (1775 –1841), Spain's most eminent "moderate" exile still abroad, charged the 1812 constitution's framers with being doctrinaire, naive admirers of French radical ideas and, even more deplorably, of Thomas Paine, who had posthumously emerged since 1811 as Spanish America's principal democratic guide. Resuming contact with his old ally, Quintana, from England, Blanco White tried to dissuade him and his colleagues from restoring the 1812 Constitution with its democratic features unaltered. He implored the revolution's leaders to dilute the Cádiz Constitution's radicalism, meaning its Franco-American republican tendency, and to opt for British-style "mixed monarchy," assuredly the correct path. Sceptical about the revived revolution's prospects, he was soon proved right with respect to the insufficiency of popular support. The *constitucionales* and enlighteners of 1820–3, he correctly predicted, would before long again be overwhelmed by "superstition" and ignorance mobilized by the Church.[22] Popular deference to the clergy was the radical revolutionaries' greatest foe. In parts of Spain, civil war erupted within the first few months, with Aragon, the Basque provinces, Navarre, and Catalonia emerging as particular centres of loyalist *absolutista* resistance.

With the Cortes's Edict of Freedom of the Press in place, and the Inquisition formally dismantled, publishers, printers, and booksellers, intoxicated with the supposed sudden advent of press freedom, and freedom to import books into the Spanish-speaking world, set to work with energy to generate a wave of publications addressing political, social, moral, and religious issues in a critical, philosophical manner that had not been permitted before 1811 and had been again forbidden between 1814 and 1820. A considerable degree of evasion and subterfuge remained necessary, however, in view of the continuing episcopal censorship machinery, which was still in place. Hence, many of the formerly clandestine – and soon again, from 1823, *definitely* clandestine – works published with an eye to the Spanish market during the years 1820–3 were published abroad rather that in Spain itself, and all these publications still often concealed the names of the Spanish translators and the distributing booksellers (*libreros*) in Spain. In Madrid, Paris, and London especially, translations banned under Fernando's rule poured out in editions intended for diffusion throughout Spain and the Spanish-speaking world.

Part of this wave carried what in other countries would be considered mainstream political thought. A five-volume translation of Montesquieu's *L'esprit de loix*, which had been placed on the papal *Index Librorum Prohibitorum* in 1751, appeared in Spanish, translated by D. Juan López de Peñalver, at Madrid, in 1820; this was followed by a three-volume edition that concealed the translator's name as Don M.V.M., Licenciado, published in three successive volumes between 1820 and 1823, in Madrid, Paris, and London.[23] In 1821, in a tenacious last stand against "philosophy," the not yet fully abolished Inquisition, entrenched where *absolutistas* prevailed, renewed its general "ban" on Montesquieu in Spanish.[24] Machiavelli's *El Principe* appeared in Spanish at Madrid, in 1821, as did John Locke's *Tratado del gobierno civil*.[25] Beccaria's classic text of 1764, translated by Juan Ribera as the *Tratado de los delitos y de las penas*, was published in successive editions at Madrid in 1820 and 1821 by the firm Fermin Villalpando, one of Spain's major presses active in Madrid between 1794 and 1830, which, precisely during the Trienio, also published Spanish versions of works by Bentham and Jean-Baptiste Say. Beccaria's *Tratado* appeared again in a new translation of 1822, and was also issued for the Spanish American market, from Philadelphia, in 1823.

Rousseau's *Contrat social* had first appeared in Spanish, translated by the "Spanish Brissotin," José Marchena y Ruiz de Cueto (1768–1821), considerably earlier. But *Émile*, *Julie*, and other key Rousseau texts appeared for the first time only during the Trienio, including the discourse on inequality published in Spanish under the title *Discurso sobre el orígen y los fundamentos de la desigualdad de condiciones entre los hombres, puesto en castellano por M.*, at Madrid, in 1822.[26] In all, no fewer than eighteen Spanish-language editions of Rousseau's principal works, mostly in translations by Marchena, were supplied to the Spanish reading public during the Trienio.[27]

If Rousseau was a radical republican in some respects but not in others, only a few of the major political thinkers of the Enlightenment could be classified as fully "radical," but among these were certainly Bentham and the great Italian theorist Gaetano Filangieri, whose work was firmly prohibited by the Spanish Inquisition in the late eighteenth century, as also for many years after 1823, but who remained, underground and behind the counter, arguably the most widely influential of all the radical political and constitutional thinkers in Spain and Spanish America. A Spanish translation of his great work rendered by D. Jaime Rubio had appeared, in ten volumes, under the title *Ciencia de la Legislación*, at Madrid in 1813, but been repressed after 1814, with many copies seized.[28] A second edition, newly translated by D. Juan Ribera, was published at Madrid in six volumes in 1821–2. A third edition, the second of Rubio's rendering, was published again in ten volumes – probably just after the ending of freedom of the press in Spain – this time at Bordeaux in 1823.[29]

In 1822 appeared Bentham's *Tratado de legislacion civil y penal*, translated by the distinguished Aragonese jurist and Salamanca professor, Ramón de Salas y Cortes (1753–1837),[30] who together with José Joaquín de Mora was one of the strongest promotors of Bentham's soon imposing reputation in Spain. Despite his vigorous promotion of Bentham's work in Spanish, Salas – a central figure in our story – was in many respects more of a disciple of Constant and especially Destutt de Tracy, whose commentary on Montesquieu (a favourite text also of Jefferson's) criticized Montesquieu for being too favourable to "mixed government" and the British system. Salas's translation of Destutt appeared in Spanish in one edition bound together with the Spanish translation of Montesquieu's *l'esprit des lois*, and in another, at Madrid, on its own as Destutt de Tracy, *Comentario sobre el Espíritu de las Leyes*, traducido por Ramón de Salas y Cortés (1821).[31]

III. The Clandestine Literature Attacking Religion

Among the foremost dilemmas faced by the Spanish Revolution of 1820–3 – and the most divisive – was that clandestine philosophical literature was spreading subversive attitudes towards religion and the Church. Initially it was an enormous boost to the revolution that leading "liberal" churchmen rallied to the cause of the restored constitution. In his capacity as Cardinal-Archbishop of Toledo and a leading figure in the revolutionary *junta*, Don Luis de Borbón had promptly issued a printed circular to his clergy, dated 15 March 1820, ordering them to instruct their flocks to support the restored 1812 constitution and obey the revolutionary *junta* and restored Cortes, and to make it clear to the faithful that the true Catholic can embrace toleration and the liberal and enlightened principles and values embodied in the constitution. Two days later, on 24 March, Borbón instructed all the curates and ecclesiastics of his archbishopric to undergo public ceremonies in which they were to swear their allegiance on the Gospel to the restored constitution.[32] The problem with Don Luis de Borbón's stance was that he simultaneously instructed his clergy that "toleration" and the principle of "freedom of the press" – the latter enacted by the revolutionary *junta*'s provisional Consultativa de Gobierno on 11 March 1820 – were allowable but were in no way to be confused with *libertinaje* (libertinage) and irreligion; and that freedom of the press was permissible and Christian as long as it remained free of "los sarcasmos y de las injurías" levelled by libertines and the irreligious at Church, clergy and Christian doctrine alike.[33] On 29 April the Cardinal-Archbishop issued an edict seeking to regulate book censorship and the prohibition of texts considered "contrary to religion".[34]

This position was bound to generate serious rifts in the 1820–3 revolution, since "freedom of the press" was not a principle that had been categorically asserted by the Cádiz Cortes. Nor did it have much support among the Spanish clergy; on the contrary, it stepped into a deep residue of outright opposition.[35] Although irreligious, anticlerical, and anti-Inquisition texts had circulated relatively freely in much of Spain during the years 1808 to 1814, a closer and clearer connection between irreligion and revolutionary republicanism became evident during the Trienio, doubtless in response to the repression of 1814–20, which had powerfully reinforced the linkage of royal absolutism with religious repression.[36] As one writer put it, in Spain the year 1820 was "el año de partida para la ideología anticlerical revolucionaria o moderna."[37] The result was a conundrum at the heart of the Revolution of 1820–3, one that would become manifest with the readoption of the Cádiz Constitution's special provisions to prevent the printing of anything detrimental to Church and religion, the *Junta Suprema de Censura* of 1813, provisions voted in again by the Cortes after it convened in June 1820. These sought precisely to balance freedom of the press against the need to prevent ironic, sarcastic, or insulting criticism of Church, clergy, and religious doctrine.[38]

But what actually was banned and what was permitted? When the Spanish Inquisition was suppressed for the second time, in 1813, having been abolished first by Napoleon in 1808, the Cortes had agreed that "escritos prohibidos, o que sean contrarios a la religion" would remain prohibited in Spain and its empire; thus it established *Tribunales protectores de la Fe* (Tribunals to protect the Faith) and assigned to them the task of drawing up a detailed list of prohibited publications. However, no such list ever appeared. Instead, the bishops and *tribunales* simply reiterated that all the books "que están prohibidos por el Santo Oficio, subsisten prohibidos."[39] Censorship then tightened markedly after 1814. Spain's Inquisitor-General between 1814 and 1818, the Bishop of Almería, Don Francisco Mier y Campillo, had a supplementary list compiled to bring the *Indice último de los libros prohibidos* of 1805 up to date.[40] When on 9 March 1820 the Spanish Inquisition was abolished for the third time, the *absolutista* bishops again issued pastoral circulars affirming that while the Inquisition itself was now in abeyance, the task of suppressing condemned writings had devolved upon the episcopate. On 14 April 1821 the Cortes confirmed that many books "prohibidos o contrarios a la Religión" were being sold in Spain publicly and petitioned the governing council to draw up a fresh list of prohibited books, in accordance with the law of 22 February 1813.[41]

The influx of Spanish translations of Montesquieu, Rousseau, Filangieri, Bentham, and other modern political thinkers banned by the Spanish Inquisition was a key phenomenon in itself. That surge also displayed on various levels inherent links with the underground literature assaulting religious authority and the Church. This is evident from the roles and life histories of the revolution's three principal translators of political thought: Salas, Mora, and Marchena. Salas had been denounced to the Inquisition in January 1792 and, on being found guilty of divulging and translating works prejudicial to religion, had been stripped of his chair at Salamanca; then on 25 September 1796 he had been sentenced to a year's imprisonment in a monastery. Not surprisingly, for Ramón de Salas, freedom of the press was "la más importante de todas la libertades." In 1808 he had joined King Joseph and the *afrancesados* and become Joseph's prefect of Guadalajara and later of Toledo. With the collapse of Joseph's regime, he had fled to France, only to return in 1820, enter the Cortes as an elected member, and play a notable part in the new revolution. He took up the task of providing a standard course in constitutional thought for Spain's schools; this was published under the title *Lecciones de Derecho público constitucional para las escuelas de España* (Madrid, 1821).

A still more striking illustration of the linkage of revolutionary politics with – in this case – an openly expressed atheistic tendency, is the life story of Marchena. A student and associate of Salas at Salamanca, by 1791 Marchena had read widely in the irreligious texts and imbibed a "razonable dosis de espíritu filosófico" (reasonable dose of *esprit philosophique*).[42] In difficulties with the Inquisition, he fled to France, where in August 1792 he emerged as an editor of the *Gaceta de la Libertad y de la Igualdad* and as one of a group of Spanish exiles introducing Brissotin revolutionary propaganda clandestinely into Spain. During 1792–93, following the Montagnard *coup d'etat* of June 1793, being a political ally of Brissot, he was imprisoned by the Robespierre regime, being released only after Thermidor. Marchena referred to the Brissotins as the "mártires de la libertad." His *Essai de théologie* (1797) was denounced by opponents, French and Spanish, as "atheistic." He returned to Spain with King Joseph in 1808 and held various posts in his administration, with the inevitable consequence that during the years 1814–20 he was again forced into exile, in Perpignan, Nîmes, and Montpellier.

During these years, Marchena translated a number of key French works into Spanish, publishing them in southern France presumably for clandestine introduction into Spain. These included his version of Rousseau's *La Nouvelle Heloise,* originally published in Spanish in 1814; *Émile,* which had first appeared at Bordeaux, in 1817; and Montesquieu's *Lettres persanes* of 1818. In 1820 he returned to Spain, where he threw himself into political debate in Seville and became notorious as a leading anticlerical urging strict subordination of the clergy to the state. His Spanish renderings of Rousseau and Montesquieu were then promptly reissued in Spain and France, under the titles *Contrato Social* (Madrid, 1820); *Emilio, ó de la educación* traducido por J. Marchena (Madrid, 2 vols, 1821); *Julia o la nueva Heloísa,* which came out in 1821 in separate editions at Bordeaux and Toulouse and then reappeared at Madrid; and the *Cartas persanas* escritas en francés por Montesquieu puesto en castellano por D. J. Marchena, nueva edicion (2 vols, Cadiz, 1821).[43] Another major work translated by Marchena, one that combined political thought with an outright attack on religion and the clergy, was Volney's *Ruines,* among the most celebrated radical works of the 1790s, which appeared under the title *Meditaciones sobre la Ruinas* in "Londres" in 1818 and then reappeared at Bordeaux in 1822.

These details concerning the influx of political thought – in the last example directly linked to an outright attack on revealed religion and the supernatural – help place in context the wave of more violently and uncompromisingly clandestine, anti-religious, and anti-ecclesiastical literature. It is noticeable that this surge of clandestine literature was dominated by the works of d'Holbach, including those of his texts that drew, largely or more residually, on elements originating in pre-1760 clandestine manuscripts and authors, in other words texts circulating in French in France and some other parts of Europe in printed versions since the 1760s at the latest. Among these latter were *La religion natural del buen cura Meslier* (also called *El buen sentido*), a copy of which was seized by the authorities in Algeciras in 1825.[44] A second version, titled *El buen-sentido fundado en la naturaleza por un cura despreocupado*, carried the subtitle "Tradúcelo y lo dedica a la Ilustración de sus compatriotas, el ciudadano S.L.M.M.J ('Lisboa' [Madrid?], Imp. Libertad, 1821"; this text was reissued in additional 1821 editions in "Londres" [Madrid?] and Bordeaux.[45]

D'Holbach had clandestinely published his *Le Bons-Sens, ou Idées naturelles opposés aux idées surnaturelles* in 1772.[46] Subsequent editions often attributed the text to the deeply subversive Jean Meslier (1664–1729), whose later notorious *Testament* had been left unpublished at his death in 1729 and whom Voltaire, in his clandestinely published *Extrait des sentiments de Jean Meslier* (1762), had purported to summarize while actually defusing his social radicalism and subverting his vehement atheism so that he ended up sounding like a providential deist. Later anonymous editions of d'Holbach's text often attributed the work to the curé Meslier – an example is the Spanish version circulating during the Trienio – though the reason for this is not altogether clear.[47] What is clear is that the text was a form of critical retaliation against Voltaire as well as religion and the Church, as was its customary post-1772 attribution to Meslier.[48]

Even more directly inspired by and drawing on sources from the past was *El Cristianismo a descubierto, ó examen de los principios y efectos de la religión Cristiana.* Escrito en Francés por Boulanger y traducido al castellano por S.D.V. ("Londres" en la emprenta de Davidson, 1821).[49] This was the Spanish version of the *L'Antiquité devoilée par ses usages*, which was genuinely based on and was already early on attributed to Nicolas-Antoine Boulanger (1722–1759), the republican friend of Diderot, Helvétius, and d'Holbach, a writer who exerted a profound influence on d'Holbach. The first clandestine French edition of this work, with a preface dated 4 May 1758, appeared at Geneva in 1761 (not 1766, as I, following Pecharroman and others, mistakenly stated in 2006).[50] Boulanger is notable for combining obvious republican tendencies with a vehement attack on organized religion.[51] D'Holbach's *Christianity Unveiled*, first published in English in 1795, appeared in Spanish only in 1821. Originally rendered from French under the title *El Cristianismo a descubierto*, supposedly in "Londres" (Madrid?) (1821), it reappeared in a second version, again supposedly in "London," under the more literal title *El Cristianismo desvelado.*[52]

Of the major works authored principally by d'Holbach himself, the *Système de la nature* (1770), appeared under the title *Sistema de la naturaleza. Los leyes del mundo físico y del mundo moral* in editions published at Paris (1822) and Gerona (1823).[53] The full Spanish versión of *La Morale Universelle ou les Devoirs de l'homme fondés sur la nature* (Amsterdam, 1776) appeared in 1820, at Madrid, under the title *La moral universal, o los deberes del hombre fundados en su naturaleza*, translated by Don Manuel Díaz Moreno, secretary of Madrid's famous Compañia de los Cinco Gremios, a corporation founded in 1667 to link the monopolies and privileges of the jewellers, silk dealers, haberdashers, clothiers, and *drogueros*; during 1821 there were two follow-up editions. Still more widely diffused was an abbreviated version of this work by the "Barón de Olbach" titled *Elementos de la moral universal, o Catecismo de la naturaleza* (Madrid, 1820), which in later versions was called *Principios de moral universal, o Manuel de los deberes del hombre fundados en su naturaleza* "traducido por" D.M.L.G., purportedly published in Valladolid.[54] In a notable incident during the post-1823 repression, following the reimposition of the Inquisition, a certain forty-six-year-old widower, D. Florencio de Imaz, a native of the Basque region in Spain, had among the confiscated forbidden books found in his possession a copy of the *Elementos*. Imaz had recently been expelled from Mexico, where he had been a royal financial official at Veracruz, by the revolutionaries there. The officer handling his case in Madrid commented that the irreligion permeating such texts was strictly forbidden, pointing to "el ansía con que los compraban los constitucionales prueba que abunda en sus ideas" (the eagerness with which the *constitucionales* buy [such works], proof that it abounds in their ideas).[55]

Other works by d'Holbach prepared for the Spanish market during the Trienio were the *Contagion sacrée, ou Histoire naturelle de la superstition* ("Londres" [Amsterdam], 1767), which appeared as *El contagion sagrado, ó Historio natural de la supersitición* (2 vols, Paris, Rodrique, 1822), and the *Lettres à Eugénie ou préservatif contre les préjugés* (1768), which first appeared in 1810 in Paris as *Cartas a Eugenia* por M. Freret and then again at Madrid in 1823.[56] The *Historia crítica de Jesús Christo, o Análysis razonado de los evangelios*, "traducido del francés por P.F. de T. ex-jesuita," appeared supposedly at "Londres" in two volumes in 1822.[57] An item directly linking this literature with one of the main figures of the revolution was d'Holbach's *Essai sur les prejugés, ou de l'influence des opinions sur les moeurs e sur le Bonheur des hommes, ouvrage contenant l'apologie d la philosophie par Mr. D.M.* (1769), which appeared under the title *Ensayo sobre las preocupaciones, escrito en francés por el Baron de Holbach, y traducido con correciones y adiciones por José Joaquín de Mora* (Madrid, 1823).[58]

José Joaquín de Mora (1783–1864), a writer, educator, and political activist from Cádiz, had at an early age become a professor of philosophy at Granada. Captured while fighting the French in 1809, he had been interned in France until 1814 and remained there subsequently, married to a French woman, until 1820. In 1820–3 he resumed his political activities in Madrid and became editor of *El Constitucional*, one of the main pro-revolution papers. With the French invasion of 1823 and the collapse of the revolution, he migrated to London, where he edited one of the main Spanish *émigré* papers, the *Correo Literario y Político de Londrés* (1823–6), then to Buenos Aires (1826–7) and Chile (1828–31). Before long Mora was one of the principal intellectual bridges to be found anywhere between the constitutional movements in Europe and Spanish America. After Chile, he moved on for a three-year spell in Peru, a country from which he was expelled. He moved on to Bolivia (1834–7), where he became a professor of literature in La Paz. After several more years of wandering, he returned to Spain in 1843.

The most prominent anti-religious items flooding in during the Trienio in Spain – items the authorities were anxious to suppress after the restoration of the Inquisition in 1823–4 – were the works of d'Holbach.[59] But of course there were numerous others. The convoluted anticlerical novel *The Monk* (1796), by Matthew G. Lewis, was published under the title *El graile ó historia del padre Ambrosio y la bella Antonia* at Madrid in 1822.[60] Diderot's *La Religieuse*, which had first been published with the blessing of the *Directoire*, in French, in 1796, which had reappeared numerous times in French, and which had been translated into English, German, and Italian by 1800, was by any reckoning a ferocious attack on what it presented as the sadism, narrowness, fanaticism, and ignorance of the life of the cloister. It appeared for the first time in a Spanish version at Paris in 1821. Although Diderot was never in fact elected to the Académie Française, and could not have been owing to the disapproval of the ecclesiastical authorities, this Spanish version was published under the title *La religiosa*, escrita en francés por M. Diderot, de la Academia Francesa. Traducida libremente al español por Don M.V.M., Licendiado.[61]

IV. Tom Paine and the Spanish-Speaking World

The early-nineteenth-century Spanish renderings of Thomas Paine's writings seem to have been directed specifically at the Spanish American milieu, rather than Spain, presumably owing to their more explicitly republican character combined with Paine's particular relevance for those seeking independence from imperial powers. When in 1821

Vicente Rocafuerte republished Paine's *Common Sense* in Spanish, at Philadelphia, supplying a prologue that loudly insisted that the American Revolution and especially Paine must be the principal guide for the Enlightenment as a political movement seeking toleration, freedom of expression, and liberty in Spanish America, he made no mention whatever of the renewed Spanish Revolution in progress at that moment.[62] This notable publication capped a process of intellectual alienation from Spain (as well as from *Robespierrisme*, which Rocafuerte loathed, and from Napoleon) that had been going on for a decade.

Manuel García de Sena (1780–1816), a Venezuelan living in Philadelphia since 1803, had rendered into Spanish numerous extracts of Thomas Paine together with the American Declaration of Independence, the United States Constitution, and the state constitutions of Massachusetts, Connecticut, New Jersey, Pennsylvania, and Virginia. The quest to forge a broader and more coherent Spanish American revolutionary consciousness by teaching the American Revolution and its constitutional outcome was reinforced further, in London, by a separate Spanish rendering of Paine's *Common Sense* that appeared in 1811, the work of the Peruvian Manuel José de Arrunátegui. García de Sena and Arrunátegui hoped to bring the entire New World, North and South, to converge in terms of republican attitudes and practices.[63] García de Sena fully embraced Paine's idea that the American Revolution represented a giant step forward in man's understanding of government and politics and that the French Revolution had carried further the American Revolution's essential principles.[64]

Five thousand copies of the Paine compilation, *La Independencia de la Costa Firme justificado por Thomas Paine treinta años ha* (The Independence of the Mainland justified by Thomas Paine Thirty Years Ago) (Philadelphia, 1811), which called for Spanish American independence from Spain and presented the turmoil gripping Spanish America as part of the wider global struggle of "liberty" against "oppression," reached Venezuela, with some seeping through to New Granada and New Spain (Mexico), besides Cuba and Puerto Rico. This was followed by García de Sena's rendering of John McCulloch's *A Concise History of the United States until 1807* (Philadelphia, 1812). Both works attracted attention in key Spanish American papers such as the *Gazeta de Caracas* (January 1812),[65] further entrenching Paine's name and ideas in the Ibero-American consciousness and before long rendering Paine the leading publicist evoking American solidarity with the Spanish American revolutions and Europe's "General Revolution." Among those contributing to discussion of Paine's ideas in the *Gazeta* was a leading Caracas republican, the journalist Juan Germán Roscio (1763–1821). In this way, Paine's arguments for republicanism and independence, rather than the rigorous constitutional monarchism of the 1812 Cádiz Constitution, began to penetrate.[66]

Until 1821, the "Tom Paine" propagated by elements of the revolutionary leadership in Spanish America was somewhat fragmentary, consisting only of *Common Sense* plus short extracts from other writings. *The Rights of Man* failed to appear in Spanish until an abbreviated version was brought out by Matthew Carey, in Philadelphia, in 1821.[67] Over several months in 1813, the ephemeral Chilean republican paper *Semanario Republicano de Chile* regularly cited Paine's republican views and pro-independence views while invoking the need for Spanish American "Washingtones." This noteworthy paper was edited by the Guatemalan Antonio José Irisarri (1786–1868), a central figure in the Chilean revolution of 1810 and commander of the Santiago National Guard. After completing his education in Europe, Irisarri had consistently figured among those Spanish American radicals claiming that republics pursue the happiness of peoples better than kings and denying that monarchy was instituted by God.[68] Reviling royalists, he rebuked fellow Spanish Americans for lamenting Napoleon's occupation of Spain as a vast calamity when they should have welcomed it as an opportunity to jettison royalty and seek independence. Deplorably, droves of ignorant loyalist Spanish Americans continued to "weep over the misfortune of Fernando."[69] Irisarri, though, also chided "moderates" of the Spanish reform party, like Joseph Blanco White, for demanding only modest changes and for obstinately championing Spain's imperial claims over Spanish America.[70]

Irisarri fully agreed with Blanco White, though, that "lack of enlightenment of the popular masses," exploited by the baseness of ambitious individuals, had "always been the reef on which republics perish."[71] Nothing illustrated this more clearly than the French Revolution. "Thus I believe that the firmest support of republics is Enlightenment and virtue; and I dread with pain in my soul that that people in which these qualities are lacking, cannot be republican," but only become more unhappy and revert to tyranny.[72] Freedom of the press itself will be "prejudicial instead of beneficial to peoples if it does not serve to purify truth and present it to men cleansed of all error, passion and interest." Enlightenment alone can yield a well-considered coherent outcome, capable of stabilizing societies, benefiting the whole, and bringing peace under a constitution like that of the United States.[73]

Events soon taught supporters of the Spanish Revolution of 1820–3 that their optimism of early 1820 was misplaced. On balance, Counter-Enlightenment opposition to the Spanish Trienio of 1820–3 did indeed mobilize greater popular support than did the revolution. In the Spanish conservative view, "la filosofía con su soberbia razón no ha hecho sino destruir: proscribió la virtud y canonizó los crimines; reinó por un instante: y quien contara los lamentos que ha causado este reinado impío? No podía ser otra cosa, por que sin Dios no hay más que injusticia, hipocresía y mentira entre los hombres" (philosophy and its proud reason has done nothing but destroy: it proscribed virtue and canonized crimes; it reigned for an instant: and who would count the laments that this impious reign has caused?).[74] For those whom Christianity was the source of all legitimate power, authority, and morality, eradicating Enlightenment philosophy in its irreligious, radical guise was a matter of society's life and death and a vital objective of the Spanish Church and people. Starting in 1821, there were populist risings against the revolution in the cities and countryside of many parts of Spain well beyond Navarre and Aragon. In 1823, in contrast to 1808, most of the populace supported the French invasion and the repression that followed.

In April 1823, 100,000 French troops poured across the Pyrenees. The Spanish army divided while the Church called on the devout not to resist Louis XVIII's "holy" invasion or in any way support the "godless" *constitucionales.* Efforts to mobilize something like the 1808 anti-French fury in reverse, behind the revolution, the Enlightenment, and the 1812 Constitution, soon came to nothing. There was simply not enough support. The common people, lamented Quintana, "obedient and submissive" by long habit, showed little ardour for the constitution and none whatever for enlightened values. The people preferred the royalist cry: "Absolute King and the Inquisition! Death to the *Liberales*!"[75] Rioting against the *constiucionales* erupted in many places. Among the victims was one of the most notable intellectual leaders of the 1808–12 revolution, Bartolomé José Gallardo (1776–1852), a peasant's son trained in philosophy at Salamanca, a passionate bibliophile avid for French books, and author of the *Diccionario Critico-Burlesco* (1811), the most anticlerical Spanish text of the age.[76] In 1814, Gallardo had fled via Lisbon to London, then remained in England until 1820, when he returned to Spain. In 1823, during popular rioting in support of the king, at Seville, a mob destroyed Gallardo's literary manuscripts, thousands of pages of his life's work, including his draft history of the Spanish theatre.

With the reactionary powers, the priesthood, and the nobles behind him, and in the New World the United States more concerned to exploit Spain's difficulties and encourage the independence movements than aid the Spanish constitutionalists, Fernando triumphed resoundingly for a second time, resuming all his former implacable rejectionism of popular sovereignty, secularism, Enlightenment, and revolution. The bishops were jubilant. The Inquisition was restored. All the books banned until 1820 were again prohibited. General Riego was publicly hanged, in Madrid, on 7 November 1823. Louis XVIII's crushing of the Spanish Revolution was endorsed by the European powers, as was its aftermath – a ferocious crackdown on *constitucionales* and all adversaries of royal and church authority.

NOTES

1 Leo Strauss, *Spinoza's Critique of Religion* (English translation [1965], original edition *Die Religionskritik Spinozas als Grundlage seiner Bibelwissenschaft* [Berlin: Akademie-Verlag, 1930]), new ed. (Chicago: University of Chicago Press, 1967), 35; Steven B. Smith, *Spinoza's Book of Life* (New Haven: Yale University Press, 2003), 191.

2 For Mühlpfortdt's republished articles from the 1970s and 1980s, see, Günter Mühlpfordt, *Halle-Leipziger Aufklärung. Kernstuck der Mitteldeutschen Aufklärung* (Halle: Mitteldeutscher Verlag, 2011).

3 Thomas Pangle, "The Light Shed on the Crucial Development of Strauss's Thought by His Correspondence with Gerhard Krűger," in *Reorientation: Leo Strauss in the 1930s*, ed. M.D. Yaffe and R.S. Ruderman (New York: Palgrave Macmillan 2014), 59–63.

4 Besides Henry F. May, *The Enlightenment in America* (New York: Oxford University Press, 1976), see Donald H. Meyer, *The Democratic Enlightenment* (New York: Capricorn Books, 1976), xiv–xxvi, and, especially, David Lundberg and Henry F. May, "The Enlightened Reader in America," *American Quarterly* 28 (1976): 262–93.

5 Jonathan Israel, *Revolutionary Ideas: An Intellectual History of the French Revolution from* The Rights of Man *to Robespierre* (Princeton: Princeton University Press, 2014), 180–203.

6 Carlos Rodríguez López-Brea, *Don Luis de Borbón. El Cardenal de los Liberales (1777–1823)* (Toledo: Junta de Comunidades de Castilla-La Mancha, 2002), 283–4; Albert Dérozier, *Manuel José Quintana y el nacimiento del liberalismo en España* (Madrid: Turner 1978), 687–8.

7 Daniel Muñoz Sempere, *La Inquisición Española como tema literario. Política, historia y ficción en el crisis del Antiguo Régimen* (Woodbridge: Tamesis, 2008), 69–70.

8 *Consejos que dirige á las Cortes y al pueblo español Jeremías Bentham: traducidos del inglés por José Joaquín de Mora* (Madrid: publisher?, 1820), prologue, 3.

9 Álvaro Flores Estrada, *Representación hecha a S.M.C. el señor Don Fernando VII* (np [London?], no publisher, London, 1818), 20–1, 38–9, 41.

10 S. Aprile, *Le Siècle des exilés. Bannis et proscrits de 1789 à la Commune* (Paris : CNRS éditions, 2010), 83–4; M. Isabella, *Risorgimento in Exile: Italian Émigrés and the Liberal International in the Post-Napoleonic Era* (Oxford: Oxford University Press, 2009), 22–30.

11 Marc Antoine Jullien, *Revue encyclopédique, ou analyse raisonnée des productions les plus remarquables dans la littérature, les sciences et les arts*, 3, 1819, 494.

12 Dérozier, *Manuel José Quintana*, 693, 700.

13 Mark Jarrett, *Congress of Vienna and Its Legacy. War and Great Power Diplomacy after Napoleon* (London: I.B.Tauris, 2014), 309–10.

14 Dérozier, *Manuel José Quintana*, 718–25.

15 *Representación que el Illmo. Dean y Cabildo de la S.ta Iglesia metropolitana de Burgos hace á S.A.S. La regencia del reyno, pidiendo,* [primero], *Que se restablezca El santo Tribunal de la Inquisición* (Burgos, 1823), 7.

16 Alejandro Agüero and Marta Lorente, "Penal Enlightenment in Spain: From Beccaria's Reception to the First Criminal Code," in *The Spanish Enlightenment Revisited*, ed. Jesús Astigarraga (Oxford: Voltaire Foundation, 2015), 235–63, here 252–6.

17 A. Martínez Garnica, "La Experiencia del Nuevo Reino de Granada," in *La Experiencias de 1808 en Iberoamérica*, ed. A. Ávila and P. Pérez Herrero (Mexico City: Universidad Nacional Autónoma de México [UNAM], 2008), 365–80, here 379–80.

18 Javier Usoz, "Political Economy and the Creation of the Public Sphere during the Spanish Enlightenment," in *The Spanish Enlightenment Revisited*, ed. Jesús Astigarraga (Oxford: Voltaire Foundation, 2015), 105–27, here 118.

19 Francisco Bethencourt, *The Inquisition: A Global History, 1478–1834* (Cambridge: Cambridge University Press, 1995) 10–15.

20 David Pantoja Morán, *El Supremo poder conservador. El diseño institucional en las primeras constituciones mexicanas* (Mexico City: Colegio de México, 2005), 535.

21 Martin Murphy, *Blanco White. Self-Exiled Spaniard* (New Haven, CT: Yale University Press, 1989), 111–12; Busaall, "Constitution," 122–3.

22 Joseph Blanco White, *Life of the Rev. Joseph Blanco White, written by himself, with portions of his Correspondence*, ed. John H. Thom (London: John Chapman, 3 vols, 1845), I: 375; Murphy, *Blanco White*, 111.
23 Manuel Torres Campos, *Bibliografía española contemporánea del derecho y de la política, 1800–1880*, 2 vols (Madrid, 1883), I: 56; Carlos Pérez Vaquero, "Introducción," in Montesquieu, *Del Espíritu de las Leyes* (Valladolid, 2008), 5–6.
24 [Jullien], *Revue Encyclopédique* X (April 1821), 170.
25 Torres Campos, *Bibliografía española contemporánea* I: 73, 84.
26 Torrres Campos, *Bibliografía española contemporánea* I: 72.
27 J.R. Spell, *Rousseau in the Spanish World before 1833. A Story in Franco-Spanish Literary Relations* (Austin: University of Texas Press, 1938), 208.
28 Concha Varela Orol, "Poder e censura: prohibitorum Libraria," in Concha Varela Orol and Martin González Fernández, *Heterodoxos e malditos. Lecturas prohibidas na Universidade de Santiago* (Santiago de Compostela: Universidad de Santiago de Compostela, 2002), 31–121, here 93, 116, 121.
29 Torres Campos, *Bibliografía española contemporánea* I: 56–7.
30 Ignacio Fernández Sarasola, "Ramón de Salas y la Nueva Ciencia Jurídica," *Teoría y Realidad constitucional* 28, 2011, 633–48, here 640–1.
31 *Boletín de la Librería* no. 23 (1895–6), no. 10, 155.
32 Rodríguez López-Brea, *Don Luis de Borbón*, 287.
33 Rodríguez López-Brea, *Don Luis de Borbón*, 286.
34 Varela Orol, "Poder e censura," 67.
35 Rodríguez López-Brea, *Don Luis de Borbón*, 302–4.
36 Muñoz Sempere, *La Inquisición Española como tema literario*, 66, 68.
37 Muñoz Sempere, *La Inquisición Española como tema literario*, 68.
38 Helena Establier Pérez, "Novela anticlerical y traducción en el Trienio Liberal. Diderot, Lewis y Radcliffe en España," *Dicenda. Cuadernos de Filología Hispánica* 30, 2012, 67–92.
39 Emilio La Parra López, *La Libertad de Prensa en la Cortes de Cadiz* (Valencia: Nau Llibres, 1984), 63–4; Varela Orol, "Poder e censura," 44.
40 Martin González Fernández, "Catálogo razoado de espíritos fortes," in Varela Orol and González Fernández, eds, *Heterodoxos e malditos*, 130.
41 Varela Orol, "Poder e censura," 46.
42 Spell, *Rousseau in the Spanish World*, 150–1.
43 *Boletín de la Librería* 22 (1894–5), no. 7, 109; Spell, *Rousseau in the Spanish World*, 206–8.
44 Gil Novales, "Notas en torno a Lecturas de Larra," in *Revisión de Larra (Protesta o Revolución?)*, in *Annales Littéraires de l'Université de Besançon*, 14, 1983, 36.

45 Gil Novales, “Notas en torno a Lecturas,” 40n12.
46 Pierre Naville, *Paul Thiry d'Holbach* (3rd ed., Paris: Gallimard, 1943), 418.
47 Naville, *Paul Thiry d'Holbach*, 134–9.
48 W.H. Wickwar, *Baron d'Holbach. A Prelude to the French Revolution* (New York: Augustus M. Kelley, 1968), 245; Jonathan Israel, *Enlightenment Contested: Philosophy, Modernity, and the Emancipation of Man 1670–1752* (Oxford: Oxford University Press, 2006), 726–7; see also the anonymous “preface de l”editeur' to d'Holbach, *Le Bon Sens du Curé J. Meslier* (Brussels: Librrairie philosophique, 1829), 5–12.
49 Max Pearson Cushing, *Baron d'Holbach: A Study of Eighteenth Century Radicalism in France* (New York: Burt Franklin, 1914), 89–90.
50 Mark Curran, *Atheism, Religion, and Enlightenment in Pre-Revolutionary Europe* (Woodbridge: The Boydell Press, 2012), 27–8, 54; O. Pecharroman, *Morals, Man, and Nature in the Enlightenment: A Study of the Baron d'Holbach's Work* (Washington, DC: University Press of America, 1977), 131.
51 Israel, *Enlightenment Contested*, 534.
52 David Holohan, “Introduction” to Paul-Henri Thiry, Baron d'Holbach, *Christianity Unveiled* (Kingston: Hodgson Press, 2008), x.
53 *Boletín de la Librería* 35, no. 7, 100.
54 Cushing, *Baron d'Holbach*, 103; González Fernández, “Catálogo razoado,” 479, 493.
55 Cushing, *Baron d'Holbach*, 103; Gil Novales, “Notas en torno a Lecturas,” 36.
56 Cushing, *Baron d'Holbach*, 93–4.
57 Cushing, *Baron d'Holbach*, 95–6.
58 *Boletín de la Librería* (Publicación mensual) XXXIV, 1906–7, 91.
59 Varela Orol, “Poder e censura,” 47, 110, 120.
60 Establier Pérez, “Novela anticlerical y traducción,” 74–5.
61 Jullien, *Revue encyclopedique* X (April 1821), 200; Establier Pérez, “Novela anticlerical y traducción,” 73.
62 Vincente Rocafuerte, “Prologo” to [Thomas Paine], *Ideas necesarias a todo pueblo Americano independiente, que quiera ser libre* [Sentido Comun (Common Sense)] (Philadelphia, 1821), 1–18.
63 G.L. Bastin, Álvaro Echeverri, and Ángela Campo, “Translation and the Emancipation of Hispanic America,” in *Translation, Resistance, Activism*, ed. M. Tymoczko (Amherst: University of Massachussetts Press, 2010), 59–61.
64 Manuel García de Sena, *La Independencia de la Costa Firme justificada por Thomas Paine Treinta Años ha* (Philadelphia: T and J. Palmer, 1811), 33.
65 A.O. Aldridge, *Early American Literature: A Comparative Approach* (Princeton: Princeton University Press, 1982), 221, 224–6.

66 Bastin, Echeverri, and Campo, "Translation and the Emancipation," 42–64, 60–1; Brewer-Carías, *Constituciones de Venezuela* I, 126–7.
67 Aldridge, *Early American Literature*, 233.
68 Antonio José Irisarri, *Semanario Republicano de Chile* (nos. 1–12, Santiago, 1813), VIII (18 September 1813), 49–50.
69 Irisarri, *Semanario Republicano* I (7 August 1813), 2–4.
70 Irisarri, *Semanario Republicano* II (14 August 1813), 9–14; Walter, "Revolution in Latin America," 120.
71 Irisarri, *Semanario Republicano* VIII (25 September 1813), 53.
72 Irisarri, *Semanario Republicano* VIII (25 September 1813), 63–4, 70.
73 Irisarri, *Semanario Republicano* XII (28 October 1813), 89.
74 *Representación que el Illmo. Dean y Cabildo de la S.ta Iglesia metropolitana de Burgos hace á S.A.S. La regencia del reyno, pidiendo,* [primero], *Que se restablezca El santo Tribunal de la Inquisición* (Burgos, 1823), 7.
75 Bethencourt, *The Inquisition*, 423.
76 Rodriguez López-Brea, *Don Luis de Borbón*, 211, 218.

Chapter Fifteen

A Clandestine Manuscript in the Vernacular: An 1822 Spanish Translation of the *Examen critique* of 1733

JOHN CHRISTIAN LAURSEN

The clandestine philosophical manuscripts of the seventeenth and eighteenth centuries sometimes had an afterlife in another language and another culture. This chapter is an analysis of a Spanish edition, published in 1822, of a French manuscript first circulated in 1733. The Spanish version was titled *Examen crítico de los apologistas del cristianismo.*[1] The place of publication, given as "Burdeos" or Bordeaux, could indicate that the translator lived in that city, but he could have lived somewhere else and simply published his book there. Or it may have been brought out somewhere else with a false publication place in order to confuse the censors. The translator's name is given as "J. B. J. G."

There is no "J. B. J. G." in the *Diccionario biográfico de España (1808–1833)*, but there is a "J. B. J.," Juan Bautista Jáuregui, for whom the entire entry is "Coronel de Ingenieros, 1823."[2] He was involved with a bridge in Guatemala in 1816 and was commander of the corps of engineers in the Kingdom of Guatemala 1820–1, and on 15 September 1821 he attended a meeting in the National Palace of Guatemala where the decision was made to declare independence from Spain.[3] In 1822 he was back in Spain, in charge of the fortifications of the town and castle of Miranda de Ebro.[4] It would not be surprising to find that a military engineer was involved in translating an anticlerical text like this one, since engineers had a scientific education, usually strongly influenced by French texts and practices, and had often travelled widely.[5] It has been pointed out that 979 of the 2,433 "afrancesados" or "Frenchified" Spaniards who supported José Bonaparte in 1813 and tended to admire revolutionary France and its anticlerical values were military men.[6] As another scholar puts it, in the years 1811–14 the Spanish military became "the first profession in which merit, rather than birth, determined entrance and advancement."[7] It has been claimed that "4000 junior officers ... had been won over to liberalism while being held as prisoners of war in France."[8] A military man translating an anti-religious text would fit with what has been described as "Spanish military liberalism."[9]

There are ten copies of the original manuscript still extant, dated to 1733 and titled *Examen critique des Apologistes de la Religion Chrétienne.*[10] The baron d'Holbach and Naigeon edited it and published it in 1766, with the author identified on the title page as "M. Fréret, Secrétaire perpétuel de l'Académie Royale des Inscriptions & Belles-Lettres."[11] Nicolas Fréret had died in 1749, so he could not be prosecuted for publishing the book, and his name could give it some prestige. When Alain Niderst brought out a modern edition in 2001, he called it "attribuable à Jean Lévesque de Burigny."[12]

There are two possible contexts for the translation, the French, where it was published, and the Spanish, presumably the intended readership. On the French side, Louis VIII had governed under a regime of moderate constitutionalism between 1816 and 1820, when an "ultra" reaction had set in. The publication of this work would not have been approved by the ultras, but it seems likely that the fact that it was a translation intended for distribution abroad probably meant it did not receive too much attention in France. Just after the publication of our book, in 1823, French troops intervened in Spain to suppress constitutionalism and restore royal authority to Fernando VII.

On the Spanish side, in 1820 a military revolt had forced Fernando VII to promise to abide by the constitution of 1808. A number of factors suggest the context: Bourdeaux was a centre of Spanish liberals in the years 1814–20, and thus local opinion might have supported such publications.[13] The years 1820 to 1823 were the years of openness: they are called the "Constitutional Triennium."[14] This was a window of opportunity for such publications.

In the Spanish context, the work was surely subversive of church and state. We have no information yet on its reception: whether it received attention from the authorities or from the Inquisition, which was suppressed in Spain in 1808–14 and again in 1820–3, but then restored and only finally abolished in 1834.

As a preliminary matter, let us return to the attribution of the manuscript. Niderst observes that some attributed the work to Voltaire (AN24). Several letters from Voltaire to friends in the months preceding its publication express his interest in seeing it, as if he had not seen it until it was published, but, as Niderst also observes, this could simply be his customary game-playing in order to be able to deny authorship (AN25–6). The case for attribution to Lévesque de Burigny is largely circumstantial (AN26). This was a writer who had published *Théologie payenne; ou Sentimens des philosophes and des Peuples Payens le plus célebres, sur Dieu, sur l'ame and sur les Devoirs de l'Homme,* 2 vols (Paris: De Bure, 1754) and has been credited with translating two of the anti-Christian works of Orobio de Castro for clandestine circulation: *La divinité de Jésus-Christ détruite* and *Dissertation sur le Messie.*[15]

We know from their other activities that when d'Holbach and Naigeon brought out the French publication of the *Examen critique* they did so with an intent to undermine Christianity. It is pretty clear that the Spanish translator intended the same. We shall proceed to analyse the apparatus he supplied with the translation: his prologue and his notes.

The "Prólogo del Traductor" defends the translated book on the ground of the importance of reason. "If reason exercised the empire that it should, things would receive attention in proportion to their importance, and the examination of the system upon the truth or falsity of which depends the unlimited happiness of mortals would occupy the first place among human considerations" (v). The problem is that both believers and unbelievers just go along with the times. "The century in which they live and the country in which they are born are the only determinants of their religious ideas" (vi). Thus, "most of the unbelievers of the nineteenth century would have followed the flag of Peter the Hermit in the eleventh century ... Some see only with the eyes of Aaron's brother or those of the son of Mary, and others think only with the understanding of the patriarch of Ferney or the philosopher of Geneva" (vi). We, on the other hand, the translator writes, "will see with our own eyes, think with our own understanding, substituting analysis and logic taken together for implicit faith" (vi). He concludes with the following: "I will finish, saying 'Since we take pride in being rational, we make use of reason; since we glory in living in the age of philosophy, we philosophize'" (vii–viii).

Now we can ask: how sincere is the translator? Is this only about rationality and philosophy, or is he really trying to undermine Christianity? The focus on reason and philosophy in the prologue could be taken as following in the tradition of d'Holbach and Naigeon. Naturally, the author had to write with care: some of his criticisms are worded ambiguously, and like Bayle and other critics of Christianity, they left room for deniability in case of accusations of heresy. The text probably belongs in the tradition of careful writing that has sometimes been associated with Leo Strauss, but can be found in many early modern texts.[16]

Is the Translator Being Ironical?

The prologue raises the question: is the translator being ironical? Irony, is, of course, the trope by which one implies the opposite of what one actually says. In the search for evidence, let us lay out another place that the question of possible irony is raised. Let us start with the last note the translator adds to the last sentence of the book (318–19). It is presented as the arguments in favour of the Christian religion that would appeal to any impartial reader. The first one is that Christianity is founded on faith, and thus that science and reason cannot undermine it. The second is that things are not always what they seem, such that reasons against Christianity might be paralogisms. The third is that perceptions of the truth are not necessarily truth, and thus that there are obscure and incomprehensible truths. The fourth is that every religion must be natural or supernatural, and since Christianity is not natural, it must be supernatural. The fifth and last is that contradictory propositions in Christianity do not prove its falsity because, as the mathematician Málesieux puts it, "there are incompatible truths" (319). To the objection that these arguments could be used in defence of any religion, he answers that "Christianity is different from the others" (319). If anyone objects to my reflections, I welcome stronger arguments, he concludes (319). Note that all of these "defences" of Christianity had been used in the Christian tradition, but that all of them are quite weak when seen from the perspective of the arguments made in the French version of the text and the arguments the translator had added in the notes. All of which suggests that this conclusion was added as protective colouring to give the translator credibility: he was not claiming to agree with the book, rather, he was merely translating it to help move rationality and philosophy forward. So, we can ask, is the translator being ironical here? Does he really mean to undermine Christianity by weak "defences" of it?

How can we answer this question? One way is to look for a pattern of irony in other notes.[17] And indeed one does emerge. The first note is to the sentence that reports that "St. Justin was the first, among the writers that we have, who had notice of the four evangelists who have come down to us"; the translator adds "And St. Irenaeus, the first and last that proved that there should be four evangelists because there are four cardinal directions. See Dupuis in his work *Origen de los cultos*, the explication of the Apocalypse" (10). This comment is perhaps ambiguous, but may be taken as an irony: the fact that Irenaeus is the last to assert something suggests that it did not find much support. The saint's reasoning is at least dubious.

The next comment is in response to the manuscript author's concession that the majority of the Christians of the early church were ready to die for Jesus. "It is necessary to concede something more, and that necessity is proved by the following reasoning of Freret," he writes (21).[18] The following reasoning is that if it is claimed that some of the early Christians were frauds and they, too, were ready to die for their false creeds, then, as the manuscript puts it, "among the first preachers of Christianity there were some who wanted to deceive their century" (21). So the translator has drawn attention to the point that if one admits that many early self-described Christians were willing to die for the religion, it must also be true that many early heretics or impostors were, too.

When "Freret" observes that St Justin had very little critical sense (*muy poca crítica*), the translator adds that "[n]or did he have much of an eye, since he transformed *Semoni Deo Sanco* into *Simoni Deo Sancto*, from which he concluded that the Romans had adored Simon Magus as God" (27). On the next page, he observes that "[i]f St. Justin had little critical sense, Tertullian was very credulous. He speaks with the most edifying confidence of the heavenly Jerusalem descending from the sky, and appearing in Judea for forty days. But then he lets us know that the apparition was at dawn, and the walls of Jerusalem faded away as the light in the sky increased" (28). This is not irony as much as direct criticism. But the translator's direct criticisms confirm the possibility of anti-Christian intentions behind the ambiguities of irony.

The translator's next intervention seems to be another irony. "If our unbelievers have denied any merit to the *canonical* Apocalypse, there have been people who were less unjust. In the East, one found the manuscript of the Apocalypse united with Aesop's fables" (37). Then there are no more interventions until page 62, where "Freret" reports that the early Christians were accused of "eating human meat" (62). The translator's note "defends" the Christians by observing that this accusation was based on "inexact information about the Eucharist" (62). Then he adds that "they had no idea about mystical *antropofagios* [maneaters]" (62). The latter certainly looks like an irony about Christian theology. On the next page he comments on Tacitus's hatred of the Christians: "Thus, we should not be surprised to see him say of the Christians: *Genus hominum superstitionis novae ac maleficae*" (63). There does not seem to be any reason to add this comment except to quote something more against the Christians.

On page 68 the translator draws attention to a dubious proof by Humphrey Ditton of Jewish recognition of the resurrection of Jesus: "proof of this was their persistence in following the law of Moses" (68). The logic was that since Jesus endorsed Judaism as the background for Christianity, the Jews should continue to observe their religion if they think he really was the Saviour and thought their religion was true as far as it went. One suspects that the translator thought that this was a dubious proof, although he does not spell it out. On the next page he observes that "Freret has not mentioned that, the incredulity of the Jews being part of the divine plan, as the Christian doctors assure us, God blinded the Jews so that they could not see the divinity of the miracles that were done" (69). This was also ambiguously simply an explanation, or an irony about the mental gymnastics that were required to include the reaction of the Jews as proof of the truth of Christianity.

In the next chapter, the number of comments increases. The French original observes that Tertullian speaks with assurance, and the translator adds a longish comment: "Assurance is very appropriate to the intrepid character of Tertullian. No one before him had said: *I believe because it is ridiculous* [*es un disparate*]; *I believe because it is absurd* [*credo quia absurdum*]. No one, probably, will repeat that. It is difficult for people to rise to that ideological sublimity [*sublimidad ideológico*] ... And, on what occasion did Tertullian have such a wandering idea? Speaking of the birth, passion, and death of J.C.! What a way to defend religion!" (77). His next comment undermines another early church father: "St. Ciprian had revelations in his dreams, and if he did not have any, he invited some children and excited them to ecstasy to instruct him, *because out of the mouth of babes comes the truth*" (78). And on the next page, Lactantius is described by the translator as "the Christian Cicero because he was not discontented concerning proofs. That which he has left us concerning the impossibility of the antipodes demonstrates this. He affirms that if they existed people would have their heads below and their legs above, which is impossible, and thus he makes maximum fun of the philosophers who maintained their existence" (79–80). We have a mix here of ironies and direct criticisms.

A few pages later, there are some slightly more ambiguous comments. The French reports that St Justin admits that pagans did exorcisms, but "affirms that Christians could expel demons that had resisted all the power of the pagan exorcists" (83). The translator observes: "Who doubts it? Only unbelievers could doubt it" (83). On the same page, when the French reports that Eusebius claimed that Apollonius's exorcist powers came from the devil, the translator adds: "This goes without saying" (83). This could be a sincere endorsement of Eusebius or an indictment of all exorcism. And on the next page, where the French says there were exorcists among the idolators, the translator comments: "How could there not be? The devil lives there more freely, as they say he lived more boldly among the Christians (Spanish and Portuguese) before the invention of the [papal] bull" (84). Is the translator affirming the Christian claims, or making fun of them by some sort of irony?

The next comments seem more obvious in their purport. When a missionary is reported to have felt sorry for the blindness of Chinese people after observing the first hour of a ceremony, the translator comments that "the bonzes were not so vain. We also have our talismans, we have holy scapulars, blessed rosaries, lambs of God, etc., etc., etc." (85). When Hippocrates is cited for the point that people have committed suicide to escape imagined spirits, the translator adds a "pitiful example of this kind of mental alienation": the Tempestarios discussed by St Agobard. Many people convinced themselves they were *tempestarias*, the causes of great storms, and persisted in this illusion although it led to their executions (87).

On the other hand, some religious people are given some credit by the translator. When it is suggested that the Jews be expelled because some Jews who had converted said they were tormented by devils sent by other Jews because they had converted, it occurred to a Jesuit that this may have been the product of a manipulation by people who wanted to confiscate the Jews' goods (91). The translator comments that "the Jesuits have been distinctive for their wisdom. The other religious institutions have remained far behind in this area" (91). The translator comments that when further investigation was conducted by means of torture, "here we have again the same faulty method of discovering the truth. It is true that in this case the declaration of guilt came after the first lashes, but the Jews could have feared the continuation" (91). So the accused might not have been guilty.

Concerning a report of a devil who could not understand much Latin during the exorcism, and thus raised the suspicion that it was really the woman who was being exorcized, the translator comments: "and why do we think there are no classes in devil society?" (93). This seems to be a transparent making fun of the anthropomorphism of the imagined world of the devils. He also quotes another unmasking of a devil who had promised to raise all unbelievers to the roof of the church: "Here you can see the service provided by the unbelievers! To throw cold water on the most entertaining ceremonies" (98).

Sometimes the translator allows himself a certain facetiousness. When it is reported that an exorcism resulted in a pregnancy, he comments that "in the end, this increases the number of Christians" (101). And when a pious prelate asserts that any bishop has seen lots of false obsessions, doubtful miracles, and fake visions that have been criticized by the malign men of the century, the translator observes: "Who is more incredulous than the most credulous?" (101). When it is said that certain words are considered an infallible remedy against certain illnesses, the translator asks: "Why not against all illnesses? Were they specific?" (103). He comments that a long list of magical words "was a complete system of magical medicine" (104). When the French reports that even the Jews cured illnesses by pronouncing the name of Jesus Christ, the translator observes that "they were luckier than many Christians of today" (105). And at the end of chapter V, when the French asserts that the emperor Valentinian had a young man who tried to cure epilepsy by pronouncing seven letters of the alphabet beheaded, he adds that "this emperor did not want cheap cures" (107). One is not sure if he is joking, or means it. A sign of good irony.

In the next chapter, the original mentions that the early enemies of the Christians called them the lowest of the low. The translator observes that "one could apply to J. C. what was said about Antisthenes: *Esurire docet, et discipulos invenit.* Nevertheless, there were very powerful reasons for preaching *so dry* a system" (109). When the French author observes that in China and Japan distinguished and literate people listened to the Christian missionaries with disgust, the translator adds that "listening to the animated discourse of our missionaries, the enlightened Chinese coolly said *if they are right, why are they angry?* In effect, the conviction belongs to the ideology, the functions of the rhetoric try to move, and not seldom to seduce ... *Declamation,* as a man of talent has said ingeniously ... *is the eloquence of error*" (113). When the author says that the Japanese who converted to Christianity were all desperately poor people who sought martyrdom to escape from their suffering, the translator disagrees: "This could have been one of the reasons ... but I do not think it was the principal one. Couldn't they have committed suicide to escape? Their religion does not prohibit suicide ... and neither do their customs. Thus the fundamental reason must have been something else" (114).

When the author brings up the alleged miracles of Deacon Paris, by which a multitude of people claimed to have been cured, the translator adds: "add to this the history of vampires, so well received by Father Calmet" (115). When the author quotes Seneca on the judgment of the people, the translator adds another citation from him: "he also says *Aestimes judicia, non numeres*" (118). When the author reports that Christianity was not accepted at first in Judaea or Rome, the translator observes that "one always observes that notorious facts are given more credit in the countries where they take place than in countries far away. That did not happen with the miracles of J. C. God wanted, in this case, to undermine the general rule" (118). It sounds to me like the translator is speaking with irony.

One of the longest of the translator's interventions comes when the author compares the early Christians with the prophets of the Dauphiné and the fanatics of the Cevennes. "There are those who say that Christianity was a religion of circumstance, and their reasoning is as follows" (119). We may summarize the reasoning the translator quotes – apparently from another anti-Christian source – as the point that most of the world was degraded and enslaved in Jesus's day, and his message appealed to the downtrodden. The translator adds: "[B]ut these reasonings should not alter our faith. The sphere of Christian faith is very high; that of human science cannot reach it" (120). As so often the case, this could be a sincere defence of Christianity, or an ironical undermining of it.

Direct Criticisms Confirm the Ironies

At this point I think we can see that most of the translator's notes are either direct criticisms of Christianity, or ironies with indirectly critical implications. When the French asserts that some Romans stopped celebrating pagan festivals in order to please the emperor, the translator adds some verse from Claudian and adds: "When Augustus drank, Poland was drunk" (124). When Constantine had the philosopher Sopatre executed, the translator adds: "This one really understood the force of the expression *compelle entrare*" (124). Some pages later, when the author has asserted that "only by employing the most violent means was paganism destroyed and completely replaced by the Christian religion," the translator adds only: "*Compelle entrare*" (132). The French asks why persecution could not have the success that it had against the Christians in Japan in other countries as well; here the translator adds: "and what the emperors did against the pagans" (135). These are direct criticisms of Christianity, again providing confirmation of the intentions behind the indirect ironies.

At the end of chapter VII the translator reinforces the observations of the original on the use of violence with the point that

> the contents of this chapter demonstrate that there is no idea or habit, no matter how deeply rooted, that can resist the logic of constant force. This logic is victorious especially against error, when it is undermined enough. Against universal and highly important truths, its victory would be ephemeral; like the Phoenix, they will be reborn from ashes, and violence itself will come to prostrate itself before their feet, abandoning the sacrilegious flags of its persecutors. See what has happened to the tyrants who persecuted the philosophers: they have been stigmatized by the queen of the world, public opinion. Their kingdom is going to end, and that of philosophy arrive. (135)

This seems to be a kind of *cri de coeur* of the translator.

When the French comments on the people who throw themselves in front of the Juggernaut in India so that they will be reborn in a happier world, the translator adds only, "Amen" (147). Irony? Hard to tell.

The translator does not hesitate to critique the author he is translating. When the French describes the barbarous spectacle of people who have preferred to die rather than to abjure, the translator adds: "*barbarous* on the part of the oppressors, *pitiable* on the part of the oppressed" (153). When the French author seems to have little respect for the Sabeans, the translator mentions him by name: "Certainly eminently erudite men did not see Sabeanism with the same disrespect as Freret, but maintained that the metaphysical systems of religion that presently divide the greater part of the world are nothing but strange degenerations of the doctrine of the Sabeans," and here he cites Volney and Dupuis (159). At another point he cites the same authors: "Freret follows the old opinion. Volney and Dupuis follow another one. See *The Ruins of Palmyra* by the first, and *The Origin of Cults* by the second" (168). And later, when the French is commenting on the Indian understanding of God, he adds that "they find, too, the trinity and the divine incarnation: a *Cris-en* or *Cris-na*, like in our evangelical books the *Cris-tos.* See the works of Volney and Dupuis" (171).

Sometimes it does seem that the translator is pious. When the French refers to wrestling with the devil to save a soul, the translator argues: "We should not reject this event as not realistic. Jacob fought with God for a whole night, and for all the former [*sic* latter?] begged him to let him go *because dawn was coming*, the son of Isaac persisted in his stance of not letting him go until he had given him his blessing, and he got it, although at the price of a limp. Genesis, esp. 32, v. 24 and following" (163). I ask again, is this serious or tongue-in-cheek?

In what appears to be making fun of scholastic language, the translator comments on a passage where the French refers to punishing persecutors that maybe "humans had a revelation that made them distinguish *inflictive* disasters from those which are *probative* or *permissive*" (166). When the French comments that Themistius and Simplicius had said that pilgrimages were unnecessary because God is everywhere, the translator adds: "It is known that Themistius and Simplicius were not in charge of any sanctuary" (and thus did not have any self-interested reason to encourage pilgrimages) (174). When the French quotes Socrates on God's omniscience, the translator observes that "the god of Noah is more popular [in the sense of adapted to the people] than Socrates's god. He descended from the heavens in person to inspect the Tower of Babel. Genesis, c. 11, v. 5" (175). This is an ironic observation on anthropomorphism.

The next few pages contain some of the translator's longest and most densely packed comments. When the French discusses Plato's view of God as wholly benevolent, the consequence being that the origin of evil must be something outside of God, the translator comments that "the coexistence of evil and a supreme Being elevated to the peak of perfection is one of the most difficult problems" (176). He observes that the problem has not been resolved, that dualism would solve the cosmological aspect of the problem but not the ontological, and that the idea of a supreme Being that was not perfect would succumb to all of these objections (176). When the French comments on Plato's view of the immortality of the soul, the translator comments that this is a very important question and that common sense or analogies would resolve the question but that philosophers think those are not good reasons (177). Under cover of pretending to comment on Plato he is really commenting on Christian theologians, and without explaining which way common sense would go, he is protected from charges of heresy. Revealing his admiration for the Enlightenment, he adds that the question of the immortality of the soul has not yet been subjected to the analytical scalpel, which was only invented in the eighteenth century (177). A couple of pages later he also appeals to "analytical heads" which cannot fathom some of the solutions offered in debates about freedom of the will (179).

When the French reports that the Greeks and Romans said that the immortality of the soul could not be disputed without impiety, he adds that "nevertheless, Caesar did not recognize the immortality of the soul in his discourse to the senate" concerning the accomplices of Catiline (178). And when the French argues that the best philosophers believed there could be no morality without freedom of the will, the translator observes that if morality means the principles of practical reason or the knowledge of well-regulated customs, there is no reason why they cannot exist without freedom of the will, but if it is defined as something that cannot exist without freedom of the will, then by definition it cannot exist, so no one would dispute it (178–9).

When the French insists that the best philosophers have always believed in an eternal moral law, the translator refers to the "unsustainable paradox" that there is no natural law (180). He claims to deduce the existence of natural law from the existence of beings who have relations with one another (180). After reporting that the moral system of our day rests on individual interests and pleasure, he asks whether we should not recognize the common good as the better basis for morals, as the Stoics did (181). To the Golden Rule that we should only do to others what we would want them to do to us, he adds the specification, "assuming those desires are just" (184). When the French comments on the rights of hospitality, the translator adds a note of rhetorical appeal: "When will civilization abandon the shameful rights of calculating morals and adopt, for philanthropic reasons, the great principles of universal fraternity? When will men rise to the heights that correspond to the monarch of the earth? ..." (184).

At one point the translator reveals his socialist ideas. "Opulence hardens the heart ... even property itself has an anti-fraternal influence. One of the most celebrated public writers of the last century called it *the original sin of society*" (185). He piously adds that "these ideas scandalize us, and we Christians are the first to look with aversion on maxims established by the first propagators of our religion" (185).

Another example of his irony is the following: where "Freret" refers to a Siamese law containing four hundred articles, the translator observes that "[t]he concision of this law is what I praise. It reminds me of a bull of Leo X against Luther in which one sentence contained more than 400 words" (189).

When the French reports that ecclesiastical ambition had come to the point of transforming states and dethroning kings, the translator gives a long restatement of the theory of Gregory VII about the indirect authority of the popes over the temporal authorities (196). He remarks that it is subtle, but he refers to the resulting papal authority as "dictadura pontífica" and claims that some years ago the Roman court had returned to its "antigua dictadura" (197). He also observes that the passive resistance of the early church is no longer to the taste of the Christians, and that Belarmine had admitted that the only reason the early Christians did not try to dethrone the emperors was that they lacked the power to do so (197). "What a pretty key for deciphering certain moral enigmas!," he exclaims (197).

When it is reported that Ravaillac assassinated Henry IV because of his disagreements with the Holy See, the translator adds that the king "was going to achieve the eminently philanthropic idea" of a federation of Europe, "without which the progressive march of the human spirit will never have all the speed and majesty possible" (201). When St Louis is quoted for recommending the execution of unbelievers and blasphemers, the translator adds: "The argument of St. Louis was, if not Christian, at least victorious. His cousin Ferdinand carried on his shoulders the firewood for burning the heretics" (202). Then, when the French says that early doctors of the church had said that "violence should never be used to support the truth," the translator adds "when it is impossible," implying of course that they would use it if they could (203). When the French observes that more powerful leaders made no distinction between rebels and those who did not blindly accept the decisions of the church, the translator adds that "the recalcitrants against the spiritual authority were hung in front of the rest of the criminals" (203). The Christians changed their tune after the Roman emperors converted and began to resort to force, on which the translator comments: "this is to know how to adapt to circumstances: *Autre temps, autre façon de voir*," he quotes in French (204). More observations on Christian violence include these exclamations: "This is how a God of mercy has been transformed into a God of vengeance by his ministers! This is how they have insulted the heavens and bloodied the earth!" (205). And when the execution of Servetus is mentioned, the translator observes that "this is the Servetus who can dispute with good reason the distinguished Harvey for the glory of having discovered the circulation of blood!" (205).

A reference in the French to the Inquisition provokes a long diatribe against it in one of the translator's footnotes. "Sensitive souls! Console yourselves: [the Inquisition] has disappeared forever ... and the names of Fernando the Catholic, of John III, and of their infamous satellites will be eternally consigned to the bloody annals of that hellish institution" (206). "But intolerance still exists! ... when will people realize that religious intolerance is the enemy of liberty, of population, of wealth, of civilization, and of public and private happiness?" (206). There are many more such exclamations. When the French refers the reader to Limborch on the Inquisition, the translator adds references to Puigblanc's *Inquisición sin máscara* and Llorente's *Historia de la Inquisición* (207; and a reference to Llorente on 215). When the French reports on the slaughter of the Albigenses, the translator comments: "And these adore a crucified God! ... No, they are not sons of Jesus, they are sons of Lucifer" (208). When the French reports that some philosophical ideas have been prohibited by the church, the translator adds that "with the celebrated Ramus intolerance went further. His singular anti-Aristotelianism cost him his life" (212). And then he quotes what some Christian peripatetics said Aristotle said about Moses: "That barbarian speaks well, but proves nothing" (213).

Patriotic Anti-Christian Irony

The translator is not anti-Spanish: he is against religious persecution wherever he finds it. So when the French praises the English for abolishing the burning of heretics, he objects that the English still deny some civil rights to Catholics: "And that nation calls itself philosophical!" (207). And he will not accept anti-Spanish exaggerations: when the French quotes Bartolomé de Las Casas to the effect that three million natives on the island of Santo Domingo were reduced to two hundred, he observes that it was probably only around a million to begin with and they may not have been reduced quite as much as to two hundred (217; and more exaggeration at 219–20). He also observes that indigenous castes do not become extinct if they are mixed with another race, but admits that Santo Domingo was the principal theatre of the atrocities of the first Europeans (217). And faced with other inaccuracies in Las Casas, he provides a substantial list of reasons for putting the missionary's views into perspective (218). He admits "the cruelty of the first conquistadors and colonists, not a systematic atrocity of the government," and he asserts that some of that cruelty was the result of religious fanaticism (218–19). And he reminds the reader that while trying to save the Indios, Las Casas was prepared to import African slaves to do their work (222). Nevertheless, when the French reports Las Casas's report that a Spanish hunter had fed a native baby to his dogs, the translator exclaims: "And nature is a passive spectator of such atrocities! ... And the sun shines on those monsters, and the earth supports them!" (222).

In another piece of criticism, when the French quotes Arnauld calling adultery a crime, the translator remarks that it is not a crime but a misdemeanour, and if a crime only a crime by positive law, not a crime by nature (230). When Orobio de Castro is quoted for explaining what will happen when the Messiah comes, the translator adds: "We will have to wait a long time, Mr. Orobio" and "it is easy to speak from behind a wall" (presumably meaning when your prediction cannot be contradicted because the outcome is in the future) (235).

The translator makes the point that if something like the first chapters of Genesis can be considered allegorical, then the Redemption can be so considered as well (237). He reports that Volney and Dupuis, whom he has cited before, give some chapters an astrological explanation, and he adds that they raise difficulties about a literal interpretation of the flood (239–40). The story of Balaam's ass and the story of the serpent, the translator comments, "are equally [just] stories" (240). The translator also supplies his own hypothetical natural explanation of the flood, with a conclusion by way of a quote from Fontenelle: "anything is possible" (241). He also supplies in a footnote some remarks about what we know about the laws of nature, and that all we can really say is that something exceeds the ordinary forces of nature (243). And he adds a Spanish epigram about Noah and the flood, and wine (244).

Other notes discuss the Chinese proofs of the age of the earth. The translator observes that "things are not always what they appear," with some remarks about sufficient grace that is not sufficient (i.e., here he is making fun of theological distinctions) (247). In one note he compares Grotius's literalism in reading Biblical texts with Father Calmet's acceptance of accounts of vampires (257). In another he makes fun of demons mentioned in the Bible (258), and in another he cites mention of the Macedonians in the Book of Esther to help document its age (260–1). When "Freret" reminds his readers that Jesus prohibited war, the translator quotes Tertullian saying that a Christian could not be a soldier, nor engage in commerce or be a magistrate (263). When "Freret" observes that Christian ascetic values are only for selected people, the translator observes that they are not convenient for political society in ordinary times, but they can be helpful in the extraordinary times of a religion being born (264).

Other notes observe that predictions of the end of the world are made *ad terrorum* (265) and that predictions of the end of the world have had to be renewed several times (266). The translator quotes Rousseau for one of his encomiums of the majesty of the Bible speaking directly to his heart, while observing that the orthodox were not usually fond of his treatment of religion (267). When "Freret" cites Jurieu, the translator remarks that Jurieu was more of a theologian than a philosopher, with the result that ignorance of basic principles led him to pitiful paralogisms (274; see also 289 questioning Jurieu's logic). When "Freret" asks us what we would think of a prince who issued obscure and confusing decrees, in analogy to God, the translator remarks that "this is reasoning in a profane mode" (276).

When the French text observes that "a religion whose proofs are not within the reach of all reasonable men cannot be the religion established by God for the simple and ignorant," the translator adds a note: "Unless the instruction of the learned is attributed to the ignorant, such that the original sin of our first ancestors has been imputed to us, their degenerate children – But which learned men should we follow? Those of the Tiber or those of the Ganges? – This is now a new difficulty" (280).

The translator questions Pierre Nicole's logic in several places (286, 290). When Nicole argues that a man who cannot know something for himself is obligated to try to know it through another, the translator adds that if he cannot know it himself or through another, he is not obligated to know it (290). He also criticizes Bossuet for a too limited sense of what due examination means (296). He cites Newton's commentary on the Apocalypse as proof that "mathematical science, without ideological spirit, does not preserve us from intellectual degradation" (298).

When the French reads that "there is nothing more absurd than to maintain that the mysteries of the Christian religion conform to our inner dispositions," the translator provides a long note criticizing Leibniz's principle that the nonconformity of the principles of Christianity with natural reason does not imply contradiction (299). When the French observes that most people take their religion from the place where they live, the translator adds that "a celebrated philosopher from the past century said that religion was a matter of geography; and he could have added, or chronology" (307). To a discussion of the mechanics of belief he adds the observation that "Helvetius said that the Christians did not believe, but that they believed they believed" (307).

When Fénelon is quoted as charging the Christians with being enthusiasts, the translator observes: "[W]asn't [Fénelon's] quietism an enthusiasm? Wasn't [his friend] Madame Guyon an enthusiast?" (310). He engages in his own philosophical distinctions when he claims that the physical order depends on the true nature of things, but the moral order depends on what we make of it: he coins the terms "existimada" and "existimación" for what seems to mean our estimate of what something is (314). When Father Maudit is cited for the principle that our interests should not weigh in our proofs of the truth of things, the translator adds that "but they usually contribute quite a bit to the persuasion of people" (315).

The notes to our text allow us to conclude that the 1822 translator of the 1733 French manuscript used a mix of direct criticism and indirect irony to undermine Christianity. The overall effect of his notes would have been to reinforce the message of Lévesque, d'Holbach, and Naigeon for Spanish readers in the nineteenth century.[19] The translation into the vernacular would have spread the message of the French author and editors into another time and place.

NOTES

1 J. B. J. G., *Examen crítico de los apologistas del cristianismo* (Burdeos: La Imprenta de Lawalle Jóven, 1822). It is clear from variant readings in the Spanish version that follow the printed version of 1766, not the manuscripts, that it was translated from one of the printed versions. Hereafter cited in the text by page number. WorldCat gives only one copy of this book extant, at the Bibliothéque Nationale, Paris, but Google Books has reproduced one from the Biblioteca de Catalunya in Barcelona.

2 "Jáuregui, Juan Bautista," in Alberto Gil Novales, ed., *Diccionario biográfico de España (1808–1833)* (Madrid: Fundación MAPFRE, 2010), vol. 2, 1569. Spaniards sometimes do and sometimes don't use their "segundo apellado," or second family name, so it would not be unusual if someone went by Juan Bautista Jáuregui for most purposes but signed something with all four initials.

3 See http://www.academiahngeohistoria.org/app/download/10109156357/3+EL+PUENTE+MALLOL.pdf?t=1439765856; Rodrigo Moreno Gutiérrez, *La Trigarancia. Fuerzas armadas en la consumación de la independencia – Nueva*

España, 1820–1821 (Mexico City: UNAM, 2016), 390; Jorge Barraza Ibarra, *Historia del Pensamiento Político en El Salvador*, vol. 1 (San Salvador: Editorial Universidad Francisco Gavidia, 2011), 110, 376–7n175. I owe the latter two sources to Javier Fernández Sebastián.

4 Carlos Diez Javiz and Alberto Otal Sáez, "El Castillo de Miranda de Ebro," *López de Gámiz: Boletín del Instituto Municipal de Historia de Miranda de Ebro* 33, 1999, 29–68. I owe this source to Javier Fernández Sebastián.

5 On some of the conditions for free-thinking in Spain in the eighteenth century, see John Christian Laursen, "When Can You Think Something?," *Daimon: Revista Internacional de filosofía*, 58, 2013, 179–84.

6 Miguel Artola, *Los afrancesados*, 2nd ed. (Madrid: Alianza Editorial, 1998), 260.

7 Carolyn Boyd, "The Military and Politics 1808–1875," in *Spanish History since 1808*, ed. J. Alvarez Junco and Adrian Shubert (New York: Oxford University Press, 2000), 66.

8 Boyd, "The Military and Politics," 67.

9 Raymond Carr, *Spain 1808–1976*, 2nd ed. (Oxford: Oxford University Press, 1982), 139.

10 Alain Niderst collated seven of them in a modern edition, *Examen critique des Apologistes de la Religion Chrétienne*, ed. Alain Niderst (Paris: Champion, 2001). Hereafter cited in the text with the initials "AN" and the page numbers. Miguel Benitez records nine in *La cara oculta de las luces* (Valencia: Biblioteca Valenciana, 2003), adding Berlin and Rouen, 49. Ira Wade recorded one in Rouen that Niderst said he could not find (AN 20). The tenth copy is in the possession of Martin Mulsow of Erfurt. Its title is "Etabilissement du Christianisme ou Réflexions critique sur les argumens employés pour prouver la Religion Chrétienne," just like the copy in the Bibliothèque d'Arsenal 2125. Mulsow reports that his copy seems never to have been in the possession of a library but always in private hands.

11 [Anon.], *Examen critique des Apologistes de la Religion Chrétienne* (N.p.: n.p., 1766). Later editions include same title, n.p., 1767 [a distinct edition]; n.p., 1768; new edition, n.p., 1775; London, 1777; Paris: Masson, 1823. Reprinted in *Oeuvres complettes de M. Fréret*, London, 1775, vol. I; *Oeuvres philosophiques de M. Freret*, London, 1776, first part; *Oeuvres de Fréret*, London, 1778, vol. I; London, 1787, vol. II; Paris, Servière et Bastien, 1792, vol. III; *Oeuvres complètes de Freret, Secrétaire de l'Académie des Inscriptions et Belles Lettres. Edition augmentée de plusieurs ouvrages inédits, et rédigée par feu M. de Septchênes*, Paris, an IV [1796], vol. XIX. There was also a German translation, which was not identified as such until recently because the title is totally different and it is only in parts a literal translation and in other parts a free German version,

with additions and partly in different order. The title of this anonymous book is *Hierokles, oder Prüfung und Verteidigung der christlichen Religion* (Halle, 1785). See Martin Mulsow, "Deutscher Deismus der Spätaufklärung. Christian Ludwig Paalzow zwischen Übersetzung, Bekenntnis, Montage und Parodie," in *Gestalten des Deismus in Europa*, ed. Winfried Schröder (Wiesbaden: Steiner, 2013), 161–202, esp. 172f.

12 AN title page.

13 Artola, *Los afrancesados*, 251.

14 Carr, *Spain 1808–1976*, 130.

15 Miguel Benitez, *Le Foyer clandestin des Lumières*, vol. 2 (Paris: Champion, 2013), 689.

16 See, for example, Winfried Schröder, ed., *Reading between the Lines: Leo Strauss and the History of Early Modern Philosophy* (Berlin: De Gruyter, 2015).

17 We can identify them because it is explicitly stated that "the alphabetical notes are from the translator" (vii).

18 Since the translator refers to the author of the manuscript as "Freret," when I am referring to his attributions to Fréret I will keep the name in quotation marks. He also wrote "Freret" without an accent mark, so I have followed his practice.

19 The translator added an "appendix" on difficulties in interpreting the book of Genesis that sustains five propositions about the Old Testament (330–5). The translator adds a note in the same form he has used in the text, suggesting that the appendix was also a translation. That note quotes Volney on misleading translations. It seems unlikely the translator would have inserted such a note in his own text; therefore the appendix must be a translation of someone else's text. I have not yet been able to identify it.

This chapter is a revised version of an article that appeared in French: "La *fortuna* d'un manuscrit clandestine. Une traduction espagnole de l'*Examen critique,*" *La Lettre clandestine*, 25, 2017, 59–81.

Afterword

JOHN CHRISTIAN LAURSEN

The chapters in this book have explored numerous heterodox clandestine philosophical manuscripts in their diverse contexts in Europe from 1620 to 1822. The history of this philosophical literature serves as a complement to the histories of philosophy and of subversive ideas that have concentrated on the main printed works. It turns out that significant philosophical and even scientific work was taking place underground, in the manuscripts that were written and circulated in this period. They were usually underground because they were subversive of church or state or both. This afterword situates this body of philosophical manuscripts in its context of other sorts of manuscript and print publication and of other reasons for clandestinity.

One thing we can emphasize here is the heterogeneity of the manuscripts and of their *fortuna.* Some were written for the exclusive use of the author, some just for friends, some were clearly written for narrow circles of elite intellectuals, some for a wider public, some for posterity perhaps conceived in decades or centuries. Some were short and some were very long. Some were occasional pieces, dashed off in a few days or weeks, some represented years of hard work, and some were the product of a lifetime of reflection. Some were quite original, and others were pastiches of other people's ideas. Some were written entirely as an intellectual or moral exercise, and some were written as potboilers for the growing market in subversive literature. Some of the authors were well aware that wealthy and influential people like Queen Christina of Sweden, Prince Eugene of Savoy, and Count Otto Thott of the Danish court had authorized agents all over Europe to purchase clandestine manuscripts for them. Some even repackaged subversive manuscripts with new titles to sell them again to the same careless buyers.

The authors were a wide range, too. Some were state officials, some churchmen, some private intellectuals, and some are unknown to us. Some were urban, some lived in small villages or country towns. Some wrote only manuscripts, and some wrote both published works and clandestine manuscripts. Some of the manuscripts were published almost immediately, some were published decades after being written and circulating in manuscript, some took centuries to appear in print, and some have never been printed. We have found them across Europe, and suspect that some may be found on other continents.

The variety is almost endless. Some of the manuscripts were quite philosophical, but others were rather superficial. If it may be asserted that the manuscripts that dealt with sexuality were not directly philosophical, it may be answered that the personal and pornographic have always been political and philosophical in their impact and implications. Even the superficial manuscripts could have an impact in making fun of church, state, traditions, and any other authorities.

And this is, in fact, one of the main things that ties the manuscripts together. They are all critical of something. An anodyne encomium to nature or celebration of a person would not count as a clandestine heterodox manuscript, even if it had a bit of philosophy in it. There has to be, at least *prima facie*, a reason why they were circulated clandestinely. And that was almost always some element of subversion, of threat to someone in a position to retaliate. If we may follow up on the theme of diversity, multiplicity, variety in the manuscripts, we see that as a whole they also promote diversity, multiplicity, and variety in social and intellectual life. As it has been felicitously put, many of them reject the "monos" of monogamy, monotheism, and monarchy. Some of the manuscripts explored some of the variety that may be found in sexuality, including polygamy. No one has yet identified the precise limits of the sexual heterogeneity found in the manuscripts taken together: we need to know how far the authors of this *corpus* were willing to go, and what their limits were. As for religion, many of the manuscripts reveal toleration of plurality, and a few even argue for atheism. There are paradoxes such as that Spinoza, the great philosophical monist who would brook no multiplicity of truths, actually encouraged multiplicity in interpretations of religion. Is it tolerant or is it intolerant to insist, as he did, that everyone agree with a list of religious truths, but then allow everyone to interpret them their own way?[1] Something similar can be said for the rejection of monarchy: was it complete, or were they just rejecting particular monarchies or forms of monarchy? When they promoted republicanism, was this a backward-looking Roman republicanism, a Christian republicanism, or some forward-looking republicanism that has yet to be described in the scholarly literature? If monarchy is rejected, is that in favour of polyarchy or anarchy? Small groups of what seem to be anarchists, known as the Levellers, existed in England during the Civil War. Did any of their ideas and practices make it into clandestine philosophical manuscripts? We still do not know the limits of the political pluralism and heterogeneity of the clandestine manuscripts.

Clandestine and Heterodox Print

Many scholars have studied the clandestine printed literature of the seventeenth and eighteenth centuries, some of which circulated underground because it might or did draw the ire of church and state authorities. So, for example, Robert Darnton has studied what he calls "the literary underground of the Old Regime" and "the forbidden bestsellers of pre-revolutionary France."[2] Many of the texts he studied owed their notoriety to pornography, not philosophy. But his idea of the "corpus of clandestine literature in France, 1769–1789" is almost entirely printed materials.[3] His specialty is "publishing and sedition," not the unpublished but sometimes widely circulated seditious manuscripts we have studied here.[4] There is no doubt that, as he puts it, state censorship "shaped literature" in the seventeenth and eighteenth centuries, but he does not consider the manuscript literature at any length, and that is what we have done here.[5]

Other genres of printed literature could be heterodox and clandestine and subject to censorship and repression just as much as our manuscripts. Simon Dickie has studied the forgotten comic literature of the eighteenth century. He found a vast *corpus* of comic novels, jestbooks, farces, and cartoons subversive of church, state, and everything else, but most of it was printed, not manuscript, and again, not very philosophical like our texts.[6]

Other Types of Manuscripts

Clandestine and heterodox philosophical manuscripts were only a subset of all manuscripts in this period. Until the invention of the printing press, of course, all writings circulated in manuscript form. The invention of the printing press by no means obliterated the continuing practice of circulating manuscripts. Harold Love provided a survey of what he called "scribal publication in seventeenth-century England" that made the point that many seventeenth-century English poets such as Donne, Corbett, Marvell, Philips, Traherne, and Rochester wrote primarily for manuscript transmission.[7] Other manuscripts in circulation included newsletters, weekly accounts of what was going on at court, and reports of the speeches in Parliament, often in multiple manuscripts.[8] These were not, of course, the philosophical manuscripts we have considered in this volume. Love's later work on satire demonstrated that printed texts and manuscripts often existed side by side, and were clandestine because of the explosive nature of their contents, but again, they were not philosophical manuscripts.[9]

The sheer numbers of manuscripts in the period are impressive. Peter Beal provided an index in four volumes of the sorts of literary manuscripts that were circulating in England in the years 1450 to 1700.[10] Presumably similar numbers could be found in French, German, Latin, and maybe other languages. If the number of manuscripts is smaller in some of the less widespread languages that does not necessarily mean they were less important for their populations.

Manuscript publication was sometimes used by women because of cultural norms that discouraged them from appearing in the masculine print sphere. But recent work has brought out the point that there were many other reasons why a woman might publish in manuscript even though she could have published in print.[11] As George Justice pointed out, scribal publication remained, even as late as the end of the eighteenth century, a viable "alternative mode of publication" alongside print.[12] It has been pointed out that manuscripts could acquire the cachet of exclusivity and elite forbidden pleasure that public print could not provide.[13]

Beyond the Core Languages

The final section of this volume consists of chapters on the reception or afterlife of the heterodox clandestine literature in Spain in the early nineteenth century. One special dimension of this section is the point that Spain may have been one of the last places anyone would have looked for heterodox literature, famous as it was for the Inquisition and monarchic government. But it turns out that given porous borders, inefficient policing, and education and travel abroad, a surprising amount of subversive literature came in during the eighteenth century, mostly from France.[14] And there were plenty of people who were eager to take advantage of what has been called the "liberal Triennium" from 1820 to 1823 in which *de facto* freedom of the press existed because of a number of political contingencies, including the Napoleonic invasion and its aftermath.

Similar work should be undertaken for all of the countries in Europe. We do not know enough about the reception, even decades later, of this literature in all of the countries outside the hotbeds of France, Germany, Britain, and the Netherlands. For example, we know that Spinoza's books and some Spinozana were held in the library of one the members of the Danish Privy Cabinet, Count Otto Thott.[15] Printed material from the period is largely abusive of Spinoza. But there may have been Spinozistic and other heterodox manuscripts circulating as well. This is one of the many open questions about the clandestine material in countries outside the central four mentioned above.

We should also look to other continents. For example, there was an Enlightenment expressed in printed texts in Nueva Granada (now Colombia).[16] Other work has foregrounded the development of subversive social and political concepts such as "Republic" and "Revolution" in the printed press in a dozen Latin American countries from 1750 to 1870.[17] This work should be supplemented by a search for manuscripts. We need to ask: did any of the clandestine literature circulate there? It could be imports, translations, or home-grown heterodoxy.

Modern Editions and Scholarship

There is an excellent series in French of modern editions of clandestine texts such as by Fontenelle, César Chesneau Du Marsais, and Abraham Gaultier edited by Antony McKenna and published by the Voltaire Foundation at Oxford.[18] Unfortunately, it has ceased publication. Fortunately, McKenna continues to edit a series with Honoré Champion in Paris that includes editions of clandestine manuscripts from time to time; it has now grown to more than seventy volumes.[19] In German there are two series edited by Winfried Schröder.[20] We need more such series to bring many of these manuscripts to wider attention. More translations of the French, German, and Latin texts into English would be an excellent idea.

As of 2017 perhaps the most important means of accessing some of the philosophical manuscripts is the collection of PDFs made available as "L'Inventaire des manuscrits philosophiques clandestins (IMPC)" at the Bibliothèque Mazarine in Paris: https://www.bibliotheque-mazarine.fr/impc. We can hope that more and more manuscripts will be made available in the near future. That will not obviate, but rather encourage, the translation into other languages of many of these manuscripts.

The latest scholarly discoveries may be found in the two periodicals dedicated to the area, *La lettre clandestine* (1992–present) and *Libertinage et philosophie au XVIIe siècle* (1996–present). Note that these are published in French, but the materials explored in this volume suggest that there should be much more attention to this area in journals published in English, German, Spanish, and other languages. New work is coming out all the time that adds to our understanding of the interplay of clandestine manuscripts and culture.[21]

The history of philosophy, the history of political ideas, the history of sexuality, the history of modernity, the history of atheism, and the history of many other things cannot be written adequately without reference to the manuscript tradition underlying the print culture of the seventeenth and eighteenth centuries. There is too much evidence that the writers of the printed texts read and thought about these manuscripts to dismiss them. The very fact that many well-known printed works circulated in manuscript for decades before being published suggests that we need to know more about their pre-print-publication impact. The essays in this volume should provide a good starting place for further work.

NOTES

1 See J.C. Laursen, "Spinoza et les 'mensonges officieux' dans les manuscrits clandestins. Une question et un programme de recherché," *La Lettre clandestine*, 26, 2018, 81–98.

2 Robert Darnton, *The Literary Underground of the Old Regime* (Cambridge, MA: Harvard University Press, 1982); Darnton, *The Forbidden Bestsellers of Pre-Revolutionary France* (New York: W.W. Norton, 1995).

3 Robert Darnton, *The Corpus of Clandestine Literature in France, 1769–1789* (New York: W.W. Norton, 1995).

4 Robert Darnton, *Edition et sédition: l'univers de la littérature clandestine au XVIIIe siècle* (Paris: Gallimard, 1991).

5 Robert Darnton, *Censors at Work: How States Shaped Literature* (New York: W.W. Norton, 2014).

6 Simon Dickie, *Cruelty and Laughter: Forgotten Comic Literature and the Unsentimental Eighteenth Century* (Chicago: University of Chicago Press, 2011).

7 Harold Love, *Scribal Publication in Seventeenth-Century England* (Oxford: Clarendon Press, 1993), 4.

8 Love, *Scribal Publication in Seventeenth-Century England*, 10–14.
9 Harold Love, *English Clandestine Satire, 1660–1702* (Oxford: Oxford University Press, 2004).
10 Peter Beal, *Index of Literary Manuscripts, 1450–1700*, 4 vols (London: Bowker and Mansell, 1980–93). See also Beal, *In Praise of Scribes: Manuscripts and Their Makers in Seventeenth-Century England* (Oxford: Clarendon Press, 1998).
11 See George Justice and Nathan Tinker, eds, *Women's Writing and the Circulation of Ideas: Manuscript Publication in England, 1550–1800* (Cambridge: Cambridge University Press, 2002).
12 George Justice, "Introduction" to Justice and Tinker, eds, *Women's Writing and the Circulation of Ideas*, 15.
13 See J.C. Laursen, "The Politics of a Publishing Event," in *Heterodoxy, Spinozism, and Freethought in Early Eighteenth-Century Europe*, ed. S. Berti, F. Charles-Daubert, and R. Popkin (Dordrecht: Kluwer, 1996), 273–96.
14 J.C. Laursen, "When Can You Think Something?," *Daimon. Revista Internacional de Filosofía* 58, 2013, 179–84.
15 See J.C. Laursen and Henrik Horstbøll, "Spinoza in Denmark: An Unknown Painting of Spinoza and the Spinoza Collection of Count Otto Thott," *Studia Spinozana* 15, 1999 [2006], 249–64.
16 See Renán Silva, *La Ilustración en el virreinato de la Nueva Granada* (Medellín: La Carreta, 2005); Renán Silva, *Nuevas perspectivas de análisis sobre el* Papel Periódico de Santafé de Bogotá, *1791–1797* (Medellín: La Carreta, 2015).
17 Javier Fernandez Sebastián, ed., *Diccionario politico y social del mundo iberoamericano*, vol. 1: *La era de las revoluciones, 1750–1850*, and vol. 2: *Conceptos políticos fundamentales, 1770–1870* (Madrid: Centro de Estudios Políticos y Constitucionales, 2009, 2014).
18 It consisted of Abraham Gaultier, *Parité de la vie et de la mort*, ed. O. Bloch (Oxford: Voltaire Foundation, 1993); Simon Tyssot de Patot, *Voyages et aventures de Jacques Massé*, ed. A. Rosenberg (Oxford: Voltaire Foundation, 1993); Guillaume Lamy, *Discours anatomiques + Explication méchanique et physique des fonctions de l'âme sensitive*, ed. A. Minerbi Belgrado (Oxford: Voltaire Foundation, 1996); *De l'examen de la religion*, attribuable à Jean Lévesque de Burigny, éd. S. Landucci (Oxford: Voltaire Foundation, 1996); *Traité de la liberté, Des Miracles, Des Oracles, La Fausseté des miracles des deux Testaments*, ed. A. Niderst (Oxford: Voltaire Foundation, 1997); Fontenelle, *Histoire des Ajaoïens*, ed. H.-G. Funke (Oxford: Voltaire Foundation, 1998); César Chesneau Du Marsais, *Doutes sur la religion, ou Examen de la religion dont on cherche l'éclaircissement de bonne foi*, ed. G. Mori (Oxford: Voltaire Foundation, 1998); Le "Traité des trois imposteurs" et "L'Esprit de Spinoza," ed. F. Charles-Daubert (Oxford: Voltaire Foundation, 1999); John

Locke, *Que la religion chrétienne est très raisonnable, Discours sur les miracles, Essai sur la nécessité d'expliquer les Epîtres de St Paul, La Vie de Cost*, ed. H. Bouchilloux and M.-C. Pitassi (Oxford: Voltaire Foundation, 1999). Another Voltaire Foundation series in English that also ceased publication included John Toland, *Nazarenus*, ed. Justin Champion (Oxford: Voltaire Foundation, 1999).

19 The catalogue for the series "Libre pensée et littérature clandestine" can be found at https://www.honorechampion.com/img/cms/pdf_catalog/2017_libre_pensee_et_litterature_clandestine.pdf.

20 "Freydenker der europäischen Aufklärung": Johann Georg Wachter, *Der Spinozismus im Jüdenthumb (1699)*, ed. W. Schröder (Stuttgart: Fromann-Holzboog, 1995); Johann Georg Wachter, *De primordiis Christiana religionis (1703/1717)*, ed. W. Schröder (Stuttgart: Frommann-Holzboog, 1995); Georg Schade, *Die unwandelbare und ewige Religion (1760)*, ed. M. Mulsow (Stuttgart: Fromann-Holzboog, 1999); [César Chesneau Du Marsais], *Die wahre Religion oder die Religionsprüfung (1747)*, ed. G. Mori (Stuttgart: Frommann-Holzboog, 2003); Balthasar Bekker, *Die bezauberte Welt (1693)*, ed. Wiep Van Bunge (Stuttgart: Frommann-Holzboog, 1997). "Philosophisches Clandestina": *Theodor Ludwig Lau*, ed. Martin Pott (Stuttgart: Frommann-Holzboog, 1992); *Friedrich Wilhelm Stosch (1648–1704)*, ed. W. Schröder (Stuttgart: Frommann-Holzboog, 1992); *Gabriel Wagner (1660–1717)*, ed. S. Wollgast (Stuttgart: Frommann-Holzboog, 1997); *Matthias Knutzen*, ed. W. Schröder (Stuttgart: Frommann-Holzboog, 2010); [Johann Joachim Müller (1661–1733)], *De Tribus Impostoribus*, ed. W. Schröder (Stuttgart: Fromann-Holzboog, 1999).

21 See, for example, Jacopo Agnesina, *The Philosophy of Anthony Collins: Free-Thought and Atheism* (Paris: Champion, 2018).

Contributors

Wiep van Bunge is Professor of the History of Philosophy at Erasmus University Rotterdam. Among his books are *From Stevin to Spinoza* (2001), *Spinoza Past and Present* (2012), and *From Bayle to the Batavian Revolution* (2019). He also (co-)edited several volumes, including *The Dictionary of Seventeenth- and Eighteenth-Century Dutch Philosophers* (2003) and *The Bloomsbury Companion to Spinoza* (2014).

Jeffrey D. Burson is Associate Professor of French History at Georgia Southern University. He is the author of *The Rise and Fall of Theological Enlightenment: Jean-Martin de Prades and Ideological Polarization in Eighteenth-Century France* (University of Notre Dame Press, 2010) and *The Culture of Enlightening: Abbé Claude Yvon and the Entangled Emergence of the Enlightenment* (University of Notre Dame Press, 2019). He is co-editor, with Ulrich L. Lehner, of *Enlightenment and Catholicism in Europe: A Transnational History* (University of Notre Dame Press, 2014), with Jonathan Wright, of *The Jesuit Suppression in Global Context: Causes, Events, and Consequences* (Cambridge University Press, 2015), and, with Anton M. Matytsin, of *The Skeptical Enlightenment: Doubt and Certainty in the Age of Reason* (Liverpool University Press on behalf of The Voltaire Foundation, 2019).

Karen Hollewand completed her DPhil at the University of Oxford in 2016. Her thesis, titled *The Banishment of Beverland: Sex, Sin, and Scholarship in the Seventeenth-Century Dutch Republic,* will be published by Brill in 2019. Her research concentrates on the social, intellectual, and cultural history of early-modern Europe, with a particular focus on sex and science. She is currently working as a postdoc at the Faculty of History of the University of Utrecht, studying the early-modern Republic of

Letters in the Skillnet Project, and finishing an English translation of Beverland's *De Peccato Originali*, together with Floris Verhaart.

Jonathan Israel taught at University College London from 1974 to 2000 and has been attached to the Institute for Advanced Study, Princeton, since 2001. He is the author of *The Dutch Republic: Its Rise, Greatness, and Fall, 1477–1806* and *Radical Enlightenment: Philosophy and the Making of Modernity, 1650–1750.* At various stages in his career, he has published a number of studies on the history of Spain and Spanish America.

Margaret C. Jacob, Distinguished Professor of History, UCLA, is author of *The Secular Enlightenment* (Princeton University Press, forthcoming December 2018), *The First Knowledge Economy* (Cambridge University Press, 2015); with Lynn Hunt and Wijnand Mijnhardt, *The Book That Changed Europe* (Harvard University Press, 2010); *The Radical Enlightenment: Pantheists, Freemasons, and Republicans* (Cornerstone, 2nd ed. 2006; 1st ed. 1981), and *Living the Enlightenment: Freemasonry and Politics in Eighteenth-Century Europe* (Oxford University Press, 1991). She is a member of the American Academy of Arts and Sciences and the American Philosophical Society and holds an honorary doctorate from the University of Utrecht (2003).

John Christian Laursen is Professor of Political Science at the University of California, Riverside. He is the co-editor of *Skepticism and Political Thought in the Seventeenth and Eighteenth Centuries* (with Gianni Paganini) (University of Toronto Press, 2015), *Paradoxes of Religious Toleration in Early Modern Political Thought* (with M.J. Villaverde) (Lexington Books, 2012), and *Monarchisms in the Age of Enlightenment* (with Hans Blom and Luisa Simonutti) (University of Toronto Press, 2007).

Inger Leemans is Professor of Cultural History at Vrije Universiteit Amsterdam and Director of ACCESS, the Amsterdam Center for Emotion and Sensory Studies. She has published on the history of pornography, emotions, the (radical) Enlightenment, cultural economy, and digital humanities. Together with Gert-Jan Johannes she published the textbook *Worm en donder. Geschiedenis van de Nederlandse literatuur 1700–1800* (Wurm and Thunder: A History of Dutch Literature 1700–1800) in the series *History of Dutch Literature* (Amsterdam: Bert Bakker / Prometheus 2011, 2nd ed. 2016). She is principal investigator of the working group "Affective Economies – Knowledge and the Market" for the international research project *Creating a Knowledge Society in a Globalizing World, 1450–1800.* Currently, she is working on the project "Affective Economies: A Cultural History of Stock Trading."

Whitney Mannies teaches political theory at California Polytechnic University in Pomona, California. Her publications include "Towards a Radical Feminist Historiography," in the edited volume, *The Invention of Female Biography,* and "The Style of Materialist Skepticism: Diderot's *Jacques le fataliste,*" in the journal *Philosophy and Literature.* Her current book projects focus on debates surrounding gender and women's status in the eighteenth-century periodical press.

John Marshall is Leonard and Helen R. Stulman Professor of Early Modern British and Early Modern British Imperial History, Early Modern European Cultural and Intellectual History, and the History of Political Thought at Johns Hopkins University. He is also director of its interdisciplinary program in Political and Moral Thought. He has written two books on the English philosopher and political theorist John Locke: *Locke: Religion, Resistance, and Responsibility* (Cambridge, 1996), and *John Locke, Toleration, and Early Enlightenment Culture* (Cambridge 2006), and co-edited with David Loewenstein *Heresy, Literature, and Politics in Early Modern English Culture* (Cambridge, 2006). He is the author of numerous articles and is currently at work on four books.

Antony McKenna, former pupil of Christ's Hospital (Horsham, Sussex) and of Brasenose College, Oxford, Emeritus Professor in French Literature at the University of Lyon (Saint-Etienne), is the author of a thesis titled *De Pascal à Voltaire. Le rôle des Pensées de Pascal dans l'histoire des idées entre 1670 et 1734,* in *SVEC,* 276–7 (Oxford, 1990). He is co-author of the *Dictionnaire de Port-Royal* (Paris, 2004) and co-directed the critical edition of the correspondence of Pierre Bayle (Oxford, 1999–2017, 15 vols) and of Voltaire's *Lettres philosophiques* (Paris, 2010), He has published monographs on Molière and on Pascal.

Martin Mulsow is Professor of Intellectual History at the University of Erfurt and director of the Gotha Research Centre. He studied philosophy in Tübingen, Berlin, and Munich. From 2005–8 he was professor of history at Rutgers University. He is a member of several German academies and was a member of the Institute for Advanced Study at Princeton (2002–3), the Wissenschaftskolleg in Berlin (2012–13), and the NIAS in Amsterdam (2017). His work on Renaissance philosophy, the history of early-modern scholarship, and the Radical Enlightenment received many prizes, among them the prize of the Berlin-Brandenburg Academy of Sciences (2012) and the Anna-Krüger-Prize (2014). Among his publications are *Enlightenment Underground* (Charlottesville, 2015); *Die unanständige Gelehrtenrepublik. Wissen, Libertinage und Komunikation in der Frühen Neuzeit* (Stuttgart, 2007); *Prekäres Wissen. Eine andere Ideengeschichte der Frühen Neuzeit* (Berlin, 2012); and *Radikale Frühaufklärung in Deutschland 1680–1720* (2 vols, Göttingen, 2018).

Gianni Paganini is Professor of History of Philosophy at the University of Piedmont. He is the author of many books on early modern philosophy, including *Pierre Bayle* (Florence, 1980); *Les Philosophies clandestines* (Paris, 2005; Rome, 2008); and *Skepsis. Le débat des modernes* (Paris, 2008). He has edited, with commentary, several texts: *Theophrastus redivivus* (1659), first and critical ed., (with G. Canziani) (2 vols, Florence, 1981–2); Voltaire, *Zadig* (Milan, 1994); Hobbes, *De motu, loco et tempore* (Turin, 2010); and Hume, *Dialogues Concerning Natural Religion* (Milan, 2013). He is also the editor of *The Return of Scepticism: From Hobbes and Descartes to Bayle* (Dordrecht, 2003); *Pierre Bayle dans la République des Lettres* (with. A. McKenna) (Paris, 2004); *Renaissance Scepticisms* (with J. Maia Neto) (Boston, 2008); *Skepticism in the Modern Age* (with C. Laursen and J. Maia Neto) (Leiden, 2009); *Skepticism and Political Thought in the Seventeenth and Eighteenth Centuries* (with C. Laursen) (Toronto, 2015); and *Early Modern Philosophy and the Renaissance Legacy* (with C. Muratori) (Berlin, 2016). For his ten years of philosophical work (2001–11) he was prized by the Accademia dei Lincei (2011). His book *Skepsis* was awarded by the Académie Française (Prix de littérature et philosophie La Bruyère, 2009).

Winfried Schröder is Professor of History of Philosophy at Philipps-Universität Marburg. He has published these books: *Spinoza in der deutschen Frühaufklärung* (1987); *Ursprünge des Atheismus* (1998, 2012); and *Athen und Jerusalem. Die philosophische Kritik am Christentum in Antike und Neuzeit* (2011, 2013). He has edited the following clandestine texts: *Symbolum sapientiae* (with G. Canziani and F. Socas) (2000); *De tribus impostoribus* (1999); *Traité des trois imposteurs* (1992, 2010). He has also edited proceedings of conferences: *Gestalten des Deismus in Europa* (2013); *Reading between the Lines: Leo Strauss and the History of Early Modern Philosophy* (2016); *The Dutch Legacy: Radical Thinkers of the 17th Century and the Enlightenment* (with Sonja Lavaert (2017); *Horkheimers und Adornos Dialek-*

tik der Aufklärung in philosophiehistorischer Perspektive (with Sonja Lavaert) (2018). He edits the series *Philosophische Clandestina* (1999 ff.).

Susana Seguin is a professor at University of Montpellier III; a Fellow at the Ecole Normale of Lyon's Institute for the History and Representation of Ideas in Modern Times (IHRIM-ENS); and a senior member of the University Institute of France (IUF). She also serves on the Executive Committee of ISECS. Her many works on the history of ideas include, in French, *Science and Religion in the Eighteenth Century: The Myth of the Universal Flood* (2001); and *La Sociabilité au temps de Robert Challe* (ed.). She is co-head of the journal "La Lettre clandestine" and is responsible for two research projects on pan-European scientific and philosophical networks (mhars.huma-num.fr and philosophie-clandestine.huma-num.fr).

Frederik Stjernfelt is Professor of Semiotics, Intellectual History, and Philosophy of Science, Aalborg University Copenhagen. His international publications include the books *Diagrammatology* (2007); *The Democratic Contradictions of Multiculturalism* (with J.M. Eriksen) (2012); *Natural Propositions* (2014); and *Mapping Frontier Research in the Humanities* (ed. with D. Budtz and C. Emmeche) (2017). He is Principal Investigator (with D. Budtz) of the Humanomics Research Center, conducting metastudies of humanities research and impact. Recent Danish books include *BUT – the History of Free Speech in Denmark* (with J. Mchangama) (2016); *The Struggle over Humanity* (ed. with D. Budtz and F. Collin, 2018); and *Your Post Has Been Removed: Tech Giants and Free Speech* (with A.M. Lauritzen) (2018). He is a member of the Royal Danish Academy of Sciences and Letters and a critic at the Danish weekly *Weekendavisen.*

Rienk Vermij is a professor in the Department of the History of Science at the University of Oklahoma. He wrote his PhD thesis on the Dutch mathematician and apologist Bernard Nieuwentijt (1654–1718). In 2002 he published *The Calvinist Copernicans: On the Reception of the New Astronomy in the Dutch Republic (1575–1750).* He has published several articles on the early modern Dutch philosophical underground.

Fabienne Vial-Bonacci, who works at the CNRS, is a collaborator in the critical edition of Pierre Bayle's correspondence and its on-line edition and is now co-director of the on-line edition of the correspondence and papers of Marc-Michel Rey, the Amsterdam bookseller and printer.

Index

THE UCLA CLARK MEMORIAL LIBRARY SERIES

1. *Wilde Writings: Contextual Conditions*, edited by Joseph Bristow
2. *Enchanted Ground: Reimagining John Dryden*, edited by Jayne Lewis and Maximillian E. Novak
3. *Culture and Authority in the Baroque*, edited by Massimo Ciavolella and Patrick Coleman
4. *Ritual, Routine, and Regime: Repetition in Early Modern British and European Cultures*, edited by Lorna Clymer
5. *Momigliano and Antiquarianism: Foundations of the Modern Cultural Sciences*, edited by Peter N. Miller
6. *Monarchisms in the Age of Enlightenment: Liberty, Patriotism, and the Common Good*, edited by Hans Blom, John Christian Laursen, and Luisa Simonetti
7. *Thinking Impossibilities: The Intellectual Legacy of Amos Funkenstein*, edited by Robert S. Westman and David Biale
8. *Discourses of Tolerance and Intolerance in the European Enlightenment*, edited by Hans Erich Bödeker, Clorinda Donato, and Peter Hanns Reill
9. *The Age of Projects*, edited by Maximillian E. Novak
10. *Acculturation and Its Discontents: The Italian Jewish Experience between Exclusion and Inclusion*, edited by David N. Myers, Massimo Ciavolella, Peter H. Reill, and Geoffrey Symcox
11. *Defoe's Footprints: Essays in Honour of Maximillian E. Novak*, edited by Robert M. Maniquis and Carl Fisher
12. *Women, Religion, and the Atlantic World (1600–1800)*, edited by Daniella Kostroun and Lisa Vollendorf
13. *Braudel Revisited: The Mediterranean World, 1600–1800*, edited by Gabriel Piterberg, Teofilo F. Ruiz, and Geoffrey Symcox

14. *Structures of Feeling in Seventeenth-Century Cultural Expression*, edited by Susan McClary
15. *Godwinian Moments*, edited by Robert M. Maniquis and Victoria Myers
16. *Vital Matters: Eighteenth-Century Views of Conception, Life, and Death*, edited by Helen Deutsch and Mary Terrall
17. *Redrawing the Map of Early Modern English Catholicism*, edited by Lowell Gallagher
18. *Space and Self in Early Modern European Cultures*, edited by David Warren Sabean and Malina Stefanovska
19. *Wilde Discoveries: Traditions, Histories, Archives*, edited by Joseph Bristow
20. *Jesuit Accounts of the Colonial Americas: Intercultural Transfers, Intellectual Disputes, and Textualities*, edited by Marc André Bernier, Clorinda Donato, and Hans-Jürgen Lüsebrink
21. *Skepticism and Political Thought in the Seventeenth and Eighteenth Centuries*, edited by John Christian Laursen and Gianni Paganini
22. *Representing Imperial Rivalry in the Early Modern Mediterranean*, edited by Barbara Fuchs and Emily Weissbourd
23. *Imagining the British Atlantic after the American Revolution*, edited by Michael Meranze and Saree Makdisi
24. *Life Forms in the Thinking of the Long Eighteenth Century*, edited by Keith Michael Baker and Jenna M. Gibbs
25. *Cultures of Communication: Theologies of Media in Early Modern Europe and Beyond*, edited by Helmut Puff, Ulrike Strasser, and Christopher Wild
26. *Curious Encounters: Voyaging, Collecting, and Making Knowledge in the Long Eighteenth Century*, edited by Adriana Craciun and Mary Terrall
27. *Clandestine Philosophy: New Studies on Subversive Manuscripts in Early Modern Europe, 1620–1823*, edited by Gianni Paganini, Margaret C. Jacob, and John Christian Laursen

www.ingramcontent.com/pod-product-compliance
Lightning Source LLC
LaVergne TN
LVHW090146080826
844660LV00013B/685/J

* 9 7 8 1 4 8 7 5 0 4 6 1 8 *